THE OFFICIAL

P

Antique & Modern

DOLLS

BY

THE HOUSE OF COLLECTIBLES, INC.

We have compiled the information contained herein through a *patented computerized process* which relies primarily on a nationwide sampling of information provided by noteworthy collectible experts, auction houses and specialized dealers. This unique retrieval system enables us to provide the reader with the most current and accurate information available.

EDITOR

THOMAS E. HUDGEONS III

FIRST EDITION

THE HOUSE OF COLLECTIBLES, INC., ORLANDO, FLORIDA 32809

IMPORTANT NOTICE. The format of **THE OFFICIAL PRICE GUIDE SERIES,** published by **THE HOUSE OF COLLECTIBLES, INC.,** is based on the following proprietary features: **ALL FACTS AND PRICES ARE COMPILED THRU A COMPUTERIZED PROCESS** which relies on a nationwide sampling of information obtained from noteworthy collectibles experts, auction houses and specialized dealers. **DETAILED "INDEXED" FORMAT** enables quick retrieval of information for positive identification. **ENCAPSULATED HISTORIES** preceed each category to acquaint the collector with the specific traits that are peculiar to that area of collecting. **VALUABLE COLLECTING INFORMATION** is provided for both the novice as well as the seasoned collector: How to begin a collection; How to buy, sell, and trade; Care and storage techniques; Tips on restoration; Grading guidelines; Lists of periodicals, clubs, museums, auction houses, dealers, etc. **AN AVERAGE PRICE RANGE** takes geographic location and condition into consideration when reporting collector value. **A SPECIAL 3rd PRICE COLUMN** enables the collector to compare the current market values with the last's years average selling price . . . indicating which items have increased in value. **INVENTORY CHECKLISTS SYSTEM** is provided for cataloging a collection. **EACH TITLE IS ANNUALLY UP-DATED** to provide the most accurate information available in the rapidly changing collectors marketplace.

All of the information, including valuations, in this book has been compiled from the most reliable sources, and every effort has been made to eliminate errors and questionable data. Nevertheless the possibility of error, in a work of such immense scope, always exists. The publisher will not be held responsible for losses which may occur, in the purchase, sale, or other transaction of items, because of information contained herein. Readers who feel they have discovered errors are invited to WRITE and inform us, so they may be corrected in subsequent editions. Those seeking further information on the topics covered in this book, are advised to refer to the complete line of Official Price Guides published by the House of Collectibles.

Published by: The House of Collectibles, Inc.
Orlando Central Park
1900 Premier Row
Orlando, FL 32809
Phone: (305) 857-9095

Printed in the United States of America

Library of Congress Catalog Card Number: 82-84638

ISBN: 0-87637-381-3 / Paperback

TABLE OF CONTENTS

Introduction 1
The History And Development Of Dolls . 2
Beginning And Building A Doll Collection 12
Condition 22
Doll Repairs 29
Doll Fakes 31
Care, Storage And Display 33
Making Money With Dolls 37
Materials 42
Mechanical Dolls 57
Doll Manufacturers Marks 60
Glossary 70
Common Abbreviations 85
Books 86
Periodicals 87
Clubs 89
Museums 89
How To Use This Book 91

LISTINGS OF MANUFACTURERS

Aboriginals 93
Emma And Marietta Adams 93
Advance Doll And Toy Company 93
Odette Aiden 93
Alexander Doll Company, Inc. 93
Allied 112
Alt, Beck, And Gottschalck 112
Amberg 113
American Character Doll Company 113
Amsco 119
Apex 119
Arlesford 119
Arranbee Doll Company 119
Arrow Novelty Company 125
Arrow Plastics 125
Art Fabric Mills 126
Artisan Novelty 126
Aspen Productions .. 126
Aunt Sarah 127
Aurora 127
Averill Manufacturing Company 127
Azark 128
Baby Berry 128
Bähr & Pröschild 129
Constance Bannister 130
Bantam 131
Bauer & Black 131
Belle 131
Belton 132
Bendee 133
Bergmann 133
Carl Bergner 136
Berman And Anderson 136
Blumberg 136
Ernst Bohne 137
Bombole Franca 137
Bonomi 137
Borden 137
George Borgfeldt 138
Madame Etena Boucher 139
Brock Candy Company 139
Brookglad 140
Brouse 140
Bru 140
Brückner 142
M.H. Buell 143
Buschow & Beck 143
Camay 144
Cameo 144
Carlson 147
Cascelloid 147
C.B.S. 148
Celtic Toys 148
Century Doll Company 148
Cey 149
Chad Valley Company 149
Chadwick-Miller 150
Chase Bag Company 150
Martha Chase 150
Chicago Tribune 151
Chiltern 151
Patti Chimera 151
Chrysler 151
Emma Clear 151
Clodrey 152
Cochran 152
Coleman 152
Columbia Toy Products 152
Comic Toy Manufacturing Company 152
Confetti 153
Co-Operative Manufacturing Company 153
Cosmopolitan 153
Crown Doll Company 154
Dakin 154
Thomas Dam 155
Danel Et Cie 156
Darrow Manufacturing Company 156
D'Autremont 156
Dee Cee 156
Dell Publishing Company 156
Deluxe 157
Deluxe Topper 158
Dennison 159
DeSoto 159
Diamond 159
Doliac Et Cie 159
Dolly's Dolls 160
Dream Dolls 160
Dreamland 161
Dream World 161
Cuno And Otto Dressel 162
Duchess 163
Dukker 164
Durham 164
Eegee 165
Effanbee 168
Einco 185
Elvis Presley Enterprises 185
Eppy 185
Erb 185
Eugene 185
Eugenia 186
Excel 186
Mark Farmer 187
F.D. 188
Fisher Price 188
Ham Fisher 189
Flagg 189
Fleischaker 189
Fleisher Studios 190
Fortune Toys 190
Freudlich 190
Fulpher 190
Fun Farm 192
Fun World 192
Furga 192
Fy 194
Gabriel 194
Gama 195
Ganda Toys Ltd. 195
Gans And Seyfarth .. 195
Gaultier 195
Gay Bob Trading Company......... 198

Gebrüder Heubach . . 199
Gebrüder Knoch 203
Gebrüder Krauss 203
Gem 204
Gem Toy Company . . 204
General Mills Fun Group 204
Georgene 204
Gera 205
Gerber 205
Sue Gibson 205
A.C. Gilbert 205
Girl's World 206
William Goebel 206
Goodyear Rubber Company 209
Gorham 209
Gotz Puppe 209
Grant's 210
Grenier 210
Gund 211
Halco 211
Hallmark Cards 211
Hall Syndicate 212
Heinrich Handwerck . 212
Larry Harmon 220
Harmus 221
Aileen Harris 221
Hasbro 221
Hazelle's 227
Gene Hazelton 227
Hedaya 227
Hedwig 227
Heico 227
Heubach-Köpplesdorf 228
Highbrow 233
Hill 233
Holiday Fair 234
Hollywood Doll Company 234
Horsman 235
Mary Hoyer 248
Hubley 248
Hugh M. Hefner Publishing Company 248
Hummel 249
Hungerford 249
Huret 249
Ideal 249
Imco 272
Imperial 273
Imperial Crown 273
IMS 274
Irwin 274
Iralocremona 274
Charles Ives 275
Jack Frost Sugar 275
Japan 275
Jerri 275
Jilmar 275
Jointed Doll Company 276
Jolly 276
Joy 277
Joyce-Miller 278
Jullien 278
Jumeau 278
Junel 289
Juro 290
Jutta 290
Kahagia 290
Kahl & Kohle 290
J.L. Kallus 291
Kamar 291
Kämmer & Reinhardt . 291
Kanto Toys 297
Kaybee 298
Kaysam 299
Kaystan 299
Keebler 299
Kellogg's 300
Kenner 300
Kerr Ghintz 305
Kestner 305
Lucille Kimsey 317
King Features 318
Kley & Hahn 319
Knickerbocker 319
Knotter 322
König And Wernicke . 322
Käthe Kruse 322
Lakeside 324
A. Lanternier 325
Lastic Plastic 325
H.D. Lee 326
Lenci 326
Lesney 331
L.H.K. 331
Libby 331
Liberty 332
Limbach 332
Limenau 333
Limoges 333
L.J.N. 333
Louis Amberg And Sons 335
Louise R. Kampes Studios 335
Lovee 335
Maison Simonne 335
Majber 336
Majestic 336
Marlon 336
Armand Marseille . . . 336
Marvel Comics Group 349
Marx 349
Mascotte 350
Mattel 350
McDonald 375
Mego 376
Metti 380
Midwestern 380
Migliorati 381
Miller Rubber Company 381
Minerva 381
Edward Moberly 381
Mollenecht 381
Mollye 382
Monica Studios 382
Montgomery Ward . . . 382
Morimura Brothers . . 383
M & S 383
My Toy 383
Nancy Ann Storybook Doll Company 384
Nasco 390
National Mask And Puppet Corporation . 390
National Periodical Publications 390
Natural Doll Company 391
Nems Enterprises . . . 391
Nestle's Chocolate . . 392
Ruth E. Newton 392
Niada 392
Nippon 392
Peggy Nisbet 393
Adelheid Nogler 395
Rose O'Neill 395
P & M 398
Parksmith 399
Adelaine Patti 399
Pauline 399
Pedigree 399
Pelham 400
J.C. Penny 400
Gutta Percha 400
Perego 400
Perfecta 400
Perfekta 401
Peter Puppet Playthings 401
Petite Portraits 401
Piacenxa 401
Pillsbury 402
Pierotti 402
Planters Peanut Company 403

Plastic Molded Arts . . 403
Plated Moulds 404
Playmates 404
Playskool 404
Playthings 405
Pocket Doll 405
Eugenie Poir 405
Politoy 405
Princess Anna 405
Princess Christina . . . 405
Product People 406
Grace Storey Putnam 406
Questar 408
Rabery & Delphieu . . . 408
Ratti 410
Bernard Ravca 410
RDF 410
Recknagel 410
Regal 411
Otto Reinecke 411
Reliable 412
Reliable Of Canada . . 412
Remco 412
Revalo 415
Rheinische Gummi And
Celluloid Fabric 415
Richard 416
Richard Bicentennial
Series 416
Rite-Lee 416
Roberta 416
Edward Rocharde . . . 417
Grace Corry Rockwell 417
Roddy 417
Rogark 417
Mademoiselle Marie
Rohmer 418
Roko 418
Ronald 418
Rosebud 418
Royal Doll Company . 419
Royal Doulton 420
Roy Design 427
R.P. 427
Rushton 427
S. & E. 428
Sakai 428
Sarco 428
Sayco 429
Schildkrot 429
Schmid 430
Bruno Schmidt 430
Franz Schmidt 430
Schoenau &
Hoffmeister 431
Schoenhut 432
Schulte 435
Schwab & Company . 435
Sears Roebuck &
Company 435
Sebino 435
S.F.B.J. 436
Shackman 441
Shannon Industries . . 442
J.B. Sheppard &
Company 442
Shimmel 442
Shindana 442
Sidney Sheldon
Productions 443
Simon & Halbig 443
Simplicity 452
Skippy 452
Ella Smith 452
Sonsco 452
Marjorie Spangler . . . 452
Stahlwood 453
Karl Standfuss 453
Street Corner
Productions 453
Steiff 453
Steiner 453
Stuart 456
Sun Rubber Company 456
Sunshine 457
Super Doll 458
Superior 458
Swedlin 459
Tecnogiocattoli 459
Teen 459
Terri Lee 459
Texaco 460
Togs And Dolls 460
Tomy 460
Tony Toy 460
Topper 461
Toy Innovations Ltd. . 461
Toy Product 461
Transogram 461
Trio Toy Company . . . 461
Uneeda 462
Unis France 468
United Features 468
Universal 469
UPA 469
Vanity 469
Verlingue 469
Video Craft 470
Virga 470
Vogue 470
Izannah Walker 479
Sheila Wallace 479
Walt Disney
Productions 479
Beverly Walter 483
Bergmann
Walterhausen 483
Warner Brothers 483
Norah Wellings 483
Adolf Wislizenus 485
Wolfpit 485
Woolworth 485
World Doll Company . 485

MANUFACTURERS UNKNOWN
Advertising 486
China Heads 488
Cloth 491
Ethnic 492
Pincushion 496
Wax 497

COLLECTIBLE DOLL ARTISTS
Ruth Arden 499
Alice Ann Beecham . . 500
Wendy Brent 501
Sonja Bryer 502
Suzanne Gibson 503
Jean Heighton 508
Sharon Lee Howard . . 511
Suzanne Marks 513
Sonia Messer 518
Sasha Morgenthaler . 521
Fae Morris 523
Carol-Lynn Waugh . . . 525

PAPER DOLLS 527

STUFFED ANIMALS
Bear Haus U.S.A. 552
Dakin 552
Ideal 552
Merry Thought 552
North American
Bears 553
Steiff 553
Miscellaneous
And Unknown
Manufacturers 560

PHOTOGRAPHIC RECOGNITION

Cover and Color Section Photographs: Photographer — Marc Hudgeons, Orlando, FL 32809

Color Separations: World Color, Ormond Beach, FL 32074

We would like to thank the East Florida Doll Collector's Guild for allowing us photographic privileges at their January 1983 Doll Show. For their cooperation we would like to thank the following: Annabelle Hahn, Venice, FL 33595; Antique Appraisal, Bill and Mary New, Holiday, FL 33590; Jean Bayl, Maitland, FL 32751; Bobi's Doll Creations, Bobi Langkau, Portage, WI 53901; Cathie Clark, Springfield, OH 45505; Dolly's Dolls, Minnie Byrd and Dollie Robbins, Jacksonville, FL 32208; The Doll Shop, Joyce Imhoff, Richmond, IN 47374; Marcia Duggins, Melbourne, FL 32935; Everett Fidler-Auctioneers, Orlando, FL 32817; The Ginny Doll Club, Lakeland, FL 33803; Olive Jolly, Delray Beach, FL 33444; Joyce's Dolls, Joyce Terry, St. Augustine, FL 32084; Lady Arden Dolls, Toledo, OH 43607; Lavonne McElroy, Great Falls, MT; Porcelain by Sonja, Bellbrook, OH 45305; Mabel C. Sousa, Punta Gorda, FL 38950; Suzanne Gibson Dolls, Auburn, NY 13021.

We would like to thank the following for submitting pictures and literature: Astro Knots Corp., St. Paul, MN 55105; Atlanta Novelty, New York, NY 10019; Carol-Lynn Rossel Waugh, Winthrop, ME 04364; Fae Morris, Les Gatos, CA 95030; Ideal, New York, NY 10016; International Playthings, Inc., Montclair, NJ 07042; Mattel Toys, Hawthorne, CA 90250; Original Dolls By Jean Heighton, San Mateo, CA 94403; Reeves International, Inc., New York, NY 10010; Shannon — Ulseth, Traverse City, MI 49684; Sharon Lee Dolls, Hesperia, CA 92345; Sonia Messer Imports, Glendale, CA 91204.

The Steiff Article appears courtesy of Sheri Hanson for Boutonniere, Huron, SD 57350.

INTRODUCTION

Most doll collectors have a personal relationship with their dolls. Rather than the owners, they feel they are the custodians of history, and it is this factor that gives collectible dolls a life of their own. Whether characterized or idealized, dolls are made in the image of mankind. They are the surviving remnants of past society. It follows that the wide diversity of human culture is mimicked in the huge variety of collectible dolls that are available. Delve into the possibilities: the bisques, chinas or newer vinyls; the elegant Jumeau, contemporary Barbie, or whimsical Kewpie. And for as many avenues that a collection can take, there are reasons why people collect dolls.

The doll collector often has a strong sense of nostalgia. The beautiful bisques of the 18th century are a call back to a gentler era. Their costumes remind us of the courtly life that has taken on the gentile glow of time gone by. These dolls often have a far away look in their startlingly realistic eyes, suggesting the wisdom of the decades they have witnessed. There are collectors that specialize in characters of the American past. The Charlie Chaplins and Shirley Temple dolls are sweet reminders of childhood, glorifying even the roughest times during the Depression. Whatever the psychological reason for the desire the collector has to keep in touch with the past, the fact is that dolls do chronicle our fashions, tastes, fads and politics. By placing all the dolls that survive from the early centuries on a time line, the historian could document a fine perspective on human development.

Many hobbyists see their collection as a legitimate reason to play with a toy as an adult. They are interested in the wardrobe and accessories that come along with the doll, often more vain about their doll's appearance than they would ever think of being themselves. Often these collectors started their collections in their childhood, carrying it with them to maturity. Dreams come true when they are older and financially able to acquire the long sought after addition to their display.

Although the number of investor/collectors are few compared to the huge number of people gathering collections of prized, emotionally invaluable dolls, some hobbyists have made investing the focus of their lives and livelihood. The values of dolls have steadily increased year by year, and there is much money to be made in this field. In January, 1983, the world record was set in Scotsdale, Arizona for an "A. Marque" bisque bebe, sold to the highest bidder for $38,000. This more than doubled the previous record set just a few short months before. Of course, dolls in this price range are the rarest in the world, but the sale shows the willingness of doll collectors to expand the market and the potential fortunes that can be made. As thousands of hobbyists enter the field each year the demand will outweigh the supply and continue this booming trend. With careful planning and realistic expectations, there is no doubt that you can maintain this profitable, lucrative hobby throughout a lifetime, upgrading your collection several times.

In this edition, we are attempting to give both the prospective hobbyist and the seasoned trader the overview necessary for making informed choices about collecting. We have listed hundreds of manufacturers and thousands of dolls of every material and description. These lists are by no means complete — it would take a multivolume encyclopedia to thoroughly document the entire history and manufacture of dolls. But whether your interest is in the antiques, the characters, the fads, or the works of art, we invite you to enjoy the world of collectible dolls.

THE HISTORY AND DEVELOPMENT OF DOLLS

The history of dolls involves so many names, dates, and developments that we can give only a brief sketch here, as this book is intended mainly as a price guide. We have included a complete bibliography of books and encyclopedias that delve deeply into this subject. It should be pointed out, though, that no COMPLETE history of doll making has ever been written, and probably never will be, as many questions remain unanswered and many facts untraced. If a hobbyist is interested in research and making fresh discoveries of his own, the field of dolls, especially antique dolls, has much to offer. It is mostly thanks to the efforts of hobbyists — past and present — that the available information has come into our hands. The doll historians are the hobbyists.

We know that dolls have existed in some form or other for a very long time, and that they evolved through very complex steps to the current dolls on today's market. And we know just as well that dolls of the 1980's do not represent the story's final chapter. The future will bring new developments — dolls that are not even dreamt of today, made possibly of wondrous space-age substances and capable of doing all kinds of human-like things. And when THOSE dolls are commonplace on the shelves, those found in today's stores will have shifted over into the antiques shops, and the next generation of hobbyists will be paying dearly for them.

Advances made in the doll industry, through the years, came via the profit motive and through advances in other industries. When new "miracle" substances were brought into the world by chemists and scientists, they naturally found their way to doll making. So too did a variety of other inventions in one form or another. The most striking example is undoubtedly the phonograph. In less than 10 years after Thomas Edison obtained a patent on the phonograph (1879), he was manufacturing talking dolls using the same principle (1887). Anything which could be accomplished in science and industry offered possible uses for doll manufacturers. Then, too, the development of doll making has been influenced by artistic and craft traditions over the years, and also merchandising techniques. When the era of large scale *mail order selling* began in the U.S., around 1880, this was a signal for doll manufacturers to cut their costs and bring out dolls which could be sold to a large segment of the population. It likewise encouraged them to look for materials that were lightweight (for shipping). By the same token, periods of economic flux have played their role in influencing doll making. The "great depression" of the 1930's caused an upheaval throughout the doll industry, as manufacturers had to slant their products to a less affluent market. This meant the downfall of bisque (replaced by composition for better-quality dolls), and the widespread use of very inexpensive materials such as celluloid and chalk for dolls to be sold in "dime stores."

Then, too, public fancy in other areas has shaped the history of dolls to some degree. Favorite celebrities have become the subjects for dolls — Jenny Lind, Shirley Temple, Margaret O'Brien, and others — and these celebrity dolls exercised some influence on the industry as a whole. A company which did not have the rights to make Shirley Temple dolls (for example), styled its dolls as closely as possible to America's Darling without using her name. Far from being any kind of new twist, this sort of thing goes back to the 19th century. Today, of course, we have yet another phenomenon on the doll scene, the TV doll based on characters from popular TV shows (either real or fictional). These have included Fonzie, Wonder Woman, The Incredible Hulk, Howdy Doody, Pinky Lee, The Man From U.N.C.L.E., Batman, Cisco Kid, and many more.

Taking the history of dolls back to the ancient world, it is not always easy to determine what was — and wasn't — considered a plaything in those remote days. Many doll-like creations have come down to us from ancient times, but it is questionable what their exact use was. For example, the graves of wealthy or noble Egyptians of 4000/2000 B.C. often contain, in addition to mountains of other articles, small painted statuettes which are easy to accept as dolls. Made of baked clay (pre-porcelain ceramic), they represent adults in various activities such as rowing boats, playing sports, herding cattle, etc. Sometimes these Egyptian "dolls" are found by the dozens, arranged in a scene, and have a great historical interest. It is not too likely that they were designed as childrens' playthings. But they may have been the equivalent of "show" or display dolls of a later era, for household ornament.

If any cloth or other fabric dolls were made in ancient times, we have no surviving record of this. Most of what we know about the classical world (Egyptian/Greek/Roman etc.) derives from actual finds made in digging out lost cities and burial places. Since cloth is so perishable, virtually no relics of this kind have been preserved. Underground burial for cloth meant destruction within a short time. Thus, we have no clothing fragments of the ancient civilizations, either, except for a few things made of hard materials. But we KNOW that these people wore clothes, even though there are no existing specimens; so it is quite possible they also made cloth or other fabric dolls.

It is a matter of recorded fact that the Romans, from the time of the Caesars, made wooden dolls. These were crudely carved little dolls strung together with strips of leather. To judge from their appearance, they could not have been intended as anything but playthings for children. Perhaps they were the first true dolls. If so, doll making in the modern accepted sense goes back about 1,900 years. Unfortunately, they are too rare to be available for collectors. You will find them occasionally in archaeological museums, and illustrated in books.

Aside from this, we know practically nothing about dolls in ancient times. But the Greeks and Romans were a fairly affluent people; they excelled at craftsmanship of all kinds; and it is reasonable to think — or at least guess — that many dolls were made.

The Roman Empire was followed by the Middle Ages. This was a period of roughly a thousand years, ending around 1500 A.D., during which the craft trades and manufacturing were at a low ebb. Although rag dolls and other home style toys were undoubtedly made and played with, none of these specimens survive to offer historical record. The dolls of 16th century Europe were not playthings but showpieces. Few were made, so far as we know, and the majority were very exquisite. They included models of enormously large size. It might be going too far to categorize all of them as dolls, but this is the label they usually receive in museums. One of the typical dolls of that era is the mounted knight in full battle armor, carrying a lance. The names of manufacturers are not known. Quite obviously they were handmade in a very limited operation. They were carved from wood and all details reflected very exacting workmanship. The original owners must have paid high prices for them. For one thing we know that there were no toyshops in the 16th century, or even in the 17th for that matter. Also, the material that revolutionized doll making — porcelain — was not yet being made in Europe. So, while dolls or objects similar to dolls were coming out 400 years ago, we could hardly compare this with the doll industry of the 1800's or 1900's.

Things progressed slowly at this early stage. Dolls continued to be made all throughout the 1600's but there was no centralized production; no real definite styles; and nothing in the way of a big public demand. Most dolls were the work of lone artisans, who put months of toil into their specimens, and, of course, no two were alike. Probably the most significant advance of the 17th century was the appearance of costume dolls in the likeness of adult women adorned with copies of the latest fashions. These, too, were very expensive and exclusive — and sometimes quite large. Most fashion dolls of this age came from France, but other countries were gradually starting to make them.

Toward the close of the 17th century some lower-priced dolls started coming out. Some were strictly amateur efforts: dolls made by mom or dad as playthings for the family's children. These are known as folk dolls. Though quite crude, they have a definite collector appeal and value. Nearly all dolls of the American colonies were folk dolls. But in Europe, which had a much larger population and a long tradition for making and selling things, commercialism was working its way into doll making. The big expensive fashion dolls served as models for smaller, less exquisite specimens — dolls that could be made faster, at a lower cost, and retailed to citizens who were not highly affluent. So we find in the latter years of the 17th century, and more especially the opening years of the 18th, a thrust toward doll making among the ordinary craftsmen of the time: potters, woodcarvers and the like. Anyone who had the tools and knowledge to manufacture things was in a position to make dolls of some kind or other. The potter, for example, could cast molds for doll heads, and sell dolls as a sideline to his normal trade in jugs and tableware. The woodcarver — who might be a specialist in ships' figureheads — could make dolls in his spare moments, or train his apprentices to make them. This is how the doll industry grew up, in no kind of organized or planned way, but through the efforts and ingenuity of many different people. There was no kind of centralized distributorship, and still no toyshops. The manufacturer was not only the creator but the seller, too. He put his dolls in his shop and hoped that some passers-by would want to buy them. Or he sold them at wholesale to itinerant merchants, who went around the streets "hawking" them. During the earlier eras of doll making, a large percentage of sales were made through these street peddlers, who brought merchandise to the people. If they did not care to buy from the doll maker, they made their own dolls. This is essentially how the "penny woodens" of the 18th century got their start. Hawkers and peddlers whittled them out of wood and sold them for a penny. Though they were not the equal of craftsman-made dolls, the potential audience for penny woodens was enormous. Thousands of children who wanted a doll could never hope to own a large, fine one. The penny wooden was accepted as a reasonable substitute. This is the same kind of thing that occurred two centuries later, when the industry's leaders were selling bisque dolls and their competition was selling celluloids.

Another type of doll made in the late 17th century and throughout the 18th was the wax doll. Wax was, of course, a very common substance in manufacturing in those days, in the era before modern plastics, clays and the like. Doll heads were made out of wax by sculpturing solid blocks of wax, or shaping wax over wooden "eggs," or by pressing wax into prepared molds. Pressing was the most inexpensive approach and dolls made in that manner were very satisfactory.

Competition increased in the doll business throughout the 18th century (1700-1800). There were no actual factories at that time, but more and more craftsmen and artisans were turning toward doll making, either fulltime or parttime. Some of them had assistants working for them, and their operations came very close to meriting the name of "factory." We all know the fairy tales about toymakers in the Black Forest of Bavaria. Doll makers of the 18th century were not too different than the pictures painted in fairy tales. Some made all sorts of toys as well as dolls. It was always a matter of what the public wanted. The local taste was the deciding factor because merchandise was sold where it was made — not shipped out for sale elsewhere. If the neighborhood wanted dolls, it got dolls. And, of course, rivalries developed in areas where the demand was strong. Each doll maker tried to make the best dolls at the best prices, or the most novel ones, or in some way draw the business away from his competitors. Even though the total quantity of dolls made during the 18th century was not overwhelming, there is extraordinary variety in materials, approaches, sizes, techniques, and in many other ways, showing the effort made to be original. If we group these craftsman or retail dolls with those of folk origin, the array of variety is really striking. And all this while the peddlers and small merchants were going along undercutting everybody, whittling their dolls from scrap wood and making plenty of sales.

The 18th century witnessed the coming of the modern type of toyshop. Before then, you could buy toys from the people who made them (if you knew where they were — there were no yellow pages), or from the street vendors. At the beginning of the 18th century there wasn't a single toyshop in all of Europe. By its close, every major town had them, in some cases many of them: shops which displayed toys made by many different artisans. These were retail shops. The owners were dealers, not craftsmen. And this innovation was the biggest step yet taken in the development of the doll industry. It encouraged more craftsmen to make toys. It also encouraged factories to turn their attention to toy manufacture. As toyshops increased, the number of doll makers increased in almost direct ratio. This brought more competition and, little by little, better dolls. It also brought greater experimentation with materials. One of these was papier mache. Manufacturers saw that papier mache could be used in the same way as wax, by pressing it into molds. It was a little less costly than wax, and the resulting doll head could take a paint job very well — since the main ingredient in papier mache was shredded or ground paper.

But at the same time that some manufacturers aimed toward the big mass market and strove to chop down their operating expenses, others took the direct opposite line of attack. There was still a discriminating element among the public which appreciated — and was willing to pay for — superbly made dolls, which could be shown in the home beside the finest furnishings and accessories. So they turned their attentions to making doll heads from porcelain (china). True porcelain was new to Europe in the 18th century, having been made previously in China and nowhere else. The Chinese had the "secret" of porcelain making — which involved a certain type of clay — and it took the westerners hundreds of years to crack that secret. Once they did, nearly everything that COULD be made from porcelain WAS made from it. Porcelain was not inexpensive but it had tremendous sales, right from the beginning. The first porcelain dolls started coming out around 1750 or shortly before. Initially they were very exclusive and hardly anyone but the social elite owned them. We do not know what they cost originally, but it was undoubtedly a steep sum. Quite likely the early manufacturers inflated the prices a bit, just to make these dolls more exclusive. Then, as always happens, the price started coming down, and the output increased. By about 1770 porcelain dolls were the rage all over Europe. They were not being made in every part of Europe, but where they were not manufactured they were imported. If you lived, for example, in Holland, you could get porcelain dolls that had been made in Germany or France. The import/export business was just as big in the 18th century as today, in terms of the geographical territory it covered. As more and more countries bought dolls, the doll making nations stepped up their output, and doll manufacturing very quickly boomed into a very lucrative enterprise. This ushered in more competition and more innovative ideas.

A list of the advances brought by the 19th century would be long. They came rapidly, one on the heels of another. Doll factories sprang up all over Europe, not to mention America and even as far away as Japan. Doll making in America was not as widespread in the 19th century as in many foreign countries, however. This was mainly because so many of the foreign producers exported their dolls to the U.S. With huge quantities of dolls coming into the country, the incentive for domestic manufacture was dampened. By around 1880 the flow of imported dolls to America had reached extraordinary proportions. Mostly they came from Germany, but a large percentage of these German dolls actually had French-made heads. The heads were made in France, wholesaled to German factories, then assembled into finished dolls and shipped over to America. The close of the 19th century also witnessed stepped-up importation of dolls from Japan. The Japanese of the 1880's and 1890's sought to become a great industrial power. They believed that their low costs of labor, much lower than of any western nation, would enable them to rule the export market. And they were very nearly correct. It was not long before Japanese dolls had surpassed those of Germany, in the volume with which they entered America. While the Japanese dolls did not aim for the high level of beauty attained by many of Germany's dolls, their prices were far lower. Thus they found a ready and eager market among the vast middle classes of Americans, for whom a German bisque doll was out of financial reach. Mail order companies and the variety chains such as Woolworth bought imported Japanese dolls by the boatload. Mainly the Japanese dolls were composition, celluloid, and chalk. There were also others of various miscellaneous materials.

At the beginning of the 19th century, the best dolls were those of china, as they had been for some years previously. But the styles in china dolls were changing. Manufacturers were looking for ways to speed production and trim costs, simply because the competition was so heavy. The objective among makers of china dolls was to continue turning out a high quality product but to increase the output and hold retail prices within line. One innovation was the pink lustre head. Painting the white porcelain head was time-consuming, yet a pure white head with enameled facial features looked garish. This problem was overcome by firing in the pink color, so that the head came out of the kiln with an overall pink color. Then, only the highlights or facial feature had to be painted, and a great deal of time was saved. In a way this also improved the quality of the product as it eliminated brush strokes and streakiness that could occur from hand painting. At the same time this was being done, some factories took the diametrically opposite approach and started selling parianware dolls, whose heads were pure white and unpainted. Walking into a toyshop in the early 1800's, the customer was greeted by quite a selection!

As competition grew more and more heated, it became obvious that the battle was not going to be won on the basis of the best-looking dolls, or the most inexpensive, or any of the old traditional ideals. The public was getting much more sophisticated and growing tired of the usual brand of doll, no matter how well put together. Around 1820 an important breakthrough came with the introduction of sleep eyes for dolls — that is, mounted eyes which operated by a weight mechanism and closed automatically when the doll was laid down on its back. This was a step toward greater realism and it made a great hit. Mostly the sleep eyes were of glass, and the glass could be colored to represent any color of eye. Though dolls with sleep eyes are still being manufactured today, they have experienced their ups and downs in the market. Following the American Civil War (1861-1865), there was a temporary decline in production of sleep eye dolls. Sleep eyes were treated as a passing novelty by the manufacturers, who did not realize that the public had come to expect this feature in good-quality dolls. When the demand was made known, sleep eyes began returning, and by 1890 were solidly entrenched throughout the industry. In the period when sleep eyes were on the decline, most fine dolls (china and bisque) had the same kind of glass eyes — but fixed in place.

Though they never became as widespread as sleep eye dolls, an even more significant innovation of the 19th century was mechanical dolls. These had their inception on a shaky trial basis around 1840 but did not reach anything approaching widespread sale until the mid 1850's. The early mechanicals were foreign-made, but just about as readily available in the U.S. as anywhere else. This was another step along the road to a doll that not only looked human but acted human. Once a motor was placed inside a doll, the possibilities were just about endless. The doll could then serve not only as an ornament or showpiece but a source of entertainment — and, even if not an actual plaything for children (which dolls were not at that stage), they could certainly keep a child amused. Since the battery-powered motor was still a long way off — electricity had not even been harnessed — early doll motors were of the spring-driven type. They were bulky and noisy, but they made the doll come alive and that was all that mattered. With a spring motor, a doll could walk or move its arms, or both. Even with a relatively small spring motor, the movement action could be sustained for at least 1½ minutes. Given a motor with a larger spring, it was possible to extend the action to 3, 4 or even 5 minutes, though actions longer than 4 minutes were rare. These motors operated by winding up the spring with a key. It was essentially the same principle as in a watch or clock, a principle known for hundreds of years but not put to its fullest use until the 19th century.

All kinds of mechanical dolls came out in the mid to later 1800's. They became a craze, to such a degree that nearly every manufacturer had to add at least a few to his line — even if he personally was not fond of mechanicals. The "walkers" were in the majority. Later, "creepers" came along, infant dolls that crept and crawled along the floor. The makers tried to get something new and different in the way of mechanical dolls on the market each year at Christmas. They even went so far as to make mechanical animal dolls: dogs, cats, elephants, etc. Mechanical dolls had a habit of springing their springs (thanks to owners who wound them too tightly), but the local watchmaker could repair them without much trouble. Mechanical dolls proved a boon in business for watch repairmen.

Among other headline-makers of the doll world, in the 19th century, was the Jenny Lind group. These dolls were modeled after the Swedish operatic soprano, who arrived in the U.S. in 1840 and made a very successful career here. The dolls bearing her likeness were just as successful and were sold throughout the world. They rank as the first true character dolls (dolls designed to represent a specific person) and opened the gates for future generations of "characters."

Musical dolls with music boxes set into the bases were made in the 1800's, as well as the first black dolls. This century also saw the introduction of swivel-head dolls, the aforementioned talking doll of Edison, and many other types, too numerous to mention. Every conceivable material was in use in the 19th century doll industry, all the way from luxurious porcelain to cloth, rags, goatskin, paper, and lithographed (printed) fabrics. It was a virtual war in the industry, to capture the public's fancy. By this time the market had grown so enormously that any doll which proved a "hit" — a best seller — could make a fabulous fortune for its innovator. It could be sold all over the world and then, if the maker chose to do so, the patent itself could be offered on the market for a high price.

Among the novelties of the 19th century was the two-headed doll. Though these are a bit too unusual for the tastes of some collectors, they do have a definite place in the history and development of dolls and can be quite valuable. The first ones were made under the name of Bartenstein and were of wax composition. Later they came out in various other materials. This was a swivel-head doll with a face on each side of the head. Sometimes the combination was crying/happy, or black/white. It was a clever concept and did especially well for play dolls, as it was like having two dolls to play with. Thanks to the continual turning of the head, the heads of two-faced dolls often parted company with their bodies.

Lithographed dolls came on the scene with a strong "press" and it looked as though they might be the doll of the future. Their success was not quite up to expectations, but these are interesting creations which many collectors find to their liking. Lithographed dolls had stiff cloth or canvas bodies, on which a design was printed — including the face. They could be manufactured very inexpensively as no molding or painting was necessary, and they were as durable as any cloth doll. Some were sold by mail, without the stuffing, for the purchaser to stuff and sew — and in that form they could be priced very low. By the early 1900's a few cereal companies were giving them away as premiums.

Celluloid dolls probably had the biggest impact of any inexpensive class of dolls on the late 19th/early 20th century market. This was another class of dolls manufactured virtually all over the world, with Japan ranking as the leader. Celluloids came with molded or cloth bodies, or, sometimes, the whole doll was celluloid and had movable arms and legs. Celluloid could be molded just like ceramic. It was tough and durable, took painting fairly well, and made for a doll that was not bad-looking — though not the equal of bisque or even composition heads. As the price was far less than bisque or composition, they had no trouble finding buyers. Millions upon millions of celluloids were sold, and they kept right on selling at a fast pace until after World War II. They would undoubtedly still be on the market, except that celluloid was banned for commercial use by the U.S. government. The substance was deemed too flammable and dangerous. The celluloid ban hit the doll industry hard, but fortunately by then a number of other materials had been introduced into doll making and the result was not disastrous.

In the early 20th century, bisque-head dolls were still coming into the U.S. in large numbers, mainly from Germany. These were the luxury dolls of their time, so far as the ordinary retail trade was concerned. Germany was the acknowledged king of the doll business in that age. It had built up a long reputation for fine dolls. American factories had the technical skills to make bisque heads, but competing against these foreign imports was a losing proposition. American manufacturers could not compete price wise with the old established German firms, and the public created a credibility gap between the young upstart firms and the imports. A doll from Germany was equivalent to a hat from Paris or caviar from Russia. Of course this did not hold true of non-bisque dolls. Anyone shopping for a lower-priced doll did not think about place of origin, so there was much more competition and activity in that direction.

With such a strong hold on the doll market, it seemed as though the Germans would reign supreme for all time, making bisques and sending them to countries throughout the globe. Fate was to direct otherwise. Just as manufacturers worked to develop a less costly substitute for china in the mid 1800's, they did the same to devise a satisfactory imitation of bisque. The result was the composition head (see entry on that subject). Many insiders in the doll market felt that composition stood a snowball's chance of toppling the bisque dynasty. But this is precisely what happened. World War I was partly responsible for this — it gave composition dolls just the boost they needed to reach the top. Germany's factories were churning out bisques in record numbers when the war clouds formed in 1914. The war destroyed, for the time being, Germany's export business with the United States — and also with its other main customer, France. The German doll makers found they could sell their products only to the domestic German and Austrian trade, a tiny fraction of the market they had been supplying. Even there the picture was bleak; with war raging, not too many Germans were buying dolls any more, or any kind of luxury merchandise. So the inevitable happened. One by one the smaller factories closed down. Even some of the big manufacturers closed their doors. Without bisques coming into the U.S., American makers of composition dolls had their golden opportunity. In the Christmas seasons of 1917, 1918, and 1919 (even after the war was over), composition dolls were the biggest sellers all over the U.S. Many of their buyers WOULD have bought bisque, if it was available. But, having purchased composition, most of them reached the conclusion that composition wasn't really bad at all. And it was less expensive than bisque in most cases (depending on the overall size of the doll and other factors). After the war, the Germans tried valiantly to recapture control of the international doll market. But whether they made dolls of bisque or composition, or any other substance, the odds were stacked against them. For several years following the war, there was general prejudice in America, England and some other nations against anything stamped "made in Germany." Additionally, the German economy became racked with runaway inflation in the 1920's. It proved impossible for the Germans to recoup their hold on the international doll industry. By the later 1920's they had given up, and went to manufacturing pressed tin mechanical toys of various kinds.

The biggest single phenomenon in the doll industry, during the first half of the 20th century, was the Shirley Temple doll — or rather Shirley Temple dolls, as they were made in every conceivable size, every material, and wearing every type of costume. Shirley Temples were not the first popular character or "star" dolls of the 20th century. Even the 19th century had such items with the Jenny Linds mentioned earlier. When the public media expanded in the late 19th and early 20th centuries, this was the signal for an onslaught of character dolls of all descriptions. First came the dolls based on comic strip characters. Comic strips started appearing in newspapers in the 1890's. At first there were just a few of them but they rapidly increased. All the favorite comic characters of this era were quickly transformed into dolls, with The Yellow Kid and Buster Brown heading the list. The Yellow Kid was ideal for a doll because he was baldheaded (no need for a wig) and wore only a long pajama-type shirt. Numerous celluloids of The Yellow Kid came out, and nobody complained — this time — about celluloid lacking class. It seemed to fit the subject perfectly! There were also Yellow Kids in chalk and other materials. These dolls were made mostly in the period from 1900 to 1910 and continued even afterward. The great comic artist Outcault was creator of both The Yellow Kid and Buster Brown — and very likely his royalties from dolls surpassed his income from doing the strips.

When motion pictures came along, the opportunity was presented for more character dolls. The first major movie star was Charlie Chaplin. Chaplin literally took the country by storm. In less than two years (1914-1916) he rose from an obscure vaudeville performer to the top celebrity in show business. Character merchandise of all kinds based on Charlie Chaplin flooded the market, including dolls. There were chalk Charlies, tin Charlies, cloth Charlies, Charlies that walked in his characteristic "tramp walk," and Charlies that twirled their walking stick just the way he did in the movies (or so the advertisements claimed). Most of them really weren't very well made. Some looked no more like their namesake than the man in the moon. But they sold — by the truckload. The doll industry firmly believed it would never again see anything to match Charlie. Just around the corner was an even bigger bombshell! By nothing more than coincidence, the clamor for Charlie Chaplin dolls was slowing down just as this new superstar was coming on the scene. When Chaplin started making serious films in the later 1920's, rather than slapstick comedies, it hurt the sales of his dolls. They declined year by year, falling off to a trickle by the mid-thirties. But then came Shirley Temple, and once again Hollywood provided a much-needed shot-in-the-arm for the doll business. With the depression in its deepest depths, neither dolls or anything else was selling very well. Shirley was the catalyst to get doll buyers back in the stores.

Nobody has yet counted the exact number of Shirley Temple dolls that were made and sold. Without any doubt, considering their long run in the market and sales volumes during the peak years (1936-1941), there were more Shirleys sold than any other doll in history. She was America's Sweetheart — a little golden-haired girl-next-door who sang, danced, and stole just about every scene in every film she made. Ronald Reagan was among her co-stars. So was another actor-turned-ploitician, George Murphy. There was a big difference between Shirley and Charlie Chaplin. The Shirley Temple dolls were cute and lovable and seemed much more realistic. In fact, they were irresistible for the little girls of America, who saw Shirley on the screen and then found these reasonable facsimiles of her at the toyshop. Millions were sold each year, and even such dire events as World War II and Shirley growing into adolescence did not halt their sales.

Shirley Temple did not prove as big a box office attraction as an adult, as she did at age 6-9. But Shirley Temple dolls had become an institution by then. By around 1950, some buyers of the dolls were probably not even aware of who Shirley Temple was. But they bought the dolls, and that was all that mattered.

Success of the Shirley Temple dolls inspired many other character and star dolls, right up to the present time. Not all of them have been successes by any means, but this is the basic thrust of the 1980's retail doll market: dolls which are recognizable to the child and its mother, which therefore have (presumably) a sales edge over nondescript dolls. In the post-Shirley Temple era — not that it ever really ended — the best selling doll representing a living person has been the Farrah Fawcett. Unlike Shirley, Farrah did not become a star until adulthood and all the Farrah dolls represent her as a grown lady.

Another market phenonama occurred when, in the early 1900's, Rose O'Neill, an actress, writer and artist, published a little story about "Kewpie," an elflike creature whose life was about love. The character soon became a doll, made by various companies in many forms, but whose impact on the children's doll market in the 1930's is undeniable. Millions of Kewpie dolls were manufactured and almost every little girl had or wanted one. Many of those original Kewpies survive in the collections of those now grown up collectors.

The comic character doll market of the 20th century was, as everyone knows, ruled by Walt Disney. It was to the credit of Disney and his associate, Kay Kamen, that the Disney character dolls were of consistently high quality, far better than the average dolls of their time. Disney would reject any samples that did not absolutely satisfy him — and he was a tough critic. He wanted every one of his dolls to precisely duplicate the character as it appeared in the comic strips and cartoons. The first Disney character doll was Mickey Mouse. Actually, Disney's first comic character was a rabbit. It wasn't successful, and his next idea was for Mickey Mouse — which he introduced in a cartoon short called "Steamboat Willie" in 1927. Mickey was a hit, and by 1930 Mickey Mouse character merchandise was on the market — not just dolls but wristwatches and many other things, which multiplied and multiplied over the years. Donald Duck came along — as a character and a doll — slightly later. Then there was Cinderella, Snow White, the Big Bad Wolf, and a long line of others. The success of the Disney dolls was partly due to the exposure they got in the media, but mostly because they were very well-made. The earlier versions of Mickey and Donald (not to mention Minnie and Daisy) are very valuable. These characters evolved over the years and ended up looking very different than Disney and his artists orginally conceived them. If you get a Mickey Mouse doll of 1930, you'll hardly recognize the millionaire mouse — and that's part of the fun of collecting Disneys, to trace their development from one stage to the next.

The current doll market is still heavily influenced by the comic and movie characters. A new avenue of collector interest opens every time a blockbuster movie creates a new American hero. The Star Wars and Star Trek sagas have produced a bevy of likenesses — of the stars and the monsters — whether in doll, figurine or stuffed animal form. Superman makes a super doll. And of course, the much beloved E.T. dollies are sure to be in prized collections in the years to come.

While artistically conceived dolls, such as the Madame Alexander's and Lenci's that are in current production, are the cornerstone of the collector market, there will always be the hobbyist who collects by cultural phenomena and historical value. These are the collectors that have created the Barbie market, which represents a fad of the 1950's turned into the multimillion dollar production of a realistic teenage ingenue. The little girls that kept their dolls through the sixties until now can turn an incredible profit on their original $3 purchase twenty years ago. There is a tremendous demand for Barbie, her friends and accessories which is not likely to diminish in the future. Current production Barbies are probably a good bet for future collector interest.

Every year doll manufacturing reaches new heights of technology. The collector of current productions has a large menu to choose from — from fads to highly realistic dolls to good old fashioned handmade works of art. The future should be as kind to doll hobbyists as the past 100 years have been — and there is certainly no sign of waning interest.

BEGINNING AND BUILDING A DOLL COLLECTION

If you become a doll collector you'll be in good company. Latest estimates place the doll collecting population in the U.S. at one million, easily ranking it as one of the most popular of all hobbies. Because of the huge scope of the doll collecting field, there are many benefits for the hobbyists, such as publications just for them and many clubs to join. Doll collecting groups and societies are scattered all across the country, within easy reach of just about everybody.

Also, the heavy demand for dolls brings more and more specimens out into the market, at antiques shops, shows, garage sales, flea markets and other sources. Collectors never need to wonder where to find dolls for sale. Instead they usually must think about how to specialize in one particular type of doll, since it would be impossible to buy everything that comes along.

Of course you can collect dolls strictly from the retail shops — currently made dolls sold at the manufacturer's list prices. Hundreds and hundreds of new dolls are available in many different types including character, novelty, and traditional dolls. There's nothing wrong with buying dolls off the current commercial market, since some of them are bound to end up climbing in value when they stop being produced. So this is a way of "investing" along with collecting. However for most hobbyists, confining a collection exclusively to the currently marketed dolls is unsatisfactory. There is a charm and appeal in the older dolls which, in the eyes of the average collector, is lacking from most new dolls. By adding older dolls to your collection, or concentrating on them exclusively, you can acquire many more different types. You can get unusual dolls and even, if your budget permits it, rarities. The older dolls are more historical and some of them — such as the chinas and bisques — surpass anything being manufactured today for sheer quality.

Fortunately the older dolls, even extremely old ones going back more than 100 years, are available for us to own and enjoy. Countless numbers of old dolls have perished through the years from breakage and other causes. But so many were manufactured, for so long a period of time, that an ample quantity has managed to survive for today's collector. Most antique shops have at least a few old dolls for sale. Some specialize in dolls and offer a selection of dozens or even hundreds. Then there are doll dealers (many of whom are collector/dealers) operating by mail, who issue lists and advertise in the hobbyist magazines. There are collector auctions at which you can find dolls and many other sources for good collectible specimens.

Yet even with all the old dolls passing through the market, going from the hands of dealers to collectors and vice-versa, there are still many awaiting discovery. America's attics continue to hold treasures untold in the way of antique dolls. Most dolls on the market have come out of attics, but the supply has been barely tapped. There are tens of thousands, possibly millions, more collectible dolls in attics right at this time. Either the owners are unaware of them, or do not know of their status as collectors' items. Dolls seem to have ended up lost in attics more often than anything else in the average home. They found their way to the attic when the little lady of the house got too old to play with them — or received a new doll and lost interest in the old one. They were just too nice to throw away, so what else could you do but "attic" them? The idea of course was that the grandchildren, when they came along, could inherit them. But often they were just forgotten. Or had gotten out of style by then, with the result that the grandkiddies received new dolls and those precious old ones just sat and sat, gathering cobwebs. Maybe you have an attic that hasn't been explored for a long while. If so, it could yield the beginnings of a doll collection!

Like any other hobby, doll collecting has its rarities and its high-priced stellar attractions: dolls which cost hundreds of dollars and some that even go into the four-digit category. This is understandable because of the large numbers of active buyers competing against each other for the better, scarcer specimens. If just 20 specimens of a particular doll are in existence and 5,000 collectors are anxious to own one, they will bid for it and boost the price up. Very possibly your local antiques shop has an early china doll in the show window — a museum-type doll that everybody who passes by falls in love with, even if they have no particular interest in old dolls. The pricetag reads $300 or $400 and that sends a chill along your spine when you think of YOURSELF collecting dolls. How could the hobby be adaptable to a week-by-week budget? Of course the answer is that this doll, or any other high priced specimens that you may see, is not representative of collectible dolls as a whole. There are rarities and super-value items in the hobby, but many others — well in the majority — which can be had for very moderate prices. Not all collectible dolls fall into the "antique" classification. Even of those which DO, many of them are fairly reasonably priced. The doll which is OLD — SCARCE — BEAUTIFULLY MADE — and FINELY PRESERVED is the exception, not the rule. Hobbyists with unlimited cash to spend WISH dolls fitting that description came along regularly. They simply don't. For every $300 or $400 doll on the open market, there are dozens priced at $10, $20 and $30. In fact you will often be spending LESS on an old collectible doll than you would pay for a brand new doll in the toyshop. This book will help to show you how the values vary from one kind of doll to the next. Chiefly, the higher priced specimens are from the ranks of china and bisque dolls. If you collect dolls of cloth, composition, celluloid, chalk, vinyl, plastic, rubber or any of numerous other substances, you will not encounter many of a high price. Just avoid china and bisque and you can adapt doll collecting to just about any budget! Of course, even with china and bisque it would be possible to collect on a tight budget, if you avoided "name" dolls and did some judicious saving-up between purchases. It's all up to you!

A collection needs a focal point, a core to build around. Nobody just buys "old dolls"; each hobbyist has his favorites, which he looks for and shuts his eyes to all other kinds. There isn't much choice but to do this, with the range of collectible dolls being so enormous. So the first step in becoming a collector is to decide what kind of dolls you're going to collect. The listings and pictures in this book should provide some help in that direction, if you don't already have a fairly good idea. Even if you DO already lean toward one kind of doll, it makes sense to take a good look at the whole market and see what's available. Quite possibly there are some types of dolls available that you are not even aware of. The best kind of dolls for you to collect are those which interest you and fall into your budgetary range.

If you're at a loss for ideas, you may get a good suggestion from your own childhood. The type of dolls that were your favorites, as a child, might be the perfect ones to collect. If doesn't matter if they're 10 years old, or 20, or 50. You will find them on the doll market and they're certain to bring back plenty of memories. You may in fact be surprised at the values attained by dolls that were just playthings to you. Or you may want to collect dolls that are the total opposites of the ones you owned as a child. If you were born in the age of vinyl and hard plastic, you might be fascinated by composition dolls. Or, by the same token, if you played with composition dolls as a child, bisque could be the collectible for you.

Of course there's no law that you have to specialize by substance. There are many other approaches to collecting. You might want to set your sights on Shirley Temple dolls or Disneys, or black dolls, or mechanicals. Don't say, "There aren't enough of them available for me to build a collection!" Unless you choose an EXTREMELY offbeat type or group of dolls, there will not only be ENOUGH to collect, but MORE than the average person could collect in a lifetime. Take 19th century mechanicals as an example. The non-collector is apt to believe that mechanical dolls were rarely made before 1900, and that he would need to do considerable shopping around before finding any. Actually, mechanicals were already about 60 years old by the time the year 1900 arrived, and thousands had been made in various parts of the world. This is true of almost any class of dolls you can think of: more of them — much more — were made than you're likely to guess. Even the antique chinas were made in far greater quantities than most people would guess.

Maybe you have a fondness for antiques as a whole and are drawn to antique dolls. This in itself, unless you break it down, is a large field. If you want to collect only dolls that qualify for the rating of "antique," the material does not matter as much as the age. Antique is technically defined as anything 100 years old or older. Thus, in 1983 any doll made in 1883 or before qualifies as an antique. In 1984 the 1884 dolls become antiques, and so on down the line. This sounds much simpler than it really is. In the first place, most dolls cannot be dated to the exact year of manufacture. If the doll falls somewhere in the 1880's, but cannot be pinned down any further, it may — or may not — deserve the designation of "antique." Quite truthfully, though, the majority of collectors are not too concerned about things like this. A doll does not go up 1¢ in price by becoming an "antique." Its value is governed by the quality, scarcity, and — above all — the popularity of that particular doll and the amount collectors are willing to pay for it. There might be a little extra charm attached to a doll which can genuinely be termed an antique, but it does nothing for the price. There are many non-antique dolls which sell for higher prices than many antique specimens. Classics like the first Shirley Temple doll and the early Mickey Mouses, only about 50 years old, sell for more than the majority of antique dolls. What this all boils down to is: if the age of a doll gives it added appeal for YOU, by all means set your sights on antique dolls. But don't fall under the "age obsession," to the point where you won't buy a doll unless you can determine for certain that it's over 100 years old. This is just plain foolishness! It does not harm a collection of antique dolls one bit, if some non-antique specimens are included. Everything is going to be an antique eventually, so what difference does it really make?

Another consideration, in choosing the type of dolls you want to collect, will probably be *space*. Dolls take up a bit more space than stamps or coins. That's fine because they also display much better — a doll collection becomes a focal point in the home and adds immeasurably to the interior decor. But if your display and/or storage area is limited, you will probably want to concentrate on small-size dolls — either that or buy rarities, which will give you a choice collection but one that does not increase too rapidly!

However you decide to specialize, you are sure to enjoy the company of your dolls, a benefit offered by few other hobbies. The following articles will help you to shape a meaningful collection as well as understand the market you are about to enter.

BUYING THROUGH ANTIQUE SHOPS

In the antique shops, you will generally find that the owners are fairly well versed on doll values and price their dolls in accordance with established market levels. This is not always the case, however. Once in a while you will come across a bargain buy in an antiques shop, which the owner simply missed by not taking the time to research the item and find its real value. He just relied on his own estimate of the value and his estimate proved to be wrong. Of course, he is still making a satisfactory profit on the doll. If he's selling a $100 doll for $40, that may seem like a giveway — but you can be sure he paid no more than $20 for it. He might actually have paid a good deal less, or received it in a consignment of miscellaneous items which cost him very little. So when you buy this doll, the dealer is just as pleased with the sale as you are with your low-priced bargain!

On the other hand, some dolls (as with merchandise in general) in antique shops are overpriced. This happens in the same way as underpricing. Instead of looking up the value, the dealer makes an estimate and his estimate is off the mark. But before you conclude that a doll is really overpriced, stop and make certain that you have correctly identified the doll; also, that the doll is in average condition for its age and type. If it happens to be a "mint" specimen, in the same condition as it came from the factory, it deserves to be priced higher than normal. It likewise deserves a higher than normal price if the dealer is also selling the original box. This gives it a special collector appeal, over and above the normal run of specimens, and the difference in market value could be 20%, 30% or even more. For a 19th century bisque or china doll in "mint" condition, a fair price could be double or even triple the normal "book" value. Whether the dealer can actually get this price is another matter. He may not be able to, if his clientele does not include any collectors who could afford the price! But he is certainly within his rights to ask a premium price.

What we're saying, basically, is that the approach to shopping in an antiques shop shouldn't be too different than shopping at a flea market or garage sale. You should not assume that the antiques dealer knows it all, and that his merchandise has passed careful scrutiny for damage, repairs, etc. Most of the dealers sell their things just as they come. You will find nicely preserved dolls in the antique shops, and others that are nothing but wrecks — along with all the various grades in between. There will be no labels on the dolls stating their condition. This is for you to determine by making your own inspection. A beginner may shudder at that prospect but it really isn't difficult — and after a while you are likely to enjoy that phase of doll-shopping more than any other. It has all the flavor of a treasure hunt in it, to find the dolls most worthy of buying. Please see the chapter on condition, in which this subject is discussed at greater length.

If you honestly believe that a dealer is charging too much for a doll that you'd like to buy, you could try to make an offer. The dealer might have had that doll in stock for months and be receptive to a sale at a slightly lower price. If you can get a discount of 10% or 20% this is a victory of no small proportions — anything greater is rare, since the dealers usually mark up their merchandise 100% and want to get a profit of at least 80% or 90% when the sale is acutally made. You cannot get something for half the marked price, in an antique shop, as this would (in most cases) amount to the dealer selling it for the price he paid — and no dealer will do that unless he's going out of business.

A little experience with the dealers in your area will reveal their pricing practices, and will also give you a clue about which ones are willing to bargain out a transaction. As you become a steady customer of any dealer, you will notice that he will probably be more willing to bend for you rather than for a stranger coming into his shop. Also, if you buy two or more dolls at the same time, you are in a better position for price consideration.

BUYING THROUGH LISTS AND ADVERTISEMENTS

Every doll collector wishes he lived within easy reach of several big, well-stocked doll shops, where he could browse and see all his purchases before making them. For most of us this is just a dream. The majority of doll collectors, no matter how they start out in the hobby, eventually reach the point of doing some buying by mail — or MOST of their buying, for that matter. The doll trade is geared toward mail-order. There might be some disadvantages in buying by mail, but one undeniable advantage is that it brings ALL the dealers closer to you, from Maine to California. The selection of dolls available to a mail-order buyer vastly exceeds the selection in any single shop or even a group of shops. If you have specialized "wants," or want rare dolls, there is really no choice but to get out the paper and pen and start corresponding. It might very well be that a dealer 3,000 miles from your home has that special doll you really want, and which would never show up for sale locally.

Most doll dealers issue lists. There's no problem finding the dealers: they advertise in the doll collecting and general hobbyist publications, which are available at most public libraries. In a publication such as ANTIQUE TRADER or HOBBIES you'll find dozens of ads from doll dealers who issue lists. You will also find detailed advertisements from dealers who print their "lists" right in the ad! Of course, some of these are not actually dealers but private collectors who want to sell duplicates from their collection. Buying through the mail is a way of doing business with them, which would probably be impossible otherwise. You would just not know about these people if you did not read their ads.

You will note that some dealers offer specialized lists, devoted to bisque dolls or character dolls or another particular kind. Others put out general lists on which a little of everything is offered. Unless you already have developed specific requirements as a collector, it may be wisest to send for all advertised lists. This gives you a feel of the market and you may make connections with some dealers who will become lifetime suppliers for you. The lists you receive from dealers will vary a great deal in other respects, too. Some will be lengthy and others brief. There will be unillustrated and illustrated lists. There will be classy-looking and very plain lists, and every type in-between. In any case they are all worth reading and great for future reference, too. Collectors never throw away a list, even if it contains nothing they choose to buy. They file it away, and build up a reference library in this fashion. Don't let yourself be fooled by the appearance of a list. The quality of the dolls is not necessarily parallel to the quality of the list. The impressiveness of a list is chiefly a matter of how deeply involved its compiler is in the doll business. Fulltime dealers with a nationwide clientele tend to put out impressive-looking lists. There are plenty of good dolls offered on these lists, but keep in mind that the overhead costs of an expensively-printed list are reflected in the prices of its merchandise. If the dealer is giving away his lists for free, he has to recoup this expense (which could run into thousands of dollars) by surcharging the prices of his dolls. On the other hand a small dealer, or a private collector selling duplicates from his collection, may have put very little cash outlay into the preparation of his list. Therefore he can sell his dolls at a lower cost and still achieve the same margin of profit as the big dealer. It doesn't work this way 100% of the time. You will occasionally get bargains from the big dealers. And the big dealers have a more diversified stock to choose from. But it's well to keep in mind, before tossing out a list that doesn't have much eye-appeal. Sometimes you will find the exact same doll in the same condition on two different lists. The price is apt to be different — maybe by as much as 20% or 30%. The more lists you receive, the better you will be able to see what is available in the market and *who to buy from.* Always read lists through from cover to cover. Often they're put together in a rush and the items are not properly grouped or alphabetized. You could miss something by skimming.

You will also discover in reading dealers' lists that they vary in terms of description. Some doll dealers are very meticulous in their descriptions, telling you everything you could possibly want to know about each doll on their list. Others — probably to save space and printing costs — use briefer descriptions, while some describe their dolls with nothing more than the manufacturer's name, the material, a reference to someone's book, and a price! They assume that you own all the hobby's reference books and can look up anything. Even if that was the case, the lack of information about *their particular specimen* would make you hesitate before sending in an order. Nothing is quite as discouraging — so far as the doll hobbyist is concerned — as a list on which no defects are mentioned. Obviously, the dolls cannot all be in perfect condition; no large group of collector dolls ever is. When defects are not mentioned for any doll, it gives the impression that ALL OF THEM are defective and that the dealer just chose not to reveal this fact! When you find defects pointed out on a list, this is definitely a confidence-builder. You can order from that dealer with some measure of assurance that the doll you receive will meet your satisfaction.

Do not look for amazing bargains on doll lists, such as dolls selling for ½ of the normal retail value. These occur very infrequently. The people who put out lists are very knowledgable about dolls and their values, being either dealers or experienced collectors. When they price a doll below its usual market value, it's because they want to make a fast sale, not because they've just guessed on the price. Even so, the discount will likely be in the range of 20% or so, which is attractive but not earth-shattering. Before assuming that the price truly does represent a discount, read the description carefully for any mention of defects. Unfortunately some dealers (quite a few, actually) are in the practice of using abbreviations on their list, to save space. This is fine if the reader is familiar with the abbreviations used by that particular dealer, but customers receiving his list for the first time may be bewildered. Look near the front of the list for a table of explanations of abbreviations. Since each dealer has his own way of making up abbreviations, do not apply the translations of one dealer to the list of another!

Try to picture how the doll would look and whether you would be satisfied with it. If a minimum of description is provided, you could get a very big — and most unlikely unpleasant — surprise when receiving the doll. When a description states nothing more than "Mickey Mouse, 8 inches," you could be getting vinyl, celluloid, cloth or who-knows-what. It could be 1940's or 1980's. There is really no way of knowing, from such a terse description, whether or not you want the doll. Why any dealers or collector/dealers put out such lists is a mystery. It can't be too profitable to mail out a list which discourages people from buying from it.

At the front of the list there should be a notice of the seller's terms. Mainly these "terms of sale" are similar from one dealer to the next. They tell you how much postage to add, and they remind residents of the state to add sales tax and other routine things of that nature. However they do vary in one major respect. Some dealers permit you to return dolls for any reason, even if there is no error in the description. Others do not mention anything about return privileges in their "terms of sale." When nothing is mentioned, you have to presume that all dolls are sold "as is" and no returns are honored — which would be a good reason for declining to do business with that dealer. If the "terms of sale" include anything that looks like a gimmick — such as, "permission to return items must be obtained by phone" — we would likewise advise against ordering from that dealer. There are so many reliable list-issuing dealers that you needn't do business with the very few questionable ones. The great majority of doll dealers are interested in selling to you TOMORROW as well as TODAY. They want to get repeat business from each of their customers, and they realize that repeat business depends on keeping the customer satisfied (and feeling secure).

When a dealer is selling dolls "as is, no returns," it gives the impression (usually correct) that they contain unmentioned defects, or are not correctly identified. In many cases such lists are put out by people who have only borderline doll knowledge and equally borderline business skills. They want to sell but don't know how to go about it.

If a list states "insurance extra," it is worthwhile to pay the additional charge. There is seldom any problem with loss or breakage in the mails, but the possibility exists. If you decline to pay for insurance, the dealer will probably not make good on the loss. When you receive a doll ordered from a list, examine it promptly. Don't put it aside for future inspection as the period for making returns will expire in the meantime. If you find that the doll was damaged in transit, stop unpacking as soon as the damage is noticed. Take the doll and the carton to the post office and fill out an insurance claim. This must be done by the recipient of a damaged parcel, since the recipient has the evidence. You can usually distinguish between damage that occurred in transit, and damage which existed beforehand, by the condition of the shipping carton. However, it is possible that a poorly-packed bisque or china head COULD break in transit without any signs of injury to the carton. This could happen if the head is not properly cushioned and the box is dropped on the street or on a concrete floor. If in doubt about whether to file a postal claim, FILE IT. If the dealer shipped you a damaged doll which was supposed to be in good condition, he's in the wrong.

BUYING THROUGH AUCTIONS

One of the most exciting and potentially lucrative ways to acquire new dolls is by buying through auctions. Whether signaling the auctioneer by raising your little finger or submitting a sealed bid through the mail, an auction offers you the opportunity to obtain dolls the way the dealers do, and often at a considerable savings over retail price. Thousands of dolls change hands every year at auctions and the opportunity to make a meaningful purchase is great for the informed buyer.

Many doll auctions are run by mail, with no in-house bidding. There are obvious advantages and disadvantages to this kind of procedure. When dealing by the mail, a national inventory is at your disposal. Sellers ship their dolls from all over the country to Kansas or New York or wherever the auction is being held. The management team then arranges the inventory into "lots" which are the parcels on which to be bid. These lots contain one or more dolls and whatever accessories and wardrobe that are included in the package. A catalogue is drawn up from photographs and descriptions of the lots. A good catalogue pictures most, if not all of the inventory. Some publications are quite professional and beautiful — works of art in themselves. These are very helpful to the prospective bidder and instill a sense of confidence in the rapidly growing practice of bidding by mail. The more information about the doll and its condition, the better judgement you can make about the top dollar figure you are willing to bid. If you are limited in the amount you can spend, some auctioneers will extend the service of limiting the purchase amount. For example, you could send in bids that total up to $500, but stipulate that you want to spend only $300. The auctioneer would automatically void any bids exceeding that sum. They offer this because they want your business and this practice increases your chances of a successful bid.

Read the catalogue carefully and select the dolls that intrigue you and will fit into your collection. After carefully reviewing your bid, and realizing that if you have the highest amount in the competition you have committed yourself to the purchase, mail it to the sellers. The auctioneers will invoice the winners after the final closing date of the sale.

After payment is received, the doll or dolls are mailed out. You can sometimes do very well buying dolls by auction. It all depends on how the sale is being operated and (of course) the competition against you, for the lots on which you're bidding. The method by which the sale is operated makes a big difference. Some sales are unreserved, which means the dolls are sold to the highest bidder regardless of the amount (with the exception of ridiculously low bids, of course). If you bid $50 on a $100 doll and nobody else bids anything, you would get the doll for ½ its value. Bargains of this sort at unreserved sales are not uncommon. However not all sales are unreserved. In many cases the auctioneer works with "minimum bids," either stated in the list or kept confidential. If a lot does not reach its minimum bid or minimum selling price, it is withdrawn. In this kind of sale there are no big bargains because all the minimum bids are scaled to at least 70% or 80% of the retail value.

Like buying through the mail order dealers, your disadvantage is the inability to personally examine the dolls on which you are bidding. Sometimes there are raised expectations and disappointments. As always, pay close attention to the terms of the sale. Many auction sales are final.

Auctioning through the mail removes an emotional trap that beginners often fall into. The excitement and competition of the in-house auction sometimes causes the bidding to go a little crazy and drives the price above the bargain level. You must have a clear idea of the bottom line and put a ceiling on your bids. But you will find you enjoy the company of other enthusiasts and going to auctions will become an important part of your hobby.

The best source for finding auctions will be your local newspaper. Try looking under the art and antique section for a listing of auctions. Most of these will be estate auctions and will only list several of the larger articles that will be on sale. Sales of antique or gift shop inventories that are closing down are not very frequent, but offer great potential for the doll collector. Most small auctions won't have a catalog, but it is worth finding out if they do since these can be a good source of information for the prospective bidder. Usually, you will run into the same problem that you can with mail order: the information will be insufficient. But still, the catalog could give you a clue to what type of dolls are available and give you enough information so you could determine whether you'll want to attend the sale. The major auction houses especially those which specialize in art objects and have sold many dolls in the past will list more complete data. Some of the auctions you can attend will have a variety of objects for sale. You may feel that your chances for winning a bid are practically non-existent when there are few dolls available. But look at it this way — there will probably be very few people present who are interested in buying the dolls.

Before the bidding starts, there will be a presale exhibit. Sometimes, this occurs the day before the sale, but arriving early on the day of the sale should give you enough time. Be sure to go prepared to a presale with notepad, pencil, and a reliable price guide. If you see an item which interests you, take your time to examine it with great care. Notice the condition and any identification marks. You will be allowed to handle any objects for sale, so check for the incised trademark or model number.

After you have noted the marks, condition and determined an accurate measurement consult a reliable price guide. Remember: there are many variations of some dolls. You need to determine exactly which variation you're considering to buy. The difference in value can be considerable. Then, you need to determine just how much you are intending to bid. How much you are willing to pay for a piece will depend on how eager you are to own a particular piece, how long you've been looking for it and how likely you are to find it again. If you want to bid under book price, that's fine. It can be exciting to purchase a fine doll at a bargain, but you shouldn't feel foolish if you're willing to bid over book price. If it's a difficult doll to locate, you may find that when the next opportunity arrives to buy it the book price will have increased beyond the price for which it sold. Whatever you decide on for your highest bid depends on your circumstances, the scarcity of the piece, and your willingness to spend.

Once you've decided on your highest bid for a particular piece, jot it down and plan to stick with this figure regardless of your feelings later on. This will prevent any errors or indiscretion on your part during the heat of competitive bidding. And don't think you can't become infected with the fever of competition. Auctioneers depend on this competitiveness of bidders to drive the prices up. Even the most experienced bidders succumb to their feelings at the moment if they don't set up limitations beforehand and stick to them. Also, you should do this for every piece you intend to bid for and not let yourself bid for any item which you did not include in your notepad. During the bidding, an item may look much more attractive to you or you may suddenly feel that you overlooked the perfect piece. This is not too likely, and besides, you won't really know what you're bidding on.

Quite often, dolls can be purchased at bargain prices at auctions, but there are many cases of pieces selling well above the market price. It all depends on a variety of circumstances. If the sale is big, chances are that the dolls will sell for more because collectors and dealers are more likely to be present.

But don't let the presence of numerous dealers discourage you from bidding. You may very well outbid the dealers and without overextending your plans. Most dealers will drop out of the bidding when 50% of the retail market value is reached. Since the dealer must leave himself enough margin to cover his costs and still make a profit, he needs to purchase his pieces well below the retail price. Occasionally, you will see a dealer bid higher than this. In such cases, the dealer usually has a customer who has authorized him to purchase the piece at a certain price or he has a waiting customer he knows he can sell the piece to immediately at a profit. It is difficult to tell the dealers apart from the crowd at first, but after 20 or more sales, you'll be able to pick them out easily. The auctioneer often reserves the front seats for dealers. They will bid cooly, showing no signs of emotion regardless as to whether they win the bid or not.

Bidding against collectors can present a problem, depending on how many collectors are present and their circumstances. Collectors are often content to pay 80% of the retail price for a piece. If it is a difficult piece to acquire and more than one wants it badly enough, they will sometimes offer prices higher than the market level. For some collectors, money is of no concern and they will go as high as necessary to outbid everyone else. Others may have been looking for a particular piece for a long time and be prepared to pay high for it. Sometimes pieces that are not rare or even scarce sell for well above market price, because the bidders just couldn't stand to lose the bid. Don't let yourself fall into this trap. You'll only regret it later. So, be very cautious and prepared to drop out of the bidding against avid collectors.

By educating yourself about the type of collection you have chosen, you expand your abilities to buy and sell in a variety of market settings with confidence and success. The auction is, perhaps, the most interesting and satisfying of these settings.

CONDITION

When considering the age, material, rarity, design and other factors that determine value do not overlook condition — the physical preservation of the doll. In most cases, condition is the most important factor in determining selling price. A damaged doll which would be worth $200 if well preserved might bring only $20 or $30. On the other hand an absolutely mint specimen of a $200 doll could realize $400, $500 or even more. The older, scarcer dolls are more subject to price-influence by condition, because they exist today in so many varying grades of condition. But even a modern doll which would be worth no more than $4 or $5 in "mint" will fluctuate in value depending on the condition.

The best advice for a beginning collector is: learn to become conscious of condition. Examine every doll you contemplate buying. Satisfy yourself that the doll is in acceptable condition. If the doll is not good condition, but you still wish to purchase it (perhaps because of rarity), be sure that the price is in line with its condition. Generally speaking, damaged dolls (which includes repaired, repainted, etc.) are not a very attractive investment unless you can get them for next to nothing. Over the years, the values of dolls in good condition rise appreciably faster than the values of "seconds," which generally remain stalled or even backslide. Yes, they can and do go down — simply because collectors become more discriminating as the years go by, and the market for damaged dolls gets thinner and thinner.

On the other hand, it is unreasonable to expect antique dolls, and dolls of the early 20th century, to be in perfect mint state. Some mint specimens are in existence and they come through the market occasionally. The vast majority of dolls in "collector condition" (sufficiently well preserved to appeal to nearly all collectors) are not mint, but deviate from mint in one way or another. This may be the result of handling, of being played with by children, or the effects of age and natural deterioration (depending on the substance from which the doll is made). Even if a doll looks perfect at first glance, a closer inspection is apt to reveal some minor damage, deterioration, or intentional change that has occurred from the original appearance. Doll collectors learn to live with these minor blemishes. Perfection would be great — but how many collectors' items, of any nature, are really perfectly preserved? If a doll is 100 years old it has likely passed through the hands of half a dozen owners and traveled across the country and back. So-called show dolls, made to be displayed rather than played with by children, tend to be (naturally) found in a better grade of preservation than play dolls. Even with show dolls, however, some allowance has to be made for the effects of age. The original owners of these dolls, back in the 1800's, did not treat them quite the same as a 1980's collector treats dolls. They were prized possessions, of course, and the owners were proud of them. But they were not as attentive to preservation as we are: and why should they really have been, when the dolls were not antiques in those days but just merchandise? One mistake they made was to display dolls in direct sunlight. They LOOKED for sunny corners of a room to displays dolls — just the opposite of what we do — as the light brought out every fine detail. Many of these dolls date before the era of modern home lighting, so they could really be enjoyed only in the daytime. You will encounter many show dolls whose facial features, skin tone and clothing are partially bleached out from long exposure to direct sunlight. This is so common that it is not considered a serious defect. Hardly anybody kept these dolls in boxes — few were even sold in boxes in the 1800's. If you owned a doll you wanted to see it and enjoy it and this of course invited damage and deterioration. If the doll was placed on a low shelf or other accessible place, the family's pet might get to it. Or the children might start playing with it. This is what brought play-type dolls on the market: the fact that children liked to play with show dolls. There could be accidents of various kinds. Some dolls show evidence of staining, possibly caused by leaky roofs or leaking water pipes. Many dolls have light scratches on the head, arms, and hands. You will find minor snags or rips on the costuming. While it would be much nicer if these defects were not present, they are not regarded as serious and they do not detract from the value. They are merely the little barriers that separate the doll from a MINT ranking.

So, essentially, the collector must develop a sensible attitude about condition: not ignoring it, but not expecting the impossible.

You should not be too concerned if you overlook some very minor blemishes before buying a doll. The object in making an inspection is to seek out any major damage — damage which, if present, would drop the doll into a lower condition category and reduce its price.

Certain kinds of damage can be looked for on virtually all old dolls. Other types are peculiar to dolls of a particular type. The type of doll to be examined — in a dealer's shop or prior to an auction sale — determines what sort of damage to look for. At first there is the initial visual inspection: looking at the doll in the shop window or on the shelf inside, before touching it. Many times you can make a "NO" decision with this initial visual inspection, but it's dangerous to make a "YES" decision. If a doll is obviously defective, just from looking at it, you can bypass it without investigating further. But even this initial visual inspection can be tricky. What happens — unless you train yourself not to LET it happen — is that you notice the positive qualities without noticing the negative aspects. You see that the doll is very old, a museum piece, with contemporary costuming — and that voice inside you says, "Buy it." Don't trust your first impression. Don't fall victim to love at first sight. It's disappointing for any collector to find a doll which looks fabulous — which he would truly like to own — then discover that some components are missing or that other serious damage is present. This is a fact of the doll collector's life. You just can't win them all, and that's what makes the successes so sweet!

Generally speaking the worst damage that can befall a doll is:

a) broken head.
b) missing parts, such as arms, legs, hands.

Obviously, some types of dolls are very vulnerable to broken heads; others are moderately vulnerable; while some (such as wooden heads) hardly ever actually break, though they can suffer damage of various other kinds. Hollow-head dolls made of ceramic substances are the most prone to breakage. These include — sadly — the two most desirable of all varieties of dolls, china and bisque. Also in this category are parian heads, stoneware, and even (though it cannot be called ceramic) composition. Composition heads are a little tougher than ceramic but they do break. Breakage of heads is the primary cause of reduction in the doll population. Most of the early owners automatically discarded a doll when the head broke, though they may not have discarded one with an arm or leg missing. If 200 specimens still exist of a doll originally manufactured in 500 specimens, you can be pretty sure that nearly ALL the 300 "extinct" ones suffered broken heads. Actually the survival rate is lower than this, on most china and bisque dolls from the 19th and early 20th century. It is closer to 1-in-10 still in existence, and in some cases probably 1-in-20 or 1-in-50. This shows you how breakable the heads were — and still are!

After these dolls started drifting into the realm of collectors' items, they received better care. But occasionally a head would still break. By then, the owners were not so willing to just throw them out. If the break was not really major, they glued the pieces back together. Thus, you will find some bisque and china (and even composition) dolls with repaired heads. If the repair job is fairly decent it may be hard to notice. This also depends on where and how the break occurred. If breakage occurred across the face, the repair will probably be rather easy to detect. If it occurred to the back of the head, it will be hidden by the doll's wig. For some reason, breakage to the back of the head and the top of the head is more common than breakage to the face. You have to examine the whole head for signs of repair. This means lifting up or possibly even removing the wig. (A word to beginners: most bisque dolls have a hole at the top of the head. They were made that way. It isn't damage!)

A doll with a repaired head is not worthless. The value may drop by 30%, 40% or more, depending on the extent and appearance of the repair, but it will not be worthless UNLESS the value for good condition (unbroken, unrepaired) is only in the $10 range. Things are worse if breakage has occurred and the repair is only partial, with a piece or pieces missing. This is rather common. If the head shattered, one or two of the small pieces might have gotten lost. Or the owner, faced with numerous small pieces to deal with, could not solve the problem of reconstructing the head. So he replaced the pieces that went into place and forgot about the others. A doll with missing head pieces is worth less than one with a fully repaired (complete) head.

You will also find some dolls with cracked heads. These dolls dropped but the head did not completely break. It merely cracked. There may be a single long crack running across the whole head, or a network of fine cracks going in various directions. A cracked head resembles a broken head which has been repaired and it may be difficult to tell them apart. If there are no visible traces of glue along the crack, it's usually taken to be a cracked head rather than a mended break. This is not necessarily true, however, as an expertly executed repair will leave no signs of glue. Of course a doll with a cracked head is undesirable. If the crack is small and the doll is rare, it will still have some collector value, but otherwise there is not likely to be any interest in it. One problem with cracked-head dolls is that they sometimes break apart at the slightest handling.

Missing components will be easily noticed on most dolls. Fully jointed dolls are the most apt to have missing parts, while non-jointed dolls are hardly ever incomplete. A joint, though it gives the doll movement and added appeal, is an automatic weak point. The children who played with these dolls 50-100 years ago sometimes exercised the joints too much or put pressure on them, and in time they just gave away. While doll manufacturers wanted the reputation of making sturdy dolls, it was not to their advantage for dolls to last forever. When a doll broke, a new one was usually purchased, and this was lucrative for the industry. Therefore they did not go to any great lengths in making the joints secure or invulnerable to damage. If a youngster got a year's worth of play out of a play doll, that was considered par for the course. The next Christmas season would bring new dolls to the shops and the child would probably want a new one anyway — whether last year's was still intact or not.

Missing components also include other things besides arms and legs. If the head is missing, you don't have a doll anymore, regardless of the body's state of preservation. If the body is all bisque, in good condition, and especially if the clothing is contemporary with it, it will have value. A suitable head can always be married up with it, since there are loose bodyless heads on the doll market, just as there are headless bodies. Finding the head that really belongs with that particular doll is just about an impossibility, but if the match is reasonable — good proportion, same skin tone, same approximate era of manufacture — you will have a collectible doll. But if you're going to buy a headless body, we would suggest that you PREVIOUSLY have lined up a source of supply for a head. Otherwise it may take a long time finding a satisfactory match-up. If an antiques shop is selling headless bodies and bodyless heads, this is probably NOT the place to do your matching, even though it seems very convenient. Chances are, if the dealer had any heads and bodies which would make a good match, he would have matched them himself. This would mean a better sale. If he has a head worth $60 alone and a body worth $40 alone, he would be anxious to match them and obtain a doll worth (perhaps) $150. The very fact that he's selling loose heads and bodies shows that he's abandoned hope of matching them. But another dealer down the street might have the perfect body for that dealer's bodyless head!

If an arm or leg is missing you will not have an easy time finding a match for the remaining one. It's really easier to replace a head, since a doll has only one head and it need not perfectly match the manufacturer's version. Of course in a case like this you could remove the remaining arm or leg and replace both of them. The larger specialized doll dealers (not general antiques shops) carry quite a supply of loose arms, legs and other doll components. They rescue these from "junk" dolls, and they build up a "spare parts bank." The specialist dealers will also perform the attachment operation for you, at a slight additional charge. A beginner is well advised to use their services, especially if the doll in question is valuable. Just getting the piece in place is not the whole objective. It must be perfectly aligned and attached by the same method as the other arm or leg, otherwise it will be shorter or longer or not operate in the same way.

A walking or talking doll might be lacking its interior mechanism or a portion of it. This is very common as the children of yesteryear were just as curious as those of today, about "what makes things work." They took the mechanism apart and — need we tell you? — were not successful getting them back together again, if they made the effort at all. So the walking doll turned into a standing doll, and the talker went silent. They can be restored by a competent doll repairer, but the cost is not low. Unless you can buy such a doll at a liberal discount from the usual value, you will end up spending more than in buying a specimen which is already intact and working. Of course there is no crime owning and displaying non-working walkers and talkers. The majority of those in existence, and even some in prestigious collections (including musuems), are not working. Given the choice between a specimen in outwardly fine condition ("display condition") which does not work, and a battered one which works, most collectors would prefer the former.

If the doll is lacking its wig, this is not considered a defect. The philosophy among collectors is that dolls (except those with rooted hair) were intended to have their wigs switched and replaced. In the case of most bisque dolls from the period 1870-1920 it is virtually impossible to say that any single wig is the "correct" one for that doll. Most of these dolls were assembled, wigged and clothed at points far removed from the place of manufacture. A factory in France would (for example) ship heads into Germany, to the doll companies there. None of the heads would have wigs on them. It then became the choice of the German company to select wig styles from its supply of wigs. If there were 3,000 identical heads coming in, it might choose to make 1,000 blonds, 1,000 brunettes and 1,000 redheads. Often the choice of wig color was determined by the market to which the dolls were destined: blond for Scandinavia, dark for southern Europe and Latin America, red for Great Britain. Because of the ethnic mixtures in the U.S., dolls with all types of wigs ended up here. The wig is certainly the easiest component to replace on any doll. Doll wigs are available just about anywhere that dolls are sold — and even some places where they aren't. Replacement wigs of real human hair are not cheap, but if you have a fine china or bisque doll with a bald dome, you can't very well display it as a Kojak. In short, if you find a good doll at a fair price and it really appeals to you, do not hesitate to buy it because the wig is missing. This is a problem you can solve. Every doll collector does some "wigging" sooner or later. Selecting and installing wigs becomes, for some doll enthusiasts, one of the enjoyable sidelines of this hobby.

When discussing missing components, wigs have to be classified as non-integral parts of dolls. They were sold with the doll originally but not actually made with it (except for rooted hair wigs). There are many other doll accessories which also rank as non-integral. They came with the doll when its original purchaser bought it, but were "add-ons," not part of the doll itself. These of course are quite often missing, since they could become detached easily or, in some cases, were already separate (such as a handbag that the doll carried). The doll's clothing comes under the heading of non-integral accessories. A fine old doll in its original clothing is what every collector wants. Some dolls, even some going back as far as the antique period (pre-1883), do still exist in their original outfits. But let's be realistic about this. Just as wigs have been changed, clothes have been changed, too. There has been much more clothes-changing than many collectors think — or would like to believe. A great deal of early doll outfits exist, but probably less than 10% of them are adorning the dolls with which they were sold. Except in cases where documentation is available (and these are rare), there is no sure way of knowing how a doll was dressed when it left the manufacturer's hands. Clues are sometimes turned up: if two or more antique dolls are found wearing the same costume, this is a fairly safe indication that it represents the original dress. But most times there is just no way of knowing, and, truthfully, what difference does it make? A serious collector will never reject a fine doll just because its clothing MAY not be original. He's in the habit of ASSUMING that the clothing is not original. Clothing, like other doll accessories, has to be judged on its merits and suitability, not on whether it can be proved to be original. To rank as desirable, the clothing should give the suggestion of being approximately contemporary with the doll (don't try to pin it down TOO closely). It should suit the doll in terms of age — a doll representing a three year old should not be wearing a ten year old's clothing. It should also suit the doll in terms of sex, but this is not as simple as it sounds. Most infant dolls, and even many post-infant dolls, can be dressed to represent either sex. They were not designed with either boy or girl in mind. However with the dolls representing older children, there was usually an effort to present them either as boys or girls. This will usually be apparent by the hair style, with dolls that have molded or rooted hair. But when a doll originally wore a wig, and the wig is now missing, it may be difficult to judge whether it was intended as a boy or girl. The rule of thumb to follow is: if the doll does not appear to lean toward boy or girl, it is suitable dressed as either — and you can redress it as the opposite sex without any qualms. Sometimes (not too often) you will run across a doll which almost certainly was intended to be a boy, but is dressed as a girl (or vice-versa). In that case you will surely want to redress it, and the cost of the redressing has to be figured in the price. It's true that most dolls in the past 150 years have been designed as girls, but there have been more boy dolls than you might imagine.

The clothing should not be overly faded or tattered. Nevertheless, even if it is, it can be replaced without too much expense. So this should not deter you from buying a fine old doll in well preserved condition. The condition of the doll is much more important than the condition of the clothing.

Accessories such as parasols, bonnets, nursing bottles or anything else with which the doll was originally marketed are likely to be missing. You will not probably be aware of this unless you are familiar with the doll, since a missing accessory seldom leaves behind any trace. Do, however, examine the doll's hands for a possible clue to a missing accessory. If the two hands are not identical to each other — if one appears to be shaped for gripping something while the other isn't — quite likely it originally held an accessory. Such dolls are certainly collectible without the accessory, but the value is not quite as high. There is always the chance that the item can be replaced, from the stock of a specialist dealer. Even if it isn't the original intended for that doll, it will be better for display purposes to have the accessory.

If a doll was sold in a suitcase, which started to become a popular approach in the 1930's and continued thereafter, its value without the suitcase will be at least 30% less and sometimes a sharper discount. When the suitcase is lacking, so are the additional accessories it contained. These may have included a handbag, change of clothing, extra pair of shoes, cosmetics, jewelry, play money, and other material. It is usually difficult to find a specimen in which ALL of the accessories are present, if the doll was sold with a great many small accessories.

There are various other kinds of defects which may be present with old dolls — or collector dolls of any age, for that matter. Their influence on the value varies. Repainting of any kind is a serious defect. Fortunately it is not common. The situation with repainted dolls is akin to that of repainted mechanical banks and most other collectibles. Hobbyists are repulsed by repaintings. Even if a doll is in perfect physical condition in terms of being free from cracks and missing parts, a repainting throws it into the undesirable category. With this kind of philosophy prevailing today, it is unthinkable that any doll will ever again be repainted! The repaintings found on the market are mostly of early vintage, going back 30, 40 or more years. Though it's impossible to say who was responsible for them, it's a fairly safe bet — in most cases — that the pioneer doll dealers were the culprits. In the earlier days of doll dealing, when the hobby was a fraction of its present size and not nearly as sophisticated, dealers worked quite a bit on their dolls before offering them to collectors. They would buy dolls in a really bad state of preservation, getting them for next to nothing, and try to refurbish them to raise the sales potential. This still goes on to a certain extent and is perfectly legitimate, but dealers are no longer repainting any dolls. Reclothing is one thing; repainting is another! It may be difficult for a beginner to recognize repaintings, especially if the work has been well done. Usually, repainting was NOT done to improve the colors of a faded doll, but rather to hide scratches and flaking. Sometimes the object was to cover a stained area. If the scratches were deep, several coats of paint are likely to have been applied, and these jobs are more easily noticed; the colors are just too thick and "heavy." Some repaintings consisted of dipping the whole head (minus the wig, of course) in a vat of paint, then, after drying, repainting the facial features as necessary. The eyes were removed before this procedure and remounted later. The trouble that went into these operations could have all been saved, if the individuals knew how future generations of collectors would feel about repainting. It was not only wasted effort, it literally destroyed the values of many, many dolls — and it cannot be reversed. Once a repainting has been carried out, there is no going back. The collector value of the doll cannot be reclaimed.

A doll's eyes are an important feature. If the eyes are not right, for one reason or another, the doll is not worth its full retail value. Obviously the worst thing that can happen with the eyes is for them to be missing. You will occasionally find fixed-eye dolls in which the eyes are missing, but it is more commonplace with sleep eyes. Fixed eyes were glued in place while sleep eyes were installed with tiny pins at either side of the eye; they could not be glued as this would prevent the opening and closing function. It was not difficult for the pins to get loose over many months or years of playing with the doll. Also, as stated earlier in connection with walkers and talkers, children sometimes could not contain their curiosity about doll mechanism and took apart the sleeping eyes to find out what made them tick. You might think that fixed eyes would have always lasted forever. They, too, suffered from the rigors of hard play. They weren't too hard to poke out with a well-directed finger! Missing eyes can be replaced, but it may be difficult to achieve a perfect match with the original. If sleep eyes are present but not operating (not opening and closing), they are either stuck or — more likely — the weight inside the head is missing. Generally the eyes were both attached to a single weight, set between them and fixed with a thin metal bar. This is a very simple mechanism and without tampering could last a thousand years — but some of them were abused and the weight came free. There is no problem replacing it. You can even use a small fishing weight, but it's important to get one of precisely the right weight. If too light, the eyes will not close all the way. If too heavy, they will close with a thud. The object is to have them in as natural a manner as possible, just as they did originally. Missing eyelashes can be replaced, too — but don't repaint painted ones that have faded.

The question of things sold originally with the doll, and now missing, brings us naturally to the *box*. In the past several years the world of doll collecting has focused greater and greater attention on boxes. As you may already know, stamp collecting has reached the point where the GUM on some rare stamps is worth *more than the stamps themselves.* It is very doubtful if doll hobbyists will ever be paying more for the original boxes than for the dolls they contained, but this is for sure: the trend is toward higher and higher premium prices for specimens in the original boxes. If the premiums continue growing at the present rate, ten years from now the boxes COULD be worth just as much as the dolls — or more. But just as there are doll collectors to whom the original box is of utmost importance, and who will pay 30% or 40% more to get it, there are others who take no interest whatsoever in the box.

Not all dolls were sold in boxes, and some of those which came in boxes were sold in boxes bearing no markings of any kind (worthless for a collector). Among the antique dolls (pre-1883) there were very few sold in printed boxes. The purpose of a printed box was to serve as an eye-catcher in the shop. It was probably felt that a doll required no sales push of this kind, since it could be easily displayed without the box and advertise itself. Later the philosophy obviously changed, as boxes with printed messages and photos came on the scene fairly extensively. The majority of doll boxes are paperboard of some kind or other. The earlier version was usually a drab plain grey box, with the printing attached to it on a piece of paper rather than printed directly on the box. All dolls that came into the U.S. from Japan were in boxes of this sort and so were most other dolls, even many made in America. Later, the boxes got more elaborate. Whereas pictures on the earlier boxes were mainly in black and white, later boxes (especially after World War II) had color pictures.

Doll boxes do have some valid reason to claim the hobbyist's attention. They carry, in some cases, information about the maker or distributor, or even the date, which is not contained on the doll itself. They also show (if they bear a picture) what the doll looked like originally, if there is any doubt about this. In this respect the interest in doll boxes is really more valid than the postage stamp collector's interest in "original gum." There are some doll boxes which rank as collectors' items in themselves, because of their artwork — such as the one in which the 1950 Bradsby "Jackie Robinson" doll was marketed. You will find this box, minus the doll, in the auction sales of sports memorabilia.

There is obviously a rarity factor in doll boxes. Most original owners made no effort to preserve the box. Even if they did, it usually got damaged along the way and was eventually discarded. If 100 specimens of a given doll are still in existence, there may be only five or six surviving boxes — or there could be none at all in some cases. When a dealer charges you a premium for a doll in the original box, he isn't gouging. It gives the doll an added rarity appeal and to SOME collectors this is important. If it isn't important to you, skip that specimen and wait for one that isn't boxed!

Just like the doll, its box can be damaged and/or repaired, and this likewise influences the value.

DOLL REPAIRS

Many collectible dolls in damaged condition have been damaged further, or utterly destroyed, through amateur repair attempts. Doll repair in its more advanced forms is an art and should be handled by professionals. There are many restorers specializing in dolls, in all parts of the country. You should be able to find one in the advertisements placed in hobby magazines, or possibly in your local area phone directory. If this does not avail, ask the local antique shops if there are doll restorers located nearby. Any museum or historical society which displays dolls among its collection will know of a competent restorer.

The fact that doll restoration is a thriving business shows that most serious collectors choose not to attempt their own repair work. Even an experienced collector who knows dolls from A to Z will usually not make any repair efforts except those of the simplest kind. One reason for this is that the professional has equipment and materials, including spare parts and matches for customers, which a collector would not be in a position to own. Also, a restorer can advise you on when repair work is apt to improve the value of the doll and when it is not, if this is of interest to you.

The types of damage found on dolls, particularly antique dolls, vary greatly. Whether restoration is worthwhile depends on the nature of the damage. There is no way that a worn or damaged doll can be made brand-new again, and the collector should not expect this. Old age in a doll is about as irreversible as old age in a human. There are many kinds of damage which should definitely be treated and which can be corrected. If, for example, you have all the parts to a strung doll and it needs restringing, it would be foolish not to have this operation performed. The doll will display much better when restrung, than as a heap of loose components! Parts that are hidden on a doll, either on the inside or hidden by clothing, are naturally more receptive to repair. On parts that show, especially the face, serious thought has to be given — will the repair accomplish the desired objective? For some forms of damage, such as chipping and flaking from the face of a painted doll, the cure is worse than the ailment. If a doll's head is sanded down and repainted, this might make it look better but the value as a collector's item will be totally lost.

Repainting the doll's face is one of the surest ways to ruin the collector value of your doll. Very few of the truly old bisques and chinas have traveled through the years with no obvious signs of wear. Sun damage and dust fades the rosy cheeks and the rich hues of painted eyes. You feel that just a dot of new rouge will bring back the youthful appearance of your treasured antique. Resist this impluse. Repainting can only be accomplished by truly artistic doll doctors and these people take days and even weeks to accomplish this task. Even when a most professional job has been done on the touch up of a doll face, the qualities of originality and age are gone, replaced with a new and sometimes modern mask. Unless the doll's appearance is seriously marred for display, and unless you feel you will never want to sell this doll on the collector's market, do not repaint the face.

The condition of the body of a doll is not usually the main indicator of value. The head far outweighs any other factor in pricing and worth. Because of the simple fact that a doll's clothing can hide a multitude of flaws and damages, the body can be somewhat marred and still carry a high collector value. In the case of structural damage, the body can be restored or repaired by a professional with a little more leeway than the head. Fingers and toes can be replaced, and some paint touch up can improve its appearance without losing too much value. Again the key here is discretion, professionalism and a respect for the original plan of the doll artist.

Instead of repainting or repairing a badly damaged body, an attempt might be made to locate a match in better condition. Loose bodies and heads are floating around the trade in great quantity, with bodies outnumbering heads. (Heads are much more apt to be damaged beyond repair.) If you decide to completely replace the body, make sure of the fit and similarity in age and skin tone. Once the transfer is made, keep a record of the change with the doll, listing all the modifications you did, and describing the old parts. It is best to keep the old pieces, if possible. The history that you are maintaining with your doll will be as valuable a sales aid as service records are to a car sale.

There are many ways a bisque, china or composition doll can be damaged. As already mentioned, paint fade should be left as is. There are a few manufacturer's flaws — for example, mold lines and pit marks (porous patches caused by excessive heat or air bubbles in the mold). If they are not too distracting they will not devalue the doll. Careless handling causes problems that can seriously reduce the price of your doll. Often chunks of bisque are missing from under the wig, caused by impatient wig removal. Abrasive cleansers cause the surface to weaken and hastens fade and wear. Hairline cracks are caused by the dreaded drop or fall. Depending on the width or position of a hairline crack, the coveted description of "excellent" is gone forever. (Forget mint. There are utterly too few dolls of any age that qualify as "mint.") No amount of repair can bring back that description, even though it improves the appearance.

Doll collectors are such purists about original condition that hidden repairs are covered under the section on Fakes and Reproductions. When dealing with a damaged doll you must ask yourself what you want to accomplish with this doll, and what place it has in your collection. If its value is questionable as is, and its appearance is marring your display, go ahead and have it restored. But realize that the new product has lost some of its old treasure.

DOLL FAKES

This is a subject you will not usually find covered in discussions of doll collecting. The doll hobby, unlike so many other collecting hobbies in current popularity, has very little problem with fakes, forgeries, counterfeits, seller swindles, and things of that nature. It is almost unnecessary to caution a collector against such dangers, as he could very likely build a large collection without ever encountering them. Nevertheless a few words on the subject should not be out of place.

In terms of out-and-out fakes of antique dolls, there are virtually none. Fakers are stopped in their tracks by the difficulty of convincingly producing a fake. There would certainly be fakers turning out copies of old dolls, if this was within the realm of possibility. The problem (for them) is that most buyers of valuable dolls, in the $300 and up region, know what an old doll is supposed to look like. They make a close examination and would spot little details revealing the fake. Someone who does not know about antique dolls would perhaps miss the telltale signs of fakery, but such an individual is not apt to be spending $300, $500 or more for a doll. Also, there would be considerable work involved in producing the fakes, which cannot be just printed on a machine like fake postage stamps. Even if the faker could successfully sell his products as the genuine original, there may not be much profit in the activity! We do not want to lull you into believing that fakes of antique dolls are absolutely non-existent. Fakes of everything turn up, now and then. On the American market they are certainly rare for the present, but we cannot speak for the foreign market; and whatever is on sale abroad can find its way here, sooner or later. There is much more fakery of antiques in certain foreign countries than in America. Hopefully the individuals responsible will not decide to turn their resources to dolls.

While fakes designed to fool collectors are rare, some honest reproductions are made of antique dolls. These mainly come from France. They are exquisitely crafted and can easily be mistaken for an 1800's doll, if you do not notice the markings. These are called "honest reproductions" because there is no intention of defrauding anyone. These dolls (mostly bisque-head) are made in the spirit of yesteryear, for buyers who want the very best that the doll marker's art can produce. The approach is the same as that of the 1880's and 1890's bisque factories and the results are just about identical. These dolls are collectors' items as soon as they reach the market, and their prices are very high, understandably. They may rise in value just as fast as the antique specimens which inspired them, but this is hard to say. The absolutely "mint" appearance of these dolls should be a clue to their modern origin, as the usual age marks of a 100-year-old specimen are missing. No attempt is made to falsely age them, as is done to fakes. They are simply made to be beautiful dolls and this is exactly what they are. The collector should not hesitate to buy them, if he finds them appealing. He will not be accused of having "fakes" in his collection.

It is not unheard of, though, that unethical dealers will try to pass off reproductions as the original. There are crooks in any profession and just because dolls are innocents does not mean the humans that handle them are perfectly honest. The best way to keep yourself out of harm's way is education, of course and perhaps most importantly, common sense. If a deal seems too good to be true, be assured, it probably is. As in any marketplace transaction it is, as always, buyer beware.

It is a matter of debate, whether repair work and restoration comes under the heading of fakery. Most forms of repair work are considered ethical. However you will find, in the shops, quite a few dolls on which extensive repairs have been performed. They might have been carried out in the best of faith, but the end product is a doll which can easily confuse the beginning collector into believing it to be older, or more valuable, than it actually is. Do not be too quick to blame the dealers for these specimens. Some of them may have been repaired under the instruction of dealers. But the great majority of modern doll dealers are not interested in handling specimens which are questionable in any way. These include dolls in which the head does not belong to the body, or in which the arms and legs are not from the original body. If the "match" is a good, close one, it can be argued that the repair was made in all honesty and that the doll is still collectible. Certainly there are many such dolls in collections.

When a repair has been made there is usually glaring evidence of it. The coloring will be slightly off the mark if the doll has been repainted, crack repairs are usually obvious, and if the body has been unsuccessfully matched it will be out of perspective with the head. Do not hesitate, before spending hundreds on a doll, to thoroughly examine the potential purchase. This includes taking off the head and wig. Peering into the skull cavity will disclose any hidden head repair, unless the shifty repairer has used today's new technology to cover the cracks with an opaque coating. Although this is very difficult to detect, the smooth matte finish and the freshly painted look can clue you in. Remember, do not be squeamish about such a complete exam. The professional doll dealer will not object. If he does, figure that nine times out of ten he is trying to hide something.

Your protection from unethical practices is education. As you progress with your collecting technique, you will find yourself less vulnerable. Set up a few rules for yourself. First of all, establish a relationship with your dealers. They will want to continue to do business with you, and will steer you away from the questionable purchase. Do not deal with sellers who will not guarantee their products, or have a no return policy. Have only as much confidence in a purchase as the seller has in the sale.

CARE, STORAGE AND DISPLAY

Dolls are definitely a "show" collectible. Most dolls of the 19th century were designed for display rather than play. But even dolls originally made as playthings are displayed as showpieces by their present owners. Thus the matter of display techniques and approaches is one of prime interest for all doll hobbyists, and this topic leads directly into the care of dolls. Care and storage are inter-related because proper display takes care and preservation into account. The first object of anyone who owns fine dolls is to preserve them in the condition in which they were acquired. If a display approach places a doll in potential danger, by (for example) exposing it to continuous direct sunlight or heat, it must be avoided. There are many ways of displaying and enjoying a doll collection while insuring the safety of its contents.

Old dolls have come down to us in various grades of condition. Often it is possible to replace missing parts and improve the appearance, and sometimes even the cash value, of a doll. Mainly, "care" involves maintenance: keeping your dolls in the best possible shape. This means keeping them from harm and deterioration, and, in some cases, cleaning them when necessary. No complicated upkeep is required. Dolls are much easier to care for, and far less prone to damage and deterioration, than many other kinds of collectors' items. Just bending the corner of a scarce postage stamp decreases its value. A collectors' doll can be handled, so long as reasonable common sense is used. And since most of the pleasure in owning dolls is just in LOOKING at them — like pictures — the hobbyist can derive 100% enjoyment from any doll he acquires. Compare this to the collector of rare mint-state phonograph records, who would not dare to play his records for fear of putting wear on them!

Most old dolls did not receive much in the way of care from their previous owners. In fact they were just about neglected in this regard, as the owners did not think of them as "collectors' items." Most of the effects of neglect can be remedied. The most common is dirt and grime, both on the doll and its clothing. A doll that has gone from collector to collector is likely to have been cleaned at some point along the road, perhaps several times. The dealers themselves will sometimes clean up a doll before offering it for sale, knowing that the sales potential will thereby be improved. But when a doll has just come out of an attic, as you will find for example at estate auctions and at flea markets, it has probably never been cleaned in its whole lifetime. The accumulated grime and dust hides the real beauty of the doll. A doll which is merely dirty and in need of cleaning can easily be mistaken for a faded doll. The condition of the clothing is really no indication of the condition of the doll as a whole, as the clothing might not be original. Or possibly the clothing has been washed and not the doll.

These dolls should unquestionably be cleaned. It improves their appearance, makes them more enjoyable to own, and, more importantly, contributes to their preservation by not allowing the dirt to become too deeply ingrained. The sooner a doll is cleaned, the less of a project it is. But it's important to take a middle-of-the-road approach to doll cleaning and not become an extremist. There are two groups of collectors who are equally mistaken in their approach to doll cleaning. The first dismisses the subject entirely and makes no effort to clean his dolls at all. This is wrong, but it is also wrong (and much worse) to get over-zealous about cleaning. The too-enthusiastic cleaner wants absolute cleanliness at all costs and is willing to sacrifice anything to get it. He uses harsh detergents, boiling water, and scrubs as if he were cleaning concrete. The doll gets clean, but its collector value is destroyed in the process. Therefore, anyone who cleans dolls needs to have an appreciation of them as collectors' items, not just decorative objects.

The approach to be taken in cleaning is determined to some extent by the nature of the doll and the condition. Some dolls are (to put it bluntly) a lot dirtier than others and need special, careful attention in cleaning. Then, too, the material from which the doll is made enters the picture, as some substances are more responsive to certain cleaning methods than others. There are some dolls which present real problems in cleaning because hardly anything can be done to them which would not harm the doll itself. Paper dolls fall into this group. Any attempt to wash paper dolls, even if by merely soaking them in water, runs the risk of bleaching out their colors and possibly leaving the doll with a stiff, unnatural appearance. Each case has to be judged individually. When the risk involved appears to be too great, there is not much choice but for the collector to forego cleaning and keep the doll "as is." This is why a knowledge of doll materials and their response to cleaning attempts is vital to the collector. It enables him to judge which dolls are a good buy and which ones fall into the questionable class. If a doll is not likely to respond well to cleaning efforts, it may be wisest not to purchase such a doll unless it is not in need of cleaning.

It is important first of all to differentiate between the ruggedness of the doll and the ruggedness of its painted color. Some dolls are made of very hard materials, which can be washed without harming the material in any way. But their coloration is vulnerable to damage in cleaning. Chalk dolls are an example. If you had a white (unpainted) chalk doll or statuette, it could be safely washed in hot soapy water. The chalk would withstand this operation without any problem, and you could get the item perfectly clean. But when chalk dolls are painted, as they almost always are, the paint is far from permanently fixed on their surfaces. Because of the powdery surface of chalk, the paint does not fix very well on it. Any kind of strenuous rubbing, or immersing in water, can loosen some of the paint. You will be able to make a better judgement of this by examining the particular doll. If the surface has a powdery feel, and some small patches of color appear to already be missing, you can be quite sure this is a delicate specimen which has to be cleaned gingerly. If, on the other hand, the surface looks hard and shiny, and there is no powdery feel upon running your fingers across it, the color is probably fairly well fixed.

Before anything else is done, the doll needs to be undressed and dusted. Undressing is essential because the clothing is always dealt with separately. Do this cautiously. It is possible that there may be hidden pins or stitches, which would cause rips or holes if the clothing is taken off in a hurry. You need to get the clothing off so do not hesitate to snip away a retaining stitch if necessary. It can always be replaced later. When the clothing has come off, put it aside and do not worry about it for the moment (its turn will come).

Quite likely a good bit of the discoloration or faded appearance of the doll is being caused by nothing more than surface dust. In any event the doll must be thoroughly dusted before anything else can be accomplished. It is usually best to remove the wig before doing this. Since you will be removing the wig anyway, further along in the cleaning process, it might as well be done at this point. Lay the doll flat on a table, face up, and go over the whole surface with a clean feather-duster. If you have one with short, closely-set feathers it will do a better job. Then turn the doll on its stomach and repeat the process. You may be surprised at how much dust billows up! And this is just the beginning. The feather-dusting will not remove all the dust. It just gets the loosest particles, which have accumulated very recently. There are still plenty of loose dust particles on the doll and they need to be removed next. You can do this with an artist's *camel-hair brush.* Don't wipe with a rag at this stage of the cleaning procedure — you will only push the dust around and accomplish nothing. A good art supply shop will have a *wide* camel hair brush. You will need one at least 1½" wide and preferably 2". Get the kind with long bristles if you have a choice. Before using it, run adhesive tape around the metal which connects the hairs to the handle — this could scratch the doll if it comes in contact with it. Then it is simply a matter of working over the whole surface area of the doll with this brush, going carefully into each crevice and detail. Wash the brush in warm soapy water afterwards, and rinse thoroughly. Hang it up to dry.

You will now be able to see just how much grime the doll carries. This is mostly the result of fingermarking from the doll being handled and played with. Just how deeply ingrained they are depends on their age and whether the fingers had ink, food, grease, etc. on them. Some of the grime on an antique doll is fixed into the surface about as solidly as the paint, and you will not be successful in removing it. Anything which would cut through it will also remove the paint — and faced with that kind of choice you are wise to settle for living with the grime. However, a good deal of the grime is probably of more recent origin and not deeply imbedded.

If the head is being cleaned separately from the rest of the doll, it is permissible to immerse the body in water. Some collectors also immerse the head (if it does not have sleep eyes), but this is a risky step which we do not recommend. Of course if the body contains any kind of mechanism, it cannot be immersed. Lukewarm water is used, without any cleaning agent. After soaking for a few minutes the body is removed and wiped over the whole surface with a cloth dipped in warm water (warmer than the soaking water). Then the body is soaked again, in fresh water. These steps can be repeated several times and the surface should get somewhat cleaner with each repetition, as the water and light rubbing breaks down the uppermost layers of grime. Don't scrub. Think of this as soaking a stamp from a piece of paper! Dry the body thereafter by patting with a dry cloth or cotton swabs and leave it in an airy place to dry further. The inside of the body (of a hollow-bodied doll) can be dried partially with a cotton swab on a stick. The remaining moisture will simply evaporate. Length of drying time will depend on how much humidity is in the air. It may range from an hour to a day or longer. Do not attempt to speed it up with a hair drier. Nature will take its course.

Instead of immersing the head, wipe it with a damp rag that has been dipped in warm water and thoroughly wrung out. This will need to be repeated several times at least. With each wiping you will dislodge some grime. The rag gets soiled quickly so it has to be rinsed out repeatedly. Be careful of the area around the eyes and the eyes themselves. In cleaning a wax or china doll you can place a few drops of household ammonia in the water, but ONLY a few drops (no more than the equivalent of one teaspoon of ammonia in a quart of water). Rubbing alcohol can also be used in the same proportion. Never use a strong solution of these substances, or any cleanser, as they could wash the paint right off the doll.

After washing and drying a wax or china head, you may want to apply a light coating of oil as a kind of "sealer." Oil (if not heavily applied) adds to the appearance and prevents dust particles, etc., from actually reaching the surface. The best kind of oil for this use is linseed oil. Soak a thin rag in it, then wring out the rag thoroughly and wipe lightly over the whole surface. Oiling a doll's head in this manner is far preferable to lacquering, which used to be recommended by some doll "experts." Collectors of yesteryear were advised to lacquer their dolls as a preventive against scratches. This is why you find some lacquered dolls on the market. The tide of present-day opinion is heavily against lacquering or anything else which provides a permanent false surface to the doll. Oil accomplishes about the same objectives as lacquer but can be easily removed at any time. Bisque dolls should not be oiled, as oil tends to give bisque an unnatural, harsh appearance and is disagreeable to most collectors. However it does not harm the doll in any way. The basic rule to follow is: if the doll is naturally glossy or shiny, oil it; if not, don't. In other words, go with the flow.

The clothing is washed separately from the doll itself. Each piece should be washed individually, not (of course) in a machine but by hand. You can use mild soap but don't rub too much. If the clothing is very old it may be quite fragile. Depending on the material, you can soak it in soapy water first to make the job easier. Several washings may be necessary to get it really clean. If there are obstinate stains you may do better leaving them as they are.

Do not redress the doll until several days after cleaning, to make sure that both the doll and its costuming has thoroughly dried. If just the slightest bit damp when redressed, this will create a situation detrimental to the doll's preservation. Humidity will build up between the clothing and the doll's body, which can lead to mold formation.

The chief danger to any doll (except cloth!) is of course breakage. So when you plan a storage and display arrangement for your collection, the first objective is to keep your dolls safe from breakage — everything else is secondary. Using care when handling a doll is one safeguard against accident, but accidents can occur in storage, too. Mostly they arise from wall shelving that has not been properly installed or is overloaded with too much weight. Breakage may also result from shelving placed too low to the floor, within reach of pets and small children. Your display arrangement must, then, be planned in consideration of your circumstances. If there are pets and youngsters in the house, some added precautions will need to be taken, but this should not cause any great inconvenience. The keynote is space. If you have wall space, the rest comes easy. In crowded, small areas, some improvising may be necessary. Do not hesitate to place shelving high up on walls, right near the ceiling, if space elsewhere is limited. Since dolls are large and bold, they can be easily viewed from a distance. There is no need to get them directly at eye level. This is one of the important advantages in displaying a doll collection. But do take into consideration the weight and strain sustained by each shelf. A shelf of dolls can be heavier than a shelf of books, if the dolls are large and positioned close together. In using long shelves, place a brace at the center to help bolster them. Also, examine the condition of your wall to determine if it will securely hold the shelf brackets. If there is any doubt, you may do better foregoing wall shelving and displaying your dolls in a standing case. A case with glass doors will provide protection against dust.

If a doll refuses to stand or sit, which is the case with some, a special prop can be used. This is an aluminum holder with two arms, which grasp the doll around its body and keep it standing. The holder is mounted on a vertical rod and fits into a pedestal base. They come in various sizes and can be purchased at the hobby shops and usually from doll dealers. If the doll dealer has none for sale he can probably tell you of a local source for them. They last forever and can be interchanged from one doll to another of similiar size.

MAKING MONEY WITH DOLLS

Most hobbyists are into doll collecting for the sheer enjoyment of it. Shopping for dolls, setting up displays, researching dolls, and meeting other collectors is a source of enormous pleasure for them and they never think in terms of financial gain. That's fine. But along with the fun of collecting dolls there is also the opportunity — for those who want to seize it — to make money with dolls, too. There are various ways in which this can be done. You need not be a dealer to profit from dolls. Millions and millions of dollars are spent in the doll hobby every year. Anyone with a knowledge of dolls and their values, and of the market, can take part in selling. Many collectors do some selling as a sideline to their hobby, using the proceeds to buy dolls that they might not otherwise have been able to afford. Some do so well that they end up becoming dealers, even though they had no such intentions at the beginning! There is also the chance to profit from your own doll collection, when and if you ever decide to sell it. The trend in doll values has been up — steadily and firmly — through the years. Nearly all doll collections increase in value while in the owner's possession, simply because the market prices go up constantly. There have been collectors who sold their dolls for twice or even three times as much as the collection cost. While there is no guarantee of profit in buying dolls, they've proven considerably better as investments than many other collectibles — better even than many stocks and bonds. Even if profit making is far from your thoughts, it's reassuring to know that the money spent on dolls is going into something with a future. That's more than can be said of cash spent on most kinds of entertainment, which brings no financial return whatsoever!

Whether you will profit from the eventual sale of your doll collection depends on several factors, some of which are under your control. A factor out of the hobbyist's control is the market itself. Values have to keep going up at a steady pace, to create a situation in which collectors can sell *today's purchases* at a profit *tomorrow.* There is no reason to suspect that this will fail to occur. The doll hobby is healthy and has been healthy for a long time. It's older than most other collecting hobbies and has a firm foundation. Antique and other fine dolls have been actively collected since the early 1900's and the number of new collectors coming into the hobby has been growing — mushrooming might be a better word — since then. They now total well over 1,000,000 individuals in the U.S. alone. This takes account only of those who buy out-of-production dolls and are collectors in the true sense of the term. If ALL doll owners were included — those who buy dolls at ordinary retail outlets — the figure would be ten times this high or more. Doll collectors' societies are at all-time highs in memberships, and the ranks of professional dealers are swelling. More and more new doll collectors' groups are starting up. And, very significantly, many more general antiques dealers are including dolls in their merchandise. There is unquestionably a doll collecting "boom" in the country. One of the MOST favorable signs is that the overall economic recession of 1982 had far less effect on doll collecting than on most other hobbies (including the two giant ones, coins and stamps). Why should this have been the case? Probably because the number of *non-collector investors* in doll collecting is much, much lower than in coins and stamps. Literally billions of dollars worth of collectible coins and stamps are purchased by individuals who are not hobbyists. They are strictly investors who buy with the intention of turning a profit. When economic storm clouds gather, these people suddenly stop buying and the market for coins and stamps feels the blow. In doll collecting, nearly everyone who buys is a hobbyist and a lover of dolls. Some are thinking in terms of profit but they still rank as collectors first and foremost. They continue buying regardless of what the national economy is doing or which political party occupies the White House.

Still, movements in the market are outside the collector's control, so he does need a certain amount of luck on his side in that respect. What he CAN control himself is the quality of his collection, which really counts even more. This means being attentive to condition. Dolls in the best grades of preservation rise in value faster than those in the "average" or lower classes. If the collector avoids space-fillers and seconds, he stands a much better chance of profiting from his collection when a sale is eventually made. The weight of numbers — and dollars — is definitely on the side of condition-conscious hobbyists. This is the case with the dealers, too, and we need not tell you that they exert an enormous influence over the market. Any dealer will buy collectible dolls in fine condition, because he has a demand for them from his customers. He may hesitate to buy defective specimens even if he can get them very, very cheaply. This is considered a gamble purchase by dealers, and dealers don't care to gamble.

Whether or not you profit from your collection may also depend, to some degree, on the type of dolls you buy. Any collectible doll in fine condition can be considered a potential "investment," but some groups do go up faster in value than others. This is not always entirely predictable because trends can develop in doll collecting, just as in any other collecting field. Dolls which are not among the most widely sought today could hit the top of the popularity list in five or ten years — or much sooner. However, the historic pattern in doll collecting, going all the way back before most of us were born, is for buying trends to surface gradually. There are very few "hotshots" in the doll hobby: groups that are popular one day and forgotten the next. Usually, when a trend develops it builds and builds over a long period of time and makes itself felt for decades. The major trend during the past 20 years of doll collecting has been bisque's emergence as the favorite among high quality molded-head dolls. It can hardly be called a trend any longer (unlike in the 1960's and early seventies), since bisque is now firmly installed at the head of the pack. The odds on any group of dolls unseating bisque as the king, within the foreseeable future, are extremely slim. But this does not mean that other groups will fail to gain in popularity.

Anyone who bought bisque dolls in the 1950's or 1960's, and sold them within the past five years, profited very handsomely on his collection. The more he originally spent, the greater his eventual profit was. Many bisque dolls were selling for $12 and $15 in the 1950's which are now in the $300, $400 and $500 categories. Even in the 1960's, some of today's $500 bisques could be picked up for around $20 or $25. Not too many investments — in anything — reflected that kind of gain in so short a period of time. It is very doubtful that the price increases on bisque dolls during the NEXT 20 years will equal those of the past. But they are almost sure to continue rising, even if the pace is not quite as rapid, and will probably return very satisfactory profits to their collectors.

All the doll-world headlines garnered by bisque in the past 20 years have, perhaps, presented a distorted picture. They've given the impression that all collectors are buying bisque and that the doll hobby revolves around bisque and nothing else. This is far from the case! Even though, unquestionably, more money is spent on bisque than on any other single class of dolls, ALL THE OTHER GROUPS have been growing in collector popularity, too! The big swing to bisque did not draw buyers away from other dolls. There were simply more new hobbyists coming into the market who wanted bisque. If someone was buying (for example) wax dolls in the 1960's, he would have no reason for regrets today. The same applies to china. Wax and china dolls are no longer getting as much publicity as bisque. They might SEEM to have diminished in collector appeal but just the reverse is actually true. These groups of dolls have risen in value at a very impressive pace in themselves. Their pace of advance has not equalled that of bisque, and you would not have profited AS MUCH by buying them in the 1960's and selling them today. But if you had purchased judiciously, going for scarce specimens and demanding top condition, you could sell such as collection profitably today. This applies to other types of dolls, too.

Some dolls have jumped in value faster than bisque within the past 20 years. This shows that the doll market is much deeper, richer, and more diverse than it might appear at the surface. The fastest rising of ALL dolls, in overall price performance, are not a *substance* group but a *subject* group. These are character dolls — dolls made in the likeness of a comic strip hero, movie star, or other identifiable person (or animal!). Very few character dolls fall into the bisque category. Most of the better ones are composition, but they run the gamut from vinyl to celluloid, hard plastic to rubber, and many other substances. They include the multitudes of Disney dolls, plus Shirley Temples, Charlie Chaplins, Popeyes, and — the fastest rising of all — dolls representing Elvis Presley and the Beatles. Increases on some of these dolls have been so immense that bisque's progress looks weak by comparison! Collectors are now paying between $600 and $800 for a set of four Beatles dolls, manufactured in 1964, which could be had for around $35 in the mid 1970's. This represents an increase of around 2,000% in less than ten years. Dolls in the likeness of Elvis Presley have registered comparable increases. (It is vital to point out, though, that current or very recently made Elvis and Beatles dolls do not have as much profit potential as those which can be termed "original.")

If someone wanted to buy with profit in mind, as well as collecting enjoyment, the currently-made character dolls representing TODAY'S personalities might be an excellent choice. The trick here would be to concentrate on characters or personalities who seem certain of gathering a strong collector following. Any dolls related to the motion picture "Extra Terrestrial" would seem ideal for investment buying at the present time. All, or most, of the original E.T. dolls can still be bought at the manufacturer's price. In light of what happened to *Star Wars* and *Star Trek* memorabilia, all E.T. merchandise is almost sure to go up in value. With character dolls, especially those of this nature, you have very heavy competition to bring up the prices: not only doll enthusiasts will buy them, but collectors of nostalgia and memorabilia. Gene Autry dolls are bought by collectors of "western movie memorabilia." Laurel and Hardy dolls are bought by collectors of "silent film comedy memorabilia." And so on. The demand widens out and out, and each new group of collectors who seize onto these dolls helps to raise the values.

There are other ways to make money on dolls, too, aside from building a fine collection and eventually putting it on the market. You can profit from dolls WHILE building your collection, too.

One way of doing this is to buy dolls far below the market value and sell them to dealers. Obviously you cannot accomplish this by buying from one doll dealer and selling to another, since the prices from one dealer to the next will be about the same. A dealer expects to buy MOST of his dolls for around 50% of their market value. Even if you could get a doll from a dealer at 70% or 80% of its usual market value, you would be losing money in reselling it to another dealer. To profit in selling to dealers, you must purchase dolls for less than half of their retail value, preferably in the range of 40% of retail or below — to give yourself a bit of leeway. If you do this, you can sell such dolls immediately to dealers and make an instant profit with no waiting involved. There are many opportunities to buy dolls at less than half the retail value, if you regularly visit the flea markets, garage sales, thrift shops and other so-called "secondary" sources of supply (a "secondary" source of supply is any source other than an antiques dealer or specialist doll dealer). You will perhaps find dolls suitable for your own collection at these sources; many hobbyists do. Even if you discover little or nothing that fits into your personal collection, there will almost surely be SOME worthwhile dolls offered at profitable prices, which can be resold to a dealer. Just about anything can turn up, and, believe it or not, even fine early bisques DO make their appearances sometimes in these out-of-the-way locations. They've come straight from attics and have never been on the collector market. The owner has no investment in them because they were bought by the owner's grandmother or great-grandmother in the far distant past. By the same token the owner has no idea of their current market value, and this is where YOU come in. To the owner they're simply old, attractive dolls, but they could be worth $20 or $2,000 as far as they know. Of course you still have to be careful about condition, which holds true whether you buy a doll for your own collection or for resale. If a doll is not in reasonably good condition (at least), it isn't worth bothering with. This applies EVEN MORE to dolls that you intend selling to a dealer. Maybe an occasional doll in sub-standard condition could "squeak by" for your own collection, if it has special appeal for you. The appeal that any doll has for a dealer is strictly SALES appeal. He is not charmed by its beauty or thrilled by age or background, and that's understandable. The doll dealer is a businessman and dolls are his merchandise. When buying them he must think in terms of whether they will be profitable for him. So, when you buy a doll with the intention of selling it to a dealer, think of whether it will be profitable to HIM. Just a little experience in the doll hobby will make this much clearer. You will soon know exactly what type of dolls are the most in demand by dealers, and which ones are in the "maybe" category. As a general rule, in buying with the motive of reselling to a dealer, we would caution against CHALK dolls unless you find something really exceptional. Some dealers regard chalk dolls as statuettes and are not interested in handling them at all. This does not diminish their appeal for collectors, but appeal and profit can sometimes do two different things. The types of dolls most wanted by most dealers are BISQUE, CHINA, and GOOD-QUALITY COMPOSITION HEADS. If you buy any character dolls, over and above those wanted for your own collection, you MAY do better selling them to a dealer in memorabilia than to a doll dealer. Names and addresses of memorabilia dealers can be found in the hobbyist publications, which are readily available at your local public library.

There is a possibility that, as you progress in collecting, your interest may switch from one type of doll to another. You may start out with Japan celluloids and advance to Shirley Temples, or begin with vinyl and shift to bisque or china. Quite a few collectors DO change direction along the way, sometimes because of a change of interest but more frequently because of financial considerations. A collector who really prefers bisque might start out collecting another type of doll because he feels bisque is too costly for him. Later, if his financial circumstances improve, or if the "bisque bug" really bites him hard, he makes the changeover. This leaves him with a number of dolls that do not fit into his collection any longer. He has the option of keeping his original collection (which some hobbyists do, as they have an absolute aversion to parting with anything), or selling it, or possibly swapping it item-by-item with fellow collectors. This is one of the ways in which dolls circulate through the market. If everybody kept on collecting the same type of doll they started with, and held their collections forever, the supply of collectible dolls in dealers' hands would dwindle down to a trickle. You have the chance to make a profit when selling one collection to begin another. However, the odds on profiting from a sale in these circumstances are somewhat lower. The problem, usually, is that little time has elapsed from purchase to sale, and *time* is one of the main ingredients in turning a profit. Say for example that you've been working on your original collection for two years, when you reach the point of switching to a different group of dolls. Even if you bought wisely and avoided any dolls in inferior condition, Father Time would be working against you in this situation. How high could the market have risen in two years? And the two-year time period would apply only to the FIRST dolls you bought, not the later additions to your collection. We will assume for the sake of making a computation that the retail value of your collection, overall, is 20% higher than the prices you paid. If you spent $1,000 on your dolls, you now have dolls worth $1,200 on the retail market (in other words, this is what it would cost to repurchase all your dolls TODAY). In going out to sell them to a dealer, the offer will be in the neighborhood of 50% of retail. It may be slightly more or less depending on the collection's nature and the dealer to whom you offer it, but 50% is the figure you will most likely be offered. On a $1,200 collection, a 50% buying offer would mean $600. Since you paid $1,000 for your dolls, there would be a considerable loss involved: $400 in actual money, and an additional sum lost because of the decline in value of the dollar. Thus, you may not consider it worthwhile to sell your no-longer-wanted collection at the time of switching to a new collecting interest. It would probably be to your advantage to retain it and sell it at some period in the future, when the market has advanced far enough to return a profit or at least allow you to break even. Five years from now, your dolls (bought for $1,000, following the above example) might have climbed to a retail value of $3,000. A dealer would then pay around $1,500 for them. Though this would not actually provide a $500 profit over your original $1,000 cost, because of inflation, it would at least bring you to the breakeven point. As logical as the foregoing advice is, most collectors do NOT wait to sell dolls in which they are no longer interested. They take their loss, just for the sake of raising some money to pour back into their collection. They're your dolls, and it's your investment, so obviously the decision is up to you. But it becomes apparent that SOME collectors sell too fast simply because they are unaware of the market's mechanics. They do not realize that waiting a few years could mean the difference between making a profit or taking a loss. They see their dolls as a source of immediate revenue, and the urge to SELL, SELL, SELL gets the best of them. If you want to take a cue from the dealers (who must be doing it right, since they make enough money selling dolls to earn a living), look at the way they handle the "time" question! When a dealer acquires a doll, he prices it to realize a reasonable profit — usually about double his cost as we have pointed out. If it fails to sell within a few months, or even a year, he does not (under most circumstances) lower his price. He does not allow himself to think in terms of *forcing a sale.* Instead, he may actually RAISE his price on the doll, to reflect the raising market. Yes — even if none of his customers has expressed the slightest interest in the doll, he may still raise its price while it's on his shelves. Why? Because he wants to sell it for the maximum fair price that he can obtain. If he holds the doll for three years, he wants to sell it for its value AT THAT TIME, not for its value at the time he purchased it. This is precisely the way a collector reasons when he thinks about selling. A bird in the hand may be great, but if you can do better in the future by saying "NO" to a sale today, then "no" is the thing to say.

MATERIALS

BISQUE

The most popular, talked-about, and heavily collected dolls on today's market are those of bisque. They are not the oldest dolls, and whether they represent the finest in workmanship and eye-appeal is a matter of some debate. Antique china dolls are at least as well made, and, possibly, a few shades better. But that hardly matters any longer. The enthusiasm of collectors has swung clearly to bisque, and there is certainly much to recommend in this area. They are more plentiful on the open market than china dolls. Bisque dolls encompass the works of more famous manufacturers than those of any other material. Since bisque dolls were produced for a long period of time, they reflect progressive changes in taste over the years. They were manufactured both here and abroad, and huge quantities exist.

Traditionally, prices of bisque dolls were not too high. China was regarded as the optimum, and a fine china would normally (up to the 1960's) outsell a bisque of equal quality by 2-to-1 or even 3-to-1. This situation has now thoroughly changed. China dolls are no longer automatically considered superior to bisque. Though an individual china doll may be more scarce than a bisque doll, this fails to have any influence on relative values in the current doll collectors' market. There are, today, more people collecting bisque dolls than china. This discrepancy in demand outweighs the fact that china dolls are rare. In many auction sales, and even in private transactions, bisque dolls are doing better than china. Obviously, one reason for this is that the current collectors are, to a large extent, specializing by manufacturer. There is simply more opportunity for collecting by manufacturer if you buy bisque.

Bisque and china are closely related as substances — so close that a beginner may be hard pressed to tell the difference. There is only one difference in the material itself. Bisque and china are made from the same clay composition. In slip (liquid) form they are identical. After manufacture, they have exactly the same vulnerability to breakage (which, unfortunately, is rather high). The difference is merely that bisque has an unglazed surface, while china (also known as porcelain) is glazed or glossy. Thus the finish of bisque is matte or dull — unreflective. A china doll has the appearance of being lacquered, or at least did have such an appearance when new; the glossiness can be dulled by age and excessive handling. There are differences of opinion on which is the more attractive finish for a doll's head. These arguments are not new, and were not initiated by collectors. Doll manufacturers of the 19th century took sides just the same, some feeling that china dolls were finer, others putting their weight behind bisque. So it was with the original buyers, too, long before these dolls fell into the sphere of collectors' items. In porcelain works in general, the glossy surface was traditionally more admired than a matte finish. But there seemed good reason to use bisque for doll heads; it might have been somewhat less handsome, but it gave the suggestion of greater realism, since human skin is not glossy like china. So far as adaptability to painting is concerned, china and bisque are equal. Bisque in its plain state (like china in the plain state) is perfectly white, like bone. Some dolls were made of plain white bisque, with enameled touches to the cheeks and facial features. These, while interesting as antiques and collectors' items, are not as lifelike as the bisque dolls to which a coloring pigment was added in the liquid slip. By placing a few drops of pink coloring in the slip, a natural skin tone can be achieved and can be lightened or darkened according to the amount of coloring added. The majority of dolls were made of this pre-colored slip. A third approach with bisque consisted of using plain white slip and painting the entire head after firing. This could bring very satisfactory results, but it was more labor-consuming. Since these dolls were designed to wear wigs, rather than having molded hair, pre-coloring the bisque was the ideal technique. No repainting had to be done afterward, except for facial features and to add some extra color to the cheeks.

Bisque was not an innovation of the doll manufacturers. It had been used in the ceramics industry for generations prior to adoption for doll making. Most of the companies that made porcelain statuettes also made others in bisque, though not on such a large scale. In statuettes, bisque was almost always left unpainted, as it was thought to give the appearance of a marble sculpture. Since classical taste ran high in the 18th and 19th centuries, many owners of ceramic statuettes preferred this look of chiseled marble. There was another selling point for bisque statuettes, too: the buyer could paint them himself, if he chose to, which was not possible with porcelain. Undoubtedly, some bisque doll heads were also painted by the owners, but it is difficult to distinguish such examples from factory work.

Though the manufacturers of bisque dolls stressed their extra realism, this was not the main reason for bisque coming into use in the doll industry. It was introduced mainly because it saved a step (glazing) in the manufacturing process, and thereby saved some cost. This allowed bisque dolls to be sold cheaper than those of china. In the 19th century, the difference of even 25¢ or 50¢ in the retail price of a doll could be very influential in its success on the market. The experimentation with bisque doll heads was carried out mostly in France and Germany. At first only a few factories were making them, but their success encouraged others to follow. By 1875, bisque had clearly taken the play away from china, wax, and all other materials for making quality dolls. Most customers believed that bisque was just as good looking as china, and the difference in price was enough to tip the scales in its favor. Later, as the rush increased to produce dolls at a lower and lower price for the mass market, bisque ironically fell into the category that china had previously occupied: "too expensive." Then came the onslaught of celluloid, vinyl, plastic, chalk and other types of dolls, all of which undercut bisque in price. Some makers of bisque tried to compete by taking shortcuts and bringing down their prices, too. More than anything else, the bisque doll market was eliminated by composition dolls (see entry on that subject), which came very close to bisque in appearance and were selling at a lower price. By 1925, composition was taking over from bisque as the substance for better-grade dolls, and within another 10 years it had just about wiped bisque out of the picture (helped along by the financial depression, which made low prices an even greater attraction than they had been before).

Still, bisque ruled the roost for about half a century. In that period of time a huge quantity of bisque dolls was made. So many in fact that the earlier generations of doll hobbyists could not conceive of any premium value being attached to them. They were too recent and too mass-produced to hold any collecting appeal for hobbyists in the 1930's and 1940's, and even into the 1950's. But this has all changed now. Some bisque dolls are now more than 100 years old; most of them are at least 50-60 years old. And while definitely mass produced, there is the breakage rate to think about when you consider current availability of *any given specimen.* On top of this, the collector must also realize that a bisque doll in very fine condition, very close to the condition in which it left the factory, can be quite a rarity. Of any particular specimen, there may be 10 or 20 in average used condition for every one that ranks as "very fine," while an absolutely mint example may not be in existence at all.

Usually, collectors of bisque dolls are specialists who buy bisque and nothing else. This is logical because it helps one to acquire a knowledge of the manufacturers and their markings, of differences in the molds, and other details necessary to intelligent buying and selling. Bisque doll collecting is an enormous field where there's always something new to learn. Even the most advanced experts do not have all the answers. Most of the questions fall into the area of the relationships between manufacturers, and it becomes a matter of *who made what?* We know that some companies, chiefly in France or Germany, made nothing but doll heads. These companies are classified as "doll manufacturers," on the strength of making heads, but they did not actually manufacture dolls. Their heads were wholesaled to other companies, which assembled the dolls and put them on the market. These "assembling companies" are also classified as doll manufacturers. With some bisque dolls, the head manufacturer and the "assembler" are both identified. This does not occur often and the hobbyist should not be overly disappointed if he cannot come up with such information. Usually, there is a fairly good chance of identifying the manufacturer of the head, through markings, since the vast majority of bisque heads DO carry a marking of one kind or another. Identifying the assembler is much trickier, since the doll body will not likely have any markings of its own. Educated guesses can be made, if one knows that a certain head maker USUALLY supplied his head to a certain assembler, but stating with 100% assurance that the doll was made by that assembler is impossible. The lack of positive attributions has not hurt the doll hobby, any more than it has hurt the market for Old Master oil paintings — most of which cannot be positively attributed, either.

Bisque dolls come in all types and varieties. The beginner who sees a few at the local antique shop, or even who sees dozens at a number of antique shops, is getting a mere taste of what exists. There are show (display) and play bisques, with play types far in the majority; walkers; talkers; adults and infants; huge bisques three feet high, and tiny ones; puppets; and just about everything else imaginable. One reason for this variety is that bisque stayed on the doll scene so long, into the era of modern or semi-modern gadgetry. Anything that could possibly be attempted in the way of a new or novel or improved doll was attempted in bisque. Very significantly, bisques were in production when the era of black dolls began, and many fine early black bisques are in existence. One focal point for a bisque collection (one of many) is to aim for variety and gather as many different styles as you can locate or afford. Try to select dolls with features totally different than any others in your collection. If this is your approach, you could build up an assemblage of hundreds without even flirting with duplication.

Also on the subject of variety, bisque dolls had many different bodies. Dolls were made entirely of bisque, with bisque torsos and limbs, but they were not common. There were drawbacks to all-bisque dolls, just as there were to all-china dolls: high cost and added danger of breakage. A soft body was, in addition to being cheaper and unbreakable, more cuddly. So the majority of bisque dolls ended up with cloth or kidskin bodies, stuffed with cotton, wood shavings or other material. Most of them had (at the least) bisque hands; others had, in addition to bisque hands, bisque forearms and forelegs — often referred to as "lower arms" and "lower legs" in the brochures of doll dealers. The better kind went a little further and used bisque for the entire arms and legs, usually with joints at the knees and elbows. Naturally all of this added to the cost, but it added somewhat to the sales appeal as well. If a doll was all bisque (aside from the torso), it could wear virtually any kind of costume. If the upper arms were, for example, not of bisque, the doll was restricted to clothing which covered its upper arms. Fortunately for doll manufacturers, the era of bisque dolls ended before dolls started wearing bikini bathing suits and other revealing fashions. This would have made all-bisque bodies a necessity, and hiked the retail prices up.

Most bisque dolls have sleep eyes. The age of sleep eyes ran right through the period of bisque (continuing up to the present), and any maker who put out a bisque doll with fixed eyes was taking a gamble on public reaction. You will find SOME with fixed eyes, and they can be very attractive. But stop and think — you're looking at things from the viewpoint as an adult collector, not as a child who wants to play with the doll. For children, sleep eyes were one of the primary attractions in a doll. So were real eyelashes, which many bisque dolls also have. And so was a natural hair wig. These things were not just aesthetic touches; they added to the realism and made it easier for the child to believe she was playing with a real baby.

CELLULOID

Anyone past the age of 40 can remember playing with celluloid toys as a child. Not just toys but a wide variety of things were made of this substance, in all phases of industry. Then, suddenly, celluloid disappeared; *nothing* was made from it anymore, and celluloid objects gradually acquired a kind of curiosity interest. In many respects, celluloid was a miracle substance. It was strong, durable, lightweight, could be molded into any shape and painted. Best of all it was inexpensive — cheaper even than the lower classes of metal. But there was one fatal flaw in celluloid, which proved its downfall: it was highly inflammable. The fire danger posed by celluloid resulted in its ban from U.S. industry.

Vast quantities of dolls were made of celluloid, over a much longer time-span than you might suspect. They still show up in abundance on the collector market and are gaining more and more acceptance. Of course they aren't as handsome or exclusive as fine bisque dolls, and for a long time this was considered a strike against them as collectors' items. They were dolls for the children of poor and middle-income families, and most hobbyists traditionally wanted the cream of the crop. With prices for fine bisque and other deluxe dolls hitting such high price levels, there are many collectors who can no longer afford them. Antique bisque is out of reach for the majority of hobbyists. Because of their much lower prices (in general), celluloids have garnered their share of collecting attention. There are probably as many active collectors for celluloids, today, as for any other class of dolls. Some undoubtedly "backed into" celluloids, looking for affordable dolls; but, once into this group, found them quite interesting and well worth collecting and displaying. One advantage of collecting celluloids, aside from the attractive prices, is the available variety. There are celluloids of every imaginable type, and in all sizes from the very small to full size.

Celluloid was not developed as a product for doll making. It came into the doll industry after being used in other trades, but it ended up being as widely used for dolls, toys and novelties as for anything else. Its use was almost universal, encompassing not only America but many foreign countries. The Japanese were very heavy users of celluloid in all kinds of manufacture, prior to World War II. Since its U.S. ban did not, of course, extend to other nations, it is still being employed in many parts of the world. However, celluloid products can no longer legally be imported into America.

Celluloid was a by-product of the great Industrial Revolution, which began in Western Europe and America around 1840. The steam engine and other mechanical advances put factory production — in all industries — at record highs. Once the ability was gained to manufacture things *rapidly,* the next step was to develop ways of manufacturing them with less costly materials. Celluloid was invented as part of the overall quest for inexpensive materials that would substitute for those already in factory use. Its inventor was an Englishman named Parkes, who announced his miracle discovery to the world in 1855. He named it after himself, calling it Parkesine — or, literally, "Parkes' clay." While the interest of chemists and scientists was aroused by Parkesine, a number of years passed before industry took any real notice of it. It was not until the 1860's that Parkesine — by then called celluloid — started to be used in manufacturing on more than an experimental basis. Its earliest use was for billiard balls. Perhaps the circular shape of billiard balls suggested to manufacturers that another more or less circular product — the heads of dolls — might also be made of celluloid. In any case, celluloid dolls were on the market not long after, and their output continued to increase through the years. It is said that in many celluloid plants there was no actual allotment of the substance for doll making; workers merely gathered the scraps left when other products were punched out of their molds, and recycled it for dolls. But celluloid dolls found a very good market and in time this became one of the chief products for the celluloid makers.

The profusion of celluloid dolls on the U.S. market reached its peak in the years from 1930 to the conclusion of World War II (1945). The depression in America and Europe, which lingered throughout the 1930's, brought about a stronger-than-usual demand for inexpensive dolls and this naturally proved a boost to celluloids. Probably more than half of those retailed in America during the thirties were of Japanese origin. Some others, but not nearly as many, came from Germany. When the war began, imports from these countries were curtailed. This left a big gap in the market, to be filled by domestic celluloid factories. Though they stepped up production, shortages of materials and labor caused by the war resulted in limited additional output.

Generally speaking, the celluloid dolls made in France are the most desirable for collectors, with those of Japan ranking at the bottom of the list. France did not turn out a great number of celluloids but the quality was quite good. Celluloid dolls were being made in France from well before 1900, and imported into the U.S. from (probably) the very earliest period. The French had a tradition for fine doll-making, and the French public certainly knew a good doll when it saw one. So the factories making celluloid dolls in that country were encouraged to keep a high standard. The French celluloids were modeled directly after French bisques, which, as the collector knows, were the best dolls in the world. It was impossible to make a celluloid doll look exactly like bisque. But, when you compare the 19th century French celluloids against those made in the 20th century in other countries, you cannot fail to be impressed by them.

Celluloid dolls normally have molded hair, since the object was to retail them cheaply and molded hair is less expensive than a wig. Some with wigs will, however, be found — usually large-size dolls. Another way to save money was to paint on the eyes, a feature found in the majority of celluloids. But, once again, you will discover some which do not fall into that classification, as sleep eyes were occasionally used. Many celluloid dolls came with molded and painted costumes, rather than fabric clothing which could be removed and replaced. This, too, was an expense-saving measure.

The possibilities in collecting celluloids are endless. Fierce competition among the manufacturers resulted in many very unusual, novel types coming on the market, and these are of course among the collectors' favorites. Quite a few black celluloids were made, mostly overseas; these are highly sought after. There were also celluloids representing various professions, and of tiny infants as well as adults and even of comic characters. One can specialize in any of these directions, or others, and build a sizable collection. To the hobbyist's great advantage is the fact that many owners of old celluloid dolls are not aware of the current demand, and sell them at prices well below the real market values. Any regular visitor to flea markets and garage sales will encounter many celluloids in the $5-15 retail range which are being sold for $1 or $2. Quite a few sellers are not even aware that the dolls are old and are made of celluloid! You will commonly hear them referred to as "plastic"!

The most common type of damage to celluloid dolls is worn paint, with the white celluloid showing through. If this is merely in the form of minor scratches, to an unimportant area of the surface, the doll is still collectible but of course it should be bought only at an appropriate price. Since these dolls are hollow, you will also find specimens with a crushed arm or leg. These of course are worthless from a collector's point of view, unless the doll is extremely scarce. A restorer may be able to make an undetectable repair, but if the doll would have minimum value, even in good condition, it would hardly be worth the cost. You will likewise find some celluloid dolls in which the two halves of the mold are starting to come apart. Always check out potential purchases for damage of all kinds.

CHALK

Chalk has been used in the manufacture of many low-priced dolls of the 20th century. Chalk dolls have been made in America but to an even greater extent in Japan and (later) Hong Kong. In the decade or so following World War II, huge quantities of chalk dolls and other chalkware were imported to the U.S. from Japan and were sold in every variety store and toyshop. The majority were "statuette dolls" which stood upright and had molded and painted hair and clothing. Original selling prices were as low as 19¢. Even the large size chalk dolls went for less than $1. That was the whole motive of making dolls from chalk — to retail them cheaply and reach a very large audience, including many customers who could not afford dolls of other types.

When the chalk dolls of the 1940's and 1950's were current, no doll collector believed they could ever attain hobbyist interest. Today, now that 30 or 40 years have passed, they're beginning to acquire a certain charm — in the view of *some* collectors. Devotees of china and bisque dolls still staunchly maintain that chalk isn't worth a second class. But, as in other hobbies, there are many doll collectors who simply cannot afford the top-of-the-market material. And there are undoubtedly others who just happen to like chalk dolls, and would specialize in them even if cost was not an object.

Chalk is used in doll making because it has a resemblance to ceramic. If someone is not too familiar with chalk and the way it's made, he could possibly mistake it for some kind of low-grade ceramic ware. Actually, chalk is not ceramic. It falls into an entirely different class. Chalk, whether made into sticks for writing or into dolls or anything else, is composed of finely powdered fish bones. For many years chalk was used in making writing sticks, before anyone got the idea of manufacturing other products from it. Regardless of the form taken by chalk, it always has the ability to write. Rub the base of a chalk doll or statuette along a blackboard, and it will write as well as a stick of chalk. But this very feature is somewhat of a detraction when chalk is made into merchandise, as it leaves a powdery film on the hands whenever the object is handled. Painting the item reduces this to some extent as it tends to seal the chalk, but there are usually some areas which aren't painted — such as the base. After standing a chalk doll on a cabinet shelf for a while, you'll discover that a layer of white powder has gathered beneath the doll.

The biggest drawback of chalk dolls is, of course, their extreme fragility. Chalk in itself is not really more breakable than bisque or china, the materials from which the finest dolls are made. However, bisque and china are molded hollow, which makes for a very light weight. If they happen to be knocked or even dropped, they stand a chance of escaping injury. Chalk on the other hand, is always molded solid and therefore heavy. This greatly increases the risk of breakage, as a dropped chalk doll hits the floor with quite an impact. Also, when chalk breaks it will usually "explode" into many small pieces and powder, making repair almost impossible.

When shopping for chalk dolls, check to see that no pieces are missing or there are no gouges or chips. Also inspect the paint for signs of wear. Paint wears off chalk very easily, as the surface is not primed before application of the paint.

CHINA

China on the whole, is a misused and misunderstood word. When applied to dolls it is even more misused and misunderstood. You will often hear of any ceramic doll — even bisque — referred to as "china." China has, in common with other ceramic substances, the fact that it derives from a clay base. Beyond that, however, it is entirely individual, in its overall ingredients, its techniques of manufactures, and, especially, the physical appearance of the finished product. It may take the novice collector some time to visually recognize the differences between china and other ceramic dolls. Until that skill has been attained, he should be very cautious of accepting a seller's claim that any particular doll is "china."

As a class, china dolls — *real* china — are the rarest, most valuable, and possibly (though sharp differences of opinion prevail on this point) the most handsome of all dolls, in terms of those available to the collector. Nearly all china dolls are bonafide antiques. That is, they were manufactured 100 or more years ago. Some are considerably older than this, going back to the 18th century, but specimens from that remote period seldom pass through the market. They are truly museum pieces and that is precisely where the majority of them are: in the museums of the world, rather than in the hands of hobbyists and dealers.

China dolls are the "classics" of this hobby, just like "pine tree shillings" are in coin collecting and "postmaster provisionals" are in the world of stamps. They were not the first dolls, since the earliest specimens were hand-carved from wooden blocks or made from wax. But they were certainly the earliest factory-made dolls, and they have the important distinction of giving birth to doll making as an industry rather than (as it had been) the occupation of lone craftsmen and peddlers.

The workmanship on china dolls, in terms of modeling and enameling, is just as fine as on the best porcelain statuettes of their era. In fact, some of the heads were manufactured by the leading porcelain factories, whose names are legendary in the world of art. In the mid 1800's, when *bisque* started coming into the doll industry, connoisseurs of dolls were unanimous in their preference for china. They considered china the "real thing" and bisque a mere imitation. Though bisque was also ceramic, it was unglazed; the surface did not have the appearance of fine porcelain, and the painted colors (for the facial features) did not stand up as sharply as on china dolls. Those who could afford china dolls continued to buy them. When doll *collecting* began in earnest, after 1900, it was these early china specimens for which the collectors of that era searched. They had extremely little enthusiasm for bisque, regarding it in about the same light as the public had when bisque dolls first appeared on the market. This point of view prevailed for a very long time. Most collectors specialized in china, and china dolls were the only ones handled by antique dealers 50 or 60 years ago. With the rise in the number of bisque collectors, the market has evened out somewhat. Still, china dolls have a nobility and grace seldom achieved outside of this medium. With the artistry comes expense and the main spark that touched off the "bisque explosion" was the lofty prices of china dolls. They became too expensive for most collectors, in an era when $100 was considered a fabulous sum for an old doll. Scores of new hobbyists were entering the market and most of them wanted to collect dolls that were readily available and not TOO costly. Bisque dolls were talked about, written about, brought into the antique shops, and took the play almost totally away from "chinas." Today, the doll hobby literally revolves around bisque dolls. Some collectors are so unaware of china dolls that they automatically believe bisque to be the supreme dolls of the 19th century.

This does not mean that china dolls are not being collected any longer, or that they go begging when offered for sale. The prices are not cheap, BUT they have not advanced at the same pace as bisque prices — nor even as rapidly as the prices of dolls made from less luxurious materials. In terms of their age, scarcity and beauty, china dolls would surely have to be considered bargains at today's prices. They may be the last remaining true bargains in the world of doll collecting!

China itself has a very lengthy history, long before its use in doll making. The Chinese were the first people to make china, which is how it got its name. China is also known as porcelain and is characterized by a hard surface and baked-in gloss or sheen, usually called "china glaze." For centuries, Europeans admired the Oriental chinaware and tried to duplicate it themselves. Their efforts met nothing but failure until the 18th century, when potters in Saxony (a province of the old kingdom of Prussia) started to turn out true porcelain. Within a few decades, porcelain factories sprang up all over Europe and porcelain-making became one of the leading industries. Although tableware was the chief product of most porcelain manufacturers, they turned out full lines of other merchandise including home decor, personal adornment, etc. Only few porcelain dolls were made at first. They were bought by the wealthy and undoubtedly were prized possessions. These were show dolls — not for children to play with. In a sense they were statuettes, carried to the point of having jointed limbs and real clothing. Gradually the output of china dolls increased. France and Germany were the early leaders in producing china dolls, and retained their supremecy during the entire period in which china dolls were manufactured (to the third quarter of the 19th century). The reason was, very simply, that France and Germany were the leading porcelain makers. Every type of porcelain produced in these countries was regarded as the best of its kind.

Doll making was never the main employment for any of the large porcelain factories. But as the 19th century progressed there was more and more demand for dolls. Manufacturers set themselves up to assemble dolls, using heads and limbs bought from the porcelain factories and attaching them to various bodies (usually cloth stuffed with more cloth!). These manufacturers put their dolls into the toy shops of Paris, London, and other great cities, and also shipped them for distribution in America. They became very popular in the U.S.

When bisque and other materials started coming into use for dolls, china went almost immediately on the decline. Even though the more astute customers still recognized china's superiority, there was a great mass of buyers to whom the price mattered more than anything else.

By around 1880 the production of china dolls had greatly declined, and those still being made were not the quality of their predecessors. They were mostly manufactured with an eye to cutting costs and putting them on a competitive footing with other dolls. Thus the collector of fine china or porcelain dolls ought to set his sights on the older examples, from before 1880 and preferably even before 1870. In terms of quality, those from about 1820 to

1850 are acknowledged to be the finest. They even have a slight edge over the earlier china dolls, of pre-1820. While the earlier ones are rarer and often sell for much higher sums, they are too unlike dolls and too suggestive of "dressed statues" to suit some collectors. By around 1820, the manufacturers had reached the stage of combining excellently modeled and enameled china with the philosophy of what a doll ought to be. The china dolls of that era are superb "little people," undoubtedly the finest dolls ever made.

You will find considerable variety in the world of china dolls. There are both *hard paste* and *soft paste* models. The hard paste are usually the more highly regarded. Soft paste china has a surface that resembles the shell of an egg, if you look closely. Because of this, it tends to become ingrained with grime and discolors faster than hard paste, which can look new after the passing of hundreds of years. Review some 1,000-year-old Chinese hard paste porcelains in museums — you'll get the feeling that they were made only yesterday!

There are also many differences in the method of construction, so far as the bodies are concerned, and the materials. Dolls made wholly of china, including the torso, were very rare. It was deemed pointless to use china for the body, since it would be covered by clothing. Also, having a china body made the doll more breakable. In order to allow the doll to wear open-collar or low-cut clothing, the shoulder head was used — that is, a head which did not terminate at the base of the neck but was continued downward to include shoulders. This was then attached to a body of a different, more durable (and cheaper) substance. If stuffed cloth was not going to be used, wood was generally the choice. Many china dolls, in fact, have carved wooden hands. When painted in a flesh tone or white with a touch of pink, they go very well with the porcelain head. If you find a china doll dating before 1870, whose body consists of pressed cardboard with fabric stuffing, the odds are good that the body is later in date than the head. It may have been added to the head by a dealer after the doll reached the collector market. An experienced collector can spot these "right head, wrong body" dolls with no trouble.

Values of china dolls hinge on many factors, which may not be easy for a beginner to fully appreciate. These are objects of art and, like other objects of art, the price can be influenced by details which may seem very minor. Everyone wants his china dolls to be antique, and in the original condition (or as close as possible to the original condition). Beyond this, there are still other matters to take into account, which go a long way toward determining the value. The fame and reputation of the manufacturer (of the doll's head) counts for a great deal in the price. Any doll with a Sevres head is automatically a premium item, as Sevres was one of the legendary French porcelain houses. The same is true of Meissen, a Saxon porcelain factory. Then we have the modeling of the head to consider: is it typical of the time and place? Above average? Not quite up to average? Is the subject common or out of the ordinary? Is there good reason to suspect that the doll is rarer than most china dolls of that time-period? The size, too, will play a part, as the largest dolls tend to realize premium prices when all else is equal. The average head circumference on a china doll of pre-1870 is 9 to 10 inches, measured around the forehead. From 11 to 12 inches is large, and anything over 13 inches is truly huge — usually with an appropriate premium in the price.

CLOTH

Cloth is one of the primary doll materials. Usually it serves for the body, but there are also many dolls with cloth heads — either cloth alone or in combination with another substance. All-cloth dolls do not date back as far as those made of carved wood or wax, which have origins in the 17th century. By the 18th century, however, all-cloth dolls were being made, both by doll makers and amateurs ("folk" dolls). Cloth has long been the favorite material among non-professional doll makers, as a cloth head can be easily sewn, stuffed, and decorated. The decoration can consist of nothing more elaborate than small buttons for facial features; or it can be drawn or painted on. Sometimes a piece of canvas or sailcloth is sewn over the face, before decoration, if painting is to be done. This proves a better surface for painting, being stiffer and less porous. Also, canvas is longer-wearing than cloth and such a doll will be more durable.

Cloth dolls have been on the retail market for a very long time. Regardless of the currently popular taste in dolls, from one generation to the next, specimens of cloth were produced and sold along with the rest. In the age when china and bisque dolls were intended mainly as showpieces, cloth dolls served the purpose of playthings — dolls that could be handled and enjoyed without any worry about breakage.

Cloth dolls come in so many varieties that it would be impossible to detail them all. Two of the most interesting for collectors are the lithographed cloth faces, and mask-face cloth dolls. Both of these represented efforts to avoid the task of painting a cloth doll's face, a job which may be very pleasurable for an amateur doll maker but rather time-consuming in factory work. After the invention of lithography in the late 1700's (a technique of printing from stone plates, which, under the term "chromolithography," allowed for beautiful color reproduction), all sorts of store merchandise was lithographed. A big industry sprang up in lithographed wallpaper, and that led to lithographed tablecloths. When manufacturers saw that they could print on cloth, and that the images would hold even after washing, the sky was the limit. Lithographed cloth dolls started coming on the scene in the late 1800's, but their big era of popularity was not reached until around 1910. Some of them had lithographed faces, with dressed bodies; others were lithographed over the entire surface of the doll, clothes, shoes and all. These (the whole-surface lithographs) are the most intriguing. Of course, when a lithographed doll was made, the fabric was always printed BEFORE the doll was sewn. Printing would have been impossible thereafter; nevertheless some collectors are under the impression that the doll was sewn, stuffed, and THEN printed! Lithographed dolls have a character all their own, which is captivating to some hobbyists. In the other mediums — china, bisque, wood, etc. — the doll maker was always limited, somewhat, by the materials he used. Certain standard approaches had to be followed. In lithographing, the manufacturer could (if he wished) work from a photograph of an actual person, which had been transformed into a lithograph. The face of such a doll was strikingly "real," though, of course, it was absolutely flat as it consisted of a picture and nothing more. Many novelty lithographed dolls were sold. One of the more valuable types was a double-faced, with a likeness of a white girl on one side and a black girl on the other. Lithographed cloth dolls are hard to find in good condition because the printing wore off as the doll was handled. Any specimen in "as new" preservation is quite a prize.

Mask-type cloth dolls had bodies and heads of cloth, like the lithographed variety. Instead of a printed face, the front of the doll's head was covered by a thin molded mask-face made from another substance — usually plastic or papier mache. This was an ideal approach for doing animal dolls of the Bugs Bunny and Mickey Mouse type. It was also used, though not quite as successfully, for dolls with human faces. The problem with human-likeness dolls was that the mask represented a very sharp contrast from the cloth head. To look satisfactory it had to be camouflaged in some way, such as by having the doll wear a bonnet that fitted close to its ears.

As you can probably guess (or have noticed, if you're already into doll collecting), the mask faces did not stay in place forever. Even with ordinary, normal handling, they could come loose in time. Many of them received a bit MORE than normal handling: their youthful owners peeled the faces right off them. Once the face is gone the doll is, of course, worthless. But if you have the face and it's detached, it can be glued back in place so that nobody will be the wiser. Most of these masks were stitched on, as well as glued. Even if you skip the stitching and just remount them with glue, they'll hold well enough for display purposes (not for play purposes!).

On the whole, cloth dolls are easier to repair than most other kinds. Most of their ills can be cured merely by sewing or adding more stuffing.

COMPOSITION

This is the one term in the whole realm of doll materials which confuses even some experienced collectors! "Composition" sounds like it could mean just about anything — and that's pretty close to correct.

Composition dolls have mainly been made in the 20th century, but some of them date back to the closing years of the 19th century. The fact that a doll is made of composition (either in whole or part) is, therefore, no clue in estimating the time of manufacture. When well-made — which is the case with most composition dolls — the doll bears a striking resemblance to bisque, and of course this is no coincidence. Composition was put into use by the doll factories as a way of imitating bisque, at a lower production cost and hence a lower retail price on the market.

When bisque dolls became the rage in the fourth quarter of the 19th century, manufacturers looked around for something as "bisque-like" as possible. As doll collectors, it might be hard for us to see this in proper perspective. Hobbyists and connoisseurs are accustomed to taking a very careful, critical look at dolls. They can spot differences in material with no trouble at all. But to the public of 1890, bisque dolls were simply *nice looking dolls.* If another substance was substituted for bisque, and the doll came out looking just about as good, nobody really cared. Especially when they received a discount in the price!

Composition dolls were made in the same way as bisque. The heads were shaped or pressed in a mold, then painted. Like bisque heads they could have painted, fixed, or sleep eyes. They could have molded, painted hair, or wear a wig. In just about every respect they were the same, except in the substance used in molding. Bisque was made from a clay slip, like porcelain. Composition was not a true pottery. It contained some clay (usually not a high grade), along with various filled materials. The filler was generally sawdust or pulped-up cardboard or both. Some glue was added so that the head would hold its shape after coming out of the mold. If this makes it sound as though composition heads are less breakable than bisque, such is not the case. Vulnerability to breakage is about the same.

To achieve a skin tone without the need for painting, pink watercolor was usually added to the ingredients while still in a soft state (before molding). This of course resulted in the entire head being pink — including the hair. But it was easier to paint over the areas not intended to be pink, than to paint the entire head from scratch. When you find a composition doll with pink eyes — which you will from time to time — this is a specimen that slipped by without getting its eyes painted white.

In terms of contours, depth, and realism, a composition head was not inferior to those made of bisque. Of course, this depended on the quality of a mold. If the manufacturer was using a good mold, he could get equally satisfactory results from bisque slip or from composition. And since he could save money with composition, this proved a strong incentive.

Composition heads were placed on dolls of all sizes and types, including marionettes and hand puppets. Any doll made between 1920 and 1950 which has a high quality, attractive face is usually made of composition. Composition just about ruled the doll industry during those years.

PAPIER MÂCHÉ

Papier mâché has not been among the most widely used doll materials, but dolls of this substance do turn up on the market and it is useful for the hobbyist to know something about them. Papier mâché has been used in making doll heads as well as bodies. You will find dolls whose heads are papier mâché, but whose bodies are cloth or another substance and vice-versa (a papier mâché body on a doll with a bisque or other kind of head). Some dolls, but not too many, have both papier mâché heads and bodies. In terms of age, there are papier mâché examples from the antique period and the 20th century, and also of many different geographical locations. It appears that many doll manufacturers experimented with papier mâché, but it did not become overly popular at any time or in any region. Chiefly the advantage of papier mâche was its cheapness. Even though the material itself was very inexpensive, it still had to be molded like bisque or composition. Once the time and labor was taken into account, the savings in using papier mâché was very little. Another "plus" was that a papier mâché head was less liable to break than one made from a ceramic substance. But if it suffered surface wear at just about the same rate, and if the mâché was thin (as was often the case), it could be easily dented if a child squeezed the head. Furthermore, papier mâché is subject to deterioration by mildew and also insect infestation. Few manufacturers added insecticide to the formula when they made papier mâché. This made it an ideal target for household pests of all kinds.

Most of us are basically familiar with papier mâché from grade-school art projects or home experimenting. Many of us have even made dolls out of papier mâché. However, the technique that we've used (and that doll artists of the present day use) are different than those employed in factory work.

When an artisan or hobbyist makes a doll from papier mache, he begins by making a clay sculpture of the head. This is covered in layers of wet mâché. When the mache dries, he saws the head in half, scoops out the clay, then glues the halves of mâché back together. The sawing is hidden by the doll's wig. If neatly done this can produce a very handsome doll, but it is not practical for mass production. In mass production, mold pressing is used instead of the clay-and-cutting approach. The molds are identical to those used for bisque dolls. The mâché is made in huge vats and poured into the molds, then pressed in place and dried. This "factory mâché" is not made of long paper strips, like artisans use, but tiny bits of paper resembling confetti. It's mixed with water and glue and, while in the liquid state, looks like mud. And it still looks like mud after drying, unless a coloring agent has been added. After drying, the head is painted.

Papier mâché dolls have been more widely made in foreign countries than in the U.S. The eastern European countries (Poland, Yugoslavia, Lithuania) have a greater affection for papier mâché, it seems, than any other people. They have also been made, but not so extensively, in China and Mexico. Production in western Europe and America has been very low. As far as currently produced dolls are concerned, there are more papier mâchés coming out of Mexico at the moment than any other country. They are extremely colorful, often unusual in design, and well worth the collector's attention. But they are not too easy to get in most parts of the U.S.

Some old papier mâché dolls from the 19th and the early 20th centuries have a wax coating over the mâché. The facial features were molded into the mâché, as if the head was designed to be painted but, instead, it was covered in a thin layer of wax. Although unpopular this was an alternative to standard wax molding and the results were satisfactory.

WAX

Wax has played an important role in the history of dolls, especially in their earlier history. The collector will find wax dolls here and there in the antique shops, but they are even more numerous in museums. Any museum with a good collection of antique dolls is certain to be showing many of wax.

In modern doll making, wax has been gradually phased out and is no longer used for commercially manufactured dolls. It is still, however, a favorite substance among amateur and craft doll makers, thanks to the fact that it can be worked with a minimum of tools and equipment. Carving in wax is similar to carving in soap. The objection to wax, in commercially made dolls, was that wax heads could not stand up to the wear and tear of play. They were fine for display-piece dolls, but when the industry changed direction and concentrated on "play" rather than "show" dolls, wax was doomed. Some play dolls were made with wax heads but these are mostly very old ones. The toy dealers kept getting complaints about dolls that wore out quickly, and these complaints filtered back to the manufacturers. Even though bisque was more breakable than wax, it did not show surface wear the way wax did. So nearly all the leading makers adopted bisque as their primarily substance, and made wax dolls only occasionally as display items.

If we say that the history of dolls begins with specimens of the 17th century (disregarding dolls of the Egyptians, Romans and other ancient civilizations), then wax specimens figure very prominently in the origin of dolls. The majority of surviving dolls from the 17th century are wax. This was apparently considered the logical material from which to make dolls, at that time. Porcelain was not yet known. Ordinary pottery heads were sometimes used, but did not have as much acceptance because of fragility. Also, pottery had to be cast in molds, whereas wax offered the opportunity for a craftsman to shape and carve as he went along. Hand carving is how all the early wax dolls were made. No molding was done at that period or for a very long time thereafter. The manufacturer could take real pride in a carved-head doll, and the purchaser knew he was getting something of which no exact duplicate existed. There was also another impetus for carving dolls from wax rather than liquifying the wax and pouring it into molds. Molding was a big operation and was suitable only if the demand for dolls was really strong. In the early days of doll making, there was no widespread demand simply because most people did not even know dolls existed! The artisans who made dolls did not earn fulltime livelihoods from them. There just weren't enough customers. These craftsmen also manufactured other things. They probably created wax designs for pottery makers, to be used in fashioning pottery molds, and similar kinds of work.

Not too many of us will ever be fortunate enough to own a 17th century wax doll. The numbers in existence are quite small, and most of those which do exist are now in museums or otherwise out of circulation. Whenever one passes through the market, the price is very high — too high for the average hobbyist. Nevertheless they are of great interest to any doll collector. They show the primitive approach to doll designing and they show, also, what was considered handsome and appealing at that time. The pioneer wax dolls have a homespun, folksy quality. We could speculate that some were made by inexperienced carvers, but we really don't know. There are no records, no catalogues, no documentation. All we have are some of the dolls themselves, and we ought to be very glad that we have *them* if nothing else.

The 17th century wax dolls are all adult dolls, and all of the showpiece variety — though many are worn to such extent that they were obviously played with by children at some point in their history. Some of the heads appear a bit small for the bodies, but this is only because we're accustomed to the practice of scaling dolls' heads a little too *large* for the bodies (which has been going on for well over 100 years). Actually the early dolls are pretty well in proportion. Some are made in the likeness of kings, noblemen, or royal ladies. There are not too many representing ordinary people, but some of that type do exist. As for 17th century dolls in the likeness of children or infants, there were probably none made, and almost certainly none in existence today. There was no motive to do this, since the dolls were intended to be displayed just like statuettes and the owners naturally wanted something grand and picturesque.

We do not know who the original purchasers of these early wax dolls were. Undoubtedly they came from the ranks of the wealthy of that time. Since each individual doll was handcrafted, with sewn garments (sometimes of luxurious materials), there is no reason to believe that the selling prices were cheap. The average citizen probably was no closer to a doll in the 17th century than the average hobbyist of today.

In terms of body construction, the early wax dolls were of various types. It is interesting to note that many of them had carved wooden hands, rather than hands of wax. Some dolls of this era also had carved wooden heads. Wood did not become as popular for doll heads as wax, simply because it was more of a chore to carve. Two or three doll heads could be made of wax, in the length of time taken to make one of wood. Also, wax had something of the color and tone of human flesh, which wood obviously did not.

The earliest wax dolls were usually made in France and England, so far as we know. However, it is not always possible to identify the country of origin of these very primitive specimens, since they carry no markings whatsoever. The style of dress is not of much help, as there is usually no assurance that the costume is original. Even if the costume absolutely dates to the 17th century, it is not necessarily original; it could have been replaced soon after the doll was manufactured, after exporting from the country of origin. More 17th century wax dolls seem to turn up in England than anywhere else, but there is a strong possibility that many of them were not manufactured there. Quite likely France was the leading producer, if the facts could really be known. As far as wax dolls coming from other countries is concerned, the only two that might have been making dolls in the 17th century are Germany and Italy. Italian wax dolls of that era were undoubtedly restricted to creche (nativity) figures, not dolls in the accepted sense.

Any object that has endured a 300-year lifespan is likely to have undergone some change along the way, both accidental and intentional. Thus we find that hardly any 17th century dolls are in a condition approximating, or even approaching, the original. Most have suffered a good deal of wear and tear, both on the head and body. Some of the people, into whose hands these dolls passed before being recognized as collectors' items, took whatever measures they saw fit to preserve or improve them. Some 17th century dolls had their heads and faces painted in the 18th and 19th centuries, when they were just "old dolls" and nobody thought about destroying their antiquarian value. Painting was a sure-fire way of hiding scratches, nicks, grime and other signs of deterioration. Either that or you will find specimens which obviously have the faces smoothed out, to remove or reduce deep scratches. This was apparently done with "OO" grade sandpaper — a very bad practice but, again, we are talking about a long era when philosophies were different. Sometimes, too, recarving was attempted, by heating up the head to soften it a bit and then using common carving tools. Any collector will surely cringe at that thought!

Wax dolls continued to be made in the 18th and the 19th centuries, but the techniques changed over the years. As the doll market expanded, and toyshops started opening up all over Europe, the carving method was too slow — and too costly. So the manufacturers switched over to molds, using liquid wax. Wax takes a mold impression very well and there was never any objection to wax dolls on that ground. For display dolls, wax was the perfect medium.

The problems encountered with wax dolls, by their owners, were often a result of their own thoughtlessness. They did not stop to realize that wax, even after being shaped into a doll's head, was still wax. Many display dolls were placed on fireplace mantelpieces and subjected to intense heat day after day. This naturally caused the wax to soften and gradually the facial features became "drawn." Then they blamed the manufacturer for producing an inferior doll, whereas even the most basic care on their part would have preserved the doll in perfect condition for many, many years.

MECHANICAL DOLLS

Probably the most intriguing class of dolls is the mechanicals — those that DO something, instead of just appealing to the visual senses. These dolls date back well over 100 years and are found among antique specimens in almost as large a quantity as in dolls of the 20th century. Antique mechanicals constitute a collectors' specialty in themselves. Many superb collections of them have been assembled. They aren't cheap. They aren't always in working order. Often the key is missing and a substitute has to be found. The parts are generally rusty and need cleaning and oiling. But these old mechanicals, reflecting the ingenuity of long-vanished generations, have a charm which you may find totally beguiling.

Mechanical dolls were produced around 1840 and their output increased almost year by year thereafter — though some manufacturers flatly refused to get into mechanicals. Traditionalists among the public and among doll makers felt there was something gimmicky about them. This was definitely the minority viewpoint. Mechanical dolls sold, and sold very well. Many mechanical dolls were bought for the sake of their novelty which would not have been bought otherwise.

The rise of mechanicals during the 19th century reflects the competitiveness in doll making during that era. A pretty face could result in a very profitable doll — but a pretty face in combination with mechanical action was a double threat. By installing a motor (or motors) in a doll, there was practically no limit to the things they could be made to do, and each new "action" was a selling point. Just like the auto manufacturers of a later period, doll makers vied with each other to bring out the most original "actions," and of course each company maintained top secrecy about the coming season's new models. They would usually be released about two months before Christmas, to take advantage of the holiday rush. A doll that proved a hot item around Christmas, even if its sales dipped sharply thereafter, could bring colossal revenues to its manufacturer. With mechanicals that was usually the case. Even the more popular ones tended to be flashes in the pan. They sold superbly for a while and then lagged on the market, as their novelty wore off. By then a rival manufacturer had come out with something more unusual, and the tide of business shifted over to him. So it went year after year, decade after decade. The result was thousands upon thousands of mechanicals coming into creation, providing a feast not only for the Victorian-era child who played with these toys but for today's doll collector.

All of the early mechanical dolls operated with spring-driven motors, wound with keys. Regardless of what the action consisted of, it was worked by such a motor — or by several of them, depending upon the size of the doll and complexity of the action. The principle of spring-driven motors is, of course, of very early origins. Watches using such motors were being made in France and Germany in the 16th century, if not earlier. Their use in other products, besides watches, came about very gradually, and for a long time their full potential was not even suspected. The direct ancestor of the mechanical doll was the *automaton,* in which spring-driven motors were used and the general principle was the same. Just like dolls, automatons were make-believe people, but they constitute a class of objects all their own and are seldom collected by doll enthusiasts. This is probably because nobody played with automatons. They were made either as showpieces for the parlor or, sometimes, in extra-large size for theatrical entertainment. Theatrical automatons were often in life size, fully as large as a human.

Automatons originated in the 18th century, at least half a century before the first mechanical dolls went on the market. Mainly they were made in France, and all the best ones were French. Just as the mechanical doll was intended as a doll that "did something," automatons were designed as statues that "did something." Their construction was very similar to that of dolls. They often had china heads and wood bodies, fully jointed, and wore real clothing. Automatons were made in the likeness of jesters, soldiers, band leaders, dancers, musicians, Arabs, and everything else under the sun. Some of them featured extremely sophisticated, intricate movements — much more intricate than anything attempted with dolls. There were musical automatons and so-called silent automatons. The musical ones had a music-box fitted in the base. A typical automaton was an organ grinder and his monkey, in which the music box played a standard organ-grinder tune while the automaton worked away. There were automatons with moving eyes, moving eyelids, moving fingers. They were considered the wonder of the age. And it was pretty wonderful, in an era without electricity or any kind of modern apparatus, that "statues" could be made to come alive. Some people were so mystified by them that they believed automatons to be possessed of magical powers. Naturally, showmen took full advantage of this. They put automatons on stage and rigged them with speakers, through which a voice spoke. Or they placed a person inside a automaton, and endowed it with the powers to play a chess game. These stage exhibitions created additional interest in the small automatons for home entertainment, even if the smaller ones were less talented.

Most of the early mechanical dolls did something which automatons hardly ever did: they walked. Mechanical walking dolls are referred to in the hobby as "walkers," and they're still being made today — more than 140 years later. The only real difference is that the modern version is battery operated, rather than key-wound. Also, some of the modern ones operate by remote control, which was impossible in the age of the spring-driven motor.

The ideal and most lifelike way for a doll to walk is by alternate movement of the legs. Some of the pioneer mechanicals were designed to do this, but it soon became clear that the approach had a serious flaw. Unless the doll's feet were enormously large, it would tip over while walking and fall flat on the floor — often breaking its china or bisque head in the process. And there it would lay, helpless, its legs still moving in a walking motion until the winding ran down. Various attempts were made to solve this problem and keep the "walkers" upright. Since the dolls of those days wore very long sweeping gowns, quite a bit of machinery could be hidden beneath the gown with nobody being any the wiser. One solution was to mount the doll on a low platform base, attached to wheels. This allowed the doll to walk without moving its legs and without running the risk of toppling over. Of course, the walking motion was lost — the doll simply moved forward without giving the appearance of actually walking.

One way to retain the moving-leg action was to provide a prop of some kind to serve as ballast. So some dolls were given dogs to walk, or carriages to push. The prop was set with wheels, and colorfully painted. These are extremely desirable dolls. Usually they aren't in working condition when found, but anyone with a touch of mechanical skills can repair them.

The number of mechanicals coming on the market greatly increased as the 19th century wore along. All sorts of experiments were made with mechanicals of very large or small size, and with different types of action. Instead of just leg movement, hand movement was added in some models, and props were added which gave the hand movement added realism (such as lifting a pair of spectacles to the face). Then in 1871 came the "Wonderful Creeping Baby," patented by Robert Clay. This rare doll — really rare when in working order — was made in the likeness of an infant which creeped along the floor on hands and knees. There were other dolls that threw kisses or fanned themselves with fans. Nobody had a monopoly on mechanicals. They were made in all parts of the world, and the patents taken out on them would probably fill a book. Quite a few of those sold in the U.S. in the 1880's came from Germany. After 1900, Japan was the leading importer of mechanical dolls to America. But the American factories likewise made a great deal of them.

All-Bisque Dolls

Bahr And Proschild

Alt, Beck And Gottschalck

Louis Amberg And Son

George Borgfeldt And Company

George Borgfeldt And Company

DANCING KEWPIE SAILOR

KEWPIE

Bru

BRU JNE R

BREVETE S.G.D.G.

Y 8 M

Cameo

Martha Chase

PAWTUCKET. R.I.
MADE IN U.S.A.

Danel et Cie

BÉBÉ FRANÇAIS

Dressel

Germany

13/0

Dressel

"Holz Masse"

Cp

C & O
Dressel

Effanbee

EFFANBEE
DURABLE
DOLLS

EFFANBEE
DOLLS
WALK-TALK-SLEEP

Franz Schimidt And Company

S
h
F. C.

F. S. & Co

Fulper

FULPER
MADE IN
USA
2B

Gauthier

F.G.

Gebruder Heubach

8192
Germany
Gebrüder Heubach
5/0 1/2
G 5/0 1/2 H

Goebel

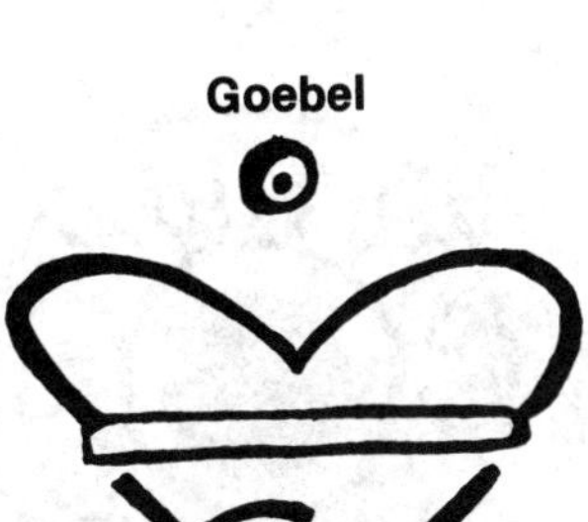

Heinrich Handwerck

Hch 6/0 H.
Germany

H HANDWERCK

Max Handwerck

Max
HANDWERCK

Germany

Heubach Koppelsdorf

E.I. Horseman

Made In USA
HORSMAN
Doll
19 © 10

Jumeau

DÉPOSÉ
TETE JUMEAU
B^TE SGDG
6

Kämmer And Reinhardt

ROYAL
K&R

K & R
SIMON & HALBIG
122
32

Kestner

JDK
Germany

Kewpie

KEWPIE
GERMANY

COPY RIGHT
ROSE ONEILL

Kewpie

KEWPIE
REG U.S.
PAT. OFF.

Lanternier

Limoges
A L

Fabrication
Francaise

AL & Cie
Limoges

Kley And Hahn

K&H
Germany

K H
Walküre

Lenci

Lenci di E. SCAVINI
TURIN (italy)
Made in ITALY
N. 159G
Pat Sept 9,1921, Pat. N. 142433
Bre 56 DG.X 87395.Brevetto 501.178

Lenci
TORINO
MADE IN ITALY

Käthe Kruse

Käthe
Kruse

Käthe Kruse

Limbach Porcelain

Metal Heads

Louis R. Kampes Studios

Armand Marseille

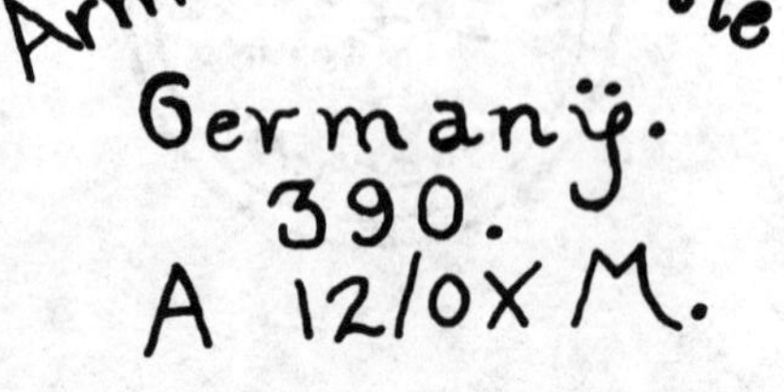

Morimura Brothers

Pierotti

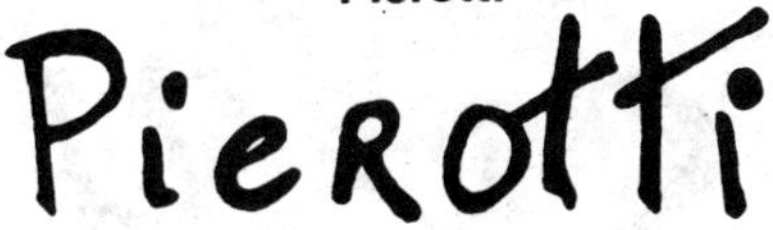

Princess Elizabeth

Rabery And Delphieu

Rawhide Dolls (Darrow Manufacturing Company)

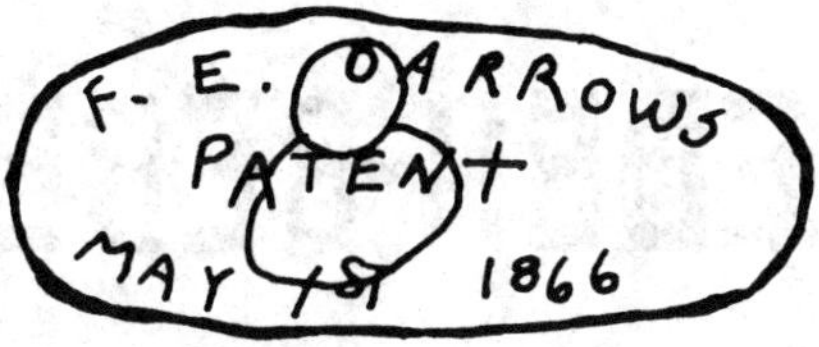

Recknagez

Rhecinische Gummit And Celluioid Fabric

Rohemer Fashion

Bruno Schmidt

Schmitt

SCH

Schoenau And Hoffmeister

S PB H

Schoenhut

H.F. Schoenhut
C
1913

Schoenhut Doll
Pat Jan 17th 1911
USA

Simon And Halbig

S&H

SFBJ

SFBJ
marque déposée

PARIS
DÉPOSÉ

EDEN-BÉBÉ

Steiff

Bouton dans l'oreille.

Herm Steiner

Herm Steiner

HS

Germany

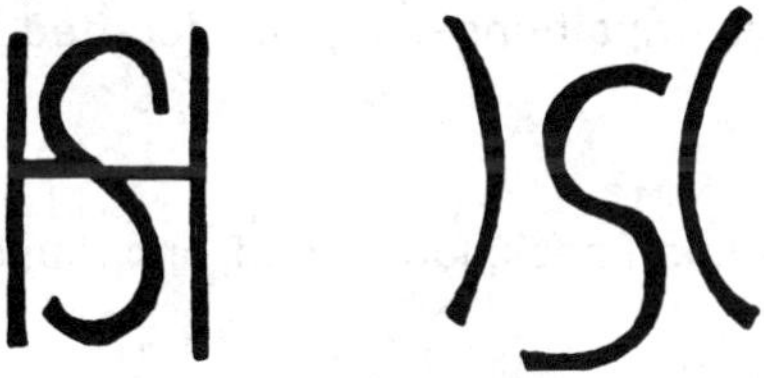

Jules Steiner

STEINER
.S.G.D.G.
PARIS
A11

Superior

M & S
Superior

Unis France

Unis
France

Adolf Wislizenus

A.W.
Set: Q/7

GLOSSARY

ACTION

Used to describe the mechanical (usually spring driven) action of a doll. The most common is walking, but action incorporated into dolls has taken numerous other forms over the years, such as raising one or both arms or creeping along the floor.

ANTIQUE

Strictly speaking, an "antique" is defined as any object 100 or more years old. Though this applies to dolls as well as to other manufactured items, collectors are loose in their interpretation of it. Any doll made before 1900 is regarded as antique by most collectors and dealers. Whether or not the designation can be properly applied to any given doll is not really a matter of much importance, since the value hinges on other factors.

ALL-BISQUE

Usually small dolls popular in the 1880's and during the Kewpie era in the 1900's. Most have shoulder joints only, but a few are fully jointed.

ALL STEEL DOLLS

Invented in 1902 by Vincent Lake, they're made entirely of thin sheet steel. Ball-jointed limbs including the wrists and the ankles; strung with steel springs.

ART DOLL

A doll based on an artist's illustrations or paintings, or a handcrafted doll designed by an artist.

BABY DOLL

A doll made to look like a baby, with a short neck, large head, and rounded limbs and torso.

BALDHEADS

Early twentieth century baldheads are dolls with painted and molded hair. In the nineteenth century, this term seemingly referred to dolls' heads whose crowns were not cut off.

BALL HEAD

A china shoulder-head without modeled or painted hair, usually having a black cloth circle on the crown of the head to which a wig may be pasted.

BALL JOINT

Ball jointed dolls were introduced around 1885 and became almost instantly popular. The ball joints were applied at the junctures where the arms and legs met the body, and sometimes also at the knees and even the wrists.

Elastic string secured the parts together, with the result that such dolls could be bent to take almost any pose. This principle had earlier been used — and was adapted from — the wooden mannakin dolls from the world of art instruction.

BÉBÉ

The French word for baby.

BÉBÉ INCASSABLE

The French used this term when describing their bisque-head, jointed, composition-bodied dolls.

BELTON-TYPE DOLLS

Dolls with bald heads made of bisque.

BENT LIMB

Baby bodies invented in Germany in 1909 that did not use ball joints.

BISQUE

Unglazed tinted or painted porcelain used for heads and sometimes for bodies, too.

BLANK OPEN MOUTH

Doll whose open mouth is painted white to suggest teeth, but in which individual teeth are not indicated.

BLOWN GLASS EYE

Stationary; used in both shoulder head and swivel-neck dolls; unusually beautiful, with great depth and naturalness with well defined irises and pupils.

BONNET DOLL

A doll with a hat or bonnet molded as part of the head. Also called a hatted doll.

BOUDOIR DOLL

A large doll intended not for children, but for the decoration of an adult bedroom.

BOXWOOD

Some Parisian dolls were made of this material in the early 1900's.

BREAST PLATE DOLLS' HEADS

An American term denoting a doll's head with shoulders attached.

BRUSH MARKS

A painted-head doll in which traces of brush marks are visible. These can occur regardless of the material, as they were the fault of the paint being too thick or the use of a too-stiff brush.

BUST HEADS

A French term denoting a doll's head with shoulders attached.

BUTTERFLY DOLL

A bonnet-type doll with molded butterfly headdress.

BYE-LO BABY

A life-sized baby doll (three days old) designed and copyrighted by Grace Storey Putnam in 1922, the first of four such copyrights.

CARNIVAL DOLL

Doll made to be given as a prize at a carnival or amusement park, either in games of chance or skill (such as knocking down metal bottles with a baseball). Usually made wholly of chalk. These date mainly from the 1930's and later and a large number are Japanese imports.

CARVED HEAD

Doll heads of carved wood have been produced in virtually every part of the world, and from the earliest times to the 20th century. They range from crude (but highly collectibles) folk specimens to the strikingly realistic wood heads of Schoenhut. Though excellent results can be obtained in this medium, not to mention the durability of carved head dolls, it is not suitable for mass production of dolls in the popular price range. Carving is a slow process and the resulting product is invariably expensive.

CELLULOID DOLLS

A synthetic material discovered in England which is composed mostly of pyroxylin and camphor. First used for making dolls in the 1860's by the Hyatt brothers.

CENTER PART

Refers to the doll's hair being parted in the center.

CHARACTER DOLL

In reference to antique dolls, this term denotes dolls modelled after real people in order to achieve realism in the features. For dolls made after 1900, this term denotes dolls modelled to look like celebrities and comic characters.

CHINA-HEAD DOLLS

Made of white clay, they are tinted, fired, dipped in glaze, and refired. First used in the 1750's, they were not used commonly until the 1840's.

CHINA-LIMB DOLLS

Dolls made during the 1840's and the 1850's had jointed wooden bodies. In later years, these dolls were made with cloth bodies which had no joints or swinging-type joints.

CLOSED/OPEN MOUTH (or OPEN/CLOSED MOUTH)

A term used occasionally, meaning a doll whose mouth is partially open. It is dropping out of the vocabulary of doll collecting, as today any doll whose mouth is not obviously closed is called "open mouth" (the approach we have adopted in the listings).

CLOSED TOP HEAD

A doll head with an opening where the crown of the head normally would be. Commonly made in wax, composition, and papier mache, the opening allowed for a wig to be tied securely, or to facilitate the insertion of the eyes.

CLOVERLEAF DOLLS

Bonnet-type doll with molded headdress in shape or cloverleaf, porcelain limbs, pink muslin body.

COMPOSITION DOLLS

A wood pulp mixture is used to make this type of doll.

CONGLOMERATE DOLL

Doll whose head was made by one factory and whose body was the work of another. Such specimens were very common in the fourth quarter of the 19th century, when German-made bisque heads were used by French doll manufacturers. They were then stamped with the French manufacturer's mark, thereby obscuring their real origin.

CORK STUFFED

Shredded cork stuffing has sometimes been used in dolls, particularly those made in Germany in the early 1900's. It was inexpensive and believed to give the doll body a more lifelike appearance.

CRECHE DOLL

Figure not made as a doll but as a component in a nativity (creche) set. Modern creche figures are usually made of chalk or hollow composition with painted bodies, and do not interest doll collectors. However in the 18th and 19th centuries, particularly in Italy, some very elaborate ones were made, just as fine as the best dolls. These are highly sought collectors' items, even when they occur for sale individually (lacking other components of the set).

DEEP SHOULDER

The older china shoulder heads were designed with more of the shoulder area being in china in order to allow for the low-cut, off-shoulder fashions popular during the first half of the 19th century.

DOLLY MADISON

A double-chinned doll head with sausage curls and center part, indicated by a white line.

DOLL-WITHIN-DOLL

A doll modeled to represent a child holding a doll. These date mainly from the 1880's and 1890's. The smaller doll is often exquisitely designed. In many specimens the smallest doll is, as would be expected, lacking, since the two were not joined together in any way (the larger doll simply cradled the smaller one in her arms).

DRESDEN

German name signifying delicate heads with elaborate decorative details.

ENAMEL BISQUE

A type of unbreakable composition used in the 1920's.

ENAMEL EYES

Fine eyes with parts of glass fastened together.

FANCIES

Any china shoulder-head in which extra details were added such as contrasting colored hair ribbons, snoods, bands, combs, guimpes, earrings (or the pierced holes for them), and necklaces.

FASHION DOLL

A doll dressed to illustrate current fashion.

FIVE PIECE BODY

A convenient way of saying that the doll's arms and legs are attached to the body, having been made separately.

FLANGE NECKS

A design where the cloth is sewn over the flange, holding the head to the body, but permitting the head to rotate from side to side.

FLANDERS BABIES

An early name for dolls with wooden bodies.

FLIRTING EYES

Name given to dolls with eyes that move from side to side. Also called flirty eyes.

FLOCK

Fibers glued or pasted onto a doll for decoration, usually made of hair or cloth — used for short, boy's type hair. As early as 1850's.

FOLLY HEADS

A whirling musical doll, complete with bells, that played a tune when whirled around.

FRENCH BISQUE

A blonde bisque head, generally associated with France, but also made in Germany.

FROZEN CHARLOTTE

A type of doll made entirely of one piece, like a statuette, usually of ceramic. They came in many sizes and poses and were popular in the late 1800's. The name derives from a New England folk tale, of a young lady who forgot to wear winter clothing on a snowy night and froze solid (the connection being, of course, that the dolls are likewise "frozen" — their bodily parts cannot be moved).

FULLY JOINTED

Doll whose body is jointed (moveable) at the shoulders, elbows, thighs, and knees.

GERMAN BISQUE

Highly colored heads; not all of these were made in Germany.

GODEY-HEAD

A blonde or brunette china-head doll, with molded headdress of vertical pointed curls.

GLUE

Used as the adhesive agent in the manufacture of papier-mache and composition dolls. Those made before World War I, using glue and flour, tended to peel and were often affected by temperature change.

GOO-GOO DOLLS

A trade name, virtually the same as Flirting-Eye dolls.

GRANDMA DOLL

Doll representing an elderly woman. These are extremely unusual.

GREINER DOLLS

Greiner (Ludwig) made papier-mache dolls' heads; he took out the first U.S. patent for a doll's head in 1858.

GUTTA-PERCHA

A popular substance for dolls in the 1850's; a rubber-like substance which is malleable in hot water, but hardens when cooled; reddish-white color.

HALF DOLL

Doll consisting of (usually) a molded head and upper body, terminating at the lower torso and lacking thighs and legs. Half dolls generally depict adult women and were intended to be dressed with a long gown which touched the ground (as the doll stood on a block or some other platform). When so displayed, the doll has a perfectly natural appearance. However, many collectors of half dolls, prizing them as a unique group, prefer to display them "as is" without this camouflage. Their heyday was from the early 1900's up to the 1920's. The majority were made in Europe.

HANDMADE DOLL

No universal agreement has yet been reached in the hobby, as to what constitutes a handmade doll. Generally speaking it means a specimen in which the head was not cast in a mold but carved or shaped by the artisan. Thus, it would be difficult, or impossible, to find two dolls identical.

HOTTENTOTS

All-celluloid Negro Kewpies which came as a pair in a blue and white blanket with wings painted white.

INSET EYES

Eyes set into the doll's head (from inside the skull), rather than being manufactured as part of the head. Inset eyes have always been considered desirable and a mark of quality, as they allow the use of a material (usually glass) different from the doll's head to achieve greater realism. Inset eyes may be either stationery or of the sleep variety.

INTAGLIO EYES

Painted eyes with concave irises and pupils.

IVORY PORCELAIN

Another name for china used to make doll's heads.

JOHNNY DOLL

These were English sailor dolls, made for baby boys in the 1890's.

JOLLY JACK

A character doll of a baby boy with composition head, molded hair, stuffed body, dressed in rompers.

KEY WOUND

Doll containing a spring-driven motor, wound with a key. Though spring-wound motors were known hundreds of years ago from the early era of clock and watch making, no attempt was made to incorporate them into playthings until the 1840's.

KEWPIE

One of the most widely known dolls in the world; designed by Rose O'Neil; patented in 1913. The earlier ones were made of bisque and celluloid, but it has been made in a large variety of substances.

KID BODY

Doll body made of kidskin (skin of young goats), stuffed with material. The stuffing may be rag, cotton, shredded cork, etc. Kid bodies were made in two duplicate pieces sewn together along the edges. The stuffing was usually worked in as the sewing progressed.

KISS BABY

A doll with a jointed composition body, whose right arm bends to the doll's mouth, then throws a kiss.

LADY DOLL

A doll made to look like an adult woman in face and figure.

LAY FIGURE

Middle Ages — 20th century. Actually not a doll but an artist's wooden model or mannequin. It is ball-jointed throughout: elbows, shoulders, wrists, and legs, and core of the head were of wood. The outer coating of the head, used to model the features, was of composition.

LONDON DOLL MARKET

Before World War I, agents selling dolls from factories in Germany made this the largest doll market in the world. In the 1920's, the market shifted to New York City.

LOWER LEGS

Used in reference to forelegs (that part of the leg from the knee to the foot).

MADE IN . . .

In 1892 a regulation was adopted in the U.S., requiring all imported products to bear a statement of their place or origin. Therefore, any doll marked "MADE IN GERMANY," "MADE IN FRANCE," etc., cannot date before 1892, though of course could be of much later origin. This is not to say that every single product was marked in conformity with the law.

MAMA DOLLS

Dolls that say "Mama."

MANNAKIN

Figure (of an adult, child or infant) intended for the display of clothing merchandise in a shop. While not manufactured as dolls, mannakins are of interest to some doll collectors because of their close relationship to dolls. The possibilities of mannakin collecting have not yet been fully explored. The older and probably better specimens are mostly of European origin, and can be found in European antique shops.

MARKS

These are usually found on the back of the doll's head or shoulders; sometimes inside the head or on the soles of the feet. In rare cases, they are on the eyeball, upper arm or upper leg, or on the pate. These marks may be pressed, incised, printed, painted, embroidered, or merely attached to the doll with a ribbon, tag, or sticker.

MARY TODD LINCOLN

The controversy still rages, among doll experts, over whether manufacturers of the 1860's (the era of Lincoln's Presidency) modeled some of their dolls after Mrs. Lincoln (Mary Todd Lincoln). For many years it was conclusively believed that they did; but this belief has been seriously questioned. Though a resemblance exists in many dolls, to the facial features of Mrs. Lincoln, this could well be coincidental.

MASK FACE

A face made of cloth stiffened with wax.

MECHANICAL

Any doll containing a mechanical mechanism. The majority are "walkers," and are operated by a spring-driven motor. Dolls featuring a voice-box are not technically referred to as mechanicals — only those in which a mechanism operates some bodily part to simulate human motion.

MEISSEN

Fine porcelain from the China Manufactory at Meissen, Germany. Many Meissen figurines exist, but few doll heads.

MENAGERIE DOLLS

Toy figures of animals, especially zoo-type animals, are often referred to as menagerie dolls. They were extremely popular in the 1800's, marketed both individually and in sets. The sets were sometimes huge and sumptuous, representing (for example) the passengers on Noah's Ark, complete with a wooden ark. As collectors' items these early sets are avidly sought and command strong prices, however, they are seldom found complete. Whether they really deserve to be called "dolls," is a point of contention.

METAL DOLLS

The French and American dollmakers made most of these just prior to the Civil War until the early 1920's.

MILLINERS' MODEL DOLLS

Early 19th century dolls with papier-mache heads and unjointed kid bodies, used to show new fashions before the printing of fashion magazines.

MISS FLAKED RICE

Lithographed cloth doll of the early 1900's, which served as an advertising vehicle for a brand of breakfast cereal manufactured at that time.

MOLDED HAIR

Doll hair which is not painted on and not applied, but is an integral part of the head itself. The contour of the hair (hairdo) is included in the head mold, therefore the origin of the term "molded hair." Molded hair is usually painted as a finishing touch.

MOLDED TEETH

Teeth molded as part of the head, rather than separately.

MONA LISA

Longer and more slender face than in most china heads. Hair, center parted, straight to tops of ears, then clustered curls. The smile is cryptic and rather mysterious.

MONTANARI DOLLS

A wax doll made in England around 1850 which had each hair individually inserted in the head.

MOVING EYES (or MOVING EYEBALLS)

This feature is different than sleep eyes (doll eyes which open and close). Moving eyes move from side to side, as if following an object. They are usually found only on ventriloquist dummies and only on the more lavish specimens. The action is regulated by a string which, attached to a loop, fits over one of the operator's fingers and is worked from the back, out of view of the audience. A famous moving eye doll was Paul Winchell's Jerry Mahoney, but the commercial versions made for sale to the public did not have this feature.

MULTI-FACED DOLLS

Dolls with two to four heads which were interchangeable; some faces lift off while others have changeable heads.

MULTI-HEAD DOLLS

Fifteen years before the Civil War, dolls were made with two heads. One head could be removed and be replaced with another while one of the two heads was concealed by clothing.

NATURE ARMS AND LEGS

Bent limbs on infant type dolls made around 1913.

NATURE SHAPED

A doll with a composition body with a molded kneecap on the lower leg and the joint above the knee, the doll could wear the short dresses popular in the 1920's.

NEEDLE MOLDING

The process of molding a cloth doll's features into three-dimensional form by stitching with a needle.

NOSTRILS

Dolls made in Japan usually have pierced nostrils. Usually, two red dots indicated the nostril.

OCCUPIED JAPAN

The marking MADE IN OCCUPIED JAPAN is found on dolls (and merchandise in general) made in Japanese factories from the conclusion of World War II (August, 1945) up to 1949. The word "occupied" was added to the traditional "made in Japan" to distinguish these items from products made before or during the war, against which some American consumers had a prejudice. When occupation of Japan by allied forces ended in 1949, the earlier "made in Japan" marking was resumed.

OPEN HEAD

The majority of bisque doll heads, on dolls made in Europe from the 1870's to the early 1900's, are of the "open" variety: there is a rather large hole at the crown. This of course would be hidden after applying the wig, but the question remains as to why it existed in the first place. Various theories have been advanced, none of which seems convincing (such as reducing the weight, to make shipment cheaper — but the open area would have accounted for less than an ounce of weight). Perhaps it had some connection with the application of the wig, though, if this was the case, its exact purpose is baffling. Another theory is that the opening assisted (in some way) with removing the bisque from its mold.

ORIGINAL BOX

Dolls still in their original manufacturer's box are always worth a premium value. In the 19th century some of the larger dolls were marketed in wooden boxes with printed labels. The majority, however, were, in cardboard boxes. In many cases it is difficult to know whether a particular doll was originally sold in a box. It can probably be assumed that most, if not all, imported dolls were originally boxed — but the very same specimens, when sold in their country of origin, may not have come with a box. Novelty boxes (in the shape of a suitcase, etc.) have been common since the 1930's.

PAPERWEIGHT EYES

Realistic-looking glass eyes that have heavy, clear corneas so the colored irises are visible from the side, giving the impression that the eyes are moving as the viewer moves.

PARIAN

A semi-vitreous paste porcelain first made by Copeland in England in 1842. It was used to made heads in the bisque form.

PATE

The crown of a doll's head which generally has a hole through which the eyes are inserted; then the hole is plugged with cork or cardboard.

PATENT DATE

The vast majority of dolls do not carry patent dates (or patent numbers, for that matter). When a patent date is present, it serves as an aid in dating the doll, but there is no assurance that the particular specimen was manufactured in the patent year or even shortly thereafter. A lapse of three, four or even five years from patent date to time of manufacture was not unusual, especially for a popular doll which was kept in production a long while.

PEDLAR (or PEDDLER) DOLLS

A class of early dolls sold by itinerant street hawkers, mostly in England, Scotland and Ireland, but to some extent elsewhere as well, including the large towns of the eastern U.S. They were intended to represent the peddlers themselves, and came equipped with tote-boxes (hung over their shoulders by straps) containing miniature versions of peddler merchandise: scissors, combs, files, ribbons, bottles, yarn, etc. In good condition with the original contents, they are highly prized. To what extent such dolls were sold in shops is questionable.

PEG DOLLS

So called because they are jointed by wooden pegs that allow the limbs to move easily, as in the Penny Woodens. "Peg" is also used to denote the shape of a primitively carved wooden head and torso. The word "carved" is almost a misnomer as the characteristic appearance of the Peg head is that of a crudely turned but otherwise flat piece of wood. Features were painted on.

PEG JOINT

The kind of joint used in carpentry and known as mortise-and-tenon.

PEG WOODEN

Carved dolls made of solid wood; the face and shoes are painted on. Smaller ones are made with peg joints while the larger are ball jointed.

PENNY WOODEN

Carved wooden dolls of small size dating from the 18th and 19th centuries. Penny woodens were the most common dolls in their time but, despite this, are by no means plentiful on today's doll collecting market. They originated in Europe but were eventually made in the U.S. as well. The majority were under six inches high and consisted of roughly carved heads and bodies to which arms and legs (usually jointed at the knee) were attached. When sold they were probably without clothing but many youthful owners fashioned clothing for them. Penny woodens were sold in toyshops and by the itinerant street peddlers. They were probably made largely by journeymen woodcarvers. The belief they were sold for a penny is not well founded, because of their differences in size.

PIERCED EARS

Female doll, generally intended to represent an adult or adolescent, with earlobes pierced for earrings. Such dolls were sometimes sold with earrings already in place, sometimes not.

PLAY DOLL

Doll intended to be used as a plaything by a child, as opposed to a "show" doll (for decoration). Of all dolls that have ever been manufactured, the play type are far in the majority.

POINTED TORSO

The bottom of the torso ends in a point. A hole, going through from side to side, is for attaching the legs.

POTTERY DOLLS

These were made in Europe and in the U.S. during the 19th century. These heads are rare and expensive when found intact.

POUPARDS

Dolls without legs; babies wrapped in long, thin bands of cloth.

POURED-WAX

A solid or nearly solid head, made by pouring wax into a mold by building up successive layers.

PRE-GREINER DOLLS

German, papier-mache heads with blown glass eyes made between the 1830's and 1850's.

PRESS ACTION

Dolls which, when pressed or squeezed, "do something." The action may consist of raising or lowering arms, turning head, etc., or they may simply emit a squeal. The squeal type, generally with a soft rubber body, is by far the most plentiful. Early versions of press action dolls contained a bellows in the body. After years of affectionate squeezing, the bellows would break — and this is the condition in which you will find most specimens on the market. Additionally, some press action dolls broke as a result of curious youngsters taking them apart, to see just how they operated.

QUEEN ANNE

There are two types of the Queen Anne dolls. One is of wood with bamboo hands having fork-like fingers. The other is also of wood but the face and shoulders are covered with a thin plaster coating and has hands that are carved more realistically. Inset glass eyes and wigs of human hair are characteristic.

QUEEN VICTORIA

A doll with straight hair parted in the center, having the front sections braided and looped down and behind the ears, to join a bun at the back of the head.

RAG DOLL

A doll made entirely of cloth, some made by hand, others mass-produced. Also called a cloth doll.

SANDERS JOINT

A type of ball and socket joint patened in 1880, used on many dolls made thereafter.

SHOULDER HEAD

Doll head which does not include merely head and neck but is continued down to the shoulders, which are of the same composition as the head and neck. The motive of course was to permit the doll to wear clothing open at the neckline. Shoulder head dolls date to the bisque era. They were usually a little more expensive, originally, than the ordinary type.

SHOW DOLL

Doll intended to be placed on a bed or otherwise displayed, rather than played with. A large proportion of early dolls were of this type, but their numbers have dwindled through the years.

SKITTLE DOLLS

Turned wooden dolls shaped like skittles (ninepins), made from 1730's to mid-1920's.

SLEEP EYES

Eyes which are open when the doll is upright, but close (turning into eyelids) when the doll is laid down. This is an automatic action controlled by small weights. The eyes are set into their sockets with pins at each side, and a level with the weight at the back. When the doll is upright, the level points downward at approximately a 45-degree angle and keeps the eye open. As the doll is tilted backward, the lever points toward the floor and causes the eye to close. The eyes of sleep eye dolls are normally made of glass or glass and ceramic, and are generally very lifelike. Such dolls have been manufactured since the third quarter of the 19th century. The principle on which they operate has been used in machinery from ancient times.

SPRINGFIELD DOLL

A jointed wooden doll made in Springfield, Vermont.

SPOON HANDS

A semi-carved wood hand with thumbs which looks like a wooden mixing spoon.

STARFISH HANDS

Doll hands with the fingers spread apart like a starfish, first 1910.

STIFF-JOINTED DOLLS

Doll limbs that moved only in a backward and forward direction.

STUMP DOLL

Very early group of dolls, made chiefly in Europe from about 1680 to the third quarter of the 18th century. Consisting of an upper body and head carved from a solid block of wood, stump dolls got their name because the body (hidden by the clothing) terminated in a flat stump, like a tree stump. Carving was minimal, consisting of little more than shaping the head and neck and giving a suggestion of facial features. Nevertheless they were the playthings of the elite in their time, as very few children owned dolls of any sort. Stump dolls seldom carry any markings. It is presumed that they were not made by toymakers, but by journeymen woodcarvers who probably sold them to the toy dealers or to peddlers.

SWIVEL HEAD

Head which can be rotated from side to side and, when rotated, remains in the position to which it was moved (rather than snapping back by itself).

TALKING DOLLS

Bellows and pipe reeds were used to make the dolls "talk." Thomas Edison invented and manufactured phonograph dolls as early as 1875-6.

TOPSY TURVY DOLLS

A head at either end of the doll, with one head hidden in the skirt while the other showed.

UNMARKED

About a quarter of all antique dolls, and a smaller percentage of those from the modern era, carry no identifying markings of any kind. There are various possible reasons for manufacturers to avoid marking their dolls, including the production of dolls that were very similar in design to those of an established patent-holder. To date, this subject has not been studied at great length by the experts and no conclusive findings have been published. Of course the absence of markings on any specimen hinders the collector seeking to make an identification. Sometimes such dolls can be assigned to a known manufacturer by similarity of details, etc.

VANITY FAIR DOLLS

China-head limbs on a muslin body. A molded gilt necklace with an oval mirror as a pendant was part of the shoulder head.

VENTRILOQUIST MOUTH

Doll whose mouth can be opened and closed like that of a ventriloquist's dummy. The mechanism may be enclosed and operate simply by a string which hangs down through a hole at the back of the head or neck. More often (and nearly always in dolls intended for actual ventriloquist use), the body of the doll is hollow and open at the back; the operator fits his hand into the doll and grasps a stick, on which the head rests. Next to the stick dangles a cord with a ring attached, through which he slips his thumb. By pulling at the ring, the mouth is made to open and close. The action is regulated by a weight attached to a lever, which in turn is attached to the mouth and jaw of the doll.

WALKER

Doll that walks as a result of mechanical action, usually a spring-driven motor. There are "independent" walkers and others which have an accessory of some kind attached, such as a baby carriage or a pet dog. The attachment helps in balancing the doll and makes its motions more fluid and natural; independent walkers tend to tremble and bounce.

WAXED

Description of a papier-mache, composition or wooden doll coated with wax.

WHEELED WALKERS

Some walkers (dolls with mechanical walking action) were designed to walk by an alternate movement of their legs in human fashion. There was a drawback to this approach, as the doll would sometimes tip over and fall, unless the mechanism was perfectly regulated and the doll was not very tall. One solution was to place the doll on a platform set with wheels, to provide the walking action. These dolls are called "wheeled walkers." The legs do not move; the doll is propelled entirely by the slow rotation of the wheels. A long gown on the doll, reaching to the ground, concealed the apparatus. These dolls did not fall down, but their movement had less appearance of real walking.

WIRE-EYED DOLLS

These were wax dolls with sleeping eyes. A wire at the waist made the eyes open and close as a substitute for counterweights.

WOOD CHIP BODY

Doll body stuffed with wood shavings. This was done occasionally in the 19th century.

COMMON ABBREVIATIONS

Alex — Madame Alexander
A.M. — Armand Marseille
Amer. Char. — American Character
BJ body — ball jointed body
BK — bent knees
bl. — blue
bld. — blonde
br. — brown
c. — circumference
cell. — celluloid
cl — cloth
c/m or clm. — closed mouth
comp. — composition
dk. — dark
E.J. — Emile Jumeau
Fr. body — French body
gl. — glass
hd mk. — head mark
H.H. — human hair
hp. — hard plastic
JCB — jointed composition body
JDK — J.D. Kestner
Jtb. — jointed
l.t. — lower teeth
m. — mohair
M.I.B. — Mint In Box
mld hair — molded hair
ml — molded lash
o/c or o cl. m — open closed mouth
o.m. — open mouth

p — pierced
P. E. — painted eye
P. L. — painted lash
ptd. — painted
p.w. eyes — paperweight eyes
rep. — repair
repl. — replacement
S&H — Simon and Halbig
SFBJ — Socrété Francaise de Fabrication de Bébés et Jouets (group of French dollmakers)
sh.pl. — shoulder plate
sl. — sleeping
stat. — stationary
sw.n. — swivel neck

BOOKS

Anderton, Johanna Gast, *More Twentieth Century Dolls, Volume One,* Wallace Homestead.

Anderton, Johanna Gast, *More Twentieth Century Dolls, Volume Two,* Wallace Homestead.

Anderton, Johanna Gast, *Sewing For Twentieth Century Dolls,* Wallace Homestead.

Anderton, Johanna Gast, *Twentieth Century Dolls,* Wallace Homestead.

Angione, Genevieve, and Judith Whorton, *All Dolls Are Collectible,* Crown Publishers, Inc.

Axe, John, *Collectible Black Dolls,* Hobby House Press, Inc.

Axe, John, *Collectible Boy Dolls,* Hobby House Press, Inc.

Axe, John, *Collectible Dolls In National Costumes,* Holly Hobby House, Inc.

Axe, John, *Collectible Patsy Dolls and Patsy-Types,* Hobby House Press, Inc.

Axe, John, *Collectible Sonja Henie,* Holly Hobby Press, Inc.

Axe, John, *Collecting Modern Dolls: How-To-Guidebook on Collecting Modern Dolls,* Hobby House Press, Inc.

Axe, John, *Encyclopedia of Celebrity Dolls,* Hobby House Press, Inc.

Axe, John, *Tammy And Dolls You Love To Dress,* Hobby House Press, Inc.

Buser, Elaine and Dan, *Guide To Schoenhut Dolls, Toys And Circus,* Collector Books.

Byfield, Magdalena, *In A Miniature Garden,* Hobby House Press, Inc.

Coleman, Dorothy S., Elizabeth A., and Evelyn J., *Collector's Encyclopedia of Dolls,* Crown Publishers, Inc.

Colton, Harold S., *Hopi Kachina Dolls,* University of New Mexico Press.

Doll Catalog, The, second edition, Hobby House Press, Inc.

Fawcett, Clara Hallard, *Dolls, A Guide For Collectors,* H.L. Lindquist Publications.

Fawcett, Clara Hallard, *Paper Dolls, A Guide To Costume,* H.L. Lindquist Publications.

Fawcett, Clara, *On Making, Mending And Dressing Dolls,* Hobby House Press, Inc.

Ferguson, Barbara, *Collecting Paper Dolls,* Wallace Homestead.

Foulke, Jan, *Focusing On Effanbee Composition Dolls,* Hobby House Press, Inc.

Foulke, Jan, *Focusing On Gebruder Heubach Dolls,* Hobby House Press, Inc.

Foulke, Jan, *Kestner, King of Dollmakers,* Hobby House Press, Inc.

Fraser, Antonia, *Dolls,* G.P. Putnam's Sons.

Haines, Frank and Elizabeth, *Early American Brides, A Study of Costume And Tradition,* Hobby House Press, Inc.
Herron, *Much Ado About Dolls,* Wallace Homestead.
Holtz, Loretta, *Developing Your Doll Collection: For Enjoyment And Investment,* Crown Publishers, Inc.
Holtz, Loretta, *The How To Book of International Dolls,* Crown Publishers, Inc.
Hoyer, Mary, *Mary Hoyer and Her Dolls,* Hobby House Press, Inc.
Jacobs, Flora Gill, *A History of Doll Houses,* Charles Scribner's Sons.
Johl, Janet Payter, *More About Dolls,* H.L. Lindquist Publications.
Jones, G.P., *An Easy To Make Godey Doll,* Dover Publications.
MacDowell, Robert and Karin, *Collector's Digest On German Character Dolls,* Hobby House Press, Inc.
Miller, Marjorie, *Nancy Ann Storybook Dolls,* Hobby House Press, Inc.
Revi, A. Christian, ed., *Spinning Wheel's Complete Book of Dolls,* Galahad Books.
Roth, Charlene, *Making Original Dolls of Composition, Bisque And Porcelain,* Crown Publishers, Inc.
Shea, Ralph A., *Doll Mark Clues,* published by the author, 489 Oak Street, Ridgefield, New Jersey 07657.
St. George, Eleanor, *The Dolls of Yesterday,* Charles Scribner's Sons.
Von Boehn, Max, *Dolls,* Dover Publications.
Waugh, Carol-Lynn Rōssel, *Miniature Doll by Contemporary American Doll Artists,* Hobby House Press, Inc.
Westfall, Marty, *Handbook of Doll Repair And Restoration,* Crown Publishers, Inc.
Woodcock, Jean, *Paper Dolls of Famous Faces,* 5369 South Owasso, Tulsa, Oklahoma.
Whitton, Margaret, *The Jumeau Doll,* Dover Publications.
Young, Mary, *Paper Dolls and Their Artists,* 1040 Greenridge Drive., Kettering, Ohio.

PERIODICALS

Antique Toy World, 3941 Belle Plains, Chicago, Illinois 60618. Publishes monthly magazine.

Bambini, P.O. Box 33, Highland, Illinois 62249, 618/675-3497. Magazine issued ten times a year.

Celebrity Doll Journal, 5 Court Place, Puyallup, Washington 98371, 206/845-0340. Quarterly mimeographed publication with pictures and information for collectors of advertising and celebrity items or dolls.

Collectors United: A Master Key to the World of Dolls, P.O. Box 1160, Chatsworth, Georgia 30705. Monthly newspaper filled with buy and sell ads and listings of shows and sales.

Costume Quarterly for Doll Collectors, c/o May Wenzel, 38 Middlesex Drive, St. Louis, Missouri 64133. An eight page quarterly newsletter offers clear pattern for a doll dress, instructions, and a photograph of the finished costume.

Doll And Craft World, 125 Eighth Street, Brooklyn, New York 11215.

Doll Castle News, P.O. Box 247, Washington, New Jersey 07882, 201/689-7512. Dolls, dollhouses, and miniatures are covered in this bimonthly magazine.

Doll Chronicle, P.O. Box 5333, Orchard Lake, Michigan 48033. Published ten times a year.

Doll Investment Newsletter, P.O. Box 1982, Centerville, Massachusetts 02632. Monthly newsletter on recent sales and auctions.

Doll Journal of Australia, c/o Mrs. Beres Lindus, Box 97, P.O. Kensington Park, South Australia 5068, 08/315073. Publishes a bimonthly magazine.

Doll News, (publication of United Fed. of Doll Clubs), 732 W. Lakeshore Drive, Lincoln, Nebraska 68528.

Doll Reader, 900 Federick Street, Cumberland, Maryland 21502, 301/759-3770. Bimonthly magazine with about 70 pages.

Doll Shop Talk, Route 1, Box 100, Evanston, Indiana 47531, 812/529-8561. Bimonthly pamphlet with about 30 pages.

Doll Talk, Kimport Dolls, P.O. Box 495, Independence, Missouri 63051, 816/461-0757.

Doll Times, P.O. Box 276, Montgomery, Illinois 60538, 312/355-0033. Monthly newspaper of about 32 pages.

International Toy and Doll Collector, P.O. Box 9, Halstead, Essex, Great Britain. A bimonthly magazine.

Kiddieland Souper Special, 11892 Bartlett Street, Garden Grove, California 92645, 714/892-5686. Bimonthly newsletter on the Campbell kids.

Midwest Paper Dolls and Toys Quarterly, P.O. Box 131, Galesburg, Kansas 66740, 316/763-2247. Quarterly illustrated mimeographed publication of over 26 pages.

National Doll World, The House of White Birches, Inc., P.O. Box 337-FX, Seabrook, New Hampshire 03874.

Paperdoll Gazette, Route-2, Box 52, Princeton, Indiana 47670, 812/385-4080. A quarterly newsletter with over 30 pages. P.D.Q. (Paper Doll and Paper Toy Quarterly Bulletin), 3135 Oakcrest Drive, Hollywood, California 90068, 213/851-2772. A quarterly illustrated magazine about paper dolls only.

Swallowhill Newsletter, P.O. Box 34, Midland, Ontario L4R 4K6 Canada, 705/526-4437. A monthly newsletter of four pages.

The Dollmaker, P.O. Box 247, Washington, New Jersey 07882, 201/689-7512. A bimonthly magazine on how to make dolls.

The Dollmasters, Auctions by Theriault, P.O. Box 151, Annapolis, Maryland 21404, 301/269-0680. A newsletter about recent auctions by Theriault and other doll market news.

The Dolls of Sunnybrook, 576 Greenlawn Avenue, Columbus, Ohio 43223. A bimonthly magazine about old dolls and paper dolls.

The Schoenhut Newsletter, 45 Louis Avenue, West Seneca, New York 14224, 716/674-6657. A mimeographed newsletter filled with information of recent shows, prices, and other events.

Yapoo's News Quarterly, Harrison Enterprises, 1045 Allesando Street, Morro Bay, California 93442, 805/772-7583.

Yesteryears Museum News, Main and River Streets, Sandwich, Massachusetts 02563, 617/563-6673 May to October, 617/888-1711 November to April. A quarterly newsletter published by Yesteryears Doll Museum.

CLUBS

Antique Toy Collectors of America
Route 2, Box 5A
Parkton, MD 21120

Doll Artisan Guild
35 Main Street
Oneonta, NY 13820
607/432-4977
The Doll Artisan published bimonthly magazine for members.

Doll Collectors of America
14 Chestnut Road
Westford, MD 01886
617/692-8392
Publishes a bimonthly bulletin for members.

Ginny Doll Club
305 West Beacon Road
Lakeland, FL 33803
813/687-8015
Publishes the *Ginny Doll Club News,* an illustrated newsletter, for members.

International Barbie Doll Collectors Club
P. O. Box 79
Bronx, NY 10464
212/885-2439
Publishes a monthly newsletter for members.

International Doll Makers' Association
3364 Pine Creek Drive
San Jose, California 95132
408/926-3077
Publishes *The Broadcaster* with membership news every four months.

The International Rose O'Neill Club
P. O. Box 668
Branson, MO 65616
417/334-3273
Publishes *The Kewpiesta Kourier* three or four times a year for members.

Madame Alexander Fan Club
P. O. Box 146
New Lenox, IL 60451
Four fan club newsletters and ten issues of *Madame Alexander Shopper* are published annually for members.

National Institute of American Doll Artists
303 Riley Street
Falls Church, VA 22046
Publishes newsletter three times a year for members.

Puppeteers of America, Inc.
2311 Connecticut Avenue
North West #501
Washington, DC 20008

Teddy Bear Club
P. O. Box 8361
Prarie Village, KS 66208

United Federation of Doll Clubs
Mrs. Edward Buchholz
Membership Chairman
2814 Herron Lane
Glenshaw, PA 15116
Publishes a monthly newsletter, *Doll News* for members.

MUSEUMS

Adirondack Center Museum
Elizabethtown, NY 12932

Aunt Len's Doll And Toy House, Inc.
New York, NY 10031

Boothbay Railway Museum
Boothbay, ME 04537

Buccleuch Mansion
New Brunswick, NJ 08901

Burt County Museum
Tekamah, NE 68061

Chattanooga Museum of Regional History
Chattanooga, TN 37404

Cornwall Historical Society
Cornwall, CT 06753

Costume And Textile Study Center
Seattle, WA 98195

Eliza Cruce Hall Doll Museum
Ardmore, OK 73401

Enchanted World Doll Museum
Mitchell, SD 57301

Eugene Field Museum
St. Louis, MO 63102

Fort Seward Historical Society, Inc.
Jamestown, ND 58401

Gadsden Museum
Mesilla, NM 80046

Gay Nineties Button And Doll Museum
Eureka Springs, AR 72632

Geuther Doll Museum
Eureka Springs, AR 72632

The Historical Society of The Tarrytowns, Inc.
Tarrytown, NY 10591

Historical Society of The Town of East Bloomfield
East Bloomfield, NY 14443

House of A Thousand Dolls
Loma, MT 59460

Ledbetter Antique Car Museum
Custer, SD 57730

Mary Merritt's Doll Museum
Douglassville, PA 19518

Milan Historical Museum, Inc.
Milan, OH 44846

Museum of Antique Dolls
Savannah, GA 31401

The New York Historical Society
New York, NY 10024

Old Brown House Doll Museum
Gothenburg, NE 69138

Old Fort Museum
Fort Smith, AR 72901

Orchard Park Historical Society
Orchard Park, NY 14127

Patee House Museum
St. Joseph, MO 64502

Perelman Antique Toy Museum
Philadelphia, PA 19106

The Playhouse Museum of Dolls And Toys
Las Cruces, NM 88005

Raggedy Ann Antique Doll And Toy Museum
Flemington, NJ 08822

The Rockwell Museum
Corning, NY 14830

South Carolina Antique Toy Museum
Pendleton, SC 29670

Town of Bethlehem Historical Association
Selkirk, NY 12158

Town of Yorktown Museum
Yorktown Heights, NY 10598

Toy Train Museum of The Train Collector's Association
Strasburg, PA 17579

Union Mills Homestead
Westminster, MD 21157

United Counties Museum
Cornwall, ON CAN

Vent Haven Museum
Fort Mitchell, KY 41011

The Washington Dolls' House And Toy Museum
Washington, DC 20015

Webster House Museum
Elkhorn, WI 53121

Wenham Historical Association And Museum, Inc.
Wenham, MA 01984

Yates County Genealogical And Historical Society, Inc.
Penn Yan, NY 14527

Yesteryears Museum
Sandwich, MA 02563

HOW TO USE THIS BOOK

Most of the listings in *The Official Price Guide to Antique and Modern Dolls* are arranged by manufacturer. If you want to look up Barbie dolls, for example, you will find them under Mattel. Ginny dolls are under Voque, and so on. The exception to this is the section on Unknown Manufactures. We have grouped these dolls according to their type — Advertising, Babies, Shirley Temples, etc. Within each grouping, the dolls are listed alphabetically, either by the name the manufacturer has given them, the type, or the material of the head. Following this title, information for positive identification is given. Whenever possible we have listed the construction material, the type of body, description of the wig, the type and color of the eyes, the costume, and manufacturer's marks when applicable. This information comes from actual specimens that have been bought and sold in the marketplace. Keep in mind that many companies made variations of their lines, and that costumes and wigs can be changed. Find the doll closest in description to yours and quite likely you will have the relative value for it at your fingertips. Another word on antique doll clothing — it was quite a common practice for owners in the olden times to make their own costumes. If the clothing is obviously contemporary with the doll, it shouldn't detract from its value even though it can't be classified as original. Measurements are always approximate — allow at least a half inch tolerance.

We have also included sections on paper dolls and stuffed animals. These are growth areas in the doll collectors market, and offer interesting opportunities and new avenues to explore. The paper doll section is alphabetized according to name or type. The stuffed animals are broken down by manufacturer, and then arranged by name and type. The final section in this edition is Accessories, which lists clothing, accents and furniture. Look up items in this classification under the group of their type.

Values. In all cases, values are current selling figures from the secondary (used/secondhand/antique) market, and are present in the form of a range with a high and low price. The use of ranges allows for the inevitable differences in prices in different parts of the country, in sales made by specialist dealers as opposed to general dealers, etc. Even so, it must be further pointed out that selling prices are influenced by factors which are often unique to that particular transaction. A seller may be stubborn or he may need money fast. He may over-value his doll or under-value it. There is no way, in a price guide, to account for the circumstances in any particular sale. Thus the values presented here should be regarded as guidelines rather than (as some people tend to regard anything printed in a book) as the voice of supreme authority. They show the average sums that dolls have brought up to the time of publication — NOT the prices they will necessarily bring at any time in the future.

As a further aid, the average *prior year* prices have also been included. A comparison of the prior year and current prices will show whether a doll has increased or decreased in value, or remained constant. It is apparent that many investors are buying dolls and this information should be useful to them — as well as to hobbyists. Anyone who is under the impression that the most valuable dolls increase the fastest in value will find, by these statistics, that this is not always the case. Of course the rates of value changes do not offer any guarantee about future price movements. One thing which IS certain from a review of this information is that doll values have, on the whole, markedly risen in the past year.

In all cases, values are DEALER SELLING PRICES — that is, the price charged by an antiques dealer or a specialist doll dealer when he sells to the public. A private owner selling TO a dealer would not receive these prices, as the dealer's operating expenses and profit margin would be figured into the transaction.

In the case of recently manufactured dolls, from the 1970's (of which many are listed), it is entirely possible that some stores still have them on sale at the retail price. The retail price might be HIGHER or LOWER than the secondary market price as indicated in the listings. If you find a doll at retail with a HIGHER price than listed in this book, you can assume that collecting interest has not yet developed and that secondhand specimens are in no great demand. On the other hand, if you find a doll selling LOWER at retail, than the value stated in this book, it means that collectors are eagerly buying it from the secondary market — unaware that it can still be found at retail. However, it would probably not be worthwhile to buy such dolls at retail, for the purpose of selling them to dealers and making a profit, unless you could obtain them for less than ½ of the secondary market value.

In any case the golden rule is to always KNOW WHAT YOU'RE BUYING (or selling). Many dolls are identical but for some slight variation, which would go unnoticed if you did not look for it. Learn to look, investigate, study and you WILL be an expert!

ABORIGINALS

	Current Price Range		Prior Year Average
☐ **Wednesday,** *cloth, unmarked, 1962, 23″ . . .*	65.00	80.00	62.00

EMMA AND MARIETTA ADAMS

☐ **Columbian Doll,** *all cloth, handpainted features, hair, bonnet, pioneer style clothing, stamped on back "Columbian Doll Emma E. Adams, Oswego, Centre, N.Y." . . . .*	550.00	650.00	550.00

ADVANCE DOLL AND TOY COMPANY

☐ **Wanda,** *walker, brown mohair wig, blue sleep eyes, pink dress, hat, 18″, c. 1949 . . . .*	175.00	225.00	185.00

ODETTE AIDEN

☐ **Mary Queen Of Scots,** *plastic, molded and painted features, dressed in reproduction of 16th century royal costume, jointed at the shoulders, unmarked, made in England in 1969, 8″ . . . .*	49.00	58.00	47.00

ALEXANDER DOLLS COMPANY INC.

When Beatrice Behrman made her first portrait doll, a tribute to her little daughter, she had no idea of the empire that had just been born. Spurred by friends and acquaintances to market her talent, she founded the Alexander Company in 1923. By the age of twenty-eight, she was a successful business woman and designer. The eager public acceptance of her products continues to be a market phenomena.

Through the years the company has grown to 600 employees in the New York factory. Big business has never compromised the high quality standards set by Beatrice Behrman, A.K.A. Madame Alexander. The 130 doll models that have been produced since the 20's are grouped by theme: historical figures, story book characters and ethnic dolls. Each doll is handpainted, hand assembled and dressed in exquisite costumes.

Madam Alexander dolls are one of the few products that appreciate immediately over retail price. Department stores and gift shops have been known to limit the number a customer can buy on any given day.

This is an attempt to keep the dolls off the scalper's market, and it is only moderately successful. Now dolls quickly turn up at flea markets and antiques shops for resale at exorbitant prices.

The lifelike but whimsical dolls created by Madam Alexander are as much a part of American nostalgia as Norman Rockwell's characters. They both have captured the innocence and wisdom of children, and the adults who collect them are in love with these qualities.

	Current Price Range		Prior Year Average
☐ **Alexanderkin,** *hard plastic, wears bathing suit, sandals, robe, square sunglasses, carries beach bag, 8″*	70.00	90.00	65.00
☐ **Alice in Wonderland,** *Madame Alexander, 12″, c. 1983*	65.00	75.00	65.00
☐ **Amy,** *plastic, sleep eyes, blonde looped curls, 14″*	95.00	110.00	80.00

Note: Amy was a character in Louisa May Alcott's Little Women.

Amy,
Little Women Series, 14″
$95.00-$110.00

	Current Price Range		Prior Year Average
☐ **Baby Doll,** *plastic head, cloth body, vinyl legs, mohair wig, lacy pink silk taffeta dress, 22″*	100.00	150.00	110.00
☐ **Baby Dolls,** *portrait series, 21″, c. 1983*	300.00	400.00	325.00
☐ **Baby Genius,** *23″*	45.00	55.00	50.00
☐ **Baby Huggums**	15.00	25.00	20.00
☐ **Baby Sister,** *blue sleep eyes, blonde hair, pink checkered dress, 14″*	50.00	60.00	52.00
☐ **Baby Sister,** *brown sleep eyes, brown wig, pink checkered dress, 14″*	50.00	60.00	52.00
☐ **Belguim,** *marked Alex, 8″*	80.00	90.00	85.00
☐ **Ballerina,** *hard plastic, sleep eyes, blond hair, wears ruffled dancing skirt, knitted top, bows on shoes, 8″*	75.00	95.00	70.00
☐ **Beth,** *bent knees, from Little Women, mint in box, #781, 8″*	100.00	150.00	110.00

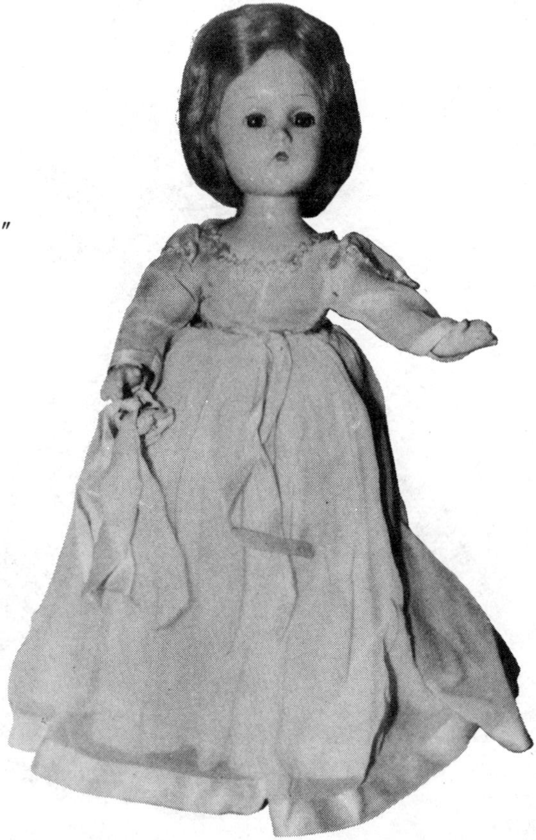

Bridesmaid,
composition body, 15″
$100.00-$125.00

	Current Price Range		Prior Year Average
☐ **Bridesmaid,** *vinyl head, composition body, vinyl wig, blue sleep eyes, high waisted gown with long bow and full sleeves, 15″*	100.00	125.00	110.00
☐ **Brigetta,** *from Sound of Music, mint in box, 11″, c. 1972*	200.00	250.00	225.00
☐ **Christening Baby,** *infant, long white baby gown and bonnet, 13″*	50.00	60.00	52.00
☐ **Cinderella,** *blue outfit, c. 1983*	70.00	80.00	75.00
☐ **Cinderella,** *brown outfit, c. 1983*	60.00	70.00	65.00
☐ **Cissette,** *bent knees, handpainted, ballerina dress, 10″*	130.00	150.00	135.00
☐ **Cissette,** *blue taffeta dress, earrings, hat, 10″*	100.00	120.00	110.00

Cissy,
hard plastic,
c. 1956, 21″
$90.00-$115.00

	Current Price Range		Prior Year Average
☐ **Cissette,** *hard plastic, sleep eyes, dressed in "Iceland" costume, 10½"*	340.00	400.00	320.00
Note: Like many of the Alexander dolls, Cissette is found in a wide variety of costumes and these have some influence on the value.			
☐ **Cissy,** *gray plush stole lined with pink*	15.00	25.00	18.00
☐ **Cissy,** *hard plastic, jointed at knees and elbows, long flowing yellow cape-style coat, sleep eyes, high heel open dress shoes, 21"*	90.00	115.00	85.00
☐ **Cissy,** *pink and yellow printed silk taffeta dress, earrings, straw hat, 20"*	300.00	400.00	310.00
☐ **Composition,** *blonde human hair wig, dimples, white satin dress, skates, cape, 15"*	300.00	350.00	310.00

Composition,
vinyl wig, 14"
$130.00-$150.00

	Current Price Range		Prior Year Average
☐ **Composition,** *head and jointed body, vinyl wig, blue sleep eyes, flared polka dot dress, velvet booties with bells, 14"*	85.00	110.00	90.00
☐ **Dionne Baby,** *composition head, yoke, arms, and lower legs, cloth torso and upper legs, marked "Dionne/Alexander," brown molded hair, brown sleep eyes with lashes, maroon and white linen dress, 17"*	275.00	325.00	280.00
☐ **Dionne Quintuplets,** *composition head, bent limb body, sleep eyes, wigs, original clothing, brass tags, 7"*	1400.00	1600.00	1450.00
☐ **Dionne Quintuplets,** *vinyl body, sleep eyes, together in terry cloth comforter, layette suits, signed by Madame Alexander*	1000.00	1250.00	1050.00
☐ **Dionne Quint, Toddler,** *auburn, mohair wig, print sunsuit, marked Alexander*	240.00	280.00	245.00
☐ **Dionne Quint, Toddler,** *molded body, pink bonnet, dress, marked Alexander*	220.00	275.00	225.00

Edith,
"The Lonely Doll" c. 1950
$200.00-$250.00

	Current Price Range		Prior Year Average
☐ **Dionne Toddler,** *composition, original lilac wool coat, hat, leggings, tag, 17"*	325.00	375.00	350.00
☐ **Ecuador Girl,** *bent knees, dark pigtails, blue sleep eyes, coin earrings, straw hat, 8", c. 1960's*	250.00	350.00	265.00
☐ **Edith,** *"The Lonely Doll," vinyl head, rubber body, blue sleep eyes, pouty mouth, party dress, c. 1950*	250.00	300.00	225.00
☐ **Elise Ballerina,** *12", c. 1983*	130.00	160.00	135.00
☐ **Elise Bride,** *12", c. 1983*	130.00	160.00	135.00
☐ **Elise Bridesmaid,** *12", c. 1983*	130.00	160.00	135.00
☐ **Elise,** *character, vinyl, jointed at elbows, knees, ankles, brown rooted hairs, blue sleep eyes, closed mouth, pink and white checked dress, white straw bonnet with flower trim, hose, high heels, 16", c. 1952*	215.00	235.00	220.00

Elise Bridesmaid,
vinyl and hard plastic,
c. 1952, 17"
$130.00-$160.00

	Current Price Range		Prior Year Average
□ **Elise,** *hard plastic head, vinyl, long brown page boy, blue sleep eyes, dressed as bridesmaid, long chintz gown, wide brimmed hat, 17", c. 1952*	150.00	200.00	175.00
□ **First Ladies,** *Series II: Angelica Van Buren, Julia Tyler, Sarah Jackson, Sara Polk, each*	115.00	145.00	125.00
□ **Gibson Girl,** *the Cissette doll in "Gibson Girl" costume, long-sleeve white shirt, floor-length full skirt, boater style hat with trim, fancy belt*	340.00	400.00	320.00
□ **Goldilocks,** *c. 1983*	60.00	70.00	65.00
□ **Gone With The Wind,** *c. 1983*	90.00	100.00	95.00
□ **Goya,** *portrait series, 21", c. 1983*	300.00	350.00	310.00
□ **India,** *marked Alex, 8"*	80.00	90.00	85.00
□ **Irish,** *doll, marked Alex, 8"*	80.00	90.00	85.00
□ **Israeli,** *doll, composition head and body, bent knee walker, intricate costume, 7"*	185.00	200.00	190.00

Jeannie Walker,
composition body, c. 1941
$500.00-$600.00

	Current Price Range		Prior Year Average
☐ **Israeli,** *doll, knee bends, 8", c. 1965*	60.00	70.00	65.00
☐ **Jacqueline,** *brown eyes and hair, blue suit and pill box hat, black heels, stockings, pearl necklace, diamond ring, 21"*	625.00	675.00	640.00
☐ **Jeannie Walker,** *composition head and body, blue sleep eyes, sundress and straw hat, 12", c. 1941*	500.00	600.00	550.00
☐ **Kathy,** *character, vinyl, blond rooted hair, brown sleep eyes, pink dress, matching bonnet, pacifier on ribbon around neck, wrist tag, 17", c. 1956*	220.00	235.00	220.00
☐ **Kathy,** *molded hair, pretty eyes, 24"*	8.00	12.00	10.00
☐ **Kathy Cry Dolly,** *vinyl, sleep eyes, rooted hair, blond or reddish blond, wears infant smock, white, frilled bonnet, holds pacifier attached to neck with elastic band, 12"*	50.00	65.00	45.00

Katie and Tommie, 12" . . . . **$1800.00-$2200.00**

	Current Price Range		Prior Year Average
☐ **Katie Greenaway,** *hard plastic head, jointed body, brown human hair wig, fringed sleep eyes, white gown with wide green velvet band, matching cap, 12"*	900.00	1000.00	950.00
☐ **Katie,** *hard plastic, original costume, with wooden rocking horse labeled "100 Years In Toys, 1862-1962, commemorative doll for 100th Anniversary of F.A.O. Schwartz Toy Co., 11", rare*	1000.00	2000.00	1100.00
☐ **Kelly,** *character, vinyl, blond rooted hair, blue sleep eyes, closed mouth, pink dress with tiers of white lace, matching bonnet, original mint, no box, wrist tag, 15", c. 1956*	185.00	210.00	185.00

Leslie Bauirje,
rare Black face, 18"
$300.00-$400.00

	Current Price Range		Prior Year Average
☐ **Laurie,** *vinyl head, sleep eyes, sad, long eyelashes, black hair, wears double-breasted jacket, plaid trousers, 12″*	15.00	22.00	14.00
Note: Laurie was a character in Louisa May Alcott's Little Women.			
☐ **Leslie Bauirje,** *composition head and jointed body, black face, brown long wig, white frilly dress with flower headband, slippers, 14″*	300.00	400.00	350.00
☐ **Lissy,** *auburn hair, red dress, flowery white hat, navy coat*	80.00	120.00	85.00

Lissy,
hard plastic, sleep eyes
$80.00-$120.00

	Current Price Range		Prior Year Average
☐ **Lissy,** *hard plastic, sleep eyes (straight-ahead staring), brown hair, long dress with waist sash, colonial style bonnet, 12″*	230.00	280.00	200.00
Note: This is a scarce costume and accounts for much of the value. "Lissy" in one of the more common costumes sells in the $75.00 to $95.00 range.			
☐ **Little Cherub,** *vinyl head, latex body, molded head, wide sleep eyes, angel suit with wings and halo, 8½″*	350.00	400.00	375.00
☐ **Little Colonel,** *composition, green sleeping eyes, lashes, blonde mohair wig with long curls, yellow and white cotton dress and bonnet, pantaloons, snap shoes, 13½″*	475.00	525.00	490.00
☐ **Little Genius,** *caracul wig, 8″*	90.00	100.00	95.00
☐ **Little Genius,** *hard plastic and vinyl, skin wig, blue-gray eyes, open mouth, white*			

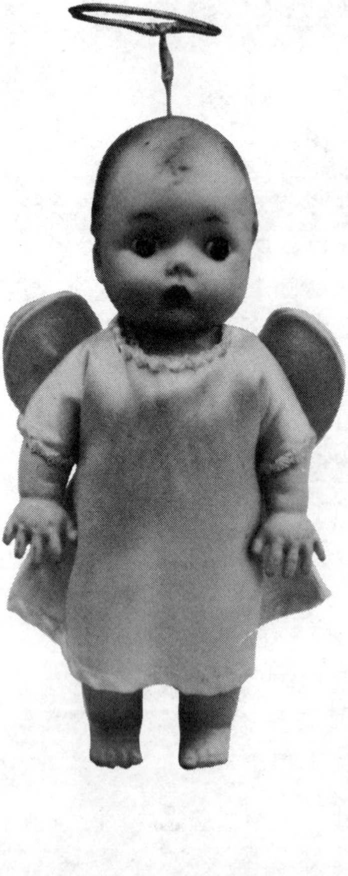

Little Cherub,
vinyl head, 1983
$350.00-$450.00

	Current Price Range		Prior Year Average
gown with lace and ribbon trim, new booties, 8"	90.00	120.00	98.00
☐ **Little Red Riding Hood,** *holds basket of fruit, marked Alex, 8"*	80.00	90.00	85.00
☐ **Little Shaver,** *vinyl, pink checked dress, 12"*	130.00	150.00	140.00
☐ **Little Tiny Billie Toddler,** *hard plastic, sleep eyes, long eyelashes, movable arms, wears diaper fastened by safety pin, 8"*	100.00	125.00	90.00
☐ **Lord Fauntleroy,** *12", c. 1983*	65.00	75.00	70.00
☐ **Lucinda,** *pink outfit, c. 1983*	80.00	100.00	85.00
☐ **Madelian Dubain,** *vinyl construction, blue sleep eyes, jointed body, 11", c. 1948*	500.00	700.00	550.00
☐ **Maggie,** *blonde hair, pink clothes, straw hat, 21"*	100.00	160.00	110.00

Madelaine DuBain, vinyl, c. 1948, 11" . . . . **$500.00-$700.00**

	Current Price Range		Prior Year Average
☐ **Maggie Walker,** *hard plastic, sleep eyes, flared printed skirt, carries suitcase with accessories inside (comb and brush, etc.) 18"*	85.00	110.00	75.00
Note: Price is for a complete specimen showing light wear only. For a Maggie Walker with suitcase but lacking the suitcase accessories, $75.00 to $95.00. For one without the suitcase, $60.00 to $80.00			
☐ **Marc Antony and Cleopatra,** *12", pair, c. 1983*	125.00	175.00	135.00
☐ **Margaret O'Brien,** *hard plastic, mohair wig in looped braids tied with silk ribbons, hat, calf-length socks, black shoes, 17"*	215.00	250.00	185.00
Note: Margaret O'Brien was a child actress in motion pictures in the early 1940's.			

Margaret O'Brien,
hard plastic, c. 1948
$215.00-$250.00

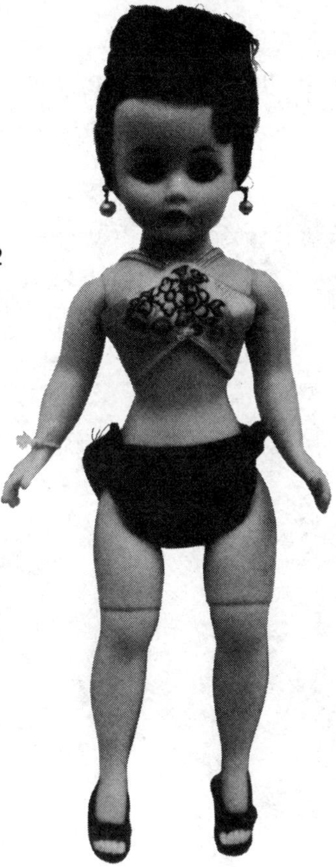

Margot,
hard plastic, 1962
$125.00-$155.00

	Current Price Range		Prior Year Average
☐ **Margot,** *hard plastic, sleep eyes, long eyelashes, long evening gown with shoulder straps, 9¼"*	125.00	155.00	110.00
☐ **Margot Ballerina,** *plastic, blonde, blue eyes, turquoise costume, satin slippers, # 1841, c. 1955*	150.00	200.00	156.00
☐ **Marlo Thomas,** *vinyl, sleep eyes, black hair, wears knee-length wool dress, strand of graduated pearls, textured stockings, boots, 16½"*	420.00	470.00	385.00

Note: A scarce doll, inspired by the TV show "That Girl" starring Marlo Thomas (daughter of Danny Thomas). It was produced only in 1967. Though Marlo and the show were hits,

	Current Price Range		Prior Year Average
the doll was not — apparently because Marlo's role on the show was too "grown up" to appeal to little girls.			
☐ **Marme,** *bent knee, walks, marked Alex, 8″* .	90.00	110.00	95.00

Marybel, "The Doll That Gets Well" . . . . **$175.00-$225.00**

☐ **Marybel,** *vinyl construction, blonde vinyl wig with bangs, sleep eyes, swivel waist, in box with hospital accessories, in coat with booties, 14″*	175.00	225.00	200.00
☐ **Mary Sunshine**	90.00	110.00	95.00
☐ **McGuffey Ana,** *composition, brown sleeping eyes, lashes, open mouth, blonde human hair braids and bangs, plaid dress, white pinafore, red high button shoes, 15″* .	245.00	285.00	260.00
☐ **McGuffey Ana,** *composition, blonde mohair braids and curly bangs, painted blue eyes, closed mouth, red and white checkered dress with organdy pinafore, black shoes, 9″*	175.00	225.00	190.00

McGuffy Ana,
composition, 12″
$250.00-$275.00

	Current Price Range		Prior Year Average
☐ **McGuffey Ana,** *c. 1983*	60.00	70.00	65.00
☐ **McGuffy Awake,** *sleep eyes, braided hair*	200.00	220.00	180.00
☐ **Mike,** *bisque head, puppet body with bisque hands, mohair wigs, painted eyes, long wool robe with rope trim, c. 1932*	175.00	250.00	200.00
☐ **Napoleon and Josephine,** *12″, pair, c. 1983*	125.00	175.00	135.00
☐ **Netherlands,** *wears wooden shoes, marked Alex, 8″*	80.00	90.00	85.00
☐ **Pamela,** *hard plastic, sleep eyes, dressed in national costume of Poland with multi-layered, boldly printed skirt, white ruffled blouse, 12″*	140.00	170.00	125.00
☐ **Pierrott,** *Wendykins, hard plastic, jointed, wig, sleep eyes, closed mouth, satin clown suit, dog on leash, mint in box, 8″*	1800.00	2200.00	1850.00

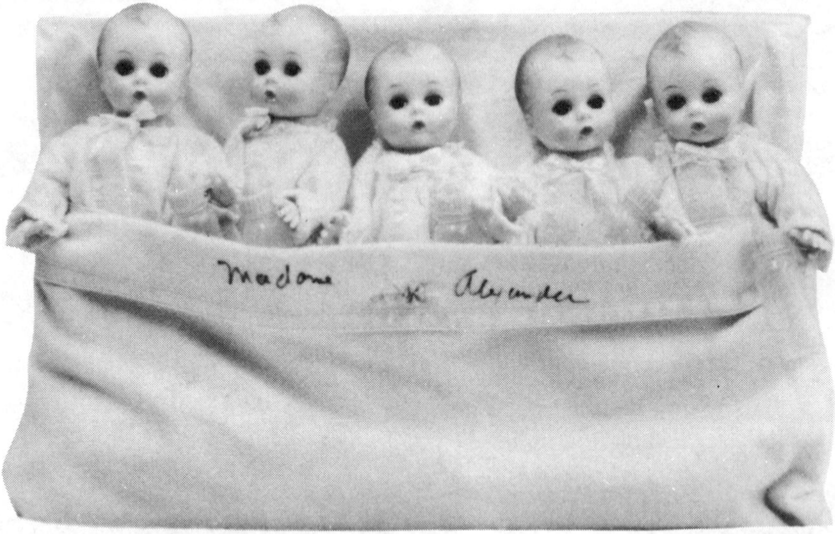

Quintuplets, vinyl, autographed . . . . **$1000.00-$1100.00**

	Current Price Range		Prior Year Average
☐ **Polly Pigtails,** *hard plastic, sleep eyes, wide-brimmed straw hat, white dress with puff sleeves, white cotton stockings, black shoes, 13⅞″* . . .	**110.00**	**140.00**	**100.00**
☐ **Portrait Queen,** *white brocade dress, mint in box, # 1186, 11″, c. 1972* . . .	**300.00**	**400.00**	**310.00**
☐ **President Ladies,** *set #2* . . .	**850.00**	**900.00**	**875.00**
☐ **Presidents Ladies,** *set # 3* . . .	**950.00**	**1000.00**	**925.00**
☐ **Princess Elizabeth,** *composition, sleep brown eyes, blonde wig, bridal dress and veil, 14″* . . .	**225.00**	**275.00**	**240.00**
☐ **Puddin,** *dark hair and eyes, checkered dress in pink and white, made in 1976, 14″* . . .	**45.00**	**55.00**	**48.00**
☐ **Pussy Cat,** *black, portrait series, 21″, c. 1983* . . .	**300.00**	**400.00**	**320.00**
☐ **Rebecca,** *c. 1983* . . .	**60.00**	**70.00**	**65.00**
☐ **Red Boy,** *jointed knees, # 740, 8″, c. 1972* . .	**120.00**	**130.00**	**125.00**
☐ **Renoir ,** *c. 1983* . . .	**60.00**	**70.00**	**65.00**
☐ **Romeo,** *12″, c. 1983* . . .	**65.00**	**75.00**	**70.00**
☐ **Scarlett,** *portrait series, 21″, c. 1983* . . .	**300.00**	**400.00**	**325.00**
☐ **Scarlet O'Hara,** *composition head and body, black human hair wig, blue sleep eyes, green taffeta dress, 17″* . . .	**450.00**	**550.00**	**475.00**
☐ **Scarlett O'Hara,** *vinyl, sleep eyes, long black glossy hair, satin gown with trimming,*			

	Current Price Range		Prior Year Average
satin bonnet, wears cameo on a chain at the neck, marked Alexander 1961, 21″	110.00	140.00	90.00
Note: Scarlett O'Hara was a character in Margaret Mitchell's "Gone With The Wind," made into a motion picture in 1939.			
☐ **Sleeping Beauty,** *Disney special edition, 1959, 9″*	200.00	500.00	180.00
☐ **M.I.B.**	450.00	500.00	400.00
☐ **Sleeping Beauty,** *c. 1983*	70.00	80.00	75.00
☐ **Smarty,** *11″*	80.00	90.00	85.00
☐ **Sonja Henie,** *composition body, blonde mohair wig, sleep eyes, short lavender skating dress, ice skates, 14″, c. 1950*	200.00	220.00	215.00
☐ **Southern Belle,** *ribbon trimmed white gown, with box, 11″, c. 1968*	350.00	450.00	400.00
☐ **Spanish Girl,** *knee bends, lacy tiered gown, labeled, 8″*	70.00	80.00	75.00

Sonja Henie,
composition
$200.00-$220.00

	Current Price Range		Prior Year Average
☐ **Toddler,** *composition head and arms, cloth body, molded hair, brown sleep eyes, open mouth, baby clothes and bonnet, 21″*	425.00	475.00	450.00
☐ **Tommy,** *hard plastic head, jointed body, short blonde human hair wig, brown sleep eyes, school boy suit with striped socks, straw hat, 12″*	900.00	1000.00	950.00
☐ **Tyrolean,** *bent knee, boy, girl, marked Alex, 8″, pair*	240.00	280.00	250.00
☐ **Tyrolean Girl,** *bent knees, mint in box, # 798, 8″*	100.00	150.00	120.00
☐ **Tyrolean Boy and Girl,** *vinyl, jointed bent knee, original, 8″*	285.00	325.00	295.00
☐ **Waac Doll,** *composition, green eyes, red hair, 14″*	375.00	425.00	395.00
☐ **Wave Doll,** *composition, blue eyes, blonde hair, 14″*	375.00	425.00	395.00
☐ **Wendy,** *hard plastic, sleep eyes, dressed as tennis player with racquet, skirt, open-toe shoes, 8″*	90.00	115.00	80.00
☐ **Wendy Ann,** *hard plastic, sleep eyes, puffy cheeks, blond hair, wears jacket and skirt of matching style, two buttons on jacket, 8″*	70.00	90.00	62.00
☐ **Wendy Bride,** *plastic, sleep blue eyes, blonde hair, white satin dress, rhinestones, veil, 21″, c. 1950's*	225.00	275.00	240.00

ALLIED

☐ **Bonnie Buttons,** *marked 39AE-1-A, 10″*	8.00	10.00	8.00
☐ **Susan,** *marked #2112, box marked Susan, 1967, made in Hong Hong*	1.50	2.25	1.50
☐ **Wendy,** *marked Allied Grand Doll Manufacturing Co., Inc., 1958, 9⅞″*	4.75	6.00	4.00

ALT, BECK AND GOTTSCHALCK

☐ **Baby,** *bisque head, five composition body, molded and painted hair, brown sleep eyes, dimples, smile, antique embroidered, tucked blouse, high waisted maize linen pants and knit boots, incised AB&G 1322, 19″ tall, 14″ circumference dome head*	500.00	550.00	520.00
☐ **Bisque Head,** *ball jointed body, blond human hair wig, set hazel eyes, white outfit, 33″*	800.00	1000.00	850.00

	Current Price Range		Prior Year Average
☐ **Bisque,** *jointed composition body, blue eyes, blonde wig, white dress, red white and blue picture hat, 24″*	325.00	375.00	340.00

AMBERG

☐ **Newborn Babe,** *bisque, sleep eyes, closed mouth, dressed in lace gown, tagged, 8″*	425.00	475.00	400.00

AMERICAN CHARACTER DOLL COMPANY

The American Character Doll Company ran from the turn of the century to 1968 when it was sold and disbanded. From their offices and factory in New York City, the company manufactured composition, rubber and later hard plastic dolls. They also operated an import division that distributed dolls from France and Italy to the American market.

The early founder, S.D. Hoffman, is credited with the "Can't Break It" process that improved composition to the point that it was more practical and cheaper than bisque for doll manufacturing. This process was later sold to the Horsman Doll and Toy Company who revolutionized the industry with it.

American Character Dolls typically have a distinct charm, whether composition or plastic, baby doll or ingenue, imported or from the New York factory. The company had a great impact on doll production in this country and their dolls enjoy avid collector interest.

☐ **American Beauty,** *plastic, blonde hair (rooted), sleep eyes (blue), unmarked, made in 1955, 21½″*	55.00	68.00	50.00
☐ **Astronut,** *vinyl, molded and painted features, rooted hair (green!), marked Amer. Doll & Toy Co., made in 1960, 18½″*	37.00	46.00	34.00
Note: It was no spelling error: "astronaut" was intentionally spelled "astronut" for the name of this doll. In 1960, when Astronut was marketed, America had not yet sent a man into space.			
☐ **Baby Lou,** *plastic, molded and painted hair (reddish), open mouth, marked Amer. Char., made in 1950, 8″*	9.00	12.00	8.00
☐ **Baby Sandy,** *composition head, rubber body, rubber arms and legs, sleep eyes (metallic), molded hair, open mouth, wears vest and bow tie, marked Petite, 18″*	140.00	170.00	130.00
☐ **Baby Tiny Tears,** *nurser, plastic head, rubber body, rubber arms and legs, sleep eyes, marked Pat. No. 2675644, American Character, 1950, 13″*	15.00	19.00	14.00

	Current Price Range		Prior Year Average
☐ **Barbara Sue,** *vinyl head and body, vinyl arms and legs, disc jointed arms, mouth closed, reddish hair with a flower at each side, frilly white dress, white stockings, marked Amer. Char. Doll, 15⅞"*	40.00	55.00	34.00
☐ **Betsy McCall,** *long gown, 14"*	90.00	100.00	94.00
☐ **Betsy McCall,** *plastic, 8"*	60.00	70.00	65.00
☐ **Bride,** *plastic/vinyl, blonde hair (rooted), sleep eyes, marked Amer. Char. Doll, 1955, 18"*	47.00	58.00	42.00
☐ **Butterball,** *vinyl, rooted hair (sandy blonde), sleep eyes (blue), marked 1961, American Doll & Toy Co., 18½"*	41.00	50.00	37.00
☐ **Chuckles,** *marked Amer. Doll & Toy Co., 1961, 23¼"*	50.00	65.00	45.00
☐ **Dandy,** *composition head and body, molded hair, marked AC, made in 1942, 11½"*	16.00	21.00	15.00
☐ **Darlin Dollface,** *vinyl head and body, vinyl arms and legs, sleep eyes, partially opened mouth with pursed lips, rooted hair, print dress, 11"*	16.00	20.00	15.00
☐ **Graduate,** *vinyl, tufted hair, painted eyes, marked Amer. Doll & Toy Co., 1960, 21"*	37.00	46.00	35.00
Note: A youth wearing a mortar board and scholar's gown. No connection with the Dustin Hoffman film.			
☐ **Hedda Get Betta,** *vinyl, molded and painted features, novelty doll with three-faced head (operated by button on top of head), representing sleep, discomfort, and comfort, marked American Doll & Toy Corp., 1961, 21"*	39.00	48.00	35.00
☐ **Little Joe Cartwright,** *vinyl, molded and painted features, molded hair, painted clothing, made in Portugal, 8"*	47.00	60.00	42.00
Note: This doll represents a character from the TV program "Bonanza," and dates probably from the early 1960's, when the show was at its height.			
☐ **Little Love,** *composition head, cloth body, composition limbs, wig attached with adhesive, marked Amer. Char. Doll, 1942, 17⅞"*	43.00	54.00	40.00
☐ **Marie Ann,** *marked American Character, 1966, 13"*	26.00	31.00	25.00
☐ **Marie Lee,** *marked 3, American Character, 1966, 13"*	26.00	31.00	25.00
☐ **Miss Chicadee,** *plastic, molded and painted hair, painted eyes, unmarked, made c. 1949, 8"*	25.00	30.00	23.00

	Current Price Range		Prior Year Average
☐ **Peek-A-Boo Toodles,** *vinyl, brown hair (rooted), sleep eyes (blue), rosy red cheeks, marked American Char. Doll, 1956, 22½″ . .*	**23.00**	**29.00**	**20.00**
☐ **Polly Pretend,** *combination vinyl and plastic, long hair, fixed eyes, partially open mouth, designed to represent a young girl dressed in her mother's or big sister's clothing, with hair roller, oversized shoes, etc. marketed in both black and white, marked A.M.S.C.O. 1974, 13½″*			
Black version:	**18.00**	**23.00**	**17.00**
White version:	**14.00**	**19.00**	**14.00**

Ricky Ricardo,
rubber, c. 1955, 15″
$45.00-$52.00

	Current Price Range		Prior Year Average
☐ **Poppi,** *plastic head, plastic body and limbs, adult doll, wears flowered skirt, white blouse, fixed eyes, called Poppi because the doll "pops" apart at the waist and chest, 11½"*	10.00	15.00	10.00
☐ **Pouty Miss Marie,** *marked Amer. Char. Inc., 1965, 13"*	25.00	29.00	24.00
☐ **Pretty Penny,** *hard plastic head and body, puffy cheeks, sleep eyes with deep-set pupils that appear to follow the viewer, arms can be posed, long black silky hair, ribbon in hair, short dress, cotton ribbed stockings, 19"*	50.00	65.00	48.00
☐ **Ricky Ricardo,** *rubber doll, 15", 1959*	45.00	52.00	40.00
☐ **Sunny Boy,** *vinyl head, vinyl arms and legs, cloth body, fixed eyes (blue), molded hair, open mouth, wears high collar and large western-style necktie, 21"*	50.00	65.00	47.00

Sweet Sue,
hard plastic, 17"
$41.00-$49.00

Terry Talks,
composition, c. 1950, 22″
$60.00-$70.00

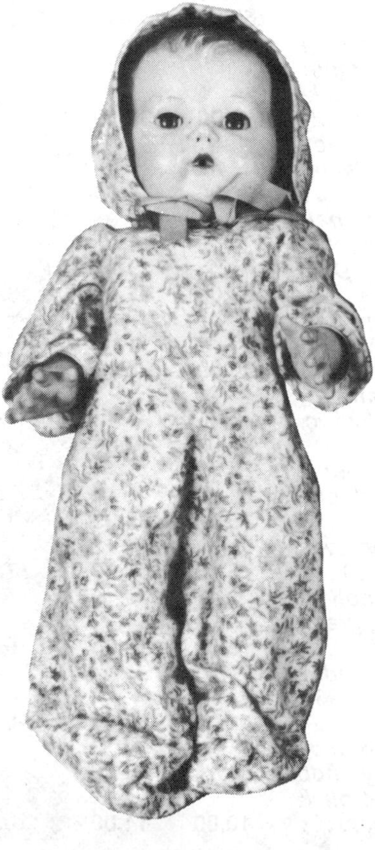

Tiny Tears,
composition and rubber,
c. 1950, 12″
$75.00-$85.00

	Current Price Range		Prior Year Average
☐ **Sweet Sue,** *bride dress, 18"*	80.00	90.00	84.00
☐ **Sweet Sue,** *plastic/vinyl, brown hair (rooted), sleep eyes, unmarked, made in 1955, 19"*	41.00	49.00	40.00
☐ **Sweet Sue,** *hard plastic, sleep eyes, long eyelashes, closed mouth with puckered lips, dark red lips, honey blond hair, wears straw bonnet, 15"*	40.00	55.00	38.00
☐ **Sweet Sue,** *hard plastic, walker, brown hair, brown sleeping eyes, lashes, peach taffeta dress with embroidered organdy, lace trim, pink straw hat, 18"*	100.00	150.00	115.00
☐ **Sweet Sue,** *hard plastic, walker, jointed at neck, arms, legs, dark blonde wig, blue sleep eyes, closed rosy lips, original printed taffeta dress with puffed sleeves, blue strap shoes, crown of pink flowers in hair, marked Amer. Char. Doll, 24"*	130.00	170.00	130.00
☐ **Sweet Sue,** *three extra outfits, 30"*	150.00	200.00	170.00
☐ **Sweet Sue (large size),** *hard plastic, roving eyes that appear to follow the observer (but actually do not move), wears beaded necklace, marked American Character, 1960, 25"*	150.00	190.00	140.00
☐ **Sweet Susanne,** *hard plastic, sleep eyes (blue), wig attached with adhesive, unmarked, made c. 1953, 17"*	36.00	45.00	35.00
☐ **Talking Marie,** *plastic/vinyl, blonde hair (rooted), sleep eyes (blue), talking mechanism in chest, marked Amer. Char. Doll, 1963, 18"*	58.00	71.00	55.00
☐ **Teeny Betsy McCall,** *plastic, brown hair (rooted), sleep eyes (blue), marked McCall Corp., made in 1958, 8"*	23.00	28.00	22.00
☐ **Terry Talks,** *composition, blonde saran wig, sleep eyes, white eyelet playdress, 22", c. 1950*	60.00	70.00	62.50
☐ **Tiny Tears,** *composition head, rubber body, molded hair, sleep eyes with tear ducts, layette suit, 12", c. 1950*	75.00	85.00	77.50
☐ **Tiny Tears,** *rubber, molded hair, sleep eyes with tear ducts, layette suit, 12", c. 1950*	75.00	85.00	77.50
☐ **Tisket -N- Basket,** *separate cloth doll in green and yellow basket with handle, green and yellow outfit, 10"*	8.00	15.00	10.00
☐ **Toodle-Loo,** *vinyl, rooted hair (blonde), painted eyes, infant doll, marked 1961, American Doll & Toy Co., 18½"*	44.00	55.00	40.00
☐ **Tressy,** *plastic/vinyl, blonde hair (rooted), with growing-hair action, operated by knob at back of body, marked American Doll & Toy Corp., 1963, 11½"*	10.00	14.00	10.00

	Current Price Range		Prior Year Average
☐ **Wee Girl,** *marked Noen, 1940, 9¾″*	25.00	29.00	23.00
☐ **Whimsie,** *vinyl, painted eyes, rooted hair (blonde), upturned eyes with angelic expression, puffy cheeks, marked Amer. Doll & Toy Co., 1960, 21″*	38.00	46.00	35.00
☐ **Whimsie,** *as a monk, plastic, brown felt habit, 21″*	25.00	35.00	30.00

AMSCO

☐ **Buffy,** *marked 1971, Amsco Ind., Inc., 12¼″*	42.00	51.00	40.00
☐ **Gramma,** *cloth (stuffed), painted features, yarn hair (grey), painted eyeglasses, sold originally with a tag reading Amsco Toys, made in Hong Kong, made in 1971, 19″*	11.00	14.00	11.00

APEX

☐ **Baby Wendy,** *vinyl head, cloth body, vinyl limbs, sleep eyes (blue), bright red lips, wears baby bonnet, marked APEX, made in 1952, 18½″*	27.00	36.00	25.00

ARLESFORD

☐ **Hilary,** *porcelain, 24″, c. 1979*	125.00	175.00	130.00
☐ **Jane,** *bisque porcelain, soft body, wigs, blown glass eyes, 24″, c. 1979*	100.00	150.00	110.00
☐ **Katherine,** *bisque, porcelain, soft body, wigs, blown glass eyes, 24″, c. 1979*	100.00	150.00	110.00
☐ **Lisa,** *bisque, porcelain, soft body, wigs, blown glass eyes, 24″, c. 1979*	100.00	150.00	110.00
☐ **William,** *porcelain, 22″, c. 1979*	100.00	150.00	110.00

ARRANBEE DOLL COMPANY

Arranbee Dolls, an American company, was started in the early 1920's and produced highly collectable dolls until it was absorbed by Vogue Doll Company in 1960. In the early years of the company, bisque heads were imported from major German and French manufacturers and assembled on American made soft bodies. When World War I disrupted trade with Europe, especially Germany, Arranbee, like most of the other doll companies turned to making their own composition heads, and their quality became famous in the industry. In the early 1950's, hard plastic replaced composition for construction and Arranbee reached its pinnacle of success. The Nancy Lee Series produced during this time is one of the most sought after collectibles in the hobby. Voque Dolls used Arranbee's molds for the initial Ginny doll issues before disbanding the company and discontinuing the use of their marks.

	Current Price Range		Prior Year Average
☐ **Angeline,** *plastic, blonde wig attached by adhesive, sleep eyes (blue), marked R & B, made in 1952, 17½"*	48.00	59.00	45.00
☐ **Army Boy,** *composition head and limbs, body stuffed with excelsior, molded hair, painted eyes, wears U.S. soldier's uniform of post-World War I era, featuring reproductions (in reduced size) of Lincoln cents for jacket buttons, 15"*	75.00	95.00	70.00
Note: The uniform style would suggest a dating of c. 1920-25, but it is believed Army Boy was made slightly later than this.			
☐ **Baby Marie,** *vinyl head, vinyl arms and legs, plastic body, sleep eyes, molded hair, partially open mouth, shaped for insertion of nursing bottle, wears diaper, quilt jacket, 8¼"*	5.00	7.00	5.00
☐ **Bottletot,** *composition head and body, sleep eyes (tin), closed mouth, bent arms, holds glass nursing bottle in one hand (celluloid hand), marked Arranbee Aug. 10, 26,*	60.00	85.00	55.00
Note: Stated value is for a specimen in the original wickerwork basket as sold by the manufacturer. The doll alone would be worth approximately 30% less.			
☐ **Bride,** *hard plastic head, hard plastic arms, legs and body, sleep eyes, closed mouth, wears bridal gown, 14"*	50.00	65.00	48.00
☐ **Carolyn The Snow Queen** *(sometimes spelled Caroline), composition head, composition arms, legs and body, sleep eyes, closed mouth, pursed lips, blonde hair with ribbon, long gown with waist sash, 20¼"*	60.00	75.00	55.00
☐ **Composition head,** *composition arms and legs, body stuffed with excelsior, molded hair, painted eyes, wears striped dress with stripes running horizontally on the upper portion and vertically on the lower portion, painted shoes, 15¼"*	70.00	90.00	68.00
☐ **Composition,** *shoulderhead with swivel neck, cloth body, composition arms and legs, brown sleep eyes, blonde human hair*			

	Current Price Range		Prior Year Average
wig, painted closed mouth, original maroon tinted plaid school dress with lace collar, marked R & B, 22″	140.00	180.00	145.00
☐ **Debu-Teen,** *composition head, cloth body, composition arms and legs, turnable head, brunette wig, attached by adhesive, sleep eyes, marked R & B, made in 1940, 18″*	43.00	52.00	40.00
☐ **Dream Bride,** *plastic, sandy blonde wig attached by adhesive, sleep eyes (blue), wears bridal gown, marked R & B, also carrying the mold mark 210, made in 1954, 21″*	43.00	55.00	40.00
☐ **Francine,** *plastic, blonde hair attached by adhesive, sleep eyes (blue), marked R & B, made in 1955, 17″*	48.00	59.00	44.00

Deanna Durbin,
composition,
c. 1938, 18″
$150.00-$200.00

	Current Price Range		Prior Year Average
☐ **Judy,** *plastic, blonde wig attached by adhesive, the wig formed into an elaborate hairdo of tightly wound braids curled into a ram's-horn and pinned against the head, sleep eyes (blue), marked with the mold number 210 and the patent number 2,537,598, made in 1951, 19"*	62.00	75.00	58.00
☐ **Littlest Angel,** *plastic, brown hair attached by adhesive, sleep eyes (blue), swivel head, jointed at the knees, marked R & B, made in 1956, 10"*	12.00	16.00	11.00
☐ **Little Angel,** *composition head, cloth body, composition arms and legs, molded hair (brunette), sleep eyes (blue), unmarked, believed to have been made c. 1940, 15½"*	29.00	37.00	27.00
☐ **My Angel,** *vinyl head, oilcloth body, vinyl arms and legs, blonde hair (rooted), sleep eyes (blue), open mouth with teeth, bright red lips, marked Arranbee, made in 1959, 22"*	45.00	56.00	42.00
☐ **Nancy,** *doll plus trunk and accessories, marked Nancy, 12", complete*	40.00	50.00	38.00
Doll only	24.00	29.00	23.00
Note: Believed to have been sold around 1933 or 1934.			
☐ **Nancy Lee,** *composition head, composition arms, legs and body, sleep eyes with long eyelashes, long blond wig, wears brightly patterned short dress with squared white collar, carries matching handbag, white stockings, black shoes, 14"*			
With handbag	50.00	65.00	45.00
Without handbag	40.00	52.00	38.00
Value of handbag alone	8.00	10.00	7.00
☐ **Nancy Lee,** *composition head and body, blonde human hair wig, brown sleep eyes, 12½"*	55.00	65.00	57.50
☐ **Nancy Lee,** *hard plastic head, hard plastic arms, legs and body, saran wig, deep flesh toned skin, short silk dress with floral pattern, tied with waist ribbon, white shoes, silk stockings, 17"*	50.00	65.00	47.00
☐ **Nanette,** *brown hair, blue sleep eyes, lashes, yellow blouse, floral print jumper, 15"*	55.00	65.00	60.00
☐ **Nanette,** *plastic, blonde mohair wig, blue sleep eyes, lashes, velvet gown, lamb jacket*	70.00	80.00	75.00
☐ **Nanette,** *plastic, brown wig, attached by adhesive, sleep eyes (blue), marked R & B, made in 1953, 14"*	46.00	55.00	45.00

Nancy Lee,
composition
$50.00-$60.00

Nanette,
hard plastic,
c. 1950, 14″
$46.00-$55.00

	Current Price Range		Prior Year Average
☐ **New Happytot,** *vinyl head and body, sleep eyes (blue), marked Arranbee, made in 1955, 16"*	24.00	30.00	23.00
☐ **Peachy,** *plastic, molded hair (brown), painted eyes, unmarked, made c. 1950, 10"*	11.00	14.00	10.00
☐ **Princess Betty Rose,** *composition head, composition arms, legs and body, sleep eyes, closed mouth with dark lipstick, full, medium-length wig, wears long dress with lace trimming, marked R & B, 17½"*	75.00	95.00	70.00
Note: Princess Betty Rose was released in the late 1930's, undoubtedly inspired by the American popularity of Britian's Princess Elizabeth.			
☐ **Prom Queen,** *walker, plastic/vinyl, brunette hair (rooted), sleep eyes (blue), marked R & B, made in 1957, 17"*	47.00	59.00	45.00
☐ **Rosie,** *composition head (swivel), composition arms and legs, cloth body, sleep eyes, molded blond hair swept down in front, long at sides, doleful expression, partially open mouth, wears long white gown, marked Arranbee, 18½"*	30.00	38.00	27.00
Note: Rosie was originally placed on the market in 1935. It was one of the better sellers among the Arranbee line.			
☐ **Scarlet,** *composition head, composition arms, legs and body, sleep eyes (green), long eyelashes, closed mouth, wears long ball gown of U.S. Civil War era and large bonnet, gown is trimmed with silk ribbons, marked R & B, 15"*	50.00	65.00	48.00
Note: Scarlet was inspired by the motion picture, "Gone With The Wind," released in 1939, and represents the character Scarlet O'Hara. It is believed that the doll went on sale in 1940. Public reaction to "Gone With The Wind" brought about a great deal of related merchandise — including quite a few Scarlet O'Hara dolls by various manufacturers.			
☐ **Skater Doll,** *bisque, blue skirt, plaid hood, jacket, skates*	150.00	200.00	175.00
☐ **Snuggle Doll,** *composition head, stuffed body, stuffed arms and legs, blonde wig attached by adhesive, fixed eyes (blue), unmarked, made in 1941, 17"*	53.00	65.00	50.00
☐ **Sonja Henie,** *composition head and body, brunette wig attached by adhesive, sleep eyes (brown), marked R & B, made in 1945, 21¼"*	49.00	58.00	47.00

	Current Price Range		Prior Year Average
Note: Sonja Henie was an Olympic ice-skating champion and, later, motion picture personality.			
☐ **Taffy,** *plastic, sleep eyes (green), marked R & B, made in 1954, 16½″*	55.00	67.00	52.00

ARROW NOVELTY COMPANY

	Current Price Range		Prior Year Average
☐ **Skookum (Indian),** *plastic, marked Trademark Registered, Skookum Indian, U.S.A., Patented 1950, 21″*	68.00	82.00	65.00
Note: This doll was actually in production well before 1950 in various early versions, but was either not patented until 1950 or (perhaps) the patent was renewed in that year. It can also be found in a number of different sizes and facial expressions. The hair is always a coarse black wig, sometimes loose, sometimes braided, but always quite long.			

ARROW PLASTICS

	Current Price Range		Prior Year Average
☐ **Baby Doo,** *vinyl, molded and painted features, molded and painted hair, (blonde), bright red lips, marked with the Arrow symbol of an arrow piercing a diamond, made in 1957, 8½″*	7.00	10.00	7.00
☐ **Bye-Bye Baby,** *vinyl, blonde hair (rooted), sleep eyes (blue), marked Arrow Plastics 18, made in 1957, 17¼″*	25.00	30.00	23.00
☐ **Candy,** *vinyl, molded and painted features, molded and painted hair, marked The Edward Moberly Co., 1958, 8″*	4.00	6.00	4.00
☐ **Cindy,** *vinyl, molded and painted features, molded and painted hair, marked 22 The Edward Moberly Co., made in 1962, 8″*	6.00	8.00	6.00
☐ **Marlene,** *vinyl, sleep eyes (blue), adult body, marked with an arrow inside a lozenge and the number 55, 24″*	40.00	48.00	38.00
☐ **My Friend,** *vinyl, molded and painted features, molded and painted hair, diapered toddler clutching a Teddy Bear, marked The Edward Moberly Co., 1964, 8″*	4.00	6.00	4.00
☐ **Playful,** *rubber, molded and painted features, marked 42, made in 1941, 11″*	21.00	27.00	20.00

	Current Price Range		Prior Year Average
☐ **Pretty Lady,** *vinyl, blonde hair (rooted), sleep eyes (blue), marked with the Arrow symbol of an arrow piercing a diamond, and additionally marked with the mold number 52, made in 1958, 31″*	27.00	36.00	25.00
☐ **Stunning,** *vinyl, sleep eyes (blue), adult body, marked with an arrow inside a lozenge and the number 55, 24″*	40.00	48.00	38.00
☐ **Sweet Judy,** *vinyl, sleep eyes (blue), adult body, marked with an arrow inside a lozenge and the number 55, 24″*	40.00	48.00	38.00

ART FABRIC MILLS

☐ **Cloth,** *lithographed face, cloth body, marked Art Fabric Mills, New York, patented February 13, 1900, 26″*	170.00	210.00	165.00
☐ **Merrie Marie,** *lithographed cloth face, cloth body, marked Art Fabric Mills, New York, 25″*	190.00	235.00	180.00

ARTISAN NOVELTY

☐ **Little Miss Gadabout,** *walker, plastic, sleep eyes (blue), unmarked, made in 1950, 18″*	31.00	39.00	30.00
☐ **Lov You,** *vinyl head, cloth body, vinyl arms and legs, unmarked, made in 1951, 22″*	33.00	39.00	30.00
☐ **Raving Beauty,** *plastic, red wig attached by adhesive, sleep eyes (brown), unmarked, made in 1953, 18½″*	45.00	55.00	42.00

ASPEN PRODUCTIONS

☐ **Alan Alda of "M.A.S.H.,"** *vinyl head, vinyl body, molded hair, has push-button in back which operates arms — putting this doll on the borderline of the puppet category, 8½″*	5.00	7.00	3.00

Note: At the same time a companion doll was made, to represent Loretta Swit. Value is about the same, but as a set they would probably bring a slight premium. Both dolls wear molded combat boots.

AUNT SARAH

	Current Price Range		Prior Year Average
☐ **Aunt Sarah,** *lithographed cloth, representing a grandmotherly woman holding bowl of pancake batter (trademark of Aunt Sarah's House of Pancakes), 18"*	4.00	6.00	3.00

AURORA

☐ **Mary Many Face (Spanish National Costume doll),** *cloth, sponsored by UNECEFF, unmarked, sold originally with a tag reading Mary Many Face, Aurora Products Corp., 17"*	15.00	19.00	14.00

AVERILL MANUFACTURING COMPANY

☐ **Baby,** *bisque head, cloth body, celluloid arms and legs, sleep eyes, open mouth, two teeth, tongue, voice box, #1005/3652/4, #1386/47, 16"*	800.00	1000.00	825.00
☐ **Baby Sweets,** *by Maude Tousey Fangel, all cloth, printed features which include blue eyes with long lashes, curly blond hair, pug nose, sweet smile, white gauze dress trimmed in lace, matching hat, 14"*	240.00	255.00	225.00
☐ **Bonnie Babe,** *bisque head, cloth body with composition arms and legs, detailed molded head, blue sleep eyes, lovely gown, rare large size, 20" body length, 13½" head circumference*	1000.00	1250.00	1000.00
☐ **Character,** *composition head and arms, cloth body and legs, painted face, wig, original clothes, tagged, 10"*	85.00	125.00	55.00
☐ **Chocolate Drop,** *black all cloth doll, painted face, three black yarn pigtails, designed by Grace G. Drayton, 11"*	195.00	220.00	195.00
☐ **Dolly Dingle,** *all cloth, jointed arms and legs, painted features, designed by Grace G. Drayton,*	185.00	210.00	175.00
☐ **Dutch Girl,** *cloth, pigtailed mohair wig, regional costume, 13"*	40.00	50.00	45.00
☐ **Indian Boy,** *painted eyes, molded hair, green felt shirt, gray felt pants, green and red moccasins, 13"*	60.00	70.00	62.00
☐ **Infant,** *bisque head, cloth body, molded hair, blue sleep eyes, open mouth, two lower teeth, white baby dress with bonnet, 18"*	1500.00	1750.00	1600.00

	Current Price Range		Prior Year Average
☐ **Italian Girl,** *cloth, yarn hair, brown eyes, print dress, white apron, 14"*	70.00	100.00	80.00
☐ **Minnehaha,** *character, cloth molded, masked face, cloth body, long black yarn pigtails, brown eyes with real eyelashes, painted features, brown skinned, colorful outfit of orange yellow, green, white moccasins, original wrist tag "Minnehaha," c. 1940's, mint, 13½*	80.00	90.00	80.00
☐ **Snowbums,** *designed by Georgene Averill from the comic strip "The Newlyweds" by George McManus, composition head, composition and cloth body, painted blue eyes, molded hair with one lock of hair, laughing mouth, playsuit, 14"*	275.00	300.00	275.00
☐ **Whistling Boy,** *composition, cloth torso, spring legs which activate a bellows, painted eyes to side, whistling mouth with hole, molded red hair, blue linen linen pants, blue striped suit, 14"*	100.00	150.00	118.00

AZARK

☐ **Calamity Jane,** *posable legs, marked Azark-Hamway, 12"*	4.00	6.00	4.00
☐ **Kit Carson,** *plastic body, plastic legs, vinyl head and arms, representing the gunfighter of the Old West, who wears a moustache, plaid shirt, striped vest, striped trousers, and tall boots, he carries a six-shooter, marked Hong Kong, c. 1974, 12"*	4.00	6.00	4.00

BABY BERRY

☐ **Christopher Robin,** *cloth body, cloth limbs, vinyl head, molded and painted hair (red), unmarked, age of manufacture unknown, representing a character from the writings of A.A. Milne*	37.00	45.00	35.00
☐ **Emmet Kelly,** *character doll, c. 1950, 20"*	125.00	150.00	120.00
☐ **Lil Abner,** *vinyl head, vinyl arms, legs and body, plaid shirt, pants patched at knees, dated 1957, 13"*	90.00	115.00	85.00

Note: Al Capp's "Lil Abner" was made into a stage play at about this time (1957), inspiring a wave of related merchandise. The

	Current Price Range		Prior Year Average
character had been introduced into comic strips in the 1930's. Baby Berry also made a matching "Daisy Mae" doll, whose market value is about the same.			
☐ **Mammy Yokum,** *vinyl head, cloth body, yarn wig, bulbous nose, square chin, large staring eyes, smokes corncob pipe, based on the character from the comic strip "Lil Abner" by Al Capp, 21"*	125.00	150.00	115.00
Note: Baby Berry also made a smaller version of Mammy Yokum, about 13", in a different style.			

BÄHR & PRÖSCHILD

The dolls of Bähr & Pröschild have gained a deservedly high reputation among collectors. Realistically modeled faces, in bisque, were standard for the dolls of this firm. The skin tones are usually as lifelike as can be achieved in bisque, and the small painted details are carefully executed. This was a German corporation founded in 1871 at Ohrdruf, Thuringia. They were neighbors of Armand Marseille in the days when Thuringia was "doll capital" of the world. Bähr & Pröschild enjoyed very good success, especially in the early 1900's, but was forced to shut down as the result of World War I.

Two different marks were used by Bähr & Pröschild. One consisted of the letters B and P enclosed within a heart. The other, somewhat more complex, consists of crossed bars resembling the letter X. On the lefthand side of this mark is the initial B; on the righthand side the initial P; at the bottom an O; and a small flourished symbol at the top. This is the more common of the two versions.

Any Bähr & Pröschild doll in good condition is likely to be quite valuable, worth several hundred dollars at minimum. So the collector should certainly learn to recognize the markings and buy if the price is right. Even if you buy only to resell to another hobbyist, or to trade, a Bähr & Pröschild doll at a fair price is a worthwhile investment.

☐ **Bisque,** *composition body (five-piece), small sleep eyes, no upper lashes, tiny painted lower lashes, bearing the factory trademark (crossed bars with a B in the left field, a P in the right field, an O beneath, and a symbol above), 16½"*	825.00	960.00	750.00
☐ **Bisque,** *composition body (five-piece), sleep eyes with eyelashes, open mouth with two teeth (large space between them), bearing the factory trademark (crossed bars with a B in the left field, a P in the right field, an O beneath, and a symbol above), marked additionally with a mold number, 585/16, 25"*	310.00	350.00	300.00

	Current Price Range		Prior Year Average
☐ **Bisque,** *socket head, fixed eyes (dark, roundish), dark narrow brows, open mouth showing teeth, dark red lips, pug nose, almost spherical head, representing a toddler, marked BP within a heart, made in Germany and with the mold identification number 585-3/0, date of manufacture unknown, based on marking evidence this doll was apparently made somewhere between the later 1890's and 1910, 10¼"*	380.00	440.00	350.00
☐ **Character Baby,** *bisque head, five piece composition body, bent leg, choppy red wig, brown sleep eyes, open mouth, frilly formal suit, booties, 14"*	700.00	750.00	725.00
☐ **Character Baby,** *bisque head, five piece ball jointed composition body, skin wig, brown sleep eyes, in white layette dress with bonnet, 7"*	200.00	300.00	225.00
☐ **Character Baby,** *bisque socket head, jointed five piece bent leg baby body, brown sleep eyes, open/closed mouth with two molded upper teeth, original blonde mohair wig, gentle smiling expression, ruffled bonnet, white infant gown, marked BP within crossed swords, 585, 5 Germany, 13"*	350.00	400.00	350.00
☐ **Character Baby,** *bisque socket head, jointed five piece bent leg baby body, brown sleep eyes, open mouth with two teeth, tremble tongue, auburn colored mohair wig, white lace trimmed gown accented with yellow silk ribbons, marked 678, 6 BP within heart, 13"*	250.00	350.00	225.00
☐ **Girl,** *bent limb, human hair wig, blue sleep eyes, open mouth, two teeth, German*	200.00	250.00	220.00

CONSTANCE BANNISTER

	Current Price Range		Prior Year Average
☐ **Bannister Baby,** *vinyl, molded and painted hair, sleep eyes (blue), nursing mouth, marked Constance Bannister, New York, date of manufacture unknown, presumably c. 1952, 17"*	70.00	88.00	65.00

Note: Constance Bannister was a professional photographer whose photos of babies were collected into several best selling books during the 1950's.

BANTAM

	Current Price Range		Prior Year Average
☐ **Sleepyhead,** *vinyl mask face, plush body, plush arms and legs, molded and painted features, molded and painted hair (blonde), sold originally with a tag reading Bantam U.S. Toys, made in 1962, 9⅞″*	5.00	7.00	5.00

BAUER & BLACK

☐ **Miss Curity,** *composition with sleep eyes, 1946, 21″*	43.00	54.00	40.00

BELLE

☐ **Baby Gem,** *vinyl, sleep eyes (blue), unmarked, believed to have been made in 1958, 8″*	6.00	8.00	6.00
☐ **Ballerina Belle,** *plastic/vinyl, brown hair (rooted), sleep eyes (blue), marked 16VW, made in 1956, 18½″*	7.00	9.00	6.00
☐ **Ballerina Belle,** *walker, marked AE 200-21, 1956, 18½″*	11.00	14.00	10.00
☐ **Belle-Lee,** *vinyl, blonde hair (rooted), sleep eyes (blue), unmarked, made in 1958, 10″*	4.00	6.00	4.00
☐ **Jackie,** *vinyl head, stuffed arms and legs, stuffed body, short molded hair swept down in front, sleep eyes with medium-length lashes, wears corduroy overalls, mold number 14 on head, 14″*	16.00	20.00	15.00
☐ **Little Miss Margie,** *hard vinyl head, hard vinyl arms, legs and body, sleep eyes, long reddish-blond hair, pearl earrings, wears print dress with white collar and cuffs, no stockings, marked with P within circle, 10″*	7.00	9.00	7.00
☐ **Melinda,** *plastic/vinyl, unmarked, 1961, 14″*	7.00	9.00	7.00
☐ **Miss B,** *vinyl, brown hair (rooted), sleep eyes (blue), unmarked, made in 1954, 11½″*	5.00	7.00	5.00
☐ **Perfect Companion,** *walker, marked AE 553, sold in 1953, 22″*	11.00	14.00	10.00
☐ **Twixie The Twisting Pixie,** *jointed waist, marked P-16, 1958, 19″*	26.00	31.00	25.00

BELTON

Beltons are among the aristocrats of the doll world. All specimens of this manufacturer rank as antiques, since the firm went out of business in 1855. Not only are they antiques, but the quality is quite high — and so, too, is the value. However, the scarcity factor with Beltons is not as extreme as with some other dolls of this general era, therefore keeping the values within more or less tolerable bounds. Some Beltons can be had for as little as $300 or $350, even in well-preserved condition: which is really saying something, for dolls of this kind of age, reputation, and visual appeal.

Belton was a French firm and was partially responsible for the worldwide acclaim achieved by French dolls in the mid 1800's. In that era, everyone acknowledged that the French were the supreme doll manufacturers. Though export into the U.S. was not nearly as heavy as it became later, well-to-do families tried to get French dolls for their children or (even more often) for display. When the Germans gradually overtook the French in doll manufacturing, they were careful to model most of their dolls along classical French lines — which meant the standard set by firms such as Belton.

Originally Belton was in partnership with Jumeau. Their company was founded at Paris in 1842. Jumeau then went off on his own and Belton carried on alone, until his death in the early 1850's, For several years thereafter his widow maintained the factory but sold out in 1855. Hence the whole history of Belton spanned only about a dozen years. None of the Belton dolls was made in large quantities, mainly because the export market was not, in the 1840's and 1850's, what it became in the 1880's and 1890's.

Belton dolls customarily bear a mold or model number but no other markings, and, in some cases, no markings whatsoever.

	Current Price Range		Prior Year Average
☐ **Bisque,** *jointed composition body, blue paper-weight eyes, closed mouth, 18″*	1400.00	2200.00	1750.00
☐ **Bisque head,** *wood body, papier mache arms and legs, fixed eyes (very large, dark), painted lashes on upper and lower eyelids, partially open mouth with no teeth showing, thin face, pug nose, pierced ears, representing an adult woman, marked with the mold number 3, date of manufacture not known, 12″*	580.00	700.00	550.00
☐ **Bisque,** *socket head, composition body, fixed eyes (wide staring), long painted eyelashes, prominent eyebrows, mouth partially open (no teeth showing), marked 137/3, 12″*	340.00	415.00	325.00
☐ **Bisque,** *socket head, fixed eyes (large, roundish), very pale painted lashes, narrow brows, closed mouth with thin pale lips, narrow nose, almost shperical head, conventional ears (pierced), representing a young woman, marked with the mold number 14, date of manufacture not known, 20½″*	700.00	850.00	650.00

	Current Price Range		Prior Year Average
☐ **Blue Bird,** *composition, moveable arms, legs, blue ribbon molded in hair, sleep eyes, closed mouth, original blue dress, apron, 14″*	115.00	130.00	115.00
☐ **Blue Boy,** *bisque head, ball jointed body, blue sleep eyes, blue velvet outfit, marked on head Bavaria 199, 16″*	475.00	500.00	480.00
☐ **China,** *cloth body, kid arms, bald with brown wig, painted eyes, contemporary lavender and silk dress with bonnet, c. 1800, 21″*	400.00	450.00	425.00
☐ **Pink Bisque,** *jointed composition body, blue eyes, red hair, closed mouth, mauve taffeta dress, 13″*	1200.00	1600.00	1350.00
☐ **Solid Dome** *bisque socket head with three holes, five piece composition body, shoes and socks, brown glass set eyes, closed mouth, light brown wig, white cotton dress, marked 200 4/0, 8″*	300.00	400.00	300.00

BENDEE

☐ **French Gendarme (policeman),** *wire encased in foam, fully posable, molded and painted features and clothing, representing a French gendarme of the 1890's, marked Bendee, date of manufacture unknown, made in England, 8¾″*	7.00	10.00	7.00

BERGMANN

Bergmann, a German firm, was a rather prolific doll producer during the early 1900's. Collectors should take note of the fact that Bergmann did not manufacture doll heads. It was strictly a maker of doll bodies and an assembler of dolls for distribution to the wholesale and export markets: that is, it bought doll heads made by other firms and attached them to its bodies. This was not, of course, a unique situation, as many other firms operated in a similar way; but companies which did not manufacture doll heads lack some of the status and glamor of firms which did. The full name of the organization was Charles M. Bergmann and Co. It was set up in 1889, when the German doll industry was rolling in high gear. Bergmann dolls are found with heads by Armand Marseille, Halbig and others. They are certainly not inferior dolls if one judges them as a whole, and the market values show that hobbyists are not exactly taking them lightly. The costumes can be very exquisite.

Bergmann did a flourishing export business, which seems to have increased steadily in the years from 1900 until the opening of World War I. The full company name usually appeared on its dolls, rather than initials, and sometimes a date as well. The name of the manufacturer of the doll's head is often indicated, too. With virtually no exceptions, the Bergmann dolls have bisque heads, sleep eyes (usually with lashes) and handsome wigs.

	Current Price Range		Prior Year Average
☐ **Bisque,** *blue set paperweight eyes, long blonde curls, open mouth, white dress with red sash, red hair bow, 25″*	425.00	475.00	440.00
☐ **Bisque,** *brown eyes, blonde wig, white and pink cotton dress, 23″*	150.00	200.00	170.00
☐ **Bisque,** *brown sleep eyes, blonde mohair wig, open mouth, long green dress embroidered in white, 32″*	725.00	750.00	740.00
☐ **Bisque,** *composition ball jointed body, blue sleep eyes, navy and white dress with hat, 25″*	600.00	700.00	625.00
☐ **Bisque,** *jointed composition body, blue eyes, brown wig, pink cotton dress and hat, 25″*	350.00	400.00	370.00
☐ **Bisque,** *original mohair wig, blue sleep eyes, open mouth, clothing, finest condition, 28″*	750.00	825.00	725.00
☐ **Bisque,** *socket head, composition body (fully jointed), sleep eyes with eyelashes, open mouth showing four teeth, marked C.M. Bergmann/BB1/Germany, 22½″*	180.00	230.00	175.00
☐ **Bisque,** *socket head, composition body, fully jointed and spring strung, sleep eyes (large), open mouth showing four teeth, pierced ears, marked C.M. Bergmann / Simon and Halbig/, 25″*	235.00	270.00	225.00
☐ **Bisque,** *socket head, composition body (fully jointed), sleep eyes, no upper eyelashes, open mouth showing four teeth, pierced ears, marked C.M. Bergmann/Simon and Halbig, 28″*	240.00	285.00	230.00
Note: The expression on this doll's face can best be described as one of apprehension.			
☐ **Bisque,** *socket head, jointed composition body, blue set eyes, long blonde wig, open mouth with four porcelain teeth, dimpled chin, pink cotton dress, eyelet pinafore, marked C.M. Bergmann, Waltershausen 1916 6½, 23″*	450.00	550.00	450.00
☐ **Bisque,** *socket head, jointed composition body, brown sleep eyes with real upper lashes, open mouth with four porcelain teeth, dimpled chin, pierced ears, dark brown wig, light salmon colored satin dress, matching lace overskirt, ruffled waist line, matching cap. marked C.M. Bergmann, Simon & Halbig 14½, 33″*	700.00	900.00	700.00

	Current Price Range		Prior Year Average
☐ **Child,** *bisque head, ball jointed composition body, brown set eyes, light brown human hair wig, closed mouth, lovely clothes, 22″ . . . . . .*	350.00	400.00	375.00
☐ **Composition,** *jointed body, closed mouth, blue eyes, lashes, dark brown wig, blue silk dress with lace, straw hat, 23″ . . . .*	250.00	300.00	270.00
☐ **Composition,** *jointed body, closed mouth, brown eyes, redish-brown wig, cotton dress, 29″ . . . .*	550.00	600.00	570.00
☐ **Composition Head,** *jointed body, blonde human hair, blue paperweight eyes, red velvet dress and hat, c. 1910, 25″ . . . .*	550.00	600.00	575.00
☐ **Girl,** *jointed composition body, gray-blue eyes, white and blue cotton dress, blue satin belt, blue ribbon in hair, 23″ . . . .*	325.00	375.00	340.00

Bisque Head,
composition body, c. 1910, 25″
$550.00-$600.00

CARL BERGNER

	Current Price Range		Prior Year Average
☐ **Bisque,** *three faced head, composition arms, cloth body, three faces depict laughing, crying, sleeping, brown glass eyes, wigged hood, lovely old dress and pantaloons, marked "C.B." on shoulder, 12"*	1000.00	1300.00	1000.00
☐ **Bisque,** *head with three faces, cloth body, composition arms, faces depict laughing, sleeping and crying, brown human hair wig, all original, 17"*	1700.00	1900.00	1700.00
☐ **Bisque,** *head, three faced character, papier mache hood, cloth and ball jointed composition body, three faces portrayed are crying with blue glass inset eyes, two molded tears, open/closed mouth, laughing, with blue glass inset eyes, similing closed mouth with white space, sleeping, original blonde wig with white lace trimmed dress and bonnet, pull string crier which functions, marks: C.B. on back of shoulder, 14½"*	1000.00	1500.00	1000.00

BERMAN & ANDERSON

☐ **Oliver Hardy,** *vinyl head, vinyl arms, legs and body, painted features, designed to represent the motion picture comedy actor Oliver Hardy (of Laurel and Hardy), dates from the 1970's, 11"*	9.00	12.00	9.00
☐ **Stan Laurel,** *vinyl head, vinyl arms, legs and body, painted features, designed to represent the motion picture comedy actor Stan Laurel (of Laurel and Hardy), dates from the 1970's, 10¼"*	9.00	12.00	9.00

BLUMBERG

☐ **Baby's First Doll,** *vinyl, molded and painted hair, sleep eyes (blue), marked 2F-3, made in 1960, 13¼"*	5.00	7.00	5.00
☐ **Jimmy,** *vinyl head, latex body, molded and painted hair, sleep eyes (bluc), unmarked, made in 1955, 15½"*	7.00	10.00	6.00
☐ **Perky Bright,** *vinyl, molded and painted hair, sleep eyes (blue), unmarked, made in 1952, 12"*	10.00	14.00	9.00

	Current Price Range		Prior Year Average
☐ **Rockabye Baby,** *vinyl, molded and painted hair, fixed eyes, unmarked, made in 1963, 14″*	6.00	8.00	5.00
☐ **Sally,** *vinyl, marked 26 AE, 1958, 15″*	8.00	11.00	7.00
☐ **Timmy,** *vinyl head, latex body, molded and painted hair, fixed eyes (blue), unmarked, made in 1954, 15″*	5.00	7.00	5.00

ERNST BOHNE

☐ **Porcelain,** *half doll, beautiful molded porcelain head and torso with arms, elaborate coiffure wreathed with flowers, molded clothing on torso, 21″*	900.00	1000.00	675.00

BOMBOLE FRANCA

☐ **Bed Doll,** *plastic head, plastic arms, legs and body, sleep eyes, wig attached by adhesive, with ribbon in hair, closed mouth with quizzical facial expression, marked Made in Italy by Bombole Franca Co., 1959, 14″*	7.00	9.00	7.00

Note: Called "bed doll" as it was designed to decorate a bed during daytime, a custom more prevalent in Europe than in the U.S.

BONOMI

☐ **Handora,** *plastic, sleep eyes (blue), jointed waist, marked Bonomi, Italy, made in the early 1960's, 22″*	33.00	39.00	30.00
☐ **Lizabetta,** *plastic, jointed waist, sleep eyes (green), strung, marked Bonomi, Italy, 19″*	37.00	47.00	35.00

BORDEN

☐ **Elsie, Borden's Cow,** *vinyl head, stuffed plush body, makes mooing sound, a premium of the Borden's Milk Co., made in 1958, 14″*	9.00	12.00	8.00

GEORGE BORGFELDT

Charlie McCarthy, composition and cloth **$250.00-$300.00**

	Current Price Range		Prior Year Average
☐ **Gladdie,** *ceramic head, fully molded and painted, composition limbs, cloth body, sleep blue eyes, original clothes and trunk with more clothes, 17″*	875.00	975.00	880.00
☐ **Gladdie,** *designed by Helen W. Jensen, ceramic head, composition legs and arms, cloth body, blue glass eyes, molded blond hair, laughing with open mouth, white bonnet with wide ruffle, white dress, shoes and socks, 20″*	825.00	875.00	800.00
☐ **Happifats,** *all bisque, jointed arms, painted black curl in middle of forehead, painted eyes with excited surprised expression, open smiling mouth, two teeth, molded clothes, 4″*	175.00	225.00	175.00

Felix the Cat,
wood, c. 1922, 10″
$225.00-$300.00

MADAME ETNA BOUCHER

	Current Price Range		Prior Year Average
☐ **Child,** *bisque head, ball jointed composition body, light brown long curls, stationary blue eyes, closed mouth, rare, 10″*	725.00	800.00	725.00

BROCK CANDY COMPANY

☐ **Sam The Scarecrow,** *cloth (printed), date of manufacture unknown, probably mid 1960's, apparently given as a premium or promotional item in connection with the purchase of Brock candy products, 17″*	13.00	17.00	12.00

BROOKGLAD

	Current Price Range		Prior Year Average
☐ **Poor Pitiful Pearl,** *vinyl, rooted hair (blonde), sleep eyes (blue), marked A Brookglad Creation, made in 1957, 13"*	25.00	30.00	23.00
☐ **Rusty,** *vinyl, molded and painted hair (red), fixed eyes (blue), marked Rusty, made in 1958, 16"*	22.00	28.00	20.00

BROUSE

☐ **Abraham Lincoln Doll,** *bisque, original clothes, 17"*	250.00	275.00	225.00

BRU

The shortest name in the doll industry, Bru, belonged to a Parisian firm of the 1800's. It survived into the 20th century, though its most collectible and valuable dolls date to the earlier period. Though this was a long-established company, its output was apparently very small, to judge by the small number of specimens that have crossed the American market (and there does not seem to be any greater quantity available in Europe, either). Standards of quality at Bru were exceptionally high. To judge from the finished results, painstaking work went into modeling of the molds. Today the Bru dolls rank among the most valuable of all antique dolls, with prices nearly always in the four-digit category for well preserved specimens.

Founder of the firm was Leon Casimir Bru, in 1867. In 1883 it was sold to a man named Chevot, who continued to operate it as Bru since the name had won considerable recognition by then. It was sold again 1890, but these changes of ownership had, surprisingly, no effect on the product's quality. The usual Bru mark consists of a dot within a circle, sometimes in a half-circle. The mark *Bru Jne,* which appears on some of the company's dolls, stands for Bru Jeune (Bru, Junior and Company — the name by which the firm was known for a while).

☐ **Bébé,** *bisque head, hands, kid body, blue paperweight eyes, blushed lids, brown human hair wig, closed mouth, pierced ears, original rose silk dress, mark: "Bébé Brévété S.G.D.G., Paris", 14"*	5000.00	6500.00	4500.00
☐ **Bébé,** *bisque head, kid body with jointed wood arms and legs, long black ringlet wig, blue paperweight eyes, ivory lace gown, leather shoes*	8000.00	9000.00	8500.00
☐ **Bébé,** *bisque head, kid body with bisque arms and legs, human hair wig, blue paper-*			

	Current Price Range		Prior Year Average
weight eyes, pierced ears, closed mouth, green and ivory silk gown and shoes, 11½″.	5000.00	6000.00	5500.00
☐ **Bébé Teteur,** *bisque head, kid body with bisque hands, curly blonde wig, blue paperweight eyes, painted eyebrows, nursing mouth, nightgown and cap, 13″ . . . .*	5000.00	6000.00	5500.00
☐ **Bisque Head,** *French ball jointed body, human hair wig, paperweight eyes, pierced ears, closed mouth, red gown . . . .*	3000.00	4000.00	3250.00
☐ **Bisque Head,** *jointed composition body, blonde wig, blue sleep eyes, open mouth with upper teeth, pierced ears, original clothes, mark: "Bru Jne R 9", 22″ . . . .*	5000.00	6000.00	5000.00
☐ **Bisque,** *bisque shoulder, head, kid lined swivel neck, blue paperweight eyes, closed mouth with red accent lines, original blonde mohair wig, cork pate, pierced ears with pearl earrings, kid body with gusset's at hips and knees, kid arms, bisque hands, green smocked silk dress with lace edged neckline and matching bonnet, dome top trunk with lithographed designs, various pieces of lace trimmed underwear, tray inset, parasol, doll purse, several doll accessories, marks: Circle Dot 3, 13″ . . . . .*	6500.00	7000.00	6000.00
☐ **Bisque,** *socket head set on bisque shoulder plate, wood body covered in kidskin, bisque forearms and forelegs, partially open mouth, pierced ears, marked Bru Jne, 17″ . .*	3250.00	3900.00	3200.00
☐ **Bisque,** *swivel head, kidskin body with bisque forearms, fixed eyes (large, staring), partially open mouth, pierced ears, marked Bébé/Brévette Paris, 20″ . . . .*	3800.00	4650.00	3750.00
☐ **Child,** *bisque head, composition jointed body, brown human hair wig, brown paperweight eyes, antique clothes and shoes, trunk with wardrobe, toys, 17″ . . . .*	6500.00	7500.00	6500.00
☐ **Child,** *bisque head on bisque shoulder plate, leather body, leather on metal upper arms and legs, bisque lower arms and wood lower legs, molded hair, brown glass stationary eyes, bebe teteur mouth, key wound feeding mechanism, antique clothing, marks: Bru Jn/3 . . . .*	3000.00	3500.00	3250.00
☐ **Child,** *bisque head, shoulder plate, leather lined, leather gusseted body, wooden upper arms and feet, bisque hands, blue paperweight eyes, brown wig, closed mouth, pierced ears, marked "Bru Jne 9," head and shoulder plate, 25″ . . . .*	6000.00	7000.00	6500.00

Fashion,
bisque and kid,
c. 1875, 18″
$2000.00-$3000.00

	Current Price Range		Prior Year Average
☐ **French Fashion,** *bisque head, kid leather body, white fashion wig, blue paperweight eyes, pierced ears, antique beige two piece Chanel suit, 18″, c. 1875*	1975.00	2200.00	2000.00
☐ **French Fashion,** *bisque head, five piece jointed body, human hair wig, blue paperweight eyes, pierced ears, elegant costume, 24″*	3000.00	3250.00	3100.00

BRUCKNER

	Current Price Range		Prior Year Average
☐ **Black Rag Doll,** *all cloth, stiffened mask face, 11″*	120.00	130.00	125.00

	Current Price Range		Prior Year Average
☐ **Rag Doll,** *printed face, original blue jumper with trimmed blouse and underwear, marked "Pat'd July 9, 1901", 12"*	60.00	70.00	60.00
☐ **Topsy-Turvy Rag Doll,** *all cloth with treated lithographed mask faces, two dolls in one, one face is white, the back side is black, cotton dress, 12"*	200.00	375.00	225.00

M. H. BUELL

☐ **Little Lulu,** *doll with mask face, height 14", c. 1944*	75.00	95.00	85.00

BUSCHOW & BECK

This German manufacturer specialized in dolls with metal heads, which it chiefly exported to the American market. It was not the only company making metal-head dolls, but it seems to have far outdone the competition in quantity. Metal-head dolls were first introduced in the 1880's (by another firm). They were supposed to solve the durability porblem, since the pretty bisque heads were breakable. Metal-head dolls could be sold at a lower price than those of bisque, and held out the promise of surviving longer than their purchaser. Indeed, they were virtually indestructible — but the popularity envisioned for them, by their promoters, never came to pass. They were simply not as good-looking as the bisque-head dolls, and the inducement of long wear was not enough to win over the public.

Buschow & Beck was in business in the later years of the 1800's and the earlier years of the present century. It did not make metal-head dolls exclusively, but also those of celluloid. On most Buschow & Beck dolls found on the U.S. market you will encounter the MINERVA trademark, which consists of that word in a semi-circle positioned atop a classical-style helmet (Minerva was of course a Greek goddess). This trademark was not used on all the firm's wares but exclusively on those alloted for export to America. Hence, if you doll-shop in the European antiques outlets, the Buschow & Beck dolls found there are not likely to have the "Minerva" marking.

For the collector these are not expensive dolls; they're old, not really bad looking, and represent something definitely "different." So you might want to consider them for your collection. Some can be found for under $100. Of course, as with any metal-head dolls, chipped paint brings down the desirability.

☐ **Metal,** *shoulder head, black, set on sateen body, muslin forelegs, black shoes, molded hair, mouth closed, marked Minerva, 12"*	150.00	190.00	140.00
☐ **Metal,** *shoulder head, set on cloth body, bisque forearms, molded reddish hair,*			

	Current Price Range		Prior Year Average
painted head, fixed eyes, open mouth showing three teeth and traces of others, marked Minerva, 18¾"	100.00	130.00	95.00
Note: This is a model of a boy about ¾ years of age.			
☐ **Metal,** *shoulder head, set on cloth body with bisque forearms and cowhide feet, fixed eyes, open mouth showing two teeth, marked Minerva, 20"*	90.00	115.00	85.00
Note: Figure of a young girl.			
☐ **Minerva,** *metal head, bisque forearms, cloth body, brown wig, blue glass eyes, open mouth, antique pale green satin dress with white lace trim, Victorian sleeves, matching bonnet, 18"*	185.00	205.00	190.00

CAMAY

☐ **Liza,** *plastic/vinyl, black hair (rooted), sleep eyes (brown), marked Made in Hong Kong, 1969, 14"*	7.00	9.00	7.00
☐ **Tim,** *plastic/vinyl, brown hair (rooted), painted eyes, marked Made in Hong Kong No. 7011, made in 1969, 10"*	5.00	7.00	5.00
☐ **Trease,** *marked Made in Taiwan 15-10, 1969, 14¼"*	6.00	8.00	6.00

CAMEO

☐ **Baby Mine,** *vinyl, marked Cameo, date of manufacture not known, 20"*	65.00	80.00	60.00
☐ **Betty Boop,** *wood and composition, painted black hair and goo-goo eyes, molded composition bathing suit, original design by J. L. Kallus, 12"*	450.00	550.00	500.00
☐ **Bye-Lo Baby,** *composition head, jointed composition body, sleep eyes, white cotton gown, ,. 1900, 12"*	350.00	450.00	355.00
☐ **Bye-Lo Baby,** *solid dome composition head with flange neck, blue sleep eyes, closed mouth, cloth body with composition hands, lace trimmed organdy dress, marks: Grace Storey Putnam, 13"*	275.00	375.00	250.00
☐ **Bye–Lo Baby,** *solid dome composition head with flange neck, molded painted brown hair, blue sleep eyes, painted closed red lips, new cloth body with bisque hands, long*			

	Current Price Range		Prior Year Average
white infant dress, marks: Grace Storey Putman, 15″	125.00	150.00	120.00
☐ **Dumbo,** *composition figure, swiveling trunk and googlie eyes, height 9″, c. 1941*	100.00	150.00	125.00
☐ **Giggles,** *composition head and body, head turns, molded hair swept downward in front, fixed eyes, 14″*	200.00	245.00	190.00
☐ **Kewpie,** *bisque, all bisque construction with jointed shoulders, head turned slightly to doll's left, felt clothing, 4″*	85.00	110.00	80.00
☐ **Kewpie,** *bisque, all bisque construction, wears Civil War-type soldier's cap, black belt (painted on), carries rifle and sabre, 4″*	110.00	140.00	100.00
☐ **Kewpie,** *bisque, all bisque construction with movable arms, wears felt "band leader" costume, 4″*	80.00	105.00	80.00
☐ **Kewpie,** *all celluloid, statuette type, in the likeness of a flapper-type girl wearing tuxedo jacket, 2″*	40.00	55.00	38.00
☐ **Kewpie,** *vinyl, molded and painted features, molded and painted hair, naked kewpie seated, legs drawn up, elbows resting on knees, chin in hands, smiling face, eyes turned to the doll's right, marked Kewpie, Rose O'Neill, Cameo, made in 1971, 3½″*	3.75	5.00	3.50
☐ **Kewpie,** *vinyl, molded and painted features, molded and painted hair, jointed, special creation from an old mold, made to celebrate the 100th anniversary of Montgomery Ward in 1972, Montgomery Ward had traditionally been one of the largest retailers of the Cameo Kewpie dolls, marked 18 Cameo, 8″*	28.00	34.00	26.00
☐ **Kewpie,** *vinyl, 14″, c. 1965*	40.00	50.00	45.00
☐ **Kewpie Gal,** *vinyl, molded and painted features, molded and painted hair, jointed at the neck and shoulders, marked Cameo JLK, made in 1971, 9″*	5.00	7.00	5.00
☐ **Margie,** *composition swivel head, jointed body, painted eyes, red dress, 10″, c. 1940*	225.00	250.00	230.00
☐ **Miss Peep,** *crier, vinyl, molded and painted hair, painted eyes, marked Cameo, made in 1957, 18″*	23.00	28.00	22.00
☐ **Newborn Miss Peep,** *vinyl, molded and painted hair, fixed eyes, marked Cameo, made in 1962, 19½″*	29.00	36.00	27.00
☐ **Plum,** *vinyl head, latex body, arms and legs, molded and painted hair, sleep eyes (blue), with a pair of "squeekers." marked Cameo, sold originally in a box which was marked*			

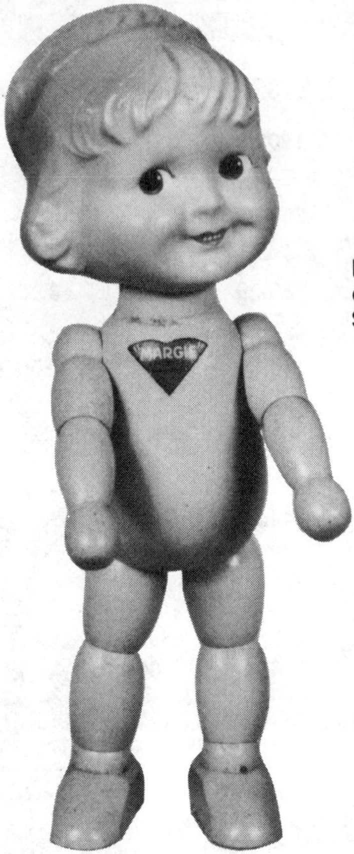

Margie,
composition, c. 1940, 10″
$225.00-$275.00

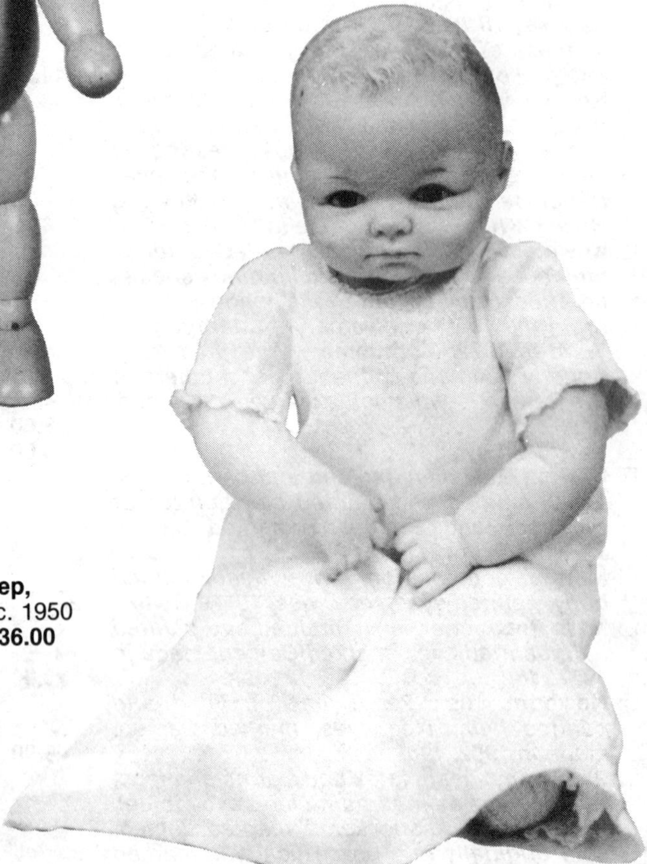

Miss Peep,
rubber, c. 1950
$29.00-$36.00

	Current Price Range		Prior Year Average
Plum, Designed and Copyrighted by JLK, specimens with the box bring a premium over the value indicated, made in 1952, 24¼"	60.00	75.00	55.00
☐ **Skootles,** *composition head, composition arms, legs and body, molded hair, painted eyes, closed mouth in broad smile, wears overalls and bright short-sleeved shirt with pattern of trees and branches, 15"*	160.00	190.00	150.00
Note: Skootles dates to the 1930's and, like many depression-era dolls, was apparently not made in very large quantities.			
☐ **Scootles,** *molded wood composition head, jointed wood composition body, painted blue eyes, closed mouth, 12"*	350.00	400.00	325.00
☐ **Scootles,** *vinyl, molded and painted hair (red), sleep eyes (blue), smiling mouth, marked Cameo, sold originally with a tag reading Designed & Copyrighted by Rose O'Neill, made in 1964, 19"*	38.00	47.00	35.00

CARLSON

☐ **George Washington,** *hard plastic, representing the first American President with a child's face and platinum blonde hair, attired in 18th century formal dress, unmarked but sold originally with a diamond-shaped tag reading Carlson Dolls, A Collector's Item, date of manufacture not known (probably around the time of the bicentennial), 7½"*	6.00	8.00	6.00

CASCELLOID

☐ **Unnamed,** *celluloid head, cloth body, sleep eyes, molded and painted hair, representing an infant, an unusual and distinguishing feature of this doll is that it has rubber ears, whose texture does not match that of the head, bisque hands, marked Pat. #535611, made in 1939, 18"*	65.00	78.00	60.00

C.B.S.

	Current Price Range		Prior Year Average
☐ **Armosandra,** *black, rubber, molded and painted features, molded and painted hair, nursing mouth, Amosandra was a character on the "Amos 'n' Andy" radio program, marked Amosandra, Columbia Broadcasting System, Inc., Designed by Ruth E. Newton, Mfg. by The Sun Rubber Co., Barberton, U.S.A., also marked with the patent numbers 2,118,682 and 2,160,739, made in 1949, 10½"*	20.00	26.00	18.00
☐ **My Fair Lady,** *vinyl head, vinyl arms, legs and body, jointed at the waist, head does not swivel, sleep eyes, brown hair in elaborate coiffure, silk dress with print pattern, carries mold mark 14R, no other markings, the box in which this doll was sold is imprinted C.B.S., Inc. and is dated 1956, 19"*	85.00	100.00	80.00

Note: Represents the character Eliza Doolittle from "My Fair Lady," which was playing on Broadway at the time this doll was manufactured.

CELTIC TOYS

☐ **Leprachaun,** *plastic head, plastic arms, painted eyes, has long white beard, felt clothing including jacket with two buttons, represents a leprachaun (tribe of tiny people who, in Irish folklore, inhabited forests), marked Made in Republic of Ireland, dated 1973, 8"*	11.00	15.00	11.00

Note: The Republic of Ireland is southern Ireland.

CENTURY DOLL COMPANY

☐ **Betty,** *composition head and hands, cloth body stuffed with excelsior, pin jointed knees, molded blond hair, painted eyes, marked Century Doll Co., 16"*	55.00	80.00	52.00

CEY

	Current Price Range		Prior Year Average
☐ **Sherri,** *vinyl, black hair (rooted), sleep eyes (blue), nursing mouth, marked J. Cey 20, made in 1961, 20¼″*	11.00	15.00	10.00
☐ **Unnamed,** *figure of young girl, plastic/vinyl, sleep eyes (blue), marked J. Cey, date of manufacture unknown, probably 1950's, 27″*	33.00	39.00	32.00

CHAD VALLEY COMPANY

	Current Price Range		Prior Year Average
☐ **Girl Doll,** *cloth head and body, painted eyes, pink and floral print, c. 1970, 14″*	20.00	25.00	22.50

Cloth Head and Body,
c. 1970, 14″
$20.00-$30.00

	Current Price Range		Prior Year Average
☐ **Little Red Riding Hood,** *character doll, all cloth, jointed neck, shoulders, hips, mohair wig, glass eyes, label, 11½"*	325.00	375.00	300.00
☐ **Prince Charles,** *Royal Children series, felt pressed head, jointed velvet body, painted features, mohair wig, original costume, 15"*	550.00	650.00	600.00

CHADWICK-MILLER

☐ **Sad Eyes,** *plastic/vinyl, blonde hair (rooted), painted eyes (brown), marked Made in Hong Kong, made in 1965, 8"*	3.00	4.00	3.00

CHASE BAG COMPANY

☐ **Eskimo Pie Boy,** *cloth (printed), foam stuffed, unmarked, made in 1962, used as a premium by the Eskimo Pie Dairy Products company, 14½"*	5.00	7.00	5.00

MARTHA CHASE

☐ **Baby,** *all cloth molded oil painted head, jointed cotton body, painted hair, brown eyes, mark: "Chase Stockinet Doll"*	375.00	400.00	350.00
☐ **Baby,** *cloth doll, molded stockinet head painted with oils, cloth body, painted facial features and hair, long gown, 16"*	450.00	650.00	425.00
☐ **Boy,** *of black rag doll, cloth, stockinet, molded painted head, painted body, short curly black wig, clothes, shoes, 17"*	800.00	1000.00	850.00
☐ **Boy,** *latex, sailor suit, 17"*	150.00	200.00	170.00
☐ **Celluloid,** *molded face set on cloth head, molded hair, very wide googly eyes, tiny eyebrows, closed smiling mouth, dimples at sides of mouth, 22"*	15.00	19.00	14.00
Note: Dating from the World War II era.			
☐ **Girl,** *molded, painted blonde hair, painted blue eyes, closed mouth, 25"*	350.00	400.00	345.00
☐ **Lady,** *all cloth, molded oil painted head, jointed cotton body, molded and painted blonde hair featuring a coiled braided bun at the nape of the neck, blue painted eyes, original dress, 15"*	950.00	1200.00	850.00

CHICAGO TRIBUNE

	Current Price Range		Prior Year Average
☐ **Dondi,** *vinyl, molded and painted features, molded and painted hair, jointed at the neck, Dondi is a character in a comic strip of the same name, created by Gus Edson and Irwin Hasen, marked 1960 Chicago Trib. NY News Syndicate, 11½″*	70.00	90.00	68.00

CHILTERN

☐ **Tricia,** *vinyl, sleep eyes (blue), marked Chiltern, Made in England, made for Marshall Fields of Chicago, in 1961, 11½″*	8.00	11.00	8.00

PATTI CHIMERA

☐ **Peddlar Woman,** *bisque head with molded grey hair, pulled back into bun, bisque arms and legs, cloth body, painted features including blue eyes, modeled features, box with trinkets, basket with miniatures, floral printed dress, red cape, black bonnet, 8½″*	25.00	35.00	25.00

CHRYSLER

☐ **Mr. Fleet,** *one-piece vinyl, a doll-bank with slot (behind head) for coins, designed to represent an auto mechanic, holding wrench, marked Chrysler Corporation 1973, 9″*	5.00	7.00	5.00

Note: Apparently made as a promotional give-away, to children of parents who visited Chrysler showrooms.

EMMA CLEAR

☐ **Emma Clear Grape Lady,** *china shoulder head has molded black hair held with elaborate gold accented snood with grape cluster at crest, blue glass inset eyes, pierced ears, china arms and legs, cloth body, lavender brocade dress, antique lace shawl, amethyst necklace, marks: back of shoulder head -Clear, 19″*	500.00	600.00	525.00

CLODREY

	Current Price Range		Prior Year Average
☐ **Edmond,** *plastic/vinyl, sleep eyes (brown), marked Clodrey 2018-6926, made in France in the early 1970's, 16″*	27.00	34.00	25.00

COCHRAN

☐ **Cindy,** *all latex, jointed, painted blue eyes, human hair wig, original costume, 15″*	650.00	725.00	625.00

COLEMAN

☐ **Dolly Walker,** *composition head and forearms, wooden body, fixed eyes glancing to doll's left, ribbons in hair, marked Harry Coleman Walking Doll, 26¼″*	140.00	185.00	135.00

COLUMBIA TOY PRODUCTS

☐ **Flip The Football Doll,** *vinyl head, rag body, vinyl hands, rag feet, molded and painted features, molded-on football helmet (with chin strap, no face-mask), marked 1961 Roko, also marked Manufactured by Columbia Toy Products, 15″*	10.00	14.00	10.00
☐ **Snuffy Smith,** *cloth/nylon, marked Copyright King Features Syndicate, Inc., 14¼″*	70.00	90.00	65.00

Note: Snuffy Smith was a character in the comic strip "Barney Google and His Horse Sparkplug" by Billy DeBeck.

COMIC TOY MANUFACTURING CORPORATION

☐ **Daisy, Dagwood and Blondie's Dog,** *rubber doll, collar and tag, swivels at neck, height 12″, c. 1940*	50.00	70.00	65.00

CONFETTI

	Current Price Range		Prior Year Average
☐ **Bride,** *composition, red wig attached by adhesive, painted eyes (blue), unmarked, made in 1947, 11″*	8.00	11.00	8.00
☐ **Cleaning Day,** *composition, blonde wig attached by adhesive, painted eyes, bright red lips, marked Confetti Doll, made in the mid 1940's, 7″*	6.00	8.00	6.00

CO-OPERATIVE MANUFACTURING COMPANY

☐ **Jointed Wooden Doll,** *painted facial features and molded hair, metal hands and feet, dressed, 12″*	650.00	800.00	650.00

COSMOPOLITAN

☐ **Emily,** *plastic head, cloth body, blonde wig attached by adhesive, sleep eyes (blue), open mouth with teeth, bright red lips, unmarked, made in 1948, 24″*	65.00	82.00	60.00
☐ **Gloria,** *plastic head, cloth body, latex arms and legs, blonde wig attached by adhesive, turnable head, sleep eyes (blue), open mouth with teeth, unmarked, made in 1948, 29″*	42.00	54.00	40.00
☐ **Japan Girl,** *all vinyl with Japanese costume, black hair, 9″*	6.00	8.00	6.00
☐ **Make-Up-Own,** *walker, a doll kit, the doll to be assembled by the purchaser, with instructions sheet, sold in 1956, height of doll when assembled, 10″*			
Kit intact as originally sold	18.00	23.00	17.00
Assembled doll	10.00	13.00	10.00
☐ **Merry,** *plastic/vinyl, marked AE 1406-41, 14″*	4.00	5.00	4.00
☐ **Mousketeer,** *vinyl, a young girl dressed in Mousketeer garb (from the TV program "The Mickey Mouse Club"), late 1950's, 8″*	10.00	14.00	10.00
☐ **Pam,** *plastic head, cloth body, vinyl arms and legs, blonde wig attached by adhesive, sleep eyes (blue), marked CDC (Cosmopolitan Doll Company), made in 1956, 22″*	28.00	35.00	25.00

CROWN DOLL COMPANY

	Current Price Range		Prior Year Average
☐ **Pinocchio,** *composition, painted white gloves*	75.00	85.00	80.00

DAKIN

	Current Price Range		Prior Year Average
☐ **Aloha Alice,** *stuffed nylon, unmarked on doll, sold originally with a tag reading Dream Dolls, R. Dakin & Co., 1956, representing a girl wearing Hawaiian native dance costume, 15″*	9.00	12.00	9.00
☐ **Elmer Fudd,** *vinyl, molded and painted features, painted eyes, jointed at the shoulders and hips, wears one-button jacket, derby hat, Elmer Fudd is a character in the comic strip "Bugs Bunny," created by R. Schlesinger, marked Warner Brothers, 1968, made in Hong Kong, 7″*	15.00	20.00	14.00
☐ **First Date,** *vinyl/plastic, blonde hair (rooted), closed eyes, long lashes, ribbon in hair, marked R. Dakin & Co., Product of Hong Kong, made in 1970, 6½″*	6.00	8.00	6.00
☐ **Funny,** *plastic/vinyl, brunette hair (rooted), painted eyes (brown), open mouth with one large tooth, marked 1965 R. Dakin & Co., Product of Hong Kong, sold originally with a tag reading Fun Farm, San Francisco, 6″*	5.00	7.00	5.00
☐ **Mickey Mouse,** *vinyl head, vinyl body, wears fabric clothing, medium-size ears, large smile on face, in addition to Dakin & Co., also bears mark of Walt Disney, made in Hong Kong, mid 1970's, 8″*	4.00	6.00	4.00
☐ **Minnie Mouse,** *vinyl head, plastic body, bow-tied ribbon on top of head, wears fabric clothing, including polka-dotted skirt, oversized shoes, in addition to Dakin's, also carries the Disney mark, almost certainly made in Hong Kong, 6″*	4.00	5.00	4.00
☐ **Pebbles,** *plastic/vinyl, marked R. Dakin Co., Product of Hong Kong, 1970, 8″*	4.00	5.00	3.00
Note: Representing a character from the comic strip "The Flintstones" created by Hanna and Barbera.			
☐ **Popeye and Olive Oil,** *all plastic, jointed*	17.00	22.00	15.00

Popeye and Olive, plastic . . . . **$17.00-$22.00**

THOMAS DAM ("DAM THINGS")

Thomas Dam of Denmark was the original manufacturer (in the mid 1960's) of the vinyl "Troll" dolls which took America by storm. They were the hottest selling dolls of the decade next to Barbies. We are not listing them individually because all are essentially the same basic doll with different hair and costuming, or with various props. Those made by Dam (all of which are marked on the back) have a current collector value in the $5.00 to $8.00 range. Imitations by other companies are of less value. Special items such as Dam's "Troll Bank" are worth a premium.

DANEL ET CIE

	Current Price Range		Prior Year Average
☐ **Bisque,** *socket head set on combination wood and composition body (fully jointed), sleep eyes, closed mouth, pierced ears, marked Paris Bébé Tête Déposé 7, accompanied by Eiffel Tower mark, 16″*	1100.00	1300.00	1000.00

DARROW MANUFACTURING COMPANY

☐ **Rawhide,** *cotton body, kid arms, painted surface, blue and white dress, red leather boots, 15″*	325.00	375.00	348.00
☐ **Rawhide,** *leather shoulder head, rawhide leather arms, cloth body, molded and painted black hair and facial features, original cotton dress, paper label, 18″*	1000.00	1500.00	500.00

D'AUTREMONT

☐ **Man,** *china head, jointed kid body, blue painted eyes, brown mohair wig, navy suit, red tie, 13″*	1300.00	1500.00	1200.00

DEE CEE

☐ **Dee Dee,** *plastic/vinyl, blonde hair (rooted), sleep eyes (blue), nursing mouth, marked Dee Cee, this was a Canadian manufacturer, the doll was made in 1961, 14″*	22.00	28.00	20.00
☐ **Jodi,** *plastic/vinyl, marked AE7, date of manufacture unknown, probably mid to late 1970's 15″*	4.00	6.00	4.00

DELL PUBLISHING COMPANY

☐ **Donald Duck,** *vinyl head, vinyl body, molded clothing, wide open mouth, hands held together as if about to dive from diving board, no movable parts, marked Dell, Walt Disney, 6″*	5.00	7.00	5.00

Note: The contract signed by Walt Disney, to use the Disney characters in Dell's "Four Color Comics," stipulated that the name "DELL" appear on character merchandise.

DELUXE

	Current Price Range		Prior Year Average
☐ **Baby Boo,** *plastic/vinyl, blonde hair (rooted), sleep eyes (blue), nursing mouth, comes with pacificer; when pacifier is removed from mouth, doll cries, battery operated, marked Deluxe Reading 1965-68, 21"*	12.00	17.00	12.00
☐ **Baby Brite,** *plastic/vinyl, blonde hair (rooted), sleep eyes (blue), partially open mouth, push-button action (2 buttons at midsection, one makes head swivel, other raises arms), marked 28 Deluxe Reading Corp., 1963, 14"*	13.00	17.00	12.00
☐ **Baby Magic,** *plastic/vinyl, blonde hair (rooted), sleep eyes (blue), changing facial expression, controlled by moving arms up and down, marked EK43 and dated 1966, 18"*	15.00	19.00	14.00
☐ **Baby Tickle Tears,** *nurser, plastic/vinyl, blonde hair (rooted), painted eyes with crying action, marked Deluxe Reading Corp., 1966, 14"*	23.00	29.00	22.00
☐ **Brenda Brush,** *vinyl, posable, hair attached by adhesive, marked Deluxe Reading Corp., 1965, 6½"*	6.00	8.00	5.00
☐ **Cool Cat,** *vinyl, posable, hair attached by adhesive, marked Deluxe Reading Corp., 1965, 6½"*	6.00	8.00	5.00
☐ **Hot Canary,** *vinyl, posable, hair attached by adhesive, marked Deluxe Reading Corp., 1965, 6½"*	6.00	8.00	5.00
☐ **Paula Marie,** *vinyl, blonde hair (rooted), sleep eyes (blue), marked VH25, made in 1959, 24"*	23.00	28.00	21.00
☐ **Penny Brite,** *vinyl, blonde hair (rooted), painted eyes, marked A9 Deluxe Reading Corp., 1963, 8"*	6.00	8.00	5.00
☐ **Schoolgirl Writing,** *plastic/vinyl, fingers on right hand shaped to hold pencil or pen, marked 1963, Deluxe Reading 2, 16"*	11.00	14.00	11.00
☐ **Slick Chick,** *vinyl, posable, hair attached by adhesive, marked Deluxe Reading Corp., 1965, 6½"*	6.00	8.00	5.00

	Current Price Range		Prior Year Average
☐ **Susie Cute,** *vinyl, rooted hair (blonde), fixed eyes (blue), action arms (arms raise when chest is pressed), marked Deluxe Reading 1964, GX, 7"*	6.00	8.00	5.00
☐ **Susie Homemaker,** *plastic/vinyl, blonde hair (rooted), sleep eyes (blue), marked 2K26, Deluxe Reading 1966, 21"*	23.00	28.00	21.00
☐ **Sweet Amy,** *vinyl/latex, marked A-1, date of manufacture unknown, probably late 1950's or early 1960's, 23"*	32.00	39.00	30.00
☐ **Sweet Janie,** *vinyl head, hard vinyl arms, legs and body, sleep eyes, long eyelashes, short hair in high-fashion cut, jointed waist, long floral print gown, wide-brimmed sun hat, mold mark 190, 25"*	22.00	27.00	20.00
Note: Copy on the box reads: "Wearing the most exclusive real embroidered party dress."			
☐ **Swinger,** *vinyl, posable, hair attached by adhesive, marked Deluxe Reading Corp., 1965, 6½"*	6.00	8.00	5.00
☐ **Tomboy,** *vinyl, posable, hair attached by adhesive, marked Deluxe Reading Corp., 1965, 6½"*	6.00	8.00	5.00
☐ **Yeah Yeah,** *vinyl, posable, hair attached by adhesive, marked Deluxe Reading Corp., 1965, 6½"*	6.00	8.00	5.00

DELUXE TOPPER

	Current Price Range		Prior Year Average
☐ **Baby Bunny,** *vinyl head, plastic body, vinyl arms, plastic legs, platinum blonde hair (rooted), fixed eyes (blue), marked 51 Deluxe Topper 1969, 20"*	15.00	19.00	14.00
☐ **Baby Catch-A-Ball,** *plastic/vinyl, rooted hair (blonde), fixed eyes (blue), holds hands in front of body in ball-catching attitude, when child throws ball to doll, dolls's arms automatically flip ball back, an ingenious design, the "secret" is in a pair of bracelets worn by Baby Catch-A-Ball, which are actually switches to activate the battery-operated mechanism, marked PB2-28 Deluxe Topper, 1969, 18"*	26.00	32.00	25.00

DENNISON

	Current Price Range		Prior Year Average
☐ **Crepe Paper,** *features printed in India ink, representing a young lady in sleeping gown and hood, 20″*	32.00	42.00	30.00

DeSOTO

	Current Price Range		Prior Year Average
☐ **Heartbeat Baby,** *plastic head, latex arms and legs, stuffed cloth body, sleep eyes, blonde hair, silk dress, equipped with a mechanism which produces the sound of a heartbeat when the doll is laid on its back, 23″*	29.00	36.00	27.00

Note: An interesting novelty doll, but it probably led many children to believe that the human heart functions only when one is lying down.

DIAMOND

	Current Price Range		Prior Year Average
☐ **Bisque,** *composition ball jointed body, human hair wig, paperweight eyes, closed mouth, blue dress, 18″*	1425.00	1600.00	1450.00
☐ **French Character,** *bisque head, composition body, dark brown paperweight eyes, human hair wig, costume, marked B-F, 17″*	1600.00	1700.00	1650.00

DISNEY, WALT
SEE WALT DISNEY

DOLIAC ET CIE

	Current Price Range		Prior Year Average
☐ **Bisque,** *socket head set on combination wood and composition body, fixed eyes, open mouth, pierced ears, marked LD DEP. 9.L., 22″*	385.00	440.00	375.00

DOLLY'S DOLLS

Howdy Dowdy,
cloth
$15.00-$20.00

	Current Price Range		Prior Year Average
☐ **Howdy Dowdy,** *plastic head, cloth body, molded hair, painted wide eyes, wool plaid shirt, blue jeans, leather belt, 18″*	15.00	20.00	17.50

DREAM DOLLS

☐ **Aloha Alice,** *stuffed Nylon, unmarked on doll, sold originally with a tag reading Dream Dolls, R. Dakin & Co., 1956, representing a girl wearing Hawaiian native dance costume, 15″*	9.00	12.00	9.00

	Current Price Range		Prior Year Average
☐ **Baby Peek 'N' Play,** *plastic/vinyl, fixed eyes (blue), one of the many interesting novelty /action dolls manufactured by this company during the 1960's, Baby Peek 'N' Play could "hear," she responded to sharp noises by raising her hands to her face, (battery operated,) marked 17EYE, New, M94, made in 1969, 18"*	22.00	28.00	20.00
☐ **Bikey,** *plastic/vinyl, blonde hair (rooted), painted eyes, arms outstrectched and hands shaped as if holding the handlebars of a bike, marked Bikey, Deluxe Topper, 1968, made in Hong Kong, 11"*	10.00	14.00	9.00
☐ **Little Miss Fussy,** *plastic/vinyl, blonde hair (rooted), fixed eyes (blue), marked K-39, Deluxe Topper, 1967, 18"*	16.00	21.00	15.00
Note: The same trademark was used on Deluxe Topper's "Party Time" doll.			
☐ **Party Time,** *plastic/vinyl, fixed eyes (blue), open mouth, "blower" action (can blow up small balloons, blow out candles on a cake, etc.), operates by battery, marked K-39, Deluxe Topper, 1967, 18"*	16.00	21.00	15.00
☐ **Tickles,** *talker, plastic/vinyl, blonde hair (rooted), sleep eyes (blue), marked 1963 Deluxe Topper 38, 20"*	14.00	18.00	13.00

DREAMLAND

☐ **To Market, To Market,** *composition, painted eyes, unmarked, date of manufacture unknown, 11"*	29.00	34.00	27.00

DREAM WORLD

☐ **Bride,** *composition, date of manufacture unknown, 10½"*	30.00	36.00	28.00
☐ **Cuba** *(national costume doll), composition, 11"*	28.00	33.00	27.00
☐ **Florence Nightingale,** *composition, representing the English nurse who became famous for her care of wounded soldiers in the Crimean War, 11"*	29.00	34.00	27.00
☐ **Flower Vendor,** *composition, unmarked on doll, sold originally with a tag reading Dream World Dolls Make Dreams Come True, 11"*	29.00	34.00	27.00

	Current Price Range		Prior Year Average
☐ **Spanish** *(national costume doll), composition, unmarked, date of manufacture unknown*	28.00	33.00	27.00

CUNO AND OTTO DRESSEL

This family owned firm began in Sonneberg, Thuringia, Germany in 1700, but the earliest record of their doll-making dates around 1863. At that time, Otto Dressel, Sr. and his sons, Otto Jr. and Cuno, were registered as dollmakers. Prior to 1863 they were known primarily as toy makers. (Indeed, the family continued to produce wooden, papier mâché, and composition toys in their Nurnberg and Grunhainichen toy factories well into the 20th century.)

The Holz Masse mark was registered in 1875. The Dressels made dolls of bisque, papier mâché, wax, and composition. They were known to have used doll heads from other firms such as Simon-Halbig and Armand Marseille. Composition was used to make dolls around the turn of the century, and in 1906 the "Jutta" trademark was registered, followed in 1909 by the "Bambina" mark. At this time they began manufacturing dolls with kid bodies. Dressel dolls with celluloid heads appeared in 1911.

	Current Price Range		Prior Year Average
☐ **Bisque,** *ball jointed body, set brown eyes, short blonde mohair wig, open mouth, flowered dress with lace trim, 25"*	425.00	475.00	445.00
☐ **Bisque,** *kid body, bisque arms, cotton lower legs, universal joints, brown sleep eyes, dark brows, long brown hair, white dress, black velvet in thread through lace, mold number 1776, 24"*	375.00	425.00	400.00
☐ **Bisque,** *shoulder head set on kidskin body, bisque forearms, fixed eyes, partially open mouth, severely slanting eyebrows that give an almost scowling facial expression, marked Holz Masse mark (winged crown within a circle), accompanied by the mold number 12/0, 12¼"*	80.00	110.00	75.00
☐ **Bisque,** *socket head, composition ball joint body, marked made in Germany, 22"*	325.00	375.00	340.00
☐ **Bisque,** *head, ball jointed composition body, human hair wig, blue sleep eyes, yellow crepe dress with bead trim, 18"*	475.00	525.00	480.00
☐ **Bisque,** *head, kid body with bisque hands, human hair wig, blue sleep eyes, pink organdy dress with antique lace trim, marked No.II, 22"*	450.00	500.00	465.00
☐ **Child,** *bisque shoulder head, jointed kid body, blue glass eyes, blonde mohair wig, open mouth, old white lace dress, 21"*	325.00	375.00	300.00
☐ **Girl,** *composition ball jointed body, blue eyes, blonde hair, 19"*	300.00	375.00	340.00

	Current Price Range		Prior Year Average
☐ **Jutta,** *composition ball jointed body, blue eyes, brown hair, marked "1349," 24"*	400.00	450.00	420.00
☐ **Papier Mâché,** *brown paperweight eyes, brown wool challis dress, marked "Holz-Masse"*	200.00	225.00	210.00
☐ **Papier Mâché,** *shoulder head, kid arms, cloth body, painted blue eyes, brown mohair wig, original cream lawn dress with lace trim, 14"*	325.00	400.00	325.00
☐ **Polar Bear,** *bisque facial mask set against plush head, plush body, one-piece construction, glass eyes with open mouth, representing a young lady in arctic attire, wholly covered in fur plush but for the face, 9"*	130.00	155.00	125.00

DUCHESS

	Current Price Range		Prior Year Average
☐ **Carmen,** *plastic, painted eyes, representing the character from the Bizet opera "Carmen," marked Duchess Doll Co., Design Copyright 1948, 7½"*	7.00	10.00	7.00
☐ **Cinderella,** *plastic, blonde hair attached by adhesive, sleep eyes (blue), marked Duchess Doll Co., Design Copyright 1948, 7½"*	4.00	6.00	4.00
☐ **Dale Evans,** *hard plastic, marked Duchess Doll Corp., 1948, representing the motion picture actress, wife of Roy Rogers, 7"*	7.00	10.00	7.00
☐ **Danny The Groom,** *plastic, molded and painted hair, painted eyes, unmarked, made in 1949, 7"*	6.00	8.00	6.00
☐ **Martha Washington,** *plastic, white hair attached by adhesive, sleep eyes (blue), representing the wife of George Washington, with a child's face, marked Duchess Doll Corp., Design Copyright 1948, 7½"*	4.00	6.00	4.00
☐ **Miss Hollywood 1949,** *plastic, brunette hair attached by adhesive, sleep eyes (blue), marked Duchess Doll Corp., Design Copyright 1949, 7¼"*	4.00	6.00	4.00
☐ **Scarlet,** *plastic, brunette hair attached by adhesive, painted eyes (blue), representing the character Scarlet O'Hara from the novel "Gone With The Wind" by Margaret Mitchell, marked Duchess Doll Corp., Design Copyright 1948, 7½"*	9.00	12.00	9.00

	Current Price Range		Prior Year Average
☐ **Scotch Miss,** *plastic, blonde hair attached by adhesive, sleep eyes (blue), a national costume doll, marked Duchess Doll Corp., Design Copyright 1948, 7½″*	4.00	6.00	4.00
☐ **Tinker Bell,** *plastic, blonde hair attached by adhesive, sleep eyes (blue), marked Duchess Doll Corp., Design Copyright 1948, 7″*	7.00	10.00	6.00

DUKKER

☐ **Lupin,** *vinyl, sleep eyes, closed smiling mouth, freckled cheeks, dressed in Norwegian peasant costume, unmarked on doll, sold originally with a tag reading Grimstad Dukker, Grimstead, Norway, date of manufacture unknown, 12″*	30.00	38.00	27.00

DURHAM

☐ **Billy The Kid,** *plastic, representing the Old West desperado, holds six-shooter in right hand, raises and points gun when button on back of doll is pushed, marked D. Durham Ind. Inc., New York, N.Y. 10010, made in Hong Kong, 8″*	3.00	4.00	3.00
☐ **Skinny Jimmy,** *vinyl, marked #1500 Durham Industries, Inc., New York, N.Y. 10010, made in Taiwan, 11″*	4.00	6.00	4.00
☐ **Wild Bill Hickok,** *plastic, representing the legendary "gunslinger" of the Old West, holds six-shooter in right hand; raises and points gun when button on back of doll is pushed, marked D. Durham Ind. Inc., New York, N.Y. 10010, made in Hong Kong, 8″*	3.00	4.00	3.00
☐ **Wyatt Earp,** *plastic, representing the legendary sheriff of Dodge City, Kansas, popularized in a TV program during the late 1950's, holds six-shooter in right hand, raises and points gun when button on back of doll is pushed, marked D. Durham Ind. Inc., New York, N.Y. 10010, made in Hong Kong, 8″*	3.00	4.00	3.00

Note: This doll is not contemporary with the Wyatt Earp TV program, but was manufactured at a much later date, in the middle 1970's.

EEGEE

	Current Price Range		Prior Year Average
☐ **Adorable,** *vinyl, blonde hair (rooted), painted eyes, nursing mouth, marked 35 Eegee Co., 1967, 12LTPE, 13″*	11.00	14.00	10.00
☐ **Andy,** *plastic/vinyl, molded and painted hair, painted eyes, dressed in military uniform, marked EG-1961, 12″*	7.00	9.00	7.00
☐ **Baby Luv,** *vinyl head, vinyl arms and legs, cloth body, blond hair, painted eyes, bearing the mold number 14BT and dates 1973, 12″*	30.00	37.00	29.00
☐ **Baby Softina,** *vinyl with dublon body, molded hair, fixed eyes, wears plush velvety child's clothing of the 1890's, marked 3-Eegee Co.-16V3, made in 1970*	7.00	9.00	7.00
☐ **Baby Susan,** *vinyl, molded and painted hair, sleep eyes (blue), marked Eegee, made in 1958, 10″*	9.00	12.00	9.00
☐ **Ballerina Sherry,** *vinyl, marked Eegee 8, 8″*	8.00	11.00	8.00
☐ **Bobby,** *vinyl, fixed eyes (blue), marked Eegee, made in 1955, 13″*	32.00	39.00	31.00
☐ **Bonnie Ballerina,** *plastic/vinyl, sleep eyes, marked Eegee 5, made in 1964, 31″*	24.00	29.00	23.00
☐ **Bundle Of Joy,** *vinyl head, cloth body, vinyl arms, plastic legs, brown hair (rooted), sleep eyes (blue), marked 19-4 Eegee Co., made in 1964, 19″*	8.00	11.00	8.00
☐ **Buster,** *plastic/vinyl, marked 1959 Eegee, 16½″*	10.00	13.00	9.00
☐ **Carol,** *plastic/vinyl, sleep eyes, marked Eegee Co., 15 PM, 1B, made in 1968, 21″*	11.00	14.00	10.00
☐ **Chikie,** *composition, sleep eyes (tin), chubby face, open mouth with teeth, unmarked on doll, sold originally with a tag reading Chikie, another Eegee Doll, date of manufacture unknown, 16″*	75.00	90.00	70.00
Note: The name should have been spelled "Chickie," as this doll represented a little girl who liked to feed chicks.			
☐ **Cuddlekins,** *plastic/vinyl, molded and painted hair, fixed eyes (blue), nursing mouth, marked Eegee Co., 13VS, made in 1970, 10″*	5.00	7.00	5.00
☐ **Darling Baby,** *plastic/vinyl, sleep eyes (blue), marked 25 10T Eegee, 10″*	4.00	6.00	4.00
☐ **Georgie,** *cloth body, vinyl head, sleep eyes (green), marked 17 RNG Eegee, 1971, 23″*	10.00	14.00	9.00
☐ **Gemette,** *plastic/vinyl, brown hair (rooted), sleep eyes (blue), marked 1963-11, 15″*	7.00	9.00	7.00

	Current Price Range		Prior Year Average
☐ **Gigi Perreaux,** *plastic/vinyl, brunette hair attached by adhesive, sleep eyes (brown), marked E.G., made in 1951, 16¾"*	50.00	64.00	47.00
☐ **Grace,** *vinyl head, latex body, latex arms and legs, blonde hair (rooted), sleep eyes (blue), marked 33H-Eegee, made in 1957, 17"*	26.00	33.00	25.00
☐ **Granny,** *plastic/vinyl, marked Eegee 3, 14"*	36.00	44.00	35.00
☐ **Howdy Doody,** *vinyl, soft body, 18"*	6.00	12.00	5.00
☐ **Kiss Me,** *plastic/vinyl, sleep eyes (blue), novelty doll whose lips performed a kissing motion when its left arm was raised and lowered, marked 14-16 Eegee, made in 1963, 17"*	7.00	10.00	7.00
☐ **Lil Susan,** *plastic/vinyl, black hair (rooted), sleep eyes (blue), marked Eegee, made in 1956, 10½"*	8.00	11.00	7.00
☐ **Little Debutante,** *plastic/vinyl, blonde hair (rooted), sleep eyes (blue), marked 20HH Eegee, made in 1958, 28"*	33.00	39.00	31.00
☐ **Little Debutante Ballerina,** *vinyl head, vinyl arms, plastic body, jointed at the waist, knees and ankles, sleep eyes, wears ballerina costume, carries the mold mark 14R*	18.00	23.00	17.00
☐ **Little Miss,** *plastic/vinyl, blonde hair (rooted), sleep eyes (blue), marked 15US, Eegee Co., made in 1962, 16"*	7.00	9.00	7.00
☐ **Luvable Baby,** *vinyl, sleep eyes (blue), marked Eegee, made in 1956, 15"*	8.00	11.00	8.00
☐ **Luvable Skin Doll,** *vinyl head and body, blonde hair (rooted), sleep eyes (blue), marked Eegee 1½-9, made in 1958, 12"*	12.00	16.00	12.00
☐ **Merry Stroller,** *vinyl head, plastic arms and legs, plastic body, sleep eyes, ribbon in hair, wears long gown, sold in suitcase, with accessories (including a change of clothing and slippers), 13", with case and accessories*	30.00	37.00	29.00
Doll alone	17.00	22.00	17.00
☐ **Miss Charming,** *composition head and body, blonde hair attached by adhesive, sleep eyes (blue), bright red lips, marked E.G., made in 1936, 19"*	53.00	66.00	51.00
☐ **Musical Baby,** *music box, vinyl head, cloth body, vinyl arms, plastic legs, blonde hair (rooted), painted eyes, marked 15, Eegee Co., 16W, made in 1967, 17"*	8.00	11.00	8.00
☐ **My Fair Lady,** *vinyl head, vinyl arms, legs and body, jointed at the waist, head does not swivel, sleep eyes, brown hair in elabo-*			

	Current Price Range		Prior Year Average
rate coiffure, silk dress with print pattern, carries mold mark 14R, no other markings on doll, the box in which this doll was sold is imprinted C.B.S., Inc., and is dated 1956, 19″	85.00	100.00	80.00
Note: Represents the character Eliza Doolittle from "My Fair Lady," which was playing on Broadway at the time this doll was manufactured.			
☐ **Newborn Baby Doll,** *vinyl head, sleep eyes, marked Eegee Co. 173, 1963, 16″*	8.00	11.00	8.00
Note: Despite the name, this doll was not designed to resemble a newborn baby but a toddler of several months.			
☐ **Nurse,** *vinyl head, vinyl arms, legs and body, painted eyes, wears white nursing cap with red cross, and fabric clothing, 4½″*	3.00	4.00	3.00
☐ **Pix-I-Posie,** *vinyl, blonde hair (rooted), sleep eyes (blue), marked Eegee Co., 1966, also marked with the patent number 3,319,370 / 24, 18″*	12.00	16.00	12.00
☐ **Playtime Susan,** *vinyl head, vinyl arms, legs and body, molded hair (short, combed down), open mouth designed to receive nursing bottle, 15″*	8.00	10.00	8.00
☐ **Posi Playmate,** *vinyl head, foam body, foam arms and legs, vinyl hands, posable, platinum blonde hair (rooted), painted eyes, marked 18LT 1/Eegee Co., made in 1969, 18″*	9.00	12.00	9.00
☐ **Robert,** *vinyl head, latex body, vinyl arms, latex legs, molded hair, sleep eyes (blue), marked Eegee, made in 1956, 21″*	43.00	52.00	41.00
☐ **Rose Red Flowerkin,** *plastic/vinyl, sleep eyes (blue), marked 8F2 Eegee, made in 1963, 15½″*	15.00	19.00	14.00
☐ **Sandi,** *plastic/vinyl, blonde hair (rooted), sleep eyes (blue), marked 12-5 Eegee Co., F2-13, made in 1963, 15″*	11.00	14.00	10.00
☐ **Sleepy,** *plastic/vinyl, painted hair, closed eyes, marked Eegee, 1967, 14″*	23.00	29.00	23.00
☐ **Sleepy Time Girl,** *vinyl head, latex body, sleep eyes (blue), marked Eegee, 18″*	14.00	18.00	14.00
☐ **Sniffles,** *plastic/vinyl, sleep eyes (blue), marked 13-14 AA Eegee Co., made in 1963, 12″*	6.00	8.00	6.00
☐ **Softina,** *vinyl, blonde hair (rooted), painted eyes, nursing mouth, marked Eegee Co.-14P., made in 1970, 13″*	6.00	8.00	6.00
☐ **Susan,** *vinyl head, plastic body, vinyl arms, plastic legs, blonde hair (rooted), sleep eyes*			

	Current Price Range		Prior Year Average
(blue), wears "mod" clothes of the 1960's, marked Eegee 1967, 17"	12.00	16.00	12.00
☐ **Tandy Talks,** *talker (pullcord action), plastic/vinyl, blonde hair (rooted), sleep eyes (blue), marked 15P, Eegee, made in 1961, 21¼"*	38.00	48.00	36.00
☐ **Tina,** *plastic/vinyl, blonde hair (rooted), sleep eyes (blue), marked S, made in 1959, 11"*	7.00	9.00	7.00

EFFANBEE

The Effanbee Doll Company was begun by B.E. Fleischaker and H. Braun in 1910, and after various corporate shifts and takeovers, is still operated by the sons of one of the founders. The reputation of this company for quality construction has never been challenged and their dolls are quite collectible.

In the early days of the company, they typically used all composition to manufacture their jointed baby dolls, usually molding and painting the hair instead of fitting the doll with a wig. Later cloth bodies appeared and by 1955, vinyl and hard plastic was the standard material for construction.

The company is famous for the movability that the jointed dolls have achieved. They have made great strides in walker doll technology as well as multi-jointed dolls with flexible mobility. The delicacy of their newer dolls and the care taken to detail in the costumes has made them instantly collectible.

☐ **Abraham Lincoln,** *black suit, stovepipe hat, limited issue, c. 1983*	70.00	80.00	73.00
☐ **Afternoon Tea,** *absolutely Abigail Collection, c. 1982, 13"*	40.00	50.00	42.00
☐ **Alice in Wonderland,** *soft body, Huggable Collection, c. 1982, 14"*	28.00	37.00	30.00
☐ **Allison,** *blue, white dress, Grandes Dames Collection, c. 1983*	50.00	62.00	52.00
☐ **Anne Shirley,** *bisque, brown human hair wig, lacy pink taffeta dress, heels, 21"*	175.00	225.00	180.00
☐ **Anne Shirley,** *composition head, composition body and legs, rubber arms, reddish hair, attached by adhesive, marked Effanbee U.S.A., made in 1939, 20"*	40.00	52.00	37.00
Note: Anne Shirley was a movie actress of the 1930's and 1940's.			
☐ **Anne Shirley,** *composition, human hair wig, sleep eyes, beige and green dress and beige shoes, c. 1935, 18"*	220.00	300.00	225.00
☐ **Atlanta,** *lavender, ribbon trimmed dress, Pride of the South, c. 1983*	40.00	50.00	42.00
☐ **Autumn,** *Four Seasons Collection, c. 1982, 15"*	35.00	45.00	37.00

Anne Shirley, composition, c. 1935, 18″ **$220.00-$300.00**

	Current Price Range		Prior Year Average
☐ **Baby Cuddle-Up,** *vinyl, molded and painted hair, sleep eyes (blue), open mouth with teeth, marked Effanbee, made in 1953, 23″* .	30.00	38.00	28.00
☐ **Baby Cupcake,** *plastic/vinyl, sleep eyes (blue), marked Effanbee, 1963, 12″*	7.00	10.00	7.00
☐ **Baby Dainty,** *cloth and composition, painted eyes, marked Effanbee, Baby Dainty, believed to have been made in the late 1930's, 15″*	65.00	80.00	62.00
☐ **Baby Face,** *plastic/vinyl, brown hair (rooted), sleep eyes (blue), marked Effanbee 1967-2600, 15″*	11.00	14.00	10.00
☐ **Baby Face,** *Granny's Corner Collection, c. 1983, 20″*	35.00	45.00	36.00
☐ **Babykin,** *vinyl, molded hair, sleep eyes (blue), nursing mouth, marked Effanbee 1964, 8½″*	6.00	8.00	6.00

Baby,
rubber, c. 1973
$10.00-$12.00

	Current Price Range		Prior Year Average
☐ **Baby Lisa,** *vinyl, jointed, fancy dress, bonnet, 11″*	20.00	30.00	21.00
☐ **Baby Sweetie Pie,** *vinyl, blonde hair (rooted), sleep eyes (blue), marked Effanbee 1963, 12″*	9.00	12.00	9.00
☐ **Baby Tinyette,** *composition, infant version, marked Effanbee Baby Tinyette, made in the mid 1930's, 8″*	60.00	75.00	55.00
Note: There was also a "standing" version of this doll; same value.			
☐ **Baby Winkie,** *Heart to Heart Collection, c. 1982, 12″*	20.00	25.00	21.00
☐ **Baby Winkie,** *with pillow, Crochet Classics Collection, c. 1982, 12″*	25.00	35.00	26.00
☐ **Baby Wonder,** *composition head, composition arms, legs and body, sleep eyes (metallic), partially open mouth, holds cel-*			

	Current Price Range		Prior Year Average
luloid nursing bottle, dressed in toddler gown and bonnet, mid 1930's, 12½"	50.00	65.00	47.00
☐ **Barbara Jean,** *from the American children series designed by Dewees Cochran, composition, marked Effanbee, Ann Shirley body, original reddish wig, clear sleep eyes, open mouth, 17"*	360.00	395.00	365.00
☐ **Betsy Ross,** *floral print dress, Women of the Ages Collection, c. 1983*	40.00	50.00	42.00
☐ **Billy Bum,** *by Faith Wick, c. 1982, 16"*	50.00	60.00	52.00
☐ **Bride,** *hard plastic, holds bouquet, 19"*	100.00	150.00	130.00
☐ **Bride,** *lacy wedding outfit, ribbon trim, flowers, Bridal Suite Collection, c. 1983, 13"*	35.00	45.00	37.00
☐ **Bride,** *lacy wedding outfit, ribbon trimmed, flowers, Bridal Suite Collection, c. 1983, 15"*	40.00	50.00	42.00
☐ **Bridesmaid,** *lacy bridesmaid outfit, ribbon trim, flowers, Bridal Suite Collection, c. 1983, 13"*	35.00	40.00	37.00

Bubbles,
compsition, c. 1910
$100.00-$150.00

	Current Price Range		Prior Year Average
☐ **Butterball,** *Granny's Corner Collection, c. 1983, 13"*	22.00	35.00	23.00
☐ **Butterball,** *with bunting, Crochet Classics Collection, c. 1982, 13"*	25.00	35.00	26.00
☐ **Butterball,** *with pillow, Heaven Sent Collection, c. 1982, 13"*	25.00	35.00	26.00
☐ **Buttercup,** *Granny's Corner Collection, c. 1983, 15"*	35.00	45.00	36.00
☐ **Buttercup,** *Heart to Heart Collection, c. 1982, 15"*	28.00	35.00	30.00
☐ **Bubbles,** *composition and cloth body, 1910*	100.00	150.00	95.00
☐ **Button Nose,** *composition, molded hair, unmarked, date of manufacture unknown, believed to date from the World War II era, 8"*	45.00	58.00	42.00
☐ **Button Nose,** *vinyl head, cloth body, vinyl arms and legs, blonde hair (rooted), sleep eyes (blue), crier, marked 15-Effanbee-1968-9508, 16½"*	23.00	28.00	21.00
☐ **Canadian Doll,** *International Collection, c. 1982, 11"*	20.00	30.00	21.00
☐ **Candy Kid,** *composition, molded and painted hair, sleep eyes (blue), marked Effanbee, made in 1946, 12"*	47.00	59.00	45.00
☐ **Captain Kidd,** *c. 1983*	20.00	30.00	21.00
☐ **Carnegie Hall,** *Grandes Dames Collection, c. 1980, 18"*	50.00	55.00	52.00
☐ **Catherine,** *composition head, composition arms, legs and body, jointed at shoulders and thighs, molded hair, painted eyes, closed mouth, bright red lips, dark flesh-tone skin, 14"*	85.00	105.00	80.00
☐ **Charleston,** *Pride of the South Collection, c. 1982, 13"*	35.00	45.00	37.00
☐ **Charlie McCarthy,** *composition body, hands (with gloves) and feet (with shoes), cloth body, molded hair, painted features, tuxedo, monocle, 13½"*	465.00	520.00	475.00
☐ **Chipper,** *Enchanted Garden Collection, c. 1982, 15"*	25.00	35.00	26.00
☐ **Chipper,** *Granny's Corner Collection, c. 1983, 15"*	30.00	40.00	32.00
☐ **Chipper,** *plastic/vinyl, brunette hair (rooted), sleep eyes (blue), marked Effanbee 1966, sold originally with a tag reading This is Chipper, an Effanbee Durable Doll, 14"*	20.00	26.00	19.00
☐ **Christina,** *lacy beige lawn dress, c. 1983*	60.00	70.00	63.00
☐ **Civil War Lady,** *c. 1979, 15"*	30.00	40.00	32.00
☐ **Claudette,** *Grandes Dames Collection, c. 1982, 15"*	45.00	55.00	47.00

Charlie McCarthy,
vinyl
$465.00-$520.00

	Current Price Range		Prior Year Average
☐ **Clown,** *vinyl, sleep eyes, jointed, white satin outfits, red pom poms, 11″*	15.00	20.00	16.00
☐ **Clown,** *vinyl, sleep eyes, jointed, white satin outfit, red pom poms, 15″*	20.00	25.00	21.00
☐ **Clown,** *vinyl, sleep eyes, soft body, white satin outfit, red pom poms, 15″*	25.00	35.00	26.00
☐ **Clown,** *vinyl, sleep eyes, soft body, white satin outfit, red pom poms, 17″*	30.00	40.00	32.00
☐ **Clown,** *vinyl, sleep eyes, jointed, white satin outfit, red pom poms, 17″*	20.00	30.00	21.00
☐ **Clown Boy,** *by Faith Wick, c. 1982, 16″*	45.00	55.00	47.00
☐ **Coco,** *brown, beige dress, Grandes Dames Collection, c. 1983, 15″*	50.00	62.00	52.00
☐ **Coco,** *Grandes Dames Collection, c. 1980, 18″*	50.00	55.00	52.00

	Current Price Range		Prior Year Average
☐ **Czechoslavakia,** *vinyl, jointed, International Collection, c. 1981*	15.00	25.00	16.00
☐ **Dallas,** *pink floral print dress, Pride of the South, c. 1983*	40.00	50.00	42.00
☐ **Danish Doll,** *International Collection, c. 1982, 11″*	20.00	30.00	21.00
☐ **Denmark,** *vinyl, jointed, International Collection, c. 1981*	15.00	25.00	16.00
☐ **Diane,** *red, pink dress, Grandes Dames Collection, c. 1983, 15″*	50.00	62.00	52.00
☐ **Dolly Dumpling,** *composition shoulder head, cork stuffed body, painted face and hair, cotton rompers, shoulder head marked "Effanbee", 15″*	150.00	200.00	150.00
☐ **Downing Square,** *Grandes Dames Collection, c. 1979, 15″*	35.00	45.00	37.00

Composition Head and Body
$95.00-$100.00

	Current Price Range		Prior Year Average
☐ **Dutch Doll,** *International Collection, c. 1982, 11"*	20.00	30.00	21.00
☐ **Dy-Dee Doll,** *fur wig, 12 accessories*	125.00	175.00	140.00
☐ **Dy Dee Baby,** *plastic head, rubber body, molded and painted hair, sleep eyes (blue), nursing mouth, marked Effanbee, made in 1950, 11½"*	13.00	16.00	13.00
☐ **Dy Dee Doll,** *vinyl, jointed, sleep eyes, 20"*	40.00	50.00	42.00
☐ **Elisabeth,** *Grandes Dames Collection, c. 1982, 11"*	30.00	40.00	32.00
☐ **Flapper,** *c. 1979, 15"*	25.00	35.00	26.00
☐ **Florence Nightingale,** *nursing outfit, Women of the Ages Collection, c. 1983*	40.00	50.00	42.00
☐ **Flossie,** *white eyelet dress, Bobbsey Twin, c. 1983*	30.00	40.00	32.00
☐ **Fluffy,** *black vinyl, jointed, sleep eyes, Girl Scout outfit, c. 1965*	10.00	15.00	11.00
☐ **Fluffy,** *vinyl, blonde hair (rooted), sleep eyes (blue), marked P-U, made in 1954, 10"*	9.00	12.00	9.00
Note: Presumably, the letters P-U were the mold's identification. Usually, Effanbee placed its name in full on its dolls and if a mold number was to be recorded, it appeared directly alongside the company's name.			
☐ **Fortune Cookies,** *Just Friends, c. 1983*	30.00	40.00	32.00
☐ **Freddie,** *tweeds, hat, Bobbsey Twin, c. 1983*	25.00	35.00	26.00
☐ **French Doll,** *International Collection, c. 1982, 11"*	20.00	30.00	21.00
☐ **Frontier Woman,** *brown gingham, c. 1979, 15"*	30.00	45.00	32.00
☐ **Frontier Woman,** *gray cotton, c. 1978, 15"*	30.00	45.00	32.00
☐ **Gay Nineties,** *c. 1979, 15"*	30.00	40.00	32.00
☐ **Garden Party,** *absolutely Abigail Collection, c. 1983*	40.00	50.00	42.00
☐ **Gay Paree,** *lacy burgandy dress, Age of Elegance Collection, c. 1983*	90.00	110.00	92.00
☐ **George Washington,** *felt outfit, three cornered hat, limited issue, c. 1983*	70.00	80.00	73.00
☐ **German Doll,** *International Collection, c. 1982, 11"*	20.00	30.00	21.00
☐ **Gibson Girl,** *c. 1979, 15"*	30.00	35.00	32.00
☐ **Girl, Boy Skater Dolls,** *black vinyl, jointed, sleep eyes, blue velvet, silk outfits, silver skates*	70.00	80.00	73.00
☐ **Girl,** *composition, jointed, blonde human hair wig, blue sleep eyes, closed mouth, blue and white checked gingham dress, Anne Shirley on back, 16"*	180.00	195.00	180.00
☐ **Greek Doll,** *c. 1983*	20.00	30.00	21.00

	Current Price Range		Prior Year Average
☐ **Gumdrop,** *plastic/vinyl, blonde hair (rooted), sleep eyes (blue), marked 1962 Effanbee, 16"*	11.00	14.00	11.00
☐ **Half-Pint,** *plastic/vinyl, blonde hair (rooted), fixed eyes, head twists, marked Effanbee 1966, 10"*	8.00	11.00	8.00
☐ **Half Pint Boy,** *Over the Rainbow Collection, c. 1981*	15.00	20.00	16.00
☐ **Hansel and Gretel,** *vinyl, jointed, c. 1981, 11"*	15.00	25.00	16.00
☐ **Hattie Holiday,** *Halloween, c. 1981, 16"*	25.00	35.00	26.00
☐ **Hattie Holiday,** *Halloween, c. 1982, 16"*	25.00	35.00	26.00
☐ **Hattie Holiday,** *July 4th, c. 1981, 16"*	25.00	35.00	26.00
☐ **Hearth Witch,** *by Faith Wick, c. 1982, 18"*	50.00	60.00	52.00
☐ **Heidi,** *Story Book Collection, c. 1982, 11"*	20.00	30.00	21.00
☐ **Hester,** *Grandes Dames Collection, c. 1982, 15"*	45.00	55.00	47.00
☐ **Historical American Children Series,** *composition head, composition jointed body, original brown human hair wig, no clothes, 17"*	400.00	500.00	425.00
☐ **Honeybun,** *vinyl head, cloth body, vinyl arms and legs, blonde hair (rooted), marked 9567J-Effanbee-1967, 17"*	15.00	19.00	15.00
☐ **Honey Girl,** *plastic, blonde hair attached by adhesive, sleep eyes (blue), marked Effanbee, introduced in the late 1940's, 13½"*	24.00	29.00	23.00
☐ **Howdy Doody,** *composition, original clothes, 19"*	70.00	80.00	75.00
☐ **Huckleberry Finn,** *limited issue, c. 1983*	60.00	70.00	63.00
☐ **Hungarian Doll,** *c. 1983*	20.00	30.00	21.00
☐ **Hyde Park,** *ruffled blue velvet gown, matching hat, Grandes Dames Collection, 15"*	35.00	45.00	36.00
☐ **Irish Doll,** *International Collection, c. 1982, 11"*	20.00	30.00	21.00
☐ **Jezebel,** *white gown, hat, Grandes Dames Collection, 15"*	35.00	45.00	38.00
☐ **John Wayne,** *Legend Series, c. 1982*	65.00	70.00	68.00
☐ **Katie,** *vinyl, molded and painted hair, sleep eyes (blue), marked Effanbee, made in 1957, 9"*	23.00	29.00	21.00
☐ **Lil Darlin,** *cloth body, vinyl head, cry box, marked Effanbee, 15¾"*	19.00	24.00	18.00
☐ **Lil Sweetie,** *vinyl, blonde hair (rooted), sleep eyes (blue), nursing mouth, wears bonnet, marked 5667 Effanbee, 1967, 15⅞"*	15.00	19.00	15.00

Note: This mold (with different clothing) was used to represent several dolls in the Effanbee line during the mid to late 1960's.

Little Lady,
composition,
c. 1938, 18″
$195.00-$215.00

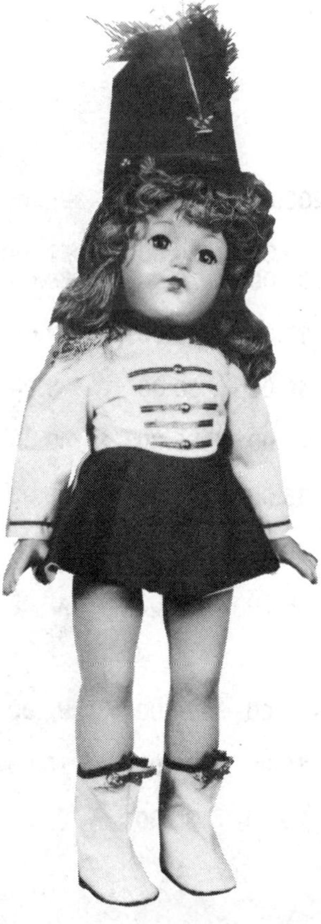

Little Lady,
composition,
c. 1941, 22″
$250.00-$300.00

	Current Price Range		Prior Year Average
☐ **Little Bo-Peep,** *soft body, Huggable Collection, c. 1982, 14″*	28.00	37.00	30.00
☐ **Little Lady,** *all composition, green sleep eyes, touseled reddish-brown mohair hair, felt pants suit, white shoes*	60.00	70.00	63.00
☐ **Little Lady,** *composition head, swivel body, brown wig, sleep eyes, beige pique dress with flower trim, marked F&B, c. 1938, 18″*	195.00	215.00	200.00
☐ **Little Lady,** *composition, yarn wig, blue sleep eyes, full drum majorette outfit, c. 1941, 22″*	250.00	300.00	275.00
☐ **Little Miss Muffet,** *c. 1983*	20.00	30.00	21.00
☐ **Little Red Riding Hood,** *soft body, Huggable Collection, c. 1982, 14″*	28.00	37.00	30.00
☐ **Little Tiger,** *c. 1983*	38.00	47.00	40.00
☐ **Lorraine,** *red, black riding outfit, Grandes Dames Collection, c. 1983, 11″*	35.00	45.00	38.00
☐ **Lotus Blossom,** *c. 1983*	40.00	50.00	42.00
☐ **Lovums,** *composition shoulder head, arms and lower legs, swivel neck, cloth body, green sleep eyes, blonde lamb's wool wig, original blue smocked romper suit, Effanbee heart necklace, laughing mouth, with two upper and lower teeth, marks: Effanbee Lovums, 21″*	200.00	225.00	195.00
☐ **Lovums,** *Heaven Sent Collection, c. 1982, 18″*	40.00	50.00	42.00
☐ **Mae West,** *Legend Series, c. 1982*	65.00	75.00	69.00
☐ **Madame Butterfly,** *multicolored kimono, 11″*	35.00	45.00	37.00
☐ **Madame Butterfly,** *multicolored kimono, c. 1983, 15″*	40.00	50.00	42.00
☐ **Madame Butterfly,** *multicolored kimono, c. 1983, 18″*	45.00	55.00	49.00
☐ **Magnolia,** *lacy pink gown, matching bonnet, Grandes Dames Collection, 15″*	35.00	45.00	38.00
☐ **Mark Twain,** *white suit, limited issue, c. 1983*	60.00	70.00	63.00
☐ **Martha Washington,** *blue dress, Women of The Ages Collection, c. 1983*	40.00	50.00	42.00
☐ **Mary Lee,** *composition, sleep eyes, open mouth, bright red lips, teeth, glossy face, marked Mary Lee, date of manufacture unknown, but presumably c. 1935, 16″*	95.00	115.00	90.00
☐ **Mary and Little Lamb,** *vinyl, jointed, c. 1981, 11″*	15.00	25.00	16.00
☐ **Mexican Doll,** *International Collection, c. 1982, 11″*	20.00	30.00	21.00

	Current Price Range		Prior Year Average
☐ **Mickey,** *vinyl, molded and painted features, wears football helmet (old style, without facemask), marked Effanbee-10, made in 1956, 11″*	8.00	11.00	8.00
☐ **Miss Black America,** *International Collection, c. 1979, 11″*	15.00	25.00	16.00
☐ **Miss Chips,** *plastic/vinyl, black hair (rooted), sleep eyes (brown), wears bridal gown, marked Effanbee 1965-1700, 18″*	22.00	28.00	21.00
Note: Has dark skin but is usually classified as "suntanned white" rather than black.			
☐ **Mobile,** *Pride of the South, c. 1982*	40.00	50.00	42.00
☐ **Mommy's Baby,** *plastic head, cloth body, plastic arms and legs, sleep eyes (blue), marked Effanbee, made in 1952, 27″*	33.00	39.00	31.00
☐ **Mother Goose,** *vinyl, jointed, c. 1981, 11″*	15.00	25.00	16.00
☐ **Musketeer,** *c. 1983*	20.00	30.00	21.00
☐ **My Fair Baby,** *vinyl, sandy blonde hair (rooted), sleep eyes (blue), nursing mouth, bright red lips, marked Effanbee, made in 1958, 17½″*	23.00	28.00	22.00
☐ **My Precious Baby,** *vinyl head, cloth body, vinyl arms and legs, blonde hair (rooted), sleep eyes (blue), crier, marked 1960 Effanbee, 20″*	14.00	19.00	14.00
☐ **New Dy Dee Baby,** *vinyl, blonde hair (rooted), nurser, sleep eyes (blue), marked Effanbee 1969, 16½″*	10.00	14.00	10.00
☐ **New Orleans,** *Pride of the South Collection, c. 1982, 13″*	35.00	45.00	38.00
☐ **Night At The Opera,** *Grandes Dames Collection, c. 1980, 18″*	50.00	60.00	52.00
☐ **Norway,** *vinyl, jointed, International Collection*	15.00	25.00	16.00
☐ **Norweigan Doll,** *International Collection, c. 1982, 11″*	20.00	30.00	21.00
☐ **Olivia,** *Grandes Dames Collection, c. 1982, 15″*	45.00	55.00	48.00
☐ **Orange Blossom,** *by Joyce Stafford, c. 1982, 13″*	40.00	45.00	42.00
☐ **Patricia,** *composition, brown sleep eyes, blonde hair, closed mouth, blue pleated dress, marked, 14″*	100.00	150.00	120.00
☐ **Patricia,** *composition, red hair attached by adhesive, sleep eyes (brown), marked Effanbee-Patricia, mid 1930's, 13½″*	68.00	83.00	65.00
☐ **Patsy,** *all composition, painted blue eyes, molded hair, original clothes*	125.00	150.00	125.00

Patricia,
composition, 15″
$68.00-$83.00

	Current Price Range		Prior Year Average
☐ **Patsy,** *composition, brown sleep eyes, real lashes, brown curly mohair wig, yellow dress with white collar, white leather shoes, 14″*	175.00	215.00	185.00
☐ **Patsy,** *mold composition body, molded hair, painted eyes, original green dress, c. 1950, 10″*	225.00	250.00	235.00
☐ **Patsy,** *two piece snow suit in red, yellow, black and white, 13″*	80.00	90.00	82.00
☐ **Patsy Ann,** *blue sleep eyes, green print dress, white socks and shoes, 19″*	100.00	150.00	120.00
☐ **Patsy Ann,** *blue sleep eyes, painted hair, sweater and blue jeans, 19″*	90.00	100.00	92.00
☐ **Patsy Ann,** *composition, 20″*	100.00	150.00	120.00

Patsy, c. 1950, 10″ . . . . **$225.00-$250.00**

	Current Price Range		Prior Year Average
☐ **Patsy Ann,** *composition, blue sleep tin eyes, molded hair, original clothes, 19″*	**225.00**	**250.00**	**225.00**
☐ **Patsy Ann,** *vinyl, blonde hair (rooted), sleep eyes (blue), bright red lips, jointed at the waist, marked Effanbee-Patsy Ann, made in 1959, 14½″*	**24.00**	**30.00**	**23.00**
☐ **Patsy Baby,** *composition head, cloth body, sleep eyes, celluloid hands, made around 1940, 10¼″*	**60.00**	**75.00**	**55.00**
☐ **Patsyette,** *as Anne Shirley in Ann Of Green Gables, brown eyes, red braids, blue suit and hat, heart bracelet, 9″*	**325.00**	**375.00**	**340.00**
☐ **Patsy Doll,** *molded, light brown hair, marked, 14″*	**105.00**	**115.00**	**110.00**

	Current Price Range		Prior Year Average
☐ **Patsy Joan,** *composition, molded and painted hair (blonde), sleep eyes (green), marked Effanbee-Patsy Joan, also bearing (originally) a wrist tag carrying the same wording. Introduced in 1927 but taken off the market soon thereafter, reintroduced about 20 years later, most of those found today are the reintroductions, for which the stated value applies; the early specimens are of higher price, 16″*	50.00	68.00	47.00
☐ **Patsy Junior,** *composition head, composition arms, legs and body, molded hair, painted eyes, marked Effanbee Patsy Jr. Doll, placed on the market in 1930 or 1931, 11″*	80.00	100.00	77.00
☐ **Patsy Ruth,** *composition head, cloth body, composition arms and legs, sleep eyes (brown), marked Effanbee, Patsy Ruth, 1935, 27″*	200.00	250.00	190.00
☐ **Pavlova,** *Storybook Collection, c. 1979, 11″*	15.00	25.00	16.00
☐ **Peaches,** *vinyl head, cloth body, vinyl arms and legs, blonde hair (rooted), sleep eyes (blue), marked Effanbee 1965, 15″*	22.00	28.00	21.00
☐ **Peddler,** *by Faith Wick, c. 1982, 16″*	75.00	85.00	79.00
☐ **Peter Pan,** *Storybook Collection, c. 1982, 11″*	20.00	30.00	21.00
☐ **Pinocchio,** *soft body, Huggable Collection, c. 1982, 14″*	28.00	37.00	29.00
☐ **Pinocchio,** *vinyl, jointed, molded nose, Storybook Series, c. 1981, 11″*	15.00	25.00	16.00
☐ **Polish Doll,** *International Collection, c. 1982, 11″*	20.00	30.00	21.00
☐ **Polka Dotty,** *vinyl, molded and painted features, molded and painted hair, open mouth, pug nose, Polka Dotty was a character from the TV puppet program "Rootie Kazootie," a Saturday morning favorite in the days of live television, marked Polka Dotty-Rootie Kazootie-Effanbee, made in 1954, 19″*	65.00	85.00	60.00
☐ **Pollyana,** *c. 1983*	20.00	30.00	21.00
☐ **Precious Baby,** *character, vinyl head, vinyl hands, legs, cloth body, blond rooted hair, sleep eyes, c. 1957, 24″*	350.00	375.00	350.00
☐ **Precious Newborn,** *vinyl head, cloth body, vinyl arms and legs, blonde hair (rooted), painted eyes, marked Effanbee 1962, 14″*	25.00	31.00	23.00
☐ **Princess Di,** *mint in box, c. 1982*	145.00	155.00	149.00
☐ **Priscilla,** *light blue dress, Grandes Dames Collection, c. 1983, 11″*	35.00	45.00	39.00

	Current Price Range		Prior Year Average
☐ **Pun'kin,** *Granny's Corner Collection, c. 1983, 11"*	25.00	30.00	26.00
☐ **Pum'kin,** *vinyl, blonde hair (rooted), sleep eyes (blue), marked Effanbee 1966, 10"*	10.00	14.00	9.00
☐ **Queen Elizabeth,** *lacy white dress, Women of The Ages Collection, c. 1983*	45.00	55.00	49.00
☐ **Rebecca of Sunnybrook Farm,** *c. 1983*	20.00	30.00	21.00
☐ **Recital Time,** *Abigail Collection, c. 1982, 13"*	40.00	50.00	42.00
☐ **Richmond,** *white and red gown, Pride of The South Collection, c. 1983*	40.00	50.00	42.00
☐ **Robyn,** *Grandes Dames Collection, c. 1982, 11"*	30.00	40.00	32.00
☐ **Roma,** *peach dress, hat, Age of Elegance Collection, c. 1983*	90.00	110.00	92.00
☐ **Romanian Doll,** *c. 1983*	20.00	30.00	21.00
☐ **Savannah,** *Pride of the South Collection, c. 1982, 13"*	35.00	45.00	37.00
☐ **Scarecrow,** *by Faith Wick, c. 1983, 18"*	65.00	75.00	69.00
☐ **Scottish Doll,** *International Collection, c. 1982, 11"*	20.00	30.00	21.00
☐ **Skippy,** *composition head, cloth body, composition arms and legs, representing the comic strip character "Skippy" created by Percy Crosby, marked Skippy, Effanbee, date of manufacture unknown but presumably c. 1935, 14"*	75.00	95.00	70.00
☐ **Spanish Doll,** *International Collection, c. 1982, 11"*	20.00	30.00	21.00
☐ **Spring,** *c. 1983*	40.00	50.00	42.00
☐ **Stephanie,** *gray, pink dress, Grandes Dames Collection, c. 1983, 15"*	50.00	62.00	55.00
☐ **Strolling in The Park,** *Abigail Collection, c. 1982, 13"*	40.00	50.00	42.00
☐ **Sugar Plum,** *Granny's Corner Collection, c. 1983, 20"*	55.00	65.00	58.00
☐ **Summer,** *Four Seasons Collection, c. 1982, 15"*	35.00	45.00	39.00
☐ **Summer,** *c. 1983*	40.00	50.00	42.00
☐ **Sunday Best,** *Abigail Collection, c. 1982, 13"*	40.00	50.00	42.00
☐ **Susan B. Anthony,** *mint in box, c. 1980*	125.00	175.00	129.00
☐ **Suzanne,** *all composition, jointed at neck, shoulder and hips, brown human hair wig, blue sleep eyes, rosebud mouth, Alice in Wonderland dress, white pinafore, wearing original Effanbee heart bracelet, head marked Effanbee Suzanne, 14"*	145.00	155.00	145.00
☐ **Suzanne,** *composition, blonde hair attached by adhesive, sleep eyes (brown), marked Suzanne-Effanbee, made in 1940, 13"*	48.00	60.00	45.00

	Current Price Range		Prior Year Average
☐ **Suzanne,** *pink, green ribbon trimmed dress, Grandes Dames Collection, c. 1983, 11"*	35.00	45.00	39.00
☐ **Suzie Sunshine,** *Granny's Corner Collection, c. 1983, 16"*	38.00	45.00	40.00
☐ **Suzie Sunshine,** *c. 1983, 18"*	45.00	55.00	49.00
☐ **Suzie Sunshine,** *plastic/vinyl, blonde hair (rooted), sleep eyes (blue), marked Effanbee 1961, 17"*	11.00	14.00	10.00
☐ **Swedish Doll,** *International Collection, c. 1982, 11"*	20.00	30.00	21.00
☐ **Sweetie Pie,** *composition, cloth, flirty eyes*	125.00	175.00	129.00
☐ **Sweetie Pie,** *Granny's Corner Collection, c. 1983, 18"*	40.00	50.00	42.00
☐ **Swiss Doll,** *International Collection, c. 1982, 11"*	20.00	30.00	21.00
☐ **Thumkin,** *vinyl head, cloth body, vinyl arms and legs, brown hair (rooted), sleep eyes (black), marked Effanbee 1965-9500U1, 18"*	12.00	16.00	11.00
☐ **Tinker Bell,** *c. 1983*	20.00	30.00	21.00
☐ **Tiny Tubber,** *black, Heart To Heart Collection, c. 1982, 11"*	15.00	20.00	16.00
☐ **Tiny Tubber,** *vinyl, blonde hair (rooted), sleep eyes (blue), nursing mouth, marked Effanbee, made in 1968, 10"*	10.00	13.00	10.00
☐ **Tiny Tubber,** *with pillow bunting, Crochet Classics Collection, c. 1981, 11"*	20.00	25.00	21.00
☐ **Tintair,** *plastic, platinum blonde hair attached by adhesive, sleep eyes (blue), marked Effanbee, made in 1951, 18"*	62.00	78.00	60.00
☐ **The 70's Woman,** *c. 1979, 15"*	30.00	40.00	31.00
☐ **Twinkie,** *vinyl, molded and painted hair (brown), sleep eyes (blue), nursing mouth, marked Effanbee 1959, 15"*	11.00	14.00	10.00
☐ **U.S.A. Doll,** *International Collection, c. 1982, 11"*	20.00	30.00	21.00
☐ **Vicki,** *Scottish outfit, Grandes Dames Collection, c. 1983, 11"*	35.00	45.00	39.00
☐ **W. C. Fields,** *vinyl, commemorative, c. 1980, 15"*	50.00	60.00	55.00
☐ **Wee Patsy,** *composition, believed to have been made around 1940, 5½"*	110.00	135.00	100.00
☐ **Wicket Witch,** *vinyl, soft body, sleep eyes, black, witch outfit, carries basket of apples*	50.00	60.00	55.00
☐ **Winter,** *Four Seasons Collection, c. 1982, 15"*	35.00	45.00	39.00
☐ **Winter,** *c. 1983*	40.00	50.00	42.00

EINCO

	Current Price Range		Prior Year Average
☐ **Character Baby,** *solid dome bisque socket head, five piece bent leg baby body, brushed stroked brown hair, blue intaglio eyes, open/closed mouth, double chin, light blue linen romper suit, scalloped white collar, cuffs, marks: Einco 1½ Germany, 13″*	600.00	750.00	600.00

ELVIS PRESLEY ENTERPRISES

☐ **Elvis Presley,** *plastic, molded and painted features, molded and painted hair, made in 1956 or 1957, wears plaid shirt and solid-color pants, has open mouth, 18″*	300.00	375.00	250.00

EPPY

☐ **Color Me,** *plastic, molded, jointed at the neck and upper arms, marked Eppy 1964, sold originally in a kit which also contained a set of crayons for coloring the doll (it could be washed and recolored at will), 12″*	6.00	8.00	6.00

ERB

☐ **Tarzan,** *plastic/vinyl, molded and painted features, fully jointed, Tarzan was created by Edgar Rice Burroughs, marked ERB Inc., 1972, (ERB, Inc., representing the estate and descendants of the late Edgar Rice Burroughs, licenses all Tarzan-related products), 8″*	5.00	7.00	5.00

EUGENE

☐ **Baby Missey,** *cloth body, vinyl head, vinyl limbs, sleep eyes (blue), marked 91/14, sold originally with a tag which read Eugene Doll Co., 91, made in Taiwan, date of manufacture unknown, probably 1970's, 9″*	3.00	4.00	3.00

	Current Price Range		Prior Year Average
☐ **Baby Sarah Lee,** *black, plastic/vinyl, rooted hair, marked Eugene, 11⅞"*	6.00	8.00	6.00
☐ **Peepers,** *vinyl, jointed, flirt eyes, mint in box, 12"*	10.00	20.00	15.00

EUGENIA

☐ **Personality Playmate,** *plastic, brunette hair attached by adhesive, sleep eyes (brown), unmarked, made in this version in 1950, 17"*	39.00	48.00	37.00
☐ **Sandra,** *plastic, blonde hair attached by adhesive, sleep eyes (blue), unmarked, made in 1950, 15"*	38.00	47.00	35.00

Note: The actual manufacturer was Ideal, which did contracting for Eugenia.

EXCEL

☐ **Admiral William F. Halsey,** *plastic/vinyl, jointed, representing the U.S. naval commander of World War II, marked Excel Toy Corp., Hong Kong, made in the 1970's, 12"*	5.00	7.00	5.00
☐ **Annie Oakley,** *plastic/vinyl, jointed, representing the female trick-shot artist who performed with Buffalo Bill's Wild West Show, holds rifle, marked Excel Toy Corp., Hong Kong, made in the 1970's, 9½"*	3.00	5.00	3.00
☐ **Belle Starr,** *plastic/vinyl, jointed, representing the noted female desperado of the Old West, marked Excel Toy Corp., Hong Kong, made in the 1970's, 9½"*	3.00	5.00	3.00
☐ **Buffalo Bill Cody,** *plastic/vinyl, representing the Old West showman and story-teller, marked Excel Toy Corp., Hong Kong, made in the 1970's, 9½"*	3.00	5.00	3.00
☐ **Cochise,** *plastic/vinyl, representing the Indian chief popularized via a TV program during the 1960's, marked Excel Toy Corp., Hong Kong, made in the 1970's*	3.00	5.00	3.00
☐ **General George S. Patton,** *plastic/vinyl, jointed, representing the U.S. army general of World War II, marked Excel Toy Corp., Hong Kong, made in the 1970's, 12"*	5.00	7.00	5.00
☐ **General John J. Pershing,** *plastic/vinyl, representing the U.S. army officer who com-*			

	Current Price Range		Prior Year Average
manded allied forces in World War I, marked Excel Toy Corp., Hong Kong, made in the 1970's, 12"	5.00	7.00	5.00
☐ **General Robert E. Lee,** *plastic/vinyl, jointed, representing the commander of Confederate forces in the Civil War, marked Excel Toy Corp., Hong Kong, made in the 1970's, 12"*	5.00	7.00	5.00
☐ **George Washington,** *plastic/vinyl, wears short jacket with brass buttons, sword, boots, tricorn hat, marked Excel Toy Corp., Hong Kong, made in the 1970's, 12"*	5.00	7.00	5.00
☐ **Jessie James,** *plastic/vinyl, jointed, representing the Old West bank robber, marked Excel Toy Corp., Hong Kong, made in the 1970's, 9"*	3.00	5.00	3.00
☐ **Lt. Col. Paul Revere,** *plastic/vinyl, representing the Boston silversmith who, according to popular legend, alerted townsfolk of a British invasion in the Revolutionary War, marked Excel Toy Corp., Hong Kong, made in the 1970's, 12"*	5.00	7.00	5.00
☐ **Lt. Col. Theodore Roosevelt,** *plastic/vinyl, representing President Roosevelt in his days as an officer in the Spanish-American War, wearing military dress with pistol in holster, marked Excel Toy Corp., Hong Kong, made in the 1970's, 12"*	5.00	7.00	5.00
☐ **Pochahontas,** *plastic/vinyl, jointed, representing the Indian princess of 17th century America who became well known through the writing of John Smith, the Virginia colonist, marked Excel Toy Corp., Hong Kong, made in the 1970's*	3.00	5.00	3.00
☐ **Ulysses S. Grant,** *plastic/vinyl, representing the Union Army general and U.S. President, wearing military dress with sword, marked Excel Toy Corp., Hong Kong, made in the 1970's, 12"*	5.00	7.00	5.00

MARK FARMER

	Current Price Range		Prior Year Average
☐ **Boy,** *bisque shoulder head, cloth body, bisque arms and legs, a modern doll made in 19th century style, date of manufacture unknown, presumably 1970's, 13"*	60.00	80.00	57.00

F.D.

	Current Price Range		Prior Year Average
☐ **Sissy,** *plastic/vinyl, brown hair (rooted), sleep eyes (blue), nursing mouth, marked F.D., made in 1963, 18"*	9.00	12.00	9.00
☐ **Winkin',** *vinyl, molded and painted features, molded and painted hair, representing the character in the Old English folk rhyme, "Winkin', Blinkin', and Nod," marked F.D., made in 1956, 8½"*	6.00	8.00	6.00

FISHER PRICE

	Current Price Range		Prior Year Average
☐ **Audrey,** *vinyl head, cloth body, rooted hair, painted eyes, blouse with small heart pattern, marked 168240, 1973, Fisher Price Toys, 14"*	11.00	15.00	10.00
☐ **Baby Ann,** *vinyl head, cloth body, rooted blond hair, painted eyes, floral print dress with large sash ribbon, marked 60, 188460, 1973, Fisher Price Toys, 13½"*	10.00	14.00	9.00
☐ **Elizabeth,** *black, vinyl head, cloth body, rooted hair, closed mouth in semi-smile, painted eyes, marked 18, 168630, 1973, Fisher Price Toys, 13½"*	11.00	15.00	10.00
☐ **Honey**	6.00	10.00	5.00
☐ **Joey**	9.00	12.00	8.00
☐ **Mary,** *vinyl head, cloth body, rooted hair, upturned eyes (painted), angelic facial expression, wears print dress and white apron, marked 168420, 1973, Fisher Price Toys, 14"*	10.00	14.00	9.00
☐ **My Friend Becky,** *vinyl, jointed brown rooted hair, blue eyes, painted features, green dress with white pinafore with floral print, white straw hat, white slippers*	20.00	30.00	25.00
☐ **My Friend Jenny,** *vinyl, jointed, dark brown rooted hair, brown sleep eyes, painted features, yellow and white gingham dress, white sleeves, white slippers, white straw hat, 17"*	20.00	30.00	25.00
☐ **My Friend Mandy,** *vinyl, jointed, blonde rooted hair, blue eyes, painted features, navy blue dress with white polka dots, red straw hat, red slippers, 17"*	20.00	30.00	25.00
☐ **My Friend Mikey,** *dark hair, bangs, freckles, pants, shirt, jacket #205*	2000	30.00	25.00

	Current Price Range		Prior Year Average
☐ **Natalie,** *vinyl head, cloth body, rooted hair, upturned eyes (painted), grinning smile, marked 168320, 1973, Fisher Price Toys, 13½"*	11.00	15.00	10.00
☐ **Susie Soft Sound,** *open, shut eyes, electronic voice, 16"*	40.00	50.00	45.00

HAM FISHER

☐ **Joan Palooka,** *vinyl head, latex body, sleep eyes, molded, painted hair, jointed arms, intended as a female counterpart of Joe Palooka, the heavyweight boxing champion of the comic strips, marked 1952, Ham Fisher, Ideal Doll, Ham Fisher was the creator of the Joe Palooka character, 14"*	20.00	25.00	18.00

FLAGG

☐ **Calypso Dancer,** *vinyl, unmarked, 7"*	10.00	13.00	9.00
☐ **Cowboy,** *vinyl, bendable, unmarked, 7"*	9.00	12.00	9.00
☐ **Cowgirl,** *vinyl, posable, unmarked, 6½"*	9.00	12.00	9.00
☐ **Dancing Doll,** *posable, vinyl, rooted hair, believed to have been made between 1955 and 1960, sold in white and black versions, which differ in costuming and minor details, 7¼", White*	7.00	9.00	7.00
Black	8.00	11.00	8.00
☐ **Egyptian Girl** *(national costume doll), vinyl, bendable, 7"*	9.00	12.00	8.00
☐ **Flagg Dancer,** *vinyl, unmarked, 7"*	10.00	13.00	10.00
☐ **Frenchman,** *vinyl, unmarked, believed to date from the mid 1940's, 7"*	9.00	11.00	8.00

FLEISCHAKER

☐ **Bi Bye,** *vinyl head, vinyl arms and legs, stuffed cloth body, painted eyes, molded and painted hair, represents a one-week-old infant with mouth wide open, crying, originally came with a tag, dated 1949, made for the Fleischaker Novelty Co. by Lastic Plastic, 16"*	14.00	18.00	13.00
☐ **Little Girl Of Today,** *vinyl head, cloth body, vinyl arms and legs, sleep eyes (blue), marked*			

	Current Price Range		Prior Year Average
Fleischaker Novelty Co. made in 1949, sold for several years thereafter, 23"	160.00	190.00	150.00
☐ **Unnamed,** *plastic, stuffed, rooted hair, sleep eyes, partially open mouth, wears checkered dress (short) with puff sleeves, two buttons on dress, arms and legs wide apart, marked Copyright 1951 Lastic Plastic, 16½"*	18.00	23.00	17.00

Note: This doll (unnamed) was manufactured by Lastic Plastic for the Fleischaker Novelty Co. The hairstyle is somewhat "afro."

FLEISHER STUDIOS

	Current Price Range		Prior Year Average
☐ **Betty Boop,** *jointed wood doll, c. 1930, 12"*	75.00	100.00	80.00

FORTUNE TOYS

	Current Price Range		Prior Year Average
☐ **Pam,** *plastic, blonde hair attached with adhesive, sleep eyes (blue), unmarked, made in 1956, 7½"*	11.00	14.00	10.00

FREUNDLICH

	Current Price Range		Prior Year Average
☐ **Baby Sandy,** *composition, molded and painted hair, sleep eyes, open mouth, bright red lips, wears bonnet, unmarked, made in 1936, 11"*	115.00	135.00	110.00
☐ **Sandy Henville,** *composition, sleep eyes, open mouth, bright red lips, date of manufacture unknown, 16"*	100.00	120.00	95.00

FULPHER (often spelled FULPER)

This Flemington, New Jersey company is well known to collectors of pottery. It was chiefly a maker of table wares and porcelain novelties of many kinds, for well over 100 years. For a few years immediately following World War I (which ended in 1918), Fulpher produced bisque doll heads. It did not manufacture whole dolls but supplied the heads on contract to assemblers. Nevertheless, any doll with a Fulpher head is called a Fulpher doll. The workmanship is of high quality and their brief period of manufacture has given them a considerable rarity factor, reflected in the values.

	Current Price Range		Prior Year Average
☐ **Bisque head,** *composition body, fixed eyes (medium size), very short painted lashes, open mouth with two teeth, bright red lips, full round face, marked Fulpher reading vertically, also marked Made in U.S.A. and with the mold number 2AA, made between 1918 and 1921, 15¼"*	305.00	345.00	300.00
☐ **Bisque Head,** *jointed body, human hair wig, brown sleep eyes, brown silk dress and hat, 19"*	450.00	500.00	460.00
☐ **Bisque,** *socket head, fixed eyes (large), painted lashes, open mouth with two teeth, puffy cheeks, marked Fulpher reading vertically within an oval, additionally marked Made in U.S.A. and with the mold number 13, made between 1918 and 1921, 17⅝"*	320.00	370.00	315.00
☐ **Bisque,** *socket head, fixed eyes (wide, staring), long thin painted lashes, open mouth, medium-dark lips, facial expression of surprise or disbelief, marked Fulpher within a square, additionally marked Made in U.S.A. and with the mold number 70, believed to have been one of the first dolls made when Fulpher began to produce dolls in 1918, 18⅞"*	210.00	240.00	200.00
☐ **Bisque,** *socket head, fixed eyes (medium large), pale painted lashes, open mouth, round jaw, prominent chin, marked Fulpher reading vertically within an oval, also marked Made in U.S.A., believed to have been among the first dolls produced by the company when it began making dolls in 1918, 17⅞"*	145.00	170.00	140.00
Note: Apparently Fulpher manufactured this doll in greater quantity than most of its others. It may have been made as a distribution sample to test the reaction of doll assembly companies (companies that would buy the bisque heads and add bodies to them).			
☐ **Boy,** *bisque head, jointed composition body, brown set eyes, brown human hair wig, open mouth, original clothes, 26"*	500.00	650.00	550.00

FUN FARM

	Current Price Range		Prior Year Average
☐ **Funny,** *plastic/vinyl, brunette hair (rooted), painted eyes (brown), open mouth with one large tooth, marked 1965 R. Dakin & Co., Product of Hong Kong, sold originally with a tag reading Fun Farm, San Francisco, 6″ . .*	5.00	7.00	5.00

FUN WORLD

☐ **Abe Lincoln,** *plastic, molded and painted features, molded and painted hair, holds hat in hand, stands on rectangular base, marked Hong Kong, made c. 1975, 8½″ . . . .*	11.00	14.00	10.00
☐ **George Washington,** *plastic, molded and painted features, molded and painted hair, arms hanging at sides, stands on rectangular base, marked Hong Kong, made c. 1975, 8½″*	11.00	14.00	10.00
☐ **Huggles,** *vinyl head, stuffed body, vinyl hands, rooted hair (reddish), painted eyes, marked Huggles by Fun World, made in 1971, 9″ . . . . .*	4.00	6.00	4.00
☐ **Sleepy Head,** *vinyl head, stuffed body, vinyl hands, rooted hair (brunette), painted eyes, marked Fun World, made in 1971, 11″ . . . . . .*	6.00	8.00	6.00
☐ **Soul Sister,** *black, plastic/vinyl, rooted hair (black), painted eyes (brown), wears large hoop earrings, short dress, boots, marked Design No. 915-664, Made in Hong Kong, made in 1971, 8″ . . . .*	9.00	12.00	9.00
☐ **Sparky,** *plastic head, plastic arms, legs and body, hair attached by adhesive, face painted as a clown, marked Made in Hong Kong, Fun World Inc., 1973, 7″ . . . .*	3.00	4.00	3.00

FURGA

☐ **Anna,** *brunette, dark sleep eyes, lashes, white, green velvet dress, pantaloons, pumps, holds hoop, Kent Collection, 18″ . . . .*	35.00	45.00	40.00
☐ **Beatrix,** *blonde curls, hazel eyes, striped skirt, white blouse, pink bonnet, 18″ . . . . . .*	45.00	55.00	50.00
☐ **Chiara,** *blonde hair, blue eyes, blue, white satin print dress, straw hat, c. 1983, 15″ . . .*	40.00	50.00	45.00
☐ **Dame Louise,** *plastic/vinyl, green eyes, pug nose, closed mouth, marked Furga, Italy, date of manufacture unknown, c. 1950's, 17″*	15.00	20.00	14.00

	Current Price Range		Prior Year Average
☐ **Furina,** *plastic/vinyl, brunette wig attached by adhesive, sleep eyes (blue), unmarked on doll, sold originally with a tag reading Furga, Made in Italy, made in 1955, 11"*	100.00	130.00	95.00
☐ **Girl,** *flowers in hair, blue sleep eyes, lashes, closed mouth, pink net, satin cape, gown*	30.00	40.00	35.00
☐ **Gretel,** *plastic/vinyl, blue eyes, marked Furga, Italy, made in 1974, 8⅞"*	18.00	25.00	17.00
☐ **Guendalina,** *plastic/vinyl, marked Furga, Italy, date of manufacture unknown, probably c. 1970, 14½"*	60.00	75.00	55.00
☐ **Isabella in Bicicletta,** *red, gray cycling outfit, matching hat, comes with bicycle, c. 1983*	75.00	85.00	80.00
☐ **Isabella El'Arpa,** *lacy white gown, harp, c. 1983*	75.00	85.00	80.00
☐ **Marabeth,** *thin plastic over mache head, similar body, henna wig attached with adhesive, sleep eyes, crier, marked Furga, Italy, 37, 15"*	25.00	30.00	23.00
☐ **Margareth,** *blonde, dark sleep eyes, long lashes, ruffly print, pantaloons, pumps, holds jumprope, Kent Collection, 18"*	35.00	45.00	40.00
☐ **Mary, Mary,** *plastic/vinyl, blue eyes, representing the storybook character "Mary, Mary Quite Contrary", marked Furga, Italy, made in 1974*	18.00	25.00	17.00
☐ **Olympia,** *white, green dress, matching hat, c. 1983*	75.00	85.00	80.00
☐ **Pettrice,** *frosted red hair, lacy green skirt, apron, beret, scarf, comes with artist's implements, c. 1983*	75.00	85.00	00.00
☐ **Plastic,** *red hair with long braids, white dress and bloomers, yellow boots, hula hoop, 14"*	40.00	50.00	44.00
☐ **Plastic,** *blue sleep eyes, silver blonde hair in large bun, pink velvet hoop dress, matching hat, white maribou trim, 16"*	40.00	50.00	44.00
☐ **Plastic,** *blue sleep eyes, short white hair, tan velvet hoop dress, white blouse, cape with hood trimmed in brown maribou, white boots, muff on gold chain, 14"*	40.00	50.00	43.00
☐ **Plastic,** *sleep blue eyes with long lashes, red hair wig, short white dress, pearl buttons, long white stockings, 22"*	50.00	60.00	53.00
☐ **Snow White,** *plastic/vinyl, blue eyes, marked Furga, Italy, made in 1974, 9"*	18.00	25.00	17.00

FY

A Japanese firm which imported large quantities of dolls and/or doll heads into the U.S. and Western Europe shortly after World War I. The heads are bisque and of rather good quality. Some specimens have marked Oriental facial characteristics, and it can probably be presumed that these are the earlier ones, before the firm learned how to make a western-looking doll.

The word "Nippon," found in the marks of this manufacturer, was an Anglo-American word (now pretty well obsolete) meaning "Japan."

	Current Price Range		Prior Year Average
☐ **Bisque,** *infant head, usually found dressed as a toddler with a bonnet, sleep eyes (large for the head size), open mouth showing two well-formed teeth, wide nose, circular face, slightly arched eyebrows, marked Fy20-8-Nippon, date of manufacture unknown, probably early to mid 1920's, 10" (but the size will vary as this head is found on various bodies)*	90.00	120.00	85.00
☐ **Bisque,** *socket head with shoulder plate, fixed eyes (medium large), barest suggestion of lashes, almost horizontal brows, partially open mouth showing teeth, medium-dark lips, puffy cheeks, marked Fy9-Nippon-402, date of manufacture unknown, probably early to mid 1920's, 19½"*	180.00	215.00	170.00
☐ **Girl,** *composition ball jointed body, brown stationary glass eyes, open mouth, teeth, long brown curls, blue satin dress with lace trim, lace cap, white shoes with bows, 25"*	325.00	375.00	340.00
☐ **Girl,** *composition ball jointed body, long blonde human hair curls, turquoise-blue velvet dress with pink lace trim, matching hat, bonnet and purse, 23"*	270.00	340.00	300.00

GABRIEL

☐ **Dan Reid,** *plastic, molded and painted features, molded and painted hair, painted eyes, Dan Reid, a fictional character, was "the Lone Ranger's long-lost brother," marked 1975 Lone Ranger, made in Hong Kong for Gabriel Industries, Inc., 8"*	11.00	14.00	10.00
☐ **Timmy,** *molded and painted features, molded and painted hair, marked 1975 Gabriel Industries, Inc., made in Hong Kong, Timmy was a character on the "Lassie" TV program, 8½"*	11.00	14.00	10.00

GAMA

	Current Price Range		Prior Year Average
☐ **Florina,** *French, in a box, 9″*	45.00	55.00	45.00
☐ **Kate,** *French, in a box, 12″*	65.00	75.00	65.00
☐ **Stephanie,** *French, in a box, 7″*	25.00	30.00	20.00
☐ **Stephanie,** *French, with suitcase, 7″*	35.00	45.00	40.00

GANDA TOYS LTD.

☐ **Poland,** *plastic head, plastic arms, legs and body, blond wig attached by adhesive, sleep eyes, represents a young girl wearing national costuming of Poland, made in Hong Kong, 7″*	4.00	5.00	4.00

Note: There were other "national costume" dolls in this Ganda series, all of which have the same value. The series was issued in 1973.

GANS AND SEYFARTH

☐ **Bisque,** *jointed composition body, brown eyes, lashes, multicolored pencil striped dress, organdy hat, 20″*	300.00	350.00	340.00
☐ **Country Girl,** *jointed composition body, brown eyes, lashes, brown wig, white dress, plaid hat, 24″*	350.00	400.00	370.00

GAULTIER

Parisian manufacturer active in the final quarter of the 19th century. Their dolls were of high quality and show considerable versatility in styling and materials. The heads were nearly always of bisque, but such components as wood, papier mache and composition were used for the bodies and limbs, sometimes all intermingled in the same doll. It is also likely that Gaultier sold bodiless heads to assembling companies. Dolls with Gaultier heads and cloth bodies were probably assembled elsewhere. A fine Gaultier in well preserved condition is a prize for the collector. They can be found in the U.S. but the prime hunting grounds are the antique shops of Paris — where they are more plentiful but VERY expensive.

☐ **Bébé,** *bisque head, jointed French composition and wood body, brown paperweight eyes, brown wig, pierced ears, closed mouth, lovely old brown velvet dress with lace trim and hat, mark: F.G. 7, 18″*	900.00	1300.00	850.00

	Current Price Range		Prior Year Average
☐ **Bébé,** *bisque head, shoulder plate, jointed French composition body, blue paperweight eyes, blond human hair wig, closed mouth, pierced ears, antique clothes, 20″*	2200.00	2500.00	2250.00
☐ **Bébé,** *bisque head, shoulder plate, jointed French composition body, blue paperweight glass eyes, blonde wig, pierced ears, closed mouth, antique dress, bonnet and undergarments, 18″*	3200.00	3800.00	3000.00
☐ **Bisque,** *big blue paperweight eyes, blonde curls, closed mouth, blue outfit, 18″*	1800.00	2400.00	2100.00
☐ **Bisque,** *socket head, fixed eyes, very large, almond-shaped, short painted lashes, heavy arching eyebrows, closed mouth, medium-dark lips, facial expression of contentment, marked with the initials F.G., and the mold number 10, date of manufacture unknown, estimated at c. 1880, 24½″*	1275.00	1550.00	1250.00
☐ **Bisque,** *socket head, fixed eyes, large and dark, very short painted lashes, thick arching eyebrows, partially open mouth with no teeth visible, round jaw, representing a child of about 3 years old, marked F.G., and also with the mold number 7, date of manufacture unknown, can probably be safely assigned to the 1880's, 17½″*	1000.00	1250.00	975.00
☐ **Bisque,** *turnable head set into shoulder plate, also made of bisque, fixed eyes, very large and dark, painted lashes, closed mouth, dark red lips, round jaw, representing a child of about 5 or 6 years old, marked with the initials F.G., recorded specimens do not bear a mold number, date of manufacture unknown, but the style would seem to suggest a dating of c. 1875, 10¾″*	480.00	565.00	475.00
☐ **Bisque head,** *repainted (long age) French wood and composition body, blue paperweight eyes, finely stroked brows, closed mouth with two-tone painted lips, antique white pantaloons, matching petticoat, antique white dress, incised F. 9 G., 20″*	2150.00	2500.00	2200.00
☐ **Bisque head,** *stockinette body, bisque hands and legs, blue paperweight eyes, light brown human hair wig with long curls, open mouth, lovely antique clothes and hat, 23″*	3300.00	3800.00	3000.00
☐ **Fashion,** *bisque head, kid body, blue glass eyes, open mouth, pierced ears, blue faille dress with hat, 16″*	450.00	550.00	425.00

	Current Price Range		Prior Year Average
☐ **Fashion,** *bisque head, kid body, blue paperweight eyes, brown mohair wig, pierced ears, lovely dress with hat, 20″*	1100.00	1600.00	1000.00
☐ **Fashion,** *bisque head, stockinette body with bisque lower arms and legs, original wig, grey blue paperweight eyes, pierced ears, two-tone smile, antique heavy rose silk two-piece ensemble with lace overlay, 16″*	2800.00	3600.00	2900.00
☐ **Fashion,** *bisque head, jointed, composition body, original mohair wig, almond shaped brown paperweight eyes, closed mouth, pierced ears, original costume and shoes, marked F. 10 G., 24″*	1900.00	2300.00	1800.00
☐ **Fashion,** *bisque head, jointed kid body, mohair wig, sleep eyes, beige and green silk dress, trimmed with fringe, c. 1870, 22″*	2500.00	2700.00	2600.00
☐ **Fashion,** *bisque head, kid body, blonde human hair wig, blue paperweight eyes, pierced ears, gathered lace gown, 38″*	2850.00	3250.00	3000.00

Fashion,
bisque, c. 1870, 22″
$2500.00-$2700.00

	Current Price Range		Prior Year Average
☐ **Fashion,** *bisque shoulder head, French kid body, blonde wig in French twist, blue set eyes, pierced ears, red long walking suit with flared skirt, 15″*	900.00	1100.00	950.00
☐ **Fashion,** *bisque shoulder head with kid lined swivel neck, blue paperweight eyes, original dark blonde mohair wig tied with original ribbon (faded), curled bangs, closed mouth with red accent lines, pierced ears, kid body with individually stitched fingers, narrow waist, well formed hips and legs, skirt with slight train and gathered front panels, fitted velveteen jacket trimmed with lace and pleated ruffles, leather shoes with tiny heels and brass flower trim, marks: F.G. on left shoulder plate under kid, 22″*	2000.00	2300.00	1800.00
☐ **Fashion Lady,** *bisque head, composition French jointed body, brown paperweight eyes, auburn French human hair wig, closed mouth, brown velvet and peach satin ensemble, marked FG in scroll, 14″*	1500.00	1950.00	1300.00
☐ **Fashion Lady,** *bisque head and shoulder plate, kid body, wired arms, kid covered fingers, blonde wig, paperweight grey eyes, closed mouth, pierced ears, beautiful wardrobe, marked F.G. on shoulder, 16″*	2500.00	2750.00	2500.00
☐ **Three Dolls,** *two children and one teacher, mechanical, bisque, wigs, closed mouth, two children turn and dance as music plays, teacher sits at piano, crank operated, base, original clothes, 12″ x 8″ x 2½″*	3100.00	3350.00	3150.00

GAY BOB TRADING COMPANY

	Current Price Range		Prior Year Average
☐ **Gay Bob,** *vinyl head, vinyl body, painted eyes, earrings, shirt, slacks and closet, c. 1982,*	8.00	12.00	10.00
☐ **Pirate,** *wax construction, brown curly wig and beard, painted brown eyes, velvet costume with high boots, three corner hat with skull and cross bones, 8½″*	150.00	200.00	175.00

Pirate,
wax
$150.00-$200.00

GEBRÜDER HEUBACH

Gebrüder Heubach ("The Heubach Brothers") operated at roughly the same time as Heubach (see below), and also in Germany, but was a different company. This was a large organization with agents and distributors virtually worldwide, and was known for ceramics of many different kinds. Today there are collectors of Gebrüder Heubach who specialize in its plates, figurines, etc. While dolls did not comprise a major portion of the firm's business, it nevertheless turned out many of them, over a long period of time. Its dolls span the era from the American Civil War right up to the Depression, and various different kinds are included. Gebrüder Heubach was one of the more innovative doll makers and designers, and for this have won a strong collector following. While most other firms were turning out dolls whose heads and facial expressions were virtual carbon copies of each other, Gebrüder Heubach inaugurated many original types, which were well ahead of their time. In terms of grandeur these dolls are not the equal of French specimens of the same age, but their originality wins for them a high ranking — and high prices, in most cases.

	Current Price Range		Prior Year Average
☐ **Baby Doll,** *brown eyes, brown wig, 19″*	300.00	350.00	340.00
☐ **Baby Doll,** *brown eyes, marked 300-20, 14″* .	200.00	250.00	220.00
☐ **Baby Stuart,** *composition ball jointed body, intaglio eyes, closed pouty mouth, molded bonnet with pink rosebuds painted on, 12″* .	900.00	1200.00	1050.00
☐ **Bisque,** *ball jointed body, set brown eyes, silver blonde human hair, open mouth, maroon dress with flowered pattern, lace trim, yellow straw hat, 17″*	150.00	200.00	172.00
☐ **Bisque,** *brown sleep eyes, brown mohair wig, open mouth, white dotted Swiss dress, white bonnet, pink shoes, 23″*	450.00	550.00	485.00
☐ **Bisque,** *composition body, molded and painted hair, painted eyes, small, thin brows, narrow pug nose, closed mouth, medium dark lips, very prominent ears, arms bent outward at the elbows, hands molded in a grasping attitude, designed to represent a boy of about 4 or 5 years of age, marked Heubach within a square, and with the numbers 10, 02/3 and the place of manufacture Germany, the numbers 02/3 refer to the mold or model number; the 10 may indicate the year 1910. In any event this doll was made no earlier than 1892 and almost certainly at least a decade thereafter, 13″*	280.00	340.00	275.00
☐ **Bisque,** *five piece body, brown paperweight eyes, wheat brown hair, 10″*	125.00	175.00	140.00
☐ **Bisque,** *jointed composition body, blue stationary eyes, blonde wig, white dress, 24″* ..	325.00	375.00	340.00
☐ **Bisque,** *jointed composition body, brown eyes, lashes, brown wig, pink cotton dress and hat, 24″*	300.00	375.00	340.00
☐ **Bisque,** *jointed composition body, brown velvet jacket, brown checkered dress, 23½″*	325.00	375.00	340.00
☐ **Bisque,** *moveable arms and legs, painted blue eyes, molded blonde hair with blue ribbon, closed mouth, low-waisted white cotton dress with lace flounce, aqua satin sash tied in bow at back, 7″*	90.00	100.00	91.00
☐ **Bisque,** *painted body, brown eyes, blonde wig, blue striped dress, 23″*	300.00	350.00	330.00
☐ **Bisque,** *socket head, papier mache body, papier mache arms and legs, fixed eyes, large, roundish, dark painted lashes on the upper and lower lids, longer on the lower,*			

	Current Price Range		Prior Year Average
closed mouth, thin lips, dark red, narrow nose, roundish jaw, puffy cheeks, prominent ears, representing a girl of about 3 or 4 years of age, marked with the mold number 3/0, printed vertically with the 3 atop the 0, and separated by a horizontal slash between them, date of manufacture unknown, believed to have been made a few years before World War I, 8″	800.00	950.00	750.00
Note: This classifies as a "character" face, even though it is basically the traditional infant doll face with just a few changes. The most recognized features of this doll are a thin upper lip and smiling mouth.			
☐ **Bisque,** *socket head, fixed eyes, large, bulging, dark, painted lashes, longer on the lower lids than on the upper, narrow brows, closed mouth with dark red lips, not smiling, narrow nose, not upturned, puffy cheeks, roundish jaw, conventional ears, representing a child of about 2 years of age, sometimes dressed as a boy, sometimes as a girl, marked Heubach within a square and also with the mold number 2/0, date of manufacture unknown, but probably made before 1900, 9½″*	390.00	480.00	375.00
☐ **Bisque head,** *jointed composition body, original curly brown mohair wig, brown sleep eyes, open mouth, smiling, two upper teeth, antique dress, M#302.15*	500.00	600.00	450.00
☐ **Bisque head,** *kid leather body, wig, brown sleep eyes, two piece suit, marked 275, 18″*	325.00	350.00	330.00
☐ **Boy,** *bisque hands, kid body, intaglio eyes, molded hair, close mouth, 19″*	675.00	725.00	690.00
☐ **Boy,** *bisque head, cloth body with celluloid hands, blue intaglio eyes, molded painted hair, closed pouty mouth, original clothes, 10½″*	460.00	500.00	440.00
☐ **Boy,** *character, bisque head, composition body, molded hair, blue intaglio eyes, closed mouth, original suit, 16″*	600.00	850.00	650.00
☐ **Character Baby,** *bisque head, composition ball jointed body, brown intaglio eyes, white cotton bassinette set with shoes and bonnet, 14½″*	250.00	300.00	275.00
☐ **Character Baby,** *blonde human hair wig, blue sleep eyes, open mouth, four upper teeth, knit dress, leggings, cap, 14″*	450.00	550.00	450.00
☐ **Character Baby,** *composition head and body, brown curly wig, blue sleep eyes, bride doll dress, marked #8413, 6″*	400.00	450.00	415.00

	Current Price Range		Prior Year Average
☐ **Character Boy,** *bisque head, ball jointed composition body, painted hair, blue intaglio eyes, navy blue suit, stockings and tie shoes, 23½″*	450.00	500.00	475.00
☐ **Character Girl,** *bisque shoulder head on kid body, bisque hands, cloth lower legs, gussets at knee, unusual molded hair drawn into a top knot, large molded curl on center of forehead, blue intaglio eyes, closed mouth, pouty expression, powder blue lace trimmed silk dress, marks: 2/0 D Heubach (in square) Germany 9042, 12″*	425.00	475.00	400.00
☐ **Character Girl,** *jointed body, blonde wig, blue sleep eyes, blue cotton dress and hat, marked 8192, 16″*	475.00	500.00	485.00
☐ **Child Character,** *bisque head, jointed composition body, blue intaglio eyes, molded hair with blue band, open-closed mouth, original white lawn dress with lace insets, 11″*	600.00	800.00	675.00
☐ **Child Character,** *bisque head, wood and composition body, molded hair, blue intaglio eyes, open mouth, lovely lace dress, 11″*	550.00	750.00	550.00
☐ **Christmas Children,** *child with sled, bisque face, cloth and wire bodies, 2½″*	100.00	150.00	120.00
☐ **Composition,** *head, ball jointed body, mohair wig, brown sleep eyes, green dress, 19″*	350.00	375.00	360.00
☐ **Composition,** *head and arms, cloth body, blonde human hair wig, brown sleep eyes, lacy hat and dress, 11″*	325.00	375.00	335.00
☐ **Composition,** *head and arms, cloth body, brown wig, brown sleep eyes, crocheted hat, lace dress, 10″*	300.00	350.00	325.00
☐ **Composition,** *head and body, five piece body, blonde ringlet curl wig, peasant dress, marked 250, 6″*	175.00	200.00	180.00
☐ **Girl,** *composition ball jointed body, blue glass eyes, closed pouty mouth, dark blonde hair, mold number 7246, 11″*	960.00	1160.00	980.00
☐ **Girl,** *jointed composition body, blue eyes, light brown hair, white lawn dress, pink bonnet, 21″*	325.00	375.00	340.00
☐ **Girl,** *jointed composition body, blue eyes, red wig, checkered dress, 14″*	150.00	210.00	175.00
☐ **Piano Baby,** *crouching, all bisque, signed, 6″*	400.00	500.00	450.00
☐ **Piano Doll,** *bisque seated toddler, molded hair and clothes, designed to sit on the piano top, 12″*	400.00	450.00	425.00

	Current Price Range		Prior Year Average
☐ **Polo Player,** *composition body and head, blond mohair wig, brown sleep eyes, red and white uniform, 16″*	400.00	425.00	410.00
☐ **Sailor Boy,** *bisque head, ball jointed composition body, molded blonde hair, blue intaglio eyes, closed mouth, navy suit and cap, marked No.6-6894, 19″*	750.00	800.00	775.00
☐ **Shoulder Head,** *blue eyes, black wig, 14½″*	125.00	175.00	140.00
☐ **Toddler,** *five-piece body, blue sleep eyes, brown human hair wig, open mouth, teeth, 14½″*	465.00	510.00	480.00
☐ **Toddler,** *jointed body, molded hair, open/closed mouth with laughing expression, molded teeth, 16″*	1000.00	1500.00	1220.00

GEBRÜDER KNOCH

☐ **Boy,** *character, bisque head, dome shaped with solid brush strokes, kid body with bisque forearms, intaglio eyes follow open-closed mouth, two teeth, small nose, old white shirt and knickers, incised symbol 143 plus "Made in Germany Gesch. 216 Gesch. 14/0, 13″*	260.00	290.00	270.00
☐ **Character Doll,** *baby, bisque head, cloth body, composition arms and legs, intaglio blue eyes, open/closed mouth, two lower teeth, painted blonde hair, long white baby dress, 10″*	475.00	525.00	495.00
☐ **Infant,** *bisque, wig, grey glass eyes, commercially dressed in 12″ sheer cotton lace paneled and trimmed dress with layers of matching slips, chemise, and panties, original accessories, bottle holder etc., Gebrüder Knoch incised, 8½″*	150.00	160.00	145.00

GEBRÜDER KRAUSS

☐ **Bisque,** *ball-jointed body, blue sleep eyes, black wig with long curls, red satin dress, 16½″*	165.00	200.00	180.00
☐ **Bisque,** *set blue eyes, feathered brows, pink dress with rose pattern, mold number 133-305, 26″*	425.00	475.00	440.00

	Current Price Range		Prior Year Average
☐ **Bisque,** *head, ball jointed composition body, human hair wig, brown sleep eyes, open mouth, pink and white dress, marked 165, 21″*	475.00	525.00	500.00
☐ **Bisque,** *socket head on fully jointed composition body, blue sleep eyes with real upper lashes, original blonde mohair wig, open mouth with four porcelain teeth, light blue sailor type dress with wide collar and lace trim, marks: 305 Gbr 165 K, 9 Germany, 26″*	275.00	350.00	300.00

GEM

☐ **Chubby Kid,** *composition, molded and painted features, molded and painted hair, unmarked, made in 1922, 12″*	70.00	90.00	65.00

GEM TOY COMPANY

☐ **Girl,** *all composition, brown glued on wool wig, large painted side glancing eyes, looks like Buddy Lee except it is girl in pigtails, blue dotted dress, matching bonnet, lace trim, made in 1910 for Sears, 13″*	65.00	80.00	65.00

GENERAL MILLS FUN GROUP

☐ **Blythe,** *plastic/vinyl, rooted hair, blonde, large sad eyes which shift from side to side and change color when pullcord is pulled, wearing a bright print dress, marked Blythe TM, Kenner Products, 1972, also marked General Mills Fun Group (the Kenner Company was a subsidiary of General Mills), 12″*	7.00	9.00	7.00

GEORGENE

☐ **Little Lulu,** *cloth, unmarked, sold originally with a tag reading Georgene Novelties Inc., Copyright 1944, 15½″*	58.00	70.00	55.00

Note: Little Lulu was a comic strip character created by Marjorie Buell.

GERA

	Current Price Range		Prior Year Average
☐ **China,** *shoulder head, cloth body, wooden arms and legs, molded hair, painted facial features, pale skin coloring, represents an adult woman in "high fashion," bearing the scrolled G mark of the Gera factory, 17″* . . .	1800.00	2300.00	1750.00
Note: This very rare doll was made around 1780, the time of the American Revolutionary War.			
☐ **China,** *figure of an adolescent boy wearing an elaborate necktie, molded and painted hair, painted facial features, bearing the scrolled G mark of the Gera factory, on combination with a scrolled F, whose significance is not yet determined, 18½″*	1600.00	2000.00	1575.00

GERBER

☐ **Baby,** *says Mama, accessories, 17″*	30.00	35.00	30.00
☐ **Gerber Baby,** *rubber, molded and painted hair, fixed eyes, nursing mouth, bright red lips, wearing a bib marked "Gerber Baby" in script letters, marked on doll Mfg. by The Sun Rubber Co., Barberton, Ohio, made in 1956, 11″*	14.00	18.00	13.00
Note: Used as a promotional item by the Gerber Foods Co., manufacturers of baby foods.			

SUE GIBSON

☐ **Little Red Riding Hood,** *bisque head and arms, cloth body, long red hood, brown set eyes, elaborate costume with cape, carrying basket, 12½″*	450.00	550.00	475.00

A. C. GILBERT

☐ **Man from U.N.C.L.E., The,** *action figures, Napoleon Solo and Illya Kuryakin, c. 1965* . .	60.00	70.00	65.00
☐ **McDare,** *vinyl head, vinyl arms, plastic legs and body, molded, painted hair, painted eyes, represents an adult man wearing*			

	Current Price Range		Prior Year Average
military style jumpsuit, zippered in front up to neck, false pockets, marked K53, K56, 11⅞″	6.00	8.00	6.00
Note: McDare was made in Hong Kong for the A. C. Gilbert Co., much better known for model railroad trains and Erector sets than dolls. The markings appear separately on each arm and represent the mold numbers for those components.			

GIRL'S WORLD

☐ **Emerald The Enchanting Witch,** *plastic/vinyl, violet colored skin, rooted hair, green, fixed eyes, wears black outfit with cone-shaped witch's hat, marked 1971, Girl's World, Pat Pend, made in Japan, 7″*	27.00	35.00	25.00

WILLIAM GOEBEL

The Goebel company, located in Germany, became internationally known in the 20th century for its Hummel figurines (which are not classified as dolls). In the 19th century this was a relatively small ceramics company which made wares of various kinds. It occasionally produced dolls, from the 1800's up to the time it began turning out Hummels in the 1930's, and even (in fact) afterward. The basic difference is that its earlier dolls are not Hummel-oriented; they utilize themes which are not connected with the artwork of Sister Hummel. Nevertheless, many of the Goebel dolls are very distinctive and are instantly recognizable as Goebel, and they even have a slight suggestion of "Hummelness" about them.

☐ **Bisque,** *ball jointed body, blue sleep eyes, reddish-gold human hair, open mouth, blue dress with rose pattern, lace trim, 14″*	225.00	275.00	245.00
☐ **Bisque head,** *ball jointed composition body, mohair wig, blue sleep eyes, open mouth, red hat and dress, 21″*	375.00	400.00	385.00
☐ **Bisque,** *head, papier mâché body, molded and painted hair, sandy red, painted eyes, large looking to the left side of the doll, short painted lashes, tiny eyebrows placed high on the forehead, closed mouth with bright red lips, almost spherical head, fingers not well defined, chunky legs, representing a very young child, marked with the letter W surmounted by the wings of a bee,*			

	Current Price Range		Prior Year Average
which later progressed into Goebel's "full bee" trademark, also marked with the mold number 12/0, date of manufacture unknown, probably first quarter of the 20th century, 6½"	125.00	145.00	120.00
☐ **Buster Brown,** *porcelain head, human hair wig, blue sleep eyes, blue satin outfit, 18"*	500.00	600.00	525.00
☐ **Chimney Sweep,** *boy, based on the work by M.I. Hummel, soft vinyl, authentic German outfit, long black coat and pants, black brimmed hat, carries cleaning tool and undersized ladder, 11"*	55.00	65.00	55.00
☐ **For Father,** *boy based on the work of M.I. Hummel, soft vinyl, authentic German outfit, blonde molded hair, dark brown shorts with straps, white shirt, red kerchief at neck, green Tyrolean hat, holds oversized foaming mug and vegetables, 11"*	55.00	65.00	55.00
☐ **Fratz,** *Redhead Dolls, soft vinyl, bright red hair, green eyes, freckles, red top with white polka dots, white baby pants, marked 1998, 9"*	45.00	55.00	45.00
☐ **Girl,** *bisque, brown dynel wig, brown sleep eyes, open mouth with teeth, green taffeta suit, black braid, flowery straw hat, 11"*	175.00	225.00	185.00
☐ **Girl,** *rubber molded brown hair in pigtails with red bows on ends, looks like goose girl, dress has red skirt, brown top, white sleeves, full bee mark on body, 16"*	215.00	235.00	220.00
☐ **Goose Girl,** *based on the work of M.I. Hummel, soft vinyl, authentic German outfit, blonde molded hair, mottled black and purple dress with white sleeves, mottled yellow apron, red kerchief around head, holds flowers, 11"*	55.00	65.00	55.00
☐ **Gretl,** *girl based on the work of M.I. Hummel, soft vinyl, authentic German outfit, blonde molded hair, mottled black and lavender dress with white sleeves, mottled yellow apron, carries small basket, 11"*	55.00	65.00	55.00
☐ **Hansel,** *boy based on the work of M.I. Hummel, soft vinyl, authentic German outfit, blonde molded hair, black shorts with straps, white shirt, black plaid jacket, red kerchief, black Tyrolean hat, 11"*	55.00	65.00	55.00
☐ **Hummel,** *rubber, jointed body, painted hair and facial features, leyderhosen, kerchief, jacket, designed by M.I. Hummel, 12"*	120.00	130.00	120.00
☐ **Lost Stocking,** *boy based on the work of M.I. Hummel, soft vinyl, authentic German out-*			

	Current Price Range		Prior Year Average
fit, blonde molded hair, mottled green overalls with cross straps, white shirt, black jacket, red kerchief at neck, Tyrolean hat, carries umbrella, 11″	55.00	65.00	55.00
☐ **Merry Wanderer,** *boy based on the work of M.I. Hummel, soft vinyl, authentic German outfit, black pants, mottled brown shirt, mottled green jacket, black brimmed*	55.00	65.00	55.00
☐ **On Secret Path,** *boy based on the work of M.I. Hummel, soft vinyl, authentic German outfit, blonde molded hair, white shirt, blue shorts with straps, red with black jacket, yellow plaid hat, carries walking stick, candles, and small bundle of sticks, 11″*	55.00	65.00	55.00
☐ **Raggedy Muffin,** *Redhead Dolls, soft vinyl, bright red hair, green eyes, freckles, green and white checkered dress, red pantaloons, red hankie pinned on front, marked 1991, 11″*	50.00	60.00	50.00
☐ **School Boy,** *boy based on the work of M.I. Hummel, soft vinyl, authentic German outfit, mottled green shorts with straps, white shirt, red kerchief at neck, bluish-gray Tyrolean hat, wears brown book bag on back, 11″*	55.00	65.00	55.00
☐ **School Girl,** *based on the work of M.I. Hummel, soft vinyl, authentic German outfit, mottled yellow dress with red bodice and white sleeves, carries book bag on her back, 11″*	55.00	65.00	55.00
☐ **Shabby O'Hair,** *Redhead Dolls, soft vinyl, bright red hair, green eyes, freckles, green overalls, checkered shirt, marked 1992, 11″*	50.00	60.00	50.00
☐ **Stitch In Time,** *girl based on the work of M.I. Hummel, soft vinyl, authentic German outfit, blonde molded hair, flowered red dress with black bodice, patterned apron, blue kerchief, knitting and needles, 11″*	55.00	65.00	55.00
☐ **Visiting An Invalid,** *girl based on the work of M.I. Hummel, soft vinyl, authentic German outfit, blonde molded hair, blue flowered apron over black dress with white sleeves, red kerchief, carries basket, flowers, and umbrella, 11″*	55.00	65.00	55.00
☐ **Weary Wanderer,** *girl based on the work of M.I. Hummel, soft vinyl, authentic German outfit, blonde molded hair, mottled green skirt, mottled red top with white sleeves, kerchief, mottled yellow apron, carries basket and polka dot knapsack, 11″*	55.00	65.00	55.00

GOODYEAR RUBBER COMPANY

	Current Price Range		Prior Year Average
☐ **Goodyear Baby,** *composition soft body, painted features, c. 1930, 13"*	75.00	85.00	78.00
☐ **Rubber Shoulder Head,** *cloth body, molded head with sausage curls, painted facial features and black hair, lovely clothes, mint, 13"*	750.00	1000.00	200.00

GORHAM

☐ **Alexandria,** *bisque, blonde, light orange dress, green velvet coat, music box, c. 1983, 19"*	250.00	300.00	260.00
☐ **Amy,** *lacy blue satin, music box, c. 1983*	200.00	250.00	220.00
☐ **Baby Doll,** *blue dress, music box, c. 1983*	125.00	175.00	130.00
☐ **Baby Doll,** *light orange dress, music box, c. 1983*	150.00	200.00	156.00
☐ **Baby Doll,** *white lace, ribbon trim, music box, c. 1983*	200.00	300.00	210.00
☐ **Benjamin and Ellice,** *toddler twins, green, white outfits, music box, c. 1983*	175.00	225.00	179.00
☐ **Beth,** *lacy yellow dress, music box, Little Women series, c. 1983*	250.00	275.00	260.00
☐ **Christina,** *music box, c. 1983, 16"*	200.00	250.00	210.00
☐ **Christopher,** *bisque, velvet outfit, music box, c. 1983, 19"*	250.00	300.00	260.00
☐ **Jeremy,** *tweed outfit, music box, c. 1983, 23"*	250.00	350.00	260.00
☐ **Jillian,** *bisque, white lacy dress, music box, c. 1983, 16"*	200.00	250.00	210.00
☐ **Jo,** *lacy blue dress, music box, Little Women series, c. 1983*	250.00	275.00	256.00
☐ **Melanie,** *bisque, white satin dress, music box, c. 1983, 23"*	250.00	350.00	260.00
☐ **Rosamond,** *bisque, lace outfit, music box, c. 1983, 19"*	225.00	300.00	230.00

GOTZ PUPPE

☐ **Gret,** *vinyl, sleep eyes, brown, marked Gotz Puppe, "Gotz Dolls," made in Germany, 1968, 16"*	15.00	19.00	14.00

GRANT'S

	Current Price Range		Prior Year Average
☐ **Bucky Bradford,** *vinyl, squeeze toy, molded and painted features, molded and painted clothing, holds sign reading "It's Yum Yum Time," stands on platform base which reads "Bucky Bradford," date of manufacture unknown, 8½"*	5.00	7.00	4.00
Note: Bucky Bradford was a symbol of the Grant restaurant chain.			
☐ **Dress Me,** *plastic/vinyl, blonde hair attached by adhesive, painted eyes, marked 1963, Grant Plastics Co., 11½"*	6.00	8.00	6.00

GREINER

	Current Price Range		Prior Year Average
☐ **Papier Mâché,** *head, cloth body with leather arms, dark glass arms, original black and brown striped dress, original leather shoes, c. 1927, 21"*	800.00	950.00	875.00
☐ **Papier Mâché,** *shoulder head, cloth body, hair molded in sausage curls, painted blonde, painted blue eyes, brown plaid taffeta dress, red leather boots and gloves*	550.00	750.00	525.00
☐ **Papier Mâché,** *shoulder head, cloth body, leather arms, blonde molded elaborate curls over ears, painted blue eyes and facial features, original black wool dress, mark: "Greiner's Label' Patent Doll Heads No.7 Pat. Mar30'58, Ext. '72", 24"*	350.00	500.00	350.00
☐ **Papier Mâché,** *shoulder head, cloth body, leather arms, molded painted head, facial features, black curly center-parted hair with ears showing, handmade clothes, mark: label on back: "Greiner's Improved Patent Heads Pat. March 30th '58"*	800.00	1000.00	800.00
☐ **Papier Mâché,** *shoulder head, cloth body, molded loose curls pulled behind ears, painted black, painted facial features, calico dress with apron, 18"*	500.00	750.00	525.00
☐ **Papier Mâché,** *shoulder head, cloth body, kid arms, blue painted eyes, black painted curly hair parted in middle and pulled behind ears, calico day dress, 30"*	750.00	850.00	725.00
☐ **Papier Mâché,** *shoulder head with molded black hair, center part, pulled behind ears in row of sausage curls, painted blue eyes with painted upper lashes, cloth body,*			

	Current Price Range		Prior Year Average
jointed at arms, legs and knees, new leather arms, with individually stitched thumbs and fingers, printed cream colored dress with ruffled hem, original black leather shoes with ties, marks: original paper label on back reads "Greiner's Improved Patent Head, Pat. March 30th, '58", 33"	450.00	550.00	450.00

GUND

☐ **Clown,** *vinyl mask face, rag body, stuffed, red hair, molded and painted features, marked Gund, made in 1964, 18"*	8.00	11.00	7.00
☐ **Jiminy Cricket,** *vinyl and cloth hand puppet, in original box, c. 1960*	7.00	12.00	9.50
☐ **Little Audrey,** *vinyl and cloth puppet in box, c. 1950*	12.00	19.00	14.00

HALCO

☐ **Miss Fluffee,** *plastic shoulder head, cloth body, vinyl arms, latex legs, sleep eyes, hair attached by adhesive, unmarked, The Halco Company was located in Pittsburgh, Pennsylvania, made in 1951, 29"*	33.00	39.00	32.00
☐ **Shirley Temple Look-Alike,** *all composition doll, jointed neck, shoulders, hips, blonde mohair wig styled in ringlets, blue sleep eyes, open mouth, turquoise printed dress, matching bonnet, original Halco box, original paper label pinned to skirt, 16"*	75.00	100.00	75.00

HALLMARK CARDS

☐ **Babe Ruth,** *Famous American series, mint in box, c. 1979*	10.00	15.00	10.00
☐ **Ben Franklin,** *cloth, Bicentennial, mint in box, c. 1976*	15.00	25.00	20.00
☐ **Beanbag Rabbit,** *cotton and flannel, yarn hair, wears striped bowtie, marked Hallmark Cards, Inc., made in Taiwan, date of manufacture unknown, c. 1974, 9"*	3.00	5.00	3.00
☐ **Betsy Clark,** *vinyl head, cloth body, vinyl hands, molded and painted features, marked*			

	Current Price Range		Prior Year Average
1975 Hallmark Cards, Inc., K.T.C., made in Taiwan, 13"	3.00	5.00	3.00
☐ **Doll toy,** *felt and cotton, stuffed, unmarked on doll, originally sold with a tag reading Hallmark Cards Inc., stock #200XDT, date of manufacture unknown, c. 1974, 6"*	3.00	4.00	3.00
☐ **Drummer Boy,** *cloth, Holiday series, with box, 7"*	4.00	8.00	5.00
☐ **Indian Girl,** *cloth, Holiday series, with box, 7"*	4.00	8.00	5.00
☐ **Santa,** *cloth, Holiday series, with box, 7"*	4.00	8.00	5.00
☐ **Snowman,** *terri, stuffed, figure of a snowman wearing a long scarf, unmarked on doll, originally sold with a tag reading Hallmark Cards, Inc., made in Taiwan, 200XDT, 6"*	3.00	5.00	3.00
☐ **Witch,** *cloth, Holiday series, with box, 7"*	4.00	8.00	5.00

HALL SYNDICATE

☐ **Margaret,** *vinyl head, cloth body, molded and painted features, molded and painted hair, marked 1968 Hall Syndicate, Inc., 15"*	22.00	28.00	21.00

HEINRICH HANDWERCK

German firm, whose name translated to English would be "Heinrich's Handcrafts." It was founded in the 1870's in Thuringia, then a part of the Prussian Empire. Heinrich Handwerck was not only a manufacturer of doll heads, but an assembling factory which made dolls with the heads of other firms. For many years they were one of the principal customers of Simon and Halbig, a maker of bisque heads, and therefore many of the Heinrich Handwerck dolls are found with "S & H" heads. By the same token, dolls of other companies will be found with Heinrich Handwerck heads, but this does not occur as often. Though its dolls are highly collectible, and nicely made, it is obvious that the company strove usually for heavy output rather than meticulous workmanship. They were very much involved in the "import war" of the 1890's, in which a number of German doll makers poured dolls by the multi thousands into the U.S., hoping to win over the American market. (No single company succeeded in winning over the American market!) For the beginning collector and especially the lover of bisque who does not have limitless funds available, dolls of Heinrich Handwerck are an attractive collecting specialty. Most of them can be had for half or third the price of French bisque dolls of the same era. Be forewarned, however, that some expensive specimens DO exist.

Bisque Head,
composition body,
c. 1905, 10″
$1100.00-$1200.00

Bisque Head,
c. 1900, 30″
$1200.00-$1300.00

	Current Price Range		Prior Year Average
☐ **Bébé Elite,** *bisque head, blonde vinyl wig, sleep eyes, blue and white floral print, c. 1860, 10½″*	25.00	30.00	27.50
☐ **Bébé Elite,** *bisque head, body, mohair wig, sleep eyes, white christening gown, c. 1894, 18″*	460.00	500.00	475.00
☐ **Bisque,** *ball-jointed body, brown sleep eyes, open mouth with separate tongue, pantaloons and a petticoats, hand embroidered cross-stitched linen dress, original openwork socks and leather shoes, incised 'Handwerck 109/11½ Germany 2½', 21″*	415.00	455.00	425.00
☐ **Bisque,** *ball jointed body, deep brown threaded sleep eyes, molded brush-stroke brows, red nostril accents, open mouth, four teeth, antique white linen dress with pleated shoulders, jabot, belt and button down cuffs embroidered in lace, feather stitched hemline, incised 109-15½, 31″*	900.00	1000.00	925.00
☐ **Bisque,** *blonde wig, blue sleep eyes, pierced ears, antique clothes, #69 12 X., 23″*	325.00	365.00	330.00
☐ **Bisque,** *brown eyes, long brown curls, open mouth, pierced ears, pink low waisted dress, with red print and lace trim, 27″*	450.00	550.00	495.00
☐ **Bisque,** *head with bisque shoulder plate, fixed eyes, large and very dark, very short painted lashes, open mouth showing three teeth, medium-dark lips, round jaw, dark arched eyebrows, representing a boy of about 4 or 5 years of age, might occasionally be found dressed as a girl, marked HcH and with the mold number 12/0, date of manufacture unknown, probably c. 1900, 14″*	175.00	220.00	165.00
☐ **Bisque,** *head with bisque shoulder plate, kidskin body, fixed eyes, large, dark, almond shaped, short painted lashes above and below, upturned pug nose, open mouth with a row of upper teeth showing, dimpled chin, dark arched eyebrows, roundish jaw, marked HcH and bearing the mold number 2, date of manufacture unknown, but it would probably be safe to place this doll at c. 1890, 22½″*	285.00	340.00	265.00
☐ **Bisque,** *head with bisque shoulder plate, fixed eyes, large, dark, not of especially good quality, partially open mouth, flattish nose, thick dark eyebrows, puffy cheeks, very prominent ears turning outward from the head, representing a boy of perhaps 5 or*			

	Current Price Range		Prior Year Average
6 years of age, marked with a four-petaled flower and the letters HcH, also marked Germany, date of manufacture unknown, but the presence of the word "Germany" in the marking places this doll no earlier than 1892, it was probably made about 10 years thereafter, 19½"	240.00	280.00	220.00
☐ **Bisque,** *head with bisque shoulder plate, fixed eyes, large, very short, pale painted lashes, partially open mouth, medium dark lips, thick dark eyebrows, puffy cheeks, roundish jaw, protruding ears, representing a child of 2 or 3 years of age, sometimes dressed as a boy, sometimes as a girl, marked with a horseshoe contained the words Made in Germany, also with the company mark HcH and the mold number 2, date of manufacture unknown but the words "Made in Germany" are a positive indication of post-1892 dating, 22½"*	215.00	245.00	200.00
☐ **Bisque,** *head with bisque shoulder plate, fixed eyes, medium large, roundish, short painted lashes above and below, open mouth with teeth showing, pastel lips, thick nose, rather prominent double chin with dimple, dark arched eyebrows, inquisitive facial expression, representing a girl of 4 or 5 years of age, marked HcH, Made in Germany, and with the mold number 9, date of manufacture unknown, but definitely after 1892 and almost certainly, on grounds of style, somewhat after 1900, probably c. 1905, 26"*	290.00	335.00	275.00
☐ **Bisque,** *head with bisque shoulder plate, fixed eyes, large, almond shaped, short painted lashes on top of eye socket, much longer painted lashes beneath, open mouth showing teeth, wide nose, thick prominent eyebrows, roundish jaw, prominent ears, marked with the letters HcH and the mold number 5/0, additionally marked with a device which resembles an airplane propeller or a flower with two petals, date of manufacture unknown, but the absence of the word "Germany" from the marking would suggest a dating of pre-1892, 17"*	230.00	280.00	210.00
☐ **Bisque,** *head with bisque shoulder plate, fixed eyes, medium large, partially open mouth showing teeth, long face with prominent cheeks and jaw, moderately arched eyebrows, representing a girl of 4 or 5 years*			

	Current Price Range		Prior Year Average
of age, marked with a four-petaled flower and the letters HcH, and also with the mold number 9/0, date of manufacture unknown, but the absence of the word "Germany" from the marking would suggest a dating of pre-1892, 14¾"	160.00	190.00	150.00
☐ **Bisque,** *jointed composition body, blue eyes, lace dress and hat, 27"*	325.00	375.00	340.00
☐ **Bisque,** *jointed composition body, blue stationary eyes, blonde wig, molded ear, mold number 99, 23"*	300.00	375.00	340.00
☐ **Bisque,** *jointed composition body, brown eyes, blonde wig, blue dress and hair ribbons, mold number 89, 25"*	400.00	450.00	430.00
☐ **Bisque,** *jointed composition body, brown eyes, brown wig, white organdy dress, blue bonnet, 28"*	450.00	500.00	465.00
☐ **Bisque,** *socket head, fixed eyes, almost circular, but not very large, applied lashes, medium-length eyebrows, open mouth showing four teeth, pastel lips, flattish nose, rounded jaw, facial expression of mild surprise, marked Germany, Heinrich Handwerck, Simon & Halbig, date of manufacture unknown, after 1892, probably around the turn of the century, this doll was assembled by Heinrich Handwerck using a head made by Simon & Halbig, the marking "Germany" means that a portion of the output, or all of it, was intended for export into America, 17½"*	220.00	265.00	205.00
☐ **Bisque,** *body, jointed composition body, blue eyes, brown wig, pink and white dress and hat, 31"*	625.00	675.00	640.00
☐ **Bisque,** *ball jointed body, brown sleep eyes, human hair wig, 22"*	495.00	550.00	450.00
☐ **Bisque,** *head, ball jointed composition body, blue sleep eyes, human hair wig, ecru print dress with hat, marked No.28 F/0/2, 21"*	650.00	700.00	675.00
☐ **Bisque,** *head, composition ball jointed body, human hair wig, brown sleep eyes with lashes, pierced ears, brocade dress, marked 69/12X, 24"*	675.00	725.00	695.00
☐ **Bisque,** *head, ball jointed body, brown curly wig, brown sleep eyes, open mouth, pierced ears, dress and hat, marked 119, 27"*	600.00	625.00	610.00
☐ **Bisque,** *head, ball jointed body, human hair wig, blue sleep eyes, pierced ears, antique white clothes, marked 119, 26"*	575.00	600.00	585.00

	Current Price Range		Prior Year Average
☐ **Bisque,** *head, ball jointed composition body, brown human hair wig, brown paperweight sleep eyes, open mouth, 33"*	950.00	1100.00	1000.00
☐ **Bisque,** *head, blue eyes, red human hair wig, original dress, 17"*	450.00	550.00	475.00
☐ **Bisque,** *head, composition body, blue sleep eyes, human hair wig, early, 24"*	475.00	575.00	475.00
☐ **Bisque,** *head, jointed composition body, blue sleep eyes, brown human hair wig, open mouth, lovely old clothes, 17"*	550.00	650.00	575.00
☐ **Bisque,** *head, cloth body, blonde mohair wig, brown sleep eyes, white gown, marked 109, 17"*	400.00	450.00	425.00
☐ **Bisque,** *head, jointed body, strawberry blond human hair wig, blue sleep eyes, molded brows, antique rose and white dress, marked Heinrich Handwerk #109, 1905, 38"*	1100.00	1200.00	1105.00
☐ **Bisque,** *socket head, fully jointed composition body, original curly blonde mohair wig, blue set eyes, open mouth with four teeth, pierced ears, white batiste dress with large puff sleeves, pink satin ribbon sash, marks: Germany Heinrich Handwerck, Simon & Halbig', 25"*	575.00	675.00	550.00
☐ **Bisque,** *socket head, jointed composition body, brown set eyes, lovely long brown human hair wig, open mouth with four porcelain teeth, pierced ears, marks: 109 Handwerck G 6½, 31"*	375.00	450.00	375.00
☐ **Bisque,** *socket head, fully jointed composition body, brown sleep eyes, original blonde mohair wig, pierced ears, open mouth with four teeth, insertion lace, matching lace petticoat, marks: Germany Heinrich Handwerck, Simon & Halbig 7, 32"*	700.00	900.00	700.00
☐ **Bisque,** *socket head, fully jointed composition body, brown sleep eyes, real upper lashes, original brown human hair wig, open mouth with four porcelain teeth, pierced ears, royal blue velveteen dress trimmed with lace, matching bonnet, marks: 109, 15DEP Germany, Handwerck, 30"*	600.00	700.00	600.00
☐ **Bisque,** *socket head, fully jointed composition body, original platinum blonde wig, brown sleep eyes, pierced ears, open mouth with four teeth, white dress with lace trimmed bodice, marks: 69 12x, Germany Handwerck 4, 24"*	550.00	650.00	550.00

	Current Price Range		Prior Year Average
☐ **Bisque,** *socket head, jointed composition body, brown sleep eyes, open mouth with four porcelain teeth, brown human hair wig styled in ringlets, pierced ears, molded eyebrows, printed pink school girl dress, marks: 119-13, Handwerck, Simon & Halbig' red stamp on body - Handwerck, 28"*	500.00	575.00	450.00
☐ **Bisque,** *socket head, fully jointed composition body, blue sleep eyes, open mouth with four porcelain teeth, pierced ears, auburn wig, lovely cream cotton dress with lace ruffles, satin sash, shoes and socks, 31"*	450.00	550.00	450.00
☐ **Child,** *bisque head, ball jointed composition body, blue glass eyes, blonde mohair wig, open mouth, 30"*	450.00	550.00	450.00
☐ **Child,** *bisque head, ball jointed composition body, brown set eyes, brown human hair wig, pierced ears, lovely clothes, mold #109, 31"*	900.00	1000.00	950.00
☐ **Child,** *bisque head, composition ball jointed body, blonde wig with bangs, blue pinafore with ribbon trim, 23"*	350.00	400.00	375.00
☐ **Child,** *bisque head, ball jointed composition body, blonde human hair wig with curly bangs, brown sleep eyes, pierced ears, brown velvet outer suit, 27"*	350.00	400.00	375.00
☐ **Child,** *bisque head, ball jointed composition body, long wavy red hair, brown sleep eyes, green velvet dress with fur trim, 28½"*	500.00	550.00	525.00
☐ **Simon Halbig,** *wood, jointed, sleep eyes, wig*	210.00	230.00	200.00

MAX HANDWERCK

German firm, whose name translated to English would be "Max's Handcrafts." It was located in Thuringia, a major center for doll manufacture. Max Handwerck went into business around the turn of the century, when the German doll trade was booming (thanks mainly to the enormous sales made to U.S. importers). Most of the dolls of this firm to be found on the antiques market date to the early 1900's.

☐ **Bisque,** *jointed composition body, blue eyes, blonde wig, white dress with red trim, 24"*	400.00	450.00	440.00
☐ **Bisque,** *jointed composition body, blue stationary eyes, brown wig, pink dress, lacy hat, 24"*	350.00	400.00	360.00

Bebe Elite,
bisque and composition,
c. 1894, 15″
$450.00-$500.00

	Current Price Range		Prior Year Average
☐ **Bisque,** *brown eyes, brown hair, white lawn dress, 24″*	450.00	500.00	460.00
☐ **Bisque,** *socket head, sleep eyes (unusual for the dolls of this firm), large dark eyes, traces of painted lashes, arched brows (dark), partially open mouth showing teeth, dark lips, puffy cheeks, thick nose with slight upturning, roundish jaw, dimpled chin, representing a girl of 5 or 6 years of age, marked Max Handwerck, Germany in incised lettering, also marked with the mold number 4½, date of manufacture unknown, presumably made just prior to World War I or possibly even following the war, 29″*	330.00	390.00	280.00

Note: The reasons for assigning a late date to this doll are its sleep eyes and large

	Current Price Range		Prior Year Average
physical size, neither of which were characteristic of Max Handwerck in the firm's early years.			
☐ **Bisque,** *socket head, fixed eyes (large, dark, slightly Oriental in shape), no eyelashes, narrow curving brows, open mouth with medium-dark lips, upturned pug nose (rather wide), double chin, representing a girl of about 3 or 4 years of age, marked with the mold number 1/0, set within a letter H, the sides of which curve outward, date of manufacture unknown, probably the first decade of the 20th century, 20¼″*	140.00	165.00	135.00
☐ **Bisque,** *socket head, fixed eyes (medium size, roundish, dark, well designed), very short painted lashes, lower eyelids heavily outlined, arched brows, open mouth showing a row of upper teeth, medium dark lips, puffy cheeks, double chin, broad nose with slight upturning, marked H/2 within a letter H, the sides of which curve outward, date of manufacture unknown, probably the first decade of the 20th century, 22¾″*	230.00	270.00	220.00
☐ **Bisque,** *socket head, fixed eyes (large, very dark, roundish), no lashes, no eyeliner (unlike some dolls of this firm), arched brows not overly thick, partially open mouth showing several teeth, medium dark lips, roundish jaw, ears not prominent, representing a girl of about 4 or 5 years of age, marked with the mold number 4 in the lower half of a letter H, the sides of which curve outward, date of manufacture unknown, probably the first decade of the 20th century, 24″*	250.00	290.00	235.00

LARRY HARMON

	Current Price Range		Prior Year Average
☐ **Oliver Hardy,** *(finger puppet), vinyl, molded and painted features, marked 1972 Larry Harmon Pictures Corp., 3″*	1.00	1.50	1.00
☐ **Stan Laurel,** *(finger puppet), vinyl, molded and painted features, marked 1972 Larry Harmon Pictures Corp., 3″*	1.00	1.50	1.00

HARMUS

	Current Price Range		Prior Year Average
☐ **Bisque,** *composition ball jointed body, mohair wig, set blue eyes, open mouth, red fashion dress with hat, marked 8, 21″*	700.00	750.00	725.00
☐ **Toddler,** *bisque head, five piece composition body, human hair wig, blue sleep eyes, two teeth in open mouth, pink and white checkered dress with hat, 13″*	670.00	700.00	675.00

AILEEN HARRIS

☐ **Little Women,** *bisque head, molded and painted hair, dressed to represent a character from the novel by Louisa May Alcott, made in 1963, 9″*	110.00	135.00	100.00

HASBRO

☐ **Adam,** *plastic/vinyl, molded, painted hair, painted features, felt clothing, represents an adult man wearing bell-bottom studded trousers, jointed at the waist, made in Hong Kong, 1971, 9″*	7.00	9.00	6.00
☐ **Aimee,** *plastic/vinyl, rooted hair, sleep eyes, long eyelashes, jointed at the waist, represents a young woman with western facial features wearing an Oriental style costume, very long earrings, 17½″*	14.00	18.00	12.00
☐ **Baby Ruth,** *vinyl head, stuffed body, vinyl hands, molded and painted features, blonde hair, rooted, sold originally with a tag reading Baby Ruth 1971, used as a premium by the Curtis Candy Co., 10″*	5.00	7.00	5.00

Note: Baby Ruth candy bars were not named for baseball player Babe Ruth, as many people believe, but for Ruth Cleveland, daughter of President Grover Cleveland. She was born while Cleveland was President and the press referred to her as " baby Ruth."

☐ **Bonnie Breck,** *plastic/vinyl, rooted hair, blond, painted eyes, jointed at the waist, two-piece matching outfit, made in Hong Kong, dated 1972, 9″*	7.00	9.00	6.00

Note: There must have been some tie-in with Breck Shampoo, but the doll itself does not carry any indication of it.

	Current Price Range		Prior Year Average
☐ **Dahlia Darling,** *vinyl head, vinyl arms, legs and body, rooted hair, painted eyes, surrounded by flowers, plastic, a doll-brooch designed to be worn on clothing, 2¼″*	3.00	4.00	3.00
☐ **Daisy Darling,** *vinyl head, vinyl arms, legs and body, rooted hair, painted eyes, surrounded by flowers, plastic, a doll-brooch designed to be worn on clothing, 3″*	3.00	4.00	3.00
☐ **Daphne Darling,** *vinyl head, vinyl arms, legs and body, rooted hair, painted eyes, surrounded by plastic flowers, a doll-brooch designed to be worn on clothing, 2¼″*	3.00	4.00	3.00
☐ **Doll House Mother,** *plastic, brunette hair attached by adhesive, painted eyes, marked Hasbro, made in 1957, 7″*	5.00	7.00	5.00
☐ **Dolly Darling,** *there were numerous variations of this doll in plastic and vinyl, all have rooted hair and painted eyes and are made in Japan, the line was introduced in the mid 1960's, in some instances the doll itself varies; in others the doll is identical but the costume and wig varies, along with the name, at this point the values are all the same, heights are from 4¼″ to 4½″*	3.00	5.00	3.00
☐ **Flying Nun,** *vinyl, brunette hair, rooted, molded and painted features, marked 1967 Hasbro, Hong Kong, 5″*	10.00	13.00	9.00
☐ **G. I. Joe.** *The G. I. Joe series by Hasbro is the second lengthiest in the world of modern dolls, in the number of issues encompassed, next only to Mattel's Barbie. It has not attracted as much hobbyist interest as Barbies, but apparently it is only a matter of time before this occurs.The series was introduced in 1964 at the beginning of U.S. involvement in the Viet Nam War, long before the war became a major political issue. Even in the days of protest marches and sit-ins, G. I. Joe continued to sell. His young purchasers were simply not politically-minded.*			
☐ **G.I. Joe,** *Action Marine, plastic, molded brown hair, brown eyes, painted, marked 7700, G.I. Joe TM Copyright by Hasbro Patent Pending, made in U.S.A., made in 1964, 11½″*	35.00	43.00	31.00
☐ **G.I. Joe,** *Action Marine, plastic, molded brown hair, brown eyes, painted, marked 7500, G.I. Joe, Copyright 1964 by Hasbro, Pat. No. 3,277,602, made in U.S.A., no problem distinguishing this 1967 version from*			

	Current Price Range		Prior Year Average
the previous: the patent is no longer pending, a patent number is shown, 11½″	21.00	25.00	19.00
☐ **G.I. Joe,** *Action Marine, plastic, molded brown hair, brown eyes, painted, marked 7700, G.I. Joe, Copyright 1964 by Hasbro Patent Pending, made in U.S.A., made in 1965, distinguished from the first issue, 1965, by the absence of the letters "TM" in the copyright notice, 11½″*	12.00	16.00	11.00
☐ **G.I. Joe,** *Action Marine, plastic, molded brown hair, brown eyes, painted, marked 7700, G.I. Joe, Copyright 1964 by Hasbro Patent Pending, made in U.S.A., this is the 1966 version, distinguished by removal of the scar which had been on the faces of previous models, 11½″*	11.00	14.00	10.00
☐ **G.I. Joe,** *Action Pilot, plastic, molded blonde hair, brown eyes, painted, marked 7800, G.I. Joe TM Copyright by Hasbro Patent Pending, made in U.S.A., made in 1964, 11½″*	35.00	43.00	31.00
☐ **G.I. Joe,** *Action Pilot, plastic, molded blonde hair, brown eyes, painted, marked 7800, G.I. Joe, Copyright 1964 by Hasbro, Pat. No. 3,277,602, made in U.S.A., no problem distinguishing this 1967 version from the previous: the patent is no longer pending, a patent number is shown, 11½″*	21.00	25.00	18.00
☐ **G.I. Joe,** *Action Pilot, plastic, molded blonde hair, brown eyes, painted, marked 7800, G.I. Joe, Copyright 1964 by Hasbro Patent Pending, made in U.S.A., made in 1965, distinguished from the first issue, 1964, by the absence of the letters "TM" in the copyright notice, 11½″*	12.00	16.00	11.00
☐ **G.I. Joe,** *Action Pilot, plastic, molded blonde hair, brown eyes, painted, marked 7800, G.I. Joe, Copyright 1964 by Hasbro Patent Pending, made in U.S.A., this is the 1966 version, distinguished by removal of the scar which had been on the faces of previous models, 11½″*	11.00	14.00	10.00
☐ **G.I. Joe,** *Action Sailor, plastic, molded brown hair, brown eyes, painted, marked 7600, G.I. Joe TM Copyright by Hasbro Patent Pending, made in U.S.A., made in 1964, 11½″*	37.00	46.00	32.00
☐ **G.I. Joe,** *Action Sailor, plastic, molded brown hair, brown eyes, painted, marked 7600, G.I. Joe, Copyright 1964 by Hasbro, Pat. No.3,277,602, made in U.S.A., no prob-*			

	Current Price Range		Prior Year Average
lem distinguishing this 1967 version from the previous: the patent is no longer pending, a patent number is shown, 11½″	20.00	26.00	18.00
☐ **G.I. Joe,** *Action Sailor, plastic, molded brown hair, brown eyes, painted, marked 7600, G.I. Joe, Copyright 1964 by Hasbro Patent Pending, made in U.S.A., made in 1965, distinguished from the first issue, 1964, by the absence of the letters "TM" in the copyright notice, 11½″*	14.00	18.00	12.00
☐ **G.I. Joe,** *Action Sailor, plastic molded brown hair, brown eyes, painted, marked 7600, G.I. Joe, Copyright 1964 by Hasbro Patent Pending, made in U.S.A., this is the 1966 version, distinguished by removal of the scar which had been on the faces of previous models, 11½″*	12.00	16.00	10.00
☐ **G.I. Joe,** *Action Soldier, plastic, molded black hair, blue eyes, painted, marked 7500, G.I. Joe TM Copyright 1964 by Hasbro Patent Pending, made in U.S.A., made in 1964, 11½″*	40.00	55.00	34.00
☐ **G.I. Joe,** *Action Soldier, plastic, molded black hair, blue eyes, painted, marked 7500, G.I. Joe, Copyright 1964 by Hasbro, Pat. No.3,277,602, made in U.S.A., no problem distinguishing this 1967 version from the previous: the patent is no longer pending, a patent number is shown, 11½″*	24.00	29.00	21.00
☐ **G.I. Joe,** *Action Soldier, plastic, molded black hair, blue eyes, painted, marked 7500, G.I. Joe, Copyright 1964 by Hasbro Patent Pending, made in U.S.A., made in 1965, distinguished from the first issue, 1964, by the absence of the letters "TM" in the copyright notice, 11½″*	18.00	23.00	16.00
☐ **G.I. Joe,** *Action Solder, plastic, molded black hair, blue eyes, painted, marked 7500, G.I. Joe, Copyright 1964 by Hasbro Patent Pending, made in U.S.A., this is the 1966 version, distinguished by removal of the scar which had been on the faces of previous models, 11½″*	16.00	20.00	14.00
☐ **G.I. Joe,** *Action Soldier, black, plastic, molded black hair, brown eyes, painted, marked 7900, G.I. Joe Copyright 1964 by Hasbro Patent Pending, made in U.S.A., made in 1965, the first black G.I. Joe, 11½″*	33.00	39.00	31.00
☐ **G.I. Joe,** *Action Soldier, black, plastic, molded black hair, brown eyes, painted, marked 7900, G.I. Joe, Copyright 1964 by Hasbro, Patent*			

	Current Price Range		Prior Year Average
Pending, made in U.S.A., this is the 1966 version, distinguished by removal of the scar which had been on the faces of previous models, 11½″	26.00	32.00	23.00
☐ **G.I. Joe,** *Action Soldier, black, plastic, molded black hair, brown eyes, painted, marked 7900, G.I. Joe, Copyright 1964 by Hasbro, Pat. No. 3,277,602; made in U.S.A., no problem distinguishing this 1967 version from the previous: the patent is no longer pending, a patent number is shown, 11½″*	18.00	24.00	17.00
☐ **G.I. Joe,** *hard plastic, blonde molded hair, marine dress uniform, c. 1964*	32.00	36.00	32.00
☐ **Goldilocks & The Three Bears,** *vinyl, molded and painted features, blonde hair, rooted, sold with figures of Mama Bear, Papa Bear and Baby Bear, which must be present to command the indicated value, sold in 1967, height of Goldilocks, 3″*	6.00	8.00	5.00
☐ **Leggy Jill,** *plastic/vinyl, rooted hair, painted eyes, represents a young woman with exaggerated Twiggy-type figure, inspired by fashion ads of the late 1960's and early 1970's, dated 1972, 10″*	5.00	7.00	4.00
☐ **Leggy Sue,** *plastic/vinyl, black, rooted hair, painted eyes, represents a young black woman with exaggerated Twiggy-type figure, inspired by fashion ads of the late 1960's and early 1970's, dated 1972, 9½″*	4.00	7.00	4.00
☐ **Lily Darling,** *vinyl head, vinyl arms, legs and body, rooted hair, painted eyes, surrounded by flowers, plastic, a doll-brooch designed to be worn on clothing, 2½″*	3.00	4.00	3.00
☐ **Little Miss No-Name,** *plasti/vinyl, blonde hair, rooted, fixed eyes, wears patched dress, has sad facial expression, marked 1965 Hasbro, probably made in Japan, but not so indicated on doll, 14½″*	23.00	29.00	21.00
☐ **Michelle,** *vinyl, molded and painted features, blonde hair, rooted, represents a member of the vocal group "The Mamas and the Papas," made in 1967, 3″*	14.00	19.00	13.00
☐ **Mother Hubbard,** *vinyl, marked 1967, Hasbro, Hong Kong, 3½″*	4.00	6.00	4.00
☐ **Music,** *plastic/vinyl, rooted hair, painted eyes, closed mouth, wide-eyed expression, representing a young woman wearing boldly printed minidress, tall boots, marked Made in Hong Kong, Hasbro U.S. Pat. Pend., dated 1971, 9″*	10.00	13.00	9.00

	Current Price Range		Prior Year Average
☐ **Poodle-Oodle,** *plastic/vinyl, wig attached by adhesive, painted features, a poodle's head with a human body, marked 1966 Hasbro, Japan, Patent Pending, 9½"*	6.00	8.00	5.00
☐ **Prince Charming,** *vinyl, molded and painted features, rooted hair, depicts the storybook character riding a horse, posable, made in 1967, 3"*	6.00	8.00	5.00
☐ **Rumpelstilskin,** *vinyl, molded and painted features including bulbous nose, rooted hair, cone-shaped hat, representing the storybook character from German folklore, marked Hasbro 1967, 3"*	6.00	8.00	5.00
☐ **Sleeping Beauty,** *vinyl, black hair, rooted, molded and painted features, made in 1967, sold with a model of a four-poster canopied bed, which must be present to command the value indicated, height of doll, 3"*	7.00	10.00	6.00
☐ **Snow White & The Seven Dwarfs,** *8 dolls, vinyl, molded and painted features, rooted hair, most of the dwarfs have beards, made in 1967, Snow White is 3" and the dwarfs are abou 1½", price is for a complete set*	10.00	14.00	8.00
Note: This product had no Disney connections.			
☐ **Soul,** *plastic/vinyl, black, rooted hair, painted eyes, closed mouth, represents a young black woman, came with two sets of clothing and a shoulder bag, 9"*	7.00	9.00	6.00
☐ **Sunday,** *vinyl, molded and painted features, molded and painted hair, partially open mouth, marked 1965 Hasbro, Japan, 4¼"*	5.00	7.00	5.00
☐ **Sweet Cookie,** *plastic/vinyl, rooted hair, very pale platinum blond cut in bangs, wide painted eyes, open mouth, freckles and pug nose, wears print dress and apron, apron carries picture of strawberry and wording "Sweet Cookie," marked Hasbro Inc., Pat. Pend., 1972, made in U.S., 18¼"*	6.00	8.00	5.00
Note: The majority of Hasbro's dolls have not been made in the U.S. but in Hong Kong, even though this is, of course, an American company.			
☐ **That Kid,** *plastic/vinyl, rooted hair, large sleep eyes, short eyelashes, pug nose, freckled face, open mouth with two teeth, talker, activated by pulling slingshot in back pocket, marked Hasbro 1967, 21¼"*	20.00	25.00	18.00
☐ **Violet Darling,** *vinyl head, vinyl arms, legs and body, rooted hair, painted eyes, sur-*			

	Current Price Range		Prior Year Average
rounded by flowers, plastic, a doll-brooch designed to be worn on clothing, 2¼″	3.00	4.00	3.00
☐ **World of Love,** *black, vinyl, molded and rooted hair painted features, black afro, jointed at the waist, marked Hasbro, U.S. Pat. Pend., probably made in Hong Kong or Japan, but not indicated on the doll, made in 1968, 9¼″ ....*	7.00	10.00	6.00

HAZELLE'S

☐ **Dagwood,** *marionette, plastic head, hands and shoes, cloth over wood body, height 14″*	20.00	25.00	22.50

GENE HAZELTON

☐ **Gas Genie,** *vinyl mask face, stuffed plush body, molded and painted features, outstretched hands, marked Gas Genie, Gene Hazelton, made in 1969, 21″ ....*	4.00	6.00	4.00

HEDAYA

☐ **Love Bug,** *vinyl, molded and painted features, painted eyes, oversize head, marked Hedaya & Co., Inc., 1966, Japan, 8″ ....*	4.00	6.00	4.00

HEDWIG

☐ **Composition,** *character doll Elin from Marguerite de Angeli's book ....*	125.00	175.00	145.00

HEICO

☐ **Heico,** *vinyl, jointed neck, platinum blonde rooted hair, representing a topless go-go dancer, marked Heico H, made in Western Germany, made in 1963, 7″ ....*	6.00	8.00	6.00

Note: Definitely not one for the kiddies.

HEUBACH-KÖPPLESDORF

	Current Price Range		Prior Year Average
☐ **Baby,** *bisque head, five piece composition body, straight redheaded wig, set blue eyes, open mouth, layette gown, toddler shoes and bonnet, 25½″*	450.00	500.00	400.00
☐ **Baby,** *character, bisque head, composition bent limb baby body, blue sleep eyes, original blonde wig, old christening gown, #342, 23″*	550.00	750.00	650.00
☐ **Baby Doll,** *unidentified, intaglio eyes, original clothes*	440.00	460.00	420.00
☐ **Bisque,** *bisque hands, kid body, blue eyes, red mohair wig, open mouth, mold number 275, 18″*	225.00	275.00	245.00
☐ **Bisque,** *head, bride, jointed arms and legs, date of manufacture unknown, 14″*	220.00	260.00	210.00

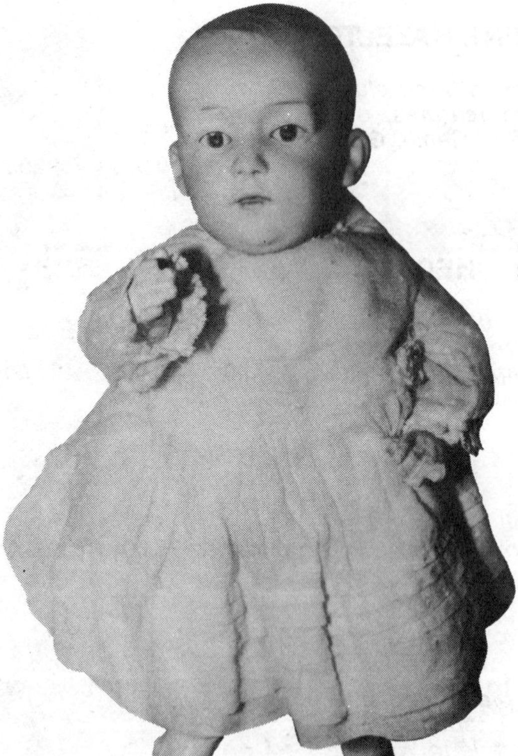

Baby,
original clothing
$440.00-$600.00

	Current Price Range		Prior Year Average
☐ **Bisque,** *head, brown body, brown sleep eyes, grass skirt, marked 399-12½ 0, 10″* . . .	**450.00**	**500.00**	**475.00**
☐ **Bisque,** *head, five-piece composition body, glass eyes, open mouth, blonde wig, original peasant costume, 6½″*	**100.00**	**110.00**	**100.00**
☐ **Bisque,** *head, five-piece composition body, open mouth, nice dress with bonnet, #342, 20″*	**550.00**	**650.00**	**600.00**
☐ **Bisque,** *head with bisque shoulder plate, fitted to a kidskin body, fixed eyes, extremely large and marble-like, and placed close together, long painted lashes on the upper and lower lids, thick arched brows, partially open mouth with teeth visible, medium thick nose, puffy cheeks, round jaw, almost spherical head, representing a girl of 3 or 4 years of age, marked with the number 3095, date of manufacture unknown, on basis of style one would have to imagine that this was among the earlier products of Heubach, dating possibly to 1890, and the absence of "Made in Germany" from the marking lends support to this, 17¾″*	**240.00**	**290.00**	**225.00**
☐ **Bisque,** *head, kidskin body, kidskin upper arms, bisque forearms, fixed, large, dark, almond-shaped eyes, painted lashes, more prominent on the lower lids than on the uppers, narrow arched brows, small open mouth with teeth visible, medium-thick nose, not upturned, prominent ears, round jaw, puffy cheeks, representing a boy of about 4 or 5 years of age, marked Made In Germany within a horseshoe, along with the date 1900 and the mold number 6/0, 14⅞″*	**100.00**	**130.00**	**90.00**
Note: Slashes in mold numbers, such as in this one, usually indicates plans to issue the doll in more than one size. Such plans were seldom put into action unless the doll sold well.			
☐ **Bisque,** *head with bisque shoulder plate, fixed large and bulging eyes almost resembling marbles, very short painted lashes, thin, slightly arched brows, open mouth showing teeth, medium-wide nose, puffy cheeks, almost spherical head, marked Germany, Heubach Köppelsdorf and with the mold identification number 275/18, date of manufacture unknown, but definitely after 1892 and most likely after 1900, 13½″*	**120.00**	**145.00**	**110.00**
Note: One of the standard dolls in the Heubach line, which, to judge from its			

	Current Price Range		Prior Year Average
relative abundance on the market, was kept in production for several years. It probably carried a very low original wholesale price.			
☐ **Bisque,** *head with bisque shoulder plate, set on a kidskin body, fixed, large, dark, almond-shaped eyes, no lashes, arched brows, small open mouth, showing a row of upper teeth, pastel lips, puffy cheeks, almost spherical head, prominent ears, quizzical facial expression, representing a youth of 3 or 4 years of age, sometimes dressed as a boy, sometimes as a girl, marked with a horseshoe and the date 1901-1, 22″ .*	230.00	270.00	215.00
Note: Why is the date given as 1901-1? Possibly this was the first mold to be introduced into the Heubach line that year. Identifying it as 1901-1 would have clearly distinguished it from other #1 molds of earlier years.			
☐ **Bisque,** *head with bisque shoulder plate, fitted on a kidskin body, fixed, bulging, almond-shaped shaped eyes, very short painted lashes, thick arching brows, open mouth, pastel colored lips, slightly upturned, broad nose, round jaw, facial expression of amazement or wonder, representing a girl of 4 or 5 years of age, marked with the date 1900, and the mold number 0½, 21½″ . . . .*	180.00	220.00	170.00
☐ **Bisque,** *shoulder head, kid body with gussets at knee, cloth lower legs, bisque, blue sleep eyes, open mouth with four porcealin teeth, authentic Sisters of Mercy nun's habit, c. 1890, marks: Made in Germany, incised horseshoe, Hch 5/10, 17″ . . . .*	175.00	225.00	165.00
☐ **Bisque,** *shoulder plate, cloth and horsehair body, composition lower arms, brown sleep eyes, brown human hari wig, 18″ . . . .*	200.00	250.00	200.00
☐ **Bisque,** *socket head, fixed, medium size, dark, almond-shaped eyes, very wispy short painted lashes, arched brows of conventional style, partially open mouth, teeth visible, pastel lips, round jaw, slight double chin, this doll is normally dressed to represent a woman or young adult, but there is really nothing recognizably adult in the face except the absence of puffy cheeks, marked with horseshoe and the date 1900, and with the mold number 3/0, 14⅞″ . . . .*	170.00	210.00	155.00
☐ **Bisque,** *socket head, fixed, large very prominent, roundish eyes, painted lashes on the*			

Bride,
bisque and composition, 14″
$220.00-$260.00

Composition,
c. 1920, 15″
$240.00-$300.00

	Current Price Range		Prior Year Average
upper and lower lids, thin brows, short thick nose, open mouth with teeth visible, bright red lips, double chin, dimpled, puffy cheeks, representing a girl of about 2 or 3 years of age but sometimes dressed in the clothing of an older child, marked Heubach Köppelsdorf and with the mold number 300-9/0, date of manufacture unknown, believed to have been made in the late 1890's or opening years of the 20th century, 12"	170.00	200.00	160.00
☐ **Bisque,** *socket head, fully jointed composition body, blue sleep eyes, brown human hair wig, open mouth with four teeth, pink silk dress, white brocade cuffs, bib front, ribbon rosettes, matching lined bonnet, original ½" mold split in rear of head at crown, marks: Heubach 250.3 Köppelsdorf Germany, 24"*	320.00	370.00	325.00
☐ **Bisque,** *socket head, very large, roundish sleep eyes, painted lashes, prominent eyelids, thick dark arched brows, partially open mouth showing three upper teeth, very dark red lips, thick lower lip, moderately broad nose, cheeks slightly puffy, ears somewhat prominent, the most recognizable characteristic of this doll is a set of lines leading downward from the lip corners, flirtatious facial expression, found dressed as a child or adult, marked Heubach Köppelsdorf, and with the mold number 250-4/0, date of manufacture unknown, 16"*	170.00	210.00	165.00
☐ **Bisque,** *socket head, large, dark, fixed eyes, painted lashes, lashes longer on the lower lid than on the upper, heavy arched brows set close together, small open mouth with teeth showing and pastel colored lips, narrow nose slightly upturned, pierced ears, puffy cheeks, double chin, round jaw, usually dressed to represent an adult woman, marked Dep-1900.6, 24"*	230.00	280.00	225.00
Note: The numeral "6" following the date is a mold number which probably meant that this was the 6th mold introduced by Heubach during 1900.			
☐ **Bisque,** *socket head, large, blue, sleep eyes, with small pupil, long painted lashes, narrow arched brows, open mouth showing two teeth, dark red lips, medium width nose, not upturned, slightly puffy cheeks, chin not*			

	Current Price Range		Prior Year Average
well defined, conventional ears, marked Heubach Köppelsdorf, Germany, and with the mold number 321.116, date of manufacture unknown, presumably made after 1900 and probably toward the beginning of World War I, this doll may be dressed to represent either a girl or boy, 13½"	140.00	170.00	135.00
☐ **Character Baby,** *bisque head, composition body, mohair wig, blue sleep eyes with fringed lashes, open smiling mouth, toddler suit with cap, 17½"*	300.00	400.00	325.00
☐ **Composition Head,** *ball jointed body, brown curly wig, brown sleep eyes, pastel hat and outfit, marked 300*	300.00	350.00	325.00
☐ **German Character Doll,** *bisque head, ball jointed composition body, human hair wig, brown sleep eyes, blue print dress, marked, 16"*	1200.00	1400.00	1150.00
☐ **Island Boy,** *character baby, very dark toned solid dome bisque socket head, molded black shaded hair, brown glass inset eyes, painted red lips, five piece dark brown composition bent leg baby body, straw skirt, hoop earrings, straw hat and ankle bracelet, marks: Heubach Köppelsdord 399.17/0 Germany, 7½"*	200.00	300.00	200.00
☐ **Scots Boy,** *bisque socket head, five piece jointed composition body, brown set eyes, open mouth, brown wig, plaid kilt, shoulder scarf, matching tam, shoes, marks: Heubach Köppelsdorf 251, 22 0 Germany, 5½"*	65.00	85.00	65.00
☐ **Toddler,** *bisque head, composition body, jonted, brown sleep eyes, baby clothes, marked 267-5, 18"*	460.00	500.00	475.00

HIGHBROW

☐ **China Doll,** *black painted hair, blue painted eyes, rose silk violet dress, 13"*	200.00	225.00	210.00

HILL

☐ **Movie Queen Natalie,** *vinyl, sleep eyes, jointed at the waist, marked Made in U.S.A., made in 1959, 21¼"*	17.00	23.00	16.00

	Current Price Range		Prior Year Average
Note: This doll was not intended to represent Natalie Wood or any movie star in particular.			

HOLIDAY FAIR

	Current Price Range		Prior Year Average
☐ **Holly,** *cloth, stuffed, painted features, blonde yarn hair, pigtails, double-faced doll, each side of head has its own face, unmarked, sold originally with a tag reading Holiday Fair, N.Y.C., 1971, made in Japan, 19″*	5.00	7.00	5.00
☐ **Luva Girl,** *plastic/vinyl, painted eyes, marked Made in Hong Kong, c. 1973, 6″*	7.00	10.00	6.00
Note: Definitely inspired by the "trolls" of Thomas Dam of Denmark.			
☐ **Terry,** *plastic/vinyl, rooted hair, marked Holiday Fair, Inc., Made in Hong Kong, c. 1973, 9″*	3.50	5.00	3.00

HOLLYWOOD DOLL COMPANY

	Current Price Range		Prior Year Average
☐ **Bonnie Blue Bell,** *composition head and body, molded and painted features, blonde hair attached by adhesive, marked Hollywood Doll, made in c. 1947, 9½″*	9.00	12.00	8.00
☐ **Composition head,** *composition arms, legs and body, swivel head, molded and painted hair, painted eyes, closed mouth, dark red lips, jointed at the shoulders and thighs, definitely an "oldie," probably from the mid 1930's, 7″*	11.00	15.00	10.00
☐ **Cowgirl,** *composition, wears button and gun, 9″*	30.00	40.00	34.00
☐ **Hollywood Baby,** *plastic, molded and painted hair, blue sleep eyes, jointed, marked Hollywood Doll, date of manufacture unknown, 4½″*	11.00	14.00	10.00
☐ **Little Miss Muffet,** *composition head and body, molded and painted features, black hair attached by adhesive, wears sunflower-print dress, marked Hollywood Doll, made in 1945, 9″*	9.00	12.00	8.00
☐ **Masquerade,** *composition head and body, molded and painted features, blonde hair attached by adhesive, marked Hollywood Doll, date of manufacture unknown, believed to be c. 1946, 9½″*	9.00	12.00	8.00

	Current Price Range		Prior Year Average
☐ **Red Riding Hood,** *composition head and body, molded and painted features, blonde hair attached by adhesive, unmarked, made in 1946, 9½"*	9.00	12.00	8.00
Note: The basic doll used for Red Riding Hood was one that served for a number of the Hollywood dolls including Masquerade and Bonnie Blue Bell. This company issued a great variety of dolls but the changes were mostly in their clothing and props.			

HORSMAN

Horsman Dolls, Inc., is an American toy and doll manufacturer of great reknown. The company has survived into the present day from the middle of the 18th century, riding the economic waves, always maintaining a clear spot at the top of the toy industry and producing a quality and collectible product.

Edward I. Horsman, in the last years of the 18th century, had a thriving toy company. He started to distribute dolls under his trademark by importing bisque parts from Germany and assembling them in his plant in New York. His first original was a cloth baby doll manufacturerd in 1902, and the quick market success of the "Babyland" line prompted new designs to be introduced.

Horman's key to success was an uncanny feeling for public interest. Time and again the company was on top of the fads of the day before their competition could turn around. The company was credited with coining the name "Teddy Bear" and with starting a rage for good luck dolls that spanned a decade.

World War I created havoc in the doll industry with the abrupt cessation of bisque imports from Europe. Horsman immediately arranged for the Fulper Pottery Company to manufacture the first American produced bisque heads.

As the years passed, Horsman has always been a pioneer of new technology. When the industry turned to composition in the early 1920's, Horsman was the first company that perfected the formula to resist breaking and pealing. When vinyl revolutionized doll design, Horsman was the first to achieve national distribution of the miraculous new product.

As science created materials that made dolls more and more life like, the Horsman Company produced line after line of realistic baby and character dolls. Their slogan was "America's best known and best loved dolls". The tight grip the company maintains on the current and collectible market is a testimony to that statement.

☐ **Alice In Wonderland,** *vinyl, jointed, dress, apron, Disney doll, 12"*	10.00	15.00	10.00
☐ **Angelove,** *vinyl, jointed, pink checked outfit, 13"*	8.00	12.00	8.00
☐ **Answer Doll,** *mechanical, vinyl, blonde hair, rooted, blue sleep eyes, doll shakes its head "yes" or "no," operated by a set of buttons,*			

	Current Price Range		Prior Year Average
marked 66-100-10 Horsman, made in 1966, to which the first two digits in the mark number refer, 10″	9.00	12.00	8.00
☐ **Anthony Pipsqueak,** *plastic/vinyl, rooted hair, painted eyes, pug nose, open mouth, marked Horsman Dolls Inc., 1967, 6712-AA, 11½″*	5.00	7.00	5.00
Note: This was one of a set of four dolls, the Pipsqueak Family, whose values are all the same.			
☐ **Athlete,** *mechanical, plastic/vinyl, molded and painted hair and features, stands on platform, operates by spring-driven motor, marked Horsman 1967, 5½″*	5.00	7.00	5.00
☐ **Babs,** *composition, blue sleep eyes, molded and painted hair, made in 1931, 10″*	63.00	75.00	55.00
☐ **Baby,** *vinyl, cloth body, white rooted hair, blue sleep eyes, open closed mouth, cryer in body, pink and white pajamas, 19″*			

Baby Doll, rubber, c. 1964, 22″ **$7.00-$10.00**

	Current Price Range		Prior Year Average
☐ **Baby,** *vinyl jointed, blonde rooted hair, blue sleep eyes, open mouth nurser, night shirt, panties, booties, pacifier, 17″*	18.00	22.00	18.00
☐ **Baby Bumps,** *composition head, cloth body, painted facial feature, molded hair, play togs, 9″*	120.00	130.00	120.00
☐ **Baby Bumps,** *negro baby, brown cotton body, 9″*	100.00	150.00	120.00
☐ **Baby Chubby,** *composition head, cloth body, composition arms and legs, molded and painted reddish blonde hair, blue sleep eyes, marked A-Horsman, made in 1940, 23″*	27.00	36.00	25.00
☐ **Baby Doll,** *unidentified, rubber, 1964, 22″*	7.00	10.00	6.00
☐ **Baby Precious,** *vinyl head, vinyl arms and legs, fabric body, stuffed, rooted hair, sleep eyes, wears gown and lace-trimmed bonnet, mold number S-175, 13, dated 1967, 17″*	5.00	7.00	5.00
☐ **Baby Tweaks,** *vinyl head, cloth body, vinyl arms and legs, blonde hair, rooted, fixed blue eyes, both legs set with squeakers, the idea was to tweak, pinch, Baby Tweaks and she would squeak, marked Horsman Doll, 1967, 07181, 20″*	24.00	29.00	22.00
☐ **Beany,** *vinyl head, stuffed body, vinyl arms, stuffed legs, platinum blonde hair, rooted, molded and painted features, marked Horsman Dolls, made in 1975, 10″*	6.00	8.00	5.00
☐ **Betty,** *vinyl, rooted blonde hair, blue sleep eyes, posable, marked Horsman, made in 1954, 14″*	22.00	27.00	20.00
☐ **Betty Ann,** *plastic head, cloth body, vinyl hands and legs, stapled red wig, blue sleep eyes, marked Horsman Doll, made in 1951, 18½″*	23.00	29.00	20.00
☐ **Black Doll,** *vinyl head, arms, and legs, cloth body, brown sleep eyes, lashes, yellow dress and panties, 16″*	40.00	50.00	43.00
☐ **Bootsie,** *black, plastic/vinyl, rooted black hair, brown sleep eyes, marked 1125-4-Horsman, made in 1969, 12″*	26.00	34.00	23.00
☐ **Buster Brown,** *bisque head, ball jointed body, human hair wig, brown sleep eyes, navy blue wool suit, 17″*	400.00	450.00	415.00
☐ **Bylow,** *vinyl, with box, pamphlet, c. 1974*	30.00	40.00	35.00
☐ **By-Low Baby,** *vinyl head and limbs, cloth body, pretty coloring, long white gown, lace trim, pink blanket with lace trim, 15″*	25.00	35.00	25.00
☐ **Campbell Kid,** *composition body and head, molded and painted hair, painted shoes and socks, 1948, 12″*	90.00	110.00	85.00

	Current Price Range		Prior Year Average
☐ **Campbell Kid,** *composition head, arms, cloth body, legs and feet, light brown, painted, molded bobbed-style hair, painted round side-glancing eyes, pug nose, watermelon mouth, original play suit, mark: label: "The Campbell Kids trademark by Joseph Campbel Mfg. by E.I. Horsman Co.", 13"*	125.00	175.00	125.00
☐ **Campbell Kid,** *shoulder head composition, pink, cotton body, romper suit, pink velvet boots, 13"*	90.00	100.00	91.00
☐ **Campbell Soup Kids,** *plastic, boy in chef hat, girl with ribbon*	25.00	32.00	22.00
☐ **Celeste Bride Doll,** *vinyl, jointed, blonde, sleep eyes, satin bridal outfit, 13"*	7.00	15.00	10.00

Campbell Soup Kids . . . . **$25.00-$32.00**

	Current Price Range		Prior Year Average
☐ **Cindy,** *plastic head, plastic arms, legs and body, swivel head, long blond rooted wig, sleep eyes, open mouth, bright red lips, puff sleeve dress with two buttons, walker, marked 170, 14½″*	22.00	27.00	20.00
Note: Cindy is dated 1953. For a Horsman doll this is considered "late" by collectors. The factory switched over to plastic, from composition, after World War II and its plastic dolls are not as valuable.			
☐ **Cindy Kay,** *plastic, blonde hair attached by adhesive, blue sleep eyes, open mouth with teeth, has the appearance of an antique doll but this was probably accidental, marked Horsman, made in 1950, 15″*	25.00	31.00	22.00
☐ **Chubby Baby,** *composition head, swivel neck, cloth body, flirty eyes, brown and gingham playsuit, c. 1930, 18″*	50.00	60.00	55.00

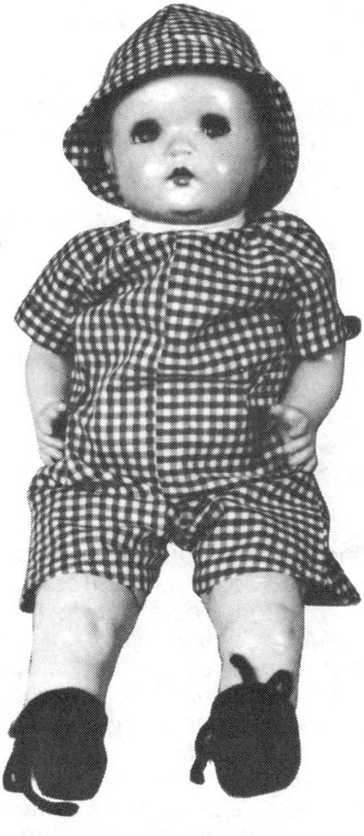

Chubby Baby,
composition and cloth,
c. 1930, 18″
$50.00-$60.00

	Current Price Range		Prior Year Average
☐ **Composition,** *brown sleep eyes, dark brown wig, red velvet dress with pink trim, matching bloomers and hat, 18"*	60.00	70.00	64.00
☐ **Dolly Dreamland,** *plastic, red hair attached by adhesive, blue sleep eyes, marked Made in U.S.A.-170, sold originally with a tag dated 1953, 15"*	32.00	42.00	30.00
☐ **Ella Cinders,** *composition head, arms, legs, cloth body, wide, painted eyes, freckles, molded painted black straight short hair, pug nose, open mouth, from the comic strip by Bill Conselman and Charlie Plumb, polka-dot dress, mark: "1925 MNS", 18"*	425.00	525.00	425.00
☐ **Fair Skin,** *vinyl, blonde rooted hair, blue sleep eyes, marked Horsman H14, also bearing an additional mold number S16, made in 1960, 15"*	15.00	20.00	13.00
☐ **Fairy Skin Doll,** *sleep eyes, marked Horsman, sold originally with a tag reading Horsman's Fairy Skin Doll, made entirely of soft vinyl plastic, 18"*	18.00	23.00	16.00
☐ **Floppy,** *vinyl head, vinyl arms, soft rubber body and legs, rooted hair, sleep eyes, closed mouth, legs are wired, marked Horsman Dolls Inc., G6175, dated 1965, 17½"*	6.00	8.00	5.00
☐ **Girl,** *babyland rag, photographic face with painted blue eyes, original red dress with large yoke and wide bonnet, 14"*	125.00	135.00	130.00
☐ **Gloria Jean,** *vinyl, blonde rooted hair, blue sleep eyes, ribbon in hair, marked Horsman, made in 1963, 10"*	6.00	8.00	5.00
☐ **Gold Medal Doll,** *vinyl, molded and painted red hair, blue sleep eyes, marked Horsman, made in 1953, 26"*	78.00	95.00	72.00
☐ **Heebee Sheebee,** *all bisque, 8"*	475.00	525.00	495.00
☐ **Heebee Sheebee,** *all bisque, jointed shoulders and hips, blue booties with ties, label on foot, 6"*	575.00	625.00	590.00
☐ **Heebee Shebee,** *character, all composition, jointed arms and legs, painted button eyes, pouty mouth, high dome forehead, heavy cheeks, molded nightshirt, blue shoes with real ties, denoting a Heebee, marks: oval label on front of nightshirt "Copyright 1925, Heebee/Shebee trademark Charles H. Twelvetrees. Horsman", tag, 10"*	300.00	650.00	600.00
☐ **Heebee Shebee,** *character, all composition, jointed arms and legs, painted button eyes, pouty mouth, high dome forehead, heavy cheeks, molded nightshirt, pink shoes with*			

	Current Price Range		Prior Year Average
real ties, denoting a Heebee, marks: oval label on front of nightshirt "Copyright 1925, Heebee/Shebee trademark Charles H. Twelvetrees. Horsman", tag, 10"	300.00	650.00	600.00
☐ **Jackie Coogan,** *composition head, hands, cloth body, painted side glancing eyes, molded blond Dutch-boy hair, closed mouth, turleneck sweater, checkered overalls, newsboy hat, mark: E.I.H. Co., 14"*	425.00	475.00	425.00
☐ **Jackie Coogan,** *composition head and hands, cloth body, painted eyes, molded hair, original clothes, marks: E.I.H. Co., 13½"*	500.00	600.00	500.00
☐ **Jody,** *plastic/vinyl, blue sleep eyes, marked Horsman Doll, 1964, T13, 15"*	12.00	16.00	11.00
☐ **Jo Jo,** *composition head and body, molded and painted features, and hair, blue eyes, marked Jo Jo 1937, Horsman, 12"*	49.00	58.00	45.00
Note: In its day this was a typical Depression-era doll, sold at a modest price. Its value is anything but depressed today.			
☐ **Joyce,** *composition head, with shoulderplate attached, composition arms and legs, stuffed fabric body, red mohair wig attached by adhesive, metallic sleep eyes, open mouth, wears silk smock, 18"*	39.00	45.00	35.00
Note: Joyce dates from the mid 1930's and represents the optimum in composition-head modeling; the head is no less fine than that of German bisque dolls of 30 or 40 year earlier. This is the sort of doll that probably will, in time, become sought-after.			
☐ **Kindergarten Kathy,** *plastic/vinyl, blonde rooted hair, blue sleep eyes, partially open mouth, braided hair, white shoes, marked Horsman T14, made in 1961, 15"*	11.00	14.00	10.00
☐ **Kindergarten Kathy,** *all vinyl, jointed blonde rooted hair, blue sleep eyes, closed mouth, pink dress with white lace trim, matching underclothes, pink bow in hair, white botards, white leather shoes, 19"*	33.00	38.00	33.00
☐ **Lifesize Baby,** *vinyl head, latex body, sleep eyes, molded hair, head stuffed with fabric, partially open mouth, showing tongue, not teeth, dated 1953, 26¼"*	22.00	27.00	20.00
Note: It's almost a shame that Horsman didn't make "Lifesize Baby" in the thirties, when it was turning out some of the best composition heads in the business.			

	Current Price Range		Prior Year Average
☐ **Lil' Softee,** *vinyl head, cloth body, vinyl arms and legs, blonde rooted hair, painted blue eyes, marked 35 Horsman Dolls Inc., 1968, 11"*	4.00	6.00	4.00
☐ **Linda,** *plastic/vinyl, rooted hair, sleep eyes, closed mouth, marked Horsman 1959, 36"*	110.00	135.00	100.00
☐ **Little Happy Fella,** *vinyl, blonde rooted hair, fixed blue eyes, marked Horsman Doll 1961, 13"*	32.00	40.00	30.00
Note: This doll started out with a low retail price and its climb to the present value represents a sharper rise than for most Horsman dolls — especially those made after 1960. It seems to be rather scarce.			
☐ **Love Me Baby,** *plastic/vinyl, platinum blonde rooted hair, blue sleep eyes, blue, nursing mouth, marked 2954-14Eye-1 Horsman, made in 1969, 16"*	5.00	7.00	5.00
☐ **Lullabye Baby,** *vinyl, blond rooted hair, blue sleep eyes, fitted with music box which plays rock-a-bye, marked M12 Horsman Doll, made in 1964, 12"*	8.00	11.00	7.00
☐ **Mama Doll,** *composition, blue sleep eyes, strawberry blonde mohair wig, aqua blue dress, white pinafore with small print, 22"*	80.00	90.00	82.00
☐ **Mary Poppings,** *vinyl, jointed, striped dress, coat, hat, carpet bag, Disney Doll, 12"*	12.00	17.00	10.00
☐ **Mary Poppins,** *walker, plastic/vinyl, sleep eyes, marked 5 Horsman Dolls, Inc., 1966, 66271, 25½"*	36.00	45.00	32.00
Note: Strangely enough, this doll bears no markings connecting it with Disney Studios, though it almost certainly must have been made under license.			
☐ **Mary Poppins,** *plastic/vinyl, black rooted hair, molded and painted features, flowered hat, marked H, licensed from Walt Disney Studios, made in 1964, 12"*	25.00	31.00	21.00
☐ **Mike Gene Carr,** *cartoon character, composition head, hands, cloth body, painted eyes, wide painted mouth, painted hair, 13"*	225.00	250.00	225.00
☐ **Mickey Mouse,** *rubber and cloth, talking doll*	45.00	65.00	40.00
☐ **Mickey Mouse,** *a boy doll blue sleep eyes, black mouse cap, blue pants, white top, black shoes, made in 1972, 8"*	18.00	24.00	20.00
☐ **Mommie's Darling,** *ma-ma crier baby, vinyl head and limbs, cloth body, blonde rooted hair, blue sleep eyes, open, closed mouth,*			

Mickey Mouse, rubber and cloth, talk box . . . . **$45.00-$65.00**

	Current Price Range		Prior Year Average
mama cryer, pink bow in hair, pink dress with white lace trim, long white, stockings and white leather shoes, 17″	**35.00**	**45.00**	**35.00**
☐ **My Baby,** *vinyl, blonde rooted hair, blue sleep eyes, marked Horsman O1, made in 1968, 9″*	**7.00**	**10.00**	**6.00**
☐ **Nipon Bisque,** *baby doll, jointed composition body, brown eyes, pierced nostrils, 19″*	**325.00**	**375.00**	**340.00**
☐ **Patty Duke,** *vinyl, posable, marked Horsman Doll 6211, 1965, representing movie actress Patty Duke, now Patty Duke Astin, as a child star, 12″*	**23.00**	**28.00**	**20.00**

	Current Price Range		Prior Year Average
☐ **Peek-A-Boo,** *composition head, composition half torso, arms, legs, cloth upper torso, molded hair, side glancing googly eyes, watermelon mouth, bathing suit, designed by Grace G. Drayton, 7½"*	90.00	100.00	90.00
☐ **Penny Penpal,** *vinyl head, plastic arms, legs and body, rooted platinum blond hair, painted eyes, jointed at shoulders, elbows, waist and thighs, holds pencil in right hand, marked 38, Horsman Dolls Inc., 1970, 17½"*	6.00	8.00	6.00
☐ **Pete,** *stuffed vinyl, molded hair, marked Horsman, made in 1957, 13"*	90.00	110.00	85.00
☐ **Pippi Long Stocking,** *vinyl, jointed red hair, c. 1972, 11"*	10.00	15.00	10.00
☐ **Polly,** *black, stuffed vinyl, molded hair, marked Horsman, made in 1957, 12¾"*	90.00	110.00	80.00
☐ **Poor Cinderella,** *plastic/vinyl, rooted blond hair, painted eyes, closed mouth, wears long dress and apron, marked H, 11½"*	6.00	8.00	5.00
Note: Representing Cinderella before her visit by the Fairy Godmother. At the same time Horsman made a "Rich Cinderella" doll, dressed in elegant ball gown. The value is the same.			
☐ **Pooty Tat,** *vinyl, rooted red hair, brown sleep eyes, marked 20SA-D, made in Hong Kong in 1969, 9"*	4.00	6.00	3.00
☐ **Pretty Betty,** *vinyl, brunette hair attached by adhesive, blue sleep eyes, closed mouth, bright red lips, marked Horsman, also bearing the mold number 1-S-5, made in 1954,*	21.00	26.00	20.00
☐ **Princess,** *plastic/vinyl, platinum blonde rooted hair, blue sleep eyes, puffy cheeks, marked 1963 Irene Szor, Horsman Doll Inc., 15½"*	44.00	55.00	40.00
☐ **Rag Doll,** *oil painted cloth head and body, painted face, brown human hair curls framing face under bonnet, cotton dress, shoes, 30"*	425.00	575.00	425.00
☐ **Renee Ballerina,** *vinyl head, vinyl arms and legs, soft vinyl body, upswept hairdo, sleep eyes, closed mouth, jointed at the elbows, 18"*	8.00	10.00	7.00
Note: Age uncertain, probably mid to late 1950's.			
☐ **Roberta,** *composition head, composition arms, legs and body, molded and painted hair, painted eyes, wears puff sleeve dress, white stockings, 14"*	41.00	47.00	38.00

	Current Price Range		Prior Year Average
☐ **Ruthie,** *vinyl, black rooted hair, with "widow's peak," black sleep eyes, marked 12-6AA, made in 1958, 12½"*	13.00	16.00	12.00
☐ **Ruth's Sister,** *plastic/vinyl, blonde rooted hair, blue sleep eyes, partially open mouth, lace trim at sleeves of dress, bow in hair, marked Horsman T27, made in 1960, 25½"*	36.00	44.00	34.00
☐ **Shadow Wave Baby,** *vinyl, blue sleep eyes, closed mouth turned down at the corners, wears short dress, marked Horsman, made in 1951, 19"*	48.00	59.00	45.00
☐ **Sherry,** *vinyl head, cloth body, vinyl arms and legs, rooted red hair, green sleep eyes, marked 2715-27-EYE, Horsman Dolls, Inc., 1967, 19"*	25.00	31.00	22.00
☐ **Softie Baby,** *vinyl head, cloth body, vinyl arms and legs, brown rooted hair, blue sleep eyes, blue, partially open mouth, marked 2515-10-Eye-S14-2, made in 1965, 14"*	6.00	8.00	5.00
Note: The soft thing about Softie Baby was its cloth body — which, of course, was hardly an innovation by the year 1965. However, so many dolls on the market had plastic or vinyl bodies that a cloth-bodied doll almost SEEMED novel.			
☐ **Songster,** *plastic/vinyl, rooted platinum blonde hair, closed eyes with long lashes, mouth wide open, singing, marked Horsman Doll, 1967, 0712,*	6.00	8.00	5.00
☐ **Sweet Memory,** *vinyl head, cloth body, vinyl hands, rooted brunette hair, blue sleep eyes, marked Horsman Dolls, 1975, 14"*	11.00	14.00	10.00
☐ **Teensie Baby,** *plastic/vinyl, molded hair, painted eyes, nursing mouth, pug nose, dressed in overalls and striped short sleeve shirt, dated 1964, 12"*	3.00	4.00	3.00
☐ **Teensie Tot,** *plastic/vinyl, sleep eyes, closed mouth, wears fur-trimmed dress, marked Horsman, made in 1973, 11¼"*	9.00	12.00	8.00
☐ **Thirstee Baby,** *plastic/vinyl, rooted brunette hair blue sleep eyes, nursing mouth, marked Horsman, made in 1963, 18"*	8.00	11.00	7.00
☐ **Topsy Turvy Girls,** *black and white oil paint over cloth face, original clothing, early American, 12"*	70.00	80.00	70.00
☐ **Topsy Turvy,** *papier mache, cotton body, black molded shoulder head with black hair, other side-white shoulder head blue-eyed blonde, black doll has red dress, white doll has pink*	225.00	275.00	240.00

	Current Price Range		Prior Year Average
☐ **Tiny Baby,** *vinyl head, vinyl arms, legs and body, fixed eyes, open mouth, pug nose, dated 1968, 6″*	3.00	4.00	3.00
☐ **Tuffie,** *vinyl, blonde rooted hair, blue sleep eyes , determined expression on face, wears fur-trimmed hood, marked Horsman Doll Inc., B19, made in 1966, 16″*	25.00	31.00	22.00
☐ **Twin Tot,** *plastic/vinyl, rooted hair, sleep eyes, open nursing mouth, puffy cheeks, wears ribbon in hair, marked 2308,3, Eye 10, Horsman Dolls Inc., 07111, 11″*	3.00	4.00	3.00
Note: Made in the 1970's.			
☐ **Twistie,** *vinyl, blonde rooted hair, molded and painted features, wears polka-dotted dress with picture of guitar on it, marked Horsman 1967, 6″*	5.00	7.00	5.00
☐ **Tynie Toddler,** *plastic/vinyl, blonde rooted hair, blue sleep eyes, marked Horsman Dolls Inc. 67165, made in 1964, 15″*	6.00	8.00	5.00

Willie Talks,
plastic and cloth, 24″
$17.50-$20.00

Willie Talks,
wood and cloth,
c. 1955, 22″
$20.00-$30.00

	Current Price Range		Prior Year Average
☐ **Walker Ruth,** *walker, plastic/vinyl, brunette rooted hair, blue sleep eyes, marked Horsman T21, made in 1967, 19½″*	10.00	14.00	9.00
Note: There was also a non-walking version of Ruth, and a doll representing Ruth's sister. But aside from these, Horsman's "Ruth family" did not get far.			
☐ **Willie Talks,** *vinyl head, cloth body, talking doll, moulded hair, painted eyes, red sweater, plaid slacks, c. 1955, 22″*	17.50	20.00	18.00
☐ **Zodiac Baby,** *vinyl, pink hair version, marked Horsman Dolls, Inc., 1968, 6″*	9.00	12.00	8.00
Note: Came with a horoscope book, which must still be present to realize the stated value. For the doll alone, $6.00 to $8.00 would be fair.			

MARY HOYER

	Current Price Range		Prior Year Average
☐ **Girl,** *composition or hard plastic, swivel neck, jointed shoulders and hips, original wig, sleep eyes with lashes, closed mouth, dressed, 14″*	120.00	130.00	120.00
☐ **Girl,** *plastic, cowboy garb*	125.00	140.00	130.00
☐ **Girl,** *plastic, majorette garb, 15″*	125.00	140.00	130.00
☐ **Julianna,** *composition, blue sleep eyes, brown wig attached by adhesive, closed mouth, marked The Mary Hoyer Doll Co., 13½″*	42.00	55.00	39.00
☐ **Peggy,** *composition, sleep eyes, black wig attached by adhesive, closed mouth, marked The Mary Hoyer Doll Co., made in 1946 and apparently sold on the retail market for several years thereafter, 13½″*	40.00	52.00	37.00
☐ **Sonja,** *composition, blue sleep eyes, brown wig attached by adhesive, closed mouth, marked The Mary Hoyer Doll Co., made in 1947, 13½″*	42.00	55.00	39.00

HUBLEY

☐ **Tonto,** *plastic head, vinyl arms, legs and body, molded, painted eyes, made in Hong Kong, dated 1973, represents the character Tonto from "The Lone Ranger", 9¾″*	7.00	9.00	6.00

HUGH M. HEFNER PUBLISHING COMPANY

☐ **Playboy Bunny,** *felt face, stuffed plush body, marked HMH Pub. Co., Inc., made in 1963, 17″*	9.00	12.00	8.00

Note: A hand puppet modeled after the famous symbol of Playboy magazine.

HUMMEL

	Current Price Range		Prior Year Average
☐ **Boy,** *rubber, felt clothes, marked, 12″*	120.00	150.00	125.00
☐ **Boy,** *rubber, molded brown hair, felt jacket, pants, white shirt, flowered tie, made in Germany, c.1950's, 11″*	115.00	145.00	120.00
☐ **Hansel,** *12″*	50.00	60.00	55.00
☐ **Radi-Bub,** *12″*	50.00	60.00	55.00

HUNGERFORD

☐ **Baby Wet,** *plastic head ("Lastic Plastic"), plastic legs, vinyl arms, vinyl body, nursing mouth, wears checked gown with ruffled neck, dated 1956, 15″*	4.00	5.00	4.00
☐ **Baby Rosie Posie,** *vinyl, molded and painted hair (blonde), sleep eyes (blue), nursing mouth, pug nose, marked Hungerford, made in 1954, 16″*	29.00	37.00	27.00

HURET

☐ **French Fashion,** *character bisque face, wood jointed body, jointed at shoulder, elbow, wrist, neck, hip, waist, knee, pewter hands, brown wig, painted eyes, original walking suit and hat, underwear and old shoes, head incised "Huret," back incised "Huret," 18″*	5000.00	8000.00	6000.00

IDEAL

☐ **Andy Gibb,** *limited issue, c. 1979, 8″*	55.00	65.00	58.00
☐ **Baby,** *jointed vinyl, blonde rooted hair, blue sleep eyes, open mouth nurser, antique white gown with tatted trim, 8½″*	12.00	15.00	12.00
☐ **Baby,** *vinyl head, cloth bodied, rooted blond hair, pull string in back and baby wiggles and clutches blanket in arms, pink pajamas, 14″*	13.00	18.00	14.00
☐ **Baby, Baby,** *vinyl, rooted hair (blonde), fixed eyes (blue), nursing mouth, marked 115 Ideal, made in Hong Kong in 1974, 7″*	7.00	10.00	6.00

	Current Price Range		Prior Year Average
☐ **Baby Belly Button,** *black, vinyl, black hair (rooted), painted features, brown eyes, smiling closed mouth, in the likeness of an infant, Baby Belly Button has a knob at its stomach which, when turned, makes the arms, legs and head move, dressed in a diaper and white lace-edged smock, marked Ideal Toy Corp., E9-2-H-165, made in Hong Kong in 1970, 9"*	5.50	7.00	5.00
☐ **Baby Big Eyes,** *vinyl, blonde hair (rooted), sleep eyes (blue), closed mouth, marked Ideal Doll, made in 1954, 21"*	45.00	56.00	42.00
☐ **Baby Flatsy,** *vinyl, rooted hair (blonde), ribbon in hair, wears scallop-edged bib, long pants, marked Ideal, 1969, Pat. Pend.*	2.75	3.75	2.50
Note: Ideal's "Flatsy Family" included a number of different dolls, sold originally in 1969 and 1970. Some came with elaborate props, which are worth more than the dolls.			
☐ **Baby Gurglee,** *plastic head, latex arms and legs, latex body, jointed arms, sleep eyes, molded and painted hair, squeeze-activity voice, 19"*	11.00	15.00	10.00
Note: Baby Gurglee (the squeeze-voice was intended to represent a gurgle) was marketed in 1951. The identical doll was placed on the market again in 1953, under the name "Touslehead."			
☐ **Baby Jo,** *plastic, molded and painted hair, sleep eyes (blue), pug nose, closed mouth, holes in nostrils, marked Ideal Doll, Made in U.S.A., 22, made in 1955, 22"*	25.00	31.00	23.00
☐ **Baby June,** *vinyl, brunette hair (rooted), sleep eyes (blue), marked Ideal Doll VS-15-2, made in 1956, 15"*	67.00	82.00	65.00
☐ **Baby Snooks,** *composition head, body, feet, cable arms and legs, molded hair, large smiling mouth, painted features, modeled after Fanny Brice, cotton print dress, large bow in hair, marked "IDEAL," 12"*	185.00	215.00	200.00
☐ **Baby Snookie,** *vinyl head, latex body, molded, painted hair, painted eyes, closed mouth, fingers spaced wide apart, wears diaper with safety pin (no other clothing), made in 1950, 9"*	5.00	7.00	5.00
Note: Obviously inspired (in name at least) from the Fanny Brice character, Baby Snooks.			
☐ **Bam Bam,** *vinyl, blonde hair (rooted), molded and painted features, painted eyes,*			

	Current Price Range		Prior Year Average
Bam Bam is a character in the comic strip "The Flintstones" by Hanna and Barbera, marked Hanna Barbera Products, Inc., BB-17, made in 1963, 15½"	12.00	16.00	11.00
☐ **Betsey Wetsey,** *plastic head, vinyl body, sheep's hair wig, blue sleep eyes, lashes, long pink gown, plastic cradle, 14"*	75.00	100.00	79.00
☐ **Betsey Wetsey,** *plastic head, vinyl body, deep eyes, bent leg, ruffled sun-suit, 14"* . . .	15.00	20.00	16.00
☐ **Betsey Wetsey,** *soft plastic, moulded hair, 1953, 13"*	16.00	21.00	15.00
☐ **Black Velvet,** *vinyl head, hard body, jointed shoulders, waist and hips, rooted black hair, smiling mouth, pull string in back that makes her twist and look around, in red and green plaid dress, blue shoes, 1972, 15"* . . .	63.00	68.00	63.00

Betsy Wetsy,
soft plastic,
c. 1953, 13"
$16.00-$21.00

	Current Price Range		Prior Year Average
☐ **Bonnie Braids,** *plastic/vinyl, reddish hair (rooted), sleep eyes (blue), open mouth with teeth, the name Bonnie Braids is adapted from a line in a ballad by 18th century Scottish poet Robert Burns, marked 1951 Chicago Tribune, 13"*	34.00	43.00	32.00
☐ **Bonnie Walker,** *walker, plastic, sleep eyes blue, open mouth with teeth, bright red lips, marked Ideal Doll W16, 17"*	23.00	28.00	21.00
☐ **Brandi,** *(sometimes spelled Brandy in dealers' lists, but incorrectly), vinyl, painted features, rooted hair (blonde), hair has "grow" feature (portion of wig is fitted inside head; when hair is pulled gently, it gives the appearance of "growing" out of the scalp), wearing a silky sleeveless gown with scooped neck, eyelet holes at the front, swivel waist, marked Ideal Toy Corp., GHB-18-H-185, made in Hong Kong in 1971*	13.00	16.00	12.00
☐ **Busy Lizy,** *plastic/vinyl, sleep eyes (blue), rooted hair (platinum blonde), pug nose, closed smiling mouth, wears dress with floral-printed cape, marked Ideal Toy Corp. HK-18, dated 1970 on the head and 1971 on the body, 17"*	26.00	32.00	25.00
☐ **Casey Flatsy,** *vinyl, painted features, molded and painted hair (red), large eyes, smiling face, dressed as a railroad motorman, marked Ideal, 1969, Pat. Pending, made in Hong Kong*	2.75	3.75	2.50
☐ **Carol Brent,** *vinyl, marked Ideal Toy Corp., M-15-L, made in 1961 for the Montgomery Ward chain, "Carol Brent" was the name used by Ward's for one of its lines of female apparel, 15"*	28.00	35.00	25.00
☐ **Charlotte,** *Victorian Lady, c. 1983, 8"*	6.00	14.00	7.00
☐ **Charlotte,** *Victorian Lady, c. 1983, 12"*	15.00	20.00	16.00
☐ **Cinnamon,** *plastic/vinyl, painted eyes (blue), open smiling mouth showing teeth, rooted hair (red), hair has "grow" feature (portion of wig is fitted inside head; when hair is gently pulled, it gives the appearance of "growing" out of the scalp), wears short lacy dress, ribbon at front, marked Ideal Toy Corp., GH-12-H-183, 12¼"*	8.00	10.00	7.00
☐ **Composition Head,** *cloth body, painted eyes, diamond mark on back, c. 1910, 19"*	60.00	65.00	62.50
☐ **Constance,** *Victorian Lady, c. 1983, 8"*	6.00	14.00	7.00
☐ **Constance,** *Victorian Lady, c. 1983, 12"*	15.00	20.00	16.00

Composition,
c. 1910, 19″
$60.00-$65.00

	Current Price Range		Prior Year Average
☐ **Cousin Sue,** *vinyl head, cloth body, vinyl arms and legs, sleep eyes (blue), unmarked, made in 1957, 17½″*	22.00	27.00	20.00
☐ **Cricket,** *plastic/vinyl, sleep eyes (brown), open smiling mouth, red hair (rooted), hair has "grow" feature (portion of wig is fitted inside head; when hair is pulled gently, it gives the appearance of "growing" out of the scalp), wears checked dress with ruffled collar and armholes, jointed at the waist, marked Ideal Toy Corp., CR-15-H-177, made in Hong Kong in 1970, 15¼″*	8.00	10.00	7.00
☐ **Creampuff,** *vinyl, red hair (rooted), sleep eyes (blue), ribbons in hair, marked Ideal Doll OB-19-2, made in 1961, 18″*	26.00	34.00	25.00
☐ **Crissy,** *talking*	20.00	25.00	21.00

	Current Price Range		Prior Year Average
☐ **Crissy,** *vinyl head, hard body, jointed shoulders, waist and hips, blue satin short dress, panties to match, 18″*	30.00	36.00	32.00
☐ **Crissy,** *vinyl head, hard body, jointed shoulders, waist and hips, rooted hair, smiling mouth, green and red plaid long dress, panties, matching shoes*	35.00	40.00	35.00
☐ **Crissy,** *vinyl head, hard body, jointed shoulders, waist and hips, rooted hair, smiling mouth, orange lace dress, panties, orange shoes, 18″*	32.00	42.00	38.00
☐ **Crissy,** *vinyl head, hard body, jointed shoulders, waist and hips, rooted hair, smiling mouth, pink fancy nightgown with matching panties, #8135-6, 18″*	38.00	46.00	40.00

Deanna Durbin, composition, c. 1950, 21″ **$200.00-$225.00**

	Current Price Range		Prior Year Average
☐ **Crissy,** *vinyl head, hard body, jointed shoulders, waist and hips, rooted hair, smiling lips, yellow pajama outfit, quilted yellow short top and matching yellow long pants with lace trim, 18″*	32.00	36.00	32.00
☐ **Cuddly Kissy,** *vinyl head, cloth body, vinyl arms and legs, blonde hair, marked Ideal Toy Corp., KB-17E, made in 1964, 16½″*	45.00	57.00	42.00
☐ **Deanna Durbin,** *all composition jointed at neck, shoulder and hips, green sleep eyes accented with eye shadow, brown human hair wig, smiling mouth with porcelain upper teeth, original blue taffeta ball gown accented with yellow ruffles at hem and neckline, original organdy hoop petticoat, marked Deanna Durbin-Ideal Doll, 24″*	425.00	475.00	400.00
☐ **Deanna Durbin,** *composition head, jointed composition body, sleep eyes, blue full length dress, c. 1950, 21″*	200.00	225.00	215.00
☐ **Deanna Durbin,** *jointed at waist, poses, marked Durbin, Ideal, U.S.A., 21″*	200.00	250.00	210.00
☐ **Dew Drop,** *plastic/vinyl, brunette hair (rooted), sleep eyes (blue), nursing mouth, crier, marked V-S-22, made in 1961, 20″*	11.00	14.00	10.00
☐ **Diana Ross,** *character, 1969 black doll, all vinyl jointed, black rooted hair, black sleep eyes, open smiling mouth with teeth, long gold evening dress with pink boa trim, hair net, 19″*	155.00	175.00	155.00
☐ **Dina,** *lacy green dress*	40.00	50.00	42.00
☐ **Dodi,** *plastic/vinyl, rooted hair (brownish blond), painted eyes, open smiling mouth with teeth, two eyelashes drawn outward at the outer corner of each eye ("Cleopatra" style — popular when this doll was made in 1964), marked DO-9-E, 9″*	9.00	11.00	8.00
☐ **Dracky, Mini Monster,** *plastic/vinyl, molded and painted features, molded and painted hair, designed as a youthful Dracula, marked 1965 Ideal Toy Corp., made in Japan, 8½″*	14.00	19.00	12.00
☐ **Dr. Evil,** *plastic, adult male model with various face changes (masks), sold in a box marked Ideal Toy Corp., and dated 1965, 11″* **Note: The stated value is for the doll plus box and accessories.**	9.00	12.00	8.00
☐ ***Emma,*** Victorian Lady, c. 1983, 8″	6.00	14.00	7.00
☐ **Emma,** Victorian Lady, c. 1983, 12″	15.00	20.00	16.00
☐ **Eric,** *plastic/vinyl, molded and painted features, molded and painted hair, model of*			

	Current Price Range		Prior Year Average
young adult, marked 1976 Ideal, made in Hong Kong, 12"	13.00	17.00	12.00
☐ **Evel Knievel,** *vinyl, posable, molded and painted hair, painted features, sold with three outfits and various props, representing the daredevil motorcycle stuntman, marked 1972 Ideal, made in Hong Kong*			
Value with all original accessories	7.00	10.00	6.00
Doll with one outfit, no props	4.00	6.00	4.00
☐ **Fannie Brice,** *composition head, stuffed wire-encased body, composition hands and feet, molded and painted features, molded and painted hair, Fannie Brice was a star of Ziegfeld's Follies and radio, made in 1939, 13"*	200.00	265.00	185.00
☐ **Flatsy Family,** *this series of dolls was placed on the market in 1970. Having run their course in the shops, they are now attracting some collector interest. Each Flatsy doll was of very small size, under 5" (some were under 3"), and came boxed with a whole array of scenery and props. For example, Cookie Flatsy (a cook) came with her own kitchen. In gereral, prices for the dolls by themselves are currently in the $2.75 to $3.75 range. When found with the original accessories, their values are much higher, up to $8.00 to $10.00*			
☐ **Franky, Mini Monster,** *plastic/vinyl, molded and painted features, molded and painted hair, designed as a youthful Frankenstein's monster, marked 1965 Ideal Toy Corp., made in Japan, 8¾"*	14.00	19.00	13.00
☐ **Flexy Soldier,** *composition over wire (posable) with wooden feet, marked Ideal Doll, believed to have been made c. 1944, 13"*	50.00	62.00	48.00
☐ **Giggle Toddler,** *plastic/vinyl, blonde hair cut in bangs, painted eyes, giggles when arms are extended, marked Ideal Toy Corp., GG18-H77-1967, 18"*	36.00	45.00	35.00
☐ **Ginger,** *composition, rooted hair, sleep eyes (brown), open mouth with teeth, bright red lips, marked with an X inside a circle, made from a Shirley Temple mold, made in 1939, 15"*	65.00	80.00	60.00

Giggles, 18″
$36.00-$45.00

	Current Price Range		Prior Year Average
☐ **Goody Two-Shoes,** *walker, plastic/vinyl, blonde hair (rooted), sleep eyes (blue), marked 1965 Ideal Toy Corp., WT18, Pat. Pending, 18″*	36.00	45.00	35.00
Note: The name "Goody Two-Shoes" was created for a character in a play by Oliver Goldsmith in the 18th century.			
☐ **Grown-Up Tammy,** *plastic/vinyl, rooted hair (blonde), painted eyes, closed mouth, bright red lips, wears heels, intended as a young-adult version of the popular Tammy doll, marked T-12-E, 11½″*	9.00	11.00	8.00
☐ **Harriet Hubbard Ayer,** *makeup doll, makeup kit and beauty table, 19″*	150.00	200.00	170.00
☐ **Honeyball,** *vinyl, rooted hair (brunette), painted eyes, marked 1966 Ideal Toy Corp., M9-H4, 9½″*	6.00	8.00	5.00

	Current Price Range		Prior Year Average
☐ **Honeysuckle,** *vinyl, brunette hair (rooted), sleep eyes (blue), pug nose, marked Ideal Doll, made in 1955, 20″*	28.00	35.00	25.00
☐ **Howdy Doody,** *plastic, cloth body, molded and painted hair, sleep eyes (blue), puppet with movable mouth, based on the TV character, marked Ideal Doll, made in 1950, 20″*	75.00	95.00	70.00
☐ **Huggee Girl,** *vinyl head, oilcloth body (stuffed), sleep eyes (blue), molded and painted hair, marked Ideal Doll BC16, 1952, 15″*	18.00	23.00	17.00
☐ **Illya Kuryakin,** *plastic/vinyl, molded and painted features, molded and painted hair, Illya Kuryakin was a character on the TV series "The Man from U.N.C.L.E.", the doll is designed to resemble the actor David McCallum, marked K-99, made in 1965, 12″*	57.00	73.00	55.00
☐ **007 James Bond,** *plastic/vinyl, molded and painted features, molded and painted hair, James Bond is a fictional detective created by Ian Fleming, this doll is made to resemble Sean Connery, who was the first actor to portray James Bond in films, marked Ideal Toy Corp., B-12½-2, made in 1965, 12″*	65.00	85.00	62.00
☐ **Joan Palooka,** *vinyl head, latex body, sleep eyes, molded, painted hair, jointed arms, intended as a female counterpart of Joe Palooka, the heavyweight boxing champion of the comic strips, marked 1952, Ham Fisher, Ideal Doll, Ham Fisher was creator of the Joe Palooka character, 14″*	20.00	25.00	18.00
☐ **Joey Stivic,** *vinyl, blonde hair, sexed*	15.00	20.00	16.00
☐ **Judy Garland,** *composition head, composition arms, legs and body, sleep eyes, open mouth, bright red lips, represents Judy Garland in the role of Dorothy in "The Wizard of Oz.," marked Ideal doll, mold number 18, dated 1939, 17½″*	120.00	150.00	110.00
Note: Has human hair wig attached by adhesive. Not a very successful resemblance to Judy Garland, this is nevertheless a very collectible doll.			
☐ **Judy Splinters,** *vinyl head, cloth body, latex limbs, marked Ideal Doll, 1951, 18″*	45.00	58.00	42.00
☐ **Katie Kachoo,** *sneezer, vinyl, marked 1968, Ideal Toy Corp., SN-17EH37, Katie sneezes when you raise her arms, 16½″*	28.00	34.00	25.00
☐ **Kerry,** *plastic/vinyl, blonde hair (rooted), hair has "grow" feature (portion of wig is fitted*			

	Current Price Range		Prior Year Average
inside head; when hair is pulled gently, it gives the appearance of "growing" out of the scalp), sleep eyes (blue), partially open mouth, marked 13 EYE, 1970, Ideal Toy Corp, NGH-18, 18"	8.00	10.00	7.00
Note: Kerry was patented in 1960 but did not get on the market until the following year.			
☐ **Kissy,** *16"*	30.00	40.00	32.00
☐ **Lemonade Flatsy (boy version),** *vinyl, painted eyes (brown), molded and painted hair (blonde), dressed as a snack vendor, wearing a chef's hat reading "15¢," and a jacket picturing a frankfurter and reading "Dogs," bendable, 2½"*	2.00	3.00	2.00
☐ **Liberty Boy,** *World War I uniform, moveable head, arms and legs, 12"*	80.00	90.00	82.00
☐ **Lindy,** *plastic, molded and painted hair, sleep eyes, closed mouth, bright red lips, unmarked, made in 1956, 8"*	5.00	7.00	5.00
☐ **Little Princess (Shirley Temple),** *composition head, composition arms, legs and body, blonde hair attached with adhesive, open mouth, bright red lips, marked Shirley Temple 18, 18"*	80.00	100.00	75.00
☐ **Look Around Velvet,** *plastic/vinyl, sleep eyes (violet blue), long lashes, blonde rooted hair, hair has "grow" feature (portion of wig is fitted inside head; when hair is pulled gently, it gives the appearance of "growing" out of the scalp), wears a brightly colored print dress, head turns by pulling a string, marked Ideal Toy Corp. GH 15-H-157, made in Hong Kong*	8.00	10.00	7.00
Note: This doll, designed in 1969, was the "action" version of Ideal's standard Velvet doll.			
☐ **Lydia,** *Victorian Lady, c. 1983, 8"*	6.00	14.00	7.00
☐ **Lydia,** *Victorian Lady, c. 1983, 12"*	15.00	20.00	16.00
☐ **Magic Lips,** *vinyl head, vinyl over cloth body, vinyl arms and legs, open mouth (which closes by pressing a button, similar to the action of a ventriloquist dummy), marked Ideal Doll T25, made in 1955, 24"*	60.00	78.00	55.00
☐ **Magic Skin Baby,** *composition head, otherwise made entirely of latex, sleep eyes, molded, painted hair, fully jointed, nursing mouth, made in 1941, 14½"*	8.00	10.00	7.00
☐ **Magic Squeezums,** *plastic head, latex body, sleep eyes, marked Ideal Doll, Made in U.S.A., 1950, 29"*	30.00	38.00	28.00

	Current Price Range		Prior Year Average
☐ **Marilyn Knowlden,** *composition, red hair, sleep eyes (blue), closed mouth, bright red lips, Marilyn Knowlden was a child actress of the 1930's, at the time when every movie studio was trying to get "another" Shirley Temple, marked USA-13, made in 1936, 13"*	140.00	170.00	130.00
☐ **Mary Hartline,** *plastic head, plastic arms, legs and body, wig attached with adhesive, sleep eyes, skirt has pattern of musical notes, wears boots with tassles, has mold number P91, dated 1952, 15"*	30.00	38.00	28.00
☐ **Mary Jane,** *composition head and body, blonde hair (wig), marked Ideal 18, believed to have been made c. 1944, 17½"*	70.00	85.00	68.00
☐ **Mia,** *plastic/vinyl, sleep eyes (blue), black eyelashes, dark brown rooted hair, hair has "grow" feature (portion of wig is fitted inside head; when hair is pulled gently, it gives the appearance of "growing" out of the scalp), striped dress with frilly collar, open mouth, showing teeth, marked Ideal Toy Corp., NGH-15-H173, made in 1970, 15¼"*	8.00	10.00	7.00
☐ **Mia,** *vinyl head, hard body, jointed shoulders, waist and hips, brown rooted grow hair, blue sleep eyes, smiling mouth, long white dress, 15"*	32.00	36.00	32.00
☐ **Mia,** *velvet outfit*	20.00	30.00	21.00
☐ **Mini-Flatsy Clock,** *two dolls with horse and cart, mint in box, 3"*	15.00	20.00	16.00
☐ **Mini Monster,** *plastic/vinyl, two-tone molded hair (grey and black), marked 1966, Ideal Toy Corp., a little girl with a ghoulish face, and a ghost printed on her dress, the dress was made in Japan, 9"*	9.00	12.00	8.00
☐ **Miss Deb Of 1942,** *composition head and body, blonde hair attached with adhesive, sleep eyes (brown), open mouth with teeth, bright red lips, marked 18, probably put on sale for the Christmas season of 1941, 18"*	30.00	38.00	28.00
☐ **Miss Revlon,** *vinyl, brunette hair (rooted), sleep eyes (blue), wears high heels, representing the symbol of the Revlon Cosmetics Co., marked Ideal Doll VT-18, made in 1956, 17"*	29.00	37.00	26.00
☐ **Miss Revlon,** *yellow striped cotton dress, c. 1955, 20"*	30.00	40.00	32.00
☐ **Mortimer Snerd,** *composition, stuffed wire-encased body, composition hands and feet, molded and painted features, molded and*			

	Current Price Range		Prior Year Average
painted hair, Mortimer Snerd was a character on the Edgar Bergen radio program, the original was a ventriloquist's dummy but this doll is a play-doll only, made in 1939, 13″	140.00	170.00	130.00
☐ **Munchie Flatsy,** *green hair, orange dotted outfit*	5.00	10.00	6.00
☐ **Munchie Time Flatsy,** *boy and girl with hot dog cart*	15.00	20.00	16.00
☐ **New Tiny Tears,** *vinyl, fixed eyes (blue), long lashes, rooted hair (blonde), puckered lips with nursing mouth, comes with nursing bottle, doll is designed in such a manner that it drinks from the nursing bottle when held upright, when lying down, the water from the bottle enters the doll through its right arm and becomes "tears," flowing out at the eyes, dressed in a paper diaper, marked Ideal Toy Corp., TNT-14-B-34, made in 1971*	5.50	7.00	5.00
☐ **Patty Playful,** *vinyl head and limbs, cloth body, white rooted hair, black pupiless sleep eyes, wide open mouth, two teeth, hand operated unit control in back clothing is body, pink pajamas, 16″*	20.00	25.00	20.00
☐ **Patti Playful,**	20.00	30.00	21.00
☐ **Patti Play Pal,** *black, c. 1982, 36″*	25.00	35.00	26.00
☐ **Pebbles,**	12.00	17.00	15.00
☐ **Penny Playpal,** *plastic/vinyl, red hair (rooted), sleep eyes (blue), marked Ideal Doll B-32-B, made in 1959, 32″*	65.00	79.00	60.00
☐ **Pepper,** *plastic/vinyl, rooted hair (blonde), painted eyes, partially open mouth, freckled cheeks, wears short dress with belt and matching collar, marked P9-3, 9″*	6.00	8.00	5.00
☐ **Pinocchio,** *composition head and body, wooden arms and legs, molded and painted hair, painted clothing, marked Ideal, originally sold with a tag reading Pinocchio, Des. & Copyright by Walt Disney, made in 1940, 11″*	90.00	110.00	85.00
☐ **Pinocchio,** *wood and composition, socket head, molded yellow cap, brown tufts of hair, long nose, painted features, white sail cloth collar with bow tie, painted molded clothing, fully jointed swivel waist, stick arms and legs, stenciled on front, Pinocchio, Des, & C. By Walt Disney, Made by Ideal Novelty & Toy Co., stenciled on back of head, Ideal Doll, USA, 7½″*	150.00	200.00	140.00

	Current Price Range		Prior Year Average
☐ **Plassie,** *composition/plastic, blonde wig attached with adhesive, sleep eyes (blue), marked P50, Ideal, Made in U.S.A., made in 1948, 17"*	24.00	29.00	22.00
Note: Ideal did more experimenting with doll materials in the 1940's than any other company. Plassie did not get her name by accident: she had a hard molded plastic head, but her arms and legs were made of standard composition. Ideal wanted to test the use of these substances in conjunction with each other. In that same year, 1948, Ideal was also experimenting with "magic skin" vinyl-plastic.			
☐ **Posie,** *walker, plastic/vinyl, sleep eyes (blue), closed mouth, bright red lips, marked Ideal Doll VP17, made in 1954, 17"*	28.00	34.00	25.00
☐ **Posie,** *vinyl head, plastic arms, legs and body, rooted hair, small sleep eyes, closed mouth, wears short smock-type gown, marked Ideal Doll VP23, not dated, apparently made in early 1950's, called Posie because the doll was fully bendable, 23"*	24.00	29.00	21.00
☐ **Pos'n Pete,** *plastic/vinyl, molded hair (short, combed down in front), painted eyes, jointed at shoulders and thighs, marked P-8 and dated 1964, 7½"*	9.00	11.00	8.00
Note: A posable doll.			
☐ **Raggedy Ann, Andy,** *porcelain, c. 1983, pair*	450.00	550.00	480.00
☐ **Real Live Lucy,** *baby, jointed vinyl body, head moves gently when lightly touched, rooted near white hair, blue sleep eyes, open rosebud mouth, fancy blue dress, lots of white lace trim matching underwear and booties, blue ribbon bow in hair, 21"*	55.00	65.00	55.00
☐ **Real Live Lucy,** *baby, jointed vinyl body, head moves gently when lightly touched, rooted near white hair, blue sleep eyes, open mouth with two teeth, red dress trimmed in white lace, buttons, rick-rack and braid, red bow in hair, 21"*	55.00	65.00	60.00
☐ **Rock Baby Coos,** *vinyl head, cloth body, rooted hair (short brownish blond), sleep eyes, wide open mouth (not nursing), wears flannel gown and terry bonnet, marked YTT-19-L-5, 20½"*	7.00	9.00	6.00
☐ **Rub-A-Dub Dollie,** *all vinyl jointed baby, blond rooted hair, painted blue eyes, pink and white flannel pajamas, 15"*	8.00	11.00	8.00
☐ **Rub-A-Dub,** *black*	20.00	30.00	21.00

	Current Price Range		Prior Year Average
☐ **Sandy McCall,** *marked McCall Corp., 1959, 36″*	110.00	140.00	100.00
☐ **Saucy Walker,** *hard plastic, blonde wig, blue sleep flirty eyes, open mouth, two teeth, floating tongue, blue dress, satin collar, blue lace trimmed blue panties with lace and bow, blue bonnet with lace trim, long white stockings, white leather shoes, marked on head, Ideal Doll WR-16, back, Ideal Doll, W-18, 17″*	75.00	95.00	75.00
☐ **Saucy Walker,** *hard plastic head, jointed walking body, sleep eyes, green and white gingham dress, c. 1950, 20″*	35.00	40.00	37.50
☐ **Saucy Walter,** *hard plastic, googly eyes, crier, 22″*	30.00	40.00	33.00

Saucy Walker,
hard plastic,
c. 1950, 20″
$35.00-$40.00

	Current Price Range		Prior Year Average
☐ **Saucy Walker,** *plastic head, plastic arms, legs and body, long blonde hair, sleep eyes, open mouth, bright red lips, ribboned hair, silk ribbons on dress, 22"*	20.00	25.00	20.00
☐ **Shirley Temple,** *Captain January, c.1982, 8"*	20.00	25.00	21.00
☐ **Shirley Temple,** *Heidi, c.1982, 8"*	20.00	25.00	22.00
☐ **Shirley Temple,** *Heidi, c.1982, 12"*	30.00	40.00	32.00
☐ **Shirley Temple,** *Little Colonel, c.1982, 8"*	20.00	25.00	21.00
☐ **Shirley Temple,** *Little Colonel, c.1982, 12"*	30.00	40.00	32.00
☐ **Shirley Temple,** *Little Miss Marker, c.1983, 8"*	10.00	15.00	11.00
☐ **Shirley Temple,** *Little Miss Marker, c.1983, 12"*	15.00	20.00	16.00
☐ **Shirley Temple,** *Littlest Rebel, c.1982, 8"*	20.00	25.00	21.00
☐ **Shirley Temple,** *Poor Little Rich Girl, c.1983, 8"*	10.00	15.00	11.00

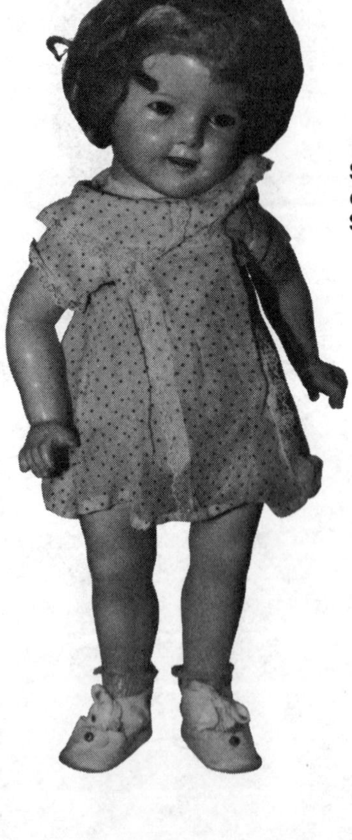

Shirley Temple,
composition, c. 1930
$550.00-$650.00

	Current Price Range		Prior Year Average
☐ **Shirley Temple,** *Poor Little Rich Girl, c.1983, 12"*	15.00	20.00	16.00
☐ **Shirley Temple,** *Rebecca of Sunnybrook Farm, c.1983, 8"*	10.00	15.00	11.00
☐ **Shirley Temple,** *Rebecca of Sunnybrook Farm, c.1983, 12"*	15.00	20.00	16.00
☐ **Shirley Temple,** *Stand Up and Cheer, c.1982, 8"*	20.00	25.00	21.00
☐ **Shirley Temple,** *Stowaway, c.1982, 8"*	20.00	25.00	21.00
☐ **Shirley Temple,** *Stowaway, c.1982, 12"*	30.00	40.00	32.00
☐ **Shirley Temple,** *Susannah of the Mounties, c.1983, 8"*	10.00	15.00	11.00
☐ **Shirley Temple,** *Susannah of the Mounties, c.1983, 12"*	15.00	20.00	16.00
☐ **Shirley Temple,** *Wee Willie Winkle, c.1983, 8"*	10.00	15.00	11.00
☐ **Shirley Temple,** *Wee Willie Winkle, c.1983, 12"*	15.00	20.00	16.00
☐ **Shirley Temple,** *all composition, 27"*	295.00	360.00	280.00
☐ **Shirley Temple,** *all composition, 25"*	170.00	205.00	160.00
☐ **Shirley Temple,** *all composition, 23"*	150.00	185.00	140.00
☐ **Shirley Temple,** *all composition, 18"*	120.00	145.00	110.00
☐ **Shirley Temple,** *all composition, 17"*	115.00	140.00	105.00
☐ **Shirley Temple,** *all composition, 16"*	112.00	135.00	100.00
☐ **Shirley Temple,** *all composition, 15"*	110.00	130.00	98.00
☐ **Shirley Temple,** *all composition, 13"*	65.00	80.00	60.00
☐ **Shirley Temple,** *all composition, 11"*	160.00	190.00	150.00
☐ **Shirley Temple,** *all composition, jointed, blonde curly mohair wig, brown sleep eyes, open mouth, six teeth, Heidi style dress and pinafore not original, c. 1938, marked on head and body: 13 SHIRLEY TEMPLE, 22"*	525.00	575.00	530.00
☐ **Shirley Temple,** *all composition jointed neck, shoulders and hips, green sleep eyes, open smiling mouth, original full blonde mohair wig styled in ringlets, original red and white polka kot dress, marked: Original Shirley Temple dress tag, head and body signed Shirley Temple, 25"*	725.00	775.00	700.00
☐ **Shirley Temple,** *character, vinyl head, plastic body, jointed shoulders and hips, rooted hair painted eyes, smiling mouth, red-polka dot dress, original, mint, 16"*	70.00	80.00	70.00
☐ **Shirley Temple,** *composition, curly top, Shirley pin, polka dotted red and white dress, c. 1935, 22"*	550.00	650.00	556.00
☐ **Shirley Temple,** *composition, jointed body, glazed eyes, blonde wig, open smiling mouth, original clothes, marked on head and body: 13 SHIRLEY TEMPLE, 13"*	450.00	550.00	475.00

	Current Price Range		Prior Year Average
☐ **Shirley Temple,** *composition, jointed body, glazed eyes, blonde wig, open smiling mouth, original clothes, marked on head and body: 13 SHIRLEY TEMPLE, 25″*	700.00	800.00	750.00
☐ **Shirley Temple,** *composition, pink organdy dress, snap dress, 15″*	275.00	325.00	290.00
☐ **Shirley Temple,** *original, ruffled lace dress, 22″*	495.00	650.00	495.00
☐ **Shirley Temple,** *vinyl and hard plastic jointed neck, shoulders and hips, rooted blonde hair, green sleep eyes, smiling mouth with four porcelain teeth, dimples, original mint condition, petite 1957 model with complete wardrobe, all clothing tagged Shirley Temple, flannel nightgown with cap, pink ballet dress, two piece plaid dress with cap, Swiss dirndl, sunglasses and Shirley Temple pin and purse, wearing a pale yellow organdy dress, marked: Ideal Doll ST-12, 12″*	215.00	225.00	210.00
☐ **Shirley Temple,** *vinyl head, jointed vinyl body, vinyl wig, sleep eyes, sheer blue gown, c. 1950, 17″*	120.00	140.00	125.00
☐ **Shirley Temple,** *vinyl, print dress, marked: Ideal, 12″*	85.00	95.00	89.00
☐ **Shirley Temple,** *vinyl, red dress, plaid trim, marked: Ideal, 12″*	70.00	80.00	73.00
☐ **Shirley Temple,** *vinyl, red dress, script pin, marked: Ideal, 15″*	100.00	150.00	105.00
☐ **Shirley Temple,** *vinyl, red, white dress, marked: Ideal, 12″*	70.00	80.00	73.00
☐ **Shirley Temple,** *vinyl, wig, red dotted dress, 15″*	60.00	70.00	63.00
☐ **Shirley Temple Baby,** *composition head, cloth body, open mouth with teeth, representing actress Shirley Temple as an infant, dressed in gown, bonnet and booties, holds teddy bear, came with a pin on the gown, bearing a picture of Shirley Temple and reading, "The World's Darling Shirley Temple Doll," 16″*	160.00	190.00	150.00
☐ **Shirley Temple Baby,** *composition head with cloth body, marked Shirley Temple, 17″*	180.00	215.00	165.00
☐ **Shirley Temple Baby,** *composition head with cloth body, marked Shirley Temple, 18″*	195.00	230.00	175.00
☐ **Shirley Temple Baby,** *composition head with cloth body, marked Shirley Temple, 22″*	210.00	240.00	200.00
☐ **Shirley Temple Baby,** *composition head with cloth body, marked Shirley Temple, 25″*	245.00	285.00	230.00
☐ **Shirley Temple Baby,** *composition head with cloth body, marked Shirley Temple, 27″*	270.00	335.00	250.00

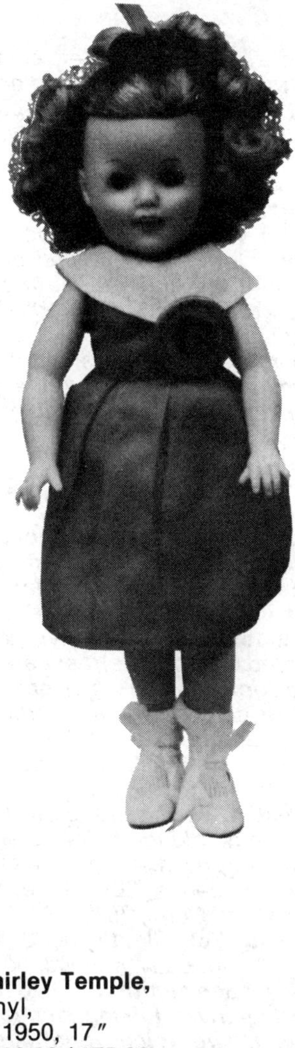

Shirley Temple,
vinyl,
c. 1957, 12″
$100.00-$125.00

Shirley Temple,
vinyl,
c. 1950, 17″
$120.00-$175.00

	Current Price Range		Prior Year Average
☐ **Shirley Temple Toddler,** *composition head, cloth body, marked #1 (some specimens do not have this marking but are marked Shirley Temple — stated value applies to both), 23″*	150.00	180.00	135.00
☐ **Shirley Temple Toddler,** *composition, marked 73 Shirley Temple, 25″*	460.00	575.00	425.00
☐ **Snow White,** *composition head, arms and legs, cloth body, molded and painted hair, molded and painted features, open mouth, eyes turned to side, marked Ideal, made c. 1939, 17½″*	70.00	85.00	65.00
☐ **Sparkle Plenty,** *plastic head, latex body, latex arms and legs, blonde hair attached by adhesive, sleep eyes (blue), Sparkle Plenty was a character in the comic strip "Dick Tracy," created by Chester Gould, marked made in U.S.A. Pat. No. 2252077, made in 1947, 15″*	50.00	65.00	45.00
Note: Competition from collectors of "comic character memorabilia" makes the price of this doll much higher than it would otherwise be.			
☐ **Spinderella Flatsy,** *vinyl, painted features, rooted hair (blonde), bendable, mounted on a platform base, to which one foot is attached, when a string is pulled, the platform turns and Spinderella "spins," made in Hong Kong, dated 1969 on the doll and 1970 on the platform*	5.50	7.00	5.00
☐ **Tabatha,** *vinyl head, cloth body, vinyl arms and legs, blonde hair (rooted), painted side-glancing eyes, Tabatha was a character in the TV series "Bewitched," marked 1966 Ideal Toy Corp., 15″*	70.00	90.00	65.00
☐ **Talking Tot,** *plastic head, vinyl arms and legs, cloth body, molded, painted hair, sleep eyes, open mouth with two teeth, talker with spring-driven talking mechanism located in chest, two voice variations: laughs when upright, cries when lying down, 22″*	16.00	19.00	15.00
☐ **Tammy,** *plastic/vinyl, rooted blonde hair, painted eyes, partially open mouth, wears two-piece bathing suit, 9″*	7.00	9.00	7.00
☐ **Tammy,** *vinyl, seran wig, painted eyes, original shorts and top, c. 1960, 12″*	12.00	14.00	12.50

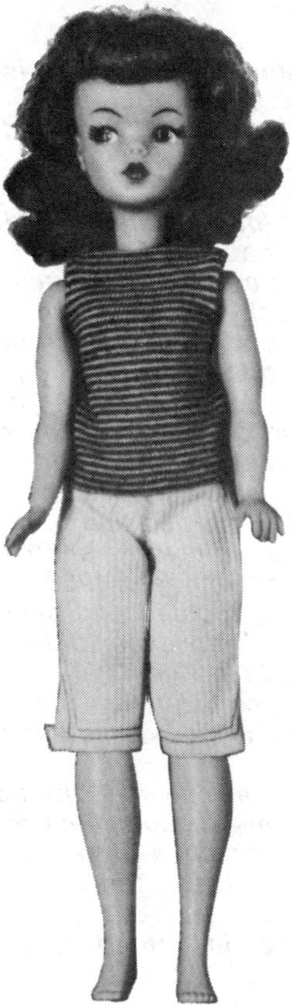

Tammy,
vinyl, 1950, 12″
$12.00-$14.00

	Current Price Range		Prior Year Average
☐ **Tammy's Mom,** *plastic/vinyl, rooted blonde hair, painted eyes looking upward, closed mouth, dressed in long gown with flowing train, marked W-18-L, also W-13 on doll body, 11⅝″*	10.00	13.00	9.00
Note: Tammy's Mom dates from the early 1960's. It came with a tag reading "Petite Fashions."			
☐ **Ted,** *plastic/vinyl, molded hair, painted eyes, closed mouth, represents an adult man (intended as Tammy's brother), marked B-12-U-2, 12″*	10.00	14.00	9.00
☐ **Theresa,** *Victorian Lady, c. 1983, 8″*	6.00	14.00	7.00
☐ **Theresa,** *Victorian Lady, c. 1983, 12″*	15.00	20.00	16.00
☐ **Thumbelina,** *molded hair, limited edition, c. 1983, 18″*	70.00	90.00	79.00

	Current Price Range		Prior Year Average
☐ **Thumbelina,** *porcelain, limited issue, c. 1983, 18″*	250.00	320.00	256.00
☐ **Thumbelina,** *rooted hair, limited edition, c. 1983, 16″*	55.00	65.00	58.00
☐ **Tickletoes,** *crier, vinyl, molded and painted hair, sleep eyes (blue), marked 16 Ideal Doll Made in U.S.A., made in 1948, 16½″*	25.00	30.00	23.00
☐ **Tiffany Taylor,** *plastic/vinyl, representing a teenage high-fashion model, wears a wig which is half blonde and half brunette, set into a revolving disc in the head; by rotating the disc Tiffany can be made to appear (from the front at least) to have either blonde or brunette hair, marked 1973, CG-19-H230 Hong Kong, 18″*	7.00	10.00	7.00
☐ **Tiny Boy,** *plastic, molded and painted hair, sleep eyes (blue), jointed at shoulders and hips, marked Ideal, made in 1960, 8″*	5.00	7.00	5.00
☐ **Tiny Girl,** *plastic, molded and painted hair (sandy blonde), sleep eyes (blue), marked Ideal Doll-9, made in 1950, 9¼″*	6.00	8.00	6.00
Note: A very good quality plastic head which most people would mistake for composition.			
☐ **Tiny Kissey,** *plastic/vinyl, blonde hair (rooted), sleep eyes (blue), jointed at the wrists, lips pucker when arms are pressed together, marked Ideal Toy Corp., K-L6-3, made in 1962, 16″*	25.00	31.00	23.00
☐ **Tiny Tears,** *porcelain, limited issue, c. 1983, 14″*	150.00	240.00	156.00
☐ **Toddler,** *hard plastic, 22″*	100.00	150.00	140.00
☐ **Toni,** *blonde hair, red striped dress, 14″*	40.00	50.00	43.00
☐ **Toni,** *character bride doll, near white wig, blue sleep eyes, closed mouth, elaborate white bridal gown with long train, five layers in skirt, brocade slip, hand beaded Victorian sleeves, tiny functional beaded buttons on cuff and down back, long veil with headpiece, 16″*	145.00	155.00	145.00
☐ **Toni,** *composition head, jointed composition body, sleep eyes, yellow dress, red shoes, c. 1950, 14″*	80.00	90.00	82.50
☐ **Toni,** *hard plastic, blonde hair, blue sleeping eyes, lashes, dress with pink bodice and green print skirt, 15″*	100.00	150.00	115.00
☐ **Toni,** *walker, plastic, blonde hair attached by adhesive, closed mouth, bright red lips, marked Ideal Doll P93, made in 1952, 21″*	65.00	80.00	60.00

Toni,
composition,
sleep eyes, c. 1950
$80.00-$90.00

	Current Price Range		Prior Year Average
☐ **Tonie,** *plastic, black hair attached by adhesive, sleep eyes (blue), marked Ideal Doll, Made in U.S.A., and additionally marked with the mold number P-90, made in 1949, 14"*	28.00	36.00	25.00
☐ **Tressy,** *vinyl head, hard body, jointed shoulders, waist, hips, rooted hair (black), blue sleep eyes, blue satin short dress and matching panties, blue original shoes, 18"*	70.00	80.00	73.00
☐ **Tressy,** *plastic/vinyl, black hair (rooted), sleep eyes (blue), pug nose, closed mouth, hair has "grow" feature (portion of wig is fitted inside head; when hair is pulled gently, it gives the appearance of "growing" out of the scalp), marked 1969, Ideal Toy Corp., GH-18, also marked (on hip) with Patent No. 3162976, made in Hong Kong*	8.00	10.00	7.00
☐ **Twins (girl),** *vinyl head, cloth body, vinyl arms and legs, blue sleep eyes, marked*			

	Current Price Range		Prior Year Average
Ideal Toy Corp., TW-14-2-U, date of manufacture not known, apparently 1960's, 15"	28.00	35.00	25.00
Note: There was also a boy version of Twins, with the same value.			
☐ **Uneeda Kid,** *composition head, arms, legs, cloth body, blue painted eyes, molded hair, hat, boots, original romper suit, yellow rain slicker with hat, carrying box of Uneeda biscuits, promotional doll for Uneeda Biscuit Co., mint, 15½"*	700.00	800.00	450.00
☐ **Upsy-Dazy,** *vinyl head with foam body, foam legs, painted features, rooted hair (blonde), Upsy-Dazy turns herself right side up, when stood on her head, marked Ideal Toy Corp., UD-H-211, made in Hong Kong in 1971, 14½"*	7.00	9.00	6.00
☐ **Velvet,** *black, vinyl, painted features, rooted hair, smiling face with closed mouth, wears white dress tied with a ribbon at the waist*	8.00	10.00	7.00
☐ **Velvet,** *white version, vinyl, painted features, rooted hair (blonde), smiling face with closed mouth, wears black dress tied at the waist with a wide white ribbon*	7.50	9.50	7.00
☐ **Velvet,** *vinyl head, hard body, jointed shoulders, waist and hips, smiling mouth, rooted hair, navy blue sailing outfit with long pants, 15"*	38.00	42.00	40.00
☐ **Velvet,** *vinyl head, hard body, jointed shoulders, waist, hips, rooted hair, smiling mouth, pink velvet blazer, plaid shirt, 15"*	35.00	38.00	35.00
☐ **Victorian Lady,** *c. 1983, 8"*	20.00	25.00	21.00
☐ **Victorian Lady,** *c. 1983, 12"*	30.00	35.00	32.00
☐ **Victorian Lady,** *vinyl stuffed head, arms, legs, oilcloth body, molded brown hair, blue sleep eyes open closed mouth, original white dress with red and dark blue stripes, large collar, red trim, cotton panties, original shoes, c. 1940's*	60.00	70.00	60.00

IMCO

	Current Price Range		Prior Year Average
☐ **Love Me,** *vinyl head and body, blonde hair (rooted), sleep eyes (blue), marked VS20, made in 1953, 19"*	23.00	29.00	21.00

IMPERIAL

	Current Price Range		Prior Year Average
☐ **Boac Airline Hostess,** *plastic/vinyl, painted features, closed mouth, rooted hair (brunette), wearing an airline hostess cap and carrying a flight bag, unmarked on doll, box marked Imperial Toy Corp., 1971, made in Hong Kong, 5″*	3.00	4.00	3.00
☐ **Heidi,** *vinyl head, plastic body, rooted blonde hair cut into bangs, painted eyes, wears peasant costume of Switzerland (Alpine region), marked Made in Hong Kong, 8″*	4.00	6.00	4.00
Note: The manufacturer's name (Imperial Toy Corp.) appears only on the box, not on the doll.			
☐ **Japan Airline (J.A.L.) Hostess,** *plastic, vinyl, painted features, closed mouth, rooted hair (black), wearing a Japanese kimono and carrying a flight bag, unmarked on doll, box marked Imperial Toy Corp., 1971, made in Hong Kong, 5″*	3.00	4.00	3.00
☐ **Linda,** *plastic/vinyl, sleep eyes (blue), closed mouth, marked Imperial, made in 1950, 17″*	25.00	31.00	23.00
☐ **Pan Am Airline Hostess,** *plastic/vinyl, painted features, closed mouth, rooted hair (blonde), wearing an airline hostess cap and carrying a flight bag, unmarked on doll, box marked Imperial Toy Corp., 1971, made in Hong Kong, 5¼″*	3.00	4.00	3.00
☐ **Sunny Surfers,** *vinyl, these small dolls (all 5″) were made in various poses and facial expressions in the mid 1970's, probably with a view to capturing the sort of market which had bought Thomas Dam's "trolls" about a decade earlier, some are marked Hong Kong, others have no marking, all products of the Imperial Toy Co., for any style*	2.50	3.50	2.50

IMPERIAL CROWN

	Current Price Range		Prior Year Average
☐ **Baby Bubbles,** *composition head, cloth body, molded and painted hair, bright red lips, glossy face, made in 1950, 21″*	16.00	21.00	15.00
☐ **Miss Pepsodent,** *vinyl, sleep eyes (blue), open mouth with "action" teeth, when lying down the doll has yellow teeth, upon rising, the yellow teeth roll back and a row of gleaming white ones appear, the message*			

	Current Price Range		Prior Year Average
was (of course) that a child who was lazy about brushing would end up with yellow teeth, this doll was apparently sold in stores but may also have been used by the Pepsodent company (makers of toothpaste) as a promotional item, date of manufacture is not known, probably early 1950's	80.00	100.00	75.00

IMS

☐ **Uncle Sam,** *bisque head, ball jointed, fixed eyes, marked IMS, date of manufacture unknown, presumably 1970's, 12″*	100.00	130.00	95.00

IRWIN

☐ **Baby,** *early plastic, jointed in old plastic high chair, 5″*	45.00	55.00	45.00
☐ **Bashful Boy,** *plastic, molded and painted features, molded and painted hair, marked Irwin, Made in U.S.A., made in 1950, 6½″*	5.00	7.00	5.00
☐ **Crib Angel,** *vinyl head, cloth body, molded and painted features, fixed eyes (blue), marked Irwin, made in 1961, 8″*	3.00	5.00	3.00
☐ **Knotts' Berry Farm,** *plastic, molded and painted features, molded and painted hair, wears broad-brimmed hat and banner reading "Knotts' Berry Farm," premium doll, date of manufacture unknown, 6½″*	3.00	4.00	3.00

ITALOCREMONA

☐ **Mirella,** *vinyl, sleep eyes, rooted hair, made in Italy for the U.S. Kresge (K-Mart) chain, 12″*	14.00	18.00	13.00
☐ **Sabrina,** *vinyl, sleep eyes, rooted hair, made in Italy for the U.S. Kresge (K-Mart) chain, 12″*	14.00	18.00	13.00
☐ **Vanessa,** *character, 1965, vinyl, jointed lady doll, brown and silver streaked hair, blue sleep eyes, closed mouth, long white sequined evening gown, matching forearms cuffs, genuine white Ermine fur complete with head and tails, 14″*	50.00	60.00	50.00

CHARLES IVES

	Current Price Range		Prior Year Average
☐ **Empress Eugenie,** *automan, French bisque head, composition body, original costume and box, one of the rarest in a series designed by Charles Hotchkiss and made by Charles Ives, 11½"*	3200.00	4000.00	3000.00

JACK FROST SUGAR

☐ **Jack Frost,** *cloth (printed), given as a premium or promotional item in connection with the purchase of Jack Frost Sugar, probably c. 1970, 20"*	8.00	11.00	8.00

JAPAN

☐ **Celluloid,** *black, painted, movable arms, large eyes, wears smock, marked Made in Japan, 8"*	45.00	60.00	42.00
☐ **Nurse,** *celluloid, movable arms, holds infant in one arm, feeding bottle in other hand, wears broad-brimmed hat, old-style nursing uniform with religious insignia, marked Made in Japan, 7"*	32.00	42.00	30.00
☐ **Shirley Temple,** *composition head and body, molded hair, closed mouth, wearing "drum majorette" uniform (sometimes referred to as "marcher"), fully jointed body, 8"*	75.00	100.00	70.00

JERRI

☐ **Blue Boy,** *c. 1983*	350.00	400.00	355.00
☐ **Melody,** *curls, lacy lilac dress, c. 1983*	300.00	350.00	310.00
☐ **Pinkie,** *c. 1983*	300.00	350.00	310.00
☐ **Virginia Dare,** *pilgrim outfit, c. 1983*	300.00	350.00	315.00

JILMAR

☐ **Praying Patti,** *talker, vinyl head, cloth body, painted eyes, recites prayers when button is pushed, unmarked on doll, sold originally*

	Current Price Range		Prior Year Average
with a tag reading TM Jilmar Co., this doll is sometimes referred to as "Sleepy Angel," 18"	19.00	23.00	18.00

JOINTED DOLL COMPANY

☐ **Composition,** *over wood head, jointed wooden body, metal hands and feet, center parted blonde coiffure, blue painted eyes, velvet dress, painted stockings and high top shoes*	425.00	575.00	425.00
☐ **Composition,** *over wood head, jointed wooden body, metal hands and feet, center parted blonde coiffure, brown painted eyes, cotton dress, painted stockings and high top shoes*	430.00	550.00	425.00
☐ **Springfield Wooden Doll,** *composition over wood head, jointed wooden body, metal hands and feet, elaborate molded and painted blonde coiffure, molded face, painted features, cotton dress, 12"*	475.00	625.00	450.00

JOLLY

☐ **Baby Angel,** *plastic/vinyl, marked Jolly Toys, Inc., made in 1961, 16"*	3.00	4.00	3.00
☐ **Cutie,** *vinyl, blonde hair (rooted), sleep eyes (blue), marked Jolly Toys, 1965, 14"*	11.00	14.00	10.00
☐ **Dixie Pixie,** *vinyl head and body, sleep eyes, closed mouth, marked FR18, made in 1963, 19¼"*	28.00	35.00	25.00
☐ **Judy Playmate,** *plastic/vinyl, marked Jolly Toy, 1968, 11½"*	4.00	6.00	4.00
☐ **Linda,** *black, plastic/vinyl, black hair (rooted), sleep eyes (brown), nursing mouth, marked Jolly Toys, Inc., 1969-16, 20"*	15.00	19.00	14.00
☐ **Little Love,** *plastic/vinyl, sleep eyes (blue), blonde hair (rooted), closed mouth, bright red lips, braided hair, Alpine-type outfit, marked Jolly Toys Inc., 1962, 13½"*	4.00	6.00	4.00
☐ **Lovely Lisa,** *vinyl head, vinyl arms and legs, cloth body, sleep eyes (blue), rooted hair (light blonde), open puckered mouth, pug nose, dressed in an infant's gown and bonnet, marked 14/4 Jolly Toys Inc., made in 1962, 14½"*	4.00	6.00	4.00

	Current Price Range		Prior Year Average
☐ **Miss Grow-Up,** *plastic/vinyl, fixed eyes, long lashes, long thin eyebrows, blonde hair (rooted), large ribbon in hair, wearing a corduroy dress with ruffled collar, marked Jolly Toys Inc., 1963, 11½″*	5.00	7.00	5.00
☐ **Mommy's Baby,** *vinyl head, cloth body, vinyl arms and legs, blonde hair (rooted), sleep eyes (blue), marked 15-6 Signature Doll Corp., Signature Doll Division, New York NY 10011, made in 1969, 19″*	6.00	8.00	6.00
Note: Whenever a doll is marked with the manufacturer's zipcode, this is positive evidence that it was made no earlier than the 1960's.			
☐ **Nikki,** *plastic/vinyl, blonde hair (rooted), sleep eyes (blue), marked Made in Hong Kong, Jolly Toys, made in 1964, 13″*	8.00	11.00	7.00
☐ **Playpen Doll,** *plastic/vinyl, blonde hair (rooted), sleep eyes (blue), marked 26 Jolly Toys, Inc., 1967, 14″*	5.00	7.00	5.00
☐ **Pretty Girl,** *plastic/vinyl, blonde hair (rooted), painted eyes, marked Jolly Toy Co., made in 1964, 17″*	9.00	12.00	8.00
☐ **Suzanna Ballerina,** *plastic/vinyl, sleep eyes (blue), marked Jolly Toy 1965, 17¼″*	7.00	10.00	7.00
☐ **Timmy,** *vinyl head, foam body, foam arms and legs, molded and painted features, painted eyes, marked Jolly Toys, Inc., 1967, 14″*	12.00	16.00	11.00
☐ **Trudy,** *plastic/vinyl, blonde hair (rooted), sleep eyes (blue), marked Jolly Toys, 1962, 13″*	11.00	14.00	10.00
☐ **Twistee,** *vinyl head, foam body, foam arms and legs, brunette hair (rooted), sleep eyes (black), marked Jolly Toy Inc., made in 1964, 16″*	6.00	8.00	6.00

JOY

☐ **Colonial Lady,** *composition head and body, sleep eyes (blue), blonde wig, unmarked, believed to have been made in the 1940's, 15″*	26.00	32.00	25.00
☐ **Prom Queen,** *composition head and body, sleep eyes (blue), red wig, made in 1939, 14½″*	30.00	37.00	28.00
☐ **Marlene Dietrich,** *composition head and body, sleep eyes (blue), blonde wig, made in 1945, 15″*	75.00	95.00	70.00

	Current Price Range		Prior Year Average
☐ **Sheila From Irleand,** *composition head, composition arms, legs and body, painted features, molded and painted hair, closed mouth, neck swivels, dressed in a native costume of Ireland, unmarked on doll, but sold with a stringed tag reading Joy Doll Corp., NYV New York World's Fair 1939, 7½″*	23.00	29.00	22.00
Note: Interest from collectors of World's Fair items contributes to the high price. However, when Sheila is lacking the tag her value is somewhat less.			

JOYCE-MILLER

☐ **Grandpa,** *cloth, unmarked on doll, sold originally with a tag reading Joyce-Miller Original, Copyright Sears Roebuck & Co., believed to date from the late 1960's, 16″* . .	22.00	28.00	22.00

JULLIEN

☐ **Bisque,** *socket head, fixed eyes (very large), painted lashes on upper and lower lids, almost straight horizontal bushy brows, closed pouting mouth, bright red lips, long narrow nose, thin face, representing a girl of 5 or 6 years of age, often dressed as an older girl or an adult, marked Jullien-2, date of manufacture unknown, c. 1885, 13″*	750.00	925.00	725.00
Note: The Jullien company was located in Paris, and was active from about the time of the American Civil War into the 20th century.			

JUMEAU

This French manufacturer produced some highly exquisite dolls. The quality, reputation and scarcity make for steep prices on the collector's market: anyone interested in Jumeau dolls needs heavy cash or the willpower to admire them behind the glass cases of museums. Jumeau went into business before 1850 and the company was still operating in the late 1800's, having won just about every award for dollmaking that existed on the face of the earth.

	Current Price Range		Prior Year Average
☐ **Bébé,** *bisque head, ball jointed composition body, long brown human hair wig, brown paperweight eyes, chiffon dress with eyelet overskirt, 16½"*	3000.00	3500.00	3250.00
☐ **Bébé,** *bisque head, composition body, blonde human hair wig, blue paperweight eyes, pierced ears, long waisted pink eyelet dress with stockings and velvet boots, 23"*	2500.00	2750.00	2600.00
☐ **Bébé,** *bisque head, composition body, brown paperweight eyes, white crochet dress, ruffled bonnet with long tie, 20½"*	2000.00	2500.00	2250.00
☐ **Bébé,** *bisque head, jointed composition body, blue paperweight eyes, blonde mohair wig, pierced ears and closed mouth, mark: Blue Jumeau Medaille d'or Paris, 12"*	2000.00	2300.00	1800.00
☐ **Bébé,** *bisque head, jointed composition body, blue paperweight eyes, brown wig, closed mouth, pierced ears, lovely antique clothes and shoes, mark: Tête Jumeau 11*	2500.00	3000.00	2200.00
☐ **Bébé,** *bisque head, jointed composition body, brown paperweight eyes, blonde mohair wig, pierced applied ears, closed mouth, rose silk antique ensemble with shoes, mark: Tête Jumeau 14, 30"*	2800.00	3500.00	2800.00
☐ **Bébé,** *bisque head, jointed wood and composition body, blue paperweight eyes, blonde wig, pierced ears, open mouth, mark: Tête Jumeau 12, Bébé Jumeau, 26"*	3200.00	4000.00	3000.00
☐ **Bébé,** *bisque head, kid body with bisque hands, brown loop curl wig, blue sleep eyes, green print dress with lace trim, straw hat, 26"*	3000.00	3500.00	3250.00
☐ **Bébé,** *bisque head, wood and composition jointed body, blue paperweight eyes, blonde mohair wig, closed mouth, pierced ears, rose silk dress and hat, 16"*	2400.00	2600.00	2400.00
☐ **Bébé,** *bisque head, wood and French composition jointed body, blue paperweight eyes, blonde mohair wig, open/closed mouth, pierced applied ears, antique green silk ensemble with shoes, mark: Déposé Jumeau 8, 18"*	3800.00	4500.00	3500.00
☐ **Bébé,** *jointed composition body, closed mouth, brown eyes, brown wig, lavender satin dress trimmed with roses, French-style bonnet*	2200.00	2800.00	2450.00
☐ **Bébé Louve,** *jointed composition body, corn-flower blue paperweight eyes, blonde mohair wig, pink dress, straw hat, made specially for the Louve Shop in Paris in 1876, 22"*	3200.00	4200.00	3600.00

	Current Price Range		Prior Year Average
□ **Bébé Parlé,** *talker, bisque, sleep eyes (roundish), painted lashes on upper and lower lids, long arching brows, partially open mouth, narrow nose, joined at the elbows, talking mechanism operated by pullcord, says two words ("mama" — "papa"), date of manufacture unknown, probably c. 1895, 32″*	900.00	1100.00	850.00

Note: The value indicated is for a specimen in working condition. This is a really impressive doll, both for its size and the fact that it was one of the early foreign talkers. It would be even more expensive but apparently Jumeau turned it out in rather large quantities.

Bisque and Composition, c. 1905, 22″ **$2000.00-$3000.00**

	Current Price Range		Prior Year Average
☐ **Bisque,** *ball jointed body, blue paperweight eyes, blonde curly wig, open mouth, pierced ears, pink dress with buttons on front, lace, pleated skirt, matching hat, 22″*	1800.00	2800.00	2250.00
☐ **Bisque,** *blue paperweight eyes, blonde wig, peach taffeta dress, marked: Jumeau, 16″*	2800.00	3600.00	3100.00
☐ **Bisque,** *blue paperweight eyes, French curls, closed mouth, head and body signed, 15″*	2000.00	2600.00	2250.00
☐ **Bisque,** *brown paperweight eyes, brown human hair wig, open mouth, pierced ears, lovely costume with hat, 19″*	2000.00	2200.00	2000.00
☐ **Bisque,** *composition body, bisque hands and feet, paperweight eyes, working mechanism, original costume, 21″*	3500.00	4500.00	3500.00
☐ **Poupee Parisienne (Paris doll),** *bisque head, wooden body, wooden arms and legs, fixed eyes (oval), painted lashes on upper and lower lids, thin brows, small closed mouth with lightly colored lips, narrow nose, squarish jaw, usually dressed to represent an adult woman, marked E, date of manufacture unknown, but probably 1890's, these are found in a variety of costumes and wearing a variety of wigs, 16″*	1375.00	1625.00	1325.00
Note: There is no doubt that the Poupee Parisienne was one of the standard Jumeau dolls for a number of years, however relatively few reached America as the firm was not (at least not at that time) export-oriented.			
☐ **Cody,** *bisque, fixed eyes (medium size, dark), lightly painted lashes on upper and lower lids, naturalistic brows (slightly arched), closed mouth, thin pale lips, narrow nose with well-defined nostrils, long thin face, found dressed as a child or adult, marked 13, date of manufacture unknown, c. 1887, one of the most famous and sought-after of the Jumeau dolls, 26″*	3200.00	3900.00	3175.00
Note: The Jumeau "Cody" doll got its name when Buffalo Bill Cody, the American showman, visited Paris in 1887 and bought a specimen of this doll. Buffalo Bill apparently had taste when it came to dolls: this long-face model represented a sharp departure from the usual mump-cheeked dolls of that era, and its facial features are very well presented.			

	Current Price Range		Prior Year Average
☐ **Bisque,** *fixed eyes (very large, roundish), painted lashes on the upper and lower lids, arched brows, partially open mouth with thin lips, narrow nose, basically thin face, applied ears (almost flat), sophisticated facial expression, may be found dressed as a young girl or an adult, marked Déposé E/9/J, on the head, additionally marked on the body: Jumeau, Medal d'Or, indicating that the Jumeau company had won gold medals for its dolls, date of manufacture unknown, probably the later 1880's or early 1890's, 20″*	1250.00	1500.00	1150.00
☐ **Bisque,** *fixed eyes (large, prominent, dark), painted lashes on the upper and lower lids, arching brows (rather bushy), partially open mouth (the lower lip much smaller than the upper), narrow nose, squarish jaw, conventional ears, representing a girl about 5 or 6 years of age, marked Déposé E-3J, date of manufacture unknown, 10½″*	950.00	1100.00	900.00
☐ **Bisque,** *French, ball-jointed body, human hair wig, blue paperweight eyes, pierced ears, open mouth, pink and green costume, c. 1907*	1900.00	2100.00	1850.00
☐ **Bisque,** *jointed composition body, blue paperweight eyes, blonde wig, closed mouth, 25″*	2200.00	2800.00	2500.00
☐ **Bisque,** *large topaz paperweight eyes, French curls, V hairline, 17″*	1200.00	2000.00	1600.00
☐ **Bisque,** *painted body, blue paperweight eyes, blonde French curls, blue organdy with embroidery, 20″*	5200.00	5800.00	5400.00
☐ **Bisque,** *socket head, walker, fixed eyes, open mouth showing teeth, head turns as doll walks, representing a young girl, marked with an X inside a circle, topped by a checkmark, date of manufacture unknown, presumed to have been made in the 1880's, 22½″*	600.00	750.00	575.00
☐ **Bisque Head,** *brown paperweight eyes, brown human hair wig, open mouth, pierced ears, lovely costume with hat, 19″*	2000.00	2200.00	2000.00
☐ **Bisque Head,** *composition body, bisque hands and feet, paperweight eyes, working mechanism, original costume, 21″*	3500.00	4500.00	3500.00
☐ **Bisque Head,** *French ball-jointed body, human hair wig, paperweight eyes, pierced ears, pink and green dress with hat, marked 1907, 25″*	2000.00	2100.00	2050.00

Lenci, Fashion Doll, *felt, painted features, c. 1940, 29″,* **$1200.00-$1500.00.**

Jumeau, *#9, bisque head, French body, paperweight eyes, c. 1910, 26"*, **$1600.00-$1800.00.**

Lanternier Et Cie, *bisque head, ball jointed composition body, sleep eyes, c. 1905, 18",* **$500.00-$600.00.**

Rabery & Delphiau, *bisque head, composition body, fixed eyes, c. 1880, 19",* **$2500.00-$2800.00.**

Simon & Halbig, *#1249 Santa Mold, bisque head, composition body, c. 1910, 26"*, **$1000.00-$1200.00.**

Grace Putnam, Bye-lo Baby, *bisque head, cloth body, sleep eyes, c. 1920, 14",* **$525.00-$575.00.**

Bisque Dome Head, *turn shoulder, fixed eyes, c. 1890, 19″,* **$875.00-$925.00.**

Ideal, Shirley Temple, *vinyl, sleep eyes, c. 1950, 17",* **$120.00-$175.00.**

	Current Price Range		Prior Year Average
☐ **Bisque Head,** *French ball-jointed body, human hair wig, paperweight eyes, open mouth, pierced ears, gold satin costume, brown trim, hat to match, 24″*	2300.00	2550.00	2350.00
☐ **Bisque Head,** *French ball-jointed body, human hair wig, blue paperweight eyes, navy blue print dress with hat, marked: No. 9, 1907, 20″*	2000.00	2250.00	2015.00
☐ **Bisque Head,** *French ball-jointed body, human hair wig, brown paperweight eyes, pierced ears, gold satin costume with brown hat, 24″*	2500.00	3000.00	2550.00

Bisque Head,
French body,
c. 1910, 26″
$1600.00-$1800.00

	Current Price Range		Prior Year Average
☐ **Bisque Head,** *jointed body, dark brown human hair wig, black paperweight eyes, open mouth, pierced ears, French blue brocade two piece dress, 1910, 26″*	1600.00	1800.00	1650.00
☐ **Bisque Head,** *jointed body, medium brown human hair wig, blue paperweight eyes, open mouth, blue silk dress and hat, shoes have "bee mark," marked: #1907, 1905, 22″*	2000.00	3000.00	2250.00
☐ **Bisque Head,** *jointed French composition body, stationary glass eyes, open mouth, pierced ears, 16″*	2500.00	2600.00	2500.00
☐ **Bisque Socket Head,** *ball-jointed wood and composition body, brown human hair wig in long curls, blue blown glass eyes with lashes, pierced ears, Austrian crystal earrings and necklace, pink fancy dress with large shoulder to waist collar, lace trimmed, matching underclothes, large matching bonnet, head marked in red mark Jumeau, body marked in red mark Jumeau, 23″*	2500.00	3000.00	2700.00
☐ **Black Doll,** *brown paperweight eyes, black wig, closed mouth, plaid taffetta dress, carries own toy, incised Jumeau, 18″*	3200.00	3800.00	3400.00
☐ **Bride,** *fashion, bisque head, lower arms and legs, kid body, blue paperweight eyes, blonde wig, pierced ears, closed mouth, lovely white lace antique bridal gown with veil, 20″*	1500.00	2000.00	1500.00
☐ **Character Doll,** *French-style body, blue eyes, mahogany wig, blue-green satin dress, matching bonnet, incised R.R., 21″*	3000.00	3600.00	3200.00
☐ **Child,** *bisque head, composition jointed body, brown glass paperweight eyes, brown wig, closed mouth, pierced ears, 21″*	3000.00	4000.00	3500.00
☐ **Child,** *bisque head, jointed French composition and wooden body, blue paperweight eyes, closed mouth, dimpled chin, applied, pierced ears, 30″*	4500.00	5500.00	5000.00
☐ **Child,** *bisque socket head, French composition and wooden jointed body, almond shaped brown glass paperweight eyes, brush stroked brows, closed mouth, pierced, applied ears, brown human hair wig, marked 10″ on head and "Jumeau Medaille d' Or" on body, 24″*	4000.00	5000.00	4000.00
☐ **Closed Mouth,** *ball-jointed composition body, brown eyes, brown hair, marked: VIII, Jumeau stamp, 17″*	1500.00	1800.00	1650.00
☐ **Closed Mouth,** *blue paperweight eyes, blonde curls, pink taffeta dress and hat, 17″*	2200.00	2800.00	2500.00

	Current Price Range		Prior Year Average
☐ **Closed Mouth,** *blue paperweight eyes, marked, 13½″*	1800.00	2600.00	2200.00
☐ **Closed Mouth,** *painted body, large blue eyes, black curls, applied ears, blue outfit, 33″*	6200.00	6800.00	6450.00
☐ **DEP,** *girl, bisque head, ball-jointed body with stiff wrists and wooden thighs, set brown eyes, six tiny teeth, red silk drop-waisted dress with lace borders and matching hat, 1894 A.M. DEP, 14″*	170.00	205.00	180.00
☐ **DEP,** *bisque head, French composition jointed body, brown sleep eyes, auburn French human hair wig, antique white dress with lace, DEP 7, 18½″*	750.00	900.00	725.00
☐ **DEP,** *bisque head, French composition ball-jointed body, human hair wig, (blonde) beautiful coloration, heirloom clothing, DEP 9, 22″*	750.00	840.00	765.00
☐ **DEP,** *bisque head, French wood jointed body, antique wig, brown sleep eyes, brush stroke brows, small, open mouth with two carved teeth, nostril accents, pierced ears, four piece ensemble of antique pantaloons, slip, petticoat and dress, all with intricate tatting trim and inserts, 2, 12″*	475.00	495.00	480.00
☐ **E.J. Bébé,** *bisque head, French composition body, brown paperweight eyes, brown human hair wig, applied, pierced ears, original clothes, marked: DÉPOSÉ E. 7 J., 18″*	4800.00	5800.00	4800.00
☐ **E.J. Bébé,** *bisque socket head, composition body with separate ball-joints, unjointed wrists, wig, paperweight eyes, applied ears, pierced ears, antique clothes, marks: head-incised "Déposé" mark and check marks, body-"Jumeau Medaille D'or," 20″*	4750.00	5500.00	4650.00
☐ **E.J. Bébé,** *bisque socket head, jointed composition body with straight wrists, blonde wig, blue paperweight eyes, closed mouth, pierced ears, unusual clothes, 19″*	6000.00	7000.00	6000.00
☐ **E.J. Bébé,** *bisque socket head, jointed composition body with straight wrists, blonde wig, brown paperweight eyes, pierced ears, closed mouth, all original clothes, mint, 20″*	7000.00	8000.00	7000.00
☐ **Fashion,** *bisque head, arms, legs, kid body, blue paperweight eyes, blonde mohair wig, pierced ears, closed mouth, original dark green silk dress with matching hat, mark: E. Jumeau, 20″*	2800.00	3200.00	2700.00

	Current Price Range		Prior Year Average
☐ **Fashion Doll,** *bisque head, kid body, swivel head, upswept wig with tendrils, blue sleep eyes, ivory silk bride suit, 15"*	1500.00	2000.00	1750.00
☐ **Fashion Lady,** *bisque, paperweight blue eyes, wig, applied pierced ears, original detailed costume, very elaborate, with her own trunk*	3500.00	4000.00	3300.00
☐ **French Fashion,** *bisque head, ball-jointed composition body, human hair wig, brown paperweight eyes, pierced ears, gold gown, 1907, 16"*	1500.00	1700.00	1550.00
☐ **French Fashion,** *bisque head, kid body, fancy blonde coiffure, brown glass eyes, watered silk dress, bow trim and bonnet, 14"*	1400.00	1500.00	1450.00
☐ **Girl,** *bisque head, jointed French composition body, brown paperweight stationary eyes, brown wig, closed mouth, pierced ears, antique clothes, marked: JUMEAU/ MEDAILLE D'OR/PARIS*	2500.00	2600.00	2500.00
☐ **Girl,** *composition ball-jointed body, brown paperweight eyes, brown human hair wig, closed mouth, marked, 22"*	2600.00	3000.00	2700.00
☐ **Girl,** *French body, blonde, human hair wig, brown paperweight eyes, closed mouth, pierced ears, silk dress, leather shoes, marked: 71EJ, 18"*	2000.00	2400.00	2100.00
☐ **Poupee Parisienne (Paris doll),** *bisque head, wooden body, wooden arms and legs, fixed eyes (oval), painted lashes on upper and lower lids, thin brows, small closed mouth with lightly colored lips, narrow nose, squarish jaw, usually dressed to represent an adult woman, marked E, date of manufacture unknown, but probably 1890's, these are found in a variety of costumes and wearing a variety of wigs, 16"*	1375.00	1625.00	1325.00
Note: There is no doubt that the Poupee Parisienne was one of the standard Jumeau dolls for a number of years, however relatively few reached America as the firm was not (at least not at that time) export-oriented.			
☐ **Papier Mâché,** *wooden body, set blue glass eyes, long brown curly wig, open mouth, blue dress with striped collar, picture hat, marked: Paris 301-12, 24"*	550.00	650.00	586.00
☐ **Phonograph Doll,** *bisque head, jointed composition body, wig, brown, blue paperweight eyes, closed mouth, voice box not working, antique clothes*	2500.00	2700.00	2500.00

	Current Price Range		Prior Year Average
☐ **Tête,** *bisque head, jointed composition body, brown paperweight eyes, brown wig, closed mouth, pierced ears, original white taffeta dress with white lace trim, shoes, mark: Tête Jumeau 5, 14½"*	2500.00	3000.00	2500.00
☐ **Poured Wax Shoulderhead,** *waxed papier mache arms, legs, cloth body, inset blue eyes, brown wig, open mouth, brown velvet lace trimmed dress, shoes, marked: E. Jumeau Med. Or 1978, Paris, 20"*	375.00	525.00	350.00
☐ **Princess Elizabeth,** *bisque head, blue sleep eyes, blonde human hair wig, blue and white print dress, blue felt coat, 17"*	1600.00	2100.00	1800.00
☐ **Tête,** *bisque head, jointed composition body, blue paperweight eyes, brown human hair wig, closed mouth, pierced ears, marked: Déposé Tête Jumeau Bte S.G.D.G. 6, 25"*	4000.00	4300.00	3900.00
☐ **Tête,** *bisque head, jointed composition body, brown wig, blue paperweight eyes, closed mouth, pierced ears, original clothes, fully signed head and body, red head, stamp: Déposé Tête Jumeau Bte S.G. D.G. 6, blue stamp or Bébé Jumeau oval sticker on body, 24"*	3800.00	4200.00	3675.00
☐ **Tête Bébé,** *bisque socket head, blue paperweight eyes, light brown human hair wig, light brown eyebrows, painted upper and lower eyelashes, open mouth with four molded teeth, and red accent lines, pierced ears, jointed composition French body, teal blue velvet dress, lace trimmed, satin bow in back, matching hat with feathers, ribbons, leather high button boots, marks: 1907 9, Body blue stamp: Bébé Jumear Bte, S.G.D.G. Déposé, 20"*	3000.00	3500.00	3000.00
☐ **Tête,** *bisque socket head, fully jointed French composition body, original cork pate, blonde human hair wig, ringlets, blue paperweight eyes, painted upper and lower lashes, closed mouth with white space between lips, red accent lines, upturned corners, pierced ears, original marked box with large Maison Jumeau label on inside of lid, original pink silk dress, lace panels with silk squares, ribbon embroidered lace, puffed sleeves, neckline with gathered lace, silk ribbon, marks: Déposé, Tête Jumeau, Bte, S.G.D.G. 12, various artist initials and check marks, body, oval paper label on back, Bébé Jumeau, Diplome D'Honneur, 26"*	4000.00	4200.00	2500.00

	Current Price Range		Prior Year Average
☐ **Tête,** *bisque socket head, jointed composition French body, brown paperweight eyes, heavy eyebrows, lavishly painted upper and lower eyelashes, closed mouth with accent lines, white space between lips, upturned edges, pierced ears, cork pate, original curly blonde mohair wig, waist length in back with curled bangs and top knot, all original, pale pink pleated dress with fitted lace trimmed coat with peplum back, frog ties in front with beaded tips, marks: Red stamp, Déposé Tête Jumeau, Bte, S.G.D.G. 6, various artist's marks, body, Blue stamp, Jumeau Medaille D'or Paris, 15″*	2400.00	3000.00	2400.00
☐ **Tête,** *bisque socket head, jointed French composition body, brown paperweight eyes, closed mouth with red accent lines, brown human hair wig styled in long ringlets, pierced ears, original cork pate, gold silk dress with lace and brown ribbon, feathered bonnet with lace and silk bow, original body finish, marks: Red stamp on head, Déposé Tête Jumeau, S.G.D.G. 12, various artist check marks, body, oval paper label reads Bébé Jumeau, Diplome, D'Honneur, 26″*	3600.00	4000.00	3400.00
☐ **Tête,** *bisque socket head, jointed French composition body, straight wrists, blue paperweight eyes, closed mouth with white line between lips, blonde human hair wig, pierced ears, original, rose colored satin dress with black lace, matching velvet bonnet, brown leather shoes, marks: head, Déposé Tête Jumeau, Bte, S.G.D.G. 4, torso, blue stamp Jumeau, Medaille D'or Paris, 13″*	2500.00	2700.00	2400.00
☐ **Tête,** *bisque socket head, jointed French composition body, wheat colored human hair wig, long braids, brown paperweight eyes, original cork pate, open mouth with row of upper molded teeth, pierced ears, heavy eyebrows that nearly meet at bridge of nose, pink taffeta two piece, fitted dress with velvet black ribbon, flowered straw hat, lace trimmed underwear, marks: red stamp, Tête Jumeau, 16″*	2500.00	3000.00	2500.00
☐ **Tête,** *blue paperweight eyes, blonde mohair wig, closed mouth, head and body marked, 15″*	2100.00	2500.00	2250.00

	Current Price Range		Prior Year Average
☐ **Tête,** *composition ball-jointed body, brown paperweight eyes, blonde mohair wig, closed mouth, head and body marked, 20″*	2800.00	3200.00	2950.00
☐ **Tête Bébé,** *bisque head, jointed composition body, blue paperweight eyes, original blonde wig, open mouth, original clothes, 17″*	2400.00	2600.00	2400.00
☐ **Tête Bébé,** *bisque head, jointed French composition body, original blonde human hair wig, blue paperweight eyes, pierced ears, earrings, closed mouth, lovely dress with matching velvet hat, marks: red stamp head, body, blue stamped mark, 24″*	3700.00	4300.00	3500.00
☐ **Tête Jumeau,** *bisque head, French composition jointed body, French human hair wig, brown sleep eyes, white antique dress, stamped: Tête Jumeau Dep 12, 27″*	1200.00	1350.00	1200.00
☐ **Walker,** *bisque head, ball-jointed composition body, talks, walks, throws kisses, human hair wig, brown sleep eyes, pierced ears, burgandy velvet dress, marked: Dep 9, 21″*	2000.00	2500.00	2250.00

JUNEL

	Current Price Range		Prior Year Average
☐ **Bonny Baby,** *mask face cloth, blonde yarn hair, red polka dot dress and hat, name on tag, 15″*	50.00	60.00	52.00
☐ **February's Birthday Gift,** *composition, brunette hair, painted eyes, jointed at the shoulders, unmarked, made in 1945, 5½″*	10.00	14.00	9.00
☐ **Isabella,** *composition, molded and painted features, wears reproduction of 15th century costume with large crucifix at neck, representing Isabella of Spain, who was instrumental in sponsoring Columbus' voyage of 1492, unmarked, made in 1946, 7½″*	14.00	19.00	13.00
☐ **Mary Lincloln,** *composition head and body, painted eyes, wears velvet dress claimed by manufacturer to be a copy of an actual fashion worn by Mary Todd Lincoln (Mrs. Abraham Lincoln), date of manufacture unknown, 11″*	25.00	31.00	23.00

JURO

	Current Price Range		Prior Year Average
☐ **Pinky Lee,** *vinyl head, cloth body, composition hands, molded and painted features, with operational arms and legs, worked by pullcord, Pinky Lee was a television personality in the 1950's, marked Juro Celebrity Products, date of manufacture unknown, c. 1956, 24"*	90.00	115.00	85.00
☐ **Charlie McCarthy,** *ventriloquist doll, jaunty black hat, eye monocle, 29"*	70.00	80.00	70.00
☐ **Charlie McCarthy,** *ventriloquist dummy, early vinyl issue*	25.00	125.00	45.00

JUTTA

☐ **Baby,** *character, bisque head, composition bent-limb baby body, blue sleep eyes, original lashes, blonde human hair wig, christening gown, 23"*	650.00	750.00	650.00

KAHAGIA

☐ **Lena,** *plastic/vinyl, sleep eyes (brown), partially open mouth, unmarked, made in Greece, probably around 1970, 12½"*	11.00	14.00	11.00

KAHL & KOHLE

☐ **Bisque,** *composition arms, legs, cloth body, wig, blue sleep eyes with lashes, black cotton costume, 23"*	655.00	725.00	650.00
☐ **Bisque,** *head with bisque shoulder plate, fixed on kidskin body, fixed eyes (large, round, dark), painted lashes on upper and lower lids, high arched bushy brows, open mouth with two upper teeth, bright red lips, narrow nose, puffy cheeks, roundish jaw, representing a girl of about three or four years of age, marked K & K and further marked with the mold numbers 38-45, date of manufacture unknown, but believed to have been made during World War I, 17"*	230.00	270.00	220.00

J.L. KALLUS

	Current Price Range		Prior Year Average
☐ **Bye-Lo Baby,** *bisque head, cloth body, celluloid hands, sleep eyes, open mouth, stamped: Bye Lo Baby, 11"*	300.00	400.00	330.00
☐ **Pinkie,** *composition, tagged dress*	70.00	80.00	75.00

KAMAR

☐ **Ana,** *vinyl, jointed at the neck, marked Japan on doll, originally sold with a tag reading 1967 Kamar, Made in Japan, 4½"*	3.00	4.00	3.00
☐ **April,** *vinyl, painted eyes, wears wig, which can be any of various colors, representing a child seated holding an armload of flowers, marked 1968 Kamar Inc., Japan, 5"*	3.00	4.00	3.00
☐ **Clown,** *vinyl head, terrycloth body, originally sold with a tag reading 1967 Kamar, Made in Japan, 10"*	3.00	4.00	3.00
☐ **Jock** *(clown), marked 1966 Kamar, Made in Japan, 12½"*	5.00	7.00	5.00
Note: Resembling Emmett Kelly.			
☐ **John F. Kennedy,** *vinyl, likeness of President Kennedy seated in rocking chair reading newspaper, fitted with a music box, which also activates the chair and makes it rock, date of manufacture unknown (post-assassination), 13"*	35.00	45.00	32.00
☐ **K-Tot,** *vinyl with furry body, sold with a tag reading 1969 Kamar Inc., Japan, 5"*	3.00	4.00	3.00
☐ **Nobo,** *vinyl with fur body, a monkey, marked 1969 Kamar Inc., Japan, 5"*	4.00	5.00	4.00
☐ **Popo,** *vinyl head, vinyl arms, legs and body, rooted hair, painted eyes, smiling closed mouth, has angel wings, marked 169, Kamar Inc., Made in Japan, dated 1969, 6¼"*	3.00	4.00	3.00
☐ **Tina Marie,** *vinyl, marked 1968 Kamar Inc., Japan, 8"*	5.00	7.00	5.00

KÄMMER & REINHARDT

☐ **Baby,** *bisque head, composition bent-limb body, molded hair, brown eyes, antique clothes, mark: K ☆ R 127, 18"*	1600.00	1800.00	1600.00

	Current Price Range		Prior Year Average
☐ **Baby,** *bisque, composition body, blue intaglio eyes, pretty gown, mark: K ☆ R 100, 11".*	475.00	575.00	450.00
☐ **Baby,** *bisque head, composition body, blue set eyes, original mohair wig, christening gown, rare huge size, 18½" head circumference, 30" length*	1200.00	1400.00	1200.00
☐ **Baby,** *character, bisque head bent-limb composition body, blue glass sleep eyes, blonde mohair wig, smiling open/closed mouth, antique white christening gown, mark: K ☆ R S & H 116 A, 18"*	1500.00	2000.00	1500.00
☐ **Baby,** *character, bisque head, composition bent-limb body, blue sleep eyes, brown wig, open mouth, old lace gown, mold No.122, 15"*	625.00	750.00	650.00
☐ **Baby,** *character, bisque head, composition bent-limb baby body, original mohair wig, blue sleep eyes, christening gown, 12" head circumference, 17" length, mark: K ☆ R 121*	750.00	900.00	750.00
☐ **Baby,** *character, bisque head, composition body, blonde mohair wig, blue sleep eyes, five piece blue knitted outfit, mark: K ☆ R 126, 17"*	485.00	575.00	475.00
☐ **Baby,** *character, bisque head, five piece composition body, blue painted eyes, molded hair, open/closed mouth, old white christening gown, mark: 36 K ☆ R 100, 14½"*	550.00	750.00	525.00
☐ **Baby Doll,** *sleep flirt eyes, two teeth showing*	360.00	380.00	320.00
☐ **Bisque,** *ball-jointed body, flirty blue eyes, brown curled wig, open mouth, pierced ears, white dress, white straw hat, 17"*	225.00	275.00	240.00
☐ **Bisque,** *jointed composition body, blue eyes, blonde wig, white dress, blue ribbon, 24"*	400.00	450.00	440.00
☐ **Bisque,** *socket head, fixed eyes (small, dark), painted lashes, arched brows (narrow), small closed mouth with bright red lips, narrow pug nose, squarish jaw, representing a girl of about four or five years of age but sometimes found dressed as an older girl or as an adult, marked with the letters KR separated by a six-pointed star enclosing a symbol at the center, also marked Simon & Halbig (the manufacturers of the head), along with the mold identification number 126, date of manufacture not known, 8"*	180.00	215.00	170.00

Baby,
bisque
$360.00-$400.00

	Current Price Range		Prior Year Average
☐ **Bisque,** *socket head, fixed eyes (large), applied lashes, small open mouth with a row of upper teeth, bright red lips, narrow nose, very puffy cheeks (rosy colored), roundish jaw, dimpled chin, high forehead, bushy eyebrows, marked with the letters KR separated by a six-pointed star enclosing a symbol at the center, additionally marked by Simon & Halbig, the manufacturers of the head, date of manufacture unknown, presumably 1890's, 16½" . . . .*	190.00	225.00	175.00
☐ **Bisque,** *molded and painted hair, painted eyes (not fully open), no lashes, very high arching brows, open mouth, puffy cheeks, distinct double chin, narrow nose, promi-*			

	Current Price Range		Prior Year Average
nent ears, marked with the letters KR separated by a six-pointed star enclosing a symbol at the center, this was one of the firm's more innovative efforts at a doll which has personality and the appearance of a real infant, date of manufacture not known	400.00	500.00	375.00
Note: The approach in designing this doll was used frequently by American manufacturers in the 20th century and even at the present time: catching a baby in "stop-action" in the midst of an appealing facial expression.			
□ **Bisque Head,** *composition ball-jointed body, blue metal flirty eyes, dress with shoes, marked: 117N, 18″*	600.00	700.00	625.00

Bisque and Composition,
c. 1890, 25″
$650.00-$750.00

	Current Price Range		Prior Year Average
☐ **Bisque Head,** *composition ball-jointed body, brown wig, blue sleep eyes with unusual original eye mechanism, open mouth with four teeth, clothes, 30″*	1715.00	2000.00	1750.00
☐ **Bisque Head,** *composition ball-jointed body, human hair wig, flirty eyes, red satin costume with hat, 30″*	2600.00	2700.00	2650.00
☐ **Bisque Head,** *composition body, full wig to middle of back, flirty, pale blue eyes, original matching drop-waist dress, slip, and pantalettes, old shoes and stockings, marked: K ☆ R FLIRTY; W on forehead, 18″*	430.00	475.00	435.00
☐ **Bisque Head,** *composition body, original wig, antique clothes, 30″*	800.00	900.00	850.00
☐ **Bisque Head,** *composition jointed body, character, brown human hair wig, beautifully dressed, mark: K ☆ 116 A, 24″*	3800.00	4000.00	3800.00
☐ **Bisque Head,** *five piece composition body, blue sleep eyes, brown human hair wig, gypsy costume, painted shoes, marked: K ☆ R-27, 8½″*	140.00	155.00	145.00
☐ **Boy,** *bisque, composition ball-jointed body, original wig, brown flirty sleep eyes, brown checked suit, straw hat, mark: K ☆ R 117N, 22″*	1400.00	1600.00	1450.00
☐ **Boy,** *bisque head, ball-jointed composition body, brown flirty eyes, green suede suit with straw hat, marked: R117N, 22″*	1600.00	1800.00	1650.00
☐ **Character Baby,** *bisque socket head, jointed composition baby bent leg body, blue sleep eyes, blonde mohair wig, fly away eyebrows, open mouth with two porcelain teeth, white lace trimmed gown, matching bonnet, mark: K ☆ R Simon & Halbig 135 32, 13″*	750.00	900.00	750.00
☐ **Character Baby,** *bisque socket head, jointed composition five piece bent-leg baby body, blue flirty sleep eyes, open mouth with two upper teeth, brown human hair wig, white lace trimmed infant dress and bonnet, marks: K ☆ R Simon & Halbig 126, 19″*	550.00	650.00	475.00
☐ **Character Baby,** *bisque socket head, jointed five piece bent leg baby body, brown human hair wig, blue set eyes, open mouth with two teeth, dimpled chin, lace trimmed dress, crochet bonnet, marks: K ☆ R Simon & Halbig 121, 22″*	550.00	650.00	525.00
☐ **Character Baby,** *bisque socket head, jointed five piece bent leg baby body, brown sleep eyes, open mouth with two porcelain teeth and tremble tongue, brown wig, dimpled*			

	Current Price Range		Prior Year Average
chin, deep modeling around mouth, embroidered white infant dress, hand knit pink jacket, lace bonnet, marks: K ☆ R Simon & Halbig 126. 22″	450.00	550.00	450.00
☐ **Character Baby,** *bisque socket head, jointed five piece bent-leg baby body, light brown mohair wig, brown sleep eyes, feathered fly away eyebrows, open mouth, tremble tongue, white lace infant dress, marks: K ☆ R Simon & Halbig 126, 25″*	750.00	900.00	700.00
☐ **Child,** *bisque head, composition and wooden ball-jointed body, intaglio grey eyes, painted features, brown human hair, pouty lips, closed mouth, lovely red dress and shoes, marked: K ☆ R 10149, 20″*	4000.00	4500.00	4000.00
☐ **Child,** *character, bisque head, jointed French composition body, grey painted eyes, blonde human hair wig, pouty, closed mouth, lovely blue dress with hand smocking and lace collar, marked: K ☆ R 114 43, 17″*	3500.00	4500.00	3500.00
☐ **Closed Mouth Baby,** *blue eyes, blonde wig, mold number 116A, 16″*	1000.00	1800.00	1300.00
☐ **Composition,** *baby girl, bent limb baby, blue eyes, brown human hair wig, open/closed mouth, mold number 116A, 10½″*	1000.00	1500.00	1200.00
☐ **Composition,** *bent limb baby, ball-jointed body, blue set eyes, brown hair, mold number 121, 20″*	650.00	700.00	665.00
☐ **Composition Head,** *weight mechanism that turns head when legs are walked, blue paperweight eyes, blonde mohair wig, blue and white contemporary outfit, c. 1890, 25″*	650.00	750.00	625.00
☐ **Flirty,** *bisque head, jointed composition body, brown human hair wig, blue glass eyes, completely matching original clothes, 18″*	425.00	525.00	450.00
☐ **Flirty Baby,** *bisque, brown sleep eyes with tin sleeping lids, multi-stroked fly-away brows, nicely formed mouth, quiver tongue, two upper teeth, incised K ☆ R Flirty Baby, 13″*	430.00	475.00	435.00
☐ **Girl,** *bisque socket head, ball-jointed composition body, rare brown eyes, blonde wig, pouty mouth, dressed, marked: K ☆ R, mold nmber 114, 17″*	3400.00	4000.00	2750.00
☐ **Kaiser Baby,** *painted bisque head, five piece bent limb composition body, intaglio eyes, open/closed mouth, marked: K ☆ R 28-100*	375.00	425.00	395.00

	Current Price Range		Prior Year Average
☐ **Marie,** *bisque, original wig, painted blue eyes, closed mouth, original underwear, antique clothes, marked: K ☆ R 101, 19″*	4300.00	4700.00	4200.00
☐ **Mein Leibling,** *bisque socket head, fully jointed composition body, brown flirty eyes, auburn human hair wig styled in braided chignon on both sides of head, open mouth with four porcelain teeth, auburn fly away eyebrows, dropped waist maroon dress trimmed with lace, two toned tie shoes, marks: K ☆ R Simon & Halbig, 117 n Germany, 19″*	1100.00	1400.00	1050.00
☐ **Pouty Girl,** *composition ball-jointed body, blue painted eyes, closed mouth, brown human hair wig with coiled braids, mold number 114, 11″*	1200.00	1600.00	1350.00
☐ **Toddler,** *bisque head, composition body, human hair wig, blue sleep eyes, brown cotton print dress, 21″*	1500.00	1600.00	1550.00
☐ **Toddler,** *bisque head, composition body, human hair wig, sleep eyes, brown cotton print costume, matching hat, marked: K ☆ R 117N, Germany, S.H., 21″*	1425.00	1600.00	1400.00
☐ **Toddler,** *bisque head, five piece composition body, brown wig, blue sleep eyes, blue rompers and cap, marked: S & H 42, 17″*	1100.00	1200.00	1150.00
☐ **Toddler,** *character, bisque head, bent limb composition body, brown sleep eyes, brown human hair wig, open mouth, mold number 122, 18″*	800.00	900.00	850.00
☐ **Toddler,** *googly eyes, jointed composition body, blue eyes, long red hair, mold number 117, 13″*	2500.00	3000.00	2700.00
☐ **Toddler Baby,** *five piece jointed body, short red wig, blue sleep eyes, in underwear, marked: 126, 9½″*	450.00	500.00	475.00

KANTO TOYS

☐ **Baby Princess,** *vinyl, walking doll, vinyl wig, sleep eyes, yellow, orange and white short dress, c. 1960, 10″*	12.00	14.00	12.50
☐ **Baby Princess,** *vinyl head, plastic body, straight blond rooted hair, painted "googly" eyes, mouth open, key-wound mechanical walker, marked Kanto Toys, Made in Japan, dated 1968, 11″*	9.00	12.00	9.00

Baby Princess,
vinyl, c. 1960, 10″
$$12.00-$14.00

KAYBEE

	Current Price Range		Prior Year Average
☐ **Judy,** *plastic/vinyl, blond hair (rooted), sleep eyes (blue), pug nose, closed mouth, marked KB within a lozenge, made in 1966, 19″*	8.00	11.00	8.00
☐ **Love-Lee,** *plastic/vinyl, blonde hair (rooted), painted eyes, closed mouth, marked KB within a lozenge, made in 1966, 15⅞″*	9.00	12.00	9.00

KAYSAM

	Current Price Range		Prior Year Average
☐ **Another Jolly Doll,** *vinyl/plastic, made in 1961, 24″*	30.00	37.00	29.00
☐ **Barbara,** *plastic/vinyl, platinum blonde hair (rooted), sleep eyes (blue), marked 4269-K27, made in 1963, 18″*	11.00	14.00	11.00
☐ **Baby Judy,** *plastic/vinyl, sleep eyes (blue), marked 6514 Kaysam, made in 1963, 14½″*	6.00	8.00	6.00
☐ **Carol Channing,** *plastic/vinyl, blonde hair (rooted), sleep eyes (blue), marked 1961 Kaysam, sold originally with a tag reading Another Jolly Toy, 24″*	220.00	270.00	210.00
Note: Carol Channing rose to fame in "Gentlemen Prefer Blondes," she later (after this doll was made) scored a bigger hit with "Hello Dolly."			
☐ **Catherine,** *plastic/vinyl, brunette hair (rooted), sleep eyes (blue), wears high heels, marked 4274-K-1961-Kay Sam Corp., 20″*	11.00	15.00	10.00
☐ **Juliet Prowse,** *plastic/vinyl, blonde hair (rooted), sleep eyes (blue), marked Kaysam 1961, Juliet Prowse, dancer and actress, was one of Fred Astaire's dancing partners in movies and TV, 15″*	100.00	130.00	95.00
☐ **Miss Sweet,** *plastic/vinyl, platinum blonde hair (rooted), sleep eyes (blue), nursing mouth, marked K11-1963, 14″*	3.75	5.00	3.50
☐ **Red Cross Nurse,** *plastic/vinyl, sleep eyes (blue), nurse's uniform, marked Kaysam, 1961, 15″*	24.00	29.00	23.00

KAYSTAN

☐ **Terry Ann Meuson,** *plastic/vinyl, painted eyes (brown), rooted hair (brunette), smiling face, dressed in long gown and wearing crown, representing Terry Ann Meuson, Miss America of 1971, marked Kaystan 1971, made in Hong Kong, 13″*	20.00	26.00	19.00

KEEBLER

☐ **Keebler Elf,** *vinyl, molded and painted features, molded and painted clothing, representing a symbol of the Keebler Bakery Co.,*

	Current Price Range		Prior Year Average
marked 1974 Keebler Co., 6½"	5.00	7.00	5.00
Note: Used as a premium by Keebler in connection with the purchase of its products.			

KELLOGG'S

	Current Price Range		Prior Year Average
☐ **Dig 'Em Frog,** *cloth (printed), marked 1973 Kellogg Co., given as a premium in connection with the purchase of Kellogg's Corn Flakes, 16⅞"*	5.00	7.00	5.00
☐ **Tony The Tiger,** *cloth (printed), marked 1973 Kellogg Co., given as a premium in connection with the purchase of Kellogg cereal products, 18"*	17.00	22.00	16.00

KENNER

	Current Price Range		Prior Year Average
☐ **Artoo Detoo,** *movable legs and a chrome top that clicks, height 2¼"*	2.00	3.00	2.00
☐ **Almond Tea,** *with Marza Panda*	8.00	11.00	8.00
☐ **Angel Cake,** *with Souffle*	8.00	11.00	8.00
☐ **Apple Dumplin,** *with tea time turtle*	8.00	11.00	8.00
☐ **Apricot,** *with Hopsalot*	8.00	11.00	8.00
☐ **Baby Alive,** *vinyl, battery-operated nurser and eater, painted eyes, marked 3564-P13 Kenner Prod., 1973, 16"*	11.00	15.00	11.00
☐ **Baby Yawnie,** *vinyl, eyes close and mouth opens in a yawn when bulb is squeezed, made in the late 1970's, 15"*	4.00	6.00	4.00
☐ **Blueberry Muffin,** *with Cheese Cake*	8.00	11.00	8.00
☐ **Blythe,** *plastic/vinyl, rooted hair (blonde), large sad eyes which shift from side to side and change color when pullcord is pulled, wearing a bright print dress, marked Blythe TM, Kenner Products, 1972, also marked General Mills Fun Group (the Kenner company was a subsidiary of General Mills), 12"*	7.00	9.00	6.00
☐ **Boba Fett,** *carries a laser with backpack, based on The Empire Strikes Back, height 13¼"*	20.00	30.00	23.00
☐ **Boba Fett,** *with laser and back pack, based on The Empire Strikes Back, height 2¼"*	2.00	3.00	2.00
☐ **Butter Cookie,** *with Jelly Bear*	8.00	11.00	8.00
☐ **Cafe Ole,** *with Burrito*	8.00	11.00	8.00
☐ **Cherry Cudler,** *with Gooseberry*	8.00	11.00	8.00

	Current Price Range		Prior Year Average
☐ **Chewbacca, The Space Wookie,** *crossbow laser fifle, ammunition cartridge is removable, height 15"*	15.00	25.00	18.00
☐ **Chewbacca,** *has ammunition belt and special laser rifle, height 4¼"*	2.00	3.00	2.00
☐ **Crepe Suzette,** *with Eclair*	8.00	11.00	8.00
☐ **Crumpet,** *plastic/vinyl, sleep eyes (blue), rooted hair (blonde), joined at the wrists and waist, pug nose, open smiling mouth with teeth, holds teapot, works by pullcord and battery, marked 1970, Kenner Products Co., 235-225, also marked with address (Cincinnati, Ohio), 18½"*	7.00	10.00	7.00
☐ **Death Star Droid,** *brilliant silver coloring and movable arms and legs, height 3¾"*	2.00	3.00	2.00
☐ **Darth Vader,** *carries light saber, detailed black armor and removable cape, height 15"*	25.00	35.00	28.00
☐ **Darth Vader,** *has retractable light saber and removable cape, height 4¼"*	2.00	3.00	2.00
Empires Strikes Back Action Figures, Series 1, *all new characters from the second movie, height 2¼" to 3¾"*			
☐ **Bespan Security Guards**	2.00	3.00	2.00
☐ **Boba Fett,** *an intergalactic*	2.00	3.00	2.00
☐ **Bossk,** *The Bounty hunter*	2.00	3.00	2.00
☐ **Bounty Hunter**	2.00	3.00	2.00
☐ **C-3P0**	2.00	3.00	2.00
☐ **Chewbacca**	2.00	3.00	2.00
☐ **Creatures From Cantina**	2.00	3.00	2.00
☐ **Darth Vader**	2.00	3.00	2.00
☐ **Ex-7,** *a multiarmed droid*	2.00	3.00	2.00
☐ **Han Solo,** *in new outfit*	2.00	3.00	2.00
☐ **IG-88,** *The Bounty hunter*	2.00	3.00	2.00
☐ **Lando Cairissian,** *main character from the movies*	2.00	3.00	2.00
☐ **Luke Skywalker,** *in new outfit*	2.00	3.00	2.00
☐ **Luke X Wing Pilot**	2.00	3.00	2.00
☐ **Obi-Wan Kenobi**	2.00	3.00	2.00
☐ **Princess Leia,** *in new outfit*	2.00	3.00	2.00
☐ **R2-D2**	2.00	3.00	2.00
☐ **Rebel Soldier**	2.00	3.00	2.00
☐ **Storm Trooper**	2.00	3.00	2.00
Empire Strikes Back Action Figures, Series 2, *all new new outfits and characters, height 2¼" to 3¾".*			
☐ **Arfive-Defour, R5-D4**	2.00	3.00	2.00
☐ **AT-AT Commander**	2.00	3.00	2.00
☐ **Bespin Security Guard**	2.00	3.00	2.00
☐ **Bib Fortuna**	2.00	3.00	2.00

	Current Price Range		Prior Year Average
☐ **Chewbacca**	2.00	3.00	2.00
☐ **Chief Chirpa**	2.00	3.00	2.00
☐ **Cloud Car Pilot**	2.00	3.00	2.00
☐ **Emperor's Royal Guard**	2.00	3.00	2.00
☐ **FX-7**	2.00	3.00	2.00
☐ **Hammerhead**	2.00	3.00	2.00
☐ **Han Solo,** *Bespin outfit*	2.00	3.00	2.00
☐ **Han Solo,** *original*	2.00	3.00	2.00
☐ **Hoth Battle Gear**	2.00	3.00	2.00
☐ **Imperial Stormtrooper,** *orginal*	2.00	3.00	2.00
☐ **Imperial TIE Fighter Pilot**	2.00	3.00	2.00
☐ **Jawa**	2.00	3.00	2.00
☐ **Lobot**	2.00	3.00	2.00
☐ **Luke Skywalker**	2.00	3.00	2.00
☐ **Luke Skywalker,** *Bespin Fatigues*	2.00	3.00	2.00
☐ **Luke Skywalker,** *Jedi Knight, outfit*	2.00	3.00	2.00
☐ **Nien Nunb**	2.00	3.00	2.00
☐ **Princess Leia Organa,** *Hoth outfit*	2.00	3.00	2.00
☐ **Princess Leia Organa,** *original*	2.00	3.00	2.00
☐ **Rebel Soldier**	2.00	3.00	2.00
☐ **Rebel Commando**	2.00	3.00	2.00
☐ **Rebel Commander**	2.00	3.00	2.00
☐ **Ree Yees**	2.00	3.00	2.00
☐ **See Threepio,** *with removable limbs*	2.00	3.00	2.00
☐ **Snaggletooth**	2.00	3.00	2.00
☐ **Squid Head**	2.00	3.00	2.00
☐ **Too Onebee**	2.00	3.00	2.00
☐ **Ugnaught**	2.00	3.00	2.00
☐ **Weequay**	2.00	3.00	2.00
☐ **Yoda, The Jedi Master**	2.00	3.00	2.00
☐ **Zuckuss**	2.00	3.00	2.00
Continuation of Kenner			
☐ **Gabbigale,** *plastic/vinyl, painted eyes (blue), rooted hair (dark blonde), talker operated by pullcord and battery, open smiling mouth with teeth, pug nose, marked 1972 Kenner Products Co., 99, 18″*	8.00	10.00	8.00
☐ **Greedo, The Cantina Creature,** *with laser pistol, movable arms and legs, based on The Return Of The Jedi, height 3¼″*	2.00	3.00	2.00
☐ **Han Solo,** *equipped with special laser pistol, height 3¼″*	2.00	3.00	2.00
☐ **Hammerhead,** *holds a laser and has movable legs and arms, based on The Empire Strikes Back, height 4″*	2.00	3.00	2.00
☐ **Huckelberry Pie,** *with Pup Cake*	8.00	11.00	8.00

	Current Price Range		Prior Year Average
☐ **Jenny The Quantas Hostess,** *vinyl, representing a hostess for Quantas (Australian) Airlines, marked 3632-189-GMFGI Kenner Products, 12"*	17.00	23.00	16.00
☐ **Lemon Meringue,** *with Frappe*	8.00	11.00	8.00
☐ **Lime Chiffon,** *with Parfait Parrot*	8.00	11.00	8.00
☐ **Luke Skywalker,** *action figure, in Tattoine desert outfit, has light saber grappling hook, removable costume, height 11¾"*	30.00	40.00	34.00
☐ **Luke Skywalker,** *with light saber ready for action with flick of special lever in his arm, height 3¾"*	2.00	3.00	2.00
☐ **Luke Skywalker, X Wing Pilot,** *battle ready in orange flight suit and laser, height 3¾"*	2.00	3.00	2.00
☐ **Meadow,** *vinyl, painted eyes (brown), rooted hair (brunette), wearing sleeveless sweater, holds watering can in right hand, in addition to the watering can, Meadow was originally sold with packets of real garden seeds, marked Garden Gal by Kenner, Hong Kong, made in 1972, 6⅞"*	5.00	7.00	5.00
Note: Don't be misled by the name Garden Gal in the marking. This was the name of a series of dolls. There was no single doll named Garden Gal.			
☐ **Mint Tulip,** *with Marsh Mallard*	8.00	11.00	8.00
☐ **Obi-Wan Kenobi,** *carries light saber with removable cape, height 12"*	25.00	35.00	28.00
☐ **Obi-Wan Kenobi,** *has retractable light saber and removable cape, height 3¼"*	2.00	3.00	2.00
☐ **Orange Blossom,** *with Marma Lade*	8.00	11.00	8.00
☐ **Princess Leia Organa,** *hair that is able to be styled, costume is removable, height 11½"*	25.00	35.00	28.00
☐ **Princess Leia Organa,** *has removable cape and laser pistol, height 3½"*	2.00	3.00	2.00
☐ **Purple Pieman,** *with Berry Bird*	8.00	11.00	8.00
☐ **Raspberry Tart,** *with Rhubarb*	8.00	11.00	8.00
☐ **R5-D4,** *red markings, makes clicking sounds, height 2½"*	2.00	3.00	2.00
Return Of The Jedi Action Figures, *new characters and costumes from the latest movie, height 2¼" to 3¾".*			
☐ **Admiral Ackbar**	2.00	3.00	2.00
☐ **AT-AT Driver**	2.00	3.00	2.00
☐ **Ben (Obi-Wan) Kenobi**	2.00	3.00	2.00
☐ **Biker Scout**	2.00	3.00	2.00
☐ **Bossk**	2.00	3.00	2.00
☐ **Boushh**	2.00	3.00	2.00
☐ **Chewbacca**	2.00	3.00	2.00
☐ **Darth Vader**	2.00	3.00	2.00

	Current Price Range		Prior Year Average
☐ **Death Star Droid**	2.00	3.00	2.00
☐ **Dengar**	2.00	3.00	2.00
☐ **FX-7**	2.00	3.00	2.00
☐ **Gamorrean Guard**	2.00	3.00	2.00
☐ **General Madine**	2.00	3.00	2.00
☐ **Greedo**	2.00	3.00	2.00
☐ **Hammerhead**	2.00	3.00	2.00
☐ **Han Solo,** *Bespin outfit*	2.00	3.00	2.00
☐ **Han Solo,** *Hoth battle gear*	2.00	3.00	2.00
☐ **IG-88**	2.00	3.00	2.00
☐ **Imperial Commander**	2.00	3.00	2.00
☐ **Imperial Stormtrooper,** *Hoth battle gear*	2.00	3.00	2.00
☐ **Jawa**	2.00	3.00	2.00
☐ **Klaatu**	2.00	3.00	2.00
☐ **Lando Cairissian**	2.00	3.00	2.00
☐ **Lando Cairissian,** *skiff guard disguise*	2.00	3.00	2.00
☐ **Lobot**	2.00	3.00	2.00
☐ **Luke Skywalker,** *Bespin fatigues*	2.00	3.00	2.00
☐ **Luke Skywalker,** *X-Wing Fighter Pilot*	2.00	3.00	2.00
☐ **Power Droid**	2.00	3.00	2.00
☐ **Princess Leia Organa,** *Bespin gown*	2.00	3.00	2.00
☐ **Princess Leia Organa,** *Hoth outfit*	2.00	3.00	2.00
☐ **Rebel Commander**	2.00	3.00	2.00
☐ **Rebel Soldier**	2.00	3.00	2.00
☐ **R5-D4**	2.00	3.00	2.00
☐ **Sandpeople**	2.00	3.00	2.00
☐ **Snaggletooth**	2.00	3.00	2.00
☐ **Star Destroyer Commander**	2.00	3.00	2.00
☐ **Two-Onebee**	2.00	3.00	2.00
☐ **Ugnaught**	2.00	3.00	2.00
☐ **Walrus Man**	2.00	3.00	2.00
☐ **Walrus Man**	2.00	3.00	2.00
☐ **Yoda**	2.00	3.00	2.00
Continuation of Kenner			
☐ **See Threeplo,** *brillant gold color, with movable arms and lips, height 3¾″*	2.00	3.00	2.00
☐ **Sippin' Sue,** *plastic/vinyl, open mouth with puckered lips into which soda straw can be inserted, marked 1972 General Mills Fun Group, Inc., 6″*	3.00	4.00	3.00
☐ **Sleep Over Dolly,** *plastic/vinyl, rooted hair, sleep eyes (blue), marked GMFGI, 1976, 16½″*	11.00	14.00	11.00
Note: There was also a black version of this doll, whose value is slightly higher.			
☐ **Snaggle Tooth,** *comes in space outfit and carries laser rifle, based on The Empire Strikes Back, height 3¾″*	2.00	3.00	2.00

	Current Price Range		Prior Year Average
☐ **Steve Scout,** *plastic/vinyl, molded and painted hair (red), painted eyes (blue), representing a youth dressed in a Boy Scout uniform, right arm moves to give scout salute, marked 1974 GMFGL, Kenner Prod., also marked with address (Cincinnati, Ohio) and zip code number (45202), 9″*	9.00	12.00	9.00
☐ **Strawberry Shortcake,** *with Custard*	8.00	11.00	8.00
☐ **Storm Trooper,** *black and white space suit and laser rifle, based on Star Wars, height 3¼″*	2.00	3.00	2.00
☐ **Storm Trooper,** *wears a white and black space suit and carries laser, based on Star Wars, height 12″*	20.00	30.00	23.00
☐ **Walrus Man,** *with rifle and articulated arms and legs, based on Return Of The Jedi, height 5¾″*	2.00	3.00	2.00

KERR GHINZ

☐ **Baby,** *bisque, painted, marked, 5″*	7.00	12.00	8.00
☐ **Bisque Babies,** *movable arms, legs, c. 1930's, marked: K & H*	8.00	10.00	8.00

KESTNER

One of the longest-surviving and most successful of the German doll companies, Kestner spanned the era from craft work to factory production, and into the age of heavy overseas exportation. Johann D. Kestner, founder of the firm, started in a very small way as a maker of papier mache novelties. In the early 1800's — while Napoleon ruled most of Europe — Kestner got the idea of making dolls, but it was many years before the firm enjoyed any real success. During the mid 1800's it was the innovator of many important doll types. By the century's close Kestner had built an export empire, supplying dolls to wholesalers in Europe and America, and is said to have employed more workers than any other doll factory of the time.

The Kestner dolls are basically of good quality and the rarity factor on most of them is not especially high, thereby bringing them within financial reach of more hobbyists than the dolls of more exclusive manufacturers. In bisque their value is usually $200.00-$400.00, in composition somewhat less.

☐ **All Bisque,** *jointed at shoulders and hips, glass eyes, human hair wig, closed mouth, lovely clothes, mold #130.7, 7″*	250.00	350.00	295.00
☐ **Baby,** *bisque head, bent limb composition body, molded hair, mold #151, 10″*	350.00	400.00	375.00

	Current Price Range		Prior Year Average
☐ **Baby,** *bisque, composition five piece baby body, wig, blue sleep eyes, white baby dress, No. 257, 18″*	650.00	720.00	640.00
☐ **Baby,** *bisque head, composition baby body, molded head, rare blue intaglio eyes, open-closed mouth, molded tongue, No. 7, 11″*	375.00	475.00	400.00
☐ **Baby,** *bisque, dome head, well modeled features, set paperweight eyes, molded closed mouth, commercial long lace trimmed gown and matched crocheted bonnet and bed jacket with bows, incised '151', 10″*	355.00	395.00	365.00
☐ **Baby,** *composition, bent limb, painted, Germany*	450.00	525.00	470.00
☐ **Baby,** *composition body, bent limb, brown painted eyes, open, closed mouth, marked: 7, 11″*	300.00	400.00	310.00
☐ **Baby,** *character, bisque head, bent limb composition body, blonde human hair wig, sleep eyes, open mouth, christening gown, #226, 23″*	750.00	850.00	800.00
☐ **Baby,** *character, bisque head, bent limb composition body, blue eyes, antique clothes, #211*	600.00	700.00	650.00
☐ **Baby,** *character, bisque head, blonde mohair wig, brown sleep eyes, facial modeling, two-tone lips, two upper teeth, quiver tongue, chunky baby body, old 33″ long christening clothes, JDK 226 BABY fully incised, 23″ tall, 16″ circumference*	620.00	685.00	630.00
☐ **Baby,** *character, bisque head, composition bent limb baby body, molded head, grey sleep eyes, dimples, open mouth, molded tongue, #151, 16″*	425.00	525.00	450.00
☐ **Baby,** *character, bisque head, composition bent limb body, molded head, grey sleep eyes, dimples, open mouth, molded tongue, #151, 13″*	375.00	450.00	350.00
☐ **Baby,** *character, bisque head, composition body, blonde original angora wig, brown sleep eyes, #257, 14″*	650.00	750.00	675.00
☐ **Bisque,** *ball-jointed body, blue sleep eyes, brown wig, open mouth, crocheted dress with ribbon around waist, painted orange shoes*	100.00	150.00	120.00
☐ **Bisque,** *brown eyes, brown hair, ecru lawn dress, hat, mold number 214, 21″*	450.00	500.00	470.00
☐ **Bisque,** *jointed composition body, blue eyes, brown hair, white lawn dress, marked: Germany, 23″*	275.00	325.00	300.00

	Current Price Range		Prior Year Average
☐ **Bisque,** *jointed composition body, blue eyes, red hair, peach taffeta dress, 25″*	325.00	375.00	340.00
☐ **Bisque,** *jointed, fancy yellow dress and bonnet, 6½″*	45.00	50.00	45.00
☐ **Bisque,** *kid body, blue sleep eyes, molded wavy blonde hair, blue school dress, trimmed in red, hair bow, 21″*	275.00	325.00	300.00
☐ **Bisque,** *kid body, set brown eyes, blonde human hair wig, open mouth, white dress, marked: C-made in Germany, 17″*	375.00	425.00	400.00
☐ **Bisque,** *leather body, brown eyes, brown wig, mold number 148, 19″*	250.00	300.00	270.00
☐ **Bisque,** *mohair wig, brown, sleeping eyes, marked Germany, 19″*	300.00	350.00	310.00
☐ **Bisque,** *mold number 150, jointed shoulders and hips, brown sleep eyes, closed mouth, brown mohair wig, white hose, blue bands, black shoes, pink crocheted dress and hat, 5¾″*	180.00	240.00	200.00
☐ **Bisque,** *set brown eyes, light brown eyebrows, closed mouth, loop strung arms and legs, pink shirred hose, black heels, 4½″*	145.00	185.00	160.00
☐ **Bisque,** *bisque shoulder and head, cloth body, with bisque arms and legs, blonde ringlet curls wig, brown flirty eyes, long suit outfit with matching hat, 23″*	200.00	250.00	225.00
☐ **Bisque,** *socket head, two upper teeth, feathered eyelashes, marked: Germany, 10″*	200.00	250.00	210.00
☐ **Bisque Body,** *crown and streamer body, brown wig, sleep eyes, short green velvet dress, marked "C", 1880, 16″*	1100.00	1400.00	1250.00
☐ **Bisque Early Turned Head,** *gussetted kid body with wood, covered arms, large brown eyes, long narrow mouth with four square teeth, incised E Germany H½, 19″*	380.00	420.00	380.00
☐ **Bisque Head And Hands,** *cloth body, black mohair wig, brown sleep eyes, plain clothes, marked 166*	500.00	600.00	525.00
☐ **Bisque Head And Hands,** *kid leather body, human hair wig, brown sleep eyes, pierced ears, navy and white costume, 16″*	480.00	490.00	485.00
☐ **Bisque Head And Hands,** *kid leather body, red human hair wig, blue sleep eyes, closed mouth, antique lace dress and hat, old shoes, 21″*	1200.00	1300.00	1250.00
☐ **Bisque Head,** *ball-jointed body, blue sleep eyes, blue crepe dress with lace trim, 30″*	1000.00	1100.00	1050.00
☐ **Bisque Head,** *ball-jointed body, mohair wig, blue sleep eyes, original gown, marked: 168*	400.00	425.00	415.00

Bisque,
c. 1880, 16″
$1100.00-$1400.00

Bisque Dome Head,
c. 1890, 19″
$875.00-$1000.00

Bisque Head,
cloth and kid body,
c. 1885, 21″
$1200.00-$1300.00

	Current Price Range		Prior Year Average
☐ **Bisque Head,** *cloth and kid body, brown human hair wig, set eyes, blue taffeta brocade dress, biege lace trim, white leather shoes, marked #10, c. 1885, 21″*	1200.00	1400.00	1250.00
☐ **Bisque,** *ball-jointed body, brown sleep eyes, reddish-brown human hair wig, open mouth, pink long sleeved dress, buttons and rosebuds down front, straw hat with lace and ribbon, marked: made in Germany E-168-9, 21″*	375.00	425.00	395.00
☐ **Bisque Head,** *composition ball-jointed body, blue sleep eyes, with lashes, furry eyebrows, elegant gown, marked: 196, 30″*	1200.00	1450.00	1250.00

	Current Price Range		Prior Year Average
☐ **Bisque Head,** *composition ball-jointed body, brown glass eyes, brown human hair wig, open mouth with teeth, silk dress, matching hat, mold #140, 29"*	700.00	900.00	750.00
☐ **Bisque Head,** *composition body, brown eyes, brown human hair wig, original clothing, #214, 21"*	800.00	900.00	750.00
☐ **Bisque Head,** *composition ball-jointed body, brown sleep eyes, closed mouth, brown human hair wig, 28"*	2300.00	2500.00	2300.00
☐ **Bisque Head,** *composition body, original wig, brown sleep eyes, antique clothes and shoes, 27"*	2000.00	2200.00	2050.00
☐ **Bisque Head,** *jointed composition body, blonde human hair wig, sleep brown eyes, open mouth with four teeth, pierced ears, silk dress, mark: K/2*	650.00	720.00	675.00
☐ **Bisque Head,** *jointed composition body, brown sleep eyes, brown human hair wig, lovely old white lace dress, mark #196, 30"*	850.00	925.00	850.00
☐ **Bisque Head,** *jointed composition body, brown wig, brown sleep eyes, open mouth with teeth, mold #215, 22"*	550.00	650.00	595.00
☐ **Bisque Head,** *jointed composition second wood body, full original heavy wig with old pink ribbons and plaster pate, blue sleep eyes, closed mouth, white heirloom dress with hand done open-work and tatting on bodice and hem with pink lining and sash, incised L Made in Germany, stamped Germany 6, 28"*	2300.00	2800.00	2350.00
☐ **Bisque Head,** *jointed composition body, straight wrists, blue paperweight eyes, French human hair wig, closed mouth, lovely dress, #7, 12½"*	1250.00	1350.00	1225.00
☐ **Bisque Head,** *kid body, mohair wig, brown sleep eyes, blue dress, marked: Kestner 154, 28"*	495.00	525.00	500.00
☐ **Bisque Head,** *kid body, with bisque arms and legs, brown sleep eyes, pink silk dress, marked No. 154, 14"*	300.00	350.00	315.00
☐ **Bisque Head,** *kid body with bisque hands, human hair wig, blue sleep eyes, pink velvet dress with hat, marked 154, Dep. 7½, 19"*	480.00	500.00	490.00
☐ **Bisque Head,** *original body, original clothes, mold #146, 24"*	900.00	1000.00	950.00
☐ **Bisque Shoulder Head,** *blue sleep eyes, open mouth with four porcelain teeth, dimpled chin, original blonde mohair wig, plaster pate, pierced ears, kid body with*			

	Current Price Range		Prior Year Average
gussets at hips and knees, bisque hands, pink calico jumper over beige linen shirt, marks: four at top rim, 246 4, 16"	300.00	400.00	300.00
☐ **Bisque Shoulder Head,** *kid body, pin jointed hips and knees, bisque hands, original blonde mohair wig, brown sleep eyes, open mouth with four porcelain teeth, well shaped hands, outlined red nails, original pale pink dress with braid, matching straw hat, marks: S 147, 18"*	375.00	500.00	350.00
☐ **Bisque Shoulder Head,** *kid lined swivel neck, kid body with gussets at hips and knees, bisque hands, original blonde mohair wig, plaster pate, large blue spiraled sleep eyes, open mouth with molded bisque upper teeth, dimpled chin, pink striped blouse, skirt with black velvet ribbon trim, marks: 14 Germany K, 26"*	575.00	675.00	575.00
☐ **Bisque Shoulder Head,** *pink kid jointed body with original composition jointed arms, full original blonde mohair wig, brown sleep eyes, lovely pointed brows, small shaded mouth, original matching ensemble of underlayers and classic ecru dress, incised '15 Made in Germany, 24"*	445.00	490.00	450.00
☐ **Bisque Shoulder Head,** *kid body with gussets at knees and hips, bisque hands, brown sleep eyes, closed mouth with red accent line between lips, auburn human hair wig, pink silk dress with smocked bodice accented with grograin ribbon, marks: 10 at top of crown, 20"*	325.00	380.00	325.00
☐ **Bisque Socket Head,** *full jointed composition body, brown sleep eyes, original blonde mohair wig, open mouth, four porcelain teeth, burgundy wool dress with lace trim and black jet buttons, marks: J Made in Germany 13, 129, 21"*	450.00	550.00	425.00
☐ **Boy Baby,** *bisque head, composition ball-jointed body, short red haired wig, brown sleep eyes, velvet bloomers and vest, satin blouse, 15"*	300.00	400.00	325.00
☐ **Character,** *bisque shoulder head, molded blonde hair, page boy style, painted blue eyes glancing to side, closed mouth, rosy cheeks, pin jointed kid body, bisque hands, pale yellow low waist dress, matching bonnet, marks: Germany, Original Crown and Steamer Kestner label, 14"*	250.00	400.00	200.00

	Current Price Range		Prior Year Average
☐ **Character,** *bisque socket head, jointed composition body, blue spiraled sleep eyes, open mouth with porcelain teeth, blonde human hair wig, molded and painted shoes and socks, original red silk dress edged with black velvet ribbon, lace bonnet, scaled lace trimmed underwear, pierced ears, marks: 209, 1, 9″*	375.00	450.00	350.00
☐ **Character Baby,** *bent limb baby body, jointed, molded and painted light brown wig, light blue sleep eyes, two piece christening gown, marked #151, c. 1915, 14″*	400.00	500.00	425.00
☐ **Character Baby,** *bent limb body, blonde mohair wig, gray sleep eyes, open mouth, four teeth, molded tongue, marked: Germany, 16″*	450.00	500.00	450.00
☐ **Character Baby,** *bisque head, five piece composition baby body, short human hair wig, blue glass eyes, open mouth, two teeth, layette outfit, 25″*	3000.00	4000.00	3500.00
☐ **Character Baby,** *bisque shoulder head, cloth body with gussets, bisque arms, blonde mohair wig, blue set eyes, open mouth, white infant gown, lace trimmed bonnet, marks: J.D.K. 235, B Made in Germany, 17″*	300.00	350.00	275.00
☐ **Character Baby,** *bisque socket head, fully jointed composition body, original blonde mohair wig, blue sleep eyes, closed mouth with red accent line and turned up corners, dimpled chin, pink linen low waisted dress trimmed with lace, original straw bonnet, marks: E Made in Germany 9, 128, 16″*	2000.00	2200.00	1800.00
☐ **Character Baby,** *bisque socket head, blue set eyes, blonde mohair wig, open mouth with molded tongue, double chin, composition jointed five piece bent leg baby body, white lace trimmed organdy infant gown, marks: 152, 9″*	300.00	400.00	275.00
☐ **Character Baby,** *bisque socket head, jointed five piece bent leg baby body, brown sleep eyes, open mouth with four porcelain teeth, light brown human hair wig, double chin with dimple, blue knitted two piece sweater and short set with matching tam, marks: Made in Germany, J.D.K. 260, 16″*	500.00	600.00	500.00

Character Body, c. 1915, 14″ . . . . **$425.00-$525.00**

	Current Price Range		Prior Year Average
☐ **Character Baby,** *solid dome bisque socket head, jointed composition five piece bent leg baby body, molded brushed stroked brown hair, blue sleep eyes, open/closed mouth, double chin, long white gown, lace trimmed front panel, tucks, paneled lace, ruffled organdy bonnet, marks: J.D.K. 7, 11″*	375.00	425.00	400.00
☐ **Character Baby,** *solid dome bisque socket head, jointed five piece bent leg baby body, blue sleep eyes, open mouth with two porcelain teeth, tremble tongue, molded*			

	Current Price Range		Prior Year Average
brush stroked hair, Victorian christening dress with embroidered lace, marks: JDK, Made in Germany 17, red stamp on body reads Made in Germany, 23"	875.00	950.00	900.00
☐ **Character Baby,** *solid dome bisque socket head, molded shaded brown hair, painted blue intaglio eyes, closed pouty mouth, jointed composition five piece bent leg baby body, white lace dress, holding a 4" china head doll, marks: Germany 178 0, 9"*	650.00	800.00	650.00
☐ **Character Baby,** *solid dome bisque socket head, pin jointed kid body with composition lower legs, bisque hands (new), brushed stroked brown hair, painted blue eyes, open/closed mouth, marks: 2, 11"*	150.00	200.00	145.00
☐ **Character Boy,** *bisque head, ball-jointed body, blue sleep eyes, navy blue wool boy suit, marked: 152, 11"*	300.00	350.00	325.00
☐ **Character Boy,** *bisque head, jointed body, brown human hair wig, blue sleep eyes, red boy outfit, marked: 152*	400.00	450.00	415.00
☐ **Character Boy,** *15-piece jointed toddler body, human hair boy wig, blue sleep eyes, navy wool suit*	600.00	650.00	615.00
☐ **Character Doll,** *bisque head, toddler body, human hair wig, blue sleep eyes, orchid and white costume with hat, 20"*	1000.00	1100.00	1050.00
☐ **Character Toddler,** *bisque head, jointed five piece body, brown human hair wig, brown sleep eyes, white school girl dress, marked: 152, 18"*	375.00	400.00	385.00
☐ **Child,** *bisque head, jointed composition body, brown sleep eyes, brown human hair wig, open mouth with teeth, lavender organdy dress with lace insets, 28"*	700.00	800.00	725.00
☐ **Child,** *bisque head with composition ball-jointed body, black wig with bangs, brown sleep eyes, open mouth, 27½"*	250.00	300.00	275.00
☐ **Child,** *bisque head, wood jointed body, long curly brown wig, brown sleep eyes, lacy tiered dress, wide brimmed bonnet, 22"*	350.00	400.00	365.00
☐ **Composition,** *five-piece body, blue glass set eyes, painted eyebrows, stroked eyelashes, dimpled chin, open mouth, upper teeth, brown bobbed mohair wig, white cotton dress, red wool coat, straw hat, 8½"*	225.00	275.00	240.00
☐ **Daisy,** *bisque, ball-jointed body, human hair wig, blue eyes, open mouth, red plaid taffeta costume, marked: 171, 28"*	950.00	1000.00	975.00

	Current Price Range		Prior Year Average
☐ **Daisy,** *character, bisque, composition ball-jointed body, human hair wig, blue sleep eyes, open mouth, red plaid taffeta dress, #171, 28″*	1000.00	1275.00	1100.00
☐ **Daisy,** *jointed composition body, brown eyes, blonde wig, white lawn dress, mold number, 31″*	725.00	775.00	740.00
☐ **Girl,** *bisque, antique ball-joint body, French human hair wig, blue sleep eyes, rosebud mouth, two teeth, incised Kestner 143, 14″*	400.00	450.00	410.00
☐ **Girl,** *bisque, platinum wig, brown sleep eyes, closed mouth, crocheted hat, dress, marked 208/4, 7″*	200.00	250.00	220.00
☐ **Girl,** *character, bisque head, jointed composition body, original mohair wig, blue sleep eyes, fur brows, white lace antique dress, #215, 26″*	650.00	800.00	675.00
☐ **Googly-Eyed Character Doll,** *bisque head, jointed composition toddler body, blue sleep side glancing eyes, watermelon mouth, 14″*	2600.00	3200.00	2500.00
☐ **Heidi,** *bisque head and body, blonde mohair wig, brown sleep eyes, blue crochet dress, 6″*	150.00	160.00	155.00
☐ **Hilda Baby,** *dome head, blue eyes, white christening dress and hat, holds rattle, 13″*	1200.00	1800.00	1300.00
☐ **Hilda,** *character baby, bisque head, molded hair, composition bent-limb body, brown sleep eyes, baby clothes, 16″*	2300.00	2700.00	2450.00
☐ **Hilda,** *character baby, bisque head, bent limb composition limbs, blonde wig, blue sleep eyes, open mouth with two teeth, original clothes*	2800.00	3000.00	2800.00
☐ **Hilda,** *rare original clothes, marked: Made in Germany (245 JDK Jr 000 1914 Hilda), 16″*	2600.00	2900.00	2600.00
☐ **Infant,** *bisque head, five piece composition body, blue sleep eyes, open mouth, four upper teeth and tongue, baby dress with coat, bonnet, marked: 152, 17″*	2000.00	2200.00	2050.00
☐ **Kewpie,** *vinyl, only head turns, side glancing eyes, painted features, wears only large red ribbon with bow around body, marks: head, Cameo, back, Cameo, left bottom of foot, JDK, 10½″*	42.00	48.00	42.00
☐ **Lady,** *bisque head, composition lady body, Gibson girl blonde wig, blue sleep eyes, open mouth with teeth, all original, mold #162, 18″*	1200.00	1300.00	1200.00

	Current Price Range		Prior Year Average
☐ **Little Red Riding Hood,** *bisque socket head, five piece jointed composition body, molded, painted heeled shoes and socks, brown set eyes, open mouth with molded teeth, original blonde mohair wig, flowered dress, red felt cape, matching bonnet, marks: 192, 8″*	100.00	125.00	90.00
☐ **Matron,** *bisque head, ball-jointed composition body, brown human hair wig, brown sleep eyes, painted brows, long navy blue flowered gown, 20″*	300.00	350.00	325.00
☐ **Oriental,** *olive tinted bisque head, black human hair wig with que, almond shaped brown glass sleep eyes, silk costume, original, with headdress, 13″*	3500.00	4000.00	3500.00

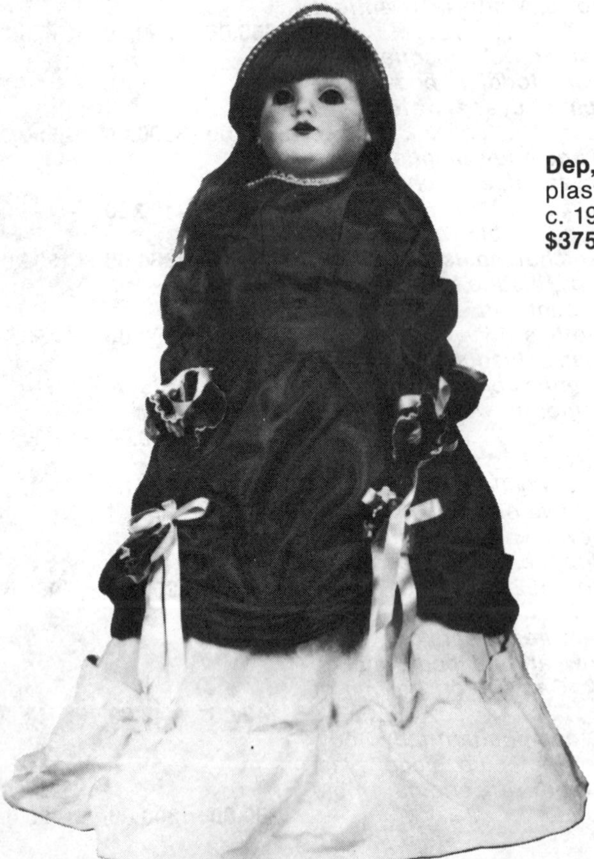

Dep,
plaster pate,
c. 1910, 18″
$375.00-$400.00

	Current Price Range		Prior Year Average
☐ **Oriental Baby,** *composition bent limb, brown sleep eyes, black human hair wig, mold number 243, 13″*	2200.00	2700.00	2400.00
☐ **Plaster Pate Head,** *kid leather body, blonde human hair wig, blue sleep eyes, closed mouth, antique white dress, marked: 698, 23″*	1000.00	1100.00	1050.00
☐ **Plaster Pate Head,** *crown and streamer body, human hair wig, human hair lashes on sleep eyes, red and biege satin dress, 1910, 18″*	375.00	400.00	395.00
☐ **Sammy,** *character baby, bisque head, composition bent limb body, molded head, blue sleep eyes, open-closed mouth, antique clothes*	450.00	550.00	475.00
☐ **Toddler,** *bisque head, composition bent limb body, blue sleep eyes, open mouth, two teeth, antique clothes, #11 JDK, Made in 20 Germany*	950.00	1000.00	975.00
☐ **Toddler,** *bisque head, composition, wood body, ball-jointed, mohair wig, blue sleep eyes, two teeth, made in Germany, 14″*	300.00	350.00	310.00
☐ **Toddler,** *bisque head, five piece ball-jointed body, brown long wig, blue flirty eyes, velvet shorts suit with tam and boots, 24½″*	300.00	325.00	315.00
☐ **Toddler,** *bisque head, wood jointed body, blonde wig, blue sleep eyes, red print dress with black trim, 26″*	200.00	250.00	225.00
☐ **Toddler Boy,** *composition head and body, human hair wig, painted eye, navy boy suit, marked: 151, 14″*	450.00	470.00	460.00
☐ **Toddler,** *character, bisque head, brown wig, blue sleep eyes, bent limb body, dressed mold #152, 19″*	500.00	600.00	510.00
☐ **Toddler Child,** *character, bisque head, jointed composition body, brown glass eyes brown human hair wig, nicely dressed, #260, 18″*	700.00	800.00	750.00

LUCILLE KIMSEY

☐ **John F. Kennedy,** *bisque head, cloth body, molded and painted hair, a likeness of President Kennedy wearing a double-breasted suit, made in 1971, 14½″*	60.00	75.00	57.00

KING FEATURES

	Current Price Range		Prior Year Average
☐ **Henry,** *vinyl, molded and painted features, molded and painted clothing, representing the character Henry from the comic strip of the same name, created by Carl Anderson, made in 1950, 9″*	22.00	28.00	20.00
Note: This doll is listed under King Features because the only marking it carries is KF. King Features was a newspaper syndicate, which owned the rights to Henry. However, the company only licensed the production of dolls, it did not manufacture them itself. The actual maker of this item is not known.			
☐ **Popeye,** *composition and wood, molded and painted features, molded and painted clothing, jointed at shoulders, hips and neck, arms bent at elbows, has tatoo on left forearm, unmarked, date of manufacture unkown, probably late 1930's, 15″*	80.00	100.00	70.00
☐ **Popeye,** *vinyl head, cloth body, vinyl arms, cloth legs, molded and painted features, representing the comic strip character created by L.C. Segar, marked 411 King Features Sy, made in 1960, 21″*	100.00	130.00	75.00
Note: The value of this doll — and most other old Popeye dolls — more than doubled in 1980, when the motion picture based on Segar's classic comic was released.			
☐ **Snuffy Smith,** *cloth/nylon, marked Copyright King Features Syndicate, Inc., 14¼″*	70.00	90.00	65.00
Note: Snuffy Smith was a character in the comic strip "Barney Google and His Horse Sparkplug" by Billy DeBeck.			
☐ **Sweet Pea,** *vinyl head, cloth body, painted eyes, wears baby bonnet (molded), Sweet Pea is a character in the comic strip "Popeye," created by L.C. Segar, marked King Features Sy. Inc., made in 1959, 10″*	45.00	60.00	35.00
Note: If this doll was 20 years older, the value would be about three times as much.			
☐ **Uncle Walt And Skeezix,** *c. 1930, pair of cheesecloth dolls, famous Gasoline Alley characters, height 12″*	70.00	80.00	75.00
☐ **Wimpy,** *vinyl, squeeze toy, molded and painted features, molded and painted clothing, Wimpy is a character in the comic strip "Popeye," created by L.C. Segar, marked King Features Syndicate, date of manufacture unknown, presumably 1960's, 6″*	7.00	10.00	5.00

KLEY & HAHN

	Current Price Range		Prior Year Average
☐ **Bisque Socket Head,** *fully jointed composition body, blue sleep eyes, open mouth with four molded teeth, light brown human hair wig, dotted Swiss dress, lace trimmed suspenders, green ribbon rosettes, original body finish, marks: 250 K H Walkure 1½, 20"*	350.00	375.00	325.00
☐ **Walkure,** *bisque socket head, fully jointed composition body, blue sleep eyes, open mouth with four porcelain teeth, long blonde wig, painted upper and lower eyelashes, printed white cotton dress, marks: 250 K H Walkure 3¼ Germany, 23"*	350.00	450.00	325.00
☐ **Walkure,** *bisque head, compositon body, ball-jointed, paperweight eyes, human hair wig, open mouth, old clothes, excellent condition, 33"*	850.00	1000.00	975.00
☐ **Walkure,** *bisque head, jointed composition body, blonde wig, brown sleep eyes, (glass) open mouth, #250, 20"*	400.00	450.00	415.00

KNICKERBOCKER

	Current Price Range		Prior Year Average
☐ **Annie Tote 'n Doll,** *rag doll, comes in cotton tote bag, 6"*	8.00	12.00	5.00
☐ **Belle Fun And Fashion Doll,** *vinyl, poseable, wears dress, bow, comes with molded Woodstock, 8"*	12.00	18.00	10.00
☐ **Campbell Kids,** *c. 1973, pair of rag dolls, in original boxes*	10.00	18.00	14.00
☐ **Carrie,** *vinyl, soft body, rooted hair, 11"*	10.00	20.00	10.00
☐ **Cowpokes,** *boy, girl rag dolls, country western, 12"*	8.00	12.00	5.00
☐ **Dennis The Menace,** *rubber head, cloth body, 14"*	9.00	12.00	8.00
☐ **Floppy Sox,** *cloth, unmarked on doll, sold originally with a tag reading Floppy Sox, Knickerbocker, 8"*	2.00	3.00	2.00
☐ **Hansel,** *cloth (painted face), stuffed body, blonde hair, wears cap, originally sold with a tag reading Hansel, Rag Doll, Knickerbocker Toy Co., made in 1969, 17"*	6.00	8.00	6.00
☐ **Holly Hobbie Tote 'n Doll,** *rag doll, comes in pink purse, 6"*	8.00	12.00	5.00
☐ **Laura,** *vinyl soft body, rooted har, 12"*	10.00	20.00	10.00

Dennis The Menace, rubber and cloth, 14″ . . . . **$9.00-$12.00**

	Current Price Range		Prior Year Average
☐ **The Magical Burger King,** *vinyl, cloth body, magic ring, multi-colored scarf, cape, boots, 19″*	**15.00**	**25.00**	**20.00**
☐ **Missy,** *vinyl, molded and painted features, closed mouth, wears wide-brimmed hat, marked KTC-1975, made in Taiwan, 11″*	**3.00**	**4.00**	**3.00**
☐ **Nancy,** *cloth (printed), unmarked on doll, sold originally with a tag reading Nancy, Knickerbocker, marked on box Copyright United Features Syndicate, Inc., 1973, 6½″*	**6.00**	**8.00**	**5.00**
Note: Nancy was a comic strip character created by Ernie Bushmiller.			
☐ **Official Levi's Rag Doll,** *denim with yarn hair, unmarked on doll, sold originally with a tag reading Levi's Denim Rag Doll, 1974, 16″*	**5.00**	**7.00**	**5.00**

	Current Price Range		Prior Year Average
☐ **Oh, Susanna,** *composition head and body, sleep eyes (brown), open mouth with teeth, marked Knickerbocker, made in 1937, 15¼″*	65.00	80.00	60.00
☐ **Orphan Annie,** *cloth doll, three dimensional, small Sandy in pocket, 16″*	12.00	17.00	10.00
☐ **Pinnochio,** *composition head and body, wooden arms and legs, molded and painted hair, painted clothing, marked: Pinnochio W.D. PR I.T. Co., paper tag on wrist, 11″*	450.00	550.00	110.00
☐ **Princess Glory Of Lilliput,** *composition head and body, sleep eyes, representing a character from the novel "Gulliver's Travels" by Jonathan Swift, date of manufacture unknown, probably mid to late 1930's, 15″*	70.00	90.00	65.00
Note: There was also a boy version of this doll, called Prince David (another character from the Swift novel), with the same value.			
☐ **Raggedy Andy,** *original label, 12″*	8.00	12.00	8.00
☐ **Raggedy Andy,** *original label, 18″*	15.00	20.00	15.00
☐ **Raggedy Andy,** *original label, 35″*	35.00	45.00	40.00
☐ **Scarecrow,** *cloth, unmarked on doll, sold originally with a tag reading Knickerbocker, 1939, 23″*	75.00	90.00	65.00
Note: Representing a character from the motion picture "The Wizard of Oz." In the movie, the Scarecrow was played by Ray Bolger.			
☐ **Sleeping Beauty,** *composition, rooted hair (reddish brown), sleep eyes, closed mouth, wearing a long taffeta nightgown, made in 1939*	60.00	75.00	55.00
☐ **Sluggo,** *cloth (printed), unmarked on doll, sold originally with a tag reading Sluggo, Knickerbocker, marked on box Copyright United Features Syndicate, Inc., 1973, 6½″*	8.00	11.00	7.00
Note: Sluggo was a character from the comic strip "Nancy," created by Ernie Bushmiller.			
☐ **Snoopy Fun And Fashion Doll,** *vinyl, jointed, jeans, T-shirt, comes with small Woodstock, 9″*	12.00	18.00	10.00
☐ **Snoopy Play Purse,** *Snoopy doll, comes in tote bag*	8.00	12.00	8.00
☐ **Snow White,** *composition head and body, black hair attached by adhesive, sleep eyes (green), marked Knickerbocker Toy Co., made in 1939, 15″*	100.00	130.00	90.00

	Current Price Range		Prior Year Average
Note: The Disney motion picture, based on this popular storybook tale, had just been released when Knickerbocker's "Snow White" went on the market. It does not carry any marks linking it with Disney.			
☐ **Sunbonnet Baby,** *vinyl, mint in box*	5.00	10.00	5.00
☐ **Soupy Sales,** *vinyl head, cloth body, marked Knickerbocker 1965, 13"*	60.00	75.00	55.00
Note: Soupy Sales hosted a daily childrens' show in the days of live TV.			
☐ **Theodore The Chipmunk,** *vinyl head, cloth body, marked Ross Bagdasarian, 14"*	23.00	29.00	21.00
Note: Ross Bagdasarian, professionally known as David Seville, created the Chipmunks as a squeaky-voiced singing group for novelty records in 1956. When the records became popular, character merchandise followed.			

KNOTTER

☐ **Girl,** *red cape, green hat, holds package, made in Japan*	30.00	40.00	30.00
☐ **Girl,** *snow suit, holds Teddy Bear*	35.00	45.00	35.00

KÖNIG AND WERNICKE

☐ **Boy,** *bisque head, ball-jointed composition body, short curly brown human hair wig, brown sleep eyes, blue velvet shirt, tie shoes, 37"*	1000.00	1100.00	1050.00

KÄTHE KRUSE

☐ **Boy,** *molded fabric head, jointed fabric body, beautifully hand painted face with brown eyes and hair, original clothes, signed on foot, 16"*	1100.00	1200.00	1000.00
☐ **Child,** *all cloth, molded cloth head, jointed body, painted features and hair, original costume, mark: Käthy Kruse on bottom of foot, 17"*	450.00	650.00	450.00
☐ **Girl,** *celluloid base with cloth overlay, human hair wig, painted eyes, c. 1957*	450.00	500.00	475.00

Celluloid and Cloth,
c. 1957, 14″
$450.00-$500.00

	Current Price Range		Prior Year Average
☐ **Girl,** *molded fabric head, jointed fabric body, painted face, original clothes, 20″ . . .*	900.00	950.00	900.00
☐ **Riekchen,** *plastic head, cloth body, painted eyes, made in Germany, 1970, 19″ . . . .*	35.00	42.00	32.00
Note: Made for the Neiman-Marcus department store of Dallas, Texas.			
☐ **Toddler,** *molded cloth head, cloth body, painted face, wig, original clothes, type Puppe VII, 14″ . . . .*	800.00	1000.00	1000.00

LAKESIDE

	Current Price Range		Prior Year Average
☐ **Gumby,** *foam over wire (posable), marked Gumby, Mfg. by Lakeside Ind., Inc., first sold in 1965, 13″*	6.00	8.00	6.00
Note: Gumby was originally a British creation, by Newfeld Ltd. It was made by Lakeside under license from Newfeld. In a sense Gumby was the English answer to G.I. Joe — a male doll wearing various "action and adventure" outfits. The outfits were sold separately.			
☐ **Lone Ranger,** *vinyl, molded and painted features, molded and painted clothing, bendable, marked 24, 1966, Lakeside Ind., Inc., sold in a box marked Wrather Corp., 6″*	4.00	6.00	4.00

Bisque and Composition,
c. 1905, 18″
$600.00-$700.00

A. LANTERNIER

	Current Price Range		Prior Year Average
☐ **Bisque Head,** *jointed body, blonde mohair wig, set eyes, molded brows, antique black and white two piece suit, velvet belt and tam, marked with anchor L.C.C., c. 1905, 18"*	600.00	700.00	625.00
☐ **Bisque Shoulder Head,** *composition and cloth body, brown stationary eyes, brown wig, closed mouth, brown wool dress with bonnet, mark: A L, 13"*	400.00	500.00	400.00
☐ **Caprice,** *French character toddler, bisque head, jointed French composition body, brown wig, blue glass eyes with black rim molded tear ducts, molded open-closed mouth, molded teeth, nice French clothes, 24½"*	1600.00	1800.00	1500.00
☐ **French Clown,** *white bisque socket head on five piece composition body, brown set eyes, light brown mohair wig, open mouth, painted clown makeup on face includes heavy black dots on forehead, cheeks and chin with green, blue and red stripes as accents, maroon and white satin clown suit with lace collar, tall maroon dunce cap, marks: LC, Anchor mark, 11"*	350.00	400.00	325.00
☐ **French Le Conte,** *bisque socket head on jointed composition French body, blue sleep eyes, light brown wig with long ringlets and curly bangs, pierced ears, open mouth with porcelain teeth, dimpled chin, molded eyebrows, painted upper and lower lashes, printed green silk dress, marks: L (Anchor) C.C. 12, 27"*	1500.00	1750.00	1350.00

LASTIC PLASTIC

	Current Price Range		Prior Year Average
☐ **Bi Bye,** *vinyl head, vinyl arms and legs, stuffed cloth body, painted eyes, molded and painted hair, represents a one-week-old infant with mouth wide open, crying, originally sold with a tag, dated 1949, made for the Fleischaker Novelty Co. by Lastic Plastic, 16"*	14.00	18.00	13.00
☐ **Plastic,** *stuffed, rooted hair, sleep eyes, partially open mouth, wears checkered dress (short) with puff sleeves, two buttons on dress, arms and legs wide apart, marked Copyright 1951 Lastic Plastic, 16½"*	18.00	23.00	17.00

	Current Price Range		Prior Year Average
Note: This doll (unnamed) was manufactured by Lastic Plastic for the Fleischaker Novelty Co. The hairstyle is somewhat "afro."			

H.D. LEE

☐ **Buddy Lee,** *all celluloid, jointed at the shoulders (legs not jointed), molded blonde hair, painted eyes, 13″*	140.00	185.00	135.00

LENCI

In 1919 the Italian doll firm of Lenci was founded by Signora Elena Konig di Scavini. Her nickname was Lenci, hence her dolls were called "Lenci's" dolls.

Madame di Scavini had been a costume designer for her husband Enrico's doll business prior to his joining the Italian military as an aviator. When he left, she began making dolls as a way of keeping busy. This need soon intensified greatly as a result of the death of their only child.

To escape from her sorrow, Madame di Scavini turned to doll making. Lenci dolls were made primarily of felt with painted faces and felt clothing and produced by local woman who cooked in their homes. Business flourished and by the late 1930's the Lenci factory was built in Turin, employing several hundred workers. Many celebrities collected her dolls including Mussolini and most of the crowned heads of Europe.

The Lenci firm continued to prosper until depression and war neccesitated diversification in the early 1940's. Classic Lenci dolls are reproduced by the company today using the same molds and processes used in the production of their dolls during the 1920's.

☐ **Amelia Earhart,** *composition body and head, jointed blonde wig, blue set eyes, flight engineer's suit, 14″*	400.00	425.00	419.00
☐ **Boy,** *character, felt mask pressed swivel head, wig, googly flifty glass eyes, original costume, Teyrolean mint, 19″*	2800.00	3500.00	2800.00
☐ **Boy,** *cloth doll, nice outfit, 10″*	35.00	45.00	40.00
☐ **Boy,** *felt construction, bent limb body, blonde short wig, brown painted eyes, floppy hat, brown riding outfit, 24½″*	500.00	600.00	525.00
☐ **Boy,** *Swiss guard, pressed felt head, jointed felt body, blue painted eyes, brown wig, striped Swiss guard felt uniform, 2nd hat, 18″*	500.00	600.00	500.00

	Current Price Range		Prior Year Average
☐ **Character Girl,** *pressed felt head, pinted felt body, swivel neck, painted features, blonde wig, Lenci tag, 19″*	700.00	800.00	650.00
☐ **Character Girl,** *pressed felt head with painted features jointed felt body, corkscrew curls, startled expression at felt, bee poised on her skirt, large bonnet, party slippers, black cloth label, 10″*	260.00	290.00	265.00
☐ **Child,** *all felt pressed head, jointed felt body, curly mohair wig, pouty faced, stitched fingers, original dress, 21″*	450.00	550.00	425.00
☐ **Child,** *bride character, all felt head with painted features, felt jointed body, brown hair, brown side glancing eyes, bridal gown in antique white, matching veil & purse, Lenci tag c. 1920's, 12″*	285.00	315.00	290.00
☐ **Child,** *felt construction, bent limb body, curly redhead, brown painted eyes, red pinafore dress with bloomers and hat, 13″*	350.00	450.00	375.00
☐ **Child,** *molded hollow, tagged, 13″*	260.00	320.00	280.00
☐ **Cloth Doll,** *elaborate peasant costume, excellent condition 10½″*	45.00	55.00	50.00
☐ **Cloth,** *pressed felt head, jointed felt body, painted features, original costume, mint, 17″*	700.00	800.00	675.00
☐ **Cowboy,** *felt construction, stationary body, brown wig, brown painted eyes, chaps, vest and shirt with wide bolero, 18″*	650.00	750.00	675.00
☐ **Girl,** *cloth, elaborate peasant costume, excellent condition 8″*	35.00	45.00	40.00
☐ **Girl,** *felt construction, arm raised, blonde wig, brown painted eyes, red dress with over skirt, 32″*	1100.00	1200.00	1050.00
☐ **Golfer,** *felt construction, bent arm body, brown wig, brown painted eyes, knickers and vest, holding golf club, 17″*	650.00	725.00	675.00
☐ **Girl,** *felt construction, bent arm body, long braided wig, blue painted eyes looking askance, diamond print dress, straw hat, 18″*	350.00	400.00	375.00
☐ **Girl,** *felt construction bent limb body, blonde mohair wig, brown painted eyes, full black ruffled dress with white lacy pantaloons, 22″*	400.00	450.00	425.00
☐ **Girl,** *felt construction, stationary body, black upswept wig, brown painted eyes, long high waisted dress, tall cylindrical hat with tassle, 18″*	350.00	400.00	375.00

	Current Price Range		Prior Year Average
☐ **Girl,** *Mascotte, pressed felt head, jointed felt body, painted blue eyes, blonde wig, original costume, cloth label, 9″*	150.00	250.00	175.00
☐ **Girl,** *red curly hair, black and red felt coat, 12″*	375.00	425.00	390.00
☐ **Fascist Youth,** *pressed felt head with painted features, jointed felt body, painted blue eyes, brown wig, wearing the black uniform and hat of Hitler's Youth, paper label, 16″*	575.00	675.00	550.00
☐ **Infant,** *felt construction, bent joint body, blonde side parted wig, blue painted eyes, modeled features, sweater over ruffled dress, 20″*	500.00	600.00	525.00
☐ **Infant,** *felt construction, bent joint body, brown curly mohair wig, brown painted eyes, modeled features, lavender ruffled chiffon dress, lacy bonnet, 20″*	500.00	600.00	525.00
☐ **Italian Girl,** *Laura Face, pressed felt head, jointed felt body, painted eyes, blonde wig, blue eyes, Italian peasant costume, 18″*	550.00	650.00	475.00
☐ **Japanese Geisha,** *Lucia Face, pressed felt head, jointed felt body, brown painted oriental eyes, brows, black wig, felt Kimono, hair ornaments, footgear, tag, 14″*	350.00	450.00	375.00
☐ **Jockey Character,** *pressed felt face with painted brown eyes, thick brown mohair wig, felt body jointed at shoulders and hips, swivel neck, individually stitched fingers, beige riding britches, yellow vest, ascot, black boots, red double breasted riding coat, black felt hat, riding crop, 12″*	350.00	450.00	375.00
☐ **Lady,** *felt construction, bent arm body, painted blue eyes, blonde fancy wig, elaborate blue ball gown with draped tiers, 17″*	350.00	400.00	375.00
☐ **Lady,** *felt construction, bent limb body, blonde human hair wig, wide blue painted eyes, long plaid dress, match tam, 19″*	450.00	500.00	475.00
☐ **Lady,** *felt construction, bent limb body, wide blue flirty glass eyes, black gown, flowered hat, 19½″*	1400.00	1600.00	1450.00
☐ **Lady,** *felt construction, stationary body, blonde curly human hair wig, blue painted eyes, elaborate ball gown with blue chiffon ruffled trim and roses, 23″*	400.00	500.00	425.00
☐ **Lady,** *felt construction, stationary body, severe blonde bun, wide surprised painted blue eyes, black watered silk gown with flowered hat, 24½″*	500.00	600.00	525.00

	Current Price Range		Prior Year Average
☐ **Lady,** *felt construction, swivel neck, blonde mohair wig, blue painted almond shaped eyes, French fashion gown, 19″*	350.00	400.00	375.00
☐ **Laura,** *child, molded felt head, jointed felt body, painted face, wig, original clothes, mint, mark: cloth and paper tags with Lenci written on them, 19″*	600.00	850.00	600.00
☐ **Marlene Dietrich,** *portrait, pressed felt face, painted features including light blue/grey eyes glancing to side, painted eyelashes, eyeshadow, original full blonde mohair wig parted in center and pulled into ringlets behind head, rouged cheeks, swivel neck, cloth body, well shaped legs with feet formed for high heels, individually stitched fingers and thumb, elaborate pale blue organdy gown, applied felt rosebuds, puffed sleeves, lace mittens, double ruffled organdy collar, yellow felt wide brimmed hat trimmed with flowers, stockings, original garters with blue felt rosebuds, original wired hoop petticoat, marks: cloth and paper labels on back of dress read Lenci, 25″*	1000.00	1200.00	1100.00
☐ **Mascott Girl,** *red and blue felt costume with lace headdress, 9″*	150.00	200.00	170.00
☐ **Paolo,** *felt pressed head, jointed felt body, painted features, original clothes and hat in perfect unplayed with condition, two Lenci toys, 14″*	600.00	750.00	650.00
☐ **Pressed,** *felt face, painted brown eyes glancing to side, original blonde mohair wig, felt body jointed at shoulders and hips, swivel neck, separately stitched fingers, original white and yellow short dress, matching cloche hat, 15″*	675.00	625.00	575.00
☐ **Pressed,** *felt molded face, painted brown eyes glancing to side, blonde mohair wig with curls on each side of head, felt body jointed at shoulders and hips, all original blue felt coat with cape collar and matching poke bonnet accented with pink felt flower, original blue shoes, 8″*	170.00	200.00	150.00
☐ **Pressed,** *felt face, painted features, swivel neck, jointed at shoulders and hips, brown eyes glancing to side, dark blonde mohair wig, felt body, individually stitched and separated fingers, candy striped pink dress, powder blue double breasted felt coat with pink edging and covered buttons, matching cloche style hat and shoes, 14″*	350.00	450.00	375.00

Fashion,
felt, c. 1940, 29″
$1400.00-$1600.00

	Current Price Range		Prior Year Average
☐ **Rag Doll,** *cloth head and body, coiled braids, painted eyes, original neopolitan red costume, c. 1940, 29″*	1400.00	1600.00	1450.00
☐ **The Sheik,** *Rudolph Valentino, character, pressed felt head jointed felt body, painted features, Sheik costume, pistol and dagger, leather boats, mint, 29″*	4500.00	5500.00	4500.00
☐ **Tennis Player,** *felt construction, bent limb body, short curly wig, brown painted eyes, red cap, brown overcoat, holding racket, 17″*	550.00	600.00	575.00

LESNEY

	Current Price Range		Prior Year Average
☐ **Alice In Wonderland,** *vinyl, blonde hair, marked Lesney 1973, made in Hong Kong, not related to Disney, 5″*	6.00	8.00	6.00
☐ **Baby,** *vinyl jointed, blonde rooted hair, painted blue eyes, open-close nurser mouth, white picque dress with matching bonnet, blue ribbon trim, 14″*	18.00	22.00	18.00
☐ **Party Patti,** *vinyl, red hair, marked Lesney 1973, made in Hong Kong*	6.00	8.00	6.00
☐ **Sailor Sue,** *vinyl, marked Lesney 1973, made in Hong Kong, 5″*	6.00	8.00	6.00

L.H.K.

☐ **Bisque,** *French body, human hair wig, brown sleep eyes, peach crepe dress with hat, 18″*	650.00	700.00	665.00
☐ **Bisque,** *blonde, goat hair wig, marked Germany, 10″*	175.00	225.00	185.00
☐ **Bisque,** *French ball-jointed body, human hair wig, blue sleep eyes, solid wrists, light blue dress and hat, 18″*	925.00	1000.00	950.00
☐ **Bisque Head,** *French jointed body, human hair wig, blue sleep eyes, light blue dress and hat*	950.00	1000.00	975.00
☐ **Bisque Head,** *French jointed composition body, brown set eyes, French human hair wig, pink velvet dress*	250.00	325.00	250.00

LIBBY

☐ **I Dream Of Jeannie (Barbara Eden),** *plastic/vinyl, sleep eyes (blue), rooted hair (blonde), closed mouth, dressed in the "Jeannie" costume from the popular TV series of the 1960's (still being shown in syndication), marked 4, 1966, Libby, box marked Sidney Sheldon Productions, (Sidney Sheldon was producer of the TV show), 20″*	23.00	29.00	22.00

LIBERTY

	Current Price Range		Prior Year Average
☐ **King,** *cloth, unmarked on doll, sold originally with a tag reading Liberty, Made in England, representing an English king wearing crown and ermine robes, but apparently no king in particular, 8½″*	23.00	29.00	22.00

LIMBACH

☐ **Bisque Head,** *French ball-jointed body, human hair wig, brown paperweight eyes, pierced ears, open mouth, blue velvet dress with antique lace trim, marked clover leaf, 16″*	600.00	650.00	620.00

Bisque and Kid,
c. 1890, 19″
$1150.00-$1400.00

	Current Price Range		Prior Year Average
☐ **Little Girl,** *bisque socket head composition chubby body, mohair glued on wig, in pigtails, black glass pupiless eyes, open mouth with four small teeth, yellow dress, matching bonnet, white pinafore, long white stockings, black leather shoes, Rauenstein Grenier trefoil mark on head, early 1800's, 9½″*	145.00	160.00	145.00

LIMENAU

	Current Price Range		Prior Year Average
☐ **Bisque Head,** *kid leather body, brown human hair wig, blue paperweight eyes, blue two piece satin suit, with maroon trim, marked 693 #6, c. 1880, 19″*	1150.00	1400.00	1250.00

LIMOGES

	Current Price Range		Prior Year Average
☐ **Bisque Head,** *French ball-jointed body, brown wig, blue paperweight eyes, pierced ears, green velvet dress, 17″*	685.00	725.00	700.00
☐ **Bisque Head,** *French wooden and composition body, brown set eyes, brown human hair wig, open mouth, lovely old clothes, 20½″*	1150.00	1275.00	1200.00
☐ **French Girl Doll,** *jointed five piece body, set blue paperweight eyes, pierced ears, frilly dress, 12″*	500.00	550.00	510.00
☐ **Francee,** *reproduction, bisque, lacy red velour dress, 22″*	100.00	150.00	125.00

L.J.N.

	Current Price Range		Prior Year Average
☐ **Mr. Action,** *plastic/vinyl, painted features, molded and painted hair, blue eyes, representing an adult male, made in 1967*	5.00	7.00	5.00
Note: Though the doll looks — and the name sounds — like something from a TV show or comic book, we cannot trace any references to a character called Mr. Action.			
☐ **Pamela,** *plastic/vinyl, painted eyes (blue), rooted hair (platinum blonde), partially open mouth, representing a high-fashion model, marked Hong Kong on doll, box marked Made exclusively for L.J.N. Toys, 1973, 17½″*	8.00	10.00	7.00

	Current Price Range		Prior Year Average
☐ **Bonnie Jean,** *plastic/vinyl, sleep eyes (blue), rooted hair (blonde), pug nose, open nursing mouth, dressed in print gown with ruffled bib, marked Lorrie Doll, 1961, 14″*	5.00	7.00	5.00
☐ **Cuddly Infant,** *vinyl head, cloth body, vinyl arms, plastic legs, molded and painted hair, sleep eyes (blue), open mouth, marked 1460T-Lorrie Doll Co., 1963, 14″*	5.00	7.00	5.00
☐ **Debbie Trix,** *black, plastic/vinyl, sleep eyes (brown), sold with red, black and brown interchangeable wigs, closed mouth, wearing a puff-sleeve dress with small floral prints, marked Lorrie Doll Co., Inc., 1964, 14½″*	9.00	12.00	9.00
☐ **Delightful,** *plastic/vinyl, brunette hair (rooted), sleep eyes (blue), ribbon in hair, partially open mouth, marked 11-Lorrie Doll, 1966, 22″*	11.00	15.00	10.00
☐ **Etty Bitty,** *vinyl head, cloth body, vinyl arms and legs, blonde hair (rooted), marked Lorrie Doll, 1968/3, made in Taiwan, 14″*	5.00	7.00	5.00
☐ **Marsha,** *vinyl, blonde hair (rooted), sleep eyes (brown), ribbons in hair, marked Lorrie Doll 1971, made in Taiwan, 11″*	6.00	8.00	6.00
☐ **Little Linda,** *vinyl, blonde hair (rooted), sleep eyes (brown), marked 9 & 11-Lorrie Doll, 1971, made in Taiwan, 9″*	6.00	8.00	5.00
☐ **Louise,** *black, plastic/vinyl, black hair (rooted), sleep eyes (brown), marked 1250-4-Lorrie, made in 1964, 12″*	13.00	17.00	12.00
☐ **Lucy,** *vinyl, sleep eyes, marked 9, Lorrie Doll, 1971, 9″*	6.00	9.00	6.00
☐ **My Baby,** *vinyl head, cloth body, vinyl arms, plastic legs, blonde hair (rooted), sleep eyes (blue), marked 1-Lorrie Doll-1960, 19″*	9.00	12.00	9.00
☐ **Pastel Miss,** *plastic/vinyl, rooted hair, sleep eyes (brown), closed mouth, marked Lorrie Doll, 1964, 22″*	6.00	8.00	6.00
☐ **Powder Puff,** *plastic/vinyl, painted eyes (blue), rooted hair (red), pug nose, open mouth, marked Lorrie Doll, 1971, 14½″*	4.00	6.00	4.00
☐ **Sandy,** *plastic/vinyl, marked 26 Lorrie Doll, 1969, made in Hong Kong, 9″*	5.00	7.00	5.00
☐ **Sweet Candy,** *plastic/vinyl, sleep eyes (blue), rooted hair (blonde), pug nose, closed mouth, wearing a toddler's gown, marked Lorrie Doll, 1964, 19″*	6.00	8.00	6.00
☐ **Sweet-ee,** *black, plastic/vinyl, marked G. Lorrie Doll Co., 1974, 12″*	23.00	29.00	21.00
☐ **Taffy,** *black, plastic/vinyl, open mouth with teeth, marked T. Lorrie Doll Co., 1974, 12″*	23.00	29.00	21.00

LOUIS AMBERG AND SONS

	Current Price Range		Prior Year Average
☐ **Charlie Chaplin,** *cloth body and head, painted face, wool hair, marked Louis Amberg & Son, Charlie Chaplin, date of manufacture unknown, 17″*	165.00	200.00	160.00

LOUISE R. KAMPES STUDIOS

☐ **Kamkins,** *pressed mask cloth face, stuffed cloth body, wig, painted features, original costume, 20″*	500.00	600.00	500.00

LOVEE

☐ **Daisy Luv,** *plastic/vinyl, marked Made in Hong Kong No. 2618, late 1960's, 11½″*	3.00	4.00	3.00
Note: Before being acquired by Lovee, the mold for this doll had been used by Mattel and the Mattel marking will still be found on the back of the doll's head. This has led some collectors and dealers into the error of classifying it as a Mattel doll.			
☐ **Unnamed,** *plastic/vinyl, nurser, painted eyes, marked 1974, Lovee Doll, 22¼″*	5.00	7.00	5.00

MAISON SIMONNE

☐ **French Fashion,** *bisque shoulder head with kid lined swivel neck, light blue glass inset eyes with dark blue outline, kid body with gussets at hips and knees, slender waist, separately stitched fingers, closed mouth with accent lines, pierced ears, rosy cheeks, blonde wig styled in ringlets and braid, original mauve colored box with Maison Simonne label, two piece deep purple velveteen dress, fitted jacket, train effect, striped silk bonnet is trimmed with flowers and plume, 18″*	2000.00	2800.00	2000.00

MAJBER

	Current Price Range		Prior Year Average
☐ **Lindy,** *plastic/vinyl, brunette hair (rooted), sleep eyes (blue), partially open mouth, marked Majber, made in 1966, 17½″*	14.00	18.00	13.00

MAJESTIC

☐ **Jack And Jill,** *printed oilcloth (stuffed), marked 1950 Majestic Dolls, 12″ each, value for pair*	2.00	3.00	2.00

MARLON

☐ **Sussy,** *vinyl, molded and painted hair, sleep eyes, nursing mouth, unmarked, made in 1968, 8″*	6.00	8.00	6.00

ARMAND MARSEILLE

Every browser among antique and semi-antique dolls has encountered specimens by Armand Marseille. The factory survived long and was, during its peak years, highly prolific, turning out dolls in large numbers for various contractors. The Armand Marseille dolls chiefly have bisque heads and run a comprehensive gamut in sizes and styles, representing infants, adults and all ages in between. Mostly they have sleep eyes. The faces are mostly very well-modeled, some with strong classical overtones, some suggesting a swing to more progressive designing. From a technical viewpoint the Armand Marseille dolls are probably as good, collectively, as any of their era. The only thing holding down their values is their lack of real scarcity on the market, owing to the large quantities manufactured. This, however, should be a bonus to the hobbyist, as it enables him to get a fine period doll at a bargain price.

Armand Marseille was a German organization. It was founded in 1865 in the town of Koppelsdorf, Thuringia, Westphalia. In its earlier years it was moderately successful but its chief growth occured after 1890. From 1900 to the onset of World War I (1914) it undoubtedly outproduced all other European doll factories. Its dolls, bearing various distributors' names, were sold in all parts of the western hemisphere. The war hindered all German doll makers, as the local market virtually collapsed and import/export business became difficult or impossible. Armand Marseille succeeded in struggling through the war. The firm was reorganized following the Armistice of 1918, with a view to reattaining the old production levels and heavily exporting into America.

This dream was never realized, for various reasons — one of which was the new influence of Japan on the export doll market. In 1927 Armand Marseille closed its doors.

	Current Price Range		Prior Year Average
☐ **Baby,** *bent limb, composition body, brown hair, blue eyes, sailor suit, mold number 990, 17″*	350.00	400.00	365.00
☐ **Baby,** *blue sleep eyes, cloth body, Germany″*	250.00	300.00	275.00
☐ **Baby,** *blue sleep eyes, dark blonde wig, open mouth, baby outfit of pink gingham checkered dress with white collar, pants to match, 12″*	175.00	225.00	185.00
☐ **Baby,** *bisque, cloth body, blue sleep eyes, closed mouth, marked Germany, 18″*	350.00	400.00	360.00
☐ **Baby,** *bisque head, composition body, blue sleep eyes, molded and painted hair, closed mouth, christening gown, mark: A.M. 341, head circumference 8″*	275.00	350.00	300.00
☐ **Baby,** *bisque head, five-piece body, sleep eyes, strong facial modeling, closed mouth, long heirloom infant dress, 341, 13″ tall, 10½″ cimcumference*	270.00	300.00	280.00
☐ **Baby,** *character, blue sleep eyes, original lashes, original blonde curly wig, pretty long dress, 20″*	475.00	575.00	450.00
☐ **Baby,** *painted, bent limb, open mouth, two bottom teeth, blue sleep eyes, Germany*	300.00	350.00	325.00
☐ **Baby Betty,** *bisque head, kid body with bisque hands, blue sleep eyes, rose plaid dress and hat, marked: 310, 16″*	600.00	625.00	605.00
☐ **Baby,** *very dark brown bisque head on black jointed bent leg baby body, brown set eyes, open mouth, pierced ears with hoop earrings, molded black hair, marks: A.M., 16″*	200.00	250.00	200.00
☐ **Betsy Baby,** *bisque, socket head, sleep eyes, open mouth with two teeth, chubby face with double chin, five-piece composition body, marked G.B. 329/A. 2 M., early 1920's. 13″*	130.00	170.00	125.00
☐ **Bisque,** *ball-jointed body, boy, set blue eyes, short blonde wig, open mouth, blue overalls, white shirt, yellow straw hat, 24″*	325.00	375.00	338.00
☐ **Bisque,** *ball-jointed body, sleep blue eyes, short blonde mohair wig, open mouth, lavender gingham dress with low waist, 17″*	225.00	275.00	240.00

	Current Price Range		Prior Year Average
☐ **Bisque,** *ball-jointed body, set blue glass eyes, long blonde human hair wig, open mouth, bridal gown with long train, bouquet, 30″*	700.00	800.00	735.00
☐ **Bisque,** *ball-jointed composition body, brown eyes, brown braids, Heidi-type outfit, mold number 390, 12″*	100.00	150.00	140.00
☐ **Bisque,** *brown sleep eyes, redish brown hair, open mouth, pierced ears, blue dress with lace trim, 18″*	325.00	375.00	340.00
☐ **Bisque,** *composition body, brown sleep eyes, brown wig, open mouth, brown velvet dress, lace trim, 7″*	100.00	150.00	120.00
☐ **Bisque,** *composition five-piece body, original wig, blue glass eyes, original white dress, 560-6/0-232, 9″*	310.00	345.00	310.00
☐ **Bisque,** *heavyweight ball-jointed composition body, blue eyes, blonde human hair with ringlets, red satin dress with dropped waist, mold number 390, 20″*	225.00	275.00	240.00
☐ **Bisque,** *heavyweight jointed composition body, blue eyes, red human hair with ringlets, dark blue velvet dress with light blue trimming, mold number, 23″*	265.00	300.00	275.00
☐ **Bisque,** *jointed composition body, blue sleeping eyes, blonde human hair wig with ringlets, white moire dress with blue lace and ribbon rimmings, mold number 390n, 26″*	300.00	350.00	320.00
☐ **Bisque,** *jointed composition body, brown bulbous eyes, dark brown human hair with ringlets, pink satin dress with ruffles and lace, mold number 390n, 23″*	275.00	325.00	290.00
☐ **Bisque,** *jointed composition body, brown eyes, blonde wig, white dress with rosebud embroidery, matching hat, mold number 390, 28½″*	375.00	430.00	400.00
☐ **Bisque,** *jointed composition body, brown human hair wig, glossy brown eyebrows, set blue eyes, open mouth, molded upper teeth, shift, black shoes and socks, 17″*	325.00	375.00	340.00
☐ **Bisque,** *jointed composition body, capri blue eyes, brown wig, navy blue dress with green pin, 22″*	200.00	250.00	215.00
☐ **Bisque,** *jointed composition body, dark brown eyes, blonde wig, blue and white print dress, white hair ribbon, 29″*	325.00	375.00	340.00

	Current Price Range		Prior Year Average
☐ **Bisque,** *jointed composition body, dark brown eyes, brown hair with ringlets, aqua blue satin dress with ecru lace trimmings, mold number 390, 26"*	300.00	350.00	318.00
☐ **Bisque,** *jointed composition body, painted, comes with crucifix, rosary, bible and religious pictures hung around neck, 17"*	125.00	175.00	140.00
☐ **Bisque,** *kid body, bisque hands, turned head to right, brown sleep eyes, heavy brows, red-brown human hair wig, open mouth, brown and black striped dress with lace trim, high top shoes, marked Germany 273, 22"*	425.00	475.00	440.00
☐ **Bisque,** *kid body, cloth and composition arms, red human hair wig, mold number 370, 21"*	245.00	285.00	260.00
☐ **Bisque,** *kidolene body, bisque hands, blue sleep eyes, pale blonde human hair wig, open mouth, teeth, blue and white striped dress, blue ribbon sash, black shoes, 18"*	275.00	325.00	300.00
☐ **Bisque,** *sleep blue eyes, long brown hair, open mouth, long brown cotton gown with flowered pattern patterns, puffed Gibson Girl sleves, brown hair bow, top boots, 24"*	350.00	450.00	385.00
☐ **Bisque Shoulder Head,** *kid body, cloth lower legs, bisque hands, blue sleep eyes, open mouth with four teeth, brown wig, original blue striped dress, marks: Armand Marseille, Germany 370 A 7/0 M, 15"*	250.00	275.00	225.00
☐ **Bisque Shoulder Head,** *kid body, pin points, celluloid arms, brown sleep eyes, open mouth with four teeth, brown wig, navy blue dress, marks: AM 7/09, 16"*	250.00	275.00	225.00
☐ **Bisque,** *socket head, bisque feet and arms, muslin body, brown eyes, brown human hair wig with ringlets, pink satin dress with dropped waist, lace, matching hat, marked: D.R.G.M. Germany, 10½"*	100.00	150.00	120.00
☐ **Bisque,** *socket head, composition body, long brown hair in curls, blue glass sleep eyes, open mouth with four small teeth, antique white dress, long, floral weave, matching bonnet, pink ribbon trim on both, 390/246/1, 11"*	170.00	190.00	170.00
☐ **Bisque,** *socket head, fully jointed composition body, original blonde human hair wig, blue set eyes with real upper lashes, open mouth with four porcelain teeth, white lace net dress, orginal, oversized pink satin bow in hair, marks: Armand Marseille, Germany, 390 A 7 M, 24"*	350.00	450.00	325.00

	Current Price Range		Prior Year Average
☐ **Bisque,** *socket head, fully jointed composition body, sleep eyes, open mouth, #14, length 33″*	250.00	350.00	225.00
☐ **Bisque,** *socket head, toddler body, sleep eyes with eyelashes, open mouth with two teeth, marked A.M. Köppelsdorf Germany/1330-A. 12 M., 21″*	190.00	235.00	180.00
Note: A large, impressive doll which would probably be more valuable, but for the fact that it seems to have been produced in rather large quantities.			
☐ **Bisque,** *socket head set on toddler body, fully jointed construction, open mouth showing two teeth, fixed eyes, marked Armand Marseille/Germany 996/A. 3 M., 16″*	180.00	225.00	170.00
☐ **Bisque,** *socket head, sleep eyes, open mouth with two teeth, five-piece body, marked G.B. 327/A. 12 M. Germany, 21″*	385.00	465.00	365.00
☐ **Bisque,** *five-piece composition body, set eyes, open mouth showing four teeth and traces of others, marked A.M. 560a/DRGM R 232/1, 14″*	330.00	380.00	315.00
☐ **Bisque,** *socket head, five-piece composition body, sleep eyes, open mouth with two teeth, marked Germany/971/A.4.M., 15″*	140.00	190.00	135.00
☐ **Bisque,** *painted head set on cloth body, sleep eyes (tin) with eyelashes, open mouth with two teeth, marked A.M./2549/9¾-3½, 16″*	85.00	110.00	80.00
Note: One of the later products of the firm, dating to the 1920's.			
☐ **Bisque,** *set on five-piece composition body, sleep "googly" eyes, closed mouth, lips turned upward at the corners, marked A.M./353/0½, 6¾″*	530.00	615.00	500.00
☐ **Bisque Head,** *ball-jointed body, human hair wig, blue sleep eyes, blue print dress with over skirt, marked 390 N, 24″*	500.00	525.00	510.00
☐ **Bisque Head,** *ball-jointed composition body, brown human hair wig, brown set eyes, open mouth with teeth, white dress, mold #390*	800.00	900.00	795.00
☐ **Bisque Head,** *ball-jointed composition body, human hair wig, brown sleep eyes, orchid costume, 32″*	1000.00	1100.00	1050.00
☐ **Bisque Head,** *ball-jointed composition body, mohair wig, blue set eyes, ecru dress, marked 560/6/0, 232, 9″*	325.00	400.00	335.00
☐ **Bisque Head,** *composition body, blonde human hair wig, blue set eyes, grey and white dotted swiss dress, 25″*	475.00	575.00	450.00

	Current Price Range		Prior Year Average
☐ **Bisque Head,** *composition ball-jointed body, reddish brown human hair wig, brown sleep eyes with lashes, open mouth, four teeth, original clothes, mold number 390, 28″*	525.00	575.00	530.00
☐ **Bisque Head,** *five-piece composition body, blue glass set eyes, white dress, marked 560-6-232, 9″*	350.00	400.00	375.00
☐ **Bisque Head,** *hands jointed, oilcloth body, brown glass eyes, brown wig, open mouth, pale green organdy dress with original underclothes, 14″*	185.00	230.00	175.00
☐ **Bisque Head,** *jointed composition body, blue set eyes, brown human hair wig, open mouth, lovely old dress, 40″*	1000.00	1200.00	1100.00

Bisque and Kid,
c. 1894, 13″
$235.00-$300.00

	Current Price Range		Prior Year Average
☐ **Bisque Head,** *jointed composition body, brown stationary eyes, brown human hair wig, mark: 1894, 14"*	275.00	325.00	250.00
☐ **Bisque Head,** *kid leather body, auburn wig, set eyes, blue dress, marked 1894 AM 8/0 Dept, 1894, 13"*	235.00	300.00	250.00
☐ **Bisque Shoulder Head,** *bisque arms, cloth body, blue sleep eyes, old wig, open mouth, lovely dress with matching hat, mold number 370, 40"*	850.00	1000.00	950.00
☐ **Bisque Shoulder Plate,** *kid body, bisque lower arms, cloth lower legs, brown set eyes, old dress and matching hat, mold number 370, 15"*	125.00	165.00	145.00

Character Baby,
bisque and composition, c. 1920, 17"
$400.00-$500.00

	Current Price Range		Prior Year Average
☐ **Black Baby,** *bisque head, five-piece composition body, brown sleep eyes, molded hair, open mouth, white christening gown, mold number 351, 13"*	425.00	550.00	400.00
☐ **Black Dream Baby A.M.,** *dark brown toned bisque solid dome head with flange neck, cloth body, brown toned composition arms, legs, brown sleep eyes, closed mouth, painted red lips, shaded brown hair, white organdy dress, marks: A.M., 10"*	375.00	500.00	375.00
☐ **Character Baby,** *bisque head, bent limb jointed body, red brown human hair wig, blue sleep eyes, short white two-piece dress with bonnet, marked mold number 990, c. 1920, 17"*	400.00	500.00	425.00
☐ **Character Baby,** *bisque socket head, jointed five-piece bent leg baby body, brown sleep eyes, original light brown mohair wig, open mouth with two porcelain teeth, dimpled chin, claret colored velvet jacket, shorts, matching beret, white satin blouse, lace collar, jabot, marks: Armand Marseille A. 975 M. Germany 12, 22"*	550.00	600.00	550.00
☐ **Character Baby,** *bisque socket head, five-piece bent leg baby body, brown sleep eyes, brown wig, open mouth with two porcelain teeth, double chin, white lace trimmed organdy gown, matching bonnet, made for Geroge Brogfeldt by Armand Marseille, marks: Germany G 327 B, A 3 M., D.R.G.M. 259, 15"*	250.00	300.00	250.00
☐ **Character Boy,** *bent limb composition body, dark brown eyes, dark brown wig, three-piece red and blue knit outfit, mold number 990, 10"*	125.00	175.00	140.00
☐ **Character Boy,** *bisque head and hands, kid body, blue intaglio eyes, fancy suit with collar, marked A 600 M, 12"*	450.00	500.00	475.00
☐ **Character Boy,** *bisque head, ball-jointed body, sleep blue eyes, navy blue suit, marked A 326 M, 12"*	400.00	450.00	425.00
☐ **Character Boy,** *bisque head, fully jointed composition body, brown sleep eyes, open mouth with two teeth, light brown human hair wig, navy striped sailor jacket with knickers, marks: Armand Marseille 971 Germany, A 1 M, 17"*	300.00	400.00	300.00

	Current Price Range		Prior Year Average
☐ **Character Boy,** *googly, molded short blonde hair, forehead curls, blue intaglio eyes, slightly smiling open/closed mouth, illusion of tongue, jointed composition body, black velvet knickers, jacket and lace shirt, marks: 210 A 6/0 M Germany, 10"*	150.00	200.00	150.00
☐ **Character Doll,** *bisque hands, kid body, intaglio eyes, closed mouth, molded hair, mold number 600, 15"*	525.00	575.00	545.00
☐ **Character Doll,** *bisque head, ball-jointed body, human hair wig, blue sleep eyes, wine colored dress and hat, marked A985M, 16"*	375.00	400.00	395.00
☐ **Character Doll,** *bisque head, ball-jointed composition body, human hair wig, brown set eyes, marked 390 N*	500.00	525.00	505.00
☐ **Character Doll,** *bisque head, composition ball-jointed body, brown glass eyes, long auburn hair, hair bows, open mouth, teeth, red dress with lace trim, matching bonnet, black patent shoes, mold number 985, 20"*	350.00	400.00	370.00
☐ **Character Doll,** *bisque head, French composition ball-jointed body, brown eyes, brown human hair wig, lovely clothes*	550.00	600.00	575.00
☐ **Child,** *bisque head, composition ball-jointed body, blue sleep eyes, open mouth, brown shorts set with suspenders, green felt hat, 23"*	300.00	350.00	310.00
☐ **Child,** *bisque head, composition hands, cloth body, blue sleep eyes, closed mouth, mold number 341*	725.00	825.00	700.00
☐ **Child,** *bisque head, wood jointed body, short straight page boy wig, blue sleep eyes, blue velvet short set with matching shoes, 28"*	350.00	400.00	375.00
☐ **Child,** *bisque, original wig, blue stationary eyes, original dress, German marking: Armand Marseille 390-A-12-M, 29"*	785.00	860.00	775.00
☐ **Child,** *bisque shoulder head, kid body with composition hands and feet, blonde ringlets, blue sleep eyes, open mouth, 23½"*	250.00	300.00	275.00
☐ **Composition** *head and body, sleep eyes, open mouth showing four teeth, marked with an S split by a horizontal bar, followed by 2966/5/0x/2/0x, 16"*	70.00	90.00	65.00

Note: Comparatively few Armand Marseille dolls had composition heads. Though this could be considered a rarity of sorts, it does not command the kind of prices paid for bisque. Date of manufacture is not determined but probably falls in the period from 1905 to the beginning of World War I.

	Current Price Range		Prior Year Average
☐ **Dream Baby,** *bisque head, composition arms and legs on cloth body, brown sleep eyes, closed mouth, toddler outfit, marked A 341 M, 10″*	340.00	360.00	345.00
☐ **Dream Baby,** *bisque head, composition bent limb body, painted blonde hair, blue sleep eyes, antique christening dress, 15″*	350.00	450.00	400.00
☐ **Dream Baby,** *solid dome bisque head with flange neck, molded shaded light brown hair, blue sleep eyes, open mouth, cloth body with composition arms, white infant dress, tiny lanundry basket, marks: AM Germany 351, 8″*	125.00	150.00	115.00
☐ **Dream Baby,** *cloth body, composition hands, set blue glass eyes, painted blonde hair, diaper, slip, long white baby dress with lace trim, 19″*	325.00	375.00	340.00
☐ **Dream Baby,** *composition head and hands, cloth body, blue sleep eyes, white christening gown, 16″*	400.00	450.00	425.00
☐ **Dream Baby,** *composition head, cloth body, blue sleep eyes, white layette suit, no hat, 10″*	300.00	350.00	325.00
☐ **Dream Baby,** *solid dome bisque head with flange neck, lightly shaded brown painted hair, cloth body, composition hands, blue set eyes, painted closed mouth, marks: Germany 16 240, 7″*	125.00	225.00	100.00
☐ **Dream Baby,** *solid dome bisque socket head with shaded blonde hair, jointed five-piece composition baby body, blue sleep eyes, closed mouth, white lace trimmed baby dress, marks: A.M. Germany 341/3½ K, 15″*	275.00	375.00	275.00
☐ **Dutchess,** *bisque head ball-jointed body, curly blonde wig, blue sleep eyes, open mouth blue velvet hat and outfit, 28″*	600.00	700.00	625.00
☐ **Fany,** *baby, bisque head, molded hair, blue glass eyes, composition toddler body, closed mouth, dressed, head incised: Fany 230 A. 3M. DRMR 248, 19″*	5800.00	6800.00	5500.00
☐ **Fany,** *character boy, bisque head, composition and wooden ball-jointed body, molded head and hair, blue glass sleep eyes, closed mouth, old clothes, c. 1915, marks: Fany 230 A 7 M.D.R.G.M., 19″*	2200.00	2500.00	2200.00
☐ **Floradora,** *bisque head, bent limb body, brown sleep eyes, short brown hair, open mouth, white dress with pink and yellow flowers, pink bonnet, 10″*	225.00	275.00	240.00

	Current Price Range		Prior Year Average
☐ **Floradora,** *bisque head, five-piece body, set blue glass eyes, brown mohair wig, open mouth, blue velvet dress with beige ribbon trim, blue shoes, 16″*	225.00	275.00	240.00
☐ **Floradora,** *bisque, leather body, 20″*	350.00	450.00	355.00
☐ **Floradora,** *bisque socket head, brown sleep eyes, brown wig, open mouth with four teeth, jointed composition stick leg body, white dress, marks: Made in Germany Floradora A 5/o m, 12″*	150.00	250.00	140.00
☐ **Floradora,** *girl, bisque socket head, jointed composition and wood body, blonde mohair wig, blue blown glass eyes, open mouth, four-teeth, antique silk velvet peach dress with antique lace trim, large matching hat, marked, 1964-AM4-Dep, 16″*	430.00	475.00	440.00
☐ **Floradora,** *jointed composition body, blue eyes, blonde hair, plaid dress, 24″*	250.00	300.00	270.00
☐ **Floradora,** *shoulder head, kid body, brown glass sleep eyes, open mouth, teeth, long blonde human hair wig, pink floral dress, straw hat with flowers, black patent shoes, 13″*	200.00	250.00	220.00
☐ **Girl,** *composition ball-jointed body, brown glass sleep eyes, lashes, open mouth, teeth, red curls, blue velvet dress and hat trimmed with lace, patent shoes, 17″*	240.00	280.00	255.00
☐ **Girl,** *composition ball-jointed body, brown, stationary glass eyes, long blonde curls, red velvet dress and hat trimmed with lace, black patent shoes, mold number 390, 17″*	240.00	280.00	250.00
☐ **Girl,** *composition body, brown stationary glass eyes, open mouth, teeth, beige velvet dress with red lace trim, mold number 390n, 22″*	250.00	300.00	270.00
☐ **Girl,** *kid body, amber stationary glass eyes, open mouth, teeth, long red human hair wig, long blue velvet gown, matching hat and purse, mold number 370, 22″*	250.00	300.00	270.00
☐ **Googly,** *bisque head, composition body, brown wig, huge blue stationary eyes, closed smiling mouth, peach silk dress with lace and ribbon, lace bonnet, marked 323 A 10 M, 11½″*	1350.00	1500.00	1300.00
☐ **Googly,** *bisque socket head, five-piece jointed composition toddler body, brown sleep eyes glancing to right, watermelon smile, brown mohair wig, blue hand knitted sweater and short set, matching beret, marks: 253 G.B. Germany A. O M., 10″*	200.00	300.00	175.00

	Current Price Range		Prior Year Average
☐ **Hoopla Girl,** *bisque, socket head set on composition body (fully jointed), fixed dark eyes, closed mouth, marked 590/A. 5 M./Germany, 20″*	415.00	470.00	400.00
Note: Hoopla Girl was made during World War I, a period of extreme recession for the factory because its main source of export trade (the U.S.) was cut off as a customer.			
☐ **Infant,** *bisque head, cloth body, composition hands and feet, molded hair, blue sleep eyes, voice box action, blue shorts outfit with suspenders, 11″*	350.00	400.00	375.00
☐ **Infant,** *mold number 342, solid dome head, blue sleeping eyes, open/closed mouth with teeth, composition hands, cloth body, crier, wears chemise, diaper and socks, 8½″*	165.00	210.00	175.00
☐ **Lilly,** *bisque head, arms and hands, kid body, universal joints, blue sleep eyes, open mouth, two piece bustle dress in brown, trimmed in red, white buttons down front, lace trim, straw hat with feather trim, 22″*	425.00	475.00	440.00
☐ **Mama Doll,** *bisque head and hands, kid body, talker, blue sleep eyes, blue gingham dress, 18″*	325.00	375.00	340.00
☐ **Mammy,** *black bisque head, jointed composition and wood body, brown sleep eyes, black mohair wig, open mouth red and white kerchief and dress, black stockings and shoes, mark: 390 A 6/0M, 11″*	250.00	375.00	225.00
☐ **Musical Marotte,** *bisque shoulder head, bisque hands, blue set eyes, black mohair wig, open mouth, original white blouse, fringed red skirt over round wooden casing which covers the musical mechanism, when doll is held by wooden handle and twirled, it plays a tune, in working order, marks: on shoulder head-3200 AM 9/0 Dep, 13″*	200.00	350.00	180.00
☐ **Oriental Baby,** *bisque head, bent limb composition body, brown oriental eyes, molded hair, silk kimono, mark: A.M. 353, 13″*	750.00	975.00	725.00
☐ **Oriental Baby,** *bisque head, bent limb composition body, brown oriental eyes, molded hair, silk kimono, mark: A.M. 353, 20″*	950.00	1500.00	950.00
☐ **Queen Louise,** *bisque head, ball-jointed body, flapper, set blue eyes, long lashes, long blonde human hair wig, open mouth, fully beaded dress, silver head band, pink feathers, silver shoes, 23″*	450.00	550.00	485.00

	Current Price Range		Prior Year Average
☐ **Queen Louise,** *bisque head, ball-jointed composition body, human hair wig, brown sleep eyes, red dress with white lace trim, 22"*	600.00	650.00	625.00
☐ **Queen Louise,** *bisque socket head on fully jointed composition body, blue sleep eyes, original brown mohair wig, open mouth, double chin, dark green printed dress with white velvet ribbon, marks: Germany, Queen Louise 10, 26"*	200.00	300.00	175.00
☐ **Queen Louise,** *bisque socket head, fully jointed composition body, brown sleep eyes, real upper lashes, open mouth with four teeth, brown wig, blue batiste dress covered with antique lace, wide lace collar, and blue embroidered satin sash, matching bonnet, marks: Queen Louise 100 Germany, 24"*	300.00	400.00	275.00
☐ **Queen Louise,** *bisque head, jointed composition body, original reddish human hair wig, brown set eyes, feathered brows, eleborate red velvet dress and matching hat, 26"*	450.00	550.00	450.00
☐ **Queen Lousie,** *composition ball-jointed body, blue sleep eyes, blonde hair, 24"*	360.00	410.00	380.00
☐ **Queen Louise,** *composition, jointed open mouth, four teeth, brown sleep eyes, German, 27"*	450.00	500.00	456.00
☐ **Queen Louise,** *jointed composition body, brown eyes, red hair, white dress and hat blue trim, 23½"*	275.00	325.00	290.00
☐ **Rockaby,** *composition head and hands, cloth body, blue sleep eyes, open mouth with two bottom teeth, 16"*	400.00	450.00	415.00
☐ **Shoulder Head,** *kid body, blonde curls, open mouth, molded teeth, pink floral dress trimmed with lace, matching bonnet, white shoes, 13"*	150.00	200.00	170.00
☐ **Shoulder Head,** *turned head, kid body, blue stationary glass eyes, lashes, brown curly hair, open mouth, teeth, blue dress and hat trimmed with lace, white shoes, mold number 370, 24"*	250.00	300.00	270.00
☐ **Toddler,** *bisque head, ball-jointed composition body, short blonde human hair wig, blue sleep eyes, open smiling mouth, velvet shorts and frilly blouse, 39"*	400.00	500.00	450.00
☐ **Toddler,** *bisque head, composition body, human hair wig, blue sleep eyes, with lashes, black and yellow print dress with hat*	500.00	600.00	510.00

	Current Price Range		Prior Year Average
☐ **Toddler,** *bisque head, jointed, bent limb, composition body, blue sleep eyes, blonde wig, white lace christening gown, mark: 980 A. 2 M, 13″*	250.00	350.00	225.00
☐ **Young Girl Character,** *bisque head, elongated limbs with high knees, long oval face with long narrow nose, diminutive sleep eyes, brush stroked brows, four teeth backed by a tongue, old soft green cotton dress, incised Armand Marsielle, Germany, 402, A O M, a very unusual unlisted mark: net a 401, 16″*	555.00	600.00	565.00

MARVEL COMICS GROUP

☐ **Spiderman,** *plastic/vinyl, molded and painted, based on the comic character from Marvel Comics Group, marked Marvel CG, 1971, 8″*	6.00	8.00	5.00

MARX

☐ **Bonnie Braids Walker,** *plastic, molded and painted features, ribbons in hair, open mouth, in the form of a walking toddler with oversized feet, operated by pullcord in stomach, marked Marx Toys, Made in Hong Kong, made in 1952, 6″*	5.00	7.00	5.00
☐ **General Custer,** *plastic, molded hair, molded features, representing Gen. George Armstrong Custer, Civil War hero and Indian-fighter who was slain at the Battle of Little Bighorn, marked Louis Marx & Co., MCMLXIII, 1963, 11½″*	4.00	6.00	4.00
☐ **Ginny Bones,** *plastic, molded and painted features, novelty doll in the form of an artist's posable mannikin with jointed plastic tubing body, sold without clothing (the doll was designed to be dressed in its owner's clothes), marked on box, Louis Marx & Co., Patent Pending, MCMLXX, 1970, 40″*	15.00	19.00	14.00
☐ **Jiminy Cricket,** *plastic, molded and painted features, clothing attached by adhesive, marked Marx Toys, Made in Hong Kong, made in 1963, 5½″*	9.00	12.00	8.00

	Current Price Range		Prior Year Average
Note: *Jiminy Cricket was an animated character from the film "Song of the South," which featured a mixture of animation and live actors.*			
☐ **Johnny West,** *plastic, representing an adult male cowboy (facial resemblance to John Wayne) wearing vest, holster, gun, marked Louis Marx & Co., Inc. MCMLXV, 1965, 12"*	4.00	6.00	4.00
☐ **Knight,** *vinyl, molded and painted features, molded clothing, marked Louis Marx & Co., MCMLXVII, 1967, 11½"*	5.00	7.00	5.00
☐ **Miss Seventeen,** *plastic, molded and painted features, closed mouth, bright red lips, the basic doll represents the winner of a teenage beauty pageant and was sold with 12 interchangeable outfits, marked U.S. Patent 2925784, British Patent 804566, made in Hong Kong, sold in the early 1960's, 18"*	10.00	14.00	10.00
☐ **Miss Toddler,** *walker, plastic, molded hair, molded features, fixed eyes, marked Louis Marx & Co., Inc. MCMLXV, 1965, 21"*	33.00	41.00	31.00
☐ **Stonewall Smith,** *vinyl, molded and painted features, molded clothing, representing a soldier, marked Marx Toys, made in 1964, 11"*	5.00	7.00	5.00
☐ **Tank Driver,** *vinyl, molded and painted features, molded clothing, marked Marx Toys, made in the 1970's*	5.00	7.00	5.00
☐ **Viking,** *vinyl, marked Louis Marx & Co. MCMLXIX, 1969, 12"*	5.00	7.00	5.00

MASCOTTE

☐ **Bisque Head,** *jointed French composition and wood body, brown human hair wig, blue paperweight eyes, original clothes*	3200.00	3500.00	3000.00

MATTEL

☐ **Baby First Step,** *plastic/vinyl, blonde hair (rooted), sleep eyes (blue), toddles (battery operated), marked 1964 Mattel, Inc., Hawthorne, Calif., 18"*	12.00	16.00	12.00
☐ **Baby Fun,** *vinyl, blonde hair (rooted), painted eyes, can blow up balloons, wears dress with three small flowers on it, marked 1968 Mattel, Inc., Hong Kong, 8"*	6.00	9.00	6.00

	Current Price Range		Prior Year Average
☐ **Baby Secret,** *talker, vinyl head, foam body, vinyl hands, stuffed legs, red hair (rooted), painted eyes, made in Japan in 1965, 17½″*	12.00	16.00	12.00
☐ **Baby Teenie Talk,** *vinyl head, cloth body, vinyl arms and legs, platinum blonde hair (rooted), painted eyes (blue), a talker with a novel feature: its mouth moves while it talks, marked Mattel, Baby Teenie Talk, 1965, 17″*	12.00	16.00	12.00
☐ **Baby Tenderlove,** *foam head and body, platinum blonde hair (rooted), painted eyes, nursing mouth, marked 652C, 1969, 15″*	5.00	7.00	5.00
☐ **Beany,** *vinyl, molded and painted features, molded hair, marked Mattel Inc. Toymakers, made in Hong Kong in 1969, 18¼″*	36.00	45.00	32.00
☐ **Big Jack,** *black, plastic/vinyl, molded and painted hair, painted eyes, fully jointed, figure of an adult black male, marked 1971 Mattel Inc., US Patent Pending, made in Hong Kong, 9½″*	7.00	10.00	7.00
☐ **Bouncy Baby,** *vinyl head, plastic body, vinyl arms and legs, blonde hair (rooted), painted eyes, set with springs to make baby bounce, marked 1968 Mattel, Inc., 11″*	5.00	7.00	5.00
☐ **Boy Baby Brother Tenderlove,** *black vinyl, rooted hair, sexed, 15″*	12.00	17.00	13.00
☐ **Buffie,** *plastic/vinyl, blonde hair (rooted), painted eyes, marked 1967 Mattel Inc., U.S. and For. Pats. Pend., 10″*	16.00	21.00	15.00
☐ **Bugs Bunny,** *vinyl face, plush body (stuffed), vinyl hands, holds carrot, marked Mattel Bugs Bunny, Warner Bros. Pictures, made in 1969, 19″*	9.00	12.00	8.00
☐ **Callisto From Jupiter,** *vinyl, posable, a space alien with corrugated arms and legs, marked 1968 Mattel, Inc., made in Hong Kong, 6″*	7.00	10.00	6.00
Note: By 1968 the "man from Mars" theme was wearing thin, so toy manufacturers turned attentions to more distant planets.			
☐ **Captain Lazer,** *plastic/vinyl, molded and painted features, molded and painted hair, wearing spaceman-type suit, carries gun, gun shoots "lazer beam" (operated by battery), marked 1967 Mattel, Inc., 12″*	11.00	15.00	10.00
Note: Investigation into the possible uses of lazer light was in its infancy when Mattel brought out "Captain Lazer."			
☐ **Character Doll,** *rubber head, cloth body*	12.00	14.00	10.00

Character Doll,
rubber and cloth
$12.00-$14.00

Chatty Cathy,
vinyl and plastic,
c. 1960
$17.00-$23.00

	Current Price Range		Prior Year Average
☐ **Charmin' Chatty,** *talker, plastic/vinyl, blonde hair (rooted), sleep eyes (blue), marked Charmin' Chatty, 1961, 25"*	35.00	46.00	33.00
☐ **Chatty Cathy,** *talker, plastic/vinyl, brunette hair (rooted), sleep eyes (brown), marked Mattel, Inc., U.S. Pat. 3,017,817. patented and first produced in 1960, continued in production for a number of years thereafter, 20"*	17.00	23.00	16.00
Note: By far the most famous and commercially successful of all talking dolls. With Chatty Cathy and silent Barbie, Mattel had a one-two punch throughout the '60's that rival doll manufacturers could not approach.			
☐ ***Chester O'Chimp (a monkey),*** *vinyl head, plush body (stuffed), bendable fingers, molded and painted features, marked Mattel, Chester O'Chimp, 1964, 14½"*	8.00	11.00	7.00
☐ **Dancerina,** *ballerina, blonde rooted hair, big blue eyes, open rosebud mouth, painted features, bright pink ballerina outfit and slippers, 24"*	25.00	30.00	25.00
☐ **Dancerina,** *mechanical (dances), plastic/vinyl, platinum blonde hair (rooted), painted eyes, operates by knob on top of head, battery powered, marked 1968 Mattel, 24"*	13.00	16.00	12.00
☐ **Doug Davis, Spaceman,** *vinyl, molded and painted features, molded and painted hair, dressed in space suit with helmet, marked Mattel, Inc., 1967, made in Hong Kong, 6"*	5.00	7.00	5.00
☐ **Dr. Doolittle,** *talker, vinyl head, cloth body, pullcord operated, says a variety of short phrases, marked Dr. Doolittle, MCMLXVII (1967), Twentieth Century Fox Film Corp., Inc. 22½"*	28.00	37.00	26.00
Note: Some added interest as "movie memorabilia."			
☐ **Gentle Ben (a bear),** *talker, all plush (stuffed), plastic eyes and nose, marked Mattel, Gentle Ben, 1967, 18"*	10.00	14.00	9.00
☐ **Liney Lou,** *sweet treats, mint in box, enclosed in spoon*	3.00	6.00	4.00
☐ **Lola Liddle,** *vinyl, blonde hair (rooted), molded and painted features, marked Mattel 1965. 3"*	6.00	8.00	6.00
☐ **Major Matt Mason,** *vinyl, posable, molded and painted features, molded and painted hair, wears space suit, marked Mattel, Inc., 1967, made in Hong Kong, 6"*	5.00	7.00	5.00

	Current Price Range		Prior Year Average
☐ **Marie Osmond,** *mannequin modeling doll, 1976, 30″*	30.00	45.00	27.00
☐ **Monkees,** *talker, hand puppet representing all four members of this singing group, plastic, molded and painted features, molded and painted hair, made in 1967*	40.00	55.00	32.00
Note: If this one wasn't collectible as "rock music memorabilia," its value would be much lower.			
☐ **Mrs Beasley,** *1967 Family Affair, vinyl head blonde rooted hair, blue cloth body, big blue eyes, painted features, yellow polk-a-dots, 22″*	22.00	28.00	22.00
☐ **Platter Pal,** *talker, printed cloth, marked Mattel, A Platter Pal, 1969, 15″*	6.00	8.00	5.00
☐ **Pioneer Daughter,** *bicentennial series, #7940*	12.00	17.00	13.00
☐ **Randy Reader,** *talker, plastic/vinyl, platinum blonde hair (rooted), operated by battery, eyes move as he reads, marked 1967 Mattel, Inc., 19″*	38.00	49.00	35.00
☐ **Raspberry Rosie,** *sweet treats, mint in box, enclosed in spoon*	3.00	6.00	4.00
☐ **Saucy,** *plastic/vinyl, rooted hair, changing facial expressions, the left arm serves as a crank, by which the doll's face changes expression, marked 1972 Mattel, Inc., 16″*	16.00	22.00	15.00
Note: One of the more imaginative novelty dolls sold by this firm.			
☐ **Sgt. Storm,** *vinyl, posable, molded and painted features, molded and painted hair, wears space suit, with oxygen tank on back, marked Mattel, Inc., 1967, made in Hong Kong, 6″*	5.00	7.00	5.00
☐ **Shrinking Violet,** *cloth head and body, blonde mop hair, sewn-on eyes, ventriloquist mouth operated by pullcord, marked Mattel Shrinking Violet, The Funny Company, made in 1962, 15″*	85.00	100.00	80.00
☐ **Singin' Chatty,** *plastic/vinyl, blonde hair (rooted), sleep eyes (blue), singing version of the Chatty Cathy doll, with which Mattel had great success, marked Singin' Chatty, 1964, Mattel, Inc., Hawthorne, Calif., 17″*	22.00	28.00	20.00
☐ **Sister Belle,** *talker (11 expressions), plastic head, cloth body, cloth arms and legs, molded and painted features, mop hair (blonde), marked Mattel, Hawthorne, Calif., made in 1961, 17″*	27.00	35.00	25.00

	Current Price Range		Prior Year Average
☐ **Sister Smallwalk,** *walker, plastic/vinyl, brunette hair (rooted), painted eyes (blue), open smiling mouth with teeth, operates by battery, marked 1967 Mattel, 11½"*	8.00	11.00	7.00
☐ **Slugger,** *vinyl head, cloth body, cloth arms and legs, holds cloth baseball bat (stuffed), red hair (rooted), molded and painted features, marked 1975 Mattel, Inc., Taiwan, 5½"*	3.00	5.00	3.00
☐ **Small Talk,** *plastic/vinyl, blonde hair (rooted), painted eyes, open mouth with teeth, pull-ring operated, marked 1967 Mattel Inc., Japan, 11"*	7.00	10.00	7.00
☐ **Sweet Sixteen,** *vinyl/plastic, molded and painted features, blonde hair, marked 1-Mattel, Inc., 1958, Korea, made in 1975 (the date in the marking refers to a mold date), 11½"*	8.00	11.00	8.00
☐ **Stephanie,** *of the Sunshine Family, print dress, made in 1973*	2.00	8.00	5.00
☐ **Talk-A-Little,** *talker, printed cloth, stuffed, cloth arms and legs, mop hair (red), pullcord operated, says several brief phrases, sold originally with a tag reading 1970 Mattel, Inc., Hawthorne, Calif., 8"*	6.00	8.00	6.00
☐ **Talking Baby First Step,** *talker/walker, plastic/vinyl, blonde hair (rooted), painted eyes, marked 1967 Mattel, Inc., 18"*	15.00	19.00	14.00
☐ **T-Bone (a dog),** *talker, head, stuffed body, molded and painted features, unmarked on doll, sold originally with a tag reading T-Bone TM 1964 Mattel Inc., 11"*	8.00	11.00	8.00
☐ **Teachy Keen,** *vinyl head, cloth body, cloth arms and legs, blonde hair (rooted), molded and painted features, closed mouth, pug nose, marked Mattel Teachy Keen, 1966, 17"*	12.00	16.00	11.00

BARBIE AND BARBIE-RELATED

THE BARBIE ERA — A CHRONOLOGY

1958

***BARBIE,** teenage fashion model is created and tested.

March, 1959

Toy Fair, New York. Toy buyers are not enthusiastic — large, life-size dolls are currently popular — a tiny fashion doll won't make it. But Barbie goes into the stores, little girls are enthused and the Barbie era begins.

1961

KEN, is introduced as Barbie's boyfriend. He is immediately accepted — first as an escort for Barbie — then as a personality in his own right.

1963

The first significant variation on the original Barbie doll is introduced this year. "Fashion Queen Barbie" has a sculptured hairstyle so that various wigs can be worn.

MIDGE, freckle-faced and impish, is brought into being as Barbie's best friend. They can wear each other's clothes. Play possibilities expand. No definite ages assigned Barbie and Midge, but little girls tend to think of the dolls as being about six years older than themselves. Barbie and her friends are receiving *fan letters* and the Barbie Fan Club is formed!

1964

***SKIPPER,** Barbie's little sister, and ***ALLAN,** Ken's buddy, join the scene. Skipper is smaller and younger than her teenage companions and is the first to be named as part of Barbie's family. Now, it's Barbie and her family and friends.

In addition, an exciting technological breakthrough — "Miss Barbie" has bendable knees and eyes that open and close! Like Fashion Queen Barbie, she has sculptured hair and comes with wigs.

1965

***SKOOTER,** and ***RICKY,** friends for Skipper, come along. Now all the dolls have bendable legs for more lifelike play. The original concept of merely posing a fashion doll in a costume is giving way to endless imaginary play situations.

1966

***FRANCIE,** Barbie's modern cousin, and ***TUTTI** and ***TODD,** tiny twin sister and brother to Barbie and Skipper, join the growing Barbie family. Francie is especially well-received.

1967

Teenage makeup and hairstyles have changed drastically since 1959. Barbie changes too — and appears with a new, more youthful face, long straight hair, AND — a major technological change — a ***TWIST 'N TURN waist!** Little girls can trade in an old Barbie on a new one. The old dolls — turned in by the millions — are given to charitable organizations.

***CASEY,** Francie's friend and ***CHRIS,** little Tutti's playmate, are introduced. (Identifying a newcomer as "friend of . . . " an existing personality indicates that he or she can wear the same clothes as the other doll.)

1968

Barbie talks! Extensive research is done to find out what kind of voice Barbie fans imagine her to have. Her newest friends are ***STACEY,** who is English and has the appropriate accent, and ***CHRISTIE,** who is black.

***TWIGGY** is introduced — the first of Barbie's friends to be copied after a real-life personality.

1969

***JULIA,** the popular TV nurse, is now a doll, with the face of Diahann Carroll.

***P.J.** is Barbie's new friend. Little girls write in: "What does P.J. stand for?" Answer: Nothing! P.J. is her name.

1970

***BRAD,** Ken's new buddy, is introduced and the world of Barbie has another black member.

***JAMIE** is a friend for Barbie made exclusively for Sears, Roebuck & Co.

1971

***FLUFF,** a playmate for Skipper, is the only new personality this year, but Barbie, Ken, Francie and Skipper bloom forth with suntans, as the ***MALIBU** versions of the dolls are introduced.

1972

***STEFFIE** is Barbie's new friend. ***TIFF** is Skipper's new playmate and ***MISS AMERICA,** in authentic gown and royal accessories, is also introduced — based on the popular national contest. Another technological breakthrough — the dolls now have hands that bend at the wrist, open and close to carry things.

1973

***KELLEY** steps on the scene with hair that can be curled without lotions, heat, water or waiting! The other dolls now have the same feature and Ken makes a dramatic change in appearance with long hair and removable beard, moustache and sideburns!

1974

BARBIE is ***SWEET 16.** Mattel celebrates with birthday parties at children's hospitals around the country. At Toy Fair 1974 in New York City, a portion of Times Square is renamed "Barbie Boulevard" during the weeks of the Fair, in honor of the famous doll's introduction in that city.

1975

Even more action is now possible with ***FREE MOVING** Barbie, Ken and P.J. dolls, who simulate the motions of swinging a golf club or tennis racket when you move a hand-held lever in the back. They are joined by two new black dolls, Free Moving ***CARA** and Free Moving ***CURTIS.**

1977

The second dramatic appearance change of Barbie's "life" — a new face with bright smile and soft complexion; longer, thicker, "sun-streaked" hair; slender movable arms bent in a model's pose and a new name: **Super Star BARBIE. Super Star CHRISTIE** has undergone a similar change.

Super Size BARBIE and **Super Size CHRISTIE** dolls each 18″ tall — with the Super Star face and a model's poseability, join the world of Barbie fashion play.

1979

Barbie greets her 20th year with a big kiss! ***BARBIE** actually tilts her head, puckers up and makes a kissing sound when the child presses a panel on her back.

Over the years, Barbie has remained a contemporary "with it" teenager, by responding not only to fashion changes, but to the changes in life style of

THE BARBIE FAMILY TREE

- **BARBIE 1959**
  - **Family**
    - Skipper 1964 (Barbie's little sister)
      - Friends
        - Ricky 1965-67
        - Skooter 1965-67
        - Fluff 1971-72
        - Tiff 1972-73
        - Ginger 1976 only
        - Scott 1980
    - Francie 1966-76 (Barbie's MODern cousin)
      - Friends
        - Casey 1967-70
    - Tutti 1966-71 (Barbie's tiny twin sister)
      - Friends
        - Chris 1967-68
    - Todd 1966-68 (Barbie's tiny twin brother)
  - **Friends**
    - Ken 1961 (Barbie's boyfriend)
      - Friends
        - Allan 1964-65 (Midge's boyfriend)
        - Brad 1970-72 (Christie's boyfriend)
        - Curtis 1975 only (Cara's boyfriend)
    - Midge 1963-67 (Barbie's best friend)
    - Christie 1968
    - (Barbie's "black is beautiful" friend)
    - Stacey 1968-70 (Barbie's British chum)
    - P.J. 1969
    - Jamie 1970-72
    - Steffie 1972-73
    - Kelley 1973-76
    - Cara 1975-78 (Black)
    - Twiggy 1967-68 (London's top teen model)
    - Truly Scrumptious 1969 only (Chitty Chitty Bang Bang movie)
    - Julia 1969-72 (Diahann Carroll TV series)
    - Miss America 1972-79 (Based on national contest)
    - Donny & Marie Osmond 1977-78
    - Jimmy Osmond 1978 only
    - TV's Star Women
      - Kitty O'Neil 1978 only
      - Kate Jackson 1978 only
      - Cheryl Ladd 1978-79
    - Debby Boone 1979 only
    - Kristy McNichol as "Buddy" 1979 only (Family TV series)
  - **Pets**
    - Dancer 1971-72 (horse)
    - Beauty 1980
    - Beauty & pups 1982 (Afghan hounds)
    - Dallas 1981 (horse)
    - Midnight 1982 (horse)

today's young women. LIFE Magazine features the doll in its November issue as reflecting 20 years of American fashions!

1980

It's an important *BARBIE doll year as the news media takes note that "Barbie" is 21 years old!

The first new personalities since 1976 join the Barbie family of dolls — ***SCOTT,** *SKIPPER's boyfriend, and ***BEAUTY,** Barbie doll's dog (a lovely Afghan hound). And, for the first time, ethnic Barbie dolls are presented — Black Barbie and Hispanic Barbie. The beginnings of an International Collection of Barbie dolls are Italian Barbie, Parisian Barbie and Royal Barbie (of England). Finally, reflecting the country's latest craze, there are new Skating Barbie and Skating Ken on roller skates.

MATTEL — BARBIE AND BARBIE-RELATED

	Current Price Range		Prior Year Average
☐ **Allan,** *fashion doll, straight leg, yachting outfit*	20.00	25.00	21.00
☐ **All Star Ken**	12.00	15.00	13.00
☐ **Angel Face Barbie,** *c. 1983*	12.00	15.00	13.00
☐ **Baby,** *(from "Barbie Babysits"), plastic, molded and painted features, blonde hair, wears an apron, marked 953, sold in 1963, 3"*	7.00	10.00	7.00
☐ **Baby,** *(from "Barbie Babysits"), plastic, molded and painted features, revised version of the doll introduced in 1963, with different hair, marked 0953, sold in 1964, 3"*	6.00	8.00	6.00
Note: Prices shown are for the doll PLUS all original accessories with which it was sold. The dolls by themselves without accessories, or with partial accessories, do not bring the full listed prices.			
☐ **Barbie,** *blonde, orange dress*	20.00	30.00	21.00
☐ **Barbie,** *blonde, white net bathing suit, orange trim*	20.00	30.00	21.00
☐ **Barbie,** *bubble cut blonde, angel outfit, c. 1963*	40.00	50.00	42.00
☐ **Barbie,** *fashion queen, red bubble cut wig, blue wool sheath*	30.00	40.00	32.00
☐ **Barbie,** *fashion queen, red flip wig, wedding outfit*	30.00	40.00	32.00
☐ **Barbie,** *live action, turquoise bathing suit*	15.00	25.00	16.00
☐ **Barbie,** *living, lavendar knit dress, elbow slit*	10.00	15.00	11.00
☐ **Barbie,** *plastic, molded and painted features, ponytail with bangs, slotted feet designed to fit in stand, loop earrings, marked 850, made in 1959, 11½"*	725.00	950.00	700.00
☐ **Barbie,** *plastic, molded and painted features, ponytail with bangs, feet NOT slotted (change in design from the original version), marked 850, made in 1960, 11½"*	650.00	825.00	600.00

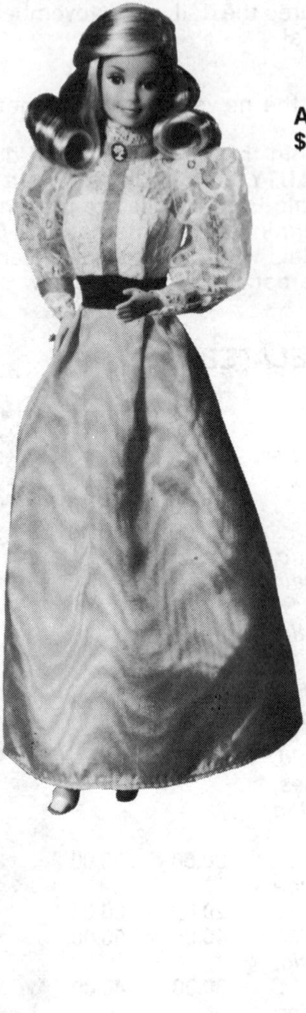

Angel Face Barbie, 1983
$12.00-$15.00

Ballerina Barbie, 1976
$10.00-$12.00

Barbie, c. 1960
$650.00-$825.00

Barbie,
bendable leg, c. 1965
$14.00-$16.00

Barbie,
sunstreaked hair
$150.00-$200.00

Black Barbie, 1980
$15.00-$20.00

Beauty Secrets Barbie, 1980
$8.00-$12.00

Bubble cut Barbie, 1963
$40.00-$60.00

Busy Barbie, 1972
$35.00-$45.00

Fashion Queen Barbie, 1963
$30.00-$40.00

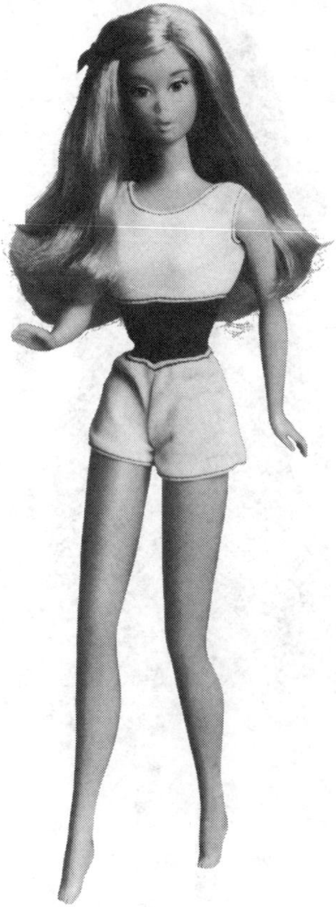

Free Moving Barbie, 1975
$25.00-$35.00

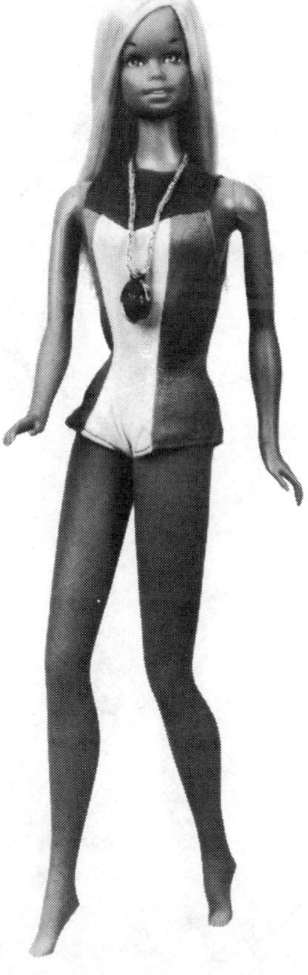

Gold Metal Barbie, 1975
$25.00-$30.00

Hispanic Barbie, 1980
$20.00-$30.00

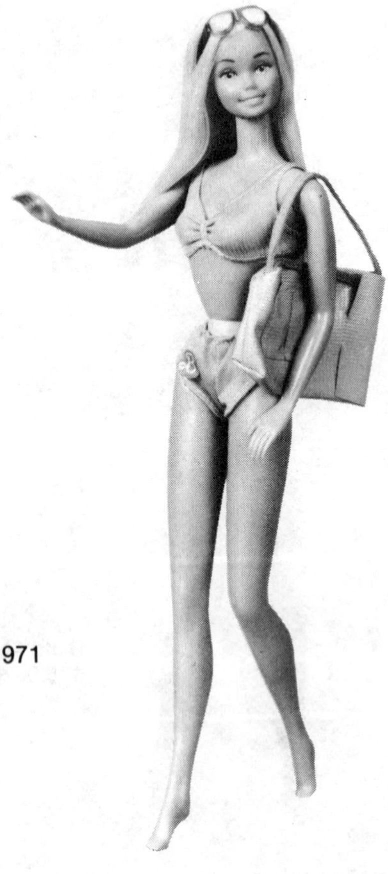

Malibu Barbie, 1971
$75.00-$95.00

Marie Osmond,
1976, 30″
$45.00-$55.00

Pretty Changes Barbie, 1979
$15.00-$17.00

	Current Price Range		Prior Year Average
☐ **Barbie's Friend Christie,** *black, plastic, molded and painted features, talker, brown hair (parted), wears knitted green shirt and red shorts, marked 1126, sold in 1968, 11½"*	120.00	150.00	100.00
Note: The first black doll in the Barbie group. The second, introduced a year later, was modeled after a living person (singer/actress Diahann Carroll).			
☐ ***Beauty Secret Barbie***	10.00	15.00	11.00
☐ **Bendable Ken,** *plastic, molded and painted features, bendable legs, wears blue jacket and red trunks, marked 1020, sold in 1965, 12"*	14.00	18.00	12.00
☐ **Bendable Legs Ken,** *plastic, molded and painted features, posable legs, painted hair (reddish brown), wears blue shorts and red jacket, marked 1010, sold in 1965, 12"*	13.00	16.00	11.00
☐ **Bendable Legs Midge,** *plastic, molded and painted features, posable legs, wears single-piece striped suit, marked 1080, sold in 1965, 11½"*	8.00	11.00	7.00
☐ **Bendable Legs Skipper,** *plastic, molded and painted features, posable legs, revised version of the original 1964 Skipper doll, which did not have posable legs, wears single-piece blue suit, marked 1030, sold in 1965, 9¼"*	12.00	15.00	11.00
☐ **Bendable Legs Skooter,** *plastic, molded and painted features, posable legs, freckled face, marked 1120, sold in 1966, 9¼"*	8.00	11.00	7.00
☐ **Birthday Barbie**	10.00	13.00	11.00
☐ **Black Barbie**	8.00	12.00	9.00
☐ **Busy Barbie,** *plastic, molded and painted features, wears checked skirt and denim sunsuit, marked 3311, sold in 1972, 11½"*	7.00	10.00	6.00
☐ **Chef Boy-Ar-Dee Barbie,** *plastic, molded and painted features, painted lashes, wears green and red suit (one piece), marked 1190, sold in 1971, 11½"*	8.00	11.00	7.00
☐ **Cheryl Ladd,** *12"*	6.00	12.00	7.00
☐ **Color Magic Barbie,** *plastic, molded and painted features, posable legs, wears harlequin bathing suit, marked 1150, sold in 1966, 11½"*	32.00	40.00	30.00
☐ **Color 'N' Curl Set Barbie,** *special set with a Barbie head and a Midge head, plastic, molded and painted features, sold with four interchangeable wigs, hair coloring and hair dryer, marked 4035, sold in 1965,*	45.00	60.00	40.00
☐ **Colored Twist 'N' Turn Francie,** *plastic, molded and painted features, waist-length dark brown hair, marked 1100, sold in 1967, 11"*	9.00	12.00	8.00

	Current Price Range		Prior Year Average
☐ **Cookin' Goodies Tutti,** *plastic, molded and painted features, marked 3559, sold in 1967, 6¼"*	5.00	7.00	4.00
☐ **Dream Date Barbie,** *c. 1983*	12.00	16.00	13.00
☐ **Dream Date Ken,** *c. 1983*	12.00	16.00	13.00
☐ **Fashion Queen Barbie,** *plastic, molded and painted features, sold with three interchangeable wigs, wears white and gold suit and scarf, marked 850, made in 1963, 11½"*	100.00	130.00	95.00
☐ **Francie, Barbie's Mod Cousin,** *plastic, molded and painted features, posable legs, wears one-piece suit, marked 1130, sold in 1966, 11"*	20.00	27.00	18.00
☐ **Francie, Barbie's Mod Cousin,** *revised version to the original 1966 doll, plastic, molded and painted features, non-posable legs, lighter pinker skin coloration, wears two-piece red and white suit, marked 1140, sold in 1966, 11"*	7.00	10.00	6.00
☐ **Francie,** *red bathing suit*	30.00	40.00	32.00
☐ **Francine's Friend Casey,** *plastic, molded and painted features, posable legs, wears white and gold outfit, marked 1180, sold in 1967, 11"*	10.00	14.00	9.00
☐ **Growin' Pretty Hair Barbie,** *plastic, molded and painted features, wears pink dress, sold with additional hair pieces, marked 1144, sold in 1971, 11½"*	28.00	34.00	26.00
☐ **Growin' Pretty Hair Francie,** *plastic, molded and painted features, wears pink dress, sold with additional hair changes, marked 1074, sold in 1971, 11"*	10.00	14.00	9.00
☐ **Growning Up Skipper,** *mint in box, #7259, c. 1974*	20.00	30.00	21.00
☐ **Hair Fair Barbie,** *plastic, molded and painted features, head only (no body), sold with additional hair pieces, marked 4044, sold in 1971*	14.00	20.00	12.00
☐ **Hair Happenin' Barbie,** *plastic, molded and painted features, wears white blouse and red skirt, came with extra hair pieces, marked 1174, sold in 1971, 11½"*	18.00	24.00	16.00
☐ **Hair Happenin' Francie,** *plastic, molded and painted features, wears blue dress, sold with additional hair pieces, marked 1122, sold in 1970, 11"*	8.00	11.00	7.00
☐ **Julia,** *black, wedding outfit*	30.00	40.00	32.00
☐ **Ken,** *blonde, flocked hair*	15.00	25.00	16.00

	Current Price Range		Prior Year Average
☐ **Ken, Barbie's Boyfriend,** *plastic, molded and painted features, woolly flocked hair, red shorts, marked 750, sold in 1961, 12,"*	30.00	40.00	27.00
Note: The first Ken doll.			
☐ **Ken, Barbie's Boyfriend,** *(revised version of original Ken doll), plastic, molded and painted features, painted hair, marked 750, sold in 1963, 12"*	14.00	18.00	12.00
☐ **Ken's Buddy Allen,** *plastic, molded and painted features, painted hair (reddish brown), non-posable legs, wears blue shorts and striped jacket, marked 1000, sold in 1964, 12"*	15.00	19.00	13.00
Note: The first Allen doll.			
☐ **Ken,** *dark flocked hair*	15.00	25.00	16.00
☐ **Ken,** *dark molded hair, business suit*	20.00	25.00	21.00
☐ **Ken,** *flocked hair, hat*	20.00	25.00	21.00
☐ **Ken,** *hard plastic, molded brown hair in crew cut #1, 11½"*	45.00	55.00	45.00
☐ **Ken,** *modern*	40.00	50.00	42.00
☐ **Ken,** *molded blonde hair, tennis outfit, racket, glasses, ball*	20.00	25.00	21.00
☐ **Ken,** *talking*	30.00	40.00	32.00
☐ **Kissing Barbie**	10.00	13.00	11.00
☐ **Little Tutti's Playmate Chris,** *plastic, molded and painted features, marked 3570, sold in 1967, 6¼"*	5.00	7.00	4.00
☐ **Live Action Christie,** *black, plastic, molded and painted features, marked 1175, sold in 1971, 11½"*	12.00	16.00	11.00
☐ **Live Action On Stage Barbie,** *plastic, molded and painted features, marked 1152, sold in 1971, 11½"*	18.00	24.00	16.00
☐ **Live Action On Stage Ken,** *plastic, molded and painted features, marked 1172, sold in 1971, 12"*	10.00	13.00	9.00
☐ **Live Action P.J., Barbie's New Friend,** *plastic, molded and painted features, marked 1156, sold in 1971, 11½"*	9.00	12.00	8.00
☐ **Living Barbie,** *plastic, molded and painted features, wearing an outfit of gold and silver with orange fishnet covering, marked 1116, sold in 1970, 11½"*	20.00	26.00	18.00
☐ **Living Skipper,** *plastic, molded and painted features, wears single-piece red, green and blue suit, marked 1117, sold in 1970, 9¼"*	8.00	10.00	7.00
☐ **Malibu Barbie,** *plastic, molded and painted features, blonde waist-length hair, wears pastel blue swimsuit, the first Barbie in "Malibu" style, with darker skin coloration, marked 1067, sold in 1971, 11½"*	75.00	95.00	65.00

	Current Price Range		Prior Year Average
☐ **Malibu Christie,** *black, plastic, molded and painted features, straight black hair (long), wears red suit, marked 7745, sold in 1973, 11½"*	12.00	15.00	11.00
Note: The purpose of the Malibu series was to show the Barbie group with suntans. Even though Christie was a black doll, it was decided to include her in the Malibu line.			
☐ **Malibu Francie,** *plastic, molded and painted features, wears one-piece red suit. With the Malibu (tan) skin coloration, marked 1068, sold in 1971, 11"*	9.00	12.00	8.00
☐ **Malibu Ken,** *plastic, molded and painted features, wears orange swim trunks, with Malibu (suntanned) skin coloration, marked 1088, sold in 1971, 12"*	11.00	14.00	10.00
☐ **Malibu P.J., Barbie's New Friend,** *plastic, molded and painted features, with Malibu skin coloration (suntan), marked 1187, sold in 1972, 11½"*	8.00	10.00	7.00
☐ **Malibu Skipper,** *plastic, molded and painted features, posable legs, wearing two-piece suit, with the Malibu (suntanned) skin coloration, marked 1069, sold in 1971, 9¼"*	9.00	12.00	8.00
☐ **Me And My Dog Tutti,** *plastic, molded and painted features, marked 3554, sold in 1966, 6¼"*	5.00	7.00	4.00
☐ **Melody In Pink Tutti,** *plastic, molded and painted features, marked 3555, sold in 1966, 6¼"*	5.00	7.00	4.00
☐ **Midge, Barbie's Best Friend,** *plastic, molded and painted features, freckles, flip-style hairdo, wears two-piece suit, marked 860, sold in 1963, 11½"*	14.00	18.00	13.00
☐ **Midge,** *blonde, hot pink lounge pants*	30.00	40.00	32.00
☐ **Midge,** *blonde, jeans and shirt*	30.00	40.00	32.00
☐ **Midge,** *dark hair, pink dress*	30.00	40.00	32.00
☐ **Midge,** *red hair*	30.00	40.00	32.00
☐ **Miss Barbie,** *plastic, molded and painted features, sleep eyes, posable legs, wears pink suit (one piece), sold with three interchangeable wigs, marked 1060, sold in 1964, 11½"*	250.00	300.00	225.00
☐ **Mod Hair Ken,** *plastic, molded and painted features, rooted hair, wears brown jacket, marked 4224, sold in 1973, 12"*	7.00	10.00	6.00
☐ **My First Barbie**	7.00	13.00	8.00

	Current Price Range		Prior Year Average
☐ **Newport Barbie,** *plastic, molded and painted features, wears yachting outfit, Malibu skintone, marked 7807, sold in 1974, 11½"*	14.00	20.00	12.00
☐ **Night Night Tutti,** *plastic, molded and painted features, marked 3553, sold in 1966, 6¼"*	5.00	7.00	4.00
☐ **Pink And Pretty Barbie**	12.00	15.00	13.00
☐ **P.J.,** *suntan, blonde hair, purple eyes*	6.00	10.00	7.00
☐ **P.J.,** *talking, necklace, ponytail advertising doll*	40.00	50.00	42.00
☐ **Pretty Change Barbie**	8.00	12.00	9.00
☐ **Quick Curl Barbie,** *plastic, molded and painted features, wears pink dress, marked 4220, sold in 1973, 11½"*	14.00	20.00	12.00
☐ **Quick Curl Francie,** *plastic, molded and painted features, wears yellow dress, marked 4222, sold in 1973, 11"*	8.00	10.00	7.00
☐ **Quick Curl Skipper,** *plastic, molded and painted features, wears blue dress, marked 4223, sold in 1973, 9¼"*	7.00	10.00	6.00
☐ **Skating Barbie**	10.00	13.00	11.00
☐ **Skating Ken**	8.00	12.00	9.00
☐ **Skipper, Barbie's Little Sister,** *plastic, molded and painted features, wears single-piece white and red suit, marked 0950, sold in 1964, 9¼"*	13.00	16.00	12.00
Note: The first Skipper doll.			
☐ ***Skipper,*** *dress and boots*	30.00	40.00	32.00
☐ **Skipper's Friend Ricky,** *plastic, molded and painted features, painted hair (reddish brown), non-posable legs, wears jacket and blue shorts, marked 1090, sold in 1965, 9¼"*	8.00	10.00	7.00
☐ **Skipper,** *Malibu, orange two-piece swimsuit*	10.00	20.00	11.00
☐ **Skooter, Skipper's Playmate,** *plastic, molded and painted features, freckled face, non-posable legs, wears two-piece red suit, marked 1040, sold in 1965, 9½"*	9.00	12.00	8.00
☐ **Spanish Talking Barbie,** *plastic, molded and painted features, wears ponytail, talker, dressed in shorts and knitted shirt, marked 8348, sold in 1968, the same as the standard talking Barbie, introduced that same year, except that she speaks Spanish, intended for sale in Spanish-speaking areas of New York, California and Texas, 11½"*	130.00	160.00	120.00
☐ **Spanish Talking Ken,** *plastic, molded and painted features, talker with bendable legs, dressed in red, Spanish-speaking version of the standard Talking Ken doll, intended for*			

	Current Price Range		Prior Year Average
sale in Spanish-speaking communities of New York, California and Texas, marked 1111, sold in 1970, 12″	70.00	90.00	65.00
☐ **Sport And Share Ken**	9.00	13.00	10.00
☐ **Stacey, Barbie's English Friend,** *plastic, molded and painted features, talker, wears to-piece striped outfit, marked 1125, sold in 1968, 11½″*	16.00	20.00	15.00
Note: The first Stacey doll.			
☐ ***Stacy,*** *red flip wig, swimsuit*	30.00	40.00	32.00
☐ **Straight Legs Francie,** *plastic, molded and painted features, non-posable legs, marked 1140, sold in 1967, 11″*	8.00	10.00	7.00
☐ **Sundae Treat Tutti,** *plastic, molded and painted features, marked 3556, sold in 1966, 6¼″*	5.00	7.00	4.00
☐ **Sunloving Barbie**	5.50	7.50	6.00
☐ **Sunloving Ken**	5.50	7.50	6.00
☐ **Sunloving Skipper**	5.50	7.50	6.00
☐ **Sun Valley Barbie,** *(with Malibu tan), plastic, molded and painted features, wears skiing outfit, marked 7806, sold in 1974, 11½″*	8.00	11.00	7.00
☐ **Sun Valley Ken,** *plastic, molded and painted features, wears skiing outfit, marked 7809, sold in 1974, 12″*	7.00	10.00	6.00
☐ **Sweet Sixteen Barbie,** *plastic, molded and painted features, waist-length blonde hair, pink gown, marked 7796, sold in 1974, 11½″*	15.00	20.00	14.00
☐ **Swing-A-Ling Tutti,** *plastic, molded and painted features, marked 3560, sold in 1967, 6¼″*	5.00	7.00	5.00
☐ **Talking Barbie,** *plastic, molded and painted features, wears ponytail, talker, dressed in shorts and knitted shirt, marked 1115, sold in 1968, 11½″*	175.00	220.00	165.00
☐ **Talking Barbie (revised version for 1970),** *plastic, molded and painted features, talker, curls at neck, new voice track mentioning P.J., marked 1115, sold in 1970, 11½″*	130.00	155.00	120.00
☐ **Talking Brad, Ken's New Buddy,** *black, molded and painted features, talker, marked 1114, sold in 1970, 12″*	75.00	95.00	70.00
Note: Brad was not placed on the market until after Christie (the Barbie group's black female doll) had been revised to look "more black." Hence the original version of Brad was in line with the more naturalistic version of Christie.			
☐ **Talking Busy Barbie,** *molded and painted features, talker, wears red top, blue shorts, marked 1195, sold in 1972, 11½″*	35.00	45.00	32.00

	Current Price Range		Prior Year Average
☐ **Talking Christie (revised version of the original 1968 Christie doll),** *black, plastic, molded and painted features, the doll was restyled to look "more black," not just a dark-skinned version of a white doll as had originally been the case, marked 1126 (same number as original version), sold in 1970, can easily be told apart by darker skin and Afro hairstyle, 11½"*	80.00	100.00	75.00
☐ **Talking Julia,** *black, plastic, molded and painted features, talker, wears silver and gold jumpsuit, marked 1128, sold in 1969, 11½"*	60.00	80.00	55.00
Note: The Julia doll was based on the TV character of that name from the Diahann Carroll show.			
☐ **Talking Ken,** *plastic, molded and painted features, talker, with bendable legs, dressed in red, marked 1111, sold in 1969, 12"*	85.00	115.00	80.00
Note: The first Talking Ken doll.			
☐ **Talking P.J., Barbie's New Friend,** *plastic, molded and painted features, talker, posable legs, marked 1113, sold in 1969, 11½"*	48.00	60.00	45.00
☐ **Ten Speeder Francie,** *plastic, molded and paitned features, rides bicycle, marked 7803, sold in 1974, 11"*	28.00	34.00	27.00
☐ **Todd, Twin To Tutti,** *plastic, molded and painted features, wears checked trousers and blue shirt, marked 3580, sold in 1966, 6¼"*	6.00	8.00	6.00
☐ **Truly Scrumptious,** *plastic, molded and painted features, talker, wears red dress, marked 1107, sold in 1969, a character from the Disney Studios film "Chitty Chitty Bang Bang," 11½"*	15.00	19.00	14.00
☐ **Tutti, Twin To Todd,** *plastic, molded and painted features, wears playsuit, marked 3550, sold in 1966, 6¼"*	5.00	7.00	5.00
☐ **Twiggy,** *plastic, molded and painted features, blonde hair, wears minidress, marked 1185, sold in 1967, 11"*	24.00	29.00	22.00
Note: Twiggy was the first character in the Barbie family who represented a living person: the London fashion model, wife of film producer Ken Russell, who became an international celebrity in the 1960's. She popularized the "starved" look for fashion models.			
☐ **Twirly Curl Barbie,** *c. 1983*	12.00	17.00	13.00

	Current Price Range		Prior Year Average
☐ **Twist 'N' Turn Barbie,** *plastic, molded and painted features, posable legs, orange fishnet suit (three piece), marked 1160, sold in 1967, 11½"*	100.00	130.00	90.00
☐ **Twist 'N' Turn Christie,** *black, plastic, molded and painted features, wears one-piece outfit, marked 1119, sold in 1970, 11½"*	19.00	24.00	17.00
☐ **Twist 'N' Turn Francie,** *plastic, molded and painted features, wears one-piece suit with red skirt, striped top, marked 1170, sold in 1967, 11"*	19.00	24.00	17.00
☐ **Twist 'N' Turn Julia,** *black, plastic, molded and painted features, wears two-piece white nurse's uniform, marked 1127, sold in 1969, 11½"*	27.00	36.00	25.00
Note: The Julia doll was based on the TV character of that name, from the Diahann Carroll show.			
☐ **Twist 'N' Turn P.J., Barbie's New Friend,** *plastic, molded and painted features, wears one-piece red outfit, marked 1118, sold in 1970, 11½"*	19.00	24.00	17.00
☐ **Twist 'N' Turn Skipper,** *plastic, molded and painted features, waist-length hair, wears single-piece blue suit, marked 1105, sold in 1968, 9¼"*	19.00	24.00	17.00
☐ **Twist 'N' Turn Stacey,** *plastic, molded and painted features, wears red suit, marked 1165, sold in 1968, 11"*	19.00	24.00	17.00
☐ **Walk Lively Barbie,** *plastic, molded and painted features, wears red jumpsuit, marked 1182, sold in 1972, 11½"*	23.00	28.00	21.00
☐ **Walking My Dolly Tutti,** *plastic, molded and painted features, marked 3552, sold in 1966, 6¼"*	5.00	7.00	5.00
☐ **Walk Lively Ken,** *plastic, molded and painted features, wears blue shirt, plaid trousers, marked 1184, sold in 1972, 12"*	7.00	10.00	7.00
☐ **Wig Wardrobe Barbie,** *plastic, molded and painted features, sold with three interchangeable wigs, marked 0871, sold in 1964, 11½"*	185.00	215.00	175.00

McDONALD

	Current Price Range		Prior Year Average
☐ **Ronald McDonald,** *printed cloth, representing the symbol of the McDonald restaurant chain, used as a promotional item, made in 1967, 17"*	4.00	6.00	4.00

MEGO

	Current Price Range		Prior Year Average
☐ **Action Figure,** *Lt. Uhura, the communications officer in red costume, 1975, 8″*	15.00	17.00	15.50
☐ **Action Figure,** *Mr. Scott, the engineer, with a phaser, full costumed, 1975, 8″*	30.00	32.00	30.00
☐ **Action Figure,** *Captain Kirk, the commander with phaser and travel pack, removable clothes, 1975, 8″*	15.00	17.00	15.00
☐ **Action Figure,** *Dr. McCoy, "Bones" in blue with phaser, 1975, 8″*	15.00	17.00	15.00
☐ **Action Figure,** *Mr. Spock with testing equipment, fully costumed, 1975, 8″*	15.00	17.00	15.00
☐ **Alien Action Figure,** *The Gorn, costumed in white robes, poseable, 1975, 8″*	30.00	35.00	31.00
☐ **Alien Action Figure,** *Andorian, fringed arms and legs with horned head, poseable, 1975, 8″*	30.00	35.00	32.00
☐ **Alien Figure,** *Arcturian, reptillian creature with yellow eyes, 3¾″*	2.00	3.00	2.00
☐ **Alien Figure,** *Betelgeusian, blue snooted sapien with black hat, 3¾″*	2.00	3.00	2.00
☐ **Alien Figure,** *Klingon, the arch villian of the Enterprise, 3¾″*	2.00	3.00	2.00
☐ **Alien Figure,** *Magarite, multilipped monster in black hood, 3¾″*	2.00	3.00	2.00
☐ **Bay Station,** *features five sound effects, flashing colors, real C.B. base station, 1976*	30.00	50.00	35.00
☐ **Buffalo Bill Cody,** *plastic, molded and painted features, marked Mego Corp., Reg. U.S. Pat. Off., made in Hong Kong in 1971, 8″*	3.00	5.00	3.00
☐ **Cochise,** *plastic, Indian chief holding rifle, marked Mego Corp., 1973, 8″*	3.00	4.00	3.00
☐ **Davy Crockett,** *plastic, holds rifle, marked Mego Corp., Reg. U.S. Pat. Off., made in Hong Kong in 1971, no connection with the Disney version of Davy Crockett, 7⅞″*	3.00	4.00	3.00
☐ **Diana Ross,** *mint in box, c. 1977, 12″*	15.00	25.00	15.00
☐ **Dorothy,** *from Wizard of Oz, basket, Toto too, mint in box, 8″*	15.00	25.00	15.00
☐ **Dorothy,** *vinyl, jointed, Wizard of Oz doll, with box, Toto, c. 1973, 8″*	5.00	10.00	5.00
☐ **Dorothy & Toto,** *plastic, molded and painted features, Dorothy and Toto were characters in "The Wizard of Oz" by L. Frank Baum, Mego's Dorothy was designed to resemble Judy Garland, who played the role in the 1939 motion picture, marked Mego Corp., MCMLXXII, 1972, also marked by M.G.M., the licenser, 8″*	6.00	8.00	6.00

	Current Price Range		Prior Year Average
☐ **Dr. Kromedome The Bionic Villain,** *plastic/vinyl, molded and painted features, molded and painted hair, wears cape, marked Mego Corp., 1975, 11½"*	15.00	19.00	14.00
☐ **Falcon,** *black, plastic/vinyl, fully jointed, molded and painted features, molded and painted hair, wears mask, marked Mego Corp., made in 1974, 8"*	7.00	10.00	7.00
☐ **Farrah-Fawcett Majors,** *plastic/vinyl, blonde hair, open mouth, marked Mego Corp., 1975, Made in Hong Kong, 12"*	14.00	19.00	12.00
Note: This was probably the best celebrity doll ever made, in terms of resembling the celebrity.			
☐ **Friar Tuck,** *plastic, molded and painted features, shaved head, sandals, monk's robe, flask at waist, carries staff, Friar Tuck was a character in the novel "Robin Hood" by Sir Walter Scott, marked Mego Corp., Reg. U.S. Pat. Off., 8"*	3.00	5.00	3.00
☐ **Glenda The Good Witch,** *plastic, molded and painted features, wears crown and carries cross-topped wand, Glenda the Good Witch was character in "The Wizard of Oz" by L. Frank Baum, marked 1974 Mego, Inc., 8"*	4.00	6.00	4.00
☐ **Good Witch,** *vinyl, jointed, Wizard of Oz doll, with box, c. 1973, 8"*	5.00	10.00	5.00
☐ **Green Goblin,** *plastic/vinyl, molded and painted features, full jointed, a character from the comic book "Spiderman," created by Stan Lee, made in c. 1974, 8"*	7.00	10.00	7.00
☐ **Incredible Hulk,** *plastic/vinyl, molded and painted features, molded and painted hair, wears tattered pants, marked Mego Corp., made in c. 1974, 7"*	18.00	24.00	14.00
Note: This doll was released before "The Incredible Hulk" became a TV program. It started out as a Marvel comic book.			
☐ **Invisible Girl,** *plastic/vinyl, blonde hair (rooted), molded and painted features, wears suit with the number 4 at the front, marked 1974 Marvel CG, made in Hong Kong, 8"*	7.00	10.00	7.00
☐ **Iron Man,** *plastic/vinyl, molded and painted features, molded and painted hair, fully jointed, wears spacesuit, made in c. 1974, 8"*	7.00	10.00	7.00
☐ **Ivanhoe,** *plastic, representing the character from the novel of the same name by Sir*			

	Current Price Range		Prior Year Average
Walter Scott, dressed in light armor with plumed helmet, heraldic lion on breastplate, holds shield with heraldic lion, carries jousting staff, marked Mego Corp., 1974, 8"	3.00	4.00	3.00
☐ **Jacklyn Smith,** *12"*	6.00	12.00	5.00
☐ **Joe Namath,** *plastic/vinyl, molded and painted features, molded and painted hair, fully jointed, marked Mego Corp., Reg. U.S. Pat. Off., Pat. Pend., made in Hong Kong in 1971, 7½"*	32.00	40.00	25.00
☐ **Jordache Cheerleader Doll,** *poseable, red, white cheerleader out fit, pom poms, baton, megaphone, pennant, book of cheers, 12"*	12.00	17.00	10.00
☐ **King Arthur,** *plastic, molded and painted features, has mustache and goatee beard, wears fleece-collared robe, metallic crown, royal seal on a link chain around his neck, marked Mego Corp, 1974, 8"*	3.00	5.00	3.00
Note: Representing the lengendary king of Britain, popularized in the writings of Thomas Mallory.			
☐ **Lion,** *vinyl, jointed, Wizard of Oz doll, with box, c. 1973, 8"*	5.00	10.00	5.00
☐ **Little John,** *plastic, molded and painted features, carries dirk in belt, Little John was character in the novel "Robin Hood" by Sir Walter Scott, marked Mego Corp., Reg. U.S. Pat. Off., made in Hong Kong, 8"*	3.00	5.00	3.00
☐ **Long John Silver,** *plastic, molded and painted features, wears tricorn hat, holds dueling pistol, tall boots, Long John Silver was a character in the novel "Treasure Island" by Robert Louis Stevenson, marked Mego Corp., Reg. U.S. Pat. Off., made in Hong Kong in 1971, 8"*	3.00	5.00	3.00
☐ **Mr. Fantastic,** *plastic/vinyl, molded and painted features, molded and painted hair, wears suit with the number 4 on the front, marked 1975 Marvel CG, 8"*	7.00	10.00	6.00
☐ **Muhammad Ali,** *black, plastic/vinyl, molded and painted features, molded and painted hair, sold with boxing gloves and other accessories, which must be present to realize the full indicated price, marked Mego Corp., New York, N.Y., Patent Pending, Made in Hong Kong, made in 1975, 9½"*	17.00	23.00	15.00
☐ **Riddler,** *plastic/vinyl, fully jointed, wears suit with question marks covering it, marked NPP Inc., 1973, the Riddler was a character from the comic strip "Batman." 8"*	4.00	6.00	4.00

	Current Price Range		Prior Year Average
☐ **Robin, The Boy Wonder,** *plastic/vinyl, molded and painted features, wears cape, Robin the Boy Wonder is a character from the comic strip "Batman," marked Mego Corp., Reg. U.S. Pat. Off., made in Hong Kong in 1971*	5.00	7.00	5.00
☐ **Scarecrow,** *vinyl, jointed, Wizard of Oz doll, with box, c. 1973, 8"*	5.00	10.00	5.00
☐ **Sir Lancelot,** *plastic, molded and painted features, wears light armor with mail sleeves and leggings, armor boots, carries shield with fleur-de-lys symbols, and a two-hand sword at his belt, represents the legendary British knight, popularized in the writings of Sir Walter Scott, marked Mego Corp., 1974, 8"*	3.00	5.00	3.00
☐ **Sitting Bull,** *plastic, molded and painted features, marked Mego Corp., Reg. U.S. Pat. Off., made in Hong Kong in 1971, 8"*	3.00	5.00	3.00
☐ **Spider Man,** *plastic/vinyl, molded and painted, based on the comic character from Marvel Comics Group, marked Marvel CG, 1971, 8"*	6.00	8.00	5.00
☐ **Superman,** *plastic/vinyl, fully jointed, wears cape, based on the Siegel & Schuster comic strip character (DC Comics), marked Mego Corp., MCMLXXI, 1971, also marked National Peroidical Publications, Inc., (the licenser), 7½"*	5.00	7.00	5.00
☐ **Tarzan,** *plastic/vinyl, molded and painted features, fully jointed, Tarzan was created by Edgar Rice Burroughs, marked ERB Inc., 1972, (ERB, Inc., representing the estate and descendants of the late Edgar Rice Burroughs, licenses all Tarzan-related products.), 8"*	5.00	7.00	5.00
☐ **The Thing,** *plastic/vinyl, molded and painted features, marked 1975 Marvel CG, made in Hong Kong, 8"*	7.00	10.00	6.00
Note: The motion picture "The Thing," in which this monster character was featured, was released in 1950 — 25 years before the doll. In the movie, the monster was played by then-unknown James Arness.			
☐ **Tin Man,** *vinyl, jointed, Wizard of Oz doll, with box, c. 1973, 8"*	5.00	10.00	5.00
☐ **Wicked Witch,** *plastic, green face and hands, wears cone-shaped, wide-brimmed hat and carries broom, the Wicked Witch was a character in "The Wizard of Oz" by L.*			

	Current Price Range		Prior Year Average
Frank Baum, marked Mego Corp., MCMLXXII, 1972, also marked by M.G.M., the licenser, 7½″	4.00	6.00	4.00
☐ **Wolfman,** *plastic/vinyl, molded and painted features with "wolf" hair, marked Mego Corp., made in c. 1974, 8″*	7.00	10.00	7.00
☐ **Wyatt Earp,** *plastic, molded and painted features, not designed to resemble Hugh O'Brien (who portrayed Wyatt Earp on a TV series), marked Mego Corp., Reg. U.S. Pat. Off., made in Hong Kong in 1971, 8″*	3.00	4.00	3.00

METTI

☐ **Bindi,** *black, vinyl, sleep eyes, open mouth with teeth, representing a child of the Australian aboriginals ("bushmen"), marked Metti, Australia, date of manufacture unknown*	70.00	90.00	65.00
☐ **Mon Cherie,** *vinyl, sleep eyes (blue), puffy cheeks, pug nose, unmarked, sold originally with a paper tag reading My Name is Mon Cheri, Made in Australia, made in 1975, 12½″*	22.00	28.00	20.00
☐ **Vanessa,** *vinyl, sleep eyes (blue), pug nose, open mouth, unmarked, sold originally with a paper tag reading My Name is Vanessa, The House of Metti, made in 1975, 24½″*	45.00	56.00	42.00

MIDWESTERN

☐ **Darleen,** *plastic/vinyl, sleep eyes (blue), marked 25-6AE, made in 1961 for the Speigel mail-order house of Chicago, 24″*	7.00	10.00	6.00
☐ **Nun Nurse,** *plastic, sleep eyes (blue), dressed as nun with hood, cape and gown, unmarked, made in 1958, 12″*	8.00	11.00	7.00
☐ **Tiny Little,** *vinyl head and body, rooted hair, nursing mouth, bright red lips, marked PTN-18, made in 1964, 15″*	4.00	6.00	4.00

MIGLIORATI

	Current Price Range		Prior Year Average
☐ **Vinyl Head,** *soft body, painted features, pink yarn hair tied with bows, pink dress and hat, known as "Nuvolette," made in Italy, 14" . . .*	35.00	45.00	38.00
☐ **Vinyl Head,** *soft body, painted features, red yarn hair tied with bows, blue dress and hat, known as "Nuvolette," made in Italy, 14" . . .*	35.00	45.00	38.00
☐ **Vinyl Head,** *hands, and feet, soft body, painted features, brown wig, lavender floor length gown, matching hat silver shoes, stand, made in Italy, 26" . . . .*	50.00	100.00	70.00

MILLER RUBBER COMPANY

☐ **Honeybunch,** *black, walker, rubber, sleep eyes (brown), made in 1956, 21½," . . . .*	55.00	70.00	52.00

MINERVA

☐ **Metal,** *shoulder head, set on cloth body with bisque forearms and cowhide feet, fixed eyes, open mouth showing two teeth, marked Minerva, 20" . . . .*	90.00	115.00	85.00
Note: Figure of a young girl.			
☐ **Metal,** *shoulder head, set on cloth body, bisque forearms, molded reddish hair, painted head, fixed eyes, open mouth showing three teeth and traces of others, marked Minerva, 18¾" . . . .*	100.00	130.00	95.00
Note: This is a model of a boy about 3 or 4 years of age.			

EDWARD MOBERLY

☐ **Candy,** *vinyl, molded and painted features, molded and painted hair, marked The Edward Moberly Co., 1958, 8" . . . .*	4.00	6.00	4.00
Note: Actually made by Arrow Plastics.			

MOLLENECHT

☐ **Gucki,** *felt with rubber head, representing an alpine peasant in traditional costuming, made in Bavaria, 12" . . . .*	11.00	14.00	10.00

MOLLYE

	Current Price Range		Prior Year Average
☐ **Angel Face,** *crier, composition head with cloth body, made in 1948, 24"*	46.00	57.00	45.00
☐ **Belgium Girl,** *cloth, marked Mollye's Doll, T.M. Reg., representing a young girl in a Belgian national costume, date of manufacture unknown, probably 1930's, 15"*	70.00	85.00	65.00
☐ **Debbie Deb,** *music box, composition, sleep eyes, blonde wig, 17½"*	350.00	425.00	330.00
Note: In working order.			
☐ **Dutch Girl,** *cloth, elaborately costumed, made in 1941, 18"*	95.00	115.00	90.00
☐ **Hi Buzzy,** *cloth, a child in cowboy outfit, made in 1949, 22"*	115.00	135.00	110.00
☐ **Irene Dunn,** *music box, composition, human hair wig, made c. 1950, 20"*	160.00	190.00	150.00
☐ **Peggy Rose The Royal Bride,** *hard plastic, sleep eyes (blue), made in 1950, 16"*	80.00	95.00	75.00
☐ **Sabu,** *composition, representing the motion picture actor Sabu dressed for his role in "The Thief of Bagdad," made c. 1948, 15"*	190.00	225.00	175.00

MONICA STUDIOS

☐ **Monica,** *composition, blue painted eyes, brown wig, red and white organdy gown with red ribbon and rickrack trim, 14½"*	225.00	275.00	240.00
☐ **Monica,** *composition, rooted hair, painted eyes, dressed as bride, unmarked, date of manufacture unknown, believed to have been made in the 1950's, 16"*	70.00	90.00	65.00

MONTGOMERY WARD

☐ **Benjamin Franklin,** *plastic/vinyl, jointed waist, representing the American printer, inventor, and diplomat, marked Made in Hong Kong, made in the 1970's, 7½"*	5.00	7.00	5.00
☐ **John Paul Jones,** *plastic/vinyl, jointed waist, representing the American naval hero of the Revolutionary War, marked Made in Hong Kong, 7½"*	5.00	7.00	5.00
☐ **Patrick Henry,** *plastic/vinyl, jointed waist, representing the American patriot of the Revolutionary War, marked Made in Hong Kong, made in the mid 1970's, 7½"*	5.00	7.00	5.00

	Current Price Range		Prior Year Average
☐ **Thomas Jefferson,** *plastic/vinyl, jointed waist, representing the American statesman and 3rd U.S. President, marked Made in Hong Kong, made in the mid 1970's, 7½″* . .	5.00	7.00	5.00

MORIMURA BROTHERS

☐ **Baby Darling,** *bisque, jointed, painted, marked Nippon*	65.00	75.00	70.00
☐ **Bisque Head,** *kid body, long red hair, blue stationary glass eyes, open mouth, teeth, green velvet dress with fur trim, feather butterfly in hair, 22″*	250.00	300.00	270.00
☐ **Bisque,** *German doll, set brown eyes, long brown hair, open mouth, white dress, baby bonnet, 30″*	550.00	650.00	588.00
☐ **Bisque Shoulder Head,** *kid body, pin jointed arms, legs, knees, bisque hands, nail detail, blue sleep eyes with real upper lashes, open mouth with four molded teeth, dimpled chin, light brown wig, white two piece suit, embroidered red lace trim, Made by Morimura Bros. marks: 5 MB within incized circle, Japan 4, 21″*	120.00	135.00	120.00
☐ **Toddler,** *nine-piece jointed body, painted eye, navy blue wool suit, 13″*	300.00	350.00	325.00

M & S

☐ **Danny,** *plastic mask face, cloth body, mop hair (red), freckles, closed smiling mouth, wears bowtie, unmarked, made in 1961, 14¾″*	8.00	11.00	7.00
☐ **Pug,** *vinyl, molded and painted features, molded and painted hair, marked M & S, made in 1961, 10½″*	9.00	12.00	8.00

MY TOY

☐ **Oh My,** *vinyl mask face, stuffed body, stuffed arms and legs, sleep eyes (brown), open mouth (yawning), marked 1967 My Toy, 16″* .	7.00	10.00	7.00

NANCY ANN STORYBOOK COMPANY

The Nancy Ann Storybook Doll Company began in San Francisco, California in 1941. It was founded by Nancy Ann Abbott and A.L. Rowland. In the beginning, they imported the bodies from various Japanese and European sources but due to the poor quality of these imports they soon began producing their own dolls.

As demand for the charming 5½" elaborately wigged and costumed dolls grew, a factory was built and dolls were produced at a rate of over 8,000 per day. The storybook dolls were originally made of bisque with painted faces, lovely wigs, one-piece head, body, legs, and jointed arms. Miss Abbott designed all the beautiful costumes herself, basing the themes on nursery rhymes, fairy tales, and her own creativity.

In the 1950's the dolls were made of hard plastic and vinyl and were fully jointed. These lovely dolls continued in production until 1960. The Nancy Ann Storybook Doll was produced again in the 1970's by Giant Consolidated Industries of Salt Lake City, Utah.

	Current Price Range		Prior Year Average
☐ **A Flower Girl For May,** *bisque, molded and painted features, blonde hair attached by adhesive, wears flowered broad-brimmed hat, long lace-trimmed dress, unmarked, sold originally in a box which gave the mold number as 191, made in 1943, 6½"*	15.00	21.00	15.00
☐ **April,** *bisque, one-piece body with jointed arms, painted eyes, wig, original costume, #190 box, 5½"*	35.00	45.00	40.00
☐ **Boy,** *bisque, jointed, blonde hair, ring bearer, one-piece pants set, bow, 4"*	45.00	55.00	50.00
☐ **Big Sister,** *hard plastic, straight leg walker, brown mohair wig, sleep blue eyes, long pink taffeta dress, white lace trim, pink matching slippers, 10"*	60.00	70.00	60.00
☐ **Big Sister And Little Sister,** *hard plastic, one-piece body with jointed arms, painted eyes, wig, original costume, 5½"*	55.00	65.00	60.00
☐ **Bisque,** *blonde hair, dotted white, yellow dress, 6"*	15.00	25.00	20.00
☐ **Bisque,** *blonde hair, white satin, flowered, pink hat*	25.00	35.00	30.00
☐ **Bisque,** *dark hair, pink satin dress, pink felt, 6"*	25.00	35.00	30.00
☐ **Bisque,** *dark hair, purple satin dress, white apron*	20.00	30.00	25.00
☐ **Bisque,** *reddish brown mohair wig, gold satin dress, black lace trim, lavender bow*	20.00	25.00	20.00
☐ **Bisque,** *straight leg, red hair, lacy white dress, pink felt hat, purple ribbons, 6"*	25.00	35.00	25.00

	Current Price Range		Prior Year Average
☐ **Bride,** *hard plastic, one-piece body with jointed arms, painted eyes, wig original brides gown with taffetta skirt and lace flock, 5½″*	25.00	35.00	30.00
☐ **Bride,** *jointed, swivel neck, hand painted, wedding outfit, veil, flowers, 6″*	20.00	30.00	25.00
☐ **Bride,** *plastic, sleep eyes, marked Nancy Ann Storybook Doll, 6″*	16.00	21.00	15.00
☐ **Bridesmaid,** *bisque, one piece body with jointed arms, painted eyes, wig, original costume blue gown, #87 box, 5½″*	45.00	55.00	50.00
☐ **Bridesmaid,** *bisque, one piece body with jointed arms, painted eyes, wig, original pink gown, #87 box, 5½″*	45.00	55.00	40.00
☐ **Christening Baby,** *plastic, molded and painted hair, sleep eyes, (blue), marked Storybook Dolls, U.S.A., made in 1952, 3½″*	13.00	17.00	12.00
☐ **Cinderella,** *hard plastic, one piece body with jointed arms, painted eyes, wig, original costume, stand, 5½″*	45.00	55.00	50.00
☐ **Commencement,** *plastic, blonde hair attached by adhesive, sleep eyes, (black), marked Storybook Dolls, U.S.A., made in 1952, 6″*	9.00	12.00	9.00
☐ **Composition,** *jointed, blonde mohair wig, pink satin dress, white lace trim, flowers*	20.00	25.00	20.00
☐ **Composition,** *jointed brown mohair wig, red full dress, yellow and green trim, large grey hat with feather*	18.00	22.00	18.00
☐ **Daffidown Dilly,** *plastic, blonde hair attached by adhesive, painted features, unmarked, sold originally in a box which gave the mold number as 171, made in 1952, 5½″*	9.00	12.00	9.00
☐ **Daisy,** *hard plastic, one piece body with jointed arms, painted eyes, wig, original costume long pink gown, 5½″*	25.00	35.00	30.00
☐ **"December,"** *bisque, one piece body with jointed arms, painted eyes, wig, original costume, 5½″, #198 box*	35.00	45.00	40.00
☐ **December,** *bisque, straight legs, blonde hair, green net gown, #198, 7″*	40.00	50.00	40.00
☐ **December,** *plastic, lacy red taffeta, matching felt, feathered hat, mint in box, #198, 7″*	30.00	40.00	35.00
☐ **Diaphanie,** *hand painted, red hair, open close eyes, multicolored floral print dress, pink apron, hat, mint in box, 6″*	30.00	60.00	35.00
☐ **Diller A Dollar,** *plastic, blonde hair attached by adhesive, sleep eyes, (blue), marked Storybook Dolls, U.S.A., made in 1952, 7½″*	9.00	12.00	9.00

	Current Price Range		Prior Year Average
☐ **Elsie Marley,** *bisque, molded and painted features, red hair attached by adhesive, unmarked, sold originally in a box which gave the mold number as 31, and carried the following couplet: "Elsie Marley's grown so fine, She won't get up 'till eight or nine," made in 1942, 5½"*	14.00	19.00	13.00
☐ **"Feb,"** *bisque, one piece body with jointed arms, painted eyes, wig, original costume, #188 box, 5½"*	35.00	45.00	40.00
☐ **Flossie Came,** *bisque, one piece body with jointed arms, painted eyes, wig, original costume, #174 box, 5½"*	45.00	55.00	50.00
☐ **Girl,** *auburn hair, yellow bow, white cotton gown, hoopskirt, staw hat, garden party #1904, 18"*	225.00	275.00	230.00
☐ **Girl,** *bisque, jointed leg, blonde hair, ruffled, pink polka dotted gown, feathered hat, 6"*	15.00	25.00	20.00
☐ **Girl,** *plastic, lacy pink nylon outfit, flowered hat, 6"*	15.00	25.00	20.00
☐ **Give Me A Lass,** *bisque, one piece body with jointed arms, painted eyes, wig, original costume, #178 box, 5½"*	35.00	45.00	40.00
☐ **Goose Girl,** *bisque, one piece body with jointed arms, painted eyes, wig, original costume, #169, box, 5½"*	35.00	45.00	40.00
☐ **Goose Girl,** *red hair, dotted red, white dress, green skirt, dotted red, white apron, mint in box*	30.00	40.00	35.00
☐ **Hard Plastic,** *jointed shoulder and neck, sleep eyes, brown mohair, white dress with pink flowers*	20.00	25.00	20.00
☐ **Hard Plastic,** *one piece, jointed arms, painted eyes, wig, original red bodice, hearts on skirt, red felt hat, 5½"*	25.00	35.00	30.00
☐ **Hard Plastic,** *one piece body with jointed arms, painted eyes, wig, original costume with green felt hat with cherries*	35.00	40.00	35.00
☐ **Hard Plastic,** *one piece body with jointed arms, painted eyes, wig, original long green gown, floral bodice and slip, 5½"*	25.00	35.00	30.00
☐ **Hard Plastic,** *one piece body, with jointed arms, painted arms, painted eyes, wig, original yellow bodice, flower, gold flower on black net, 5½"*	20.00	30.00	25.00
☐ **Hard Plastic,** *sleep eyes, dressed as a nun, black habit, white collar, cross*	22.00	28.00	25.00
☐ **Jennie,** *swivel neck, jointed, open close eyes, blue, white striped dress, purple bows, lacy white hat, mint in box, 6"*	30.00	40.00	35.00

	Current Price Range		Prior Year Average
☐ **Jointed,** *hand painted, swivel neck, painted eyes, dark hair, white satin floral dress, felt hat*	20.00	30.00	25.00
☐ **"July,"** *bisque, one piece body with jointed arms, painted eyes, wig, original costume, #193 box, 5½"*	35.00	45.00	40.00
☐ **July,** *bisque, socket head, straight legs, red, white, blue outfit, mint in box, #193, 7"*	45.00	55.00	45.00
☐ **June,** *bisque, one piece body with jointed arms, painted eyes, wig, original costume, #192 box, 5½"*	35.00	45.00	40.00
☐ **Lily Of The Valley,** *hard plastic, one piece body with jointed arms, painted eyes, wig, original costume, long pink gown, 5½"*	25.00	35.00	30.00
☐ **Little Betty Blue,** *bisque, blonde, blue floral print dress, blue felt hat, white feather, mint in box, 6"*	40.00	50.00	45.00
☐ **Little Betty Blue,** *hard plastic one piece body with jointed arms, painted eyes, wig, original costume, 5½"*	35.00	45.00	40.00
☐ **Little Joan,** *bisque, molded and painted features, blonde hair attached by adhesive, made in 1941, 5"*	14.00	19.00	13.00
☐ **Little Miss Muffet,** *bisque, straight leg, flowery print dress, bloomers, ruffled cap, ribbon trim, 6"*	25.00	35.00	25.00
☐ **Little Miss, Sweet Miss,** *swivel neck, jointed, hand painted, open close eyes, pink dress, black trim, pink feathered hat, mint in box, 6"*	30.00	40.00	35.00
☐ **Little Sister,** *black, plastic, black hair attached by adhesive, sleep eyes, (black), marked Storybook Doll, made in 1952, 5½"* **Note: The word sister had no special ethnic meaning in 1952 when this doll was made. But the name was certainly well chosen, and lends extra collecting appeal today.**	17.00	22.00	16.00
☐ **Margie Ann,** *hard plastic one piece body with jointed arms, painted eyes, original school girl costume, 5½"*	50.00	60.00	55.00
☐ **"May,"** *bisque, one piece body with jointed arms, painted eyes, wig, original costume, #191, box, 5½"*	35.00	45.00	40.00
☐ **Miss Muffet,** *plastic, blonde hair attached by adhesive, sleep eyes, (blue), unmarked, originally sold with a tag reading Styled by Nancy Ann, Nancy Ann Storybook Dolls, San Francisco, made in 1956, 6½"*	9.00	12.00	9.00

	Current Price Range		Prior Year Average
☐ **Muffie,** *plastic, brunette hair attached by adhesive, sleep eyes, blue, marked Storybook Dolls, California, made in 1952, 7″* . . .	9.00	12.00	9.00
☐ **Muffie,** *vinyl, a female version of Daniel Boone, made in 1956, 8″* . . .	22.00	27.00	20.00
☐ **Muffie,** *walker, dark pigtails, blue eyes, molded lashes* . . .	60.00	70.00	60.00
☐ **Muffie Around The World,** *hard plastic. This was a series released in the 1970's, showing the basic Muffie doll in various national costumes. Each came in a colorfully printed display package. All are 8″ tall and the values are $11.00-$14.00.*			
☐ **Nellie Bird,** *swivel neck, jointed, open close eyes, red hair, purple, blue floral print dress, blue apron, lacy white hat, mint in box, 6″* . .	30.00	40.00	35.00
☐ **Nun,** *hard plastic, one piece body with jointed arms, painted eyes, wig, original costume, 5½″* . . .	45.00	55.00	50.00
☐ **October,** *hard plastic, one piece body with jointed arms, painted eyes, wig, original costume, 5½″* . . .	30.00	40.00	35.00

October,
hard plastic, 5½″
$30.00-$40.00

	Current Price Range		Prior Year Average
☐ **One Two Button My Shoe,** *hard plastic, one piece body with jointed arms, painted eyes, wig, original costume, 5½"*	30.00	40.00	35.00
☐ **On Two, Button My Shoe,** *bisque, brunette hair attached by adhesive, painted eyes, (blue), closed mouth, marked Storybook Doll, U.S.A., made in 1941, 5"*	19.00	24.00	18.00
☐ **Operetta-Bittersweet,** *bisque, one piece body with jointed arms, painted eyes, wig, original costume, #311 box, 5½"*	35.00	45.00	40.00
☐ **Polly Put The Kettle On,** *bisque, brunette hair attached by adhesive, painted eyes, (blue), holds ceramic kettle, marked Storybook Doll, U.S.A., made in 1941, 5"*	18.00	24.00	17.00
☐ **Queen Of Hearts,** *bisque, molded and painted features, brunette hair attached by adhesive, unmarked, sold originally with a tag reading 117, Queen of Hearts, made in 1942, 5"*	14.00	19.00	14.00
☐ **Rain Rain,** *bisque, one piece body with jointed arms, painted eyes, wig, original costume, #170 box, 5½"*	45.00	55.00	50.00
☐ **Ring Around The Roses,** *bisque, one piece body with jointed arms, painted eyes, wig, original costume, #159 box, 5½"*	35.00	45.00	40.00
☐ **Ring Bearer And Flower Girl,** *hard plastic, one piece bodies with jointed arms, painted eyes, wigs, original costumes, 5½" tallest figure*	90.00	110.00	100.00
☐ **"September,"** *bisque, one piece body with jointed arms, painted eyes, wig, original costume, #195 box, 5½"*	35.00	45.00	40.00
☐ **Spring,** *bisque, painted, green, net gown, flower motif, seasons series, #90, 6"*	30.00	40.00	35.00
☐ **Star Light-Star Bright,** *hard plastic, one piece body with jointed arms, painted eyes, wig, original costume, stand, 5½"*	45.00	55.00	50.00
☐ **Sugar And Spice,** *hard plastic, one piece body with jointed arms, painted eyes, wig, original costume, 5½"*	35.00	45.00	40.00
☐ **Valentine,** *bisque, painted, lacy gown with red heart, lacy bonnet, 5½"*	17.00	22.00	16.00
☐ **Wester Miss,** *American Girl series bisque, one-piece body with jointed arms, painted eyes, wig, original costume, #58 box, 5½"*	35.00	45.00	40.00
☐ **Winter,** *plastic, brunette hair attached by adhesive, molded and painted features, marked Storybook Dolls USA., made in 1952, 5¾"*	9.00	12.00	9.00

	Current Price Range		Prior Year Average
Note: From a series of "seasons" dolls, all of which have the same retail value. Each is dressed appropriately for the season she represents.			

NASCO

	Current Price Range		Prior Year Average
☐ **Andy,** *vinyl/plastic, yarn hair, marked Nasco Dolls Inc., The Bobbs-Merrill Co., Inc., Bobbs-Merrill was the publishing company that owned the rights to Raggedy Ann and Andy, made in 1973, 24"*	11.00	14.00	11.00
☐ **Debbie Lou,** *composition head and body, sleep eyes, (blue), closed mouth, blonde hair, fully jointed, made in 1944, 14"*	31.00	37.00	30.00
☐ **Raggedy Ann,** *vinyl/plastic, yarn hair, marked Nasco Dolls Inc., The Bobbs-Merrill Co., Inc., Bobbs-Merrill was the publishing company that owned the rights to Raggedy Ann, made in 1973, 24"*	11.00	14.00	11.00
☐ **Stumbles,** *walker, vinyl head, cloth body, vinyl hands, representing a toddler just learning to walk, who takes many "stumbles," marked Nasco Doll Co., Inc., Taiwan, date of manufacture unknown, probably c. 1973, 13"*	10.00	14.00	10.00

NATIONAL MASK & PUPPET CORPORATION

	Current Price Range		Prior Year Average
☐ **Joan Palooka,** *vinyl head, cloth body, vinyl hands and feet, a hand puppet, Joan Palooka was a character from the comic strip "Joe Palooka," created by Ham Fisher, unmarked, made in 1952, 11½"*	19.00	25.00	18.00

NATIONAL PERIODICAL PUBLICATIONS

☐ **Superman,** *plastic/vinyl, fully jointed, wears cape, based on the Siegel & Schuster comic strip character (DC Comics), marked Mego*

	Current Price Range		Prior Year Average
Corp. MCMLXXI, 1971, also marked National Periodical Publications, Inc., the licenser, 7½"	5.00	7.00	5.00

NATURAL DOLL COMPANY

☐ **Baby,** *plastic/vinyl, painted eyes, unmarked, made in 1967, 13"*	11.00	14.00	10.00
☐ **Baby Jasmine,** *crier, vinyl head, cloth body, vinyl arms and legs, marked N52, made in 1952, 23"*	30.00	38.00	27.00
☐ **Dolly Ann,** *plastic/vinyl, red hair, (rooted), sleep eyes, (green), partially open mouth, marked Linda Williams, the same mold was used as that of Natural's Linda Williams doll, made in 1963, 14"*	14.00	19.00	13.00
☐ **Linda Williams,** *plastic/vinyl, brunette hair, (rooted), sleep eyes, (blue), open mouth with teeth, marked Linda Williams, which many collectors mistakenly take to be the manufacturer's name, made in 1959, 13½"*	18.00	24.00	16.00
☐ **Miss Ritzi,** *vinyl, sleep eyes, (blue), marked A/14RA, believed to be the first doll made by a U.S. company with a naturalistic adult female body, made in 1959, 17"*	13.00	17.00	12.00

NEMS ENTERPRISES

☐ **George,** *vinyl, hair attached by adhesive, molded and painted features, representing George Harrison of the Beatles, marked NEMS ENT. Ltd. 1964, 5"*	210.00	250.00	200.00
☐ **John,** *hard plastic, hair attached by adhesive, molded and painted features, representing John Lennon of the Beatles, marked NEMS ENT. Ltd. 1964, 5"*	290.00	345.00	275.00
☐ **Paul,** *vinyl, hair attached by adhesive, molded and painted features, representing Paul McCartney of the Beatles, marked NEMS ENT. Ltd. 1964, 5"*	240.00	280.00	230.00
☐ **Ringo,** *hard plastic, hair attached by adhesive, molded and painted features, representing Ringo Starr of the Beatles, marked NEMS ENT. Ltd. 1964, 5"*	1100.00	1350.00	915.00

NESTLE'S CHOCOLATE

	Current Price Range		Prior Year Average
☐ **Chocolate Man,** *cloth (printed), given as a premium in connection with the purchase of Nestle's Chocolate, date of manufacture unknown, c. 1970*	7.00	9.00	7.00

RUTH E. NEWTON

☐ **Babee Bee,** *vinyl, molded and painted hair (blonde), sleep eyes (blue), nursing mouth, marked Sunbabe, Babee Bee, Ruth E. Newton, New York, NY, made in 1954, 12″*	11.00	14.00	11.00
☐ **So-Wee,** *plastic, baby doll, comes with bottle, booties, jacket, towel and soap*	30.00	40.00	35.00

NIADA

☐ **Gibson Girl,** *bisque shoulder head, darkd blue set eyes with painted upper and lower lashes, faintly roughed cheeks, pierced ears, strawberry blonde human hair wig pulled on top of head in bouffant hairdo, cloth body with pin jointed bisque lowerd arms, exquisite lace dress consisting of embroidered white lace, pattern lace insert lace, extraordinary brown velveteen hat trimmed with pleated silk ribbon rosettes and plume, marks: Marianne De Nunez, 19″*	600.00	700.00	575.00
☐ **Mischief,** *bisque, by artist Ellery Thorpe, executed by Marion Mosser, 12″*	325.00	375.00	350.00
☐ **Set of Henry VIII And His Six Wives,** *paper painted faces, wire armature court dress by artist Bernard Ravca*	500.00	600.00	500.00

NIPPON

☐ **Baby,** *bisque, brown sleep eyes, christening gown, 13″*	125.00	175.00	150.00
☐ **Baby,** *five-piece body, painted blue eyes, blonde hair, closed mouth, white baby dress, 7″*	80.00	90.00	83.00
☐ **Baby Bud,** *painted brown eyes, molded old-fashioned blue bathing suit, 3¾″*	60.00	70.00	63.00

	Current Price Range		Prior Year Average
☐ **Bisque Head,** *ball-jointed body, mohair wig, brown sleep eyes, brown velvet suit*	300.00	350.00	320.00
☐ **Bisque Shoulder Head,** *China arms, legs, cloth body, flowered dress with tiny rick-rack trim, blue cape and matching bonnet, head marked Nippon*	90.00	100.00	90.00
☐ **Character Baby,** *bisque socket head, jointed composition bent leg baby body, brown sleep eyes, open mouth with four porcelain teeth, brown wig, lace trimmed baby dress, marks: S over H within circle, Nippon, 14″*	125.00	135.00	100.00
☐ **Girl,** *bisque head, articulated bisque fore-arms with long hands, pin-jointed kid body with composition lower legs, original braided human hair wig, blue sleep eyes, brush-stroke brows, rosebud mouth with four teeth, 27″*	360.00	400.00	375.00
☐ **Girl,** *bisque, jointed arms, painted features, hair, marked Nippon, 5″*	40.00	50.00	42.00
☐ **Lady,** *bisque socket head, wood and composition ball-jointed body, blonde mohair wig, brown blown glass eyes, long antique white dress with black velvet sleeves, black lace trim, full white lace collar, large black hat with black feather and ribbon, head marked: Nippon, M-405-FY., 24″*	430.00	475.00	440.00
☐ **Oriental Toddler,** *bisque head, five-piece composition body, black wig, black sleep eyes, red plaid shirt and slacks, 13″*	625.00	650.00	630.00

PEGGY NISBET

☐ **Anwar Sadat,** *white uniform, c. 1983*	45.00	55.00	50.00
☐ **Bob Hope**	30.00	40.00	35.00
☐ **Captain Cook**	20.00	30.00	25.00
☐ **Clark Gable**	30.00	40.00	35.00
☐ **Duchess Of Windsor**	30.00	40.00	35.00
☐ **Elizabethian Lady**	20.00	30.00	25.00
☐ **Flower Girl,** *plastic, removable clothing, representing an itinerant flower seller of Old London, from Peggy Nisbet's "Cries of London" series, made in England, marked BR309, 8″*	30.00	38.00	28.00
☐ **Hengrist, Chief Of The Angles,** *plastic, removable clothing, representing a leader of one of the ancient barbarian tribes which ruled Britain, made in England, 8″*	45.00	60.00	42.00
☐ **Henry VIII And Six Wives,** *c. 1983*	350.00	450.00	375.00

	Current Price Range		Prior Year Average
☐ **Lavender Girl,** *plastic, removable clothing, representing an itinerant seller of violets ("lavenders") of Old London, from Peggy Nisbet's "Cries of London" series, made in England, marked BR304, 8"*	30.00	38.00	27.00
☐ **Lord Mayor Of London**	20.00	30.00	25.00
☐ **Lord Nelson,** *plastic, removable clothing, representing the British naval hero who was slain in the Napoleonic Wars, made in England, 8"*	45.00	60.00	42.00
☐ **Margaret Thatcher**	30.00	40.00	35.00
☐ **Nell Gwyn,** *costume doll, hard plastic, jointed at shoulder, painted features, red hair, orange satin skirt, chiffon overskirt, basket of oranges, original box, mark: Peggy Nesbitt, made in England, 7½"*	20.00	30.00	20.00
☐ **Pearly Queen,** *Peggy Nisbit Costume Doll, hard plastic, jointed at shoulders, painted features, blonde mohair wig, two-piece black belvet suit sewn with white sequins, original box signed Peggy Nesbit, made in England, 7½"*	45.00	55.00	50.00
☐ **Pope John Paul II,** *c. 1983*	55.00	65.00	60.00
☐ **Prince, Princess Of Wales,** *wedding outfit, c. 1983*	100.00	150.00	110.00
☐ **Queen Anne,** *plastic, removable clothing, representing the Queen of England who ruled from 1702 to 1714, made in England, 8"*	45.00	60.00	42.00
☐ **Queen Catherine,** *plastic, removable clothing, representing Catherine of Aragon, first wife of King Henry VIII, made in England, 8"*	45.00	60.00	42.00
☐ **Queen Isabella,** *plastic, removable clothing, representing the Spanish queen who was instrumental in sponsoring Columbus' voyage of 1492, made in England, 8"*	45.00	60.00	42.00
☐ **Richard III,** *plastic, removable clothing, representing the medieval king of Britain, made in England, 8"*	45.00	60.00	42.00
☐ **Robert Burns,** *plastic, removable clothing, representing the Scottish national poet of the 18th century, 8"*	50.00	65.00	48.00
☐ **Ronald And Nancy Reagan,** *c. 1983*	80.00	110.00	95.00
☐ **Royal Baby Christening Set,** *c. 1983*	100.00	150.00	110.00
☐ **Santa Claus,** *c. 1983*	45.00	55.00	50.00
☐ **Scots Laddi,** *plaid Kilt, stockings, jacket, tam*	20.00	30.00	25.00
☐ **Teddy Roosevelt And Friend,** *vinyl, jointed, dressed in his Rough Riders outfit, carrying a minature Teddy Bear, inspired by the famous Berryman cartoon published in the*			

	Current Price Range		Prior Year Average
Washington Post, special signature commemorative for the 125th anniversary of Roosevelt's birth, limited to 7,500, 8"	70.00	80.00	75.00
☐ **Vivian Leigh**	30.00	40.00	30.00
☐ **William The Conqueror,** *plastic, removable clothing, representing the Norman general who conquered Britain in 1066, made in England, 8"*	45.00	60.00	42.00
☐ **Winston Churchill,** *c. 1983*	45.00	55.00	45.00

ADELHEID NOGLER

☐ **Friedel,** *celluloid, molded and painted features, brown hair attached by adhesive, representing a youth in Alpine costume, made in Innsbruck, Austria, in 1937, 9"*	35.00	45.00	33.00

Note: Scarce, without any doubt. Foreign dolls in national costumes of their land of manufacture were almost always intended for local sale — as souvenirs for tourists — rather than for wholesale export. Considering that not too many Americans were visting Austria in the troubled late '30's, only a relatively few specimens could have been brought to this country.

ROSE O'NEILL

☐ **Kewpie,** *bisque head, jointed arms and neck, stationary legs, marked on foot, 4½"*	150.00	200.00	175.00
☐ **Kewpie,** *composition, all one molded piece torso and legs on rounded base, jointed arms, starfish hands, molded blonde top forelock, two side curls, blue wings, mischievious, painted, brown eyes glancing to side, marks: round paper label on bottom reads Rose O'Neill c. 1913, 12"*	100.00	175.00	75.00
☐ **Kewpie,** *composition doll with moveable arms, tiny blue tipped wing buds on back, decal intact, height 11"*	80.00	90.00	85.00
☐ **Kewpie,** *composition head and jointed arm body, molded hair, painted googly eyes, closed mouth, open fingers, 11"*	150.00	200.00	175.00

Kewpie Boy,
composition,
painted features,
c. 1920, 12″
$120.00-$130.00

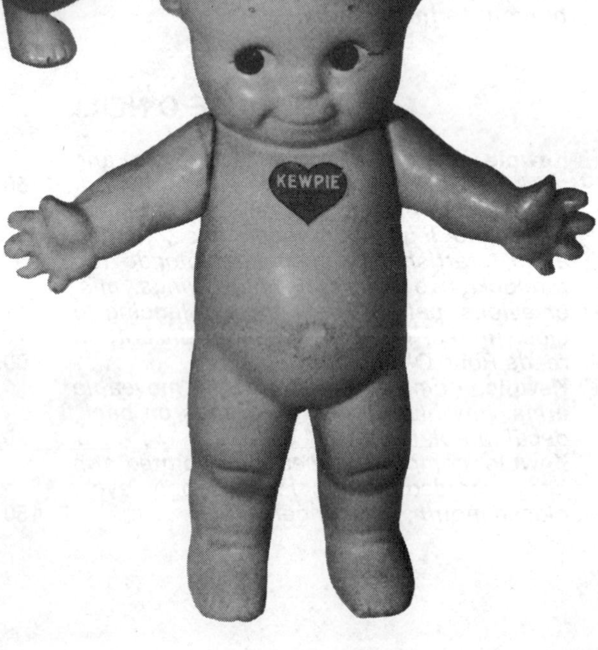

Kewpie,
composition, 11″
$120.00-$130.00

Kewpie Girl, composition, painted features, c. 1920, 12″ **$120.00-$130.00**

	Current Price Range		Prior Year Average
☐ **Kewpie,** *composition, head turns, jointed shoulder, hips, side glaring eyes, molded blonde hair peaked on top, painted features, smiling face, pink sunsuit trimmed in lace, 13″*	120.00	130.00	120.00
☐ **Kewpie,** *composition, jointed at head, shoulders, hips, side glancing eyes, exceptional facial coloring, blue dress with white polka dots, 13″*	145.00	155.00	145.00
☐ **Kewpie,** *female, composition head, molded composition body, painted eyes, red and white dress, c. 1920, 12″*	120.00	130.00	120.00
☐ **Kewpie,** *male, composition head, fixed composition body, painted eyes, red pants, white shirt, c. 1920, 12″*	130.00	140.00	150.00

P & M

	Current Price Range		Prior Year Average
☐ **Belinda,** *black, plastic/vinyl, black hair, (rooted), sleep eyes, (brown), marked P & M Sales, Inc., 1966, marked additionally with a mold number BD19, 23"*	14.00	19.00	13.00
☐ **Lotus Blossom,** *vinyl, sleep eyes, (brown), oriental features and costuming, made in 1966, 12"*	7.00	10.00	7.00
☐ **Royal Princess,** *plastic/vinyl, brunette hair, (rooted), sleep eyes, (blue), nursing mouth with teeth, marked 17EYE, 1967, P&M Doll Co., 17"*	8.00	11.00	7.00

Note: The idea for a Royal Princess doll might have been inspired by Caroline of Monaco, who in 1967 was about the age of the girl represented by this doll.

China Head,
cloth body,
painted features,
c. 1850, 23"
$400.00-475.00

PARKSMITH

	Current Price Range		Prior Year Average
☐ **Googly,** *vinyl, eyes spin when squeezed, a boy wearing horn-rimmed eyeglasses, holding an ice cream cone, marked U.S. Pat. No.3451160, made in Japan in 1969, 6″*	4.00	6.00	4.00

ADELAINE PATTI

☐ **Lady,** *china head, porcelain arms and legs, desirable hairdo, centerpart, swept back at temples, 12 vertical curls at sides, raised pompador over forehead, red eye lines, circular nostrils, full molded lips with painted separation lines, stylish black lace trimmed walking suit, 21″*	375.00	415.00	385.00

PAULINE

☐ **Ling-Ling,** *oriental character, vinyl head and limbs, cloth body, black rooted long hair with bangs, brown sleep eyes, skin looks like wax, long white dress matching pantaloons, lace trim, 16″*	45.00	55.00	45.00

PEDIGREE

☐ **Martha,** *walker, plastic, brunette hair attached by adhesive, sleep eyes, (blue), marked Pedigree, made in England in 1952, 12½″*	23.00	29.00	21.00
☐ **Saucy Walker,** *black, sleep eyes, (brown), forearms bent outward at elbows, marked Pedigree, International Aircraft Ltd., made in England in 1957, 15″*	110.00	135.00	100.00

Note: Reproduction of an antique, apparently made in small quantity.

PELHAM

	Current Price Range		Prior Year Average
☐ **Poodle,** *(marionette puppet), wood and fur, fully jointed, a more or less naturalistic figure of a poodle, with a ribbon in its hair, unmarked, made in 1958, 7″*	12.00	16.00	11.00

J.C. PENNEY

	Current Price Range		Prior Year Average
☐ **Mariclaire,** *fashion doll representing an adult woman, vinyl head, vinyl arms and legs, plastic body, rooted blond hair, painted eyes, marked 155, Made in Hong Kong, 12″* . . . . **Note: Apparently dates from the early or middle 1960's.**	5.00	7.00	5.00

GUTTA PERCHA

	Current Price Range		Prior Year Average
☐ **Bisque,** *shoulder head, cloth body, painted black eyes and hair, original dress, 21″*	425.00	550.00	425.00

PEREGO

	Current Price Range		Prior Year Average
☐ **Topo Gigio,** *(a mouse), vinyl head, cloth body, vinyl hands, rooted hair, marked 1963 Maria Perego, 12⅞″* . . . . **Note: Topo Gigio, a puppet-mouse, was featured many times on the Ed Sullivan TV program.**	11.00	14.00	10.00

PERFECTA

	Current Price Range		Prior Year Average
☐ **Sad Song,** *vinyl, brunette hair, (rooted), molded and painted features, teardrop emerging from left eye, holds hands clasped, marked Perfecta, Made in Hong Kong, made in 1965, 6½″*	5.00	7.00	5.00

PERFEKTA

	Current Price Range		Prior Year Average
☐ **Pregnant Doll,** *plastic/vinyl, sleep eyes, (blue), rooted hair, marked Perfekta, Made in Hong Kong, 14″*	10.00	14.00	10.00

Note: We have been unable to locate any information on the Perfekta Doll Co., which almost certainly was not located in Hong Kong even though this doll was made there. To judge from the progressive nature of the doll it was possibly a West German product.

PETER PUPPET PLAYTHINGS

☐ **Princess Summerfall Winterspring,** *(marionette puppet), composition head, wood body, composition hands and feet, wears Indian-style clothing, Princess Summerfall Winterspring was a character on the "Howdy Doody" TV program, unmarked, made in 1950, 13½″*	50.00	65.00	45.00

PETITE PORTRAITS

☐ **Campbell Kid,** *composition, 12″*	325.00	375.00	340.00
☐ **Liz Taylor,** *bisque head, cloth body, bisque arms and legs, painted features, black wig, marked Petite Portraits and L.W., for the sculptor, Lita Wilson, date of manufacture unknown, c. 1970, 15½″*	500.00	650.00	475.00
☐ **Prince Ranier Of Monaco,** *bisque head, cloth body, bisque arms and legs, molded and painted hair, marked Petite Portraits and L.W., for the sculptor, Lita Wilson, made in 1971, 16″*	325.00	400.00	300.00

PIACENXA

☐ **Athena,** *plastic, sleep eyes, (blue), bright red lips, marked Athena, Piacenxa, 40P, date of manufacture unknown, 18″*	90.00	115.00	90.00

Note: The manufacturer's name is pronounced Piacen-ZA.

PILLSBURY

	Current Price Range		Prior Year Average
☐ **Doughboy,** *printed cloth, (stuffed), wearing a chef's hat with the Pillsbury logo, used as a premium, made in the 1960's, 13″*	7.00	10.00	7.00
☐ **Poppin' Fresh,** *vinyl, molded features, all one piece, representing the symbol of the Pillsbury Flour Co., marked 1971, The Pillsbury Co., Minneapolis, Minn., undoubtedly a premium or promotional item, 7″*	5.00	7.00	5.00

PIEROTTI

Wax,
human hair wig,
marked 1875,
$500.00-$600.00

	Current Price Range		Prior Year Average
☐ **Shoulder Head,** *poured wax head, arms, legs, cloth body, blonde mohair inset hair, blue glass inset eyes, original navy blue taffeta dress, 19″*	900.00	1250.00	925.00
☐ **Wax Head,** *ball jointed body, blue sleep eyes, floral yoked dress with straw hat, marked 1875*	500.00	600.00	530.00

PLANTERS PEANUT COMPANY

☐ **Mr. Peanut,** *printed cloth, stuffed, representing the symbol of the Planters Peanut Co., used as a premium, date of manufacture unknown, believed to be early 1960's, 19½″*	11.00	15.00	10.00

PLASTIC MOLDED ARTS

☐ **Alice In Wonderland,** *hard plastic, blonde wig attached with adhesive, sleep eyes, not connected with Disney, 7″*	3.00	4.00	3.00
☐ **Captain Hook,** *plastic, molded and painted features, molded and painted hair, Captain Hook was a character from "Peter Pan," unmarked, made in 1949, 7½″*	8.00	11.00	8.00
☐ **Crusader,** *molded and painted hair, sleep eyes, (blue), roughly, (very roughly), representing a medieval knight from the era of the Crusades, marked Plastic Molded Arts, made in 1950, 7″*	5.00	7.00	5.00
☐ **Debbie Cakes,** *plastic, unmarked, representing the character from "Little Debbie" baked goods, apparently used as a premium, date of manufacture unknown, probably early 1970's, 7½″*	5.00	7.00	5.00
☐ **Greenbrier Maid,** *black, plastic, sleep eyes, wears bracelet and earrings, unmarked, made in 1955, 7″*	8.00	11.00	7.00
☐ **Polish Girl,** *(national costume doll), plastic, blonde hair attached by adhesive, sleep eyes, (blue), unmarked, made in 1952, 7″*	5.00	7.00	5.00
☐ **Scotch Groom,** *plastic, molded and painted hair, sleep eyes, (blue), dressed as a Scottish bridegroom of the 19th century, unmarked, made in 1955, 7″*	5.00	7.00	5.00

	Current Price Range		Prior Year Average
☐ **Suzy Walker,** *walker, hard plastic, sleep eyes, unmarked, date of manufacture unknown, probably c. 1970, 8"*	5.00	7.00	5.00

PLATED MOULDS

To judge from the spelling of the name — a "u" in "molds" — this was either a British or Canadian company. We have been unable to locate any information on them. They apparently made very few dolls.

☐ **Nelly,** *vinyl head, cloth body, plastic arms and legs, painted eyes, marked U-Plated Moulds Inc., 1961, 15"*	7.00	10.00	7.00
☐ **New Baby,** *vinyl head, cloth body, vinyl arms and legs, blonde hair, (rooted), sleep eyes, (blue), nursing mouth, marked Plated Moulds Inc., 1961, 20"*	14.00	19.00	13.00

PLAYMATES

☐ **Baby,** *rubber one piece, head turns, brown molded hair, painted on blue eyes, open mouth nurser, diaper, booties, long fancy gown, blue blanket trimmed with lace, 7"*	8.00	12.00	8.00
☐ **Little Belle,** *vinyl jointed, blonde rooted hair in pigtails and bangs, blue sleep eyes, closed mouth, fancy white dress and bloomers, flowered trim, comb and brush set, 7"*	14.00	18.00	14.00
☐ **Shelley,** *plastic/vinyl, brunette hair, unmarked, date of manufacture unknown, probably c. 1970, 14"*	6.00	8.00	6.00
☐ **Toddler Twin,** *girl, plastic/vinyl, marked Hong Kong, premium doll used in a promotion by a cereal company in 1974, 8"*	3.00	4.00	3.00

PLAYSKOOL

☐ **Dressy Bessy,** *cloth, mop hair, (red), fixed eyes, unmarked on doll, sold originally with a tag reading Dressy Bessy, Teaching Doll, Playskool, Inc., made in Hong Kong in 1970, Playskool was a subsidiary of the Milton Bradley games company, 19½"*	4.00	6.00	4.00

PLAYTHINGS

	Current Price Range		Prior Year Average
☐ **Nancy,** *vinyl, sleep eyes, (blue), blonde rooted hair, marked 25 Playthings, made in 1954, 20″*	6.00	8.00	6.00

POCKET DOLL

☐ **Brave Cowboy,** *stockinette with cloth body, marked Pocket Doll, 1962, Wolfpit Enterprises, Inc., 7¼″*	12.00	16.00	12.00

EUGENIE POIR

☐ **French Doll,** *cloth, painted brown eyes, reddish brown mohair wig with braids rolled at sides, yellow dotted dress with white apron, 18″*	325.00	375.00	340.00

POLITOY

☐ **Glasgow Scotland,** *hard plastic, sleep eyes, (brown), representing a youth in Scottish dress, marked Politoy 35, Made in England, 14″*	19.00	24.00	18.00

PRINCESS ANNA

☐ **Nun,** *composition, 6″*	15.00	20.00	18.00
☐ **Pert Pierette,** *plastic, molded and painted features, blonde hair attached by adhesive, marked PA1951, 7½″*	5.00	7.00	5.00
☐ **Polish Girl,** *(national costume doll), plastic, blonde hair, attached by adhesive, painted eyes, marked PA-1949, 7½″*	8.00	11.00	8.00
☐ **Red Riding Hood,** *plastic, blonde hair attached by adhesive, molded and painted features, marked PA, made in 1950, 7½″*	5.00	7.00	5.00

PRINCESS CHRISTINA

☐ **Chiffon,** *vinyl head, cloth body, vinyl hands, long blonde hair tied with ribbons, floral*

	Current Price Range		Prior Year Average
print dress, white stockings, black shoes, unmarked on doll, made in France in 1974, 12″	22.00	28.00	20.00
☐ **Corina,** *black vinyl, jointed, mint in box, West Germany, 12″*	40.00	50.00	40.00
☐ **Sweet Sue,** *vinyl, jointed, mint in box, 16″*	40.00	50.00	40.00

PRODUCT PEOPLE

☐ **Charlie The Tuna,** *vinyl, molded and painted, representing the symbol of the StarKist Tuna Co., a tuna wearing cap and eyeglasses, made in 1973, 7″*	4.00	6.00	4.00

GRACE STOREY PUTNAM

☐ **Bye-Lo Baby,** *all bisque, human hair, brown eyes, painted shoes and socks, rare, 6″*	750.00	825.00	750.00

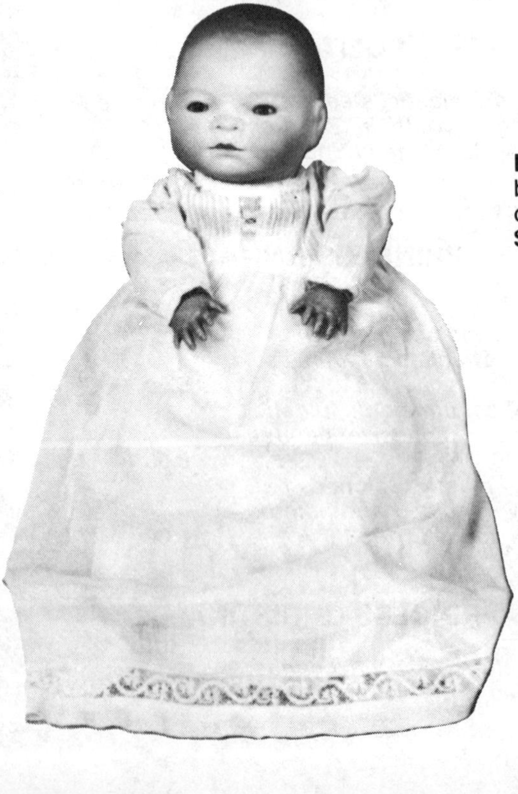

Bye-lo,
bisque and cloth,
c. 1920, 14″
$525.00-$600.00

	Current Price Range		Prior Year Average
☐ **Bye-Lo Baby,** *all bisque infant, comes with cradle and toy, 5½*	260.00	300.00	270.00
☐ **Bye-Lo Baby,** *all bisque, jointed limbs, painted features, incised mark on back, 3½*	250.00	300.00	265.00
☐ **Bye-Lo Baby,** *bisque head, celluloid body, blue sleep eyes, white dress with bonnet, 12½"*	550.00	600.00	575.00
☐ **Bye-Lo Baby,** *bisque head, celluloid body, painted skin head, brown sleep eyes, closed mouth, long christening gown, 13½"*	400.00	500.00	425.00
☐ **Bye-Lo Baby,** *bisque head, celluloid hands, cloth body, 11½"*	425.00	475.00	440.00
☐ **Bye-Lo Baby,** *bisque head, cloth body, celluloid hands, sleep blue eyes, long white baby dress with lace trim, 12"*	625.00	675.00	640.00

Bye-lo,
composition,
c. 1900, 14"
$225.00-$300.00

	Current Price Range		Prior Year Average
☐ **Bye-Lo Baby,** *bisque head, composition bent limb, jointed body, molded painted hair, 14"*	650.00	750.00	650.00
☐ **Bye-Lo Baby,** *bisque head, original body, blue sleep eyes, beautiful antique dress, large size 14" head circumference*	675.00	775.00	650.00
☐ **Bye-Lo Baby,** *black, bisque, long white baby gown, 23"*	250.00	300.00	270.00
☐ **Bye-Lo Baby,** *blue sleep eyes, christening gown, rare extra large size, original marked head and body, 16" head circumference*	850.00	1250.00	1000.00
☐ **Bye-Lo Baby,** *brown sleep eyes, straight legs*	375.00	450.00	350.00
☐ **Bye-Lo Baby,** *celluloid head and hands, cloth body, brown set eyes, ruffling hat and clothes, 11"*	600.00	650.00	625.00
☐ **Bye-Lo Baby,** *cloth body, blue sleep eyes*	390.00	500.00	375.00
☐ **Bye-Lo Baby,** *sleep eyes, bent limb body, 17"*	550.00	650.00	550.00

QUESTER

☐ **Cinderella,** *all cloth, printed face, open mouth, (smiling), sold with mop, pail and extra skirt, 9½"* **Note: Not a Disney product.**	8.00	10.00	7.00

RABERY & DELPHIEU

☐ **Bébé,** *bisque head, ball-jointed composition body, brown glass eyes, brown human hair wig, pierced ears, closed mouth, elaborately costumed, 25"*	2800.00	3300.00	2800.00
☐ **Bébé,** *bisque head, jointed composition body, blue paperweight eyes, closed mouth, blonde wig, pierced ears, original ecru lace dress, mark "R & D," 14"*	1800.00	2000.00	1700.00
☐ **Bisque Head,** *French ball jointed body, human hair wig, blue paperweight eyes, pierced ears, purple dress with purple violet hat, 20"*	2000.00	2200.00	2050.00
☐ **Bisque Head,** *jointed arms and legs, fixed eyes, peach hat and coat, brown and beige dress, c. 1880, 19"*	2500.00	2800.00	2650.00
☐ **Deana Durbin,** *composition and cloth, mohair wig, sleep eyes, navy and white jumper, fur jacket, 1938, 18"*	150.00	200.00	175.00

Bisque Head, composition body, c. 1880, 19″
$2500.00-$2800.00

	Current Price Range		Prior Year Average
☐ **French Bisque Head,** *composition ball-jointed body, blue paperweight eyes, human hair wig, closed mouth, dressed, 17″*	1650.00	1850.00	1600.00
☐ **Sonia Henie Type,** *all composition, jointed, red human hair, blue sleep eyes, original lavender dress with white lace trim, R & B, 16″*	100.00	110.00	100.00
☐ **Young Girl,** *composition, all jointed, blonde human hair wig, brown glass sleep eyes, pensive look, lovely coloring, lavender dotted swiss dress with matching bonnet, R & B, 17″*	130.00	145.00	130.00

RATTI

	Current Price Range		Prior Year Average
☐ **Girl,** *brown mohair wig, goo goo, sleep, blue eyes, lashes, green corduroy dress, 18″ . . .*	150.00	200.00	160.00
☐ **Happy Andrina,** *vinyl head, vinyl arms, legs and body, rooted hair, sleep eyes, open mouth with broad smile, freckled cheeks, wears short-sleeved dress with floral appliques, marked Ratti, made in Italy, date 1964, 11″ . . . .*	14.00	18.00	14.00
Note: The mark of the Ratti Co., which its dolls carry, is a pair of seated rats.			
☐ **Plastic,** *flat finish, googly blue eyes, long black braids, red and white satin costume, made in Italy, c. 1960's . . . .*	30.00	40.00	35.00

BERNARD RAVCA

☐ **Elderly Dutch Couple,** *cloth stockinette faces sculptured with needle stitching, hand painted features, white hair, individually stitched fingers, stuffed bodies, working clothes, wearing painted Dutch type shoes, marks, both have paper labels reading "Original Ravca-Paris," cloth label attached to clothing - Made in France, 13″ .*	75.00	150.00	100.00
☐ **Old Fisherman,** *all cloth doll has hand painted stockinet needle stitched face, white mohair wig, beard, black felt beret, wine colored trousers, shirt, carries a "fishing net," marks, paper label reads -Original Ravca, Fabrication Francaise, cloth label on clothing reads - Made in France, 9½″ . . .*	65.00	85.00	55.00

RDF

☐ **Tiny Tim,** *vinyl, grotesque caricature, marked RDF 67, 3½″ . . . .*	13.00	17.00	12.00

RECKNAGEL

☐ **Bisque,** *ball jointed body, blue eyes, long red curls, blue satin dress, 14″ . . . .*	150.00	175.00	160.00

	Current Price Range		Prior Year Average
☐ **Bisque,** *ball-jointed body, dark brown eyes, dark brown wig with wavy hair, blue satin dress, 12″*	100.00	140.00	118.00
☐ **Bisque,** *brown eyes, brown wig, white and blue dress, 21″*	300.00	350.00	340.00
☐ **Bisque,** *jointed composition body, blue eyes, black curls, pink dress and hat, 21″*	350.00	400.00	370.00
☐ **Bisque Socket Head,** *jointed five piece jointed papier mache composition body, molded socks and shoes, blue sleep eyes, open mouth with four teeth, red lace trimmed dress, original brown wig, marks, 1907 R/A DEP, 6½″*	50.00	75.00	50.00
☐ **Bisque,** *stick figure, set blue glass eyes, blonde wig, open mouth, pink patterned taffeta dress with black stripes and lace, 15″*	150.00	200.00	170.00
☐ **Composition,** *five-piece composition body, brown eyes, brown hair, molded hair*	100.00	150.00	120.00
☐ **Googlie,** *boy, bisque head, five piece composition body, molded blonde hair, blue intaglio eyes, closed watermelon mouth, marked R49A, 8″*	600.00	700.00	625.00
☐ **Googlie,** *five piece body, blue sleep eyes, 11″*	625.00	675.00	640.00

REGAL

☐ **Eskimo,** *vinyl head, plush body stuffed with excelsior, black hair, (rooted), fixed eyes, marked Regal, Made in Canada, 1965, 16″*	23.00	29.00	21.00
☐ **Louise,** *vinyl head, plastic body, sleep eyes, rooted hair, puffy cheeks, partially open mouth, wide-eyed facial expression, wears white dress with small floral print, marked Regal Toy, Made in Canada, 1962, 13″*	6.00	8.00	6.00

OTTO REINECKE

☐ **Baby Name Doll Grete,** *bisque, long blonde curls, grey sleep eyes, two upper teeth, commercial organdy dress with lace tatting on sleeves, "GRETE," 12″*	310.00	340.00	320.00

☐ **Character Baby,** *bisque head, five piece bent-limb composition body, original wig, blue sleep eyes, brush-stroke brows, two upper teeth, molded tongue, old pink cotton*

	Current Price Range		Prior Year Average
striped play dress with matching full romper, knit socks, incised "P. M. 914, Germany 9," 16"	365.00	400.00	375.00
☐ **Character Baby,** *bisque socket head, jointed bent leg body, brown wig, brown sleep eyes, open smiling mouth with two porcelain teeth, illusion of tongue, dimples, lace trimmed white gown, hand made crochet yellow sweater, matching bonnet, made by Otto Reinecke, marks P. M. 914 12, 28"*	375.00	450.00	375.00

RELIABLE

☐ **Mary Baby,** *plastic head, plastic arms, legs and body, rooted hair in elaborate high-fashion coiffure, sleep eyes with thick long eyelashes, 13½"*	4.00	6.00	4.00

RELIABLE OF CANADA

☐ **Barbara Ann Scott,** *composition, sleep eyes, (blue), open mouth, marked Reliable of Canada, 14"*	90.00	115.00	85.00

REMCO

☐ **Baby Crawl-Along,** *mechanical crawler, plastic/vinyl, rooted hair, (blonde), sleep eyes, (blue), ribbon in hair, marked New R11 Remco Ind., 67, made in 1967, 20"*	13.00	17.00	12.00
☐ **Baby Grow-A-Tooth,** *plastic/vinyl, rooted hair, (blonde), sleep eyes, green, open mouth, comes with playpen, this was the first and probably the only doll that ever "grew" a tooth, the tooth was spring-mounted and snapped into the doll's head when its thumb was inserted into its mouth, upon removing the thumb, the tooth appeared, a pacifier could be used in place of the thumb, marked Remco Ind., Inc., 1969, 14"*	17.00	23.00	17.00

	Current Price Range		Prior Year Average
☐ **Baby Know It All,** *plastic/vinyl, fixed eyes, marked Remco Ind., Inc., 1969, 16½"*	8.00	11.00	8.00
☐ **Baby Laugh A Lot,** *vocal, (laugher), vinyl head, cloth body, vinyl hands, red hair, (rooted), painted eyes, (blue), pullcord operated, marked 3066-33 Remco Ind., Inc., made in 1970, 16"*	11.00	14.00	11.00
☐ **Baby Polly PUff,** *vinyl, jointed, c. 1970, 9"*	8.00	12.00	8.00
☐ **Baby Sad & Glad,** *plastic/vinyl, platinum blonde hair, (rooted), painted eyes, blue, mouth opens and closes by mechanism connected to leg, not battery operated, marked Remco Ind., Inc., 1966-1M, 13½"*	9.00	12.00	9.00
☐ **Baby Stroll-A-Long,** *walker, plastic/vinyl, platinum blonde hair, (rooted), sleep eyes, (blue), marked S2 Remco Ind., Inc., E177, made in 1966, 15"*	8.00	11.00	8.00
☐ **Birthday Party Mickey Mouse,** *vinyl, green outfit, limited anniversary issue, mint in box, c. 1978, 16"*	25.00	35.00	30.00
☐ **Bottle Baby,** *vinyl, molded and painted features, wears scarf around neck, six-shooter and diaper, Bottle Baby was packaged inside a bottle, marked Remco, 1967, 4"*	6.00	8.00	6.00
☐ **Same as above,** *but alone*	4.00	6.00	4.00
☐ **Dr. John Littlechap,** *plastic/vinyl, molded and painted features, molded and painted hair, closed mouth, unmarked, made in Hong Kong in 1963, 15"*	18.00	23.00	17.00
☐ **Heidi,** *growing, vinyl head and body, painted features, "growing" action consists of a telescope waist, marked Remco Ind., Inc., 1966, doll is 6" and can grow to 7"*	5.00	7.00	5.00
☐ **Jan,** *vinyl head and body, black hair, (rooted), painted eyes, dressed in Oriental costume, pressing a button on the body causes arms to raise, marked 2-FJ2-112 Remco, 1965, 5½"*	5.00	7.00	5.00
☐ **Judy Littlechap,** *plastic/vinyl, brunette hair, (rooted), painted eyes, closed mouth, marked Judy Littlechap, Remco Industries, 1963, 13"*	14.00	18.00	13.00
☐ **Jumpsy,** *mechanical, vinyl/plastic, blonde hair, (rooted), painted eyes, (blue), pug nose, puffy cheeks, closed mouth, battery-operated, (jumps as if skipping rope), marked Remco Ind., Inc., 1970, 14"*	10.00	14.00	10.00
☐ **Laurie Partridge,** *plastic/vinyl, molded and painted features, closed mouth, Laurie Partridge was a character on the TV program*			

	Current Price Range		Prior Year Average
"The Partridge Family," marked 1973 Remco Industries, Inc., Harrison, N.J., made in Hong Kong, 18½"	26.00	33.00	23.00
☐ **L.B.J.,** *Lyndon B. Johnson, vinyl, molded and painted features, molded and painted clothing, wears button reading "LBJ," marked with the mold number 74, made in 1964, (the year after Johnson assumed the Presidency, following the assassination of John F. Kennedy), 5½"*	37.00	48.00	35.00
Note: The high price results mostly from competition by collectors of political memorabilia.			
☐ **Libby Littlechap,** *plastic/vinyl, brunette hair, (rooted), molded and painted features, closed mouth, marked Libby Littlechap, Remco Ind., made in Hong Kong in 1963, 10½"*	14.00	18.00	13.00
☐ **Little Orphan Annie,** *printed cloth, mop hair, (red), wearing a shirt reading "Kiss 'n Hug Me," sold originally with a tag reading 1967 Remco Ind., Inc., 16"*	28.00	37.00	25.00
Note: Little Orphan Annie started out in life as a comic strip character, created by Harold Gray.			
☐ **Liza Littlechap,** *plastic/vinyl, molded and painted features, molded and painted hair, closed mouth, marked Liza Littlechap, Remco Industries, 1963, also bearing the mold numbers B92 and B95 on the legs, 14"*	14.00	18.00	13.00
☐ **Snugglebun,** *all vinyl, crier, green sleep eyes, blonde hair, red two-piece outfit, made in 1966, 15"*	25.00	35.00	28.00
☐ **Snugglebun,** *vinyl head, plastic body, vinyl arms, plastic legs, blonde hair, (rooted), sleep eyes, (blue), partially open mouth, marked Remco Ind., Inc., 1965, 16"*	11.00	15.00	10.00
☐ **Sweet April,** *vinyl, arms move when back button is pressed, wears diaper, sits in pink plastic walker on wheels, made in 1972, 5"*	2.00	6.00	4.00
☐ **Sweet April,** *vinyl, blonde hair, (rooted), fixed eyes, (blue), nursing mouth, arms raise and lower by pushing button on back of doll, marked 3339 Remco Ind., Inc., 1971, 5½"*	5.00	7.00	5.00
☐ **Tippy Tumbles,** *mechanical, plastic/vinyl, red hair, (rooted), fixed eyes, (blue), remote-control battery operated, marked SM-E32-Remco Ind., Inc., 1966, 16"*	9.00	12.00	9.00

	Current Price Range		Prior Year Average
☐ **Tumbling Tomboy,** *plastic/vinyl, platinum blonde hair, (rooted), pigtails, fixed eyes, (green), closed smiling mouth, wears a shirt reading "Tumbling Tomboy," checkered slacks, white shoes, marked 2000-17EYE-New-E27, made in 1969, 15½"*	9.00	12.00	9.00
☐ **Whistler,** *vinyl head, stuffed body, vinyl hands, molded and painted features, blonde hair, (rooted), lips pursed as if whistling, marked Remco Ind., Inc., 1970, 14"*	6.00	8.00	6.00

REVALO

☐ **Bisque Socket Head,** *jointed compositon body, blonde wig, blue sleep eyes, open mouth, striped sailor dress, marks: Revalo 5, 16"*	300.00	400.00	300.00
☐ **Character Doll,** *jointed composition body, molded blonde hair with blue molded hair ribbon, close mouth, 13"*	525.00	575.00	540.00
☐ **Girl,** *marked 150/Germany, jointed composition body, blonde human hair wig, brush stroked eyebrows, painted lower lashes, open mouth, molded upper teeth, blue cotton dress with flocking, black shoes and socks, 18"*	450.00	500.00	465.00
☐ **Infant Bisque Head,** *five-piece composition body, human hair wig, blue sleep eyes, white baby dress, 14"*	700.00	750.00	725.00

RHEINISCHE GUMMI & CELLULOID FABRIC

☐ **Isabell,** *plastic head, plastic arms, legs and body, (strung), long blonde wig attached by adhesive, sleep eyes with metallic eyelids, open mouth, marked Turtle 35, made in Germany, 14½*	14.00	18.00	13.00

Note: The Rheinische Gummi & Celluloid Fabric is or was a factory in Mannheim, Germany. The name would translate as "Rhineland Plastic and Celluloid Factory." The word "turtle" in the mark is probably a code relating to the mold, possibly to keep the name of the mold-maker secret from competitors.

RICHARD

	Current Price Range		Prior Year Average
☐ **Colonist 1740,** *vinyl, dressed as a female American colonist, marked Hong Kong, made in 1975, 8″*	3.00	4.00	3.00
☐ **First Lady 1789,** *plastic/vinyl, representing Martha Washington with a child's face, marked Hong Kong, made in 1979, 8″*	3.00	5.00	3.00
☐ **Flapper 1925,** *plastic/vinyl, marked Hong Kong, made in 1975, 8″*	3.00	5.00	3.00
☐ **Pilgrim 1620,** *vinyl, female pilgrim in puritan attire, marked Hong Kong, made in 1975, 8″*	3.00	4.00	3.00
☐ **Southern Belle 1861,** *plastic/vinyl, a girl dressed in a Civil War era gown, marked Hong Kong, made in 1975, 8″*	3.00	5.00	3.00
☐ **Toni Tot,** *plastic/vinyl, painted eyes, marked Hong Kong, 6″*	3.00	4.00	3.00

RICHARD BICENTENNIAL SERIES

In 1975 the Richard Toy Co., Ltd. issued a series of 8″ dolls showing the evolution in women's fashions in America from the earliest times to the 20th century. They were inspired by the Bicentennial, to be observed the following year. At the present time these dolls are just beginning to appear on the secondary market, thus their modest values may not be a true reflection of the opinion collectors hold of them.

RITE-LEE

	Current Price Range		Prior Year Average
☐ **Baby Lynne,** *vinyl, molded and painted hair, sleep eyes, (blue), nursing mouth, unmarked, date of manufacture unknown, 7″*	5.00	7.00	5.00

ROBERTA

	Current Price Range		Prior Year Average
☐ **Dr. Ben Casey's Nurse,** *plastic/vinyl, brunette hair, (rooted), sleep eyes, (blue), unmarked, made in 1963, 16½″*	8.00	11.00	8.00
Note: A portion of the value derives from its status as "TV memorabilia."			
☐ **Haleloke,** *walker, plastic, sleep eyes, wears Hawaiian native costume, Haleloke, (pronounced Holly-low-key), a Hawaiian entertainer, was a regular on the TV program 'Arthur Godfrey and His Friends" in the 1950's, this doll must have been made around 1954 or 1955, 17″*	70.00	90.00	65.00

	Current Price Range		Prior Year Average
☐ **Roberta Ann,** *plastic, brunette wig attached by adhesive, sleep eyes, (blue), open mouth, bright red lips, sold originally with a paper tag reading Your Roberta Ann has Saran Hair that can be washed, combed, curled, waved and set, came with hair rollers on the tag, made in 1952, 15″*	30.00	38.00	28.00
☐ **Tear Drop,** *plastic/vinyl, sleep eyes, marked 14-5W, made in 1966, 15½″*	6.00	8.00	6.00

EDWARD ROCHARDE

☐ **Fashion Doll,** *bisque head, lower arms, gussetted kid body, threaded blue glass eyes, brown mohair wig, closed mouth, pierced ears, original blue dress with lace insets, ruffled pleats, matching hat, very elaborate, mark: Edward Rocharde Depose, 29″*	5000.00	7500.00	5500.00

GRACE CORRY ROCKWELL

☐ **Girl,** *character, bisque head, cloth body, composition limbs, molded hair, sleeping eyes, closed mouth, voice box, 14½″*	3000.00	3500.00	2500.00

RODDY

☐ **Janie,** *plastic, reddish hair attached by adhesive, sleep eyes, (blue), marked Roddy, made in England, made in 1951, 11½″*	27.00	36.00	25.00

ROGARK

☐ **Highlander,** *plastic head, plastic arms, legs and body, sleep eyes, molded, painted hair, represents a Scottish highlander in national costume, with bagpipes, marked Rogark Made in Wales U.K., 6″*	9.00	12.00	8.00

MADEMOISELLE MANE ROHMER

	Current Price Range		Prior Year Average
☐ **Rohmer Fashion Doll,** *China head, arms, jointed kid body, blue set glass eyes, brown wig, pierced ears, closed mouth, original elaborate green silk costume with matching cape and hat trimmed in ribbon and lace, mark: Mae Rohmer, Brevtte SGDG Paris, 15″*	4000.00	6000.00	4500.00

ROKO

☐ **Flip The Football Doll,** *vinyl head, rag body, vinyl hands, rag feet, molded and painted features, molded-on football helmet, (with chin strap, no face-mask), marked 1961 Roko, 15″ .*	10.00	14.00	9.00

RONALD

☐ **Gramps,** *vinyl head, cloth body, (painted), marked Hong Kong, made in the mid or late 1970's, 8″ ....*	2.00	3.00	2.00
Note: There was a companion doll called "Granny," worth the same price.			
☐ **Granddaughter,** *vinyl head, cloth body, blonde rooted hair, marked Hong Kong, made in the mid or late 1970's, 7″ ....*	2.00	3.00	2.00

ROSEBUD

☐ **Mariann,** *plastic/vinyl, brown hair, (rooted), sleep eyes, (blue), marked Rosebud, made in 1959, 19″ ....*	13.00	17.00	12.00
☐ **Rosette,** *plastic/vinyl, platinum blonde hair, (rooted), sleep eyes, (blue), wears high-heel shoes, marked Rosebud, made in Great Britain in 1958, 14″ ....*	49.00	60.00	47.00
☐ **Rose Of 1963,** *plastic/vinyl, reddish brown hair, (rooted), sleep eyes, (blue), marked Rosebud, made in England, 14″ ....*	24.00	29.00	23.00

ROYAL DOLL COMPANY

	Current Price Range		Prior Year Average
☐ **Joy,** *vinyl, blonde hair, (rooted), painted eyes, (brown), ribbon in hair, white shoes, marked A Royal Doll-65, made in 1965, 11″*	23.00	29.00	21.00
☐ **Lonely Liza,** *vinyl head, cloth and foam body, vinyl arms and legs, posable, blonde hair, (rooted), painted eyes, closed mouth, marked 1964 Royal Doll, 20″*	38.00	47.00	36.00
☐ **Debbie,** *vinyl, blonde hair, (rooted), sleep eyes, (blue), closed mouth, ribbons in hair, marked Royal Doll, 1961, 14½″*	23.00	28.00	21.00
☐ **Granny,** *vinyl, rooted hair, (black and grey), sleep eyes, (blue), marked 40B-SG, date of manufacture unknown, c. 1968, 18½″*	35.00	43.00	33.00
Note: One of the few grandmother dolls in which there was no attempt at caricature or humor.			
☐ **Jodi,** *plastic/vinyl, blonde hair, sleep eyes (blue), nursing mouth, marked 1964 Royal Doll-10, 12″,*	22.00	28.00	21.00
☐ **Lilo,** *vinyl, rooted hair, sleep eyes, closed mouth, marked Royal Doll, made in 1958, 19″,*	30.00	38.00	28.00
☐ **Merry Lee,** *vinyl, molded and painted hair, sleep eyes (blue), marked Royal Doll Co., 1964, 12″*	16.00	21.00	15.00
☐ **California,** *fiesta outfit, c. 1982*	30.00	40.00	35.00
☐ **Florida,** *early 1930's outfit, fruit basket, c. 1982*	30.00	40.00	35.00
☐ **Georgia,** *blonde curls, long light orange gown, c. 1983*	30.00	40.00	35.00
☐ **Hawaii,** *black hair, holoku dress, c. 1982*	30.00	40.00	35.00
☐ **Iowa,** *straw hat, holds carrots, c. 1983*	30.00	40.00	35.00
☐ **Louisiana,** *clown outfit, c. 1983*	30.00	40.00	35.00
☐ **New Jersey,** *red poodle skirt, white blouse, c. 1983*	30.00	40.00	35.00
☐ **New York,** *early 1900's, outfit, plumed hat, comes with stand, state flag, c. 1982*	30.00	40.00	35.00
☐ **North Carolinia,** *late 1800's garb, apron, bonnet, c. 1982*	30.00	40.00	35.00
☐ **Oklahoma,** *froniter outfit, c. 1983*	30.00	40.00	35.00
☐ **Royal Deb,** *black, white dress, matching black cape, c. 1983, 15″*	55.00	65.00	60.00
☐ **Royal Deb,** *ivory, burgandy, cameo necklace, c. 1983, 15″*	55.00	65.00	60.00
☐ **Royal Deb,** *lacy white wedding outfit, bouquet, c. 1983, 17″*	55.00	65.00	60.00
☐ **Royal Deb,** *white brocade, matching boa, hat, c. 1983, 15″*	55.00	65.00	60.00

	Current Price Range		Prior Year Average
☐ **South Carolina,** *lacy white dress, matching hat, c. 1983*	30.00	40.00	35.00
☐ **Tennessee,** *country, western gingham square dance outfit, scarf, crinolines, bow, c. 1982*	30.00	40.00	35.00
☐ **Texas,** *brunette, suede outfit, boots, stetson, c. 1982*	30.00	40.00	35.00
☐ **Virginia,** *colonial blue floral dress, white cap, c. 1983*	30.00	40.00	35.00

ROYAL DOULTON

HEIRLOOM DOLLS

☐ **Firstborn,** *this baby doll is a beautiful blue-eyed infant in a basket crib trimmed in lace, the infant is dressed in a traditional christening robe of white figured cotton with a lace front panel, bonnet is of white satin and lace*	175.00	225.00	195.00
☐ **Little Bridesmaid,** *dress in cream satin, trimmed with cream lace which matches the lace on the bride (Wedding Day), flowers are yellow, orange and white, hair is light auburn, and headdress is a ringlet of similar flowers*	150.00	200.00	170.00

First Born,
Heirloom series
$175.00-$225.00

Wedding Day and Little Bridesmaid, pair ....**$450.00-$550.00**

	Current Price Range		Prior Year Average
☐ **Royal Baby Doll,** *to commemorate the birth of His Royal Highness Prince William of Wales, born June 21, 1982, baby wears a dress and bonnet of cream lace and net over taffeta, underneath are cream cotton bloomers, bonnet is cream trimmed in matching lace and ribbons, the canopied crib is draped with a white and cream figured cotton, trimmed with baby blue, the face, hands and feet are a delicate baby tone, limited edition of 2,500*	275.00	325.00	295.00
☐ **Wedding Day,** *bride wears a wedding dress of ivory silk which is almost entirely covered with ivory lace, the veil is matching lace and pink and cream flowers accenturate her brunette reall hair, she carries a miniature bouquet of yellow, orange and white flowers, height 14"*	200.00	250.00	220.00

Royal Baby Doll,
Heirloom series
$275.00-$325.00

KATE GREENAWAY SERIES

	Current Price Range		Prior Year Average
☐ **Big Sister,** *white dress with lacey under-skirt, royal blue ribbon at the waist, hat is white trimmed in same color blue, slippers white, carrying dark brown basket with white and red flowers, limited edition of 5,000, height 12"*	150.00	200.00	170.00
☐ **Little Model,** *gown is light beige with blue ribbon at waist, hat is blue matching ribbon on dress with deep maroon ties, cape is maroon, limited edition of 5,000, height, 12"*	150.00	200.00	170.00
☐ **The Muff,** *dressed in tailored full length coat with a fur cape collar and carrying a fur muff, the coat has a pink lining, dress is maroon satin, hat is plum colored and trimmed with chocolate and pink feathers, hair is auburn, limited edition of 5,000, height 12"*	175.00	225.00	195.00

Wedding Day, Heirloom series . . . . **$200.00-$250.00**

	Current Price Range		Prior Year Average
☐ **Pink Ribbon,** *dress is white taffeta line with pink underskit, hat white pink satin ribbon and white feathers, carrying a miniature bouquet of silk rosebuds, limited edition of 5,000, height 12″*	175.00	225.00	195.00
☐ **Pink Sash,** *dressed in white taffeta over a pink underskirt, wearing white hat decorated with feathers and pink ribbon, over blonde hair, carrying a miniature bouquet of silk rosebuds, limited edition of 5,000, height 10″*	125.00	175.00	140.00

The Muff, Kate Greenaway series .... **$175.00-$225.00**

	Current Price Range		Prior Year Average
☐ **Small Sister,** *small child has all white dress with white shoes tied with pink ribbons, bonnet is white with pink bows over dark blonde hair, limited edition of 5,000, height 8″*	**100.00**	**150.00**	**120.00**
☐ **Swansdown,** *dressed in a white figured satin fur trimmed coat over a white satin dress, she carries a white fur muff and wears a lace trimmed hat over her blonde curyl hair, decorated with Swansdown and yellow ribbons, limited edition of 5,000, height 12″*	**175.00**	**225.00**	**195.00**

Pink Sash,
Kate Greenaway series
$175.00-$225.00

	Current Price Range		Prior Year Average
☐ **Vera,** *deep beige dress with matching color overdress, hat matches dress, light auburn hair, carrying basket of pink flowers, limited edition of 5,000, height 12″*	150.00	200.00	170.00
☐ **Waiting,** *simple white gown of silk with frilled neckline and cuff, wide sash of orange satin ribbon at waistline, matching the lining of her dark brown lace and feather hat, under the hat is a white linen cap trimmed in lace, limited edition of 5,000, height 12″*	175.00	225.00	195.00
☐ **Winter,** *costume is scarlet red trimmed with black fur, carrying fur muff, beautiful black hat showing underneath is her red hair,black shoes, limited edition of 5,000, height 12″*	150.00	200.00	170.00

VICTORIAN BIRTHDAY DOLLS

The well remembered nursey rhyme inspired this charming new collection. While each Day's child is represented by a boy and girl doll, each girl has a hairpiece while the boys hair is sculptured in the ceramic. Their costumes follow the 19th century tradition. This is a non-limited edition.

	Current Price Range		Prior Year Average
☐ **Monday's Child,** *is fair of face*	120.00	160.00	140.00
☐ **Tuesday's Child,** *is full of grace*	120.00	160.00	140.00
☐ **Wednesday's Child,** *is full of woe*	120.00	160.00	140.00
☐ **Thursday's Child,** *has far to go*	120.00	160.00	140.00
☐ **Friday's Child,** *is loving and giving*	120.00	160.00	140.00
☐ **Saturday's Child,** *works hard for a living*	120.00	160.00	140.00
☐ **Sunday's Child,** *a child that is born on the Sabbath Day is bonny and blithe and good and gay*	120.00	160.00	140.00

Monday's Child,
Heirloom series
$120.00-$160.00

ROY DESIGN

	Current Price Range		Prior Year Average
☐ **Clown,** *vinyl, molded and painted features, mohair hair, marked Roy Design of Florida, date of manufacture unknown, presumably 1970's, 5⅞″*	3.00	4.00	3.00

R.P.

☐ **Purina Scarecrow,** *vinyl head, printed cloth body, molded and painted featrues, used as a premium product by the Purina pet food company, marked R.P. Co., made in 1965, 23″*	11.00	14.00	10.00
Note: Bears a close resemblance to the scarecrow in "The Wizard of Oz," but there is no connection between them.			

RUSHTON

☐ **Connie,** *vinyl facemask, cloth body, vinyl hands and feet, yarn hair (blonde), marked White Provision Co., date of manufacture unknown, 13½″*	34.00	41.00	32.00
Note: So far as we can determine, the mark White Provision Co. does not appear on any other Rushton doll and very likely has no connection at all with Rushton. Quite likely this was a company which provided materials with which the doll was made.			
☐ **Howdy Doody,** *his shaggy dog in doll form, has "Howdy Doody" sailor hat on, height 16″*	40.00	50.00	45.00
☐ **Musical Mistress Mary,** *music box, vinyl head, cloth body, music box located in body, wound with key, unmarked, made in 1964, 15½″*	18.00	23.00	17.00
☐ **Naptime Pal,** *vinyl face mask, plush body, this was literally a teddy bear with a human face, marked Rushton Co., made in 1961, 19″*	5.00	7.00	5.00
☐ **Santa Claus,** *vinyl mask face, foam-stuffed body, vinyl hands, Santa smiles while holding a bottle of Coca-Cola in his right hand, marked The Rushton Co., made in 1956, 15″*	55.00	75.00	52.00
Note: Why is Santa holding a Coke bottle? Could this have been a store display doll,			

	Current Price Range		Prior Year Average
not intended for sale? We tend to doubt this because the Coke bottle is so small that the name can be seen only at VERY close range.			
☐ **Sleepy,** *vinyl head, plush body, with squeeker, marked with a C within a circle (symbol for copyright), no other markings, date of manufacture unknown, probably mid to late 1960's, 21½"*	6.00	8.00	6.00

S & E

	Current Price Range		Prior Year Average
☐ **Easter Bonnet Toddler,** *plastic, brunette hair attached by adhesive, painted eyes, wears bonnet with ribbon tied under chin, silk dress with small floral prints, white shoes, marked S & E, made in 1953, 5½"*	11.00	14.00	11.00
☐ **St. Pat's Day Bonnet Toddler,** *plastic, blonde hair attached by adhesive, painted eyes, wears bonnet with ribbon tied under chin, print dress (lace trimmed), white shoes, marked S & E, made in 1953, 5½"*	11.00	14.00	11.00
☐ **Valentine Bonnet Toddler,** *plastic, blonde hair attached by adhesive, painted eyes, wears bonnet tied with ribbon under chin, long lace-trimmed dress, white shoes, marked S & E, made in 1952, 5½"*	11.00	14.00	11.00

SAKAI

	Current Price Range		Prior Year Average
☐ **Sucking Thumb Baby,** *cloth body, vinyl head, vinyl hands, unmarked on doll, sold originally with a tag reading Sakai & Co. Ltd., Japan, this doll was made for the F.A.O. Schwarz toy chain in 1975, 12½"*	28.00	35.00	27.00

SARCO

	Current Price Range		Prior Year Average
☐ **Robin Good,** *vinyl head with felt body, representing the legendary character Robin Hood, whose name is here changed to Robin Good, unmarked, sold originally with a tag reading Sarco, Japan, probably made in the 1970's*	3.00	4.00	3.00

SAYCO

	Current Price Range		Prior Year Average
☐ **Adorable,** *plastic/vinyl, blonde hair (rooted), sleep eyes (blue), ribbons in hair, wears shorts and bib, marked K27 Sayco Doll Corp., date of manufacture unknown, 11″*	6.00	8.00	6.00
☐ **Billy Joe,** *vinyl head, latex body, molded and painted hair, sleep eyes (blue), open mouth with two teeth, marked Sayco 25F-1950, 25″*	39.00	49.00	37.00
☐ **Bride,** *vinyl head and body, jointed at the waist, made in 1957, 14″*	22.00	28.00	20.00
☐ **Bubble Bath Baby,** *plastic/vinyl, blonde hair (rooted), sleep eyes (blue), open mouth, marked Sayco Doll Corp., made in 1964, 15″*	7.00	10.00	7.00
☐ **Melissa,** *vinyl head, cloth body, vinyl limbs, sleep eyes (brown), marked Sayco 18-D, 20″*	60.00	75.00	60.00
☐ **Mommy's Baby,** *vinyl head, cloth body, vinyl arms and legs, blonde hair (rooted), sleep eyes (blue), wears gown with a drawing of a dog on it, marked Sayco Doll Corp., 1961, 18″*	13.00	17.00	12.00
☐ **New Hampshire Baby,** *vinyl head, latex body, brunette hair (rooted), sleep eyes (blue), marked B17 Sayco, made in 1965, 18″*	11.00	14.00	11.00
Note: How this doll relates to New Hampshire is an unsettled question, possibly it was modeled after an antique original made in that state.			
☐ **Pouty Paul,** *plastic/vinyl, sleep eyes (blue), closed mouth, marked Sayco Doll Corp., NY, 1964, 20″*	16.00	22.00	15.00
☐ **Sherry Ann,** *vinyl head and body, sleep eyes (blue), bright red lips, closed mouth, marked 74, made in 1956, 20″*	30.00	38.00	27.00
☐ **Walking Bride,** *walker, plastic/vinyl, blonde hair (rooted), sleep eyes (blue), pug nose, closed mouth, bright red lips, also cries, unmarked, made in 1956*	14.00	19.00	13.00

SCHILDKROT

☐ **Cleodine,** *black, vinyl, sleep eyes, squeeker, nurser, marked Schildkrot, Germany, 1958, mold #63, 12″*	80.00	100.00	75.00
☐ **Gret,** *vinyl, sleep eyes (blue), blonde hair, marked Turtle, Schildkrot, Germany, 40, made in 1963, 14⅞″*	13.00	17.00	12.00

SCHMID

	Current Price Range		Prior Year Average
☐ **Clown,** *musical, cloth, brown yarn hair, red and white clown outfit with polka dots, plays "Send In The Clowns," marked 286-009, 10"*	30.00	40.00	30.00
☐ **Duck,** *musical, cloth, yellow fur, pink checkered bonnet, plays "Raindrops," marked 286-005, 8½"*	30.00	40.00	30.00
☐ **Nurse,** *musical, cloth, yellow yarn hair, white dress and nurse's cap, plays "Spoonful Of Sugar," marked 286-008, 8½"*	30.00	40.00	30.00
☐ **Tennis Player,** *musical, cloth, brown yarn hair, holds small cloth tennis racquet, plays "It's A Small World," marked 286-001, 8½"*	30.00	40.00	30.00

BRUNO SCHMIDT

☐ **Baby,** *bisque head, five piece composition body, short black wig, blue flirty eyes, long layette gown, lacy bonnet, 26"*	400.00	500.00	450.00
☐ **Character Doll,** *bisque head, ball-jointed body, human hair wig, brown sleep eyes, pierced ears, corduroy print dress, 20"*	500.00	550.00	515.00

FRANZ SCHMIDT

☐ **Baby,** *character, composition baby body, molded head, brown set eyes, breather, long gown, 27" length, 18½ head circumference*	1250.00	1375.00	1275.00
☐ **Bisque Socket Head,** *on jointed French composition body, straight wrists, brown sleep eyes, closed mouth with white space between lips and red accent lines, plump face, light brown mohair wig, red velvet dress and straw bonnet, possibly Schmitt, marks: 8, 15"*	1200.00	1500.00	1100.00
☐ **Little Lord Fauntleroy,** *solid dome head, ball-jointed body, sleep blue eyes, black velvet suit, marked 1272/282, 14"*	500.00	525.00	515.00

SCHOENAU & HOFFMEISTER

Bisque Head,
kid body,
c. 1880, 16″
$265.00-$325.00

Bisque Head,
composition body,
c. 1900, 14″
$450.00-$600.00

	Current Price Range		Prior Year Average
☐ **Baby,** *character, bisque head, five-piece composition body, blue sleep eyes, blonde mohair wig, open mouth, original christening gown, 14"*	450.00	600.00	450.00
☐ **Bisque Head,** *ball-jointed composition body, brown set eyes auburn wig, old white dress, 36½"*	1200.00	1300.00	1200.00
☐ **Bisque Head,** *jointed body, red mohair wig, brown sleep eyes, dark green watered taffeta dress and hat, 19"*	450.00	500.00	460.00
☐ **Bisque Head,** *kid body, jointed, blonde wig, sleep eyes, navy and violet dress, biege lace trim, marked "Germany S.H. 1800 '/0,' 1880, 16"*	265.00	325.00	275.00
☐ **Bisque Head,** *wooden body, original thick blonde wig, large wide eyed set brown eyes, four porcelain teeth, SPBH 5800, 24½"*	380.00	420.00	395.00
☐ **Bisque Socket Head,** *on jointed composition body, straight wrists, hands, and torso brown sleep eyes, brown human hair wig, open mouth with four porcelain teeth, white dotted Swiss low waisted dress trimmed with pink satin ribbon, marks: 4500 SH PB Boywithin star, 21"*	325.00	400.00	325.00
☐ **Toddler,** *bisque head, jointed composition toddler body, original blonde mohair wig, original lashes, old outfit, 169 P & B, 15"*	575.00	675.00	575.00
☐ **Child Doll,** *bisque head, ball-jointed composition body, black wig in a stylish bun, black sleep eyes, open smiling mouth, chinize gown with black lace cape, 26"*	350.00	400.00	375.00
☐ **Hanna Baby,** *brown mohair wig, brown sleep eyes, open mouth, two upper teeth, chemise, pink skirt*	400.00	500.00	425.00

SCHOENHUT

When Albert Schoenhut arrived in America from Wurttenberg Gernamy at the age of 17, he was already an accomplished wood carver. The Schoenhut family in Germany had been wood carvers for generations. Albert continued this family tradition, teaching the trade to his six sons and, in the 1870's, the Schoenhut family opened a toy factory in Philadelphia, Pennsylvania. However, it was not until 1911 that he began to market his unique all wood dolls. These first Schoenhut dolls had swivel necks, spring jointed bodies with a hole in the bottom of each foot which permitted the use of a stand for display purposes.

When Albert Schoenhut died in 1912, his sons carried on the Schoenhut doll and toy business. In 1913, Albert's oldest son designed a bent-limb baby and or toddler doll, and in the 1920's a less expensive elastic jointed doll was introduced into production. Before it ceased operation in the 1930's, Schoenhut also marketed a fully jointed, all composition doll.

	Current Price Range		Prior Year Average
☐ **Acrobat,** *wooden toy man, hinged at hips, tall molded red fez and tassel, goatee and moustache, two-piece brown patterned cotton suit, 7″*	**60.00**	**70.00**	**63.00**
☐ **Baby,** *all wood, molded wooden head, doweled bent limb wooden body, painted blue eyes, open/closed moth, 12″*	**350.00**	**450.00**	**350.00**
☐ **Baby,** *bent limb, blonde skin wig, closed mouth, 11″*	**350.00**	**400.00**	**365.00**
☐ **Baby Character,** *wooden head, jointed wooden body, brown intaglio eyes, original wig, pouty mouth, original clothes and shoes, 21″*	**1200.00**	**1300.00**	**1200.00**

Baby,
all wood,
c. 1911, 12″
$300.00-$400.00

	Current Price Range		Prior Year Average
☐ **Baby,** *wooden construction carved features, ball-joint body, painted eyes, open mouth, layette suit with bonnet, c. 1911, 12"*	300.00	400.00	325.00
☐ **Boy,** *carved wooden head and spring jointed wood body, painted brown eyes, with blonde wig, two-piece black velvet suit and white shirt, paint peeling across face, marks: Schoenhut Doll Pat. Jan. 17'11, USA, 14"*	95.00	100.00	200.00
☐ **Boy,** *sombre face, blonde wig, sailor suit, 16"*	350.00	400.00	365.00
☐ **Boy,** *spring jointed, bald, painted blue eyes, partially open mouth*	400.00	450.00	410.00
☐ **Boy,** *wooden, blue painted eyes, closed pouty mouth, striped woolen suit, marked head and marked incised body*	550.00	650.00	550.00
☐ **Circus Clown,** *wooden, striped cotton suit in green, pink, and white, large red feet, 8"*	90.00	100.00	92.00
☐ **Dolly Face,** *brown mohair wig, 22"*	275.00	325.00	295.00
☐ **Dolly Face,** *red pigtail mohair wig, sticker, 17"*	225.00	275.00	240.00
☐ **Dolly Face,** *15½"*	400.00	450.00	420.00
☐ **Girl,** *all-wood, jointed wooden body, blue intaglio eyes, brown wig, dressed in sailor suit, 16"*	625.00	725.00	600.00
☐ **Girl,** *character, wooden head, jointed wooden body, pouty, brown wig, painted features, original clothes, 16"*	900.00	1000.00	950.00
☐ **Girl,** *molded brown pulled over ears and tied in back with molded blue ribbon, fully jointed wooden body, painted blue eyes, pink gingham dress, 16"*	975.00	1175.00	900.00
☐ **Girl,** *sombre face, blonde wig, 15"*	350.00	400.00	360.00
☐ **Lady Bareback Rider,** *bisque head, painted blue eyes, brown hair, pink and green outfit, 7½"*	425.00	475.00	440.00
☐ **Pouty,** *wooden head on spring jointed wooden body, painted blue intaglio eyes, new blonde human hair wig, wearing pink checked pinafore over white lace trimmed blouse, nose rub, discreet retouching of face, marks: oval label reads "Schoenhut Doll, Pat. Jan. 17th, 1911 U.S.A., 14"*	275.00	300.00	270.00
☐ **Rolly Dollys,** *clown, 9"*	100.00	150.00	120.00
☐ **Rolly Dollys,** *policeman, 7"*	90.00	110.00	98.00
☐ **Toddler,** *brown, mohair wig, painted eyes, partially open mouth, 11"*	350.00	450.00	365.00
☐ **Walker,** *wooden head, jointed wooden five piece body, painted blue eyes, blonde mohair wig, open/closed mouth, sailor suit, paper label*	400.00	575.00	425.00

Item	Current Price Range		Prior Year Average
☐ **Walker,** *wooden, original mohair wig, blue painted eyes, closed pouty mouth, walker body, cute sailor suite, marked head and body, 16½″*	695.00	850.00	650.00
☐ **Walker,** *wood, spring jointed, carved head, blue ribbon headband with bow in back, brown intaglio eyes, Schoenhut stick in back, original sailor suit, underwear and shoes, 14″*	1500.00	1700.00	1450.00

SCHULTE

Item	Current Price Range		Prior Year Average
☐ **Turtle Girl,** *celluloid head, bisque hands, cloth body, brown sleep eyes, blue stripe print dress with hat, 23″*	275.00	325.00	300.00

SCHWAB & COMPANY

Item	Current Price Range		Prior Year Average
☐ **Lissy O,** *lady, bisque shoulder head and arms, oil cloth hinged body, brown glued on wig, human hair, blown glass blue eyes, open mouth with four teeth, long blue lace with blue velvet sleeves and border on hem of dress, full antique off white lace collar, matching bonnet in blue velvet, feather, marked Lissy-O, made in Germany (early 1900's), 27″*	335.00	365.00	340.00

SEARS ROEBUCK & CO.

Item	Current Price Range		Prior Year Average
☐ **Dennis The Menace,** *promotion doll, vinyl and cloth, in original box, c. 1967*	60.00	70.00	65.00
☐ **Grandpa,** *cloth, unmarked on doll, sold originally with a tag reading Joyce-Miller Original, Copyright Sears Roebuck & Co., believed to date from the late 1960's, 16″*	22.00	28.00	22.00

SEBINO

Item	Current Price Range		Prior Year Average
☐ **Ciondolina,** *vinyl head, cloth body, plastic limbs, painted eyes (black), mop-type hair (reddish), marked: Sebino, Made in Italy, made in 1975, 10″*	8.00	11.00	8.00

	Current Price Range		Prior Year Average
☐ **Cosetta,** *vinyl head, cloth body, vinyl hands, black hair, painted eyes, marked: Sebino, Made in Italy, made in 1975, 17"*	11.00	14.00	11.00
☐ **Dudu,** *vinyl head, vinyl body and limbs, sleep eyes, tongue moves in and out, marked: 143, Sebino, Made in Italy, made in 1975, 14"*	48.00	60.00	47.00
☐ **Melita,** *plastic, black hair attached by adhesive, molded and painted features, marked: Sebino, Made in Italy, made in 1971, 12½"*	2.00	3.00	2.00

S.F.B.J.

The initials S.F.B.J. stand for Société Française de Bébés et Jouets. This society was organized in 1899 by the leading dollmakers of France and was headed by Herr Fleischmann of Fleischmann and Blodel. Jumeau, Rabery and Delphieu, Bru, Danel and Cie, and Jullien were among the prominent members of this prestigious group.

This society produced some of the most highly prized dolls sought by collectors to this day. Their character dolls with bisque heads on composition bodies are in great demand. These dolls are marked S.F.B.J. and generally have a mold number in the 200's.

The Société Francaise de Bébés et Jouets was active until the 1950's when it finally disbanded after more than 50 years of production.

☐ **Baby,** *character, bisque head, jointed composition and wooden toddler body, blue sleep eyes, brown human hair wig, pouty closed mouth, antique lace dress, marks: 21 S.F.B.J. 252 Paris 12, 28"*	7000.00	8000.00	7000.00
☐ **Bébé,** *bisque head, ball-jointed composition, long dark curls, brown sleep eyes, pierced ears, velvet and eyelet day dress, wide rim satin hat, 22"*	475.00	500.00	485.00
☐ **Bébé,** *bisque head, jointed wood and composition body, blue paperweight eyes, brown human hair wig, open mouth, pierced ears, green silk dress trimmed in black lace with black velvet hat, 18"*	750.00	1000.00	700.00
☐ **Bébé Jumeau Type,** *bisque head, composition jointed body, blue set eyes, French human hair wig, pink dress and hat, 23"*	850.00	975.00	875.00
☐ **Bisque,** *domed head, composition ball-jointed body, brown jewel eyes, open/closed mouth, mold number 226, 14"*	1000.00	1500.00	1200.00

	Current Price Range		Prior Year Average
☐ **Bisque,** *French ball-jointed body, human hair wig, blue flirty sleep eyes, eyelashes, open mouth, pierced ears, walker, rose satin costume, hat to match, plume decoration on hat, 23″*	2000.00	2600.00	2000.00
☐ **Bisque,** *French ball-jointed body, human hair wig, blue sleep eyes, movable tongue, open mouth, original white costume, marked: SFBJ 251, 13″*	1750.00	1900.00	1750.00
☐ **Bisque,** *swivel neck, jointed shoulders, hips, and neck, brown sleep eyes, closed mouth, brown mohair wig, brown shoe with pompoms, 5¾″*	250.00	300.00	260.00
☐ **Bisque Head,** *composition body, human hair wig, blue flirty sleep eyes, with lashes, pierced ears, rose satin costume with plumed hat*	2200.00	2300.00	2250.00

Bisque Head,
composition body,
c. 1890, 25″
$700.00-$750.00

	Current Price Range		Prior Year Average
☐ **Bisque Head,** *composition jointed body, blue sleep eyes, French human hair wig, old costume, 29"*	1850.00	1950.00	1795.00
☐ **Bisque Head,** *composition ball-jointed body, human hair wig, blue sleep eyes with human hair lashes, open mouth, red and white flowered dress with hat, marked: 251, 20"*	2000.00	2200.00	2050.00
☐ **Bisque Head,** *French ball-jointed body, human hair wig, blue sleep eyes, open mouth, movable tongue, light blue dress and hat, 13"*	1800.00	2000.00	1850.00
☐ **Bisque Head,** *jointed composition body, human hair wig, paperweight eyes, pink and white gingham dress, marked: SH1009, c. 1890, 25"*	700.00	750.00	725.00
☐ **Bisque Head,** *long blonde human hair wig, sleep eyes with eyelashes, open mouth with teeth, original costume, 10½"*	400.00	450.00	400.00
☐ **Bisque Socket Head,** *jointed composition body, blue set eyes, open mouth with four molded teeth, brown wig, pierced ears, original pale yellow silk dress trimmed with green ribbon and gold braid, wearing a quilted feather bonnet, one finger reglued, marks: France S.F.B.J. 301 Paris, red stamp, Tête Jumeau Body, blue stamp, Bébé Jumeau, Bte S.G.D.G. deposé, 27"*	1300.00	1400.00	1100.00
☐ **Bisque Socket Head,** *jointed composition body, blue spiraled set eyes, auburn human hair wig styled in ringlets, open mouth with molded teeth, rosy cheeks, pale peach dress with smocking, ruffled hem, peplum back, beige grosgrain ribbon, delightful open bell sleeves, matching bonnet, marks: 24 S.F.B.J. 60 Paris 4, body, blue and red round label reads Fabrication Française, Paris S.F.B.J., 20"*	575.00	625.00	500.00
☐ **Bisque Socket Head,** *jointed composition body, brown sleep eyes, brown human hair wig styled in ringlets, open mouth with molded teeth, painted upper and lower lashes, pink striped lace trimmed dress, marks: S.F.B.J. 60 Paris 2/0, 16"*	600.00	675.00	550.00
☐ **Boy,** *bisque composition jointed body, brown jewel glass eyes, open closed mouth with two teeth, inoperative voice box, marked: No. 235, 20"*	2400.00	2600.00	2300.00

	Current Price Range		Prior Year Average
☐ **Boy,** *character, bisque eyes, jointed composition body, blue paperweight eyes, brown wig, closed mouth, mark: S.F.B.J. 239 Paris Poulbot, 14″*	6000.00	7500.00	5500.00
☐ **Boy,** *character, bisque head, jointed French composition body, brown paperweight eyes, molded hair, open mouth, old clothes, 18″*	1200.00	1500.00	950.00
☐ **Boy,** *paper mâché, blonde wig, blue glass eyes, alsace clothing, 13″*	100.00	150.00	120.00
☐ **Character Boy,** *bisque head, composition body, jeweled eyes, open mouth with inset teeth, formal dress, corduroy tam with tassel, marked: 235*	800.00	1000.00	950.00

Character Boy,
bisque and composition,
marked 235
$2400.00-$2600.00

	Current Price Range		Prior Year Average
□ **Character Boy,** *solid dome bisque socket head, jointed composition French body, brown paperweight eyes, molded and brushed stroked brown hair, open smiling mouth with molded bisque upper teeth, deep facial modeling, S.F.B.J. French Characters by Marlowe Cooper, two-piece sailor type outfit marked: 227, 19½″*	1850.00	1950.00	1750.00
□ **Character Girl,** *bisque head, composition ball-jointed body, human hair wig, blue paperweight eyes, open mouth with teeth, marked: 235*	800.00	900.00	825.00
□ **Character Toddler,** *bisque socket head, brown sleep eyes, real upper lashes, dark brown wig, jointed toddler body, laughing open/closed mouth with molded upper teeth, pink silk smocked dress, pink bonnet, marked: S.F.B.J. 236, Paris, 18″*	1400.00	1500.00	1450.00
□ **Child,** *bisque head, jointed composition body, brown sleep eyes, brown wig, open mouth, 24″*	225.00	325.00	200.00
□ **Child,** *bisque head, wood and composition body, short brown wig, brown sleep eyes, pierced ears and open mouth, brown tailored suit, 21″*	300.00	350.00	325.00
□ **Child,** *character, bisque head, jointed French composition body, blue sleep eyes, blonde wig, open mouth, original costume, hat, and shoes, 19″*	800.00	975.00	850.00
□ **Girl,** *jointed, brown vinyl bru wig, brown sleep eyes, open mouth with upper teeth, crocheted dress, 10″*	500.00	600.00	525.00
□ **Girl,** *paper mâché, blonde wig, blue glass eyes, alsace clothes, 12½″*	100.00	150.00	120.00
□ **Laughing Boy In Baseball Suit,** *bisque head, jointed composition body, wig, original costume, No. 256*	2300.00	3000.00	2500.00
□ **Fashion,** *French, bisque head, jointed wood and composition body, stationary brown eyes, blonde wig, open mouth, pierced ears, 27″*	725.00	1200.00	750.00
□ **French Character,** *composition, wood, molded brown hair, stationary black eyes, open mouth, four upper teeth, soldier costume, mold, No. 237, 17″*	1200.00	1900.00	1250.00
□ **Parisian Doll,** *bisque head, French ball-jointed body, human hair wig, brown paperweight eyes, pierced ears, open mouth, taffeta dress and hat, marked: 301*	2000.00	2250.00	2050.00

	Current Price Range		Prior Year Average
☐ **Toddler,** *bisque head, French ball-jointed body, human hair wig, blue sleep eyes, open mouth, yellow and white checkered dress with hat, marked: 251, 13″*	2600.00	3000.00	2650.00
☐ **Toddler,** *brown hair, blue eyes, jointed body, sailor suit, mold, No. 251, 15½″*	1000.00	1500.00	1200.00
☐ **Toddler,** *character, bisque head, ball-jointed wood and composition body, blue sleep eyes, brown wig, open/closed mouth, two teeth, 18″*	2200.00	2400.00	2100.00

SHACKMAN

☐ **Amy From Little Women,** *bisque head, bisque forearms, legs, cloth body, blonde hair, blue eyes, pink hair bow, long pink dress, pink lace trim, two full slips, camisole, lace trimmed pantaloons, painted on boots, 18″*	70.00	80.00	75.00
☐ **Beth From Little Women,** *bisque shoulder head, arms, legs, cloth body, light brown molded hair with braids going around head, blue eyes, long yellow and white checked dress, ruffled trim at hem, white high necked collar, 18th century styling, matching full slip, pantaloons, painted on high boots, 18″*	70.00	80.00	75.00
☐ **Bye-Low Baby,** *bisque head, hands, feet, cloth body, light blue christening gown with white lace and ribbon trim, fancy matching bonnet, 13″*	70.00	80.00	70.00
☐ **Jo From Little Women,** *bisque shoulder head, arms and legs, cloth body, black molded hair, blue eyes, long red dress, full circle sleeves, lace trim, full slip, pantaloons, painted on high boots, 18″*	70.00	80.00	75.00
☐ **Mannikin,** *bisque head, all wood body, jointed at shoulders, thighs and knees, molded hair, painted eyes, represents an adult woman with fashionable coiffure, sold without clothing, made in Japan, dated 1964, the body is a reproduction of the "penny wooden" style of antique times, 9″*	7.00	9.00	7.00
☐ **Skeetle,** *all bisque, continuous one-piece construction except for arms (jointed at shoulders, can be moved up and down), painted eyes, molded and painted hair, marked Copyright Shackman, Made in Japan, box carries the date 1972, 5″*	8.00	10.00	8.00

SHANNON INDUSTRIES

	Current Price Range		Prior Year Average
☐ **Erin,** *vinyl head, vinyl arms, plastic legs, plastic body, rooted reddish-brunette hair, sleep eyes, wears short dress with kerchief tied over head, 14″*	8.00	10.00	8.00
Note: Made in Ireland, chiefly for sale to tourists to that country rather than for export.			

J.B. SHEPPARD AND COMPANY

☐ **Philadelphia Baby,** *all cloth, molded treated head, arms and legs, molded painted facial features and hair, molded ears, old dress, 21″*	800.00	1000.00	800.00

SHIMMEL

☐ **Betty Boop,** *plastic/vinyl, molded and painted features, marked King Features Syndicate, Inc., made by Shimmel under license from King Features Syndicate (Betty Boop was originally a comic strip), made in 1976, 9″*	10.00	14.00	9.00

SHINDANA

☐ **Baby Janie,** *black, plastic/vinyl, black hair (rooted), painted eyes, nursing mouth, marked Div. of Operation Bootstrap, made in 1968, 13″*	22.00	28.00	17.00
☐ **Li'l Soul,** *black, printed cloth, yarn hair (black), arms spread apart, wearing a shirt printed with various slogans such as "Right On," "Learn Baby Learn," etc., marked 1970 Shindana Toys, 9½″*	10.00	14.00	8.00
☐ **Flip Wilson/Geraldine,** *(two-sided doll), black, talker, printed cloth, one side pictures comic Flip Wilson as himself, the other as "Geraldine," marked 1970, Street Corner Productions, 16″*	42.00	53.00	36.00
☐ **Marla Gibbs,** *black vinyl, jointed, 15″*	10.00	15.00	10.00
☐ **O.J. Simpson,** *boxed with accessories, action figure, 9½″*	15.00	25.00	13.00

SIDNEY SHELDON PRODUCTIONS

	Current Price Range		Prior Year Average
☐ **I Dream Of Jeannie,** *(Barbara Eden), plastic/vinyl, blue sleep eyes, blonde rooted hair, closed mouth, dressed in the "Jeannie" costume from the popular TV series of the 1960's (still being shown in syndication), marked 4, 1966, Libby, box marked Sidney Sheldon Productions, Sidney Sheldon was producer of the TV show, 20"*	23.00	29.00	22.00

SIMON & HALBIG

The German firm of Simon & Halbig produced dolls of the highest caliber at their Grafenheim Thuringia factory, which operated continuously from the 1870's through 1935. During this period they produced thousands of bisque heads of every kind which were used in the production of French, German and American dolls. The doll parts were fired in the factory kilns and then turned over to the doll making cottage industry of Thuringia for painting and assembly. Everyone contributed to the completion of the dolls, even small children. Each person had their own specialty such as painting eyebrows, eyelashes, or lips.

Simon & Halbig also produced complete dolls for their own firm as well as Kammer and Reinhardt, Jumeau, C.M. Bergmann, Fleischmann and Blodel, George Borgfeldt and Company and many more. In 1890 they introduced the moveable eye which had a tremendous impact on the doll industry of the day.

"S & H" also manufactured thousands of dolls and doll heads of lesser quality as it was their goal to provide dolls in every price range in order to corner a lions share of the market.

☐ **American Indian Character Doll,** *bisque head, wooden ball-jointed body, painted eyes, mohair long black wig, original costume, 22"*	5000.00	6000.00	3000.00
☐ **Baby,** *bisque head, composition body, blue sleep eyes, open mouth, handmade christening dress, marked 1294 No. 60, 24"*	1775.00	1950.00	1750.00
☐ **Baby,** *bisque head, five piece composition body, blonde human hair wig with curls, blue sleep eyes, blue sweater and pantaloons, 24"*	350.00	400.00	360.00
☐ **Baby,** *bisque head, jointed composition body, blue sleep eyes, blonde French human hair wig, 33" tall, 16½" head circumference*	1100.00	1200.00	1050.00
☐ **Baby,** *character, bisque head composition bent-limb toddler body, sleep blue eyes, wig, closed mouth, old clothes, extremely rare, incised 1428-6, 13"*	1450.00	1850.00	1650.00

	Current Price Range		Prior Year Average
☐ **Baby,** *composition, jointed, open mouth, four teeth, brown sleep eyes, silk dress, 21″*	475.00	525.00	485.00
☐ **Baby,** *jointed composition body, brown eyes, lashes, strawberry-blonde wig, pink baby dress, mold number 914, 29″*	600.00	650.00	620.00
☐ **Bisque,** *ball-jointed body, black skin, brown wig, brown paperweight eyes, open mouth, pierced ears, print dress, bonnet, 13″*	1100.00	1200.00	1150.00
☐ **Bisque,** *cloth body, bisque arms, cloth feet, set blue glass eyes, blonde mohair wig, brown skirt, velvet vest, lace trim, black shoes, mold number 1010, 11″*	425.00	475.00	430.00
☐ **Bisque,** *composition, ball-jointed, blonde mohair wig, brown eyes, raised eyebrows, marked with manufacture's name, 23″*	500.00	550.00	510.00
☐ **Bisque,** *composition body, ball-jointed, blue sleep eyes, marked Germany*	500.00	525.00	500.00
☐ **Bisque,** *five-piece body, blue sleep eyes, blonde human hair, open mouth, pierced ears, brown and black striped silk dress with lace trim, 10″*	325.00	375.00	340.00
☐ **Bisque,** *jointed composition body, blue eyes, blue satin dress and bonnet, 29½″*	650.00	700.00	660.00
☐ **Bisque,** *jointed composition body, bronze-brown eyes, light brown wig, blue and pink cotton print dress with lace ecru trim, 29″*	550.00	600.00	570.00
☐ **Bisque,** *jointed composition body, brown stationary eyes, brown wig, dotted Swiss white dress, 24″*	350.00	400.00	370.00
☐ **Bisque,** *jointed composition body, brown eyes, brown wig, pink and green plaid dress, pink hair bow, mark at back of head, 22″*	275.00	325.00	300.00
☐ **Bisque,** *jointed composition body, brown eyes, yellow curls, mint green-taffeta with ecru lace, matching hat, 25″*	450.00	500.00	470.00
☐ **Bisque,** *original blonde ringlet wig, gray sleep eyes with original lashes, original underwear and blue dotted dress with lace collar and cuffs, waistband ties in back, patterned socks and black leather shoes, incised KR Simon Halbig, 70 with W on forehead*	800.00	900.00	825.00
☐ **Bisque,** *original stamped ball-jointed body, original blonde wig, threaded sleep eyes with original wax, Simon Halbig 570, 22″*	260.00	290.00	270.00
☐ **Bisque,** *wig, original clothes, S And H 1160, 6″*	140.00	160.00	130.00
☐ **Bisque Head,** *ball-jointed body, brown set eyes, open mouth, brown checkered suit and straw hat, marked 66, 24″*	975.00	1100.00	1000.00

Bisque Head,
composition body,
c. 1910, 26″
$1000.00-$1100.00

	Current Price Range		Prior Year Average
☐ **Bisque Head,** *ball-jointed body, human hair wig, blue sleep eyes, original lace clothes, marked K and R, 34″*	1000.00	1200.00	1050.00
☐ **Bisque Head,** *ball-jointed body with straight wrists of wood and composition, fine hairline to forehead, brown paperweight eyes, pierced ears, two upper and lower square cut teeth, old clothes and shoes, 949, 584, 15″*	320.00	345.00	330.00
☐ **Bisque Head,** *ball-jointed composition body, blonde curly wig, green glass eyes, open mouth, tailored dress, 34″*	450.00	500.00	475.00
☐ **Bisque Head,** *ball-jointed composition body, human hair wig, blue sleep eyes, blue taffeta with blue velvet over skirt and hat, marked with star, 21″*	485.00	525.00	500.00
☐ **Bisque Head,** *ball-jointed composition body, human hair wig, brown sleep eyes, pierced ears, green and white lace dress, marked 1249, 24″*	1000.00	1100.00	1050.00

	Current Price Range		Prior Year Average
☐ **Bisque Head,** *cloth body, human hair wig, brown glass eyes, ecru dress, marked 1160/9/0, 6½″*	465.00	500.00	475.00
☐ **Bisque Head,** *cloth body with bisque arms and legs, brown glass eyes, dress and slippers, Little Women series, marked 1160, 7″*	400.00	500.00	425.00
☐ **Bisque Head,** *composition body, blonde wig, blue sleep eyes, white lace christening gown, c. 1900, 14″*	250.00	300.00	265.00
☐ **Bisque Head,** *composition body, brown stationery eyes, open mouth, pierced ears, dressed, marked: K ☆ R, 36″*	1525.00	1675.00	1500.00
☐ **Bisque Head,** *composition body, light brown human hair, sleep brown eyes, open mouth, pierced ears, authentic clothing, white batiste bonnet dress, coat, hand embroidered, 32″*	1255.00	1375.00	1250.00
☐ **Bisque Head,** *composition jointed body, blue sleep eyes, brown wig, closed mouth, antique clothes, marked: K ☆ R Simon & Halbig, 117″*	2800.00	3200.00	2850.00
☐ **Bisque Head,** *composition and wood, jonted body, sleep eyes, open mouth, pierced ears number 1079, 9″*	250.00	325.00	220.00
☐ **Bisque Head,** *jointed body, light blonde mohair wig, blue sleep eyes, molded brows, biege viole dress and hat with maroon trim brown leather shorts, marked Heinrick Handweick, 1900, 30″*	1200.00	1300.00	1250.00
☐ **Bisque Head,** *jointed body, brown sleep eyes, pierced ears, antique white dress and straw hat, marked 1249 Santa mold, c. 1910, 26″*	1000.00	1100.00	1050.00
☐ **Bisque Head,** *jointed body, upswept wig, human hair lashes on sleep eyes, slim waisted brown and blue two-piece suit, marked 1159, 1910, 16″*	1400.00	1600.00	1350.00
☐ **Bisque Head,** *jointed body with swivel neck, brown curly wig, brown sleep eyes, pierced ears, brown velvet gown and ruffled hat, 22″*	474.00	500.00	485.00
☐ **Bisque Head,** *jointed composition body, blue sleep eyes, blonde human hair wig, white dress, number 1079, 33″*	950.00	1150.00	975.00
☐ **Bisque Head,** *jointed composition body, brown sleep eyes, original lashes, brown French human hair wig, lace dress number 1078, 33″*	950.00	1100.00	975.00
☐ **Bisque Head,** *jointed composition body, human hair wig, brown sleep eyes, pierced ears, high forehead, antique costume, number 1009 23″*	650.00	700.00	625.00

Bisque Head,
wood body, 18″
$400.00-$500.00

	Current Price Range		Prior Year Average
☐ **Bisque Head,** *kid body, bisque arms and legs, blonde wig, paperweight eyes, pierced ears, blue taffetta wig, marked SH 950, 19″* .	1000.00	1200.00	1050.00
☐ **Bisque Head,** *kid body with bisque hands and feet, blue paperweight eyes, open mouth, wine colored striped silk dress, 19″* .	1000.00	1100.00	1050.00
☐ **Bisque Head,** *Schmitt type body, biege brown human hair wig, open/closed mouth, 20″*	925.00	975.00	900.00
☐ **Bisque Head,** *sleep eyes, open mouth, four teeth*	275.00	325.00	240.00
☐ **Bisque Shoulder Head,** *cloth body with bisque arms, blue flirty staring eyes, yoke top gown eith eyelet trim, 20½″*	275.00	300.00	280.00

	Current Price Range		Prior Year Average
☐ **Bisque Shoulder Head,** *kid body with composition hands, blonde short curly wig, brown threaded eyes, peach, chintze old fashioned dress, 23½"*	350.00	400.00	375.00
☐ **Bisque Socket Head,** *ball-jointed body, brown human hair wig, brown blown glass eyes, open mouth, four teeth, blue velvet dress with lace and embroidered flowers, real white fur hat with matching, muff, head marked Simon Helbig, body marked Heinick Handwerck, number 4, 24"*	475.00	525.00	485.00
☐ **Black Baby,** *wig, stationary brown eyes, open mouth, six teeth, 19"*	450.00	500.00	450.00
☐ **Black Bisque Head,** *jointed composition body, mulatto coloring, brown sleep eyes, curly black human hair wig, pierced ears, 13½"*	750.00	825.00	750.00
☐ **Black Child,** *black fired-in-bisque head, ball-jointed black composition body, brown sleep eyes, brown curly short wig, pierced ears, open mouth, cream silk dress, mark S 10 H 739 Dep, 18"*	425.00	525.00	425.00
☐ **Black Doll,** *bisque head, composition ball-jointed body, black human hair wig, black set eyes, red and white check dress with hat, 14"*	520.00	600.00	525.00
☐ **Black Fired In Bisque Head,** *composition jointed body, brown glass set eyes, open mouth, pierced ears, original clothes*	3500.00	4500.00	3650.00
☐ **Boy,** *character, bisque head, jointed composition body, brown eyes, blonde human hair wig, open mouth with two upper teeth, original clothes, number 1279, 15"*	1600.00	1750.00	1650.00
☐ **Character,** *bisque shoulder head, pin-jointed pink-tinted kid body, composition arms with joints at elbow and wrists, original blonde mohair wig, brown sleep eyes, open mouth with four porcelain teeth, marks: S And H 1260 Dep, Germany 4, 14"*	400.00	500.00	400.00
☐ **Character,** *bisque socket head, blue set eyes, open mouth with two molded teeth, light brown mohair wig, molded brown heeled shoes, painted white socks, five piece jointed composition body, detailed on hands and feet, marks: 1078, Simon And Halbig, S And H Germany 3/0, 8½"*	125.00	140.00	130.00
☐ **Bisque Socket Head,** *jointed composition body, brown set eyes, real upper lashes, dark blonde human hair wig, open mouth with four teeth, pierced ears, two-piece red*			

	Current Price Range		Prior Year Average
velvet outfit accented with white mink, white mink hat and muff, white high button boots, marks: Germany, Henrich Handwerck, Simon And Halibig, 23"	400.00	500.00	400.00
☐ **Child,** *bisque head ball-jointed composition body, long blonde human hair wig with bangs, brown flirty eyes, net overskirt on long dress, bow trim, 41"*	350.00	400.00	375.00
☐ **Child,** *bisque head, ball-jointed composition body, human hair blonde wig, brown sleep eyes, open mouth with four teeth, number 540, 21"*	400.00	440.00	420.00
☐ **Child,** *bisque head, ball-jointed composition body, short black wig, brown sleep eyes, closed mouth buster brown suit, 20½"*	200.00	300.00	225.00
☐ **Child,** *bisque head, ball-jointed composition body, straight blonde wig, blue sleep eyes, short dotted swiss dress, matching bonnet, kid boots, 22"*	350.00	400.00	375.00
☐ **Child,** *bisque head, composition and wood body, blue sleep eyes, brown human hair wig, open mouth, lovely old dress, 16"*	375.00	500.00	375.00
☐ **Clown,** *bisque, jointed composition body, painted clown face, wig, open mouth, original clown costume and hat, 26"*	1200.00	1300.00	1200.00
☐ **Composition,** *jointed, painted, brown sleep eyes, open mouth, four teeth*	450.00	500.0	450.00
☐ **Character,** *bisque head, composition body, human hair wig, blue flirty eyes, lovely white dress, number 1039, 19"*	650.00	750.00	625.00
☐ **Character,** *bisque head, jonted composition body, flirty blue eyes, original lashes, blonde French human hair wig, antique clothes, 22"*	875.00	975.00	850.00
☐ **Character Baby,** *bisque head, jointed body, red human hair wig, sleep eyes, smiling, marked 116, 15"*	2000.00	2250.00	2100.00
☐ **Character Boy,** *composition head, ball-jointed body, blue sleep eyes, wool check knicker suit, marked 126*	400.00	450.00	415.00
☐ **Character Girl,** *bisque head, ball-jointed composition body, blonde ringlet curls, green paperweight eyes, painted lashes, green silk drss, closely ruffled dress, 28"*	3000.00	3500.00	3250.00
☐ **Doll House Lady,** *cloth body, bisque arms and legs, brown glass eyes, blonde mohair wig, period costume of tan jacquard satin, wood frame under skirt, 6"*	200.00	250.00	215.00

Fashion,
bisque and composition,
c. 1910, 16″
$1400.00-$1600.00

	Current Price Range		Prior Year Average
☐ **English Lady,** *bisque head jointed body, blonde mohair wig, blue sleep eyes, molded brown, biege and maroon dress and hat, leather shoes, marked Heinrick Handwerk, 1900, 30″*	700.00	800.00	725.00
☐ **Girl,** *bisque head, composition ball-jointed body, blue set eyes, brown human hair wig, lovely white organdy dress, #1079, 22″*	425.00	550.00	450.00
☐ **Girl,** *bisque head, jointed composition body, blonde wig, blue stationary eyes, open mouth, four teeth, antique clothing, K + R Simon And Halbig 117/70*	1900.00	2000.00	1850.00
☐ **Girl,** *composition, jointed body, blonde mohair wig, dark brown sleeping eyes, open mouth, four middle upper teeth, marked Germany, 18″*	500.00	600.00	500.00
☐ **Girl,** *jointed composition body, brown hair, brown eyes, orange chemise dress, 12″*	350.00	400.00	370.00

	Current Price Range		Prior Year Average
☐ **Infant,** *bisque head, compositon jointed body, short red headed wig, brown flirty eyes, smiling open mouth, crochet bonnet, white cotton layette dress, 19″*	450.00	500.00	475.00
☐ **Ingenue,** *bisque head, ball-jointed composition body, long curly red headed wig, brown flirty eyes, 19½″*	300.00	350.00	320.00
☐ **Ingenue,** *bisque head, cloth body and and bisque hands, brown bun wig, brown sleep eyes, cotton gown with sinched waist, ruffled sleeves, 20″*	300.00	325.00	310.00
☐ **Lady Doll,** *ball-jointed body, blue paperweight eyes, black silk suit, marked 5/0, 15″*	900.00	1000.00	925.00
☐ **Lady Doll,** *bisque head, composition lady body, brown human hair wig, brown sleep eyes, open mouth, pierced ears, beautiful clothes, 19″*	1500.00	1700.00	1600.00
☐ **Little Lord Fauntleroy,** *ball-jointed body, blonde mohair wig, blue sleep eyes, black velvet suit, marked 540, 20″*	500.00	50.00	515.00
☐ **Morocean,** *bisque, ball-jointed body, wig, brown paper weight eyes, open mouth, pierced ears dressed, 13″*	1050.00	1200.00	1075.00
☐ **Oriental,** *bisque, human hair lashes, olive complexion*	1500.00	2500.00	2000.00
☐ **Sailor Boy,** *bisque head, ball-jointed composition body, blonde pageboy wig, brown set eyes, navy blue sailor suit with white piping, 20″*	400.00	500.00	425.00
☐ **Toddler,** *bisque head, five-piece composition body, blue sleep eyes, open mouth, two teeth and tongue, black velvet suit and cap, marked 121-62, 25″*	1800.00	2000.00	1900.00
☐ **Toddler,** *bisque head, five-piece composition body, pageboy style wig, blue sleep eyes, bib and pantaloons, 9½″*	300.00	400.00	350.00
☐ **Toddler,** *character, bisque head composition and wooden ball-jointed body, blue glass eyes, real lashes, blonde human hair wig, pouty mouth, c. 1915, old long gown, marks K + R Simon and Halbig, 115 A 72, 27″*	2800.00	2900.00	2700.00
☐ **Turned Head,** *blue eyes, blonde wig, 23″*	250.00	320.00	285.00
☐ **Young girl,** *Bisque shoulder head, jointed kid body, blonde chignon wig, blue sleep eyes, dotted swiss garden dress*	350.00	400.00	360.00
☐ **Walking doll,** *Bisque head, joined composition body, blue eyes, flirty, brown mohair wig, head moves from side to side as legs move, lovely old costume shoes and hat, 16″*	750.00	950.00	725.00

SIMPLICITY

	Current Price Range		Prior Year Average
☐ **Holly Hobbie,** *sew-it-yourself cloth doll, simplicity pattern #6248, 17″*	4.00	6.00	4.00

SKIPPY

	Current Price Range		Prior Year Average
☐ **Baby Ellen,** *vinyl head, cloth body, vinyl arms and legs, blonde hair (rooted), sleep eyes (blue), open mouth with two teeth, marked S1968 Skippy Doll, 21″*	9.00	12.00	8.00
☐ **Julia,** *plastic/vinyl, sleep eyes (blue), marked A Skippy Doll, 1967, 17″*	9.00	12.00	8.00

ELLA SMITH

	Current Price Range		Prior Year Average
☐ **Alabama Indestructible Doll,** *all cloth, molded oil painted head, painted features and shoes, cotton dress, 25″*	600.00	750.00	600.00

SONSCO

	Current Price Range		Prior Year Average
☐ **Bonnie Dee,** *talker, plastic/vinyl, blonde hair, sleep eyes (blue), battery operated, unmarked, made in 1973, 14″*	11.00	14.00	10.00
☐ **Lady Baseball Player,** *stockinette, posable, representing an adult woman holding a baseball bat, unmarked on doll, sold originally with a tag reading Sonsco Toys, Japan, believed to date from about 1967, 12¼″*	22.00	27.00	21.00

MAJORIE SPANGLER

	Current Price Range		Prior Year Average
☐ **Cynthia,** *vinyl, jointed, blonde pigtails, blue sleep eyes, pink dotted swiss party dress, white leotards, black patent leather shoes, 13″*	45.00	50.00	45.00
☐ **Emerald Isle Doll,** *long blue dress, bonnet, commemorative collection, c. 1980, 15″*	45.00	55.00	50.00

STAHLWOOD

	Current Price Range		Prior Year Average
☐ **Buck,** *vinyl, squeeze toy, molded and painted features, made of scented vinyl, marked Buck, Soft Standing, Scented, made in 1955, 8″*	4.00	6.00	4.00

KARL STANDFUSS

☐ **Juno,** *metal head, kid body, cloth arms and legs, painted features, pink and green floral print dress, straw bonnet with flowers, made in Germany, 18″*	50.00	100.00	70.00

STREET CORNER PRODUCTIONS

☐ **Flip Wilson/Geraldine,** *(two-sided doll), black, talker, printed cloth, one side pictures comic Flip Wilson as himself, the other as "Geraldine," marked 1970, Street Corner Productions, 16″*	42.00	53.00	36.00

STEIFF

☐ **Fireman,** *plastic face, helmet, felt clothes, c. 1960's, 12″*	137.00	168.00	135.00
☐ **Man,** *farmer, character, cloth, wig, glass eyes, large hands and feet, original costume, 20th century, 14″*	650.00	800.00	700.00
☐ **Shepherd Doll,** *velvet outfit, 8″*	25.00	35.00	30.00

STEINER

☐ **Bébé,** *bisque head, composition body, blonde shoulder length curls, blue paperweight eyes, aqua chiffon day dress with pearl detail, 22″*	3000.00	3200.00	3000.00
☐ **Bébé,** *bisque head, composition body, blue paperweight eyes, brown wig, pierced ears, closed mouth, mark, Bébé Steiner, Medaille d'Or, Paris, 17″*	2200.00	2800.00	2000.00

	Current Price Range		Prior Year Average
☐ **Bébé,** *bisque head, French ball jointed composition body, long straight blonde hair, blue paperweight eyes, velvet skirt, white silk shirt, bonnet, 18½"*	2500.00	3000.00	2950.00
☐ **Bébé,** *bisque head, French composition body, black long curly wig, brown flirty eyes, long lacy flapper dress, sandals and cap, 20"*	2000.00	2500.00	2250.00
☐ **Bébé,** *bisque head, jointed composition body, blue eyes, brown wig, pierced ears, open/closed mouth, original navy blue walking suit with red hat, 11"*	3000.00	3800.00	3000.00
☐ **Bébé,** *bisque head, Motschmann-type body, blue paperweight eyes, long blonde wig, closed mouth, pierced ears, voice box, lovely original costume bonnet and shoes, 17"*	3300.00	3600.00	3200.00
☐ **Bébé,** *bisque head, composition body, redheaded ringlet curl wig, turquoise sleep eyes, pierced ears, long ball gown, 20"*	3000.00	3500.00	3250.00
☐ **Bisque Head,** *arms, cloth body, blue paperweight eyes, brown wig, open mouth, original wine silk dress, 26"*	4000.00	5000.00	4200.00
☐ **Bisque Head,** *ball jointed composition body, human hair wig, blue googlie eyes, open mouth with teeth, pierced ears, rose taffeta costume, 18"*	2200.00	2600.00	2250.00
☐ **Bisque Head,** *composition jointed body, blue paperweight eyes, closed mouth, antique clothes, 17"*	2800.00	3000.00	2800.00
☐ **Bisque Socket Head,** *jointed composition body, straight wrists, almond shaped dark blue paperweight eyes, painted upper and lower lashes, original blonde human hair wig, closed mouth, pierced ears, brushed stroked eyebrows, mauve colored taffeta dress, matching plumed bonnet, marks, J. Steiner, Bte. S.G.D.G. Paris F 1 re A 15, body, original paper label of little girl carrying a flag reads "Le Petite Parisien, Bébé J. Steiner, Medaille D'or Paris 1889, 23"*	4200.00	4500.00	4000.00
☐ **Bisque Socket Head,** *jointed composition body, straight wrists, blue paperweight eyes, closed mouth, pierced ears, blonde mohair wig pulled softly back from face into pigtails pinned on back of head, beige silk dress with pleated hem, lapels, lace trimmed underwear, marks, Head - Steiner. Paris Fre A 5, 13"*	2200.00	2600.00	1900.00
☐ **Bisque Socket Head,** *jointed composition body, straight wrists, brown set eyes, closed*			

	Current Price Range		Prior Year Average
mouth with white space between lips and red accent lines, pierced ears, lamb's wool platinum blonde wig, blue silk two piece dress, lace overlay, matching straw bonnet, marks, Head - A 3 "Le Parisien"; body, blue stamp — Bébé Le Parisien Medaille D'or, Paris, 10½"	2000.00	2200.00	1750.00
☐ **Black Baby,** *black fired-in-bisque head, light brown cloth body, brown sleep eyes, closed mouth, 9" head circumference, 12" length*	350.00	450.00	375.00
☐ **Closed Mouth,** *brown eyes, brown hair, blue dress, 19½"*	2400.00	3000.00	2600.00
☐ **Composition Head And Body,** *blonde lambs wool wig, blue paperweight eyes, blue velvet Steiner dress, marked B.S., c. 1880, 15"*	3600.00	3800.00	3675.00
☐ **Girl,** *A series, composition ball jointed body, blue paperweight eyes, blonde hair, closed mouth, 16"*	2400.00	2800.00	2575.00
☐ **Girl,** *jointed composition body, lavender-blue paperweight eyes, yellow French curls, closed mouth, outfit and hat with pink roses, 25"*	2800.00	3400.00	3100.00
☐ **Girl,** *walker, bisque head, composition arms and legs, brown wig, blue eyes, blushed lids, open mouth with two rows of tiny teeth, key and lever mechanism working, 22"*	2500.00	2600.00	2000.00
☐ **Infant,** *bisque, celluloid hands, full cheeks, sleepy face, big dome head, fine 20" long old lace paneled christening gown and bonnet, HERM STEINER INFANT, 12"*	295.00	335.00	310.00
☐ **Infant,** *bisque head, bye-lo body, celluloid hands, blue sleep eyes, white baby dress*	400.00	450.00	410.00
☐ **Talker,** *bisque head, French ball jointed body, pull string voice box, human hair, brown sleep eyes, open mouth, pierced ears, blue French costume, marked A-15, 23"*	3000.00	3250.00	3050.00
☐ **"Le Petit Parisien,"** *bisque head, jointed composition body, blue paperweight eyes, blonde mohair wing, closed mouth, pierced ears, peach silk dress with matching hat, shoes, mark, label, "Le Petit Parisien, Bébé Steiner, Medaille d'Or, Paris, 1889," 17"*	3000.00	4000.00	3200.00
☐ **Talking Child,** *bisque head, French wood and composition jointed body, blue paperweight eyes, closed mouth, pierced ears, working mechanism, 29"*	4000.00	5000.00	3800.00
☐ **Walker,** *bisque head, jointed composition body, brown paperweight eyes, brown wig, open mouth, pierced ears, inoperative walking mechanism, 22"*	3500.00	4000.00	3500.00

	Current Price Range		Prior Year Average
☐ **Walking Doll,** *bisque head, composition body, blue glass eyes, blonde wig, open mouth, antique costume, 21"*	950.00	1400.00	1000.00

STUART

☐ **Baby's Doll,** *vinyl head, cloth body, cloth arms and legs, molded and painted hair, fixed eyes (blue), partially open mouth, marked Styled by Stuart, St. Paul, Minn., made in 1961, 8"*	6.00	8.00	5.00
☐ **Muff Doll,** *cloth mask-type face, painted, yarn hair, stuffed body, unmarked, made in 1939, 10"*	16.00	21.00	15.00

SUN RUBBER COMPANY

☐ **Amosandra,** *black, rubber, molded and painted features, molded and painted hair, nursing mouth, Amosandra was a character on the "Amos 'n Andy" radio program, marked Amosandra, Columbia Broadcasting System Inc., Designed by Ruth E. Newton, Mfg. by The Sun Rubber Co., Barberton, U.S.A., also marked with the patent numbers 2,118,682 and 2,160,739, made in 1949, 10½"*	20.00	26.00	18.00
☐ **Annie,** *squeezer, rubber, fixed eyes, molded and painted hair, marked The Sun Rubber Co., 1965, 9"*	4.00	6.00	4.00
Note: Not "Little Orphan Annie."			
☐ **Babee Bee,** *vinyl, molded and painted hair (blonde), sleep eyes (blue), nursing mouth, marked Sunbabe, Babee Bee, Ruth E. Newton, New York, NY, made in 1954, 12"*	11.00	14.00	11.00
Note: Ruth E. Newton designed a number of dolls for the Sun Rubber Company.			
☐ **Baby,** *vinyl, molded and painted hair, molded and painted features, molded diaper and shoes, painted eyes, designed by Ruth E. Newton, marked with her name and that of the Sun Rubber Co., made in 1956, 8"*	5.00	7.00	5.00
☐ **Bannister Baby,** *vinyl, molded and painted hair, sleep eyes (blue), nursing mouth, marked Constance Bannister New York, date of manufacture unknown, presumably c. 1952, 17"*	70.00	88.00	65.00

	Current Price Range		Prior Year Average
Note: Constance Bannister was a professional photographer whose photos of babies were collected into several best selling books during the 1950's.			
☐ **Betty Bows,** *rubber/vinyl, molded and painted hair, sleep eyes (blue), nursing mouth, bow in hair, marked Betty Bows, The Sun Rubber Co., made in 1953, 12"*	9.00	12.00	9.00
☐ **Chunky,** *vinyl, molded and painted hair, painted eyes, partially open mouth, molded clothing (short sun dress), marked Mfg. by The Sun Rubber Co., Barberton, Ohio, made in 1954, 8"*	5.00	7.00	5.00
Note: Chunky was designed by Ruth E. Newton.			
☐ **Dotty,** *vinyl, molded and painted features, molded and painted clothing, partially open mouth, jointed at the neck, marked Ruth E. Newton, the Sun Rubber Co., made in 1955, 8"*	4.00	6.00	4.00
☐ **Gerber Baby,** *rubber, molded and painted hair, fixed eyes, nursing mouth, bright red lips, wearing a bib marked "Gerber Baby" in scrip letters, marked: Mfg. by The Sun Rubber Co., Barberton, Ohio, made in 1956, 11"*	14.00	18.00	13.00
Note: Used as a promotional item by the Gerber Foods Company, manufacturers of baby foods.			
☐ **Little Natalia,** *rubber, molded and painted features, molded hair, open mouth with teeth, marked Little Natalia, Sun Rubber Co., date of manufacture unknown, believed to be pre-World War II, 7"*	50.00	65.00	48.00
☐ **So Wee,** *vinyl, molded and painted hair, fixed eyes (blue), open mouth, designed by Ruth Newton, marked Sunbabe, made in 1957, 10"*	7.00	10.00	7.00
☐ **Sun Dee,** *vinyl, rooted hair, sleep eyes (blue), nursing mouth, marked Sun Dee, Sun Rubber Co., 1956, Barberton, Ohio, 13"*	9.00	12.00	9.00
☐ **Tod-L-Tee,** *vinyl, molded and painted hair, fixed eyes (blue), wears sunsuit (molded), shoes and socks, marked Sun Rubber Co., 1956, 10"*	5.00	7.00	5.00

SUNSHINE

☐ **Happy,** *vinyl, brunette hair (rooted), sleep eyes, marked: c. 1964, 14"*	9.00	12.00	9.00

SUPER DOLL

	Current Price Range		Prior Year Average
☐ **Baby Debbi,** *black, vinyl head, cloth body, vinyl arms and legs, rooted hair (black), sleep eyes (brown), partially open mouth, unmarked, made in 1965, 15⅞"*	24.00	29.00	23.00
☐ **Little Debbi Eve,** *plastic/vinyl, blonde hair (rooted), sleep eyes (blue), closed smiling mouth, flower in hair, marked Super Doll, Inc., 1963, 15½"*	12.00	16.00	11.00
☐ **Melody Baby Debbi,** *music box, vinyl head, cloth body, vinyl arms and legs, blonde hair (rooted), sleep eyes (blue), partially open mouth, marked SD, made in 1965, 17¼"*	11.00	14.00	10.00

SUPERIOR

☐ **China Doll,** *painted blonde hair and blue eyes, blue wool dress, 20"*	300.00	350.00	325.00
☐ **China Doll,** *painted blonde hair and blue eyes, white lawn dress with rose trim, 20"*	300.00	325.00	310.00
☐ **Girl,** *molded blonde hair, painted blue eyes, fashion mitt hands, 15"*	125.00	175.00	130.00
☐ **Lady,** *papier mâché molded shoulder head, cloth body, kid arms, molded painted hair, painted eyes, old fashioned clothing, mark: label on shoulder head, 17"*	275.00	375.00	325.00
☐ **Papier Mâché Head And Body,** *painted eyes, white pique dress and cape, c. 1850, 32"*	600.00	700.00	650.00
☐ **Papier Mâché Head,** *molded painted hair, painted face original, lovely clothes, label, 17"*	400.00	600.00	500.00
☐ **Papier Mâché Shoulder Head,** *cloth body, molded and painted head, facial features and black hair, original cotton dress, marked: label on back "M&S Superior 2015," 24"*	325.00	375.00	325.00
☐ **Papier Mâché Shoulder Head,** *Goldsmith leather body, painted black, elaborately molded hairstyle with curls covering ears, painted facial features, blue taffeta plaid dress, 22"*	375.00	550.00	350.00

SWEDLIN

	Current Price Range		Prior Year Average
☐ **Mimi The Martian,** *vinyl head, vinyl arms, legs and body, rooted hair, painted eyes, marked J. Swedlin, Inc., 1967, Made in Japan, 4⅞"*	4.00	6.00	4.00

TECNOGIOCATTOLI

☐ **Bettina,** *vinyl head, plastic body, rooted hair, sleep eyes, strung doll made to represent an adolescent girl, made in Italy, marked Sebino, 16¼"*	14.00	18.00	13.00

TEEN

☐ **Calamity Jane,** *posable legs, marked Azark-Hamway, 12"*	4.00	6.00	4.00
☐ **Emma Peel,** *plastic/vinyl, painted eyes, representing a character from the TV program "The Avengers," marked Made in Hong Kong, presumably c. 1965, 11½"*	26.00	33.00	25.00

TERRI LEE

☐ **Benji,** *black, walker, vinyl, brown sleep eyes unmarked, date of manufacture unknown, believed to have been made in the late 1950's or early 1960's, 10"*	90.00	115.00	85.00
☐ **Connie Lynn,** *plastic, red hair, blue sleep eyes, partially open mouth, unmarked, made in 1955, 18½"*	65.00	80.00	60.00
☐ **Gene Autry,** *plastic, molded and painted, wears Gene Autry button, marked Terri Lee, Pats. Pending, date of manufacture unknown, presumably c. 1950, 16"*	225.00	275.00	220.00
☐ **Terri Lee,** *composition body, blonde wig, tin eyes, closed mouth, original clothes, 12"*	215.00	235.00	220.00
☐ **Terri Lee,** *plastic, dark hair, hairnet, two piece pink play suit, 16"*	100.00	165.00	105.00

TEXACO

	Current Price Range		Prior Year Average
☐ **Cheerleader,** *vinyl head, plastic arms, legs and body, blonde long rooted hair, painted eyes, wears sweater and short shirt with tall boots, marked 56, Hong Kong, 12″ ....* **Note: The number 56 in the marking is not a reference to 1956 but to a mold number. This doll was made in 1973 and used as part of a promotion for Texaco filling stations.**	6.00	8.00	6.00

TOGS AND DOLLS

☐ **Penny Walker,** *walker, plastic, blue sleep eyes, hair attached with adhesive, marked Pat. Pend., made in 1951, 12″ ....* **Note: Togs and Dolls was a New York City company whose manufacturing was done in Greensboro, North Carolina. They didn't make very many dolls.**	12.00	16.00	12.00

TOMY

☐ **Ricky,** *walker, vinyl head, metallic body, plastic shoes, holds bell, molded and painted hair, painted eyes, made in Japan, date of manufacture unknown, 12″ ....*	11.00	14.00	11.00
☐ **Ricky,** *plastic and tin, with vinyl arms, made in Japan, date of manufacture not known, apparently c. 1970, 12″ ....*	12.00	16.00	12.00

TONY TOY

☐ **Baby Sleep Amber,** *black, vinyl head, cloth body, vinyl arms and legs, black rooted hair, brown sleep eyes, closed mouth, marked Tony Toy, 1970, made in Hong Kong, 11″ ...* **Note: Actually made by the Uneeda Doll Company.**	14.00	18.00	13.00

TOPPER

	Current Price Range		Prior Year Average
☐ **Dawn,** *vinyl, blonde rooted hair, painted eyes, jointed at the waist, marked 11A, made in Hong Kong in 1970, 6″*	5.00	7.00	5.00

TOY INNOVATIONS LTD.

☐ **Mailman,** *cloth printed, unmarked, sold originally with a tag reading Toy Innovations Ltd., Family Friends, 15″*	3.00	5.00	3.00

TOY PRODUCT

☐ **Lil Sis,** *composition, molded and painted features, molded and painted hair, marked Lil Sis, A Toy Product, made in the 1930's, 12″*	10.00	14.00	10.00

TRANSOGRAM

☐ **Mannequin,** *composition, molded and painted blonde hair, painted eyes, comes in carrying case with clothing, marked Transogram Co., Inc., New York, made in 1947, 10″, stated value is for the doll plus the original container*	28.00	37.00	26.00

TRIO TOY COMPANY

☐ **Boy,** *composition head, straw stuffed body, blonde molded hair, blue painted eyes, closed mouth, red and white romper suit, 12″*	125.00	150.00	135.00
☐ **Boy,** *composition, original straw stuffed body, blonde molded hair, blue painted eyes, closed mouth, original pink and white romper suit, 12″*	115.00	130.00	115.00

UNEEDA

	Current Price Range		Prior Year Average
☐ **Angeltime,** *vinyl, blonde hair, molded and painted features, closed mouth, marked Uneeda Doll Co., Inc., 1965, 3½″*	1.50	2.00	1.50
☐ **Antebellum Southern Belle,** *(Uneeda's 50th Anniversary Doll), plastic/vinyl, red rooted hair, brown sleep eyes, closed mouth, marked 8 Uneeda Doll Co., 1967, 25″*	45.00	52.00	42.00
☐ **Baby Dana,** *plastic/vinyl, blonde hair, blue sleep eyes, nursing mouth, pug nose, marked Uneeda Doll Co., Inc., MCMLXXIII, 1973, 20″*	7.00	9.00	7.00
☐ **Baby Peewee,** *plastic/vinyl, blonde rooted hair, molded and painted features, pug nose, partially open mouth, no shoes, made in 1966, 3″*	2.75	3.50	2.75
☐ **Baby Sleep Amber,** *black, vinyl head, cloth body, vinyl arms and legs, black rooted hair, brown sleep eyes, closed mouth, marked Tony Toy, 1970, made in Hong Kong, 11″*	11.00	14.00	11.00
☐ **Beau Time,** *(Tiny Teen), plastic/vinyl, blonde rooted hair, brown eyes, closed mouth, marked Uneeda Doll Co., Inc., 1967, made in Hong Kong, 5″*	4.00	6.00	4.00
☐ **Blabby,** *crier, vinyl, rooted brunette hair, blue sleep eyes, pug nose, ribbon in hair, when stomach is pressed the doll opens its mouth and cries, marked Uneeda Doll Co., Inc., made in 1962, 18″*	25.00	31.00	23.00
☐ **Blue Fairy,** *plastic/vinyl, platinum blonde rooted hair, blue sleep eyes, wears high heels, marked Uneeda, made in 1960, 10″*	5.00	7.00	4.00
☐ **Bob**	8.00	12.00	8.00
☐ **Carolina,** *vinyl, platinum blonde hair, blue eyes, closed mouth, from the American Gem Collection, marked Uneeda Doll Co., Inc., MCMLXXI, Made in Hong Kong, though dated 1971, this doll was not on the market until several years thereafter, 8″*	3.00	4.00	3.00
☐ **Clover,** *plastic/vinyl, brunette rooted hair, made in Hong Kong, date of manufacture unknown, believed to be c. 1976, 10″*	3.00	5.00	3.00
☐ **Connie,** *vinyl, red rooted hair, blue sleep eyes, nursing mouth, marked Uneeda Doll Corp., 1968-69, 14½″*	8.00	11.00	7.00
☐ **Country Girl,** *plastic/vinyl, rooted hair, painted eyes, pug nose, partially open mouth, wears polka-dotted dress, marked Uneeda, made in 1956, 22″*	21.00	27.00	20.00

	Current Price Range		Prior Year Average
☐ **Cuddly Baby,** *vinyl head, plush stuffed body, plush stuffed arms and legs, vinyl hands, rooted blonde hair, fixed eyes, closed mouth, pensive expression, wears woollen skullcap, marked Uneeda Doll, made in 1961, 9¼″*	6.00	8.00	6.00
☐ **Dance Time Pee Wee,** *vinyl, blonde molded hair and painted features, pug nose, closed mouth, marked Pee Wee TM, United Doll Co., Inc., 1965, made in Hong Kong, 3½″*	2.00	3.00	2.00
☐ **First Born Baby,** *vinyl head, cloth body, plastic arms and legs, molded and painted hair, blue sleep eyes, marked Uneeda Doll Co., Inc., 1968, 1468, 13″*	5.00	7.00	5.00
☐ **Freckles,** *plastic/vinyl, red rooted hair, blue sleep eyes, pug nose, partially open mouth, ribbon in hair, marked 22, made in 1960, 32″*	27.00	36.00	26.00
☐ **Fun Time,** *(Tiny Teen), plastic/vinyl, brunette rooted hair, brown eyes, closed mouth, marked Uneeda Doll Co., Inc., 1967, Hong Kong, 5″*	6.00	8.00	6.00
☐ **Georgia,** *vinyl, platinum blonde hair, blue eyes, closed mouth, from the American Gem Collection, marked Uneeda Doll Co., Inc., MCMLXXI, Made in Hong Kong, though dated 1971, this doll was not on the market until several years thereafter, 8″*	3.00	4.00	3.00
☐ **Georgina, Little Sophisticate,** *plastic, vinyl, rooted hair, closed eyes, closed mouth, marked Uneeda Doll Co., Inc., 1967, made in Japan, 8″*	5.00	7.00	5.00
☐ **Grannykins,** *plastic/vinyl, black hair streaked with grey, blue painted eyes, wears eyeglasses and shawl, open mouth, marked Uneeda Doll Co., Inc., MCMLXXIV, 1974, 6″*	3.00	4.00	3.00
☐ **Hee Wee,** *vinyl, molded and painted features, molded and painted hair, marked Uneeda Doll Co., Inc., 1965, 3½″*	4.00	6.00	4.00
☐ **Jennifer,** *plastic/vinyl, brown rooted hair, painted eyes, short dress, marked Made in Taiwan, made in 1971, 18″*	9.00	12.00	9.00
☐ **Kim,** *vinyl, red rooted hair, painted eyes, long painted lashes, short dress, marked UD Co., Inc. MCMLXX, 1970, made in Hong Kong, 5″*	3.00	4.00	3.00
☐ **Lin,** *vinyl, rooted hair, painted eyes, pug nose, nursing mouth, marked Uneeda Doll Co., Inc., MCMLXXI, 1971, made in Hong Kong, 4″*	4.00	6.00	4.00

	Current Price Range		Prior Year Average
☐ **Little Coquette,** *plastic/vinyl, platinum blonde rooted hair, blue sleep eyes, bow in hair, marked Uneeda Doll Co., 1964, 11″*	6.00	8.00	6.00
☐ **Little Sophisticate Kristina,** *plastic/vinyl, brunette rooted hair, closed eyes, closed mouth, marked Uneeda Doll Co., Inc., 1967, made in Japan, 8″*	5.00	7.00	5.00
☐ **Magic Meg,** *plastic/vinyl, blonde rooted hair, blue sleep eyes, closed mouth, marked Uneeda Doll Co., Inc., MCMLXXI, 616, made in Hong Kong, 16″*	9.00	12.00	9.00
☐ **Marika, Little Sophisticate,** *plastic/vinyl, rooted hair, closed eyes, closed mouth, marked Uneeda Doll Co., Inc., 1967, Made in Japan, 8″*	5.00	7.00	5.00
☐ **Mini Time,** *(Tiny Teen), rooted hair, painted eyes, closed mouth, marked Uneeda Doll Co., Inc., 1967, Made in Hong Kong, 5″*	6.00	8.00	6.00
☐ **Miss Debteen,** *plastic/vinyl, blonde rooted hair, blue sleep eyes, closed mouth, ribbon in hair, marked U., made in 1962, 23″*	11.00	14.00	11.00
☐ **Moonmaid,** *plastic/vinyl, blonde rooted hair, molded and painted features, closed mouth, pug nose, marked Uneeda Doll Co., Inc., 1966, 11″*	16.00	21.00	14.00
☐ **Needa Toddles,** *plastic/vinyl, blonde rooted hairblue sleep eyes, pug nose, closed mouth, wears short-sleeve print dress, marked Uneeda 1964, 19″*	6.00	8.00	6.00
☐ **New Born Yummy,** *vinyl head, cloth body, vinyl arms and legs, platinum blonde rooted hairblue painted eyes, partially open mouth, puffy cheeks, marked UD Co., Inc., made in Hong Kong in 1970, 6¼″*	3.00	4.00	3.00
☐ **Patience,** *vinyl, brunette hair, blue eyes, closed mouth, from the American Gem Collection, marked Uneeda Doll Co., Inc., MCMLXXI, Made in Hong Kong, though dated 1971, this doll was not on the market until several years thereafter, 8″*	3.00	4.00	3.00
☐ **Penelope, Little Sophisticate,** *plastic, vinyl, brown rooted hair, closed eyes, bow in hair, marked Uneeda Doll Co., Inc., made in Japan in 1967, 8″*	5.00	7.00	5.00
☐ **Pollyanna,** *plastic/vinyl, platinum blonde rooted hair, blue sleep eyes, pug nose, open mouth with teeth, marked Walt Disney Prod., Mfd, by Uneeda, made in 1960, 31″*	36.00	45.00	33.00
☐ **Posable Baby Trix,** *vinyl head, foam body, blonde rooted hair, blue sleep eyes, marked*			

	Current Price Range		Prior Year Average
Uneeda Doll Co., Inc., also marked with the mold number 3, made in 1964, 10″	6.00	8.00	6.00
☐ **Posin' Elfy,** *vinyl, molded and painted red hair, molded and painted features, elf-like eyes drawn up and out at the corners, marked Uneeda Doll Co., Inc., made in 1964, 10″*	5.00	7.00	5.00
☐ **Pretty Portrait,** *plastic/vinyl, blonde rooted hair, molded and painted features, doll is mounted in a picture frame to be hung on a wall, marked Uneeda Doll Co., Inc., 1966, total height, 11″*	7.00	10.00	7.00
☐ **Princess Bride,** *plastic/vinyl, blonde rooted hair, blue sleep eyes, wears bridal gown, marked with the mold number 3, made in 1955, 20¼″*	14.00	19.00	13.00
☐ **Priscilla,** *vinyl, brunette hair, blue eyes, closed mouth, from the American Gem Collection, marked Uneeda Doll Co., Inc., MCMLXXI, Made in Hong Kong, though dated 1971, this doll was not on the market until several years thereafter, 8″*	3.00	4.00	3.00
☐ **Pri-Thilla,** *vinyl, blonde rooted hair, blue sleep eyes, open mouth, can suck thumb, wears polka-dotted shirt, marked 4, made in 1958, 12″*	12.00	16.00	11.00
Note: Pri-Thilla was redesigned and released again in 1961 as a balloon inflater.			
☐ **Prom Time,** *(Tiny Teen), rooted hair, painted eyes, closed mouth, marked Uneeda Doll Co., 1967, Made in Hong Kong, 5″*	6.00	8.00	6.00
☐ **Prudence,** *vinyl, red hair, blue eyes, closed mouth, from the American Gem Collection, marked Uneeda Doll Co., Inc. MCMLXXI, Made in Hong Kong, though dated 1971, this doll was not on the market until several years thereafter. 8″*	3.00	4.00	3.00
☐ **Purty,** *vinyl, molded and painted hair, blue fixed eyes, nursing mouth, puffy cheeks, pug nose, eyes squint when doll is squeezed, marked 516-42 Uneeda, made in 1961, 15¼″*	23.00	29.00	22.00
☐ **Rita Hayworth As Carmen,** *composition head and body, red hair attached by adhesive, sleep eyes, elaborate clothing (19th century Spanish senorita), unmarked on doll, sold in a box marked The Carmen Doll, W.I. Gould & Co., Inc., made in 1948, 14″*	170.00	210.00	150.00
Note: Rita Hayworth never sang opera; she played Carmen in a non-operatic motion picture adaptation of the Bizet classic.			

	Current Price Range		Prior Year Average
☐ **Rosanne, Little Sophisticate,** *plastic, vinyl, rooted hair, closed eyes, closed mouth, marked Uneeda Doll Co., Inc., 1967, Made in Japan, 8″*	5.00	7.00	5.00
☐ **Schooltime,** *vinyl, brunette molded hair and painted features, pug nose, closed mouth, wears glasses, marked Uneeda Doll Co., Inc., 1965, 3½″*	2.00	3.00	2.00
☐ **Secret Sue, The Girl From U.N.E.E.D.A,** *plastic/vinyl, red rooted hair, painted eyes, wears trenchcoat, marked Uneeda Doll Co., Inc., made in 1966, 11½″*	11.00	14.00	10.00
Note: The name was a parody of the TV program, "The Man From U.N.C.L.E.," a private-eye show (which explains why Secret Sue wears a trenchcoat).			
☐ **Shower Time** *(Tiny Teen), rooted hair, painted eyes, closed mouth, marked Uneeda Doll Co., Inc., 1967, Made in Hong Kong, 5″*	6.00	8.00	6.00
☐ **Sunny Face,** *vinyl, blonde rooted hair, blue fixed eyes, pug nose, open mouth, marked Uneeda Doll Co., Inc., made in 1963, 14½″*	14.00	18.00	14.00
☐ **Surprise Doll,** *vinyl, brunette rooted hair, blue sleep eyes, nursing mouth, the "surprise" was that Surprise Doll kicked its feet and flailed its arms when its stomach was pressed, marked Uneeda, made in 1954, 16″*	33.00	39.00	32.00
☐ **Sweetum,** *vinyl head, latex body, blonde rooted hair, blue sleep eyes, partially open mouth, marked Uneeda, made in 1953, 22″*	26.00	34.00	25.00
☐ **Tea Time** *(Tiny Teen), rooted hair, painted eyes, closed mouth, marked Uneeda Doll Co., Inc., 1967, Made in Hong Kong, 5″*	6.00	8.00	6.00
☐ **Tina Tiny Teen,** *vinyl, blonde vinyl wig, sleep eyes, blue and white floral print dress, c. 1960, 10½″*	25.00	30.00	27.50
☐ **Tinyteen,** *plastic/vinyl, blonde rooted hair, blue sleep eyes, closed mouth, bright red lips, carries handbag, wears boots, marked Uneeda, made in 1960, 10″*	7.00	10.00	7.00
☐ **Tiny Trix,** *vinyl head, stuffed body, stuffed arms and legs, blonde rooted hair, blue painted eyes, partially open mouth, marked UD, Inc., Made in Japan, made in 1970, 7″*	3.00	4.00	3.00
☐ **Troll Wishnik,** *vinyl, violet hair, jointed at the neck, marked Uneeda Wish-Nik TM, Patent No., date of manufacture unknown, 6″*	3.00	4.00	3.00
☐ **Twinkle Tears,** *crier, vinyl, blonde hair, blue sleep eyes, open mouth, unmarked, made in 1961, 11½″*	5.00	7.00	5.00

Tina,
vinyl, sleep eyes,
c. 1960, 10½"
$25.00-$30.00

	Current Price Range		Prior Year Average
☐ **Teenie Toddles,** *plastic/vinyl, brunette hair, brown sleep eyes, closed mouth, marked Uneeda, made in 1965, 11½"*	3.00	4.00	3.00
☐ **Vacation Time,** *(Tiny Teen), plastic/vinyl, black rooted hair, blue eyes, closed mouth, marked Uneeda Doll Co., Inc., 1967, Made in Hong Kong, 5"*	6.00	8.00	6.00
☐ **Virginia,** *vinyl, blonde hair, blue eyes, closed mouth, from the American Gem Collection, marked Uneeda Doll Co., Inc., MCMLXI, Made in Hong Kong, though dated 1971, this doll was not on the market until several years thereafter, 8"*	3.00	4.00	3.00
☐ **Weepsy,** *crier, plastic/vinyl, molded, painted hair and features, marked Uneeda Doll Co., Inc., MCMLXXII 1972, made in Hong Kong, 4"*	2.00	3.00	2.00
☐ **Wiggles,** *vinyl, brown rooted hair, molded and painted features, pug nose, open*			

	Current Price Range		Prior Year Average
mouth, wears bonnet with silk strings, marked Uneeda Doll NF21, made in 1959, 19″	67.00	83.00	65.00
☐ **Wish-Nik,** *vinyl, brunette rooted hair and painted features, outstretched arms, marked Uneeda Wish-Nik, Patented, made in 1964, 7″*	3.00	4.00	3.00
☐ **Yummy,** *vinyl, brunette rooted hair, blue sleep eyes, open mouth, mouth moves when stomach is pressed (button on dress indicates place to be pressed), unmarked, made in 1951, 12″*	23.00	28.00	22.00

UNIS FRANCE

☐ **Bisque,** *composition body, five pieces, blue painted eyes, closed mouth, blonde mohair wig, painted boots, crocheted dress, pink satin ribbon, 5½″*	75.00	100.00	80.00
☐ **Bisque Head,** *jointed composition body, blue paperweight eyes, blonde wig, open mouth, blue taffeta dress, mark: "Unis France 301 E.T.", 18″*	325.00	450.00	300.00
☐ **Composition Body,** *five pieces, blue glass eyes, open mouth, teeth, red mohair hair, painted shoes and socks, blue romper suit, 6½″*	125.00	175.00	140.00
☐ **French Character Doll,** *composition head and body, black set eyes, tall hat and long plaid gown, 10″*	200.00	315.00	305.00
☐ **French Child,** *jointed composition body, big blue eyes, dark blonde wig, 31″*	900.00	1100.00	990.00
☐ **Bisque Head,** *French ball jointed body, human hair wig, blue sleep eyes, open mouth, pierced ears, ecru dress, 21″*	1500.00	2000.00	1750.00

UNITED FEATURES

☐ **Charlie Brown,** *inflated doll, marked 1969 United Features Syndicate Co., Inc., 16″ when inflated*	4.00	6.00	4.00

Note: Charlie Brown is a character in the comic strip "Peanuts," created by Charles M. Schultz. The actual maker of this doll is not known; United Features Syndicate was merely the licenser.

	Current Price Range		Prior Year Average
☐ **Honest Abe Yokum,** *vinyl head, rubber body, molded and painted hair, molded and painted features, Honest Abe Yokum is a character in the comic strip "Lil' Abner," created by Al Capp, marked United Features Syndicate, Inc., 1953, 11"*	38.00	47.00	32.00

UNIVERSAL

☐ **British Soldier,** *plastic/vinyl, molded and painted features, representing a British infantryman at the time of America's War of Independence, marked Product of Universal, Hong Kong, date of manufacture unknown, believed to have been made in 1976, 8"*	8.00	11.00	8.00
☐ **Continental Soldier,** *plastic/vinyl, molded and painted features, representing an infantryman of the Continental Army at the time of America's Revolutionary War, marked Product of Universal, Hong Kong, date of manufacture unknown, believed to have been made in 1976, 8"*	8.00	11.00	8.00

UPA

☐ **Mr. Magoo,** *vinyl head, stuffed rag body, stuffed arms and legs, molded and painted features, wears three-button vest, marked 1962 UPA Pictures, Inc., 16"*	12.00	16.00	11.00

VANITY

☐ **Big Girl,** *black, plastic head, cloth body, latex arms and legs, black hair, sleep eyes (brown), wears a baby bonnet, unmarked, made in 1949, 23"*	58.00	70.00	55.00

VERLINGUE

☐ **Girl,** *five piece body, brown eyes, closed mouth, dark hair, molded shoes and socks, 8"*	100.00	150.00	120.00

VIDEO CRAFT

	Current Price Range		Prior Year Average
☐ **Pinocchio,** *vinyl head, cloth body, cloth arms and legs, molded and painted features, molded and painted hair, painted eyes, marked Video Craft Ltd., 1962, made in Japan, 13″*	8.00	11.00	7.00
Note: No connection with the Disney version of Pinocchio.			

VIRGA

☐ **Lucy,** *plastic, walker, comes in plaid suitcase, 8″*	40.00	50.00	45.00

VOGUE

Vogue was founded by doll costume designer Jennie Graves in 1937 but it wasn't until the advent of the Ginny doll in 1948 that Vogue really got off the ground. From that point on, however, Vogue was firmly established in the doll world. The 1948 Ginny was a 7″ jointed composition doll with mohair wig, painted facial features and various charming costumes. She was later made of hard plastic, and then vinyl, and acquired a complete wardrobe, jewelry and accessories as well as a family.

The Vogue company has introduced many dolls over the years such as Ginny's little sister, Baby Ginnette, Teenage Jill, Baby Dear, Star Brite, Posie Pixie, Lil Imp, Too Dear, Bunny Hug, Jama Baby and Love Me Linda to name but a few.

Vogue absorbed Arranbee in 1959 and was itself acquired by Ilonka Corporation in 1973. Lesnoy bought Vogue from Tonka and is in current production.

☐ **Baby Dear One,** *vinyl head and limbs, cloth body, blonde rooted hair, blue sleep eyes, closed mouth, mama cryer, blue dress with white pinafore, blue booties, 21″*	55.00	65.00	55.00
☐ **Ballerina,** *brown eyes, brown mohair hair, pink tutu with green and gold trim, flowers in hair*	125.00	175.00	140.00
☐ **Becky,** *strung, brown eyes, red hair, velvet top, organdy skirt, straw hat*	120.00	160.00	138.00
☐ **Boy,** *strung, blue eyes, red hair, aqua corderoy overalls, knitted hat*	110.00	160.00	128.00
☐ **Brickette,** *plastic/vinyl, reddish hair (rooted), sleep eyes (green), closed smiling mouth, white shoes, unmarked, made in 1960, 22″*	38.00	48.00	35.00
☐ **Bride,** *strung, brown eyes, blonde*	200.00	250.00	220.00

	Current Price Range		Prior Year Average
☐ **Bridegroom,** *strung, blue sleep eyes, dark blonde hair*	200.00	250.00	220.00
☐ **Bridesmaid,** *strung, blue eyes, red hair*	200.00	250.00	220.00
☐ **Cheryl,** *redhead, mold number 44*	190.00	230.00	205.00
☐ **Cinderella,** *strung, hazel eyes, blonde wig*	200.00	250.00	240.00
☐ **Dutch Boy,** *strung, brown eyes, blonde hair*	125.00	175.00	140.00
☐ **Fairy Godmother,** *strung, light brown eyes, blonde wig*	200.00	250.00	240.00
☐ **Ginny,** *ballerina, blue eyes, molded lashes, blonde wig, pink and white tutu, flowers in hair, braid leather shoes*	150.00	200.00	170.00
☐ **Ginny,** *ballerina, blue eyes, molded lashes, brown hair, pink taffeta top, white net, pearl crown*	110.00	160.00	128.00
☐ **Ginny,** *ballerina, strung, dark brown eyes, golden blonde hair, multicolored ribbon trimmed with silver, flowers on dress and in hair*	200.00	260.00	228.00
☐ **Ginny,** *beryl, strung, brown eyes, red hair*	200.00	250.00	220.00
☐ **Ginny,** *blonde pigtails, c. 1950*	70.00	80.00	75.00
☐ **Ginny,** *blonde poodle hair cut, organdy dress embroidered with flowers, center snap shoes*	150.00	200.00	170.00
☐ **Ginny,** *blue eyes, molded lashes, blonde hair, black print dress with yellow flowers, yellow straw hat*	60.00	70.00	62.00
☐ **Ginny,** *blue eyes, molded lashes, blonde hair, yellow and black two-piece outfit, matching hat*	80.00	90.00	83.00
☐ **Ginny,** *blue eyes, molded lashes, golden blonde hair, white organdy, matching hat*	80.00	90.00	84.00
☐ **Ginny,** *blue eyes, molded lashes, platinum blonde wig, blue flower print with organdy black velvet trim, matching hat*	70.00	80.00	73.00
☐ **Ginny,** *blue eyes, red braids, yellow cotton two piece outfit trimmed with white and black, hair band, pocketbook*	175.00	225.00	195.00
☐ **Ginny,** *bon bon, strung, dark brown eyes, blonde hair, pink organdy with flocked flowers, pink straw hat*	160.00	210.00	180.00
☐ **Ginny,** *brown poodle cut, c. 1950's*	70.00	80.00	75.00
☐ **Ginny,** *clown, dark blue braids, molded lashes, brown braids, peach and pink clown, outfit*	160.00	210.00	180.00
☐ **Ginny,** *clown, walker, blue eyes, painted lashes, brown braids*	160.00	190.00	175.00
☐ **Ginny,** *clown, walker, blue eyes, painted lashes, red braids, large ruffle around neck*	150.00	200.00	170.00
☐ **Ginny,** *cowgirl, blue eyes, molded lashes, red hair, gun*	160.00	210.00	180.00

	Current Price Range		Prior Year Average
☐ **Ginny,** *early hard plastic straight leg non walker, painted lash, blue lace dress, 7½".*	85.00	95.00	85.00
☐ **Ginny,** *glad doll, strung, blue eyes, red hair, red cotton dress with cherries, green straw hat, mold number 42*	225.00	275.00	240.00
☐ **Ginny,** *Girl Scout, walker, navy blue eyes, painted lashes, red hair*	150.00	200.00	170.00
☐ **Ginny,** *hard plastic, blonde hair, blue sleep eyes, green jump suit, white shirt and shoes, 8", c. 1978*	15.00	20.00	15.00
☐ **Ginny,** *hard plastic, dark brown hair, blue sleep eyes, white tennis shoes, c. 1978*	15.00	20.00	15.00
☐ **Ginny,** *hard plastic, dark brown hair, blue sleep eyes, red and white striped jacket with hood, 8"*	15.00	20.00	15.00
☐ **Ginny,** *hard plastic, painted eyes, blonde mohair wig, cotton red polka dot dress, matching pants, pink straw hat, center snap shoes*	120.00	160.00	128.00
☐ **Ginny,** *hard plastic, painted eyes, blonde mohair wig, white organdy and plaid outfit, red straw hat*	150.00	200.00	170.00
☐ **Ginny,** *hard plastic, painted eyes, red dress, heart in hair*	200.00	250.00	215.00
☐ **Ginny,** *hard plastic, painted eyes, white mohair ringlets, pink taffeta, net gown with gold tinsel*	300.00	350.00	320.00
☐ **Ginny,** *hard plastic, strung, painted eyes, brown mohair hair, white organdy dress with embroidery, black velvet top, matching hat*	150.00	200.00	170.00
☐ **Ginny,** *hard plastic, walker, blue sleep eyes, blonde wig, original blue cotton floor length dress, white organdy pinafore, with rosebuds, matching white straw hat, rosebuds on each side, pink metal signed Ginny trunk, plastic Ginny dotted rain cape, two hangers, marks: Head - Vogue; Body -Ginny, dress tag, Vogue Dolls, Inc., 7"*	85.00	110.00	85.00
☐ **Ginny,** *ice skater, strung, blue eyes, blonde wig, red velvet skater outfit with gold trim and white fur*	225.00	275.00	242.00
☐ **Ginny,** *mistress Mary, dark brown eyes, blonde hair, watering pail*	275.00	325.00	290.00
☐ **Ginny,** *plastic, brown hair, brown sleep eyes, blue velvet swede, gold fringe dress, pants, hat, roller skates*	45.00	55.00	50.00
☐ **Ginny,** *plastic, jointed knees, blue sleep eyes, blonde hair, striped blouse, red skirt, black plastic shoes, made c. 1950's*	55.00	65.00	59.00

	Current Price Range		Prior Year Average
☐ **Ginny,** *plastic, walker, blonde wig, blue sleep eyes, painted lashes, majorette outfit, boots, c. 1954*	70.00	100.00	70.00
☐ **Ginny,** *red wig with poodle style cut, lavender organdy dress, big hair bow*	150.00	200.00	170.00
☐ **Ginny,** *Scottish girl, walker, blue eyes, blonde hair, molded lash*	50.00	60.00	54.00
☐ **Ginny,** *Southern Belle, strung, brown hair, blue eyes, hat and purse*	150.00	200.00	170.00
☐ **Ginny,** *strung, blue eyes, blonde braids, blue print dress, bunny coat, matching hat*	80.00	90.00	84.00
☐ **Ginny,** *strung, blue eyes, blonde braids, white dress trimmed with red flowers, red straw hat*	100.00	150.00	120.00
☐ **Ginny,** *strung, blue eyes, blonde braids, yellow organdy party dress trimmed with lace, matching bloomers*	125.00	175.00	140.00
☐ **Ginny,** *strung, blue eyes, blonde braids, yellow print dress with green patent leather belt, green straw hat*	100.00	150.00	120.00
☐ **Ginny,** *strung, blue eyes, blonde hair, red cloth dress trimmed with lace, large red bow*	175.00	225.00	190.00
☐ **Ginny,** *strung, blue eyes, blonde hair, yellow organdy with aqua velvet, trimmed in gold, hat, gold shoes*	100.00	160.00	130.00
☐ **Ginny,** *strung, blue eyes, blonde wig, aqua taffeta trimmed with lace, matching hat and pants*	80.00	90.00	83.00
☐ **Ginny,** *strung, blue eyes, blonde wig, blue taffeta net party dress with gold trim, gold hair bow, gold shoes, gold heart hanging from wrist*	275.00	325.00	300.00
☐ **Ginny,** *strung, blue eyes, blonde wig, white organdy, matching hat with red trim*	125.00	175.00	140.00
☐ **Ginny,** *strung, blue eyes, brown braids, roller skating outfit in gray and pink, matching hat, skates*	160.00	210.00	172.00
☐ **Ginny,** *strung, blue eyes, brown braids, see through rain hat and boots*	60.00	70.00	63.00
☐ **Ginny,** *strung, blue eyes, brown hair, navy blue dress with bunny coat, hat, muff, and gloves*	150.00	210.00	170.00
☐ **Ginny,** *strung, blue eyes, brown hair, print top, organdy pink skirt trimmed with gold, gold shoes*	90.00	110.00	98.00
☐ **Ginny,** *strung, blue eyes, brown wig, aqua polka dot dress with gold trim, aqua glasses*	90.00	130.00	105.00
☐ **Ginny,** *strung, blue eyes, golden blonde wig, yellow organdy skirt with aqua velvet top trimmed with gold, matching hat, gold sleppers*	175.00	225.00	195.00

	Current Price Range		Prior Year Average
☐ **Ginny,** *strung, blue eyes, multicolored print dress, lilac velvet top, lilac straw hat*	125.00	175.00	140.00
☐ **Ginny,** *strung, blue eyes, pink and gray organdy dress, straw hat*	80.00	90.00	83.00
☐ **Ginny,** *strung, blue eyes, poodle cut red hair, brown and white gingham, trimmed with green and yellow, green hair bow, green center snap shoes*	225.00	275.00	240.00
☐ **Ginny,** *strung, blue eyes, red wig, bridal dress, bouquet*	200.00	250.00	220.00
☐ **Ginny,** *strung, blue eyes, red wig, pink and blue striped overalls, matching blouse*	90.00	130.00	105.00
☐ **Ginny,** *strung, blue eyes, taffy blonde hair, yellow organdy dress trimmed with lace and flower print, green satin belt, yellow straw hat with matching flowers*	200.00	250.00	218.00
☐ **Ginny,** *strung, brown eyes, blonde hair, mint green cotton dress with black and white, green straw hat*	140.00	180.00	155.00
☐ **Ginny,** *strung, brown eyes, blonde wig, blue dotted Swiss, white straw hat trimmed with blue*	140.00	190.00	160.00
☐ **Ginny,** *strung, brown eyes, brown braids, pink print with pink organdy apron, matching hat*	100.00	150.00	120.00
☐ **Ginny,** *strung, brown eyes, brown hair, red organdy dress trimmed with white rick-rack and red tinsel bow*	90.00	140.00	110.00
☐ **Ginny,** *strung, brown eyes, golden blonde hair, flower print cotton dress, pink and green rose satin trim, pink straw with flower trim*	150.00	200.00	190.00
☐ **Ginny,** *strung, brown eyes, red hair, organdy garden dress, trimmed with embroidered chickens, pink straw hat*	90.00	100.00	94.00
☐ **Ginny Doll,** *strung, brown eyes, painted lash, blonde wig, cowgirl outfit of purple skirt and hat, gold trim, belt, wristlets and boots*	100.00	150.00	120.00
☐ **Ginny,** *strung, brown eyes, red hair, gray dress with pink organdy, pink straw hat*	140.00	180.00	158.00
☐ **Ginny,** *strung, brown eyes, red hair, pink cotton dress, pink straw hat and pocketbook*	140.00	180.00	155.00
☐ **Ginny,** *strung, brown eyes, strawberry-blonde hair, pineapple dress, matching straw hat*	160.00	210.00	175.00
☐ **Ginny,** *strung, dark blue eyes, blonde braids, pink cotton dress, matching hat*	120.00	160.00	138.00

	Current Price Range		Prior Year Average
☐ **Ginny,** *strung, dark brown eyes, blonde braids, pink cotton dress with flower trim, pink straw hat*	125.00	175.00	140.00
☐ **Ginny,** *strung, dark brown eyes, blonde hair, black and white gingham, white straw hat with gingham trim*	140.00	180.00	155.00
☐ **Ginny,** *strung, dark brown eyes, blonde hair, pink romper, pink and white coat with matching picture hat, pocketbook, gloves and mirror*	140.00	190.00	160.00
☐ **Ginny,** *strung, dark blue eyes, blonde wig, blue cotton dress, straw hat*	120.00	160.00	135.00
☐ **Ginny,** *strung, dark brown eyes, brown hair, purple print dress, purple straw hat*	140.00	180.00	155.00
☐ **Ginny,** *strung, dark brown eyes, golden blonde hair with gretchen haircomb, white sheer party dress, trimmed with pink flowers, matching flowers in hair*	150.00	200.00	170.00
☐ **Ginny,** *strung, dark brown eyes, red braids, two piece pink and gray ski outfit with zipper, matching hat with pompom, skies*	250.00	300.00	270.00
☐ **Ginny,** *strung, dark blue eyes, red hair, pink dotted Swiss, pink bow*	125.00	175.00	140.00
☐ **Ginny,** *strung, golden brown hair, blue eyes, blue and white cotton sailor dress, matching pants, straw hat*	100.00	150.00	140.00
☐ **Ginny,** *strung, hard plastic, painted eyes, blonde mohair, two piece coral dress with organdy zippered apron, coral bow*	150.00	200.00	170.00
☐ **Ginny,** *strung, hazel eyes, gold hair, pink print blouse, gray flannel jumper, straw hat with black velvet trim*	200.00	250.00	220.00
☐ **Ginny,** *strung, ice skater, brown eyes, brown braids, yellow felt ice skater skirt, black hat, leotard, skates*	175.00	225.00	195.00
☐ **Ginny,** *strung, pink coloring, hazel eyes, light brown mohair wig, pink and green print dress, pink felt bower hat*	150.00	200.00	170.00
☐ **Ginny,** *strung, skater, blue eyes, strawberry blonde hair, emerald green outfit with gold trim, matching hat with two pompoms, roller skates*	200.00	250.00	220.00
☐ **Ginny,** *tennis player, strung, brown eyes, brown braids, tennis racquet*	150.00	200.00	170.00
☐ **Ginny,** *T.V. hostess, strung, hazel eyes, red hair*	200.00	250.00	218.00
☐ **Ginny,** *vinyl, blonde hair, blue sleep eyes, beige tunic top, dark brown velvet pants, all original, mint in box, 8″ c. 1977*	17.00	20.00	17.00

	Current Price Range		Prior Year Average
☐ **Ginny,** *walker, bent knee, blue eyes, blonde braids, pink velvet dress, bunny coat and hat*	80.00	90.00	84.00
☐ **Ginny,** *walker, bent knee, blue eyes, blonde wig, plaid outfit with matching tam*	70.00	80.00	73.00
☐ **Ginny,** *walker, bent knee, blue eyes, silver blonde hair, pink taffeta and lace with hat*	52.00	62.00	57.00
☐ **Ginny,** *walker, bent knee, blue eyes, brown hair, mold number 1007*	100.00	160.00	128.00
☐ **Ginny,** *walker, bent knee, blue eyes, molded lash, brown braids, ballerina outfit of pink satin and white net, pink satin ballerina slippers*	80.00	90.00	82.00
☐ **Ginny,** *bent knees, blue sleep eyes, molded lash, rosy cheeks, short curly red hair, plaid dress of turquoise, yellow, and white, yellow straw hat, blue socks and shoes, marked*	80.00	90.00	82.00
☐ **Ginny,** *walker, bent knee, dark blue eyes, ginger pixie hair, aqua print dress*	50.00	60.00	52.00
☐ **Ginny,** *walker, blue eyes, brown wig with bangs, molded lash, pink cotton dress, turquoise velvet coat, pink pompoms, pink fur hat, pink shoes*	80.00	120.00	90.00
☐ **Ginny,** *walker, blue eyes, molded lash, auburn hair, gingham pink sunsuit*	60.00	70.00	62.00
☐ **Ginny,** *walker, blue eyes, molded lash, blonde wig, pink dress, straw hat*	45.00	55.00	48.00
☐ **Ginny,** *walker, blue eyes, painted lashes, blonde wig, cowboy with matching hat, gun*	140.00	180.00	155.00
☐ **Ginny,** *walker, blue eyes, painted lashes, blonde wig, red and white gingham dress with black plastic fishes*	70.00	80.00	74.00
☐ **Ginny,** *walker, blue eyes, painted lashes, organdy dress trimmed with gold, pin bow*	100.00	150.00	120.00
☐ **Ginny,** *walker, blue eyes, painted lashes, red hair, emerald green taffeta dress, straw hat*	125.00	175.00	140.00
☐ **Ginny,** *walker, blue eyes, painted lashes, brown braids, pink print with overskirt of white organdy, pink hat*	80.00	90.00	83.00
☐ **Ginny,** *walker, blue eyes, painted lashes, red braids, lime green ski outfit, matching hat, ski poles*	160.00	200.00	175.00
☐ **Ginny,** *walker, blue eyes, painted lashes, red braids, yellow outfit and hat, with extra outfits*	90.00	100.00	92.00
☐ **Ginny,** *walker, blue eyes, painted lashes, red hair, white organdy dress, blue satin bow and belt*	150.00	200.00	170.00

	Current Price Range		Prior Year Average
☐ **Ginny,** *walker, blue eyes, painted lashes, white blonde hair, white organdy with pink roses trimmed with lavender velvet, lavender straw hat*	150.00	200.00	170.00
☐ **Ginny,** *walker, brow eyes, painted lashes, brown braids, red, white and blue suit with plastic dog and belt, beenie hat*	80.00	120.00	98.00
☐ **Ginny,** *walker, brown eyes, red hair, painted lash, black velvet and pink taffeta, black straw hat*	80.00	90.00	83.00
☐ **Ginny,** *walker, brown eyes, painted lashes, brown braids, gold cotton blouse, multicolored skirt, gold straw hat*	100.00	150.00	118.00
☐ **Ginny,** *walker, brown eyes, painted lashes, golden blonde hair, yellow cotton dress trimmed with blue and pink, matching bow*	150.00	200.00	170.00
☐ **Ginny,** *walker, brown eyes, painted lashes, red hair, taffeta top, red pants trimmed with gold, gold-silver belt and shoes*	150.00	200.00	170.00
☐ **Ginny,** *walker, dark blue eyes, molded lashes, silver blonde hair, black print dress, straw hat*	70.00	80.00	74.00
☐ **Ginny,** *walker, dark brown eyes, painted lashes, red braids, plaids cotton skirt, white blouse, blue felt vest, blue straw hat*	200.00	250.00	220.00
☐ **Ginny,** *walker, molded lashes, blonde, blue gingham blouse, green skirt, straw hat*	60.00	70.00	62.00
☐ **Ginny,** *walker, molded lashes, blonde braids, green and white gingham sunsuit with matching hat*	140.00	190.00	160.00
☐ **Ginny,** *walker, molded lashes, blonde wig, blue plaid dress and hat*	50.00	60.00	52.00
☐ **Ginny,** *walker, navy blue eyes, painted lashes*	60.00	70.00	63.00
☐ **Ginny,** *walker, nurse, navy blue eyes, painted lashes, red hair, hot water bottle*	200.00	250.00	220.00
☐ **Ginny,** *walker, painted lashes, brown braids, aqua party dress, pink net with gold, gold crown, gold shoes*	275.00	325.00	295.00
☐ **Ginny,** *walker, painted lashes, brown braids, yellow jersey blouse, green checkered jumper*	150.00	200.00	170.00
☐ **Ginny,** *walker, painted lashes, red hair, pink sweater and skirt, beenie*	140.00	180.00	155.00
☐ **Giny,** *walker, blue eyes, red braids, painted lashes, graysilk dress with white ruffled organdy hat*	110.00	160.00	125.00
☐ **Ginny,** *walker, straight leg, majorette outfit, marked Ginny Vogue Dolls, 8″*	70.00	80.00	75.00
☐ **Ginny of Foreign Lands,** *hard plastic, Polish outfit, 8″, c. 1972*	22.00	28.00	23.00

	Current Price Range		Prior Year Average
☐ **Jan,** *auburn hair, blue sleep eyes, lashes, skating outfit, skates, cap #3364, c. 1958*	40.00	50.00	45.00
☐ **Jill,** *blonde hair, wedding outfit, earrings, necklace, flowers*	45.00	55.00	47.00
☐ **Jill,** *composition body, black curly wig, painted eyes, 10″*	125.00	140.00	135.00
☐ **Jill,** *golden blonde hair in angel hairstyle, black exercise outfit, pearl earrings and necklace*	60.00	70.00	62.00
☐ **Jill,** *plastic, brunette hair attached by adhesive, blue sleep eyes, jointed at the knees, dressed in bridal gown, marked Jill-Vogue Doll-Made in U.S.A., 1957, 10″*	10.00	14.00	10.00
☐ **Jill,** *strawberry blonde ponytail, knit top, pleated skirt, navy blazer, gold earrings, straw purse*	40.00	50.00	45.00

Jill,
walker, c. 1960
$8.00-$12.00

	Current Price Range		Prior Year Average
☐ **Jill,** *strawberry blonde wig, beige taffeta dress with lace trim, stand, head band, pocketbook*	160.00	210.00	175.00
☐ **Jill,** *underwerar, earrings with box, #3013*	30.00	40.00	30.00
☐ **Prince Charming,** *strung, brown eyes, blonde wig*	200.00	250.00	240.00
☐ **Red Riding Hood,** *strung, brown eyes, golden blonde hair, carries basket*	125.00	175.00	140.00
☐ **Skier,** *walker, blue eyes, painted lashes, red and white sweater, blue pants, skis and poles*	170.00	220.00	190.00
☐ **Toodles Sailor Boy,** *composition, molded and painted features, molded and painted hair, wears sailor suit, marked Vogue, date of manufacture unknown, 7½″*	38.00	46.00	35.00
☐ **Wanda,** *brown eyes, brown hair, white cotton dress with yellow flowers, matching shoes and straw hat*	160.00	210.00	178.00
☐ **Wee Imp,** *green eyes, blonde braids, freckles, pink taffeta with lace*	100.00	150.00	120.00

IZANNAH WALKER

☐ **Lady,** *fabric, pressed head, oil painted face and hair, applied ears, original outfit*	3000.00	4000.00	2800.00
☐ **Rag Doll,** *all cloth, stockinet molded oil painted head, cloth body, painted hair, eyes, arms, legs, stitched toes, original cotton dress, 17″*	1700.00	2300.00	1500.00
☐ **Rag Doll,** *stockinet molded oil painted head, cloth body, painted hair, eyes, shoes, original cotton dress, early, 19″*	2000.00	2500.00	2000.00

SHEILA WALLACE

☐ **Jenny Jerome Churchild,** *wax, 21″, c. 1979*	500.00	550.00	515.00

WALT DISNEY PRODUCTIONS

☐ **Bashful (one of the Seven Dwarfs),** *composition, molded and painted features, beard attached by adhesive, unmarked, made in 1939, 8½″*	58.00	72.00	55.00

	Current Price Range		Prior Year Average
☐ **Christopher Robin,** *polyfoam-covered wire, molded and painted features, molded and painted hair, posable, marked Made in England, Walt Disney Productions, 1966, 10″*	15.00	19.00	14.00
Note: Christopher Robin was a character from A.A. Milne's "Winnie the Pooh."			
☐ **Donald Duck,** *hard plastic, musical roly-poly, closed mouth, molded clothing, coat has two buttons, carries no markings, believed to date from the late 1960's or early 1970's and probably made in Hong Kong, 11″*	8.00	10.00	8.00
☐ **Donald Duck,** *vinyl head, plastic body, arms spread wide apart, wears felt jacket with four buttons, made in Hong Kong, 8″*	4.00	6.00	4.00
Note: Don't let this one fool you. It looks much older than it is. It was made in the mid 1970's but was designed to show Donald as he appeared about 40 years earlier, very different than the modern version.			
☐ **Donald Duck,** *vinyl head, vinyl body, molded clothing, wide open mouth, hands held together (as if about to dive from diving board), no movable parts, marked Dell, Walt Disney, 6″*	5.00	7.00	5.00
☐ **Dopey (of the Seven Dwarfs),** *vinyl head, plush body (stuffed), two buttons at front, arms wide apart, wide open eyes looking upward, 8½″*	8.00	10.00	7.00
Note: Dopey was a character in "Snow White and the Seven Dwarfs," a Disney animated film.			
☐ **Ferdinand The Bull,** *composition head and body, fully jointed, marked Walt Disney Enterprises, Ideal Novelty & Toy Co., 9″*	65.00	80.00	62.00
Note: Ferdinand was the docile bull who refused to charge matadors or do other bullish things.			
☐ **Grumpy,** *rubber, molded and painted features, marked Gund, W.D.P., 1938*	40.00	55.00	37.00
Note: Representing a character from Disney's animated film, "Snow White and the Seven Dwarfs,"			
☐ **Jiminy Cricket,** *plastic, molded and painted features, clothing attached by adhesive, marked Marx Toys, Made in Hong Kong, made in 1963, 5½″*	9.00	12.00	8.00
Note: Jiminy Cricket was an animated character from the film, "Pinnochio."			

Mickey and Minnie, cloth, c. 1920 .... **$45.00-$85.00**

	Current Price Range		Prior Year Average
☐ **Mickey Mouse,** *rubber, molded and painted features, marked 50 Walt Disney Prod., Sun Rubber Co., Barberton, Ohio, believed to have been manufactured in the mid 1940's, 11″*	**32.00**	**38.00**	**30.00**
☐ **Mickey Mouse,** *roly-poly, vinyl face mask and vinyl ears over stuffed head, stuffed body with fabric clothing, Mickey smiles and holds his hands wide apart, age uncertain (but not particularly early), 10″*	**12.00**	**16.00**	**11.00**
☐ **Mickey Mouse,** *vinyl head, vinyl body, wears fabric clothing, medium-size ears, large smile on face, in addition to Disney, also bears mark of Dakin and Co., made in Hong Kong mid 1970's, 8″*	**4.00**	**6.00**	**4.00**
☐ **Mickey Mouse,** *vinyl (posable), molded clothing, molded gloves and shoes, marked © Walt Disney Productions, Hong Kong, believed to date from the late 1960's or early 1970's, 5½″*	**3.00**	**4.00**	**3.00**

	Current Price Range		Prior Year Average
☐ **Mickey Mouse,** *wood, painted, stump hands without fingers, large bulbous nose, marked Mickey Mouse, Copyright By Walt Disney, 3″*	80.00	110.00	75.00
Note: Mickey's primitive appearance in this doll places it in the early 1930's. A companion piece, MINNIE MOUSE, was also issued, and is worth about the same price.			
☐ **Mickey Mouse Hobo,** *vinyl head, all vinyl body, molded clothing (including a shirt with two buttons, the letter M and a crown atop it), squeaks when squeezed, 10″*	5.00	7.00	5.00
☐ **Minnie Mouse,** *vinyl swivel head, plastic body, molded clothing, a wheeler doll (wheel in each foot, but no walking mechanism — doll had to be pushed manually), marked Walt Disney Productions, 11″*	10.00	14.00	10.00
☐ **Minnie Mouse,** *vinyl head, plastic body, bow-tied ribbon on top of head, wears fabric clothing, including polka-dotted skirt, oversized shoes, in addition to Disney mark, also carries mark of Dakin and Co., almost certainly made in Hong Kong but not marked to that effect, 6″*	4.00	5.00	4.00
☐ **Peter Pan,** *seated vinyl figurine with cloth jacket, c. 1950*	22.00	35.00	27.50
☐ **Pinocchio,** *composition head and body, wooden arms and legs, molded and painted hair, painted clothing, marked Ideal, originally sold with a tag reading Pinocchio, Des. & Copyright By Walt Disney, made in 1940, 11″*	90.00	110.00	85.00
Note: The Disney film, "Pinocchio," was released in 1937, three years before this doll came out.			
☐ **Pinocchio,** *composition head, composition arms, legs and body, painted eyes, wears Tyrolean-style (or mountain climber) cap, marked Pinocchio, Walt Disney Pr., Knickerbocker Toy Co., 12″*	80.00	100.00	75.00
☐ **Pluto Pulltoy,** *all wood construction overlaid with printed paper, set with wheels, equipped with a leash with which Pluto could be "walked," as the toy was pulled along, the wheels activated its front and hind legs and set them in walking motion, length, 15″*	120.00	150.00	110.00
Note: First placed on the market around 1946, still being sold at retail in 1950 and possibly later — but these have nevertheless become scarce, when complete and in good operating condition.			

BEVERLY WALTER

	Current Price Range		Prior Year Average
☐ **Bisque Father Christmas,** *dressed as Daniel Boone, bisque shoulder head, hands, black boots, cloth body, 1980 UFDC Souvenir doll from the Washington, D.C. Convention made by Beverly Walter, molded white hair, beard, moustache, eyebrows, blue intaglio eyes, detailed facial modeling, sombre expression, Daniel Boone tan fringed velveteen hunting suit, mink hat, marks: Father Christmas, Beverly Walter, 1980, 16½″*	225.00	250.00	230.00

BERGMAN WALTERSHAUSEN

☐ **Bisque,** *spring-jointed body, original wig, blue-grey sleep eyes, two tone lips, four porcelain teeth, incised CM Bergman Walters Hausen 1916 6½″*	295.00	330.00	300.00
☐ **Girl,** *bisque head, spring, jointed body, original long brown wig, fine antique cotton dress with elaborate panelling and embroidered white on white flowers, original slip, shoes, incised Bergman Waltershausen, 1916, 6, 22″*	360.00	395.00	365.00

WARNER BROTHERS

☐ **Elmer Fudd,** *vinyl, molded and painted features, painted eyes, jointed at the shoulders and hips, wears one-button jacket, derby hat, Elmer Fudd is a character in the comic strip "Bugs Bunny," created by R. Schlesinger, marked Warner Brothers, 1968, made in Hong Kong, 7″*	15.00	20.00	14.00

NORAH WELLINGS

☐ **American Indian Character,** *English doll, 19″*	220.00	240.00	200.00
☐ **Dutch Boy,** *jointed body, velvet body, 8″* ...	60.00	70.00	65.00
☐ **Fellow,** *comic, very expressive, perfect clothes, 8″*	35.00	40.00	35.00
☐ **Native Boy,** *brown red wig, brown glass eyes, 15″*	100.00	120.00	110.00

American Indian,
19″
$220.00-$240.00

	Current Price Range		Prior Year Average
☐ **Norah Sue,** *mask face, stuffed body, painted facial features, human hair wig, wears bowtie, unmarked on doll, sold originally with a tag reading Made in England by Norah Wellings, date of manufacture unknown, 15½″*	50.00	65.00	47.00
☐ **Queens Guard Character,** *all cloth, molded painted features, authentic queens guard uniform, cloth tag on foot, made in England by Norah Wellings, 9″*	60.00	65.00	60.00
☐ **Royal Air Force Parachutist Character,** *all cloth, molded, painted features, helmet, gogles, harness strap with comfort pouch attached, red, white, blue parachute in open position with display string, mark: cloth tag under collar "Royal Air Force, Comforts End, UK" 7½″*	60.00	65.00	60.00

	Current Price Range		Prior Year Average
☐ **Royal Air Force Character,** *all cloth, molded painted features, RAF dress uniform mark: cloth tag on foot, made in England by Norah Wellings, 10″*	60.00	65.00	60.00

ADOLF WISLIZENUS

☐ **Bisque Head,** *jointed composition body, dark blonde human hair wig, blue sleep eyes, original lashes, antique white dress, 23½″*	450.00	550.00	425.00

WOLFPIT

☐ **Brave Cowboy,** *stockinette with cloth body, marked Pocket Doll, 1962, Wolfpit Enterprises, Inc., 7¼″*	12.00	16.00	12.00

WOOLWORTH

☐ **Simple Simon,** *vinyl head, plastic body, blonde rooted hair, represents the character Simple Simon from the old English nursery rhyme, there is no reference to Woolworth on the doll itself, but the name appears on the box, marked Made in Hong Kong, 7″*	4.00	6.00	4.00

WORLD DOLL COMPANY

☐ **Marilyn Monroe Portrait Doll,** *porcelain, wig, painted features, white seguin gown, high heeled shoes, nylon stocking, string of pearls, sculpted by Joyce Christopher, numbered and dated, certificate of authenticity, collector registration, 16½″, c. 1983*	375.00	425.00	400.00
☐ **Marilyn Monroe Portrait Doll,** *vinyl, red jersey knit gown, white marabon feather boa, red high heeled shoes, nylon stockings, rhinestone necklace, certificate of authenticity, c. 1983*	75.00	150.00	80.00

MANUFACTURER UNKNOWN

There are approximately 1,000 dolls listed in this section. Every effort has been made to include the widest possible range of dolls of an unknown origin. Many high quality, collectible dolls were produced without marks, however this has not decreased their value.

To aid the reader, the dolls in this section have been grouped, when possible, according to their most obvious characteristic. For example, if the reader wished to find a listing for an unmarked Charlie Chaplin doll, they would first refer to the Celebrity section under C. If there is no specific category which would include the doll in question, the reader could then refer to the alphabetized miscellaneous section.

ADVERTISING	Current Price Range		Prior Year Average
☐ **Ben Franklin,** *blue vest, advertising*	8.00	14.00	9.00
☐ **Ben Franklin,** *orange vest, advertising*	8.00	14.00	9.00
☐ **Big Boy Bank,** *big, advertising*	6.00	12.00	7.00
☐ **Big Boy Bank,** *small, advertising*	6.00	12.00	7.00

The Burger King,
all cloth, 18″
$10.00-$12.00

Ronald McDonald,
all cloth, 15″
$6.00-$12.00

	Current Price Range		Prior Year Average
☐ **Burger King,** *cloth one piece construction, painted decoration and feature, made for advertisement, 18″*	10.00	12.00	15.00
☐ **Burger King,** *fat, advertising*	6.00	12.00	7.00
☐ **Burger King,** *tall, advertising*	6.00	12.00	7.00
☐ **Campell Kids,** *bisque dolls, jointed head, arms and legs, dressed in red and white, 9″*	100.00	200.00	150.00
☐ **Campbell Kid,** *painted socks, shoes, c. 1948, 12″*	125.00	175.00	130.00
☐ **Campbell Kids,** *pair of bicentennial boy and girl dolls, in box, 10″, c. 1976*	55.00	75.00	65.00
☐ **Colonel Sanders Bank,** *short, advertising*	10.00	15.00	11.00
☐ **Cowardly Lion,** *from Wizard of Oz, advertising*	8.00	14.00	9.00

	Current Price Range		Prior Year Average
☐ **Count Chocolate,** *General Mills, advertising*	10.00	15.00	11.00
☐ **Dough Boy,** *advertising*	6.00	12.00	7.00
☐ **Elsie The Cow,** *advertising*	25.00	35.00	28.00
☐ **Gerber Baby,** *comes with glass baby bottles, funnel, baby brush, bracelet, rattle, leatherette suitcase, made in 1940's*	90.00	120.00	105.00
☐ **Hamburgerlar,** *advertising*	6.00	12.00	7.00
☐ **Holland, America Line,** *cloth and plastic sailor doll, an advertising promotional item for this steamship line, 12", c. 1950*	14.00	19.00	16.00
☐ **Miss Sunbeam,** *advertising*	30.00	40.00	32.00
☐ **Mr. Peanut,** *advertising*	8.00	14.00	9.00
☐ **My Name Is Miss Corn-Krisp,** *cloth, dark hair, rosy cheeks, blue stockings, red shoes; printed in red and black, 26"*	100.00	150.00	120.00
☐ **Ronald McDonald,** *advertising, 13"*	6.00	12.00	7.00
☐ **Ronald McDonald,** *advertising, 16"*	6.00	12.00	7.00
☐ **Scarecrow,** *from Wizard of Oz, advertising*	8.00	14.00	9.00
☐ **Sippin Sue,** *General Mills, advertising*	10.00	15.00	11.00
☐ **Sweet Heart Soap Baby,** *mechanical*	200.00	300.00	225.00
☐ **Sweet Nell,** *Texas Dairy Queen, advertising*	8.00	12.00	9.00
☐ **Trailways Bus Hostess,** *advertising*	8.00	12.00	9.00
☐ **Woodsey Owl,** *advertising*	10.00	15.00	11.00

CHINA HEADS

☐ **Adelina Patte,** *china head, cloth body, molded hair, painted eyes, blue silk dress, lace trim, c. 1850, 23"*	350.00	450.00	360.00
☐ **Agnes,** *china head, kid body with cloth arms and legs, molded hair, painted eyes, closed mouth, 15"*	500.00	600.00	525.00
☐ **Alice,** *shoulder head doll, bisque forearms and feet, cloth body, blue sleep eyes, blonde wig, pink tafetta dress, 10½"*	115.00	155.00	130.00
☐ **Bald China Shoulder head,** *arms, legs, cloth body, brown painted eyes, brown mohair wig, black silk dress with matching black bonnet, 13"*	325.00	475.00	350.00
☐ **Bisque,** *molded pink frilly bonnet, sewed-on lace dress, green bow and boots, 3"*	20.00	30.00	24.00
☐ **Bisque Shoulder Head,** *cloth body with bisque arms and legs, molded blonde hairdo with ribbon headband, blue glass eyes, pierced ears, original costume, 16½"*	850.00	950.00	900.00
☐ **Black,** *china head, long ringlets, red print dress, 16"*	120.00	160.00	135.00
☐ **Blonde Parian Child,** *pink cotton body, composition hands, black and white striped taffeta dress, organdy apron, paper shoes*	60.00	70.00	62.00

Agnes,
china and kid, 15″
$500.00-$600.00

China,
painted features, 18″
$300.00-$350.00

	Current Price Range		Prior Year Average
☐ **Blonde Parian,** *china, cotton body, painted eyes, closed mouth, green dress with pink flowers, leather boots*	325.00	375.00	340.00
☐ **Boy,** *china head, cloth body, black hair, maroon felt pants, blue wool jacket, black high top shoes, 23″*	100.00	150.00	120.00
☐ **Boy,** *china shoulder head, kid arms, cloth body, painted blue eyes, black painted, molded, side parted hair, pierced ears, black jacket, grey vest, trousers, black leather shoes, 15″*	450.00	650.00	425.00
☐ **Boy Doll,** *china head, cloth body, porcelain hands and feet, sailor outfit with white pantaloons, blue beret, 8″*	12.00	18.00	14.00
☐ **China Shoulder Head,** *cloth body with china arms and legs, molded hair with curls, painted blue eyes, tailored school marm dress, black boots, 20″*	300.00	400.00	325.00
☐ **China Shoulder Head,** *cloth body with kid arms, jointed construction, molded black hair, painted black eyes, 14½″*	450.00	500.00	460.00
☐ **China Shoulder Head,** *forearms, legs, cloth body, blond molded hair pulled away from face with braid coming across forehead, braids draped across back of head, pale coloring, delicate, lavender calico long dress matching undies, leather shoes, 18″*	175.00	195.00	180.00
☐ **China Shoulder Head,** *hands, cloth body, molded ringlets, painted facial features with brown eyes, Spanish custome, 8″*	250.00	325.00	250.00
☐ **China Shoulder Head,** *kid body, wooden arms and legs, molded black hairstyle with soft short curls, delicately painted features, 11″*	325.00	425.00	300.00
☐ **Highland Mary,** *molded blonde hair, painted features, original cloth body with bisque hands and feet, 8″*	35.00	45.00	40.00
☐ **Highland Mary Parian,** *composition head, leather body, molded wig, set blue eyes, red dress, red kid boots, 26″*	600.00	700.00	610.00
☐ **Highland Mary,** *parian head and body, painted hair and eyes, long dark gown with lace trim, 10″*	200.00	215.00	210.00
☐ **Lady,** *china head, leather body, extreme center part hairdo, three high horizontal curls each side, flat back of head, red eye lines, exposed ears, stitching on hands to resemble gloves, original green two piece dress, elaborate bustle, matching green silk heeled pumps with large rosettes, many layers of underwear, 19½″*	400.00	445.00	415.00

	Current Price Range		Prior Year Average
☐ **Parian Bisque Shoulder Head,** *arms, cloth body, elaborately molded blonde coiffure with rows of curls, black molded, ribbon, wearing cream silk dress with black detail work, 16″*	325.00	450.00	300.00

CLOTH

	Current Price Range		Prior Year Average
☐ **American Black Rag Doll,** *wooled hair, button eyes, embroidered mouth, stitched nose, homespun cotton floral play-suit, 13″, c. 1900*	120.00	135.00	120.00
☐ **Boudoir Doll,** *all cloth, long skinny body and limbs, painted face, blonde pigtails, blue pajamas, 3′*	20.00	30.00	24.00
☐ **Cloth Boy,** *stitched features, shirt, shoes, hat, hair, home made, 13″, c. 1900*	30.00	40.00	30.00
☐ **Porcelain Half Doll,** *elaborate molded hairdo with molded bust, fingers cupped behind ears, marks: 6785 Germany, 4″*	30.00	35.00	30.00
☐ **Princess Eugenie Lady,** *parian, bisque head, original cloth body, detailed painting throughout, exquisite sculptured nose and mouth, glazed feather and purple lustre plum with green snood, with some old clothes, 20″*	425.00	465.00	435.00
☐ **Cloth,** *painted face, short blonde mohair, 1920 style, 22″*	30.00	40.00	33.00
☐ **Clown Doll,** *crocheted, blue yarn with light yellow, 13″*	8.00	12.00	9.00
☐ **Lenci-Type,** *molded felt face with painted brown eyes, black mohair wig, felt body, Italian peasant, dark blue felt dress decorated with gold braiding, red apron and felt cap from which falls a lace kerchief, necklace, matching dangle earrings and a whimsical felt rooster, marks: cloth tag on dress, A. Alberani Vecchiutti, Milano, made in Italy, 12″*	50.00	75.00	50.00
☐ **Lenci-Type,** *pressed felt masked face, painted blue button eyes glancing to side, white mohair wig, all felt body, original yellow felt skirt trimmed with applied flowers, lace shawl and felt tricorn black hat, 9″*	30.00	40.00	35.00
☐ **Lenci-Type,** *pressed felt masked face with painted brown eyes glancing to the side, black mohair bangs and side curls peeking out from red turban on head, cloth and felt body with stitched fingers, jointed at arms*			

	Current Price Range		Prior Year Average
and legs, gypsy-like costume consisting of red skirt with felt appliques, fringed shawl, black felt boots decorated with orange felt rosettes, basket of felt fruit, beaded necklase and hoop earrings, marks: cloth tag - Bahiama Doll, handmade in Brazil, 20"	200.00	300.00	200.00
☐ **Oilcloth Doll,** *painted features, blonde yarn hair, 16"*	40.00	50.00	43.00
☐ **Rag Doll,** *all cloth head, body, arms, and legs; yarn hair tied into ponytail with ribbon, floor length dress with printed flowers, lace at nack and sleeves, 10"*	2.00	8.00	4.00
☐ **Rag Doll,** *all cloth, yellow yarn hair, green checkered dress, white ruffled hat, 6"*	2.00	6.00	3.00
☐ **Rag Doll,** *round painted eyes, watermelon mouth, yellow yarn hair, blue print dress, matching bonnet, blue apron, 27"*	12.00	18.00	14.00
☐ **Rag Doll,** *round painted eyes, watermelon mouth, yellow yarn hair, pink print dress, matching bonnet, pink apron, 27"*	12.00	18.00	14.00
☐ **Sock Doll,** *soft, fine yellow yarn hair styled in pony tail and tied with pink ribbon, pink dress with ruffles and lace trim, 6"*	5.00	10.00	7.00
☐ **Tea Cozy Doll,** *molded stockinette face with hand painted blue eyes, blonde mohair wig styled in braid, cloth torso and arms, calico print skirt over heavily quilted "tea cozy", marks: cloth tag, made in Soviet Union, peasant girl, 10"*	15.00	25.00	20.00

ETHNIC

	Current Price Range		Prior Year Average
☐ **American Indian,** *pair, celluloid, girl has black mohair wig, boy has molded black hair, brown sleep eyes, girl wears buckskins, boy wears red wool suit, 5½", c. 1940's*	13.00	18.00	13.00
☐ **American Indian Character,** *bisque head, jointed composition body, brown glass eyes, black human hair wig with braids, closed mouth, original costume moccasins, 12"*	500.00	650.00	550.00
☐ **Amish Boy,** *German, authentic costume, with literature, 11"*	80.00	90.00	83.00
☐ **Amish Girl,** *German, authentic costume, with literature, 11"*	80.00	90.00	83.00
☐ **Arabic Couple,** *composition heads, wooden bodies, painted features, native costumes, handmade in country of origin, 7", c. 1940's*	25.00	35.00	25.00
☐ **Austrian Alp Doll,** *felt, handmade, hand-painted features, suede Lederhosen, plaid*			

Amish girl,
plastic
$80.00-$90.00

	Current Price Range		Prior Year Average
shirt, green felt alpine hat, molded facial features, brown straw hair, 9″	10.00	15.00	10.00
☐ **Black Pickaninny,** *bisque, sits in play pen with rattle, 3½″*	45.00	55.00	48.00
☐ **Brazilian Doll,** *hard plastic, sleep eyes, mohair wig, 9″*	10.00	15.00	12.00
☐ **Bulgarian,** *pair, molded composition faces with painted features, cloth bodies, stitched fingers, lady is 8½″, man is 9″, embroidered peasant outfit, dark mohair wig tied with babushka, holds tools with carding wool, man wears a dark green Cossack type uniform, black boots, black lambs wool hat, marked: on both N.E.F. Sofia, Bulgaria*	20.00	25.00	20.00

	Current Price Range		Prior Year Average
☐ **Chinese Baby,** *paper mâché, crier, black silk braids, ebony brown glass eyes, gold and orange brocade costume, 8″*	60.00	70.00	64.00
☐ **Chinese Character Doll,** *man, authentic Chinese costume, 6½″*	20.00	30.00	23.00
☐ **Chine Character Doll,** *woman, authentic Chinese costume, 6½″*	20.00	30.00	23.00
☐ **Chinese Couple,** *papier mâché heads, cardboard torso with papier mâché hands, brown glass inset eyes, painted wig on man, coarse black wig on woman, painted features, eggshell colored kimono, 12½″*	75.00	80.00	75.00
☐ **Chinese Doll,** *paper mâché, glass eyes, six changeable paper mâché masks, wooden box, 7″*	60.00	70.00	63.00
☐ **Chinese Lady,** *composition head and hands, lovely detail and costume, stands on wooden base, 12″*	50.00	60.00	50.00
☐ **Chinese Man,** *composition, deep modeling, original silk clothes, 10″*	35.00	40.00	30.00
☐ **Colonial Doll,** *hard plastic, sleep eyes, mohair wig, 9″*	10.00	15.00	12.00
☐ **Dutch Girl,** *alma, bisque head, ball jointed arms, set brown eyes, open mouth, violet high waisted dress, lace cap, wooden shoes, 12″*	125.00	175.00	140.00
☐ **Dutch Girl,** *composition, decal eyes, molded blonde hair, black Dutch outfit with red, blue, and white trim, wooden Dutch shoes, 10″*	80.00	90.00	83.00
☐ **Early American Dolls,** *hard plastic, sleep eyes, mohair wig, 9″*	10.00	15.00	12.00
☐ **French Flower Girl,** *composition, authentic costume, 8½″*	30.00	40.00	33.00
☐ **Geisha,** *composition and cloth from Japan, three separate wigs, glass eyes, closed mouth, fancy flowered red and gold kimono, 8″*	25.00	35.00	30.00
☐ **Geisha Girl,** *cloth head and body, silk screened features, blue silk oriental costume, 15″*	125.00	145.00	120.00
☐ **German,** *celluloid, moveable arms and legs, 10″*	30.00	40.00	33.00
☐ **German,** *jointed composition body, brown eyes, brown hair, ecru dress, straw hat with blue trim, mold number 63, 24″*	325.00	375.00	340.00
☐ **German Girl,** *celluloid, blonde mohair wig, unmarked*	45.00	55.00	49.00
☐ **German Girl,** *painted blue eyes, blonde hair with blue band, open closed mouth, moveable arms, red and white silk dress trimmed with red silk ribbon, 4½″*	60.00	70.00	63.00

	Current Price Range		Prior Year Average
☐ **Guatemalan Couple,** *handmade in Guatemala, have handsome facial features, both wear national peasant costume, woman carries a baby, 10″*	22.00	28.00	22.00
☐ **Gypsy,** *china head, cloth body, molded wig and hat with feather, colorful costume, 8¼″*	500.00	600.00	550.00
☐ **Hungarian Bride and Groom,** *papier mache shoulder heads, cloth bodies, jointed arms, legs, authentic molded brown hair on man, brown wig styled in braids on woman, Hungarian wedding clothes, 11″*	175.00	250.00	200.00
☐ **Hungarian,** *papier mache shoulder head, jointed cloth body, blonde mohair wig, painted features, wedding party clothes, crown of flowers with ribbon streamers, 11″*	100.00	110.00	100.00
☐ **Indian,** *all bisque, molded black hair, goo goo eyes, watermelon smile, feather fits in head, 4½″*	80.00	95.00	84.00
☐ **Indian,** *bisque head, ball jointed body, set black eyes, black hair, open mouth loin cloth, fringe, 7½″*	100.00	150.00	120.00
☐ **Indian,** *bisque head, five piece ball jointed body, set brown eyes, black hair, open mouth, two piece tan felt Indian suit, 6½″*	100.00	150.00	120.00
☐ **Indian,** *bisque, papier mache body, felt, frinze costume, marked Germany, scowls, 10″*	150.00	200.00	156.00
☐ **Indian Boy,** *celluloid, 5″*	8.00	15.00	12.00
☐ **Indian Girl,** *celluloid, 5″*	8.00	15.00	12.00
☐ **Indian Boy,** *ceramic, cloth body, blue jeans, plaid flannel shirt, 20″*	30.00	60.00	35.00
☐ **Italian Doll,** *composition head, arms, and legs, cardboard body, brown glass eyes, long brown curls, beige print dress, white apron, made about 1918, 13″*	45.00	55.00	48.00
☐ **Japan,** *plastic, 8″*	10.00	20.00	11.00
☐ **Japanese Girl,** *painted features, bobbed molded blonde hair, jointed at arms and legs, blue gingham dress, painted white socks and black shoes, 5½″*	45.00	55.00	48.00
☐ **Japanese Girl,** *papier mache, dark hair, glass eyes, red kimono*	70.00	80.00	73.00
☐ **Korean Character Man,** *composition, fur mustache, two piece silk outfit, made in 1930's, 9½″*	70.00	80.00	74.00
☐ **Mexican Doll,** *four, husband, wife, baby, daughter with bucket*	10.00	20.00	11.00
☐ **Mountain Boy,** *celluloid head and jointed body, molded blonde hair, sleep eyes, green velvet suspender shorts, Austrian cap*	40.00	50.00	42.50

	Current Price Range		Prior Year Average
☐ **Mountain Girl,** *celluloid head and jointed body, vinyl wig with bangs and long braids, blue sleep eyes, flowered dress with apron, 17″*	50.00	60.00	52.50
☐ **Oriental Baby,** *composition, glass eyes, 6″*	10.00	15.00	12.00
☐ **Oriental Boy,** *composition head and ball jointed, six different wigs, dark brown eyes, oriental costume, 6″*	125.00	135.00	128.50
☐ **Oriental Lady,** *papier mache, glass eyes, silk outfit, with stands, 9″*	15.00	18.00	16.00
☐ **Oriental Man,** *bisque, cloth body, pierced nostrils, satin and silk outfit of coat, hat, and boots, 13″*	200.00	250.00	220.00
☐ **Russian Doll,** *wooden, painted, blonde plaited mohair wig, long striped skirt, white blouse, 7″*	5.00	10.00	6.00
☐ **Scotchman,** *bisque head, cardboard body, composition arms and legs, set blue eyes, short brown mohair wig, open mouth, red plaid kilts, black velvet jacket, marked 12/0, 12″*	125.00	175.00	144.00
☐ **Scots Boy,** *all composition, jointed neck, arms, legs, molded blonde hair, painted features, original Scots Highlander costume including bag pipes, 10½″*	20.00	30.00	20.00
☐ **Scottish Girl,** *bisque head, five piece composition body, red wig, tam and shawl, 8″*	775.00	200.00	195.00
☐ **Spanish Dancers,** *all cloth, authentic Spanish dress, 10″*	20.00	30.00	23.00
☐ **Spanish Girl,** *vinyl, moves head, sucks pacifier, pink, pleated dress, booties, comes in wicker basket, battery operated, 23″*	85.00	95.00	89.00

PINCUSHION

☐ **Pincushion Doll,** *boy clown head, blonde hair, neck ruffle, molded cap with pompom, 1⅞″*	30.00	40.00	32.00
☐ **Pincushion Doll,** *colonial lady, gray haired, black ribbon at throat, white chemise top, made in Germany, 3″*	90.00	100.00	92.00
☐ **Pincushion Doll,** *eau de nil skirt, Pompadour hairstyle, flowers in hair, holding bouquet of flowers, marked: Germany*	45.00	55.00	48.00
☐ **Pincushion Doll,** *flapper, blonde curly hair, molded rose on side, pink bodice, hands on waist, probably made in Japan, 3¼″*	30.00	40.00	33.00
☐ **Pincushion Doll,** *flapper head, slight smile, spit curls and bun at back of head, 1⅜″*	30.00	40.00	32.00

	Current Price Range		Prior Year Average
☐ **Pincushion Doll,** *lady with blonde mohair wig, molded blue dress, holding fan and rose, 4¾″*	100.00	150.00	118.00
☐ **Pincushion Doll,** *lady with mohair wig, black choker, 4″*	80.00	90.00	82.00
☐ **Pincushion Doll,** *lady with molded ribbons in hair, silk bodice trimmed with flowers, 3½″*	80.00	90.00	82.00
☐ **Pincushion Doll,** *lady with red-orange hat and blue plume, blue fan, mold number 345, Germany, 3¾″*	30.00	40.00	33.00
☐ **Pincushion Doll,** *porcelain, polyester-filled, silk-like skirt, trimmed with ecru lace and rosebuds, satin ribbon at waist, 5″*	30.00	40.00	33.00
☐ **Pincushion Doll,** *porcelain, polyester-filled, skirt, silk-like skirt and blouse, 2″*	18.00	24.00	19.00

WAX

☐ **Poured Wax Doll,** *wax head, cloth body, blue glass eyes, blonde mohair wig, original blue taffeta dress with matching hat, boots, 16″, c. 1875*	500.00	700.00	475.00
☐ **Wax,** *composition hands and booted feet, blue glass paperweight eyes, braided mohair wig, long two piece silk taffeta dress with ruffles, 20″*	475.00	525.00	488.00
☐ **Wax,** *cotton body, composition hands and blue booted feet, fashionable lady, sleep cobalt eyes, blonde mohair wig, closed mouth, two piece blue dress with black trim, tan velvet hat, pink trim and flowers, 19″*	275.00	325.00	298.00
☐ **Wax,** *leather arms, blue eyes, molded blonde hair, white dress with lace trim, red wool stockings, green shoes, 26″*	200.00	250.00	220.00
☐ **Wax,** *model of a farmer with a pitchfork, amateurishly shaped head painted over the wax, (most of the coloring faded or rubbed), bleached wool imbedded for hair and long beard, painted eyes, long nose, closed mouth, smokes corncob pipe, wears plaid shirt and grey baggy trousers, (the clothing is probably not original, but old), two fingers broken from one hand, the legs bolstered by wire stripping held in place with wire bands, (an old repair effort), place and date of manufacture unknown, thought to be American from the 1850's or slightly later, 14½″*	400.00	525.00	385.00

	Current Price Range		Prior Year Average
☐ **Wax Over Papier Mache,** *shoulder head, papier mache arms, cloth body, blue glass eyes, brown mohair wig, original lace trimmed pink silk dress, 22″*	375.00	475.00	350.00
☐ **Wax Over Porcelain Head,** *hands, and feet, soft body, shoulder head, brown mohair wig with curls, white print dress, matching hat with flowers, red hair bows, white satin slippers, 18″*	40.00	50.00	42.00
☐ **Wax Over Porcelain Head,** *hands, and feet, soft body, shoulder head, painted features, red mohair wig with long curls, orange lace dress with ecru lace, straw hat, black shoes, heart necklace, 12″*	30.00	40.00	32.00
☐ **Wax,** *poured wax head, hands, and lower legs, cotton body, painted blue eyes, blonde mohair wig, rose taffeta and net dress, made in the 1920's, 18″*	60.00	70.00	63.00
☐ **Wax,** *set blue glass eyes, blonde short curl mohair wig, blue striped dress, red wool cape, 19″*	225.00	275.00	240.00
☐ **Wax Shoulder Head,** *waxed composition arms, cloth body, original gauze and silk dress, 49″*	1000.00	2000.00	1200.00
☐ **Wax,** *stuffed body, wooden arms and legs, a grey-haired man with smiling mouth, small set eyes, narrow brows, very long dangling arms, thin legs, (entirely misproportioned, in the manner of a folk doll, but quite likely a commercial production), wears a striped white shirt, dark vest with frills, long stockings and knee-pants, believed to have been made in Bavaria in the early part of the 19th century, 6½″*	100.00	130.00	95.00
☐ **Wax,** *with cloth body (stuffed), figure of a toddler wearing a strawberry colored bonnet, celluloid eyes, rosy cheeks, closed mouth which at one time was painted, nearly all the paint now worn away, double chin, squared jaw, prominent ears, (some damage to one), at one time the head was lacquered by a former owner and most of the lacquering has peeled away, wearing toddler's clothing which appears to be either original or contemporary, has carved and painted wooden white hands, in good condition, place and date of manufacture unknown, thought to be English or Scottish and date from the third quarter of the 19th century, 12½″*	275.00	330.00	260.00

COLLECTIBLE DOLL ARTISTS

RUTH ARDEN

Ruth Arden has mastered many mediums of art-ceramics, glass blowing, pottery, drawing and painting, but it wasn't until 1978 that she first turned her talents to doll making. Since then, after intensive training and effort, she has become one of the most famous of the current doll artists. Her medium is porcelain and her ability to capture pathos in the human face has made her line coveted on the collector's market.

Karmie,
Lady Arden Series, porcelain
$175.00-$225.00

	Current Price Range		Prior Year Average
☐ **Angel,** *Ohio, porcelain, Lady Arden doll*	100.00	125.00	125.00
☐ **Bag Lady,** *Ohio, porcelain, one of a kind, Lady Arden doll*	1400.00	1600.00	1500.00
☐ **Fairy,** *Ohio, porcelain, Lady Arden doll*	100.00	125.00	125.00
☐ **Karmie,** *Ohio, porcelain, Lady Arden doll* . .	175.00	225.00	200.00

	Current Price Range		Prior Year Average
☐ **Lady Arden,** *Ohio, porcelain, limited edition*	125.00	175.00	150.00
☐ **Lady Arden Series II,** *Ohio, porcelain, limited edition*	75.00	125.00	100.00

ALICE ANN BEECHAM

☐ **Annie,** *Astro Knots Corporation, Kurly Kuddly Kids, Minnesota, black cloth, crocheted curls, gingham dress, white pinafore, bow, pattern available, 9″*	15.00	20.00	16.00
☐ **Aunt Maude,** *Astro Knots Corporation, Kurly Kuddly Kids, Minnesota, cloth, crocheted curls, jointed structure, poke bonnet, matching dress, umbrella, pattern available, 12″*	16.00	22.00	17.00
☐ **Baby Beth,** *Astro Knots Corporation, Kurly Kuddly Kids, Minnesota, cloth, crocheted curls, kit available, 22″*	58.00	65.00	60.00
☐ **Dotty Clown Doll,** *Astro Knots Corporation, Kurly Kuddly Kids, Minnesota, cloth, red, white, green, dotted jumpsuit, pointed cap, kit available, 18″*	35.00	50.00	37.00
☐ **Ginnelle,** *Astro Knots Corporation, Kurly Kuddly Kids, Minnesota, cloth, crocheted curls, dress, pinafore, pattern available, 18″*	15.00	20.00	16.00
☐ **Julie,** *Astro Knots Corporation, Kurly Kuddly Kids, Minnesota, cloth, crocheted curls, full skirted, lacey dress, pattern available, 9″*	15.00	20.00	16.00
☐ **Kelly,** *Astro Knots Corporation, Kurly Kuddly Kids, Minnesota, cloth, crocheted curls, white dress, green pinafore, kit available, 13″*	35.00	50.00	37.00
☐ **Little Alice,** *Astro Knots Corporation, Kurly Kuddly Kids, Minnesota, cloth, knit dress, bonnet, pattern available, 9″*	5.00	10.00	6.00
☐ **Mari,** *Astro Knots Corporation, Kurly Kuddly Kids, Minnesota, cloth, Eurasian, black crocheted curls, Oriental outfit, pattern available, 15″*	10.00	15.00	11.00
☐ **Mary Jo,** *Astro Knots Corporation, Kurly Kuddly Kids, Minnesota, cloth, crocheted curls, skating outfit, pattern available, 14″*	5.00	10.00	6.00
☐ **Melissa,** *Astro Knots Corporation, Kurly Kuddly Kids, Minnesota, cloth, crocheted curls, early American outfit, pattern available, 14″*	10.00	15.00	11.00
☐ **Michelle,** *Astro Knots Corporation, Kurly Kuddly Kids, Minnesota, cloth, crocheted curls, full skirted print dress, apron, kit available, 18″*	15.00	20.00	16.00
☐ **Teeny Arline,** *Astro Knots Corporation, Kurly Kuddly Kids, Minnesota, cloth, dress, bonnet, booties, kit available, 7½″*	10.00	15.00	11.00

Kelly,
cloth, 13″
$35.00-$50.00

WENDY BRENT

	Current Price Range		Prior Year Average
☐ **Cat Angel,** *California, rose petal composition, c. 1981*	475.00	525.00	500.00
☐ **Cat Jester,** *California, rose petal composition, c. 1981*	475.00	525.00	500.00
☐ **Fairy Godmother,** *California, rose petal composition, c. 1981*	475.00	525.00	500.00
☐ **Flower Fairy,** *California, rose petal composition, c. 1981*	475.00	525.00	500.00
☐ **Rabbit Jester,** *California, rose petal composition, c. 1981*	475.00	525.00	500.00
☐ **Wood Elf,** *California, rose petal composition, c. 1981*	475.00	525.00	500.00

SONJA BRYER

Sonja Bryer is an accomplished doll artist and member of The Original Doll Artist Council of America. After many courses in art and sewing, and after teaching ceramics for 12 years, Sonja turned her attentions to doll making. At first she followed the general trend of making reproductions of the grand old French dolls. Her own creativity shown through and soon she was making limited editions of cloth and wire dolls of her own invention. After numerous blue ribbons at doll shows, she is firmly entrenched in doll artist society.

	Current Price Range		Prior Year Average
☐ **Beth,** *Ohio, cloth, wire armature, blonde pigtails, red pants, white shirt, limited edition, signed, miniature*	100.00	130.00	110.00
☐ **Beth,** *Ohio, cloth, wire armature, Victorian style dress, limited edition, swivel head on bisque shoulder plate, signed, miniature*	125.00	150.00	130.00
☐ **Billy,** *Ohio, cloth, wire armature, coat and knit cap, limited edition, signed, miniature*	85.00	105.00	89.00

Christmas Group, Beth, Billy and Santa . . . . **$350.00-$400.00**

	Current Price Range		Prior Year Average
☐ **Billy,** *Ohio, cloth, wire armature, sailor top and knickers, limited edition, signed, miniature*	85.00	95.00	89.00
☐ **Cindy,** *Ohio, porcelain, limited edition, signed, c. 1980, 15″*	175.00	225.00	179.00
☐ **Elf,** *Ohio, cloth, wire armature, red, white, green suit, leather apron, red stocking cap with bell, limited edition, signed, miniature*	80.00	90.00	84.00
☐ **Little Dumpling,** *Ohio, porcelain, limited edition, signed, c. 1980, 12″*	150.00	180.00	156.00
☐ **Mammy,** *Ohio, cloth, wire armature, black dress, white apron, limited edition, signed, miniature*	130.00	150.00	136.00
☐ **Santa,** *Ohio, cloth, wire armature, red suit and cap, limited edition, signed, miniature*	85.00	110.00	89.00
☐ **Sara,** *Ohio, bisque, swivel head, jointed body, pastel taffeta dress, closed edition, signed, miniature*	145.00	165.00	149.00

SUZANNE GIBSON

	Current Price Range		Prior Year Average
☐ **Amanda,** *Reeves International, drink and wet, floral print dress, bonnet, 16″, c. 1983*	38.00	45.00	40.00
☐ **Barbara,** *Reeves International, brunette, pigtails, pajamas, signed, c. 1983, 24″*	45.00	55.00	49.00
☐ **Belinda,** *Reeves International, blonde, nightgown, 20″, c. 1983*	40.00	45.00	42.00
☐ **Billy,** *Reeves International, blonde, sailor suit, tam, 24″, c. 1983*	45.00	55.00	49.00
☐ **Blyth,** *Reeves International, blonde, coat with fur lined hood, dress, muff, 24″, c. 1983*	55.00	65.00	59.00
☐ **Bobby,** *Reeves International, brunette, sailor suit, tam, 24″, c. 1983*	45.00	55.00	49.00
☐ **Bonnie,** *Reeves International, nightgown, 14″, c. 1983*	20.00	25.00	21.00
☐ **Camila,** *Reeves International, blonde, floral print dress, 20″, c. 1983*	45.00	55.00	47.00
☐ **Carole,** *Reeves International, blonde, velvet dress, hat, 20″, c. 1983*	60.00	65.00	63.00
☐ **Carrie,** *Reeves International, dotted Swiss christening gown, 20″, c. 1983*	60.00	65.00	60.00
☐ **Chelsey,** *Reeves International, drink and wet, ash blonde, striped pastel dress, bonnet, 16″, c. 1983*	45.00	55.00	47.00
☐ **Cherie,** *Reeves International, brunette, nightgown, 14″, c. 1983*	22.00	28.00	25.00
☐ **Clarissa,** *Reeves International, brunette, pigtails, raincoat, dress, cap, pantaloons, 24″, c. 1983*	55.00	65.00	60.00

Billy and Darcy, 1983, (each) .... **$50.00-$60.00**

	Current Price Range		Prior Year Average
☐ **Colette,** *Reeves International, drink and wet, red head, floral print dress, bonnet, 16", c. 1983*	**40.00**	**60.00**	**45.00**
☐ **Corine,** *Reeves International, blonde, pigtails, pajamas, 24", c. 1983*	**40.00**	**48.00**	**45.00**
☐ **Czechoslovakian Doll,** *Reeves International, elaborate trimmed costume, beribboned head dress, signed, 8", c. 1983*	**48.00**	**60.00**	**50.00**
☐ **Danny And Danielle,** *Reeves International, blonde, velvet dress, suit, caps, signed, 24", c. 1983*	**125.00**	**175.00**	**127.00**
☐ **Darcy,** *Reeves International, brunette, floral print dress, cap, 24", c. 1983*	**50.00**	**60.00**	**55.00**
☐ **Darlene,** *Reeves International, blonde, pigtails, robe, nightgown, slippers, 24", c. 1983*	**45.00**	**55.00**	**47.00**
☐ **Dawn,** *Reeves International, brunette, eyelet dress, cap, 14", c. 1983*	**25.00**	**35.00**	**26.00**
☐ **Dulcie,** *Reeves International, drink and wet, brunette, red striped dress, bonnet, 16", c. 1983*	**40.00**	**60.00**	**42.00**
☐ **Dutch Doll,** *Reeves International, blonde braids, dressed in elaborate folk costume, conical cap, signed, 8", c. 1983*	**48.00**	**60.00**	**50.00**

	Current Price Range		Prior Year Average
☐ **Eileen,** *Reeves International, blonde, pigtails, raincoat, dress, cap, pantaloons, 24″, c. 1983*	55.00	65.00	58.00
☐ **Electra,** *Reeves International, blonde, pastel striped dress, 20″, c. 1983*	55.00	65.00	58.00
☐ **Elsbeth,** *Reeves International, blonde, nightgown, 14″, c. 1983*	22.00	28.00	25.00
☐ **Emily,** *Reeves International, blonde, pastel striped dress, 14″, c. 1983*	30.00	38.00	32.00
☐ **German Doll,** *Reeves International, full skirted dress, red apron, hat, signed, 8″, c. 1983*	48.00	60.00	50.00
☐ **Gloria,** *Reeves International, nightgown, booties, 20″, c. 1983*	35.00	55.00	38.00
☐ **Grandma, Red Riding Hood,** *Reeves International, limited edtion, 21″ and 16″, c. 1983*	210.00	250.00	230.00
☐ **Irish Doll,** *Reeves International, bodice, blouse, apron, cap, signed, 8″, c. 1983*	48.00	60.00	50.00
☐ **Italian Doll,** *Reeves International, elaborate folk costume, headdress, signed, 8″, c. 1983*	48.00	60.00	50.00
☐ **Jack,** *Reeves International, c. 1983*	65.00	75.00	69.00
☐ **Japanese Doll,** *Reeves International, black bob hairdo, traditional kimono, signed, 8″, c. 1983*	48.00	60.00	50.00
☐ **Jill,** *Reeves International, c. 1983*	78.00	85.00	80.00
☐ **Kalico Kid, Annie Lou,** *Reeves International, strawberry blonde, floral print dress, apron, 18″, c. 1983*	55.00	65.00	58.00
☐ **Kalico Kid, Lillian,** *Reeves International, brunette, gingham dress, white smock, booted, 18″, c. 1983*	55.00	65.00	58.00
☐ **Kalico Kid, Millicent,** *Reeves International, ash blonde, purple bow, gingham dress, floral print pinafore, 18″, c. 1983*	55.00	65.00	58.00
☐ **Kalico Kid, Molly,** *Reeves International, brunette, lacey gingham dress, attached apron, 14″, c. 1983*	50.00	60.00	55.00
☐ **Kalico Kid, Muffin,** *Reeves International, blonde, lacey gingham dress, attached apron, 14″, c. 1983*	50.00	65.00	55.00
☐ **Kalico Kid, Sarah Jane,** *Reeves International, long auburn braids, freckles, dress, apron, 18″, c. 1983*	55.00	65.00	60.00
☐ **Kalico Kid, Toby,** *Reeves International, strawberry blonde, patched knickers, striped shirt, suspenders, freckles, 18″, c. 1983*	55.00	65.00	60.00
☐ **Kalico Mother,** *Reeves International, blonde bun, polka dotted dress, floral print apron, signed, 21″, c. 1983*	78.00	85.00	80.00

Eileen,
1983, 24″
$55.00-$65.00

	Current Price Range		Prior Year Average
☐ **Little Bo Peep,** *Reeves International, floral print dress, puffs out at hips, pantaloon, hat, staff, 16″, c. 1983*	78.00	85.00	80.00
☐ **Little Girl With a Curl,** *Reeves International, auburn ringlets, floral print, trimmed, dress, pantaloons, hat, parasol, 16″, c. 1983*	78.00	85.00	80.00
☐ **Little Miss Muffet,** *Reeves International, black hair, floral print dress, puffs out at hips, pantaloons, hat, stuffed spider, 16″, c. 1983*	78.00	85.00	80.00
☐ **Lucy Locket,** *Reeves International, c. 1983*	78.00	85.00	80.00
☐ **Madelon,** *Reeves International, brunette, pigtails, white dress, cap, 24″, c. 1983*	50.00	60.00	55.00

Megan and Mamie, 1983, 16″, (each) .... **$45.00-$55.00**

	Current Price Range		Prior Year Average
☐ **Mamie,** *Reeves International, drink and wet, dotted Swiss christening gown, 16″, c. 1983*	**45.00**	**55.00**	**50.00**
☐ **Mary Had a Little Lamb,** *Reeves International, blonde ringlets, floral print dress, pantaloon, lamb, 16″, c. 1983*	**78.00**	**85.00**	**80.00**
☐ **Mary Mary Quite Contrary,** *Reeves International, platinum ringlets, floral print dress, pantaloons, hat, watering can, 16″, c. 1983* .	**78.00**	**85.00**	**80.00**
☐ **Megan,** *Reeves International, drink and wet, dotted Swiss nightgown, 16″, c. 1983*	**45.00**	**55.00**	**50.00**
☐ **Miss Abigail,** *Reeves International, platinum curls, colonial gown, striped, floral velvet touches, lace hat, 21″, c. 1983*	**95.00**	**110.00**	**100.00**
☐ **Miss Felicity,** *Reeves International, ash blonde curls, colonial gown, jacket, velvet sash, hat, 21″, c. 1983*	**95.00**	**110.00**	**100.00**

	Current Price Range		Prior Year Average
☐ **Miss Penelope,** *Reeves International, auburn curls, colonial gown, straw hat, 21", c. 1983*	95.00	110.00	100.00
☐ **Mother Goose,** *Reeves International, floral print dress, shawl, cap, apron, goose, 21", c. 1983*	100.00	110.00	120.00
☐ **Polish Doll,** *Reeves International, elaborate folk costume, kerchief, signed, 8", c. 1983*	48.00	60.00	50.00
☐ **Scottish Doll,** *Reeves International, dressed in kilt, tam, signed, 8", c. 1983*	48.00	60.00	50.00
☐ **Selena,** *Reeves International, brunette, nightgown, 20", c. 1983*	40.00	45.00	42.00
☐ **Sharon,** *Reeves International, blonde, christening gown, cap, pillow, 14", c. 1983*	35.00	45.00	37.00
☐ **Shirley,** *Reeves International, brunette, floral print dress, 20", c. 1983*	50.00	55.00	52.00
☐ **Sydney,** *Reeves International, blonde, floral print dress, cap, 24", c. 1983*	50.00	60.00	55.00
☐ **Tabitha,** *Reeves International, drink and wet, floral print nightgown, 16", c. 1983*	30.00	35.00	32.00

JEAN HEIGHTON

Jean Heighton started her professional life as a custom milliner with her own hat shop for 18 years. When she retired from the retail life to raise her son, she found she needed to keep working with her hands and her talent and started making dolls. Her part-time hobby became a full time job as her boy grew and she is now one of the most prolific of the doll artists. Each of her creations is an original, no two are identical and she still has plenty of fantasy folk in her head waiting to be born.

☐ **Alice in Wonderland,** *Fantasy Folk, California, porcelain, blonde, dress, ribbon, pinafore, limited edition, 7½", c. 1981*	85.00	95.00	89.00
☐ **Billy The Kid,** *Fantasy Folk, California, porcelain, leather cowboy hat, vest, chaps, blue jeans, checked shirt, tie, two gun holsters, horns, limited edition, 8", c. 1982*	85.00	95.00	89.00
☐ **Easter Rabbits,** *Fantasy Folk, porcelain parts, wood wire, cloth body, real fur, male wears frock coat, vest, collar, tie, holds basket of eggs, female wears frilly dress, slip, bonnet, holds basket of eggs, limited edition, 8", c. 1980, (each)*	75.00	85.00	80.00
☐ **Froggy By The Sea,** *Fantasy Folk, California, ceramic, green, girl, old fashioned, blue sailor suit, pleated skirt, pantaloon swim suit, hat, 8", c. 1978*	60.00	70.00	63.00

Easter Rabbits, porcelain, 1980, (each) . . . . **$75.00-$85.00**

	Current Price Range		Prior Year Average
☐ **Ivan The Bearable,** *Fantasy Folk, California, porcelain, brown, bear, fur pants, wool hat, red coat trimmed in fur, limited edition, 8", c. 1981*	75.00	85.00	79.00
☐ **Little Red Riding Rat,** *Fantasy Folk, California, porcelain, gray, girl, short dress, slip, pantaloons, holds basket of cheese, bread, fruit, limited edition, 8", c. 1983*	75.00	85.00	79.00
☐ **Ma Ma Bear,** *Fantasy Folk, California, brown, peasant style dress, dust cap, holds baby cub, limited edition, 8", c. 1981*	75.00	85.00	79.00
☐ **Mother Goose,** *Fantasy Folk, California*	70.00	80.00	79.00
☐ **Nanny Goat and Kid,** *Fantasy Folk, California, porcelain, mother goat holds kid, long dress, apron, dust cap, limited edition, 8", c. 1980*	75.00	85.00	79.00
☐ **Nun,** *Fantasy Folk, California*	70.00	80.00	79.00

	Current Price Range		Prior Year Average
☐ **Old Goat,** *Fantasy Folk, California, porcelain, cloth, wire, male goat, horned, bearded, holds basket of vegetables, straw hat, checked shirt, overalls, limited edition, 8″*	75.00	85.00	79.00
☐ **Puss and Boots,** *Fantasy Folk, California, porcelain, orange, velvet coat, large brim hat, feather trim, knee pants, boots, leather baldock with sword, limited edition, 8″, c. 1983*	90.00	100.00	93.00
☐ **Rabbi,** *Fantasy Folk, California*	70.00	80.00	74.00
☐ **Sherlock Holmes,** *Fantasy Folk, California, porcelain parts, cloth, wire body, black, white hounds tooth check cape coat, deer stalker cap, holds lit match, pipe, black shoes, gray spats, 18″, c. 1983*	170.00	210.00	175.00
☐ **Tabatha and Kit Kat,** *Fantasy Folk, California, mother cat, porcelain parts, china painted orange markings, porcelain kitten, fully dressed, flower trimmed straw bonnet, striped tails, blue eyes, 8″, c. 1983*	85.00	95.00	89.00

Tabatha and Kit Kat,
porcelain and cloth
$85.00-$95.00

	Current Price Range		Prior Year Average
☐ **The Dutchess,** *Fantasy Folk, California, porcelain, long dress with train, fur lined brocade coat, gold hat, gauze veil, holds baby pig, limited edition, 9", c. 1979*	85.00	95.00	89.00
☐ **The White Rabbit,** *Fantasy Folk, California, porcelain, checked blue, green frock coat, green velvet dress, watch, watch chain, fur legs, tail, limited edition, 8", c. 1980*	85.00	95.00	89.00

SHARON LEE HOWARD

Sharon Howard is a free lance doll artist from California and member of the Original Doll Artist Council of America. She produces hand-sculpted dolls of fimo clay, wax and cloth.

Fimo clay is a low fire oven baked clay which is imported from Germany. When it is fired it looks like wax but is much more durable. These dolls have either cloth or ball jointed bodies. Sharon uses glass eyes or she sculps them and especially loves to make dolls with buck teeth and glasses.

The wax dolls Sharon Howard makes are hand-sculpted wax over papier mache with glass eyes, cloth body and fimo clay hands and feet.

Miss Howard also makes about fifty different cloth dolls. Each doll is a handmade original of muslin, stretch knit or felt with handpainted faces and elaborate costumes. She has recently produced a line of original doll patterns as well.

All Sharon Lee Howard dolls are signed and dated.

☐ **Angela,** *California, cloth, pattern available*	38.00	50.00	40.00
☐ **Apple Betty,** *Yum Kid, California, stretch knit, pattern available, 6"*	20.00	25.00	21.00
☐ **Baby Mouse,** *California, cloth, pattern available*	12.00	17.00	15.00
☐ **Banana Split,** *Yum Kid, California, stretch knit, pattern available, 6"*	20.00	25.00	21.00
☐ **Bear,** *California, cloth, jointed, pattern available*	20.00	30.00	21.00
Colonial Lady, *California, fimo clay, ball jointed, with baby.*			
☐ *Lady*	115.00	140.00	130.00
☐ *Baby*	55.00	75.00	65.00
☐ **Cookie,** *California, cloth, holds rabbit, pattern available*	30.00	40.00	32.00
☐ **Fanny,** *California, cloth, pattern available*	20.00	25.00	21.00
☐ **Geng Sing,** *California, felt, mohair hair, kimono, lotus blossom, pattern available*	12.00	17.00	15.00
☐ **Gibson Girl,** *California, cloth, pattern available*	48.00	52.00	50.00
☐ **Humbug Witch,** *California cloth, pattern available*	40.00	50.00	42.00
☐ **Jody,** *California, cloth, with rabbit, pattern available*	25.00	35.00	26.00

Leanne,
cloth and wool, 12″
$15.00-$20.00

	Current Price Range		Prior Year Average
☐ **Kipper,** *California, stretch knit, holds doll, pattern available, 11″*	15.00	20.00	16.00
☐ **Lady,** *California, wax over papier mache, glass eyes, period clothing, mohair wig, 20″*	180.00	225.00	200.00
☐ **Mouse,** *California, cloth, dressed, pattern available*	15.00	20.00	16.00
☐ **Nellie,** *California, cloth, pattern available*	25.00	30.00	26.00
☐ **Pamela Pig,** *California, cloth, pattern available*	10.00	15.00	11.00
☐ **Purple Popover,** *Yum Kid, California, cloth, pattern available*	15.00	20.00	16.00
☐ **Rosey,** *California, cloth, pattern available*	22.00	28.00	25.00
☐ **Sally Thumb Sucker,** *California, pattern available*	32.00	37.00	35.00
☐ **Santa Set,** *California, cloth, Santa, little girl, teddy bear, bag of gifts, pattern available*	55.00	65.00	58.00

	Current Price Range		Prior Year Average
Sara and Jake, *California, cloth, pattern available.*			
☐ *Each*	40.00	55.00	42.00
☐ *Set*	90.00	100.00	94.00
☐ **Shauntie,** *California, cloth, pattern available*	25.00	32.00	26.00
☐ **Small Baby,** *California, cloth, pattern available*	10.00	12.00	11.00
☐ **Snookims,** *California, stretch knit, baby doll, cries, pattern available, 15"*	20.00	25.00	22.00
☐ **Standly Stub-a-Toe,** *California, cloth, pattern available*	32.00	37.00	35.00
☐ **Strawberry Clown,** *Yum Kid, California, stretch knit, pattern available, 6"*	20.00	25.00	21.00
☐ **Sugar,** *Yum Kid, California, cloth, pattern available*	15.00	20.00	16.00
Tall Tom, Tall Betty, *California, cloth, pattern available.*			
☐ *Each*	35.00	45.00	37.00
☐ *Set*	68.00	80.00	70.00
☐ **Teeny Mouse,** *California, cloth, pattern available*	5.00	7.00	6.00
☐ **The Kids,** *California, muslin, dressed in old clothes, barefoot, messy hair, pattern available, 14"*	24.00	28.00	25.00
☐ **Tillie,** *California, cloth, pattern available*	25.00	30.00	26.00
☐ **Treasure Chest Doll,** *California, cloth, pattern available, soft box*	25.00	30.00	26.00
☐ **Ugly Baby,** *California, cloth, pattern available*	25.00	30.00	26.00
☐ **Victoria,** *California, muslin, scanty costume, with male partner, pattern available, 12"*	21.00	26.00	22.00

SUZANNE MARKS

Suzanne Marks of California, member of the Original Doll Artists Council of America, designs and makes dolls in her own unmistakable style. The subject of her dolls is children, in all their infinite playful variety.

Mrs. Marks began her interest in art as a child and took up oil painting again when her children were small. She then tried her hand at sculpting and found that she preferred the three-dimensional expression it afforded her.

Her professional career began when she was asked to make miniatures for doll house hobbyists. She began to distribute her miniatures in California and determined that there was a real need for miniature, jointed, porcelain dolls.

Mrs. Marks began professional doll making with a few lessons in doll making and a lot of trial and error. The end results are fully jointed miniature porcelain dolls with hand sculpted hair, hand painted faces and intricate hand sewn clothing, which is removable.

	Current Price Range		Prior Year Average
☐ **Annie,** *California, porcelain, auburn hair, ringlets, brown eyes, boots, rust paint dress, ribbons, sculpted white roses in hair, c. 1980, 4″*	165.00	175.00	170.00
☐ **Clown,** *California, porcelain, boy, molded strawberry blonde hair, brown eyes, black slippers, multi-colored costume and hat, beret with feathers, c. 1983, 6″*	225.00	275.00	250.00
☐ **Clown,** *California, porcelain, girl, molded strawberry blonde pigtails, pink, rust dress, lacy bloomers, molded black slippers, c. 1983*	225.00	275.00	250.00
☐ **Daughter,** *California, porcelain, molded brown hair, molded black shoes, lacy pink pinafore dress, ribbon, c. 1980, 4″*	165.00	175.00	170.00
☐ **Eric,** *California, porcelain, brown hair, blue eyes, brown boots, blue print shirt, knickers, lace collar, c. 1908, 4″*	165.00	175.00	170.00
☐ **Ingrid,** *California, porcelain, light brown hair, blue eyes, boots, hand sculpted roses in hair w/blue ribbons, blue dress, off white lace, ribbon, c. 1980, 4″*	165.00	175.00	170.00
☐ **Jenny,** *Califonia, porcelain, tea party girl, auburn hair, brown eyes, brown eyelet pinafore dress, brown ribbons in hair, sculpted, red, high heeled shoes, blue bead necklace, red straw hat, feather, c. 1981, 4″*	150.00	225.00	165.00
☐ **Kiko,** *California, porcelain, Oriental, molded black hair, brown eyes, molded black slippers, multi-colored, embroidered Kimono, matching obi, sculpted pink roses in hair, c. 1982, 4″*	195.00	225.00	200.00
☐ **La Comedie,** *California, porcelain, girl clown, painted matte white, brown eyes, molded slippers, lacy silk costume, blue satin clown hat, c. 1981, 6″*	250.00	300.00	260.00
☐ **Le Tragedie,** *California, porcelain, boy clown, painted white matte, blue eyes, molded black slippers, lacy, navy blue dress, gold beads, lavender hat, c. 1981, 6″*	250.00	300.00	260.00
☐ **Lizabeth,** *California, porcelain, black doll, molded black hair, dark brown eyes, blue hair ribbon, lacy blue, white checked dress, lacy white bloomers, black molded shoes, socks, c. 1981, 5″*	180.00	220.00	200.00

Le Tragedie,
c. 1981, 6″
$250.00-$300.00

	Current Price Range		Prior Year Average
☐ **Maggie,** *California, porcelain, tea party girl, blonde molded hair, blue eyes, molded socks, red, white dress, blue bow, beige straw hat, pink robbon, feathers, black, sculpted high heel shoes, white pearl necklace, c. 1981, 4″*	180.00	220.00	200.00
☐ **Mahalia,** *California, porcelain, black doll, brown eyes, molded shoes, socks, molded black pigtails, pink ribbons, gold earrings, pink, white paisley dress, embroidered, buttoned, c. 1981, 5″*	200.00	250.00	215.00
☐ **Meg,** *California, porcelain, blonde, brown eyes, boots, dark brown dotted dress, lace trim, lacy pinafore, brown bow, c. 1981, 4″*	165.00	175.00	170.00

	Current Price Range		Prior Year Average
☐ **Mother,** *California, porcelain, molded brown hair, sculpted rose, brown eyes, off white, lacy dress, slip, pantaloons, molded brown boots, c. 1980, 6″*	225.00	275.00	250.00
☐ **Ned,** *California, porcelain, molded blonde hair, molded shoes, socks, red, white, blue sailor suit, red beret sculpted lollipop, c. 1981, 4″*	180.00	210.00	190.00
☐ **Nicole,** *California, porcelain, barefoot, flower girl, molded long blonde hair, blue eyes, lacy blue voile dress, beige straw hat, sculpted roses in front, carries basket with pink hand, sculpted roses, holds rose in her right hand, c. 1983, 6″*	200.00	250.00	210.00

Nicole,
c. 1983, 6″
$200.00-$250.00

Oriental Dolls, 4″-6″ .... **$500.00-$600.00**

	Current Price Range		Prior Year Average
☐ **Sachiko,** *California, porcelain, Oriental, black matte hair, sculpted pink roses, brown eyes, black shoes, pink, black trimmed Kimono, matching obi, c. 1980, 4″*	165.00	175.00	170.00
☐ **Son,** *California, porcelain, molded brown hair, brown eyes, black shoes, molded socks, dotted white, navy jumper suit, short sleeve shirt, lace collar, navy thread bow, c. 1980, 4″*	160.00	180.00	170.00
☐ **Stefan,** *California, porcelain, blonde, brown eyes, brown boots, pink shirt, knickers, lace collar, c. 1980, 4″*	165.00	175.00	170.00
☐ **Sue,** *California, porcelain, molded brown hair, blue sculpted high heeled shoes, layered eyelet dress, bow, pink ribbon belt, blue felt handbag, c. 1981, 4″*	180.00	210.00	190.00
☐ **Suzy,** *California, porcelain, brunette, pigtails, brown eyes, black shoes, dotted red dress, white lace trim, red ribbons, c. 1980, 4″*	165.00	175.00	170.00

	Current Price Range		Prior Year Average
☐ **Taro,** *California, porcelain, Oriental, molded short, black hair, brown eyes, molded black slippers, multi-colored patterned Kimono, matching obi, c. 1982, 4"*	180.00	225.00	190.00
☐ **Taki,** *California, porcelain, Oriental, molded black slippers, flowered Kimono, matching obi, trimmed white ribbon, red and white hair ribbons, c. 1982, 5"*	195.00	225.00	200.00
☐ **William,** *California, porcelain, black doll, molded curly, black hair, red dotted shirt, red embroidered collar, blue denium overalls, molded socks, shoes, c. 1981, 4"*	180.00	220.00	190.00

SONIA MESSER

Sonia Messer is a California doll artist whose creations are famous nationwide. The Smithsonian has selected her hand-fired porcelain dolls for their catalog two years in a row, a distinction that proves her treasures are tomorrow's heirlooms. All dolls are handpainted and the costumes are specially designed of the finest silks, velvets, laces and satins, Her elegant dolls are superb in every detail.

☐ **Albert,** *musical clown, on porcelain base, "Send In The Clowns." Costumed in white satin with black trim, 14"*	70.00	80.00	72.50
☐ **Baby Love,** *marked AM352, costumed in an elaborate christening gown of satin and laces, cloth body, 12"*	75.00	90.00	80.00
☐ **The Bride,** *reproduction of Kestner fashion doll, marked F162.10 German, c. 1910, lavish gown of French embroidered lace and silk embellished with seed peals, two petticoats of moire taffeta and lace cover silk bloomers with point d'esprit lace, 11"*	400.00	500.00	425.00
☐ **Chang,** *Oriental boy, marked JDK243, costumed in traditional Chinese brocade and satin with matching hat, 12"*	90.00	110.00	95.00
☐ **Elizabeth I,** *elegantly dressed in a queen's costume of wine velvet, trained dress with full skirt and silk brocade sleeves, dress has beautiful trims of metallic threads and laces, moire taffeta and lace bouffant petticoat, human hair wig coiffeured in a stately English style, headdress of lace and seed pearls, 16"*	200.00	300.00	225.00
☐ **Emmett Kelly,** *clown, costume of colorful raw silk, hand-made derby hat, 13"*	90.00	100.00	95.00
☐ **Googly Boy,** *costumed in the European tradition with beige shirt, velvet trousers, straw hat, 14"*	90.00	100.00	95.00

	Current Price Range		Prior Year Average
☐ **Googly Girl,** *Windsor Rose lace dress streamered with ribbons, matching hat and bloomers, 14″*	110.00	125.00	115.00
☐ **Gretchen,** *costumed in delicate seafoam silk and contrasting velvet, 12″*	95.00	110.00	100.00
☐ **Hans,** *costumed in seafoam velvet with silk and lace trims, matching velvet hat, 12″*	95.00	110.00	100.00
☐ **Hilda,** *toddler, marked JDK Jr. German, costumed in lavender print eyelet with matching pinafore trimmed with satin ribbons, 14″*	85.00	100.00	90.00
☐ **Just Me,** *costumed in yellow dotted swiss and eyelet, with matching ribbon bonnet, 9″*	70.00	80.00	75.00
☐ **Laughing Jumeau,** *costumed in lavender silk, lavished with embroidered flowers and laces, matching silk handbag, 14″*	90.00	100.00	95.00
☐ **Lily,** *costumed in a sumptuous gown of pale turquoise, original design detail in the lavish ruffles and laces, matching parasol, and hat trimmed with ostrich feathers, handmade matching slippers with pearl button, human hair wig, ball-jointed, 18″*	225.00	250.00	230.00
☐ **Mein Liebling Boy,** *ball-jointed, costumed in luscious brown velvet, 16″*	145.00	150.00	147.00
☐ **Mein Liebling Girl,** *ball-jointed, costumed in exquisite moss green moire taffeta, hat lavished with laces and silk flowers, 16″*	160.00	180.00	165.00
☐ **Monica,** *dress made in moire taffeta with imported braid trims adding touches of silk and gold, velvet jacket trimmed with mink, and gold braid, coiffured human hair, costume and beautiful ostrich-trimmed hat all designed in the Victorian period, ball-jointed, 16″*	225.00	250.00	245.00
☐ **Paris Pouty,** *marked SFBJ252, costumed in French blue silks and imported French laces, a matching French silk bonnet with an abundance of lace trims, 11″*	90.00	110.00	95.00
☐ **Pouty Boy,** *costumed in Wedgewood blue velvet, 12″*	85.00	100.00	90.00
☐ **Pouty Girl,** *costumed in Wedgewood blue velvet, 12″*	85.00	100.00	90.00
☐ **Shih Chieh,** *silk pleated gown, Princess headdress, pearl necklace, hand-made silver lame slippers, 16″*	150.00	160.00	155.00
☐ **Shih Chieh's Robe,** *made of silk threads and hand-beaded*	100.00	120.00	110.00
☐ **Twirp,** *adorably costumed in a white dress, all-over embroidered with pink flowers and touches of soft green, 12″*	95.00	100.00	97.50

	Current Price Range		Prior Year Average
☐ **Twirp,** *costumed in peach silk with French lace detail, studded with hand-made silk flowers and seed pearls, 16″*	145.00	160.00	150.00
☐ **Winston,** *an original clown designed by Sonia Messer, black, silver, and gold lame costume, hand-made gold lame hat and shoes, hand-painted eyes, 16″*	150.00	175.00	155.00

Winston,
porcelain, 1983, 16″
$150.00-$175.00

SASHA MORGENTHALER

Sasha Morgenthaler was a Swiss doll artist who spent most of her life creating incredibly beautiful cloth and bisque dolls for her family and a chosen few collectors. She was a private person, and as intensely talented woman who was used to making her dolls by hand for a tiny market. In the late 1960's, when the Doggart's of London wanted to manufacture her dolls at their doll factory, Sasha was very suspicious of the quality of a mass produced product. After friendship and trust was established between them, the long, arduous process of inventing a manufactruing system that preserved the Sasha magic began. It was eventually perfected and most of the owners of these dolls feel that Sashas are real.

Sasha Morgenthaler died in 1975, leaving a legacy of enchanted dolls that will live forever.

Sasha, 1980, 16″ . . . . **$150.00-$160.00**

	Current Price Range		Prior Year Average
☐ **Baby,** *black*	35.00	45.00	37.00
☐ **Baby,** *blonde, nighdress*	35.00	45.00	37.00
☐ **Baby,** *brunette, wears denim*	40.00	50.00	42.00
☐ **Baby,** *blonde, wears sundress*	35.00	45.00	37.00
☐ **Baby,** *brunette, with white bird*	35.00	45.00	37.00
☐ **Baby,** *honey blonde*	35.00	45.00	37.00
☐ **Baby Bear,** *baby, white travelling outfit, holds teddy bear, c. 1982, #512, 12″*	40.00	50.00	44.00
☐ **Blonde,** *gingham outfit*	45.00	55.00	47.00
☐ **Blonde,** *sail smock*	45.00	55.00	47.00
☐ **Brunette,** *pink dress*	45.00	55.00	47.00
☐ **Brunette, red pinafore**	45.00	55.00	47.00
☐ **Caleb**	45.00	55.00	47.00
☐ **Cora**	45.00	55.00	47.00
☐ **Gregor Jeans**	45.00	55.00	47.00
☐ **Gregor Jump Suit,** *blonde*	45.00	55.00	47.00

Sasha, 1982, 16″ . . . . **$45.00-$50.00**

	Current Price Range		Prior Year Average
☐ **Gregor Redhead,** *T-shirt, pants, jacket, shoes, #312, c. 1982, 16″*	45.00	55.00	47.00
☐ **Marina,** *brunette*	45.00	55.00	47.00
☐ **McGuffy Anna,** *c. 1983*	60.00	70.00	63.00
☐ **Redhead,** *white dress*	45.00	55.00	47.00
☐ **Sasha,** *real blonde hair, brown eyes, white dress, white socks, green velvet shoes, limited edition, c. 1982*	100.00	150.00	130.00
☐ **Sasha,** *blonde short hair, cinched sweater, knee length skirt, knee socks, white shoes, #112, c. 1982, 16″*	45.00	50.00	49.00

FAE MORRIS

Chloe,
porcelain bisque, 22″
$465.00-$500.00

Fae Morris, like many doll artists, started her career when her children were grown and she needed something as wonderful as childrearing to fill her time. Starting with portrait painting, switching to sculpture and finally resolving the two into doll making, Fae creates porcelain dolls modelled from real life people. Her attention to detail is meticulous, and her dedication to the art of hand made dolls has made her limited editions instantly collectible.

	Current Price Range		Prior Year Average
☐ **Chloe,** *California, porcelain bisque, evening gown, 22″*	465.00	500.00	480.00
☐ **Danny,** *California, porcelain bisque, cloth body, limited edition, 24″*	425.00	500.00	445.00
☐ **Patty,** *California, porcelain bisque, cloth body, limited edition, 21″*	325.00	375.00	330.00
☐ **Petite Chloe,** *California, porcelain bisque, limited edition, 19″*	375.00	450.00	385.00
☐ **Wendy,** *California, porcelain, jointed, limited edition, 13″*	170.00	200.00	165.00

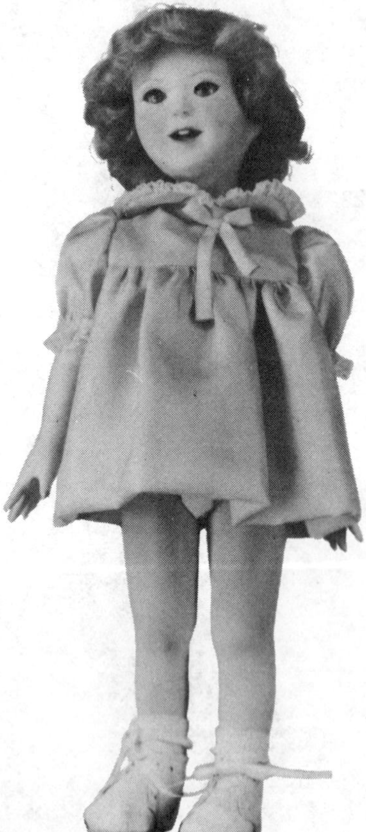

Wendy,
porcelain, jointed, 13″
$175.00-$200.00

CAROL LYNN WAUGH

	Current Price Range		Prior Year Average
☐ **Bearishnikov,** *Maine, composition, brown, molded leotard, tights, ballet shoes, jointed, 6″*	45.00	55.00	49.00
☐ **Bearishnikov,** *Maine, composition, yellow, molded foe shoes, ballet costume, roses at neckline, jointed, 6″*	45.00	55.00	49.00
☐ **Bearlock And The Super Sleuth,** *Maine, composition, jointed, molded Sherlock Holmes collar, pierced hands, 5″*	45.00	55.00	49.00
☐ **Beartram,** *Maine, latex swivel head, velour body, wire armature, limited edition, c. 1982, 7″*	75.00	85.00	79.00
☐ **Cedric,** *Maine, composition, jointed, molded shoes, spats*	55.00	65.00	59.00

Cedric,
porcelain, c. 1980
$55.00-$65.00

Honey Apple and Beartram, 1982 .... **$150.00-$300.00**

	Current Price Range		Prior Year Average
☐ **Honey Apple,** *Maine, latex swivel heads, velour body, wire armature, limited edition, c. 1982, 7"*	75.00	85.00	79.00
☐ **Ms. Bear,** *Maine, composition, jointed, molded collar, bow, 5"*	45.00	55.00	48.00
☐ **Santa Bear,** *Maine, composition, jointed, molded jacket, boots, mittens, 5"*	45.00	55.00	48.00

PAPERDOLLS

Alice in Wonderland, Disney, c. 1951 . . . . **$75.00-$100.00**
(photo by Hake's Americana, York, Pa.)

	Current Price Range		Prior Year Average
☐ **Air Hostess,** *1947 Saalfield*	**12.00**	**18.00**	**14.00**
☐ **Airline Stewardess,** *1957 Samuel Lowe* . . .	**2.00**	**8.00**	**5.00**
☐ **Alice Faye,** *1941 Merrill #4800, three dolls, forty-three pieces of clothing*	**70.00**	**80.00**	**74.00**
☐ **A Little French Doll Cut-Out,** *with dresses like those Queen Marie Antonnette wore, 1931, newspaper doll, assorted clothes, uncut*	**8.00**	**12.00**	**9.00**
☐ **All Aboard For Shut-Eye-Town,** *Dionne Quints, 1937, uncut*	**30.00**	**40.00**	**34.00**
☐ **All Nations Paper Doll Book,** *reproduction of 1900 book, four dolls, 8", assorted clothes*	**2.00**	**6.00**	**4.00**
☐ **American Colonial Brides,** *by Peggy Jo Rosamond, six historic brides, wedding dresses and assorted outfits, uncut*	**2.00**	**6.00**	**4.00**
☐ **Amy,** *c.1970's, former President Carter's daughter, magic touch clothes, uncut*	**12.00**	**20.00**	**15.00**
☐ **Amy Jo,** *1972 Saalfield*	**2.00**	**6.00**	**4.00**
☐ **Angel Babies,** *1943, Merrill book #4833, ten dolls, cut*	**5.00**	**10.00**	**7.00**
☐ **Annie Oakley With Tagg And Lofty,** *1956 Whitman book #1960, statuette dolls, eight pages of Western outfits, uncut*	**45.00**	**55.00**	**48.00**

	Current Price Range		Prior Year Average
☐ **Ann Southern,** *1943 Saalfield #2483, three dolls, twenty-three outfits, eighteen accessories, cut*	20.00	30.00	22.00
☐ **Antique Dolls Go To A Paper Doll Wedding,** *by Peggy Jo Rosamond, reproductions of four dolls in authentic wedding outfits, uncut*	2.00	6.00	4.00
☐ **Antique French Doll Paper Dolls,** *by Peggy Jo Rosamond, authentic antique costumes, uncut*	2.00	6.00	4.00
☐ **Antique German Bisque Paper Dolls,** *by Janet Nason, four paper dolls based on German bisque dolls, four pages of clothing, uncut*	2.00	6.00	4.00
☐ **Archie Paperdolls,** *1969 Whitman #4743, four statuette dolls, clothes and stands, cut*	2.00	8.00	4.00
☐ **Around The Clock With Sue And Dot,** *1951 Merrill*	2.00	6.00	4.00
☐ **Artistic Series #750A,** *by Raphael Tuck, one dress, tabs fit around hair*	30.00	40.00	34.00
☐ **Artist's Models,** *1945 Saalfield book #2489, four dolls, assorted outfits, uncut*	15.00	20.00	17.00
☐ **At Our House,** *Saalfield book, Jacqueline Kennedy and Caroline, uncut*	12.00	18.00	14.00
☐ **Ava Gardner,** *1952 Whitman #1192, two dolls, fifteen outfits, cut*	10.00	18.00	14.00
☐ **Ava Gardner,** *1953 Whitman #2108, two dolls, assorted outfits, folder, cut*	10.00	18.00	14.00
☐ **A World Of Costumes In Cutout,** *by Rosemary Lowndes and Claude Kailer, instructions and pieces for three-dimensional paper dolls, three-dimensional costumes from the Middle Ages to 1905, backgrounds, fashion plates, background booklet on costumes, 9" x 11½", uncut*	8.00	12.00	9.00
☐ **Badgett Quadruplets,** *1941 Saalfield*	50.00	60.00	52.00
☐ **Ballet Dancing Dolls,** *1955 Whitman, four dolls*	2.00	7.00	4.00
☐ **Ballet Dolls,** *two little dancers, assorted ballet costumes*	5.00	10.00	7.00
☐ **Ballerinas,** *1967 Whitman book #1995, four dolls, assorted costumes, comes in folder, cut*	4.00	10.00	6.00
☐ **Ballet Dancers,** *1968 Whitman book #1962, three dolls — Jennifer, Marilyn, and Claudia, assorted costumes, cut*	2.00	8.00	4.00
☐ **Ballet,** *two dolls — one blonde, the other brunette, punch-outs, assorted costumes, uncut*	8.00	12.00	9.00

Cat and Owl,
cardboard stand-ups,
McLoughlin Brothers, 12″
$30.00-$40.00

	Current Price Range		Prior Year Average
☐ **Ballet Stars,** *six dolls — Chris, Tania, Andre, Laura, John, and Alice, assorted costumes, pink and blue cover, uncut*	8.00	12.00	9.00
☐ **Barbara Britton,** *1954 Saalfield, uncut*	25.00	35.00	29.00
☐ **Barbie Doll,** *1962 Whitman book #1963, one doll, assorted outfits including wedding gown, folder, cut*	2.00	8.00	4.00
☐ **Barboir's Irish Flax,** *1895, ad doll, blonde, peach-colored dress trimmed in flowers, cut*	8.00	12.00	9.00
☐ **Bambi,** *#966, punch-out, cut*	20.00	30.00	24.00
☐ **Beauty Dolls To Dress,** *1930's, tall doll with red hair, two outfits, cut*	8.00	12.00	9.00
☐ **Becky And Betsy,** *1952 Merrill book #345210, four dolls, wrap around Civil War era dresses, uncut*	30.00	40.00	32.00
☐ **Bedknobs And Broomsticks,** *1971 Whitman*	2.00	8.00	5.00
☐ **Beth Ann,** *by Kathy Laurence, (Queen Holden's daughter), 1970 Whitman book #1955, one doll, assorted clothes, cut*	8.00	12.00	9.00
☐ **Betsy McCall,** *1965-66 Saalfield book #1370, reprint, uncut*	12.00	18.00	14.00
☐ **Betsy McCall,** *1971 Whitman box #4744, one doll, assorted clothes, boxed, uncut*	12.00	18.00	14.00
☐ **Betsy Ross,** *by Queen Holden, 1963 Platt and Munk book #224B, assorted dresses, uncut*	25.00	35.00	29.00

	Current Price Range		Prior Year Average
☐ **Betsy Ross And Her Friends,** *by Queen Holden, 1969 Platt and Munk #1251, Tom, Betsy, Dolly, and John, Colonial costumes, boxed, uncut*	8.00	12.00	9.00
☐ **Betty And Bob,** *by Queen Holden, 1952, #991, large dolls — boy is a brunette, the girl is a blonde, assorted outfits, cut*	15.00	25.00	18.00
☐ **Betty Blue And Patty Pink,** *1958 Merrill, wrap-around clothes*	12.00	18.00	14.00
☐ **Betty Bobbs Baby Brother Buddy Bobbs,** *(Pictorial Review), February 1925, cut*	4.00	8.00	5.00
☐ **Betty Bonnett Paper Dolls,** *by Sheila Young, includes sixteen original Betty Bonnet sheets*	2.00	6.00	4.00
☐ **Bettina And Her Playmate Rosalie,** *1931 Saalfield, uncut*	25.00	35.00	27.00
☐ **Betty Davis,** *1942 Merrill, uncut*	55.00	65.00	56.00
☐ **Betty Field,** *1943 Saalfield book #332, two large dolls, gowns and assorted clothes, jewelry and jewelry box, cut*	45.00	55.00	48.00
☐ **Betty Grable,** *1953 Merrill, uncut*	40.00	50.00	43.00
☐ **Betty Grable,** *1941 Whitman #989, two dolls, thirty-six outfits, twenty-eight accessories, cut*	12.00	18.00	13.00
☐ **Betty Grable,** *1943 Whitman #976, two dolls, twenty-five outfits, fourteen accessories, cut*	20.00	30.00	23.00
☐ **Betty Grable,** *1951 Merrill*	75.00	125.00	90.00
☐ **Betty Hutton And Daughters,** *1958 Saalfield book #4423, three statuette dolls, assorted outfits, cut*	30.00	40.00	32.00
☐ **Big And Little Dolls,** *1954 Whitman book #4081, four dolls, assorted outfits, scissors, comes in folder, uncut*	20.00	30.00	24.00
☐ **Big Baby,** *c.1950's, Abbott book #1326, large toddler in diapers, assorted baby clothes, die cut, uncut*	40.00	50.00	43.00
☐ **Big, Big Doll Book — Two Little Girls,** *by Queen Holden, 1964 Lowe book #9045, large dolls, punch-out clothes, uncut*	40.00	50.00	44.00
☐ **Big Jim And Big Jack,** *1976 Whitman, Mattel Dolls*	2.00	8.00	5.00
☐ **Big 'N' Little Sister,** *1951 Merrill*	2.00	6.00	4.00
☐ **Big Doll Betty,** *1960 Samuel Lowe, uncut*	2.00	6.00	4.00
☐ **Big 'N' Easy,** *1949 Merrill, uncut*	5.00	10.00	7.00
☐ **Big Sister,** *Reuben Lilja Company book #921, four dolls, dolls in green striped suits, additional matching outfits, thin cover, uncut*	10.00	15.00	11.00

Betty Grable, Merrill, c. 1951 . . . . **$75.00-$125.00**
(photo by Hakes's Americana, York, Pa.)

	Current Price Range		Prior Year Average
☐ **Bild-A-Set,** *by Pachter, Chicago, 1943, eight dolls with front and back uniforms, cut*	40.00	50.00	43.00
☐ **Billy Boy,** *Samuel Lowe, uncut*	2.00	6.00	4.00
☐ **B Is For Betsy,** *1954 Merrill*	2.00	6.00	4.00
☐ **Blondie,** *1944 Whitman book #981, four dolls — Blondie, Dagwood, Cookie, and Alexander, assorted outfits, cut*	30.00	40.00	34.00
☐ **Blondie,** *1945 King Features book #987, Blondie, Dagwood, Alexander, Cookie, and Daisy, assorted outfits, cut*	30.00	40.00	32.00
☐ **Blondie,** *from the T.V. show, Saalfield book #1334, Comic characters also, uncut*	20.00	30.00	23.00
☐ **Blonde Doll,** *by Betty Campbell, numerous front and back outfits, cut*	8.00	12.00	9.00
☐ **Buffy,** *from the T.V. show (Family Affair), 1968 Whitman book #1995, carries Mrs. Beasley, assorted outfits*	20.00	30.00	22.00
☐ **Buffy And Jody,** *from the T.V. show (Family Affair), 1970, statuette dolls, assorted clothes, boxed, uncut*	16.00	24.00	19.00

	Current Price Range		Prior Year Average
☐ **Buffy With Little Mrs. Beasley,** *1968 Whitman #1985, folder, cut*	2.00	8.00	5.00
☐ **Busy Days,** *Abbott book #1359, four dolls — two older children and two younger, assorted outfits, uncut*	18.00	22.00	19.00
☐ **Butterfly Ballet,** *Saalfield, five dolls, assorted costumes, uncut*	12.00	18.00	14.00
☐ **Bye Baby Bunting,** *1956 Samuel Lowe, uncut*	2.00	6.00	4.00
☐ **Candy,** *1964 Watkins, four dolls, clothes for teenagers, such as prom dresses, outfits for tennis and luaus*	5.00	10.00	7.00
☐ **Candy Queens,** *1950's, #2632, reprint of Gale Storm, three dolls — Miss Candy Kiss, Miss Lollipop, and Miss Peppermint, assorted outfits, uncut*	12.00	18.00	14.00
☐ **Cathy Goes To Camp,** *1954 Merrill, uncut*	2.00	6.00	3.00
☐ **Cecilia My Kissing Cousin,** *1960 Lowe book #9985, one doll with kissing disc, assorted clothes, cut*	12.00	18.00	14.00
☐ **Century Dolls,** *by Queen Holden, eight dolls, costumes from Civil War era, cut*	8.00	12.00	9.00
☐ **Characters For Punch And Judy,** *from magazine (The Metropolitan), May 15, 1901, uncut*	20.00	30.00	22.00
☐ **Charlie McCarthy,** *by Queen Holden, 1938 Whitman book #995, one doll, another head, assorted outfits, cut*	12.00	18.00	14.00
☐ **Charming,** *Saalfield book #1323, three ladies, assorted clothes, uncut*	8.00	12.00	9.00
☐ **Chatty Cathy,** *1964 Whitman book #1961, Mattel doll, blonde hair, uncut*	16.00	24.00	19.00
☐ **Children Around The World,** *1955 Merrill, wrap-around clothing*	5.00	10.00	7.00
☐ **Chitty Chitty Bang Bang,** *1968 Whitman book #1982, five large dolls, assorted costumes, uncut*	30.00	40.00	33.00
☐ **Cinderella,** *book, #1731, four die-cut dolls, medieval costumes, thin book, uncut*	8.00	12.00	9.00
☐ **Cinderella,** *1950 Saalfield, four dolls, 6½" x 12" book*	5.00	10.00	7.00
☐ **Cinderella Steps Out,** *1948 Samuel Lowe, uncut*	10.00	18.00	13.00
☐ **Cindy,** *1964 Samuel Lowe, uncut*	2.00	6.00	4.00
☐ **Circus Time,** *1952 Samuel Lowe, cut*	2.00	4.00	3.00
☐ **Circus Twins,** *c.1940's, front and back dolls, uncut*	2.00	6.00	4.00
☐ **Cowboy And Cowgirl,** *1950 Merrill, uncut*	2.00	6.00	4.00
☐ **Cowboys And Cowgirls,** *1950 Samuel Lowe, uncut*	5.00	8.00	7.00

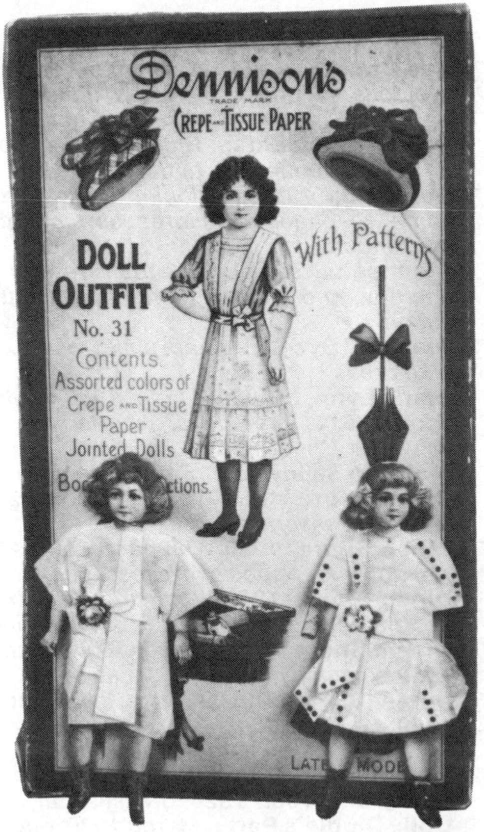

Dennisons,
Crepe and Tissue Doll Outfit
$30.00-$40.00

	Current Price Range		Prior Year Average
☐ **Cradle Tots,** *1945 Merrill, uncut*	10.00	18.00	13.00
☐ **Crepe Paper Doll Outfit,** *Mrs. A.A. Gutgesell, Inc., Dennison-type doll, crepe paper clothes, folder, cut*	20.00	30.00	24.00
☐ **Cuddles And Rags,** *1950's Bonnie Books #2738, reprint of #1283, assorted clothes, uncut*	30.00	40.00	33.00
☐ **Curiosity Shop,** *1971 Saalfield, uncut*	2.00	6.00	4.00
☐ **Curious George Paper Dolls,** *by Margaret Rey and Kathy Allert, two dolls, forty-eight costumes showing George as a pirate, Indian chief, fireman, window washer, and more, thirty-two pages, uncut*	2.00	6.00	3.00
☐ **Curley McDimple,** *colored forms, boxed set*	20.00	30.00	24.00
☐ **Curtain Time,** *#1733, reprint of Diana Lynn, two dolls, four pages of outfits, uncut*	8.00	12.00	9.00

	Current Price Range		Prior Year Average
☐ **Cyd Charisse,** *1956 Whitman book #2084, two dolls, six pages of clothes, uncut*	80.00	90.00	81.00
☐ **Daddy's Girl,** *1974 Saalfield, uncut*	2.00	6.00	4.00
☐ **Debbie Reynolds,** *1960 Whitman book #1956, statuette doll, folder, cut*	20.00	30.00	23.00
☐ **Deerfield,** *1919, Colonial home, Indian home, six pages of children, six story booklets, uncut*	45.00	55.00	48.00
☐ **Dennisons,** *set of three dolls — one girl, one boy, and a baby, handmade outfits for girl only*	30.00	40.00	32.00
☐ **Diamond Dye Girl,** *wears pink dress, extra blue dress*	8.00	12.00	10.00
☐ **Diana Lynn,** *by Judy Stang, 1953 Saalfield book #2611, three dolls, assorted dresses, uncut*	20.00	30.00	24.00
☐ **Dick The Sailor,** *1941 Samuel Lowe, uncut*	8.00	12.00	9.00
☐ **Dinah Shore,** *1954 Whitman book #2042, two dolls, assorted outfits, cut*	30.00	40.00	34.00
☐ **Dinah Shore,** *1956 Whitman book #2060, two dolls, six pages of dresses, uncut*	70.00	80.00	73.00
☐ **Dinah Shore,** *1958 Whitman book #1963, two statuette dolls, assorted outfits, uncut*	60.00	70.00	64.00
☐ **Dinah Shore And George Montgomery,** *1959 Whitman book #1970, cut*	40.00	50.00	43.00
☐ **Dinah Shore And George Montgomery,** *1959 Whitman book #1970, statuette dolls, assorted clothes, folder, uncut*	60.00	70.00	63.00
☐ **Dolly Dingle's Paper Dolls And Her Little Friend Julie,** *July 1924, dresses, cut*	2.00	6.00	4.00
☐ **Dolly Dingle's Party,** *March 1930, one doll, clothes, dog Comfy, uncut*	8.00	12.00	9.00
☐ **Dolly Dingle's Playmates,** *May 1929, matching Raggedy Andy costume, uncut*	8.00	12.00	9.00
☐ **Dolly Dingle's Sammy Snooks,** *December 1921, one doll, coat and hat, cut*	2.00	6.00	3.00
☐ **Dolly Dingle's Sweetheart,** *July 1929, uncut*	8.00	12.00	9.00
☐ **Dolly Dingle's Sweetheart,** *July 1929, cut*	4.00	8.00	6.00
☐ **Dolly Dingle's Travels,** *September 1929, alsace costume, day dress, uncut*	8.00	12.00	9.00
☐ **Dolly Dingle's Trip Around The World — Somewhere In France,** *August 1917, small doll, cut*	2.00	8.00	4.00
☐ **Dolly Dingle's Vacation,** *September 1927, story, playsuit, backed, cut*	5.00	10.00	7.00
☐ **Dolly Dingle's Weekend Paper,** *August 1929, Colonial costume, uncut*	8.00	12.00	9.00
☐ **Dolly Dingle's Weekend,** *August 1929, one doll, assorted outfits, cut*	6.00	10.00	8.00

	Current Price Range		Prior Year Average
☐ **Dolly Dingle's Weekend Guest Virginia,** *November 1926, one doll, gown, hat, purse, and flower, cut*	8.00	12.00	9.00
☐ **Dotty Double,** *1933, 13" front and back doll, cut*	6.00	10.00	7.00
☐ **Double Date,** *1957 Saalfield, uncut*	5.00	10.00	7.00
☐ **Double Dolls,** *five dolls — two girls and three boys, dressed in different styles, no outfits*	18.00	22.00	19.00
☐ **Double Wedding,** *1939 Merrill, uncut*	25.00	35.00	28.00
☐ **Down On The Farm,** *Samuel Lowe, uncut*	10.00	18.00	13.00
☐ **Dream Girl,** *1947 Merrill, uncut*	10.00	18.00	13.00
☐ **Dresses Worn By The First Ladies Of The White House,** *by Mabelle Mercer, 1939 Saalfield book #2164, three dolls, assorted costumes, cut*	16.00	24.00	19.00
☐ **Dress Me,** *by Queen Holden, 1950 Whitman book #972, nude baby, one suit and several other outfits, cut*	12.00	18.00	14.00
☐ **Elaine Stewart,** *1955 Whitman book #2048, two dolls, assorted outfits, cut*	30.00	40.00	34.00
☐ **Elizabeth,** *1963 Samuel Lowe, uncut*	2.00	6.00	4.00
☐ **Elizabeth Taylor,** *1949 Whitman book #968, assorted outfits, cut*	40.00	50.00	44.00
☐ **Elizabeth Taylor,** *1955 Whitman book #1951, two large dolls, cut*	30.00	40.00	34.00
☐ **Elly May,** *1963 Watkins/Strathmore book #1819A, small book, two dolls, eight pages of clothes, uncut*	40.00	50.00	43.00
☐ **Emilie,** *Merrill*	45.00	55.00	48.00
☐ **Emily And Mimi,** *by Queen Holden, 1971 James and Jonathan book #2711, assorted dresses, uncut*	8.00	12.00	9.00
☐ **Esther Williams,** *1950 Merrill book #1563, three dolls, numerous outfits, uncut*	55.00	65.00	58.00
☐ **Esther Williams,** *1950 Merrill book #1563, two dolls, several outfits, cut*	35.00	45.00	38.00
☐ **Erte' Fashion Paper Dolls Of The Twenties,** *by Erte', six paper dolls, forty-three costumes including gowns, coats, hats, and accessories with elaborate details, book production supervised by Erte', thirty-two pages, 9¼" x 12¼"*	2.00	6.00	4.00
☐ **Eve Arden,** *1953 Saalfield, uncut*	25.00	35.00	28.00
☐ **Evelyn Rudie,** *1958 Saalfield book #1745, four front and back dolls, four pages of clothes, thin cover, uncut*	20.00	30.00	23.00
☐ **Evelyn Rudie,** *1958 Saalfield book #1745, signed by Aralo, four dolls, four pages of outfits, soft cover, cut*	10.00	20.00	14.00

Elizabeth Taylor, Whitman, 1949 . . . . **$40.00-$50.00**
(photo by Hakes's Americana, York, Pa.)

	Current Price Range		Prior Year Average
☐ **Fairy Princess,** *Samuel Lowe Co., book #125515, large dolls, assorted costumes, uncut*	**30.00**	**40.00**	**33.00**
☐ **Family Affair,** *from the T.V. show, 1968 Whitman #4767, five statuette dolls, uncut*	**20.00**	**30.00**	**24.00**
☐ **Family Reunion** — *Grandmother And Grandfather, by Tina Lee, 1941, Jack and Jill set, uncut*	**8.00**	**12.00**	**9.00**
☐ **Farmer Fred,** *1943 Samuel Lowe, uncut* . . .	**5.00**	**10.00**	**7.00**
☐ **Fashion Art Dolls,** *four 10" dolls, six fashion sheets, two fabric sheets, eight fashion colors, artist brush, scissors, fifty fashions to make, uncut*	**2.00**	**6.00**	**3.00**
☐ **Fashion Book Of Round About Dolls,** *by Betty Campbell, 1936 McLaughlin book #540, four dolls, assorted dresses, cut*	**20.00**	**30.00**	**24.00**

	Current Price Range		Prior Year Average
☐ **Fashion Paper Dolls From Godey's Lady's Book,** *by Susan Johnston, seven fashion paper dolls, fifty costumes, published in the magazine between 1840-1854, uncut*	3.00	9.00	6.00
☐ **Fashion Previews,** *1949 Samuel Lowe, uncut*	10.00	18.00	14.00
☐ **Faye Emerson,** *1952 Saalfield book #1557, large dolls, cut*	20.00	30.00	23.00
☐ **Feeding The Swans,** *from newspaper (Boston Sunday Globe), 1906, doll with swans, uncut*	12.00	18.00	15.00
☐ **Folk Festival Pictures — Mexico,** *by Janet Smalley, December 1950, uncut*	2.00	8.00	4.00
☐ **Folk Festivals — Philadelphia's Mummers,** *by Janey Smalley, January 1951, Jack and Jill set, uncut*	2.00	6.00	4.00
☐ **Four Ballet Dancing Dolls,** *1955 Whitman book #1957, assorted costumes, cut*	2.00	8.00	5.00
☐ **Four Cousins Paperdolls,** *1941 Saalfield book #1952, reprint of Princess Paperdolls, set of four dolls, assorted outfits, cut*	20.00	30.00	24.00
☐ **Four Gems,** *Artcraft, reprint of Hootnany, four dolls — Donna, Peg, Wanda, and Kim, assorted outfits, uncut*	8.00	12.00	9.00
☐ **Four Little Girls From School,** *1957 Merrill, wrap-around clothes*	12.00	18.00	14.00
☐ **Four Mothers, Lane Sisters And Gale Page,** *1941 Whitman book #968, four dolls, assorted clothes, cut*	18.00	24.00	21.00
☐ **French Doll,** *front and back doll, front and back clothes, uncut*	8.00	12.00	9.00
☐ **Fritze Ritz,** *by Ernie Bushmiller, Lowe book #1259, two dolls, wrap-around dresses, based on the comics, uncut*	30.00	40.00	33.00
☐ **Gaby Harp,** *1954 Samuel Lowe*	2.00	6.00	4.00
☐ **Gale Storm,** *1958 book #2061, two dolls, assorted outfits, uncut*	40.00	50.00	44.00
☐ **Gisele MacKenzie,** *1957 Saalfield book #4421, two dolls, assorted clothes, uncut*	40.00	50.00	42.00
☐ **Gisele MacKenzie,** *1957 Saalfield, cut*	15.00	25.00	18.00
☐ **Gisele MacKenzie,** *1958 book #4475, uncut*	30.00	40.00	33.00
☐ **Glamour Parade,** *c.early 1950's, Stevens*	2.00	6.00	4.00
☐ **Glamorous Movie Stars Of The Thirties Paper Dolls,** *by Tom Tierney, eight famous actresses, thirty-eight authentic costumes from films; includes Garbo, Harlow, Crawford, Lombard and others, thirty-two pages, 9¼" x 12¼"*	3.00	9.00	6.00
☐ **Gloria Jean,** *1940 Saalfield #1661, two dolls, fifteen outfits, four accessories, cut*	10.00	18.00	14.00

Gloria Jean, Saalfield, 1941 . . . . **$50.00-$75.00**
(photo by Hakes's Americana, York, Pa.)

	Current Price Range		Prior Year Average
☐ **Gloria Jean,** *1941 Saalfield #223, uncut* . . .	**35.00**	**45.00**	**38.00**
☐ **Gloria's Make Up,** *1952 book #2585, later became Rosemary Clooney, one doll, assorted outfits, cut* . . .	**16.00**	**24.00**	**20.00**
☐ **Golden Book Of Dolls And Toys,** *by Miloche and Kane, five dolls — two are babies, assorted clothes, cut* . . .	**18.00**	**22.00**	**19.00**
☐ **Golden Girl,** *1953 Merrill book #1543, two dolls, large assortment of clothes, cut* . . .	**25.00**	**35.00**	**28.00**
☐ **Goldilocks And The Three Bears,** *1939 Saalfield, uncut* . . .	**35.00**	**45.00**	**38.00**
☐ **Gone With The Wind,** *1940 Merrill #3405, uncut* . . .	**85.00**	**95.00**	**88.00**
☐ **Gone With The Wind,** *1940 Merrill, eighteen dolls, assorted clothes, cut* . . .	**125.00**	**175.00**	**140.00**
☐ **Gone With The Wind,** *1940 Merrill #3404, uncut* . . .	**85.00**	**95.00**	**88.00**

	Current Price Range		Prior Year Average
☐ **Gone With The Wind,** *by Charlotte Whatley, two dolls — Rhett 13" and Scarlette 11", sixteen authentic movie costumes, black and white, limited edition of 500*	8.00	12.00	10.00
☐ **Gone With The Wind,** *characters from the movie: Scarlette, Rhett, Melanine, Carreen, Ellen Suellen, Aunt Pittypat, Mammy, and Gerald, assorted outfits*	35.00	45.00	38.00
☐ **Good Little Dolls,** *1941 Saalfield, uncut*	15.00	25.00	18.00
☐ **Good Neighbor,** *1944 Saalfield, uncut*	10.00	18.00	13.00
☐ **Grace Kelly,** *1955 Whitman book #2049, dolls punch out and put back in, assorted outfits, uncut*	90.00	100.00	92.00
☐ **Grace Kelly, 1956 Whitman book** *#2064, assorted outfits, cut*	30.00	40.00	33.00

Grayce Kelly, Whitman, 1956 .... **$30.00-$40.00**
(photo by Hakes's Americana, York, Pa.)

	Current Price Range		Prior Year Average
☐ **Great Ballet Paper Dolls,** *by Nancie Swanberg, two paper dolls in color — male and female dancer, numerous costumes to be colored, short history of each ballet represented, 10" x 12½", uncut*	5.00	10.00	7.00
☐ **Great Empresses And Queens,** *by Tom Tierney, sixteen dolls including Queen Nefertiti, Grace Kelly, Marie Antoinette, Queen Victoria, and Cleopatra, uncut*	2.00	6.00	3.00
☐ **Great Fashion Designs Of The Belle Epoque Paper Dolls,** *by Tom Tierney, two dolls, thirty authentic costumes from the fasion of the late Victorian period, the Edwardian era, and the First World War, thirty-two pages, uncut*	2.00	6.00	3.00
☐ **Great Women Paper Dolls,** *Bellerophon, includes outstanding women such as Susan B. Anthony, Madame Curie, and Golda Meir, to be colored, uncut*	2.00	6.00	3.00
☐ **Green Acres,** *Eddie Albert and Ava Gabor, 1967 Whitman book #1979, two dolls, assorted outfits, cut*	16.00	24.00	20.00
☐ **Greer Garson,** *Merrill #3858, two dolls, cut*	5.00	10.00	7.00
☐ **Growing Up Skipper,** *1976 Whitman book #1990, uncut*	4.00	10.00	6.00
☐ **Grown-Up,** *1936 Merrill, uncut*	20.00	30.00	23.00
☐ **Gulliver's Travels,** *1939 Saalfield, uncut*	45.00	55.00	48.00
☐ **Hair-Do Dolls,** *by Queen Holden, 1948 Whitman book #991, three dolls, cut*	16.00	24.00	19.99
☐ **Heidi And Peter,** *c.1950's Saalfield, 6½" x 12" book*	2.00	8.00	5.00
☐ **Henry And Henrietta,** *1938 Saalfield, uncut*	20.00	30.00	24.00
☐ **Henry VIII And His Wives,** *Bellerophon, authentic costumes for each, to color, uncut*	2.00	6.00	4.00
☐ **Here's Mary,** *Miloche wooden doll, real blonde mohair curls, large assortment of dresses, uncut*	10.00	16.00	12.00
☐ **Here's Sally — Here's Sunny,** *by Beatrice Mallet, 1939 Whitman book #915, large dolls, cartoon-like children, uncut*	60.00	70.00	62.00
☐ **Here's The Bride,** *1953 Whitman #2109, bridal doll, assorted outfits, folder, cut*	8.00	12.00	9.00
☐ **High School,** *1940 Merrill, uncut*	20.00	30.00	24.00
☐ **High School Dolls,** *1948 Merrill, uncut*	10.00	18.00	13.00
☐ **Historic Costume,** *by Rachel Taft Dixon, 1934 Whitman book #905, four dolls, costumes from the Empire, Colonial and Victorian eras, cut*	12.00	18.00	14.00
☐ **Honey-Hair Bow Doll,** *chubby dolls, assorted outfits, cut*	12.00	18.00	14.00

	Current Price Range		Prior Year Average
☐ **Honeymoon,** *1961 Saalfield book #2724, two dolls, assorted outfits, uncut*	8.00	12.00	9.00
☐ **Honeymooners,** *1956 Samuel Lowe, uncut*	25.00	35.00	28.00
☐ **Hood's Family,** *one doll, blonde, three outfits, one hat*	18.00	22.00	20.00
☐ **Hoody Doody,** *four dolls, margerine premium, cut*	12.00	18.00	14.00
☐ **Ice Festival,** *by Lucille Wallace, Saalfield book #2711, four dolls, assorted costumes, uncut*	16.00	24.00	19.00
☐ **Ice Skating Dolls,** *1960 Merrill, three dolls*	12.00	18.00	14.00
☐ **I Love Lucy,** *1953 Whitman #2101, two dolls, assorted clothes, folder, cut*	10.00	18.00	14.00
☐ **Infamous Women Paper Dolls,** *Bellerophon, includes such women as Mata Hari, George Sand and Lucrezia Borgia, to be colored, uncut*	2.00	6.00	4.00
☐ **Jane Powell,** *1957 Whitman book #2085, two dolls, six pages of clothes, uncut*	70.00	80.00	73.00
☐ **Jane Powell,** *1957 Whitman book #2085, one doll in red and white striped suit, assorted outfits, cut*	12.00	18.00	14.00
☐ **Jane Withers,** *1938 Whitman book #996, four dresses, cut*	15.00	20.00	17.00
☐ **Jane Withers,** *1940 Whitman book #989, one doll in blue shorts and green blouse, five dresses, cut*	15.00	20.00	17.00
☐ **Jeanette MacDonald,** *1941 Merrill book #3460, two dolls — one backed, assorted costumes, cut*	45.00	55.00	48.00
☐ **Jeannie And Gene,** *1975 Samuel Lowe, uncut*	2.00	6.00	4.00
☐ **Jill,** *1963 Samuel Lowe, uncut*	15.00	25.00	18.00
☐ **Jill Makes Doll Clothes From Christmas Papers,** *by Tina Lee and Rita Oliver, Jack and Jill, 1940, uncut*	8.00	12.00	9.00
☐ **Jill's Christmas Doll,** *by Tina Lee, December 1941, Jack and Jill set, uncut*	8.00	12.00	9.00
☐ **Jill With The Kissing Lips,** *by Queen Holden, 1963 James and Jonathan, large doll, assorted outfits, uncut*	40.00	50.00	43.00
☐ **Jimmy And Jane Visit Gene Autry At Melody Ranch,** *1951 Whitman book #1184115, western outfits, uncut*	60.00	70.00	63.00
☐ **Joan,** *by Miloche, statuette doll, five outfits, cut*	4.00	10.00	6.00
☐ **Kiddies Koasting Karnival,** *by Durand Chapman, January 1915, assortment of dolls, sleds, uncut*	12.00	18.00	14.00

	Current Price Range		Prior Year Average
☐ **Kim Novak Paperdolls And Colorbook,** *1957 Saalfield book #4459, two dolls, four pages of dresses, coloring book, uncut*	55.00	65.00	58.00
☐ **Kim Novak,** *1958 Saalfield, uncut*	25.00	35.00	28.00
☐ **Kissey,** *1963 Saalfield, Ideal doll, has kissing disc on mouth, large doll, uncut*	15.00	25.00	18.00
☐ **Kit,** *by Queen Holden, 1952 Whitman book #210625, one doll, large assortment of clothes and toys, cut*	30.00	40.00	33.00
☐ **Kitchen Play,** *1938 Saalfield, uncut*	10.00	18.00	13.00
☐ **Kitty Goes To Kindergarden,** *1956 Merrill, uncut*	2.00	6.00	4.00
☐ **Lace And Dress Puppy,** *1975 Samuel lowe, uncut*	2.00	4.00	3.00
☐ **Lady And Girl,** *World War I, Decalco Lithography Co. set #, costumes, uncut*	6.00	12.00	8.00
☐ **Lana Turner,** *1942 Whitman #988, uncut*	30.00	40.00	33.00
☐ **Lana Turner,** *1945 Whitman #975, uncut*	30.00	40.00	33.00
☐ **Lana Turner,** *1945 Whitman #975, two dolls, twenty-seven outfits, nineteen accessories, cut*	20.00	30.00	24.00
☐ **Large Babies,** *c.early 1950's, three dolls, thirty-one pieces of clothing*	2.00	8.00	5.00
☐ **Large-Sized Doll,** *Raphael Tuck, white top, lavender petticoat, three dresses, two coats — one brown and one red*	45.00	55.00	50.00
☐ **Laugh-In,** *1969 Saalfield book #6045, assorted clothes and punchlines, uncut*	12.00	18.00	14.00
☐ **Laugh-In Party,** *1969 Saalfield, cut*	2.00	4.00	3.00
☐ **Lennon Sisters,** *1957 Whitman book #1979, four dolls, assorted outfits, uncut*	40.00	50.00	42.00
☐ **Lennon Sisters,** *1959 Whitman book #1991, four dolls, assorted clothes, tri-folder, uncut*	45.00	55.00	48.00
☐ **Lennon Sisters,** *1961 Whitman book #1983, assorted dresses, tri-folder, uncut*	45.00	55.00	48.00
☐ **Lennon Sisters,** *1963 Whitman book #1991, statuette dolls, assorted clothes, tri-folder, uncut*	40.00	50.00	42.00
☐ **Lettie Lane Paper Dolls,** *by Shelia Young, reproduction of twenty-four antique paper dolls published in Ladies Home Journal 1908-1910, assorted outfits — evening dress, summer wear, and haute couture, thirty-two pages, 9¼" x 12¼", uncut*	3.00	9.00	6.00
☐ **Let's Play House,** *by Robert Bezucha, 1932 Whitman book #W968B, three rooms, uncut*	45.00	55.00	48.00
☐ **Let's Play Store,** *by Fran Bisel Peat, 1933 Saalfield book #971, grocery store, uncut*	70.00	80.00	74.00

	Current Price Range		Prior Year Average
☐ **Let's Play With The Baby,** *1948 Merrill book #1550, cut*	4.00	8.00	5.00
☐ **Liberty Belles,** *1943 Merrill, uncut*	15.00	20.00	17.00
☐ **Lieutenant Greene J.G.,** *by Tina Lee, May 1941, Jack and Jill set, uncut*	8.00	12.00	9.00
☐ **Life Size Doll,** *by Queen Holden, 1936 Whitman book #958, large blonde toddler, assorted outfits, cut*	40.00	50.00	43.00
☐ **Lilac Time,** *1959 Saalfield, uncut*	5.00	10.00	7.00
☐ **Linda Darnell,** *1953 Saalfield book #1584, two dolls, assorted costumes and clothes, cut*	55.00	65.00	58.00
☐ **Lindy-Lou 'N' Cindy-Sue,** *1954 Merrill, uncut*	8.00	12.00	9.00
☐ **Lito-Paris,** *two statuette dolls, assorted outfits, uncut*	5.00	10.00	7.00
☐ **Little Ballerina,** *1953 Merrill #1542, woman and girl, assorted costumes, uncut*	12.00	18.00	14.00

Mary Martin, Saalfield, c. 1942 .... **$40.00-$50.00**
(photo by Hakes's Americana, York, Pa.)

	Current Price Range		Prior Year Average
☐ **Melody Four,** *#1358, reprint set of Martha Hyer, uncut*	12.00	18.00	14.00
☐ **Mickey Mouse,** *1971 Whitman book #1918, punch-outs, Mickey, Donald, Goofy, and Pluto, uncut*	12.00	18.00	14.00
☐ **Mimi From Paree,** *1960 Samuel Lowe, uncut*	2.00	6.00	4.00
☐ **Mini Mods,** *1969 Saalfield, uncut*	2.00	4.00	3.00
☐ **Miss America,** *by Betty Campbell, 1941, thirty-one pieces of clothing*	5.00	10.00	7.00
☐ **Miss Holly Day,** *by Quida, c.1950's, DeJournette Co. #2201, traveling doll set, numerous outfits, tickets, and travel box, cut*	8.00	12.00	9.00
☐ **Miss Molly Munsing,** *1909, various outfits, uncut*	40.00	50.00	44.00
☐ **Mod Fashions — Jane Fonda,** *1966 Saalfield book #1369, assorted clothes, uncut*	18.00	24.00	20.00
☐ **Mods,** *1967 Milton Bradley #4727, large headed dolls — one boy and one girl, mod clothes from the 1960's, cut*	2.00	8.00	4.00
☐ **Molly Bee,** *1962 Whitman book #2091, one doll, assorted clothes, tall thin book, uncut*	20.00	30.00	22.00
☐ **Molly Bee,** *1962 Whitman book #2091, one doll, assorted outfits, cut*	10.00	18.00	13.00
☐ **Mother Goose Rhyme Punch Out,** *1965, four scenes to punch out and put together*	2.00	6.00	4.00
☐ **Munsing Family,** *1909, set of eight dolls, with accessories, cut*	40.00	50.00	42.00
☐ **My Bonnie Lassie,** *1957 Saalfield*	5.00	10.00	7.00
☐ **My Book Of Paper Dolls,** *Frances Brundage, three dolls — two girls and one boy with one girl on back cover, assorted outfits*	15.00	20.00	16.00
☐ **My Doll House Family,** *1967 Whitman book #1985, house and family members, uncut*	20.00	30.00	22.00
☐ **My Farm,** *Whitman book #1967, farm, Farmer Brown, Mrs. Brown, Tom and Linda, front and back dolls, uncut*	20.00	30.00	22.00
☐ **My First Cut Out Book,** *1952 Merrill book #345110, large dolls, uncut*	20.00	30.00	24.00
☐ **My Fish And Mrs. Crab Each Summer Smile With Glee When Little Girls And Little Boys Play With Them By The Sea,** *by Barbara Hale, (McCalls), July 1920, uncut*	8.00	12.00	9.00
☐ **My Little Margie,** *by Aralo, 1954, Gale Storm, three dolls, four pages of clothes, soft cover, uncut*	30.00	40.00	33.00
☐ **My Twin's,** *by Yvonne Perrin, Saalfield book, uncut*	4.00	10.00	6.00

	Current Price Range		Prior Year Average
☐ **My Very Own Baby Doll,** *by Queen Holden, 1974 James and Jonathan book #3719, baby, assorted outfits, uncut*	12.00	18.00	14.00
☐ **Nanny And The Professor,** *1970/1971 Artcraft book #5114, window on Prudence, five dolls and a dog, punch-out clothes, uncut*	30.00	40.00	32.00
☐ **Natalie Wood,** *1958 Whitman book #2086, assorted outfits, cut*	40.00	50.00	43.00
☐ **National Velvet,** *1961 Whitman book #1958, from the T.V. show, folder, uncut*	20.00	30.00	23.00
☐ **National Velvet,** *1962 Whitman book #1948, one doll, assorted clothes, uncut*	30.00	40.00	33.00
☐ **Nurse And Doctor Paper Dolls,** *from T.V. Show, by Betty Campbell, Saalfield book #2777, five doll set, uncut*	30.00	40.00	34.00
☐ **Nurse And Doctors,** *by Betty Campbell, 1952 Saalfield*	5.00	10.00	7.00
☐ **Nursery Rhyme Party Dolls In Costume,** *McLoughlin Brothers, #574, cut*	30.00	40.00	33.00
☐ **Nurses Three,** *1964 Whitman book #1964, based on T.V. show, three dolls — Penny, Kelly, and Tracy, assorted outfits, uncut*	12.00	18.00	14.00
☐ **Official New York World's Fair Paper Doll Book,** *1964-1965 Spertus book #700-59, assorted foreign costumes, pictures of fair buildings, uncut*	8.00	12.00	9.00
☐ **Oklahoma,** *1956 Whitman book #1954, Gordon MacRae, Shirley Jones, assorted costumes, uncut*	70.00	80.00	73.00
☐ **Once Upon A Time,** *c.1960's Saalfield, ten dolls, ninety-four costumes from Mother Goose, reprint of The Old Woman Who Lived In A Shoe, uncut*	12.00	18.00	14.00
☐ **Once Upon A Wedding Day,** *Saalfield, cut*	2.00	6.00	3.00
☐ **One Hundred And One Dalmations,** *Walt Disney, Whitman book #1993:59, twenty-five stand up figures, fifteen costumes, accessories, tri-folder, uncut*	60.00	70.00	63.00
☐ **Our Little Pet,** *Raphael Tuck Artistic Series #106, one doll, two dresses*	18.00	22.00	20.00
☐ **Our New Baby,** *1937 Merrill, uncut*	15.00	25.00	19.00
☐ **Our Wave Joan,** *by Miloche and Kane, 1943 Whitman book #1012, die cut cover, four pages of clothes, uncut*	30.00	40.00	34.00
☐ **Outdoor Paper Dolls,** *1941 Saalfield book #1958, fourteen dolls, outdoor outfits, thin covers, uncut*	8.00	12.00	9.00
☐ **Ozzie And Harriett,** *1954 Saalfield, uncut*	15.00	25.00	19.00

	Current Price Range		Prior Year Average
☐ **Pageant,** *#4412, reprint of Brenda Starr (faces changed), assorted outfits same as Brenda Starr, uncut*	8.00	12.00	9.00
☐ **Palmer Cox Brownies,** *1895, jointed, uncut*	55.00	65.00	58.00
☐ **Pam And Her Dolly,** *Saalfield #1010, blonde doll — Dolly Ellen, assorted outfits, punch outs, uncut*	10.00	18.00	14.00
☐ **Pavlova And Nijinsky Paper Dolls,** *by Tom Tierney, two dolls of two famous Russian dancers, thirty authentic costumes, uncut*	2.00	6.00	4.00
☐ **Peasant Costumes Of Europe,** *1934 Whitman #900, uncut*	15.00	25.00	18.00
☐ **Peek-A-Boo,** *1955 Whitman, four babies, 6"*	5.00	10.00	7.00
☐ **PeePul Pals,** *1967 Whitman book #4758, four statuette dolls — Brenda Bride, Betty Ballerina, Nina Nurse, and Sally Stewardess, numerous outfits, cut*	2.00	8.00	6.00
☐ **Pee Wee,** *1967 Whitman book #1963, four dolls, Uneeda doll, uncut*	8.00	12.00	9.00
☐ **Peggy,** *1951 Saalfield book #1552, front and back doll, clothes, uncut*	12.00	18.00	14.00
☐ **Peggy And Peter,** *by Queen Holden, 1962 Lowe book #9041, two toddlers, numerous outfits, cut*	12.00	18.00	14.00
☐ **Peggy Pryde's Athletic Brother Phil,** *1926, three suits, hat, cut*	5.00	10.00	7.00
☐ **Penny's Party,** *1952 Samuel Lowe, uncut*	2.00	4.00	3.00
☐ **Penny,** *1964 Saalfield, uncut*	5.00	10.00	7.00
☐ **Penny's Party,** *1952 Bonnie book #4207, two dolls, assorted outfits, cut*	4.00	10.00	6.00
☐ **Peggy Pryde's Cousin Carrie,** *(Pictorial Review), March 1926, uncut*	12.00	18.00	14.00
☐ **Peggy Pryde's Little Brother Peter,** *(Pictorial Review), February 1926, uncut*	12.00	18.00	13.00
☐ **Pepe And The Senoritas,** *1961, four dolls, assorted costumes are reprints of Rita Hayworth's Carmen, uncut*	18.00	22.00	19.00
☐ **Pert And Pretty,** *1950's Saalfield, four teenagers*	5.00	10.00	7.00
☐ **Peter And Pam Twins,** *1961 Whitman, front and back dolls*	5.00	10.00	7.00
☐ **Peter Pumpkin's House,** *1955 Merrill, cut*	2.00	6.00	4.00
☐ **Peter Rabbit Paper Dolls,** *by Kathy Albert, Peter Rabbit doll, twenty eight outfits showing Peter in various occupations, such as magician, astronaut, rock star, football player, detective, and scuba diver, uncut*	2.00	6.00	3.00
☐ **Petticoat Junction,** *1964 Whitman book #1954, four dolls, assorted clothes, cut*	20.00	30.00	25.00
☐ **Petunia And Patches,** *1937 Saalfield, uncut*	35.00	45.00	38.00

	Current Price Range		Prior Year Average
☐ **Picnic,** *1952 Saalfield, uncut*	10.00	16.00	12.00
☐ **Pig-Tails,** *1949 Merrill, uncut*	5.00	10.00	7.00
☐ **Pink Prom Twins,** *1956 Merrill, uncut*	5.00	10.00	7.00
☐ **Pink Wedding,** *1952 Merrill book #1559, five dolls, numerous outfits, cut*	8.00	12.00	9.00
☐ **Piper Laurie,** *1953 Merrill, uncut*	40.00	50.00	44.00
☐ **Pixie And Pup,** *by Queen Holden, 1968 James Jonathan, punch outs, Pixie, toys, and clothes, uncut*	20.00	30.00	23.00
☐ **Playmate,** *DeJournette #800, one doll, three dresses, cut*	10.00	16.00	12.00
☐ **Playmates,** *1958 Whitman, four dolls, cut*	3.00	9.00	6.00
☐ **Playtime Pages,** *Circus Sam, by Stella Delcosta, July 1952, Jack and Jill set, uncut*	2.00	6.00	3.00
☐ **Playtime Pals,** *1946 Lowe book #1045, six dolls — two of them toddlers, several outfits, cut*	8.00	12.00	10.00
☐ **Playtime Playhouse,** *1968 Whitman, dolls, house, furniture*	2.00	6.00	4.00
☐ **Play Train,** *Saalfield book #4322:25, punch-out train, pictures to cover, railroad trademarks, uncut*	8.00	12.00	9.00
☐ **Polly And Her Playmates,** *1951 Merrill, uncut*	5.00	10.00	7.00
☐ **Polly Bergman,** *1958 Saalfield book #4442, two statuette dolls in red and green suits, assorted outfits, uncut*	45.00	55.00	48.00
☐ **Rock-A-Bye Baby,** *1945 Saalfield, uncut*	8.00	12.00	9.00
☐ **Rock Hudson,** *1957 Whitman book #2087, two dolls, assorted outfits, uncut*	40.00	50.00	43.00
☐ **Roller Rhythm,** *1944 Merrill, uncut*	15.00	25.00	18.00
☐ **Roly Poly Twins,** *Whitman #4123, two dolls — Sue and Skippy, red check sunsuits, uncut*	12.00	18.00	14.00
☐ **Romance,** *Saalfield book #1741, reprint of Diana Lynn, soft cover, uncut*	18.00	24.00	20.00
☐ **Rosemary Clooney,** *1956 Samuel Lowe, uncut*	40.00	50.00	42.00
☐ **Rosemary Clooney,** *1950 Abbott book #1806, two dolls, four pages of clothes, thin cover, uncut*	20.00	30.00	22.00
☐ **Rosita,** *c.1950's Saalfield, one dancing doll with spanish costumes and fans*	5.00	10.00	7.00
☐ **Roy Rogers And Dale Evans,** *1950 Whitman book #1186-15, dolls and Trigger, reproduction of Roy's autograph, uncut*	60.00	70.00	63.00
☐ **Roy Rogers And Dale Evans,** *1954 Whitman book #1950, statuette dolls, western outfits, brown leather-like cover, uncut*	45.00	55.00	48.00

	Current Price Range		Prior Year Average
☐ **Roy Rogers And Dale Evans,** *1956 Whitman book #1950, assorted western outfits, uncut*	45.00	55.00	48.00
☐ **Roy Rogers, Dale Evans And Dusty At The Double R-Bar Ranch,** *1957 Whitman book #1950, three statuette dolls, western outfits, uncut*	45.00	55.00	48.00
☐ **Royal Family,** *by Charlotte Whatley, three dolls — Prince Charles, Princess Diana, and baby; nineteen pages, thirty-five costumes, black and white, limited edition of 500*	8.00	12.00	10.00
☐ **Royal Wedding, Lady Diana And Prince Charles,** *made in England, book 12" x 18"*	14.00	20.00	17.00
☐ **Rub A Dub Dolly,** *1977 Whitman*	2.00	6.00	4.00

Sailor Boy, C. I. Hood and Company, c. 1894, 7" . . . . **$100.00-$150.00**

	Current Price Range		Prior Year Average
☐ **Sally,** *1951 Saalfield book #1553, front and back doll and clothes, small size, uncut*	12.00	18.00	14.00
☐ **Sally And Sue,** *#2945, called wood dolls, numerous outfits, cut*	2.00	8.00	4.00
☐ **Sally And Sunny,** *by Beatrice Mallet, 1939 Whitman book #915, two large dolls, seven outfits, accessories, cut*	12.00	1800	14.00
☐ **Sally Ann,** *1960 Samuel Lowe, uncut*	5.00	10.00	7.00
☐ **Sally Ann,** *1960 Samuel Lowe, cut*	2.00	6.00	4.00
☐ **Sally Lou,** *1931 Saalfield book #956, assorted outfits, cut*	30.00	40.00	34.00
☐ **Sally, Sandra, And Sue,** *1950-54 book #3460, assorted outfits, uncut*	12.00	18.00	14.00
☐ **Sally, Sue, And Sherry,** *1969 Samuel Lowe, uncut*	2.00	4.00	3.00
☐ **Sandra Dee,** *1959 Saalfield book #4417, two statuette dolls, assorted clothes, uncut*	30.00	40.00	33.00
☐ **Santa's Band,** *1962 Samuel Lowe, uncut*	2.00	4.00	3.00
☐ **Sarah-Ann,** *reproduction from the Castle Museum in England, one front and back doll, several front and back outfits from the 1880's, uncut*	2.00	6.00	4.00
☐ **School Chums,** *c.1950's, four dolls, assorted clothes*	3.00	8.00	5.00
☐ **Shirley Temple Playhouse,** *1935 Saalfield book #1739, carriage, assorted outfits, cut*	45.00	55.00	46.00
☐ **Shirley Temple Snap-On Paper Dolls,** *1958, boxed set*	40.00	50.00	42.00
☐ **Shirley Temple Standing Doll,** *1935, small statuette doll, assorted outfits, uncut*	80.00	90.00	81.00
☐ **Shirley Temple Standing Doll,** *1935 Saalfield book #1727, one doll, six pages of clothes, cut*	55.00	65.00	57.00
☐ **Six And Sweet Sixteen,** *1955 Merrill, uncut*	5.00	10.00	7.00
☐ **Six Little Steppers,** *by Charlotte Bejj, 1953 Merrill book #345310, uncut*	30.00	40.00	33.00
☐ **Six Reely Trooly Dolls,** *six dolls, faces, hands, and feet mounted on cloth, boxed*	40.00	50.00	43.00
☐ **Sixteen Two Date Girls And Their Clothes,** *assorted outfits, uncut*	20.00	30.00	22.00
☐ **Sleepy Doll,** *1971 Saalfield #6027, baby with sleeping eyes, punch-out clothes, uncut*	10.00	18.00	13.00
☐ **Slumber Party,** *1943 Merrill, uncut*	15.00	25.00	18.00
☐ **Snow White And The Seven Dwarfs,** *by Queen Holden, 1938 Whitman book #970, assorted costumes, cut*	30.00	40.00	33.00
☐ **Sonja Henie,** *1939 Merrill book #3475, three dolls, numerous costumes and clothes, cut*	60.00	70.00	64.00

	Current Price Range		Prior Year Average
☐ **Sonja Henie,** *1941 Merrill #3418, two dolls, twenty-two outfits, six accessories, uncut*	35.00	45.00	38.00
☐ **Sonja Henie,** *1941 Merrill book #3418, one doll in blue skating outfit, costumes, cut*	25.00	35.00	28.00
☐ **Sweet Sixteen,** *1944 Merrill book #4862, sixteen dolls, cut*	8.00	12.00	9.00
☐ **Swinging In The Hammock Is The Best Of Summer Joys For Dotty, Jim, Babe Ruth, And Tim, Their Pup And Cat, And Toys,** *by Barbara Hale, (McCalls), September 1920, uncut*	8.00	12.00	9.00
☐ **Tommy And Betty,** *large dolls, cut*	4.00	10.00	6.00
☐ **Teen Boutique,** *1973 Saalfield, uncut*	2.00	4.00	3.00
☐ **Teen Shop,** *1948 Saalfield, uncut*	5.00	10.00	7.00
☐ **Teri And Tonya,** *1967-1970 Saalfield book #4247, reprint of Jane Fonda, uncut*	8.00	12.00	9.00
☐ **Texas Rose,** *1959 Saalfield, uncut*	10.00	18.00	13.00
☐ **Thirteen Children,** *by Queen Holden, numerous outfits, cut*	20.00	30.00	24.00
☐ **This Is Bunny,** *1939 Whitman, reprint of Dionne Quints, one of five "Dolly Sisters," cut*	18.00	24.00	21.00
☐ **Three Baby Dolls,** *Saalfield book #4438, three statuette dolls, metal scissors, uncut*	6.00	10.00	7.00
☐ **Three Darling Dolls,** *1964 Saalfield, uncut*	5.00	10.00	7.00
☐ **Three Dolls In One — Trudy,** *1947 A.T.R. Publishing Co., one doll with three jointed heads which move, assorted outfits, cut*	45.00	55.00	48.00
☐ **Three Ice Skating Dolls,** *1960 Merrill book #1552, assorted costumes, uncut*	12.00	18.00	14.00
☐ **Three Lady Tucks,** *Belle of Saratoga, Belle of the West, and Belle of Newport, eight gowns*	125.00	175.00	140.00
☐ **Three Little Girls And How They Grew,** *by Hilda Miloche and Wilma Kane, 1944, cut*	16.00	24.00	20.00
☐ **Three Little Nixons,** *Pat, Julie, and Tricia, uncut*	8.00	12.00	10.00
☐ **Three Little Pigs Push Out Book,** *1958 Whitman*	10.00	18.00	14.00
☐ **Thumbelina,** *1969 Whitman book #1967, Ideal toy baby, one doll and assorted outfits, uncut*	8.00	12.00	9.00
☐ **Timmy,** *1956 Samuel Lowe, uncut*	2.00	4.00	3.00
☐ **Tina And Tony,** *1940 Samuel Lowe, uncut*	15.00	25.00	18.00
☐ **Tiny Thumbelina,** *1963 Western Publishers book #1885E, two dolls, assorted, cut*	6.00	10.00	7.00
☐ **Tiny Tots,** *c.1950's, two hard dolls, 6½", twenty-three pieces of clothing, cut*	2.00	5.00	3.00

	Current Price Range		Prior Year Average
☐ **Tiny Tot Shop,** *by Kathy Laurence (Queen Holden's daughter), 1969 Whitman book #1965, uncut*	16.00	24.00	19.00
☐ **Tippy Tumbles,** *1969 Whitman book #4760, Remco doll, assorted outfits, uncut*	4.00	10.00	6.00
☐ **Tom And His Toys,** *1943 Samuel Lowe, uncut*	5.00	10.00	7.00
☐ **Tom And The Aviator,** *1941 Samuel Lowe, uncut*	15.00	25.00	18.00
☐ **Tom Corbett Space Cadet,** *book #4304, push-out, dolls, planes, and guns, uncut*	18.00	22.00	19.00
☐ **Toni Hair-Do Cut-Out Dolls,** *1950 Samuel Lowe, uncut*	15.00	25.00	18.00
☐ **Toodles,** *1977, one walking doll, 9"*	2.00	6.00	4.00
☐ **Town And Country,** *1954 Saalfield, uncut*	10.00	18.00	13.00
☐ **Tracy,** *one 11" doll, three-dimensional, sculptured and contoured, assorted glamorous clothes*	5.00	10.00	7.00
☐ **Tricia Nixon,** *White House Tour Game, by Jeanne Voelz, 1970 Saalfield book #4248, one doll, assorted outfits, uncut*	10.00	18.00	13.00
☐ **Trinket,** *1953 Samuel Lowe, uncut*	2.00	4.00	3.00
☐ **Vivien Leigh Paper Dolls,** *by Tom Tierney, one doll, twenty-eight costumes from twelve films, on heavy stock*	2.00	6.00	4.00
☐ **Walt Disney's Mary Poppins,** *1964 Whitman book #1982:59, four dolls, assorted costumes, uncut*	40.00	50.00	43.00
☐ **Watch Me Grow,** *1944 Merrill, uncut*	15.00	25.00	19.00
☐ **Wedding Day,** *1964-1968 Saalfield Artcraft book, seven front and back dolls, uncut*	12.00	18.00	14.00
☐ **Wedding Day,** *Saalfield book #5128, punch-outs, uncut*	12.00	18.00	14.00
☐ **Wedding Paper Dolls,** *by Irene Griger, 1971, five dolls, assorted outfits, uncut*	8.00	12.00	9.00
☐ **Wedding Party,** *1964-1967 Saalfield book #1389, seven dolls, assorted outfits, uncut*	8.00	12.00	9.00
☐ **Wee Wee Baby Doll Book,** *1945 Samuel Lowe, uncut*	15.00	25.00	18.00
☐ **Well-Dressed Girl,** *1949 Saalfield, adult doll*	12.00	18.00	14.00
☐ **When We Grow Up,** *1971 Samuel Lowe, uncut*	2.00	4.00	3.00
☐ **Whishnik,** *1965 Whitman, trolls, numerous costumes, uncut*	8.00	12.00	9.00
☐ **Ziegfield Girls,** *c.1941, six famous movie stars, ten models, cut*	125.00	175.00	140.00
☐ **Zoo Revue,** *1974 Saalfield, uncut*	2.00	6.00	4.00
☐ **Yogi Bear And Cindy,** *1974 Wonder book*	2.00	8.00	5.00
☐ **You Are A Doll,** *Saalfield, uncut*	10.00	18.00	13.00
☐ **Yvonne,** *Merrill, uncut*	45.00	55.00	48.00

STUFFED ANIMALS

	Current Price Range		Prior Year Average
BEAR HAUS USA			
☐ **Baby Bear,** *tan, jointed, #3019, 10″*	10.00	15.00	11.00
☐ **Bear,** *tan, jointed, #1301, 14″*	12.00	15.00	13.00
☐ **Big Bear,** *tan, jointed, #2314, 16″*	15.00	20.00	16.00
☐ **Brownie Bear,** *jointed, #6005, 14″*	15.00	20.00	16.00
☐ **Junior Bear,** *tan, jointed, #2303, 10″*	9.00	12.00	10.00
☐ **Junior Snow Bear,** *white, jointed #2017, 10″*	10.00	15.00	11.00
☐ **Little Bear,** *tan, jointed, #1502, 12″*	11.00	16.00	12.00
☐ **Mama Bear,** *tan, jointed, #3100, 14″*	15.00	20.00	16.00
☐ **Papa Bear,** *tan, jointed, #3008, 16″*	15.00	20.00	16.00
☐ **Snow Bear,** *white, jointed, #2006, 16″*	15.00	20.00	16.00
DAKIN			
☐ **Bentley Bear,** *jointed, growls, 21″*	35.00	45.00	37.00
☐ **Garfield,** *7″*	6.00	12.00	8.00
☐ **Garfield,** *9″*	10.00	15.00	11.00
☐ **Mama and Baby Kittens,** *18″*	20.00	25.00	22.00
☐ **Odie,** *12″*	8.00	12.00	9.00
☐ **Odie,** *18″*	18.00	25.00	20.00
☐ **Teddy Bear,** *Theodore, jointed, 12″*	8.00	12.00	9.00
☐ **Teddy Bear,** *Theodore, jointed 15″*	11.00	18.00	12.00
☐ **Unicorn,** *little Utopia, lying, 13″*	15.00	25.00	16.00
☐ **Unicorn,** *Utopia, standing, 22″*	30.00	40.00	32.00
IDEAL			
☐ **Kisses,** *Hershey bear, plush, wears T-shirt, chocolate scent, 6″*	2.00	4.00	3.00
☐ **Kisses,** *Hershey bear, plush, wears T-shirt, chocolate scent, 10″*	5.00	8.00	6.00
☐ **Kisses,** *Hershey bear, plush, wears T-shirt, chocolate scent, 17″*	11.00	13.00	12.00
MERRY THOUGHT			
☐ **Anniversary Bear,** *commemorative,, 50th, off white, with growler, 16″*	100.00	150.00	105.00
☐ **Anniversary Bear,** *plush tan, RS14*	75.00	85.00	79.00
☐ **Cheeky Bear,** *gold mohair,jointed, TR18*	60.00	70.00	65.00
☐ **Cheeky Bear,** *gold, mohair, wool blend, jointed, music box, GT14*	65.00	75.00	70.00
☐ **Cheeky Bear,** *off white, jointed, bib, growler, LM16*	80.00	100.00	90.00
☐ **Cheeky Bear,** *plush, pink or blue, Pk12*	50.00	60.00	55.00
☐ **Edwardian Bear,** *mohair, jointed, with growler, HE18*	80.00	110.00	84.00
☐ **Gargey Bear,** *wool, plaid jumper, comes with cassette, 6″*	35.00	45.00	37.00

	Current Price Range		Prior Year Average
☐ **Merry Bear,** *mohair, embroidered green scarf, MY14*	50.00	60.00	55.00
☐ **Teddy Bear,** *music box*	65.00	75.00	69.00

NORTH AMERICAN BEARS

☐ **Aloysius,** *brown bear, plaid ribbon, 20″*	35.00	45.00	37.00
☐ **Bialosky Bear,** *golfer, hand-knit sweater, 13″*	25.00	35.00	26.00
☐ **Bialosky Bear,** *golfer, hand-knit sweater, 18″*	45.00	55.00	47.00
☐ **Bialosky Bear,** *sailor middy, 13″*	25.00	35.00	26.00
☐ **Bialosky Bear,** *sailor middy, 18″*	45.00	55.00	47.00
☐ **Bialosky Bear,** *tuxedo, satin bow tie, 13″*	25.00	35.00	26.00
☐ **Bialosky Bear,** *tuxedo, satin, bow tie, 18″*	45.00	55.00	47.00
☐ **Humphrey Beargart,** *grown bear, beige trench coat, brown hat, 19″*	40.00	50.00	42.00

STEIFF

Steiff (pronounced stif) is a name that has become synonymous with quality stuffed toys and teddy bears. The history of Steiff dates back to 1880 in the small village of Geigen, West Germany. It was there that Margarete Steiff, a seamstress, created the first Steiff toy — an elephant pincushion constructed out of felt scraps. This small gray elephant became a much coveted toy by the village children. In 1880 Margarete Steiff made eight of these little elephants and by 1885 she had sold 596 of these treasures.

In 1893 Margarete's brother Fritz took a sampling of toys to the Leipzig Trade Fair. It was in this same year that the firm was entered in the official Trade register.

In 1894 the first Steiff catalog was introduced and each new production acquired the company's trademark. A metal button was attached to the ear of the stuffed animals, and though the button has changed over the years, it is still found attached to each and every animal produced. This button serves to identify the product, and is a statement of quality that meets the Steiff motto, "For our children the best is just good enough."

As the popularity of the felt toys grew, the line was expanded to include monkeys, dogs, pigs and camels. Today, it is almost impossible to think of an animal that has not been produced by Steiff at one time or another.

Any history of Steiff would be incomplete if dolls and bears were not discussed. Early Steiff dolls were felt faced with seams — these dolls were produced from 1908 to 1922. The array of character dolls is almost too extensive to even attempt to list. They ranged from policemen, firemen, soldiers, bavarian couples, and chinesemen to everyday folks and children. Many collectors credit the creation of the teddy bear in 1903 to Steiff, although many companies in America make this claim. The first Steiff bears were based on sketches made by Richard Steiff at the Stuttgart Zoo. Early Steiff bears are typified by their shoe button eyes, long arms with curved paws and distinctive humps on their back.

The Stieff company celebrated their 100th Anniversary in 1980. To commemorate this milestone, the firm offered 11,000 Anniversary Bears. Each bear was numbered and offered in a box with a signed certificate by Han Otto Steiff. Today, this is one of the more sought after limited editions — originally selling for $150, this bear today is valued at $495. Another limited edition commemorative piece is the Richard Steiff Bear of 1983 — marking the 80th Anniversary of the Steiff Teddy Bear.

	Current Price Range		Prior Year Average
☐ **Albert The Running Bear,** *jogging outfit, 12″*	10.00	20.00	11.00
☐ **Arco,** *German shepherd, mohair, lying down, #2335,00, c.1950's, 10″*	126.00	137.00	130.00
☐ **Baby Petsy,** *acrylic bear, #5740/16, c.1970's, 6″*	54.00	65.00	58.00
☐ **Baby Rabbit,** *voice box, pink, #5686/28*	50.00	60.00	55.00
☐ **Baby Teddy,** *bear, voice box, pink, #5683/26*	50.00	60.00	55.00
☐ **Bessy,** *cow, mohair, felt udder, #1325,00, c.1950's, 10″*	126.00	142.00	130.00
☐ **Bison,** *c.1982*	20.00	30.00	25.00
☐ **Cockie,** *spaniel, mohair, #4273/12, c.1974, 4″*	30.00	42.00	32.00
☐ **Colt,** *brown velvet, glass eyes, #56/6414, c.1957, 6″*	45.00	55.00	48.00
☐ **Cora Baby Gorilla,** *c.1981*	70.00	80.00	73.00
☐ **Cosy Fiep,** *mouse, blue, #5390/15, 6″*	35.00	45.00	37.00
☐ **Cosy Flossy,** *fish, green, yellow felt fins, #5385/25, 10″*	65.00	75.00	68.00
☐ **Cosy Grissy,** *donkey, gray, #5470/27*	55.00	65.00	58.00
☐ **Cosy Issy,** *polar bear, white, #5405/30, 12″*	65.00	85.00	68.00
☐ **Cosy Joggi,** *hedgehog, beige, brown, #5397/15*	55.00	65.00	58.00
☐ **Cosy Lamby,** *#5140/22, c.1976*	35.00	45.00	38.00
☐ **Cosy Manni,** *rabbit, #5361/24, 5″*	40.00	50.00	42.00
☐ **Cosy Mobby,** *whale, gray, white, #5387/27*	40.00	50.00	42.00
☐ **Cosy Nessy,** *dragon, brown, yellow, #5430/50, 20″*	70.00	100.00	73.00
☐ **Cosy Piccy,** *duck, yellow, felt beak, #5377/12, 5″*	35.00	45.00	37.00
☐ **Cosy Pig,** *pinkish, beige, #5415/28, 11″*	60.00	80.00	63.00
☐ **Cosy Pony,** *brown, #5360/25*	80.00	110.00	84.00
☐ **Cosy Robby,** *seal, brown, #5375/57, 8″*	45.00	55.00	47.00
☐ **Cosy Snuffy,** *rabbit, beige, #5363/16, 6″*	40.00	50.00	42.00
☐ **Cosy Snuffy,** *rabbit, brown, #5365/16, 6″*	40.00	50.00	42.00
☐ **Cosy Snuffy,** *rabbit, caramel, #5364/16, 6″*	40.00	50.00	42.00
☐ **Cosy Trampy,** *elephant, acrylic, gray, pink, #6620,00, c.1950's, 8″*	47.00	63.00	50.00
☐ **Cosy Waggi,** *duck, blue, yellow, felt beak, voice box, #5380/26, 5″*	40.00	50.00	42.00

	Current Price Range		Prior Year Average
☐ **Cosy Waldi,** *dog, brown, #5460/35*	40.00	60.00	42.00
☐ **Cuddly Dog,** *beige and brown, #5530/25, 10″*	60.00	70.00	63.00
☐ **Cuddly Rabbit,** *brown, red ribbon bow, #5525/25, 10″*	60.00	70.00	63.00
☐ **Dalle,** *guinea pig, #2252/10, 4″*	35.00	45.00	37.00
☐ **Dangling Cat,** *#6286/50, 20″*	80.00	110.00	84.00
☐ **Deer,** *mohair, felt antlers, #1335,00, c.1950's, 14″*	127.00	156.00	135.00
☐ **Diggy,** *badger, mohair, #840,00, c.1960's*	60.00	70.00	63.00
☐ **Diggy Elephant,** *gray, #0505/18, 7″*	60.00	70.00	63.00
☐ **Diva,** *persian cat, acrylic, sitting, #2835/35, c.1970, 25″*	100.00	126.00	105.00
☐ **Dog,** *cocker spaniel, black and white, mohair, swivel head, flirty black and white eyes, #4276/29, c.1960's*	80.00	90.00	85.00

Fireman,
12″
$135.00-$165.00

	Current Price Range		Prior Year Average
☐ **Dog Scotty,** *black mohair, #1322,00, c.1940's, 9"*	96.00	115.00	100.00
☐ **Dolphin,** *c.1982*	10.00	20.00	11.00
☐ **Donkey,** *c.1982*	35.00	45.00	37.00
☐ **Duck,** *music, yellow, green, felt beak, #6372/18, 7"*	60.00	70.00	63.00
☐ **Ferdy,** *pony, brown and white mohair, #3750/16, c.1980, 7"*	45.00	55.00	49.00
☐ **Fish,** *green, c.1980*	25.00	30.00	26.00
☐ **Floppy Cockie,** *mohair, #29/7317, c.1957*	40.00	50.00	42.00
☐ **Floppy Cockie,** *mohair, felt eyes, sleeping, #29/7328, c.1957*	20.00	30.00	22.00
☐ **Floppy Zotty,** *mohair, felt eyes, sleeping, #12/7317, c.1974*	50.00	60.00	54.00
☐ **Flora,** *cow, white, beige, #3792/25, 10"*	60.00	80.00	63.00
☐ **Flossy,** *fish, mohair, felt lips, #2322,00, c.1950's, 11"*	68.00	89.00	70.00
☐ **Foxy,** *fox terrier, red collar, standing, #1322,00, c.1950's, 9"*	79.00	89.00	82.00
☐ **Gaty,** *alligator, mohair, #0980/15, c.1960's, 14"*	40.00	50.00	42.00
☐ **Hango,** *gibbon, dangling, #0040/45, 18"*	60.00	80.00	63.00
☐ **Hango,** *monkey, tan, bendable, c.1960's*	40.00	50.00	42.00
☐ **Hopsi,** *squirrel handpuppet, #6900/18, c.1970's, 4"*	46.00	67.00	50.00
☐ **Husky,** *Molly, c.1981*	85.00	95.00	89.00
☐ **Jocko,** *chimpanzee, brown mohair, jointed, #9/5325, c.1957, 10"*	35.00	45.00	38.00
☐ **Jocko,** *chimpanzee, jointed, felt face, brown, mohair, #5325,00, c.1950's, 8"*	56.00	79.00	60.00
☐ **Jocko,** *chimpanzee, jointed, felt face, brown mohair, #5325,00, c.1950's, 12"*	89.00	110.00	92.00
☐ **Joggi,** *hedge hog, music, beige, brown, #6373/18, 7"*	60.00	70.00	63.00
☐ **Jolly Skunk,** *acrylic arm puppet, four legs, #3476/40, c.1970's, 16"*	96.00	120.00	100.00
☐ **Jumbo,** *elephant, mohair, red bib, sits, #0520/35, c.1960's, 14"*	100.00	115.00	105.00
☐ **Jumbo,** *elephant, squeaker, bell, begging, #0520/22, c.1957, 9"*	125.00	175.00	129.00
☐ **Junior Schnauzer,** *c.1980*	60.00	70.00	63.00
☐ **King Louie,** *from the Jungle book, acrylic, #0050/25, c.1960's, 10"*	66.00	79.00	68.00
☐ **Knoepfchen,** *bear, #0218/16*	45.00	55.00	48.00
☐ **Lady Bug,** *c.1982*	5.00	10.00	6.00
☐ **Laika,** *space dog, mohair, #1325,00, c.1950's, 10"*	156.00	166.00	160.00
☐ **Leo,** *lion, mohair, standing, #0800/17, c.1974, 7"*	70.00	80.00	73.00
☐ **Leopard,** *c.1982*	80.00	85.00	82.00

	Current Price Range		Prior Year Average
☐ **Leopard,** *mohair, lying down, #2317,1, c.1960's*	60.00	70.00	63.00
☐ **Linda,** *hippopotamus, green, #5517/25, 10"*	50.00	60.00	55.00
☐ **Linda,** *kangaroo with baby, mohair, #0700/14, c.1957, 6"*	70.00	80.00	74.00
☐ **Lion,** *yellow, c.1981*	40.00	45.00	42.00
☐ **Lizzy Cat,** *c.1982*	35.00	45.00	37.00
☐ **Lizzy Lizard,** *cotton, green, yellow stomach, #1406,00, c.1950's, 2"*	65.00	79.00	68.00
☐ **Lulac,** *dangling rabbit, #6283/50, 20"*	80.00	110.00	84.00
☐ **Lulac,** *rabbit, mohair, yellow chest, #6343,01, c.1950's, 17"*	126.00	169.00	131.00
☐ **Lully Bear,** *mohair, jointed head, felt mouth, #0350/22, c.1960's, 9"*	46.00	62.00	50.00
☐ **Lynx,** *molly, c.1981*	150.00	200.00	156.00
☐ **Manschli,** *bear, brown, #0310/19*	50.00	60.00	55.00
☐ **Mecki,** *mohair, #7627/17, c.1974, 7"*	35.00	45.00	39.00
☐ **Micki,** *mohair, #7628/17, c.1974, 7"*	35.00	45.00	39.00
☐ **Molly Koala,** *acrylic, #0331/22, c.1970's, 11"*	49.00	63.00	51.00
☐ **Molly Piff,** *marmot, #0346/30, 12"*	50.00	60.00	55.00
☐ **Molly Terrier,** *mohair, jointed head, curly brown and white, #3322,2, 11"*	110.00	130.00	115.00
☐ **Mother And Baby Bear Set,** *jointed, c.1981, 15", 7"*	125.00	175.00	129.00
☐ **Mouse,** *gray wool, c.1982*	5.00	10.00	6.00
☐ **Nagy,** *beaver, mohair, #2120/10, c.1974, 4"*	25.00	35.00	26.00
☐ **Naggy Beaver,** *brown mohair, felt tooth, #4310,00, c.1950's, 4"*	39.00	48.00	42.00
☐ **Niki,** *baby dolphin, orange, yellow, #6434/13*	30.00	40.00	35.00
☐ **Niki,** *baby giraffe, yellow, blue, #6432/13*	30.00	40.00	35.00
☐ **Nikili,** *dressed rabbits, mohair, #736, c.1950's, 10"*	110.00	150.00	120.00
☐ **Nosy Rhino,** *mohair, felt tusk, #1100,14, c.1950's, 6"*	46.00	62.00	50.00
☐ **Ossi,** *rabbit, brown mohair, standing, #2940/23, c.1973, 10"*	90.00	110.00	93.00
☐ **Otter,** *c.1981*	28.00	37.00	30.00
☐ **Paddy,** *walrus, mohair, plastic tusks, #4310,00, c.1950's, 4"*	45.00	70.00	49.00
☐ **Panda Bear,** *mohair, jointed, #5322,2, c.1957, 9"*	275.00	350.00	295.00
☐ **Peggy Penquin,** *mohair, felt beak, #4310, 00, c.1950's, 4"*	26.00	37.00	28.00
☐ **Peggy Penquin,** *mohair, felt beak, #4314, 00, c.1950's, 6"*	46.00	57.00	50.00
☐ **Peggy Penguin,** *mohair, felt beak, #4322, 00, c.1950's, 9"*	56.00	67.00	60.00

	Current Price Range		Prior Year Average
☐ **Peggy Penquin,** *mohair, felt beak, #4335, 00, c.1950's, 14"*	67.00	77.00	70.00
☐ **Peips,** *mohair, gray, white, #4308,00, c.1950's, 3"*	40.00	45.00	44.00
☐ **Petsy,** *acrylic bear, fat tummy, #0241/24, c.1960's, 9"*	92.00	110.00	95.00
☐ **Peips Bear,** *yellow, voice squeezer, #6410/13*	60.00	80.00	63.00
☐ **Polar Bear Collection,** *limited edition*	215.00	245.00	230.00
☐ **Pomeranian,** *rust color, c.1981*	80.00	85.00	82.00
☐ **Puma,** *lying, c.1981*	70.00	80.00	73.00
☐ **Pummy,** *rabbit, mohair, crouched position, #2960/25, c.1960's, 10"*	65.00	79.00	69.00
☐ **Rabbit,** *sitting, c.1982*	30.00	40.00	32.00
☐ **Recorder Peter,** *monkey, mohair, pumping cart, wooden wheels, #325, 10"*	115.00	130.00	120.00
☐ **Renny,** *reindeer, mohair, felt antlers, #1314,00, c.1950's, 5"*	66.00	83.00	68.00
☐ **Richard Steiff Bear,** *copy of original Teddy Bear, mohair, silver gray, jointed, felt paws, voice box, limited edition, c.1983, 12"*	85.00	9500	89.00
☐ **Rico Horse,** *brown, white, red harness, rein, #3760/25, 10"*	60.00	80.00	63.00
☐ **Running Rabbit,** *mohair, #1314,00, c.1950's, 6"*	66.00	84.00	68.00
☐ **Running Rabbit,** *mohair, #1317,00, c.1950's 7"*	100.00	130.00	105.00
☐ **Sigi,** *sea horse, acrylic blue, yellow, #4628, 00, c.1950's, 11"*	126.00	148.00	130.00
☐ **Sigi Leopard,** *c.1982*	35.00	45.00	37.00
☐ **Sissi Cat,** *gray, white tiger stripes, #2726/17*	40.00	50.00	45.00
☐ **Slo,** *turtle, mohair head, rubber back, #2450/10, c.1957*	35.00	45.00	38.00
☐ **Snobby Poodle,** *black, gray, white mohair, #5313,04, c.1950's, 5"*	48.00	62.00	50.00
☐ **Snobby Poodle,** *black, gray, white mohair, #5343,04, 17"*	130.00	165.00	136.00
☐ **Snucki,** *mountain goat, white, black face, legs, #1317,00, c.1950's, 6"*	70.00	85.00	73.00
☐ **Sonny Rabbit,** *brown, sitting, #2960/17, c.1960's, 7"*	45.00	65.00	49.00
☐ **Starli,** *kakadu, acrylic, pink comb, #2545/30, c.1970's, 12"*	85.00	99.00	89.00
☐ **Sulla Lioness,** *c.1982*	35.00	45.00	37.00
☐ **Swapl,** *lamb, black mohair, #6510,00, c.1950's, 4"*	100.00	120.00	105.00
☐ **Swinny,** *guinea pig, dralon, cotton, #2250/12, c.1960's*	20.00	30.00	21.00

Margaret Strong Teddy Bear, mohair, voice box
$185.00-$200.00

	Current Price Range		Prior Year Average
☐ **Tea Party Set,** *four bears, mohair, white, brown, honey, caramel, jointed, comes with porcelain tea set, limited edition, 7″*	160.00	200.00	165.00
☐ **Teddy,** *brown mohair, jointed, #5315, c.1957, 6″*	250.00	310.00	256.00
☐ **Teddy,** *brown mohair, jointed, #5335,2, c.1940's, 13″*	320.00	440.00	330.00
☐ **Teddy,** *brown plush, swivel neck, jointed at arms and legs, long snout with embroidered black nose, brown glass eyes, individually stitched ears, brown felt paws, 12″*	185.00	200.00	195.00
☐ **Teddy,** *golden plush, swivel neck, jointed at arms and legs, amber glass eyes, long snout with embroidered nose, 17″*	110.00	130.00	120.00
☐ **Teddy,** *gold plush, brown button eyes, long snout with embroidered nose, swivel neck, jointed at shoulders and hips, separately stitched ears, 6″*	160.00	100.00	170.00
☐ **Teddy,** *mohair, jointed, #0201/36, c.1960's, 14″*	126.00	154.00	130.00

	Current Price Range		Prior Year Average
☐ **Teddy Bear Purse,** *plush, glass eyes, 10"*	15.00	20.00	16.00
☐ **Teddy Roosevelt Commemorative Set,** *three bears, jointed, mohair, white, gold, caramel, voice box, hunter's outfits, limited edition, 9"*	180.00	220.00	189.00
☐ **Theodore Bearington,** *beige sweater, cap, 20"*	50.00	60.00	52.00
☐ **Terrier,** *Yorkshire, acrylic, #4085/28, c.1970's, 11"*	77.00	100.00	79.00
☐ **Tiger,** *#1314,0, c.1957*	60.00	70.00	63.00
☐ **Tiger,** *mohair, lying down, #2317,00, c.1950's*	60.00	70.00	63.00
☐ **Toldi Dog,** *brown, wears bib, #6244/30, 12"*	60.00	80.00	63.00
☐ **Toldi Bear,** *brown, #6242/30, 12"*	65.00	80.00	68.00
☐ **White Teddy Bear Series,** *four bears, 5", 10", 14", 16"*	150.00	200.00	156.00
☐ **Wild Boar,** *c.1982*	18.00	25.00	20.00
☐ **Woodchuck,** *c.1982*	25.00	35.00	26.00
☐ **Young Owl,** *furry brown, white, #2591/22*	50.00	60.00	55.00
☐ **Zotty,** *mohair, bendable #0305/22, 9"*	35.00	45.00	38.00
☐ **Zotty,** *swivel neck, 9"*	70.00	80.00	74.00
☐ **Zotty,** *swivel neck, growler, 20"*	220.00	270.00	226.00
☐ **Zotty,** *swivel neck, white bib, c.1920's ballerina outfit, 12"*	85.00	95.00	89.00
☐ **Zotty,** *swivel neck, white bib, squeaker, 7"*	70.00	80.00	74.00
☐ **Zotty,** *swivel neck, white bib, 18"*	120.00	140.00	126.00

MISCELLANEOUS AND UNKNOWN MANUFACTURERS

☐ **Anniversary Bear,** *brown wool, mohair, jointed, voice box, limited edition, by Dean, c.1983, 16"*	68.00	80.00	70.00
☐ **Big Fox,** *riding outfit, by Little Folks*	95.00	105.00	100.00
☐ **Brown Bear,** *28"*	9.00	12.00	10.00
☐ **Colonel Teddy,** *blue uniform, holds flag*	30.00	35.00	32.00
☐ **Colonel Teddy,** *khaki, holds flag*	30.00	35.00	32.00
☐ **Colonel Teddy,** *plush, eyeglasses, 18"*	28.00	35.00	30.00
☐ **Elephant,** *limited series, by Kammer*	75.00	85.00	79.00
☐ **Flamingo,** *pink satin*	75.00	85.00	79.00
☐ **Horses,** *by S. T. Clydesdale*	75.00	85.00	79.00
☐ **Koala Bear,** *real fur, 16"*	20.00	30.00	21.00
☐ **Koala,** *small*	6.00	12.00	7.00
☐ **Little Fox,** *riding outfit, by Little Folk*	35.00	45.00	40.00
☐ **Monkey,** *brown fur, climbs*	80.00	105.00	84.00
☐ **Monkey,** *brown fur, plays drums, windup, mint in box, c.1938*	20.00	30.00	25.00
☐ **Pig,** *brown and white*	35.00	45.00	40.00

	Current Price Range		Prior Year Average
☐ **The Porridge Bear,** *jointed, voice box, wears nightshirt, comes with box, limited edition, by Projects International, 17"*	80.00	100.00	84.00
☐ **President Teddy,** *in tuxedo*	30.00	35.00	32.00
☐ **Rabbit,** *lambs wool, key wind, hops, French, 10"*	250.00	300.00	295.00
☐ **Sailor Bear,** *brown alpaca, jointed, limited edition, signed, #5024, by Nisbet, c.1983, 16"*	50.00	60.00	55.00
☐ **Teddy Bear,** *champagne colored plush bear has long snout with embroidered nose, straw stuffed, hump on back, felt pads on paws, separately stitched ears, 9"*	280.00	310.00	285.00
☐ **Teddy Bear On Wheels,** *dark brown bruin has short mohair fur, black shoe button eyes, felt paws, hump on back, separately stitched ears, embroidered black nose and stands on a red metal scooter with black rubber wheels, red wooden handle on this unusual scooter, bear is attached to front wheel mechanism and turns side to side enabling child sitting on bear's back to steer, 22"*	95.00	110.00	100.00
☐ **Teddy Bear,** *dark brown plush mohair, swivel neck, jointed at arms and legs, tan velveteen paws, amber glass eyes, tan snout with embroidered black nose, individually stitched ears, 14"*	35.00	45.00	40.00
☐ **Teddy Bear,** *early brown plus bear has blue glass eyes, short embroidered snout, swivel neck, jointed at arms and legs, felt paws, separately stitched ears, hump on back, 17½"*	145.00	160.00	150.00
☐ **Teddy Bear,** *gold colored plush, brown glass eyes, jointed at shoulders and hips, worn spots on back of head, 5"*	30.00	40.00	35.00
☐ **Wise Owl,** *horse rider, jockey outfit, cap, holds crop*	95.00	105.00	99.00
☐ **Wise Owl,** *huntsman, hunting outfit*	100.00	120.00	105.00
☐ **Wise Owl,** *jogger*	95.00	105.00	100.00
☐ **Wise Owl,** *judge, official outfit, wig*	95.00	105.00	99.00
☐ **Wise Owl,** *Lady Barrister, official outfit*	95.00	105.00	99.00
☐ **Wise Owl,** *lady doctor, lab coat*	95.00	105.00	99.00
☐ **Wise Owl,** *lady golfer*	100.00	120.00	105.00
☐ **Wise Owl,** *professor, mortar board, tassle, academic robe*	95.00	105.00	99.00
☐ **Wise Owl,** *skier*	100.00	120.00	105.00
☐ **Wise Owl,** *tennis player, tennis whites, visor, holds racket*	100.00	120.00	110.00
☐ **Wise Owl,** *yachtsman*	100.00	120.00	105.00

FOR IMMEDIATE DELIVERY

VISA & MASTER CARD CUSTOMERS

ORDER TOLL FREE!

1-800-327-1384

This number is for orders only, it is not tied into the customer service or business office. Customers not using charge cards must use mail for ordering since payment is required with the order — sorry no C.O.D.'s. Florida residents call (305) 857-9095 — ask for order department.

OR SEND ORDERS TO

THE HOUSE OF COLLECTIBLES, *ORLANDO CENTRAL PARK*
1900 PREMIER ROW, ORLANDO, FL 32809 PHONE (305) 857-9095

☐ *Please send me the following price guides—(don't forget to add postage & handling):*

☐ *I would like the most current edition of the books listed below.*

☐ 184-5 @ 9.95	☐ 324-4 @ 9.95	☐ 394-5 @ 9.95	☐ 391-0 @ 2.95	☐ 379-1 @ 2.95
☐ 364-3 @ 9.95	☐ 349-X @ 9.95	☐ 188-8 @ 9.95	☐ 345-7 @ 2.50	☐ 319-8 @ 2.95
☐ 381-3 @ 9.95	☐ 189-6 @ 9.95	☐ 356-2 @ 9.95	☐ 316-3 @ 2.95	☐ 317-1 @ 2.95
☐ 363-5 @ 9.95	☐ 353-8 @ 9.95	☐ 355-4 @ 9.95	☐ 388-0 @ 2.95	☐ 385-6 @ 2.95
☐ 354-6 @ 9.95	☐ 125-X @ 9.95	☐ 348-1 @ 9.95	☐ 396-1 @ 2.95	☐ 387-2 @ 2.95
☐ 374-0 @ 9.95	☐ 352-X @ 9.95	☐ 365-1 @ 9.95	☐ 318-X @ 2.95	☐ 386-4 @ 2.95
☐ 350-3 @ 9.95	☐ 371-6 @ 9.95	☐ 369-4 @ 9.95	☐ 378-3 @ 2.95	☐ 171-3 @ 6.95
☐ 383-X @ 9.95	☐ 398-8 @ 9.95	☐ 308-2 @ 2.50	☐ 315-5 @ 2.50	☐ 300-7 @ 6.95
☐ 384-8 @ 9.95	☐ 187-X @ 9.95	☐ 373-2 @ 2.95	☐ 372-4 @ 2.95	☐ 301-5 @ 6.95
☐ 357-0 @ 9.95	☐ 351-1 @ 9.95	☐ 376-7 @ 2.95	☐ 400-3 @ 2.95	☐ 302-3 @ 6.95
☐ 367-8 @ 9.95	☐ 375-9 @ 9.95	☐ 377-5 @ 2.95	☐ 314-7 @ 2.50	

Add $1.00 postage and handling for the first book and 50¢ for each additional book. Add $2.50 to each order for insurance and special handling. Florida residents add 5% sales tax.

☐ Check or money order enclosed $________(include postage and handling)

☐ Please charge $________________ to my: ☐ MASTERCARD ☐ VISA

Charge Card Customers Not Using Our Toll Free Number Please Fill Out The Information Below.

Account No. (All Digits)________________ Expiration Date________

Signature________________________________

NAME (please print)______________________ PHONE ____________

ADDRESS ______________________________ APT. # ________

CITY ______________________ STATE ________ ZIP ________

10